PI

Project M

Professional Exam

Study Guide

Fifth Edition

PMP®

Project Management Professional Exam

Study Guide

Fifth Edition

Kim Heldman

Wiley India Pvt. Ltd.

PMP: Project Management Professional Exam
Study Guide, Fifth Edition

Authorized reprint by Wiley India Pvt. Ltd., 4435-36/7, Ansari Road, Daryaganj, New Delhi – 110002.

Cover Designer: Ryan Sneed

Reprint: 2010

Printed at: *Kay Kay Printers, Delhi*

ISBN : 978-81-265-2189-0

Dear Reader,

Thank you for choosing *PMP: Project Management Professional Exam Study Guide, Fifth Edition*. This book is part of a family of premium-quality Sybex books, all of which are written by outstanding authors who combine practical experience with a gift for teaching.

Sybex was founded in 1976. More than thirty years later, we're still committed to producing consistently exceptional books. With each of our titles we're working hard to set a new standard for the industry. From the paper we print on, to the authors we work with, our goal is to bring you the best books available.

I hope you see all that reflected in these pages. I'd be very interested to hear your comments and get your feedback on how we're doing. Feel free to let me know what you think about this or any other Sybex book by sending me an email at `nedde@wiley.com`, or if you think you've found a technical error in this book, please visit `http://sybex.custhelp.com`. Customer feedback is critical to our efforts at Sybex.

Best regards,

Neil Edde
Vice President and Publisher
Sybex, an Imprint of Wiley

To BB, my forever love

—Kimmie

Acknowledgments

Thank you for buying the PMP Project Management Professional Study Guide Fifth Edition to help you study and prepare for the PMP® exam. Thousands of readers worldwide have used previous editions of this book to help them study for and pass the exam. Because of their success and their recommendations to friends and co-workers, we've been able to keep this study guide up-to-date to match the changes made in the PMBOK® Guide Fourth Edition.

I would also like to thank the countless instructors who use my book in their PMP prep classes. I've heard from many of you over the past few months wondering when this edition would be available. Thank you for your continued interest in using the Study Guide in your classes. A big thanks to all the PMI chapters who use this book in their classes as well.

A huge thank you goes to Neil Edde, vice president and publisher at Sybex, for giving me the opportunity to revise and update this edition. Neil took a chance way back when on the first edition of this book. I can't thank him enough for having the foresight at that time to believe in this little known exam.

This book clearly fits the definition of a project, and the team at Sybex is one of the best project teams you'll ever find. I appreciate all the hard work and dedication everyone on the team put into producing this book. A special thanks goes to Jeff Kellum, acquisitions editor. Jeff and I have worked on several editions of this book together and I appreciate his diligence and insightful ideas for updates to the book over the years. It's always a pleasure to work with Jeff.

Next I'd like to thank Alexa Murphy, development editor, for her diligent work in helping me make this edition the best it can be. Her recommendations and clarifications helped make the text much stronger. A big thanks also goes to Christine O'Connor, production editor, for her insightful suggestions and comments and for keeping the latter stages of the book on track. And thanks also to Judy Flynn, copyeditor, for all her help.

There were many folks involved behind the scenes who also deserve my thanks. They are Publication Services, Inc., proofreaders, and Nancy Guenther, indexer.

Next I'd like to thank Terri Wagner, technical editor, for her keen eye and valuable suggestions for improvements to the text. Terri is the president of Mentor Source, Inc. and uses this book in her classes. Her suggestions came from years of classroom exposure and student questions and suggestions. I have had the pleasure of working with Terri on several occasions and would recommend her classes. Thanks, Terri, for helping make this the best edition of the Study Guide ever!

I have a special heartfelt thanks for Brett Feddersen, who served as the final technical editor on the book. I have had the great pleasure of working with Brett over the last several years and have delighted in our friendship and in watching him stretch and grow professionally while dealing with the many challenges that came his way. If you are ever in need of the best project manager in the world, Brett is your man (but you can't have him because he works for me!).

Last, but always the first on my list, is my best friend for a couple of decades and counting, BB. I love you and I would never have accomplished what I have to date without your love and support. You're the best! And I'd be remiss if I didn't also thank Jason and Leah, Noelle, Amanda and Steve, and of course the two best granddaughters on the planet, Kate and Juliette, for their support and understanding.

About the Author

Kim Heldman, MBA, PMP, is the deputy enterprise architect for the state of Colorado and the chief information officer for the Colorado Department of Transportation. Kim is responsible for managing projects with IT components ranging from small in scope and budget to multimillion dollar, multiyear projects. She has over 19 years experience in information technology project management. Kim has served in a senior leadership role for over 11 years and is regarded as a strategic visionary with an innate ability to collaborate with diverse groups and organizations, instill hope, improve morale, and lead her teams in achieving goals they never thought possible.

Kim has extensive experience in the government sector managing projects of various size and scope. Currently, Kim is working with the governor's Office of Information Technology assisting in the oversight of one of the largest projects ever undertaken in the state of Colorado. She is also about to kick off a major upgrade project for the Department of Transportation's ERP system.

In addition to her project management experience, Kim also has experience managing application development, web development, network operations, infrastructure, security, and customer service teams.

Kim wrote the first edition of the PMP Project Management Professional Study Guide, published by Sybex, in 2002. Since then, thousands of people worldwide have used the Study Guide in preparation for the PMP® Exam. Kim is also the author of Project Management JumpStart 2nd Edition and Project Manager's Spotlight on Risk Management and co-author of Excel 2007 for Project Managers. Kim has also published several articles and is currently working on a leadership book.

Most of the Real World Scenarios in the Study Guide are based on Kim's real life experiences. The names and circumstances have been changed to protect the innocent.

Kim continues to write on project management best practices and leadership topics and she speaks frequently at conferences and events. You can contact Kim at `Kim.Heldman@comcast.net`. She personally answers all her email.

Contents at a Glance

Contents

Introduction

This book was designed for anyone thinking of taking the Project Management Professional (PMP®) exam sponsored by the Project Management Institute (PMI®). This certification is growing in popularity and demand in all areas of business. PMI has experienced explosive growth in membership over the last few years, and more and more organizations are recognizing the importance of project management certification.

> **NOTE** Although this book is written primarily for those of you taking the PMP® exam, you can also use this book to study for the Certified Associate in Project Management (CAPM®) exam. The exams are similar in style, and the information covered in this book will help you with either exam.

This book has been updated to reflect the latest edition of *A Guide to the Project Management Body of Knowledge (PMBOK® Guide), Fourth Edition.* It assumes you have knowledge of general project management practices, although not necessarily specific to the *PMBOK® Guide.* It's written so that you can skim through areas you are already familiar with, picking up the specific *PMBOK® Guide* terminology where needed to pass the exam. You'll find that the project management processes and techniques discussed in this book are defined in such a way that you'll recognize tasks you've always done and be able to identify them with the *PMBOK® Guide* process names or methodologies.

PMI offers the most recognized certification in the field of project management, and this book deals exclusively with its procedures and methods. Project management consists of many methods, each with its own terminology, tools, and procedures. If you're familiar with another organized project management methodology, don't assume you already know the *PMBOK® Guide* processes. I strongly recommend that you learn all of the processes—their key inputs, tools and techniques, and outputs. Take the time to memorize the key terms found at the end of every chapter as well. Sometimes just understanding the definition of a term will help you answer a question. It might be that you've always done that particular task or used the methodology described but called it by another name. Know the name of each process and its primary purpose.

> **NOTE** All of the process group names—including their inputs, tools and techniques, outputs, and descriptions—found throughout this book are from the *PMBOK® Guide.*

What Is the PMP Certification?

The PMI is the leader and the most widely recognized organization in terms of promoting project management best practices. The PMI strives to maintain and endorse standards and ethics in this field and offers publications, training, seminars, chapters, special interest groups, and colleges to further the project management discipline.

The PMI was founded in 1969 and first started offering the PMP® certification exam in 1984. PMI is accredited as an American National Standards Institute (ANSI) standards developer and also has the distinction of being the first organization to have its certification program attain International Organization for Standardization (ISO) 9001 recognition.

The PMI boasts a worldwide membership of more than 265,000, with members from 170 different countries. Local PMI chapters meet regularly and allow project managers to exchange information and learn about new tools and techniques of project management or new ways to use established techniques. I encourage you to join a local chapter and get to know other professionals in your field.

Why Become PMP Certified?

The following benefits are associated with becoming PMP certified:

- It demonstrates proof of professional achievement.
- It increases your marketability.
- It provides greater opportunity for advancement in your field.
- It raises customer confidence in you and in your company's services.

Demonstrates Proof of Professional Achievement

PMP® certification is a rigorous process that documents your achievements in the field of project management. The exam tests your knowledge of the disciplined approaches, methodologies, and project management practices as described in the *PMBOK® Guide*.

You are required to have several years of experience in project management before sitting for the exam, as well as 35 hours of formal project management education. Your certification assures employers and customers that you are well grounded in project management practices and disciplines. It shows that you have the hands-on experience and a mastery of the processes and disciplines to manage projects effectively and motivate teams to produce successful results.

Increases Your Marketability

Many industries are realizing the importance of project management and its role in the organization. They are also seeing that simply proclaiming a head technician to be a "project manager" does not make it so. Project management, just like engineering, information technology, and a host of other trades, has its own specific qualifications and skills. Certification tells potential employers that you have the skills, experience, and knowledge to drive successful projects and ultimately improve the company's bottom line.

A certification will always make you stand out above the competition. If you're certified and you're competing against a project manager without certification, chances are you'll come out as the top pick. As a hiring manager, all other things being equal, I will usually opt for the candidate who has certification over the candidate who doesn't have it. Certification tells potential employers you have gone the extra mile. You've spent time studying techniques and methods as well as employing them in practice. It shows dedication to your own professional growth and enhancement and to adhering to and advancing professional standards.

Provides Opportunity for Advancement

PMP® certification displays your willingness to pursue growth in your professional career and shows that you're not afraid of a little hard work to get what you want. Potential employers will interpret your pursuit of this certification as a high-energy, success-driven, can-do attitude on your part. They'll see that you're likely to display these same characteristics on the job, which will help make the company successful. Your certification displays a success-oriented, motivated attitude that will open up opportunities for future career advancements in your current field as well as in new areas you might want to explore.

Raises Customer Confidence

Just as the PMP certification assures employers that you've got the background and experience to handle project management, it assures customers that they have a competent, experienced project manager at the helm. Certification will help your organization sell customers on your ability to manage their projects. Customers, like potential employers, want the reassurance that those working for them have the knowledge and skills necessary to carry out the duties of the position and that professionalism and personal integrity are of utmost importance. Individuals who hold these ideals will translate their ethics and professionalism to their work. This enhances the trust customers will have in you, which in turn will give you the ability to influence them on important project issues.

How to Become PMP Certified

You need to fulfill several requirements in order to sit for the PMP exam. The PMI has detailed the certification process quite extensively at its website. Go to `www.pmi.org`, and click the Professional Development and Careers tab to reveal the Certifications selection and get the latest information on certification procedures and requirements.

As of this writing, you are required to fill out an application to sit for the PMP exam. You can submit this application online at the PMI's website. You also need to document 35 hours of formal project management education. This might include college classes, seminars, workshops, and training sessions. Be prepared to list the class titles, location, date, and content.

In addition to filling out the application and documenting your formal project management training, there is one set of criteria you'll need to meet to sit for the exam. The criteria in this set fall into two categories. You need to meet the requirements for only one of these categories:

- Category 1 is for those who have a baccalaureate degree. You'll need to provide proof, via transcripts, of your degree with your application. In addition, you'll need to complete verification forms—found at the PMI website—that show 4,500 hours of project management experience that spans a minimum of three years and no more than six years.
- Category 2 is for those who do not have a baccalaureate degree but do hold a high school diploma or equivalent. You'll need to complete verification forms documenting 7,500 hours of project management experience that spans a minimum of five years and no more than eight years.

The exam fee at the time this book is being published is $405 for PMI members in good standing and $555 for non-PMI members. Testing is conducted at Thomson Prometric centers. You can find a center near you on the PMI website. You have six months from the time PMI receives and approves your completed application to take the exam. You'll need to bring a form of identification such as a driver's license with you to the Thomson Prometric center on the test day. You will not be allowed to take anything with you into the testing center. You will be given a calculator, pencils, and scrap paper. You will turn in all scrap paper, including the notes and squiggles you've jotted during the test, to the center upon completion of the exam.

The exam is scored immediately, so you will know whether you've passed at the conclusion of the test. You're given four hours to complete the exam, which consists of 200 randomly generated questions. Only 175 of the 200 questions are scored. A passing score requires you to answer 106 of the 175 questions correctly. Twenty-five of the 200 questions are "pretest" questions that will appear randomly throughout the exam. These 25 questions are used by PMI to determine statistical information and to determine whether they can or should be used on future exams. The questions on the exam cover the following process groups and areas:

- Initiating
- Planning
- Executing
- Monitoring and Controlling
- Closing
- Professional Responsibility

All unanswered questions are scored as wrong answers, so it benefits you to guess at an answer if you're stumped on a question.

After you've received your certification, you'll be required to earn 60 professional development units (PDUs) every three years to maintain certification. Approximately one hour of structured learning translates to one PDU. The PMI website details what activities constitute a PDU, how many PDUs each activity earns, and how to register your PDUs with PMI to maintain your certification. As an example, attendance at a local chapter meeting earns one PDU.

How to Become CAPM Certified

If you find you don't have quite enough experience or education to sit for the PMP exam, you should consider sitting for the Certified Associate in Project Management (CAPM) exam. The CAPM exam is structured like the PMP exam only the requirements are not as strict as they are for the PMP. CAPM candidates typically work in a supporting role with a project manager or as a subproject manager. Like the PMP, CAPM has two categories of requirements; each category requires 23 hours of project management education:

- Category 1 is for those who have a baccalaureate degree. You'll need to provide proof, via transcripts, of your degree with your application. In addition, you'll need to complete verification forms that show 1,500 hours of project management experience that spans a minimum of two years and no more than three years.
- Category 2 is for those who do not have a baccalaureate degree but do have a high school diploma or equivalent. You'll need to complete verification forms documenting 2,500 hours of project management experience that spans a minimum of two years and no more than three years.

The CAPM® exam fee at the time of this publication is $225 for PMI members in good standing and $300 for non-PMI members.

Included on the CD with this book is a sample CAPM exam. If you're sitting for the CAPM exam, I encourage you to answer all of the end-of-chapter questions and take the bonus exams in addition to the sample CAPM exam. You'll get a much broader sense of the types of questions and the topics you'll encounter on the actual exam by using all of the sample questions provided in this book and on the CD.

Who Should Buy This Book?

If you are serious about passing the PMP exam (or the CAPM exam for that matter), you should buy this book and use it to study for the exam. This book is unique in that it walks you through the project processes from beginning to end, just as projects are performed in practice. When you read this book, you will benefit by learning specific *PMBOK® Guide* processes and techniques coupled with real-life scenarios that describe how project managers in different situations handle problems and the various issues all project managers are bound to encounter during their career. This study guide describes in detail the exam objective topics in each chapter and has attempted to cover all of the important project management concepts.

How to Use This Book and CD

We've included several testing features, both in the book and on the companion CD. Following this introduction is an assessment test that you can use to check your readiness for the actual exam. Take this test before you start reading the book. It will help you identify the areas you may need to brush up on. The answers to the assessment test appear after the last question of the test. Each answer includes an explanation and a note telling you in which chapter this material appears.

An Exam Essentials section appears at the end of every chapter to highlight the topics you'll most likely find on the exam and help you focus on the most important material covered in the chapter so that you'll have a solid understanding of those concepts. However, it isn't possible to predict what questions will be covered on your particular exam, so be sure to study everything in the chapter.

NOTE

Like the exam itself, this Study Guide is organized in terms of process groups and the natural sequence of events a project goes through in its life cycle. By contrast, in other study guides, material is organized by Knowledge Area—Human Resource Management, Communications Management, and so on—and it can be confusing when studying for the exam to map the processes in each Knowledge Area to process groups.

Review questions are also provided at the end of every chapter. You can use these to gauge your understanding of the subject matter before reading the chapter and to point out the areas in which you need to concentrate your study time. As you finish each chapter, answer the review questions and then check to see whether your answers are right—the correct answers appear on the pages following the last question. You can go back to reread the section that deals with each question you got wrong to ensure that you answer the question correctly the next time you are tested on the material. If you can answer at least 80 percent of the review questions correctly, you can probably feel comfortable moving on to the next chapter. If you can't answer that many correctly, reread the chapter, or the section that seems to be giving you trouble, and try the questions again. You'll also find more than 200 flashcard questions on the CD for on-the-go review. Download them right onto your PDA device for quick and convenient reviewing.

NOTE

Don't rely on studying the review questions exclusively as your study method. The questions you'll see on the exam will be different from the questions presented in the book. There are 200 randomly generated questions on the PMP exam and 150 on the CAPM, so it isn't possible to cover every potential exam question in the Review Questions section of each chapter. Make sure you understand the concepts behind the material presented in each chapter and memorize all the formulas as well.

In addition to the assessment test and the review questions, you'll find bonus exams on the CD. Take these practice exams just as if you were actually taking the exam (that is, without any reference material). When you have finished the first exam, move on to the next exam to solidify your test-taking skills. If you get more than 85 percent of the answers correct, you're ready to take the real exam.

The CD also contains an audio file that you can download to your favorite MP3 player to hear a recap of the key elements covered in each chapter.

Finally, you will notice various Real-World Scenario sidebars throughout each chapter. These are designed to give you insight into how the various processes and topic areas apply to real-world situations.

Additionally, if you are going to travel but still need to study for the PMP exam and you have a laptop with a CD drive, you can take this entire book with you just by taking the CD. This book is available in PDF (Adobe Acrobat), so it can be easily read on any computer.

NOTE: Also on the CD in PDF is the appendix, "Process Inputs and Outputs."

For those of you who purchased the Deluxe Edition, you'll find a series of scenarios and exercises that map to each chapter. These workbook exercises are designed to help you put the theories you've learned in each chapter into practice.

The Exam Objectives

Behind every certification exam, you can be sure to find exam objectives—the broad topics in which the exam developers want to ensure your competency. The official PMP exam objectives are listed at the beginning of every chapter in this book.

NOTE: Exam objectives are subject to change at any time without prior notice and at PMI's sole discretion. Please visit the Certification page of the PMI's website, www.pmi.org, for the most current listing of exam objectives.

How to Contact the Author

I welcome your feedback about this book or about books you'd like to see from me in the future. You can reach me at Kim.Heldman@comcast.net. For more information about my work, please visit my website at KimHeldman.com.

Sybex strives to keep you supplied with the latest tools and information you need for your work. Please check the website at `www.sybex.com`, where we'll post additional content and updates that supplement this book if the need arises. Enter ***PMP Project Management Professional Study Guide*** in the Search box (or type the book's ISBN—9780470455586), and click Go to get to the book's update page.

Assessment Test

1. The project sponsor has approached you with a dilemma. The CEO announced at the annual stockholders meeting that the project you're managing will be completed by the end of this year. The problem is that this is six months prior to the scheduled completion date. It's too late to go back and correct her mistake, and stockholders are expecting implementation by the announced date. You must speed up the delivery date of this project. Your primary constraint before this occurred was the budget. Choose the best action from the options listed to speed up the project.

   A. Hire more resources to get the work completed faster.

   B. Ask for more money so that you can contract out one of the phases you had planned to do with in-house resources.

   C. Utilize negotiation and influencing skills to convince the project sponsor to speak with the CEO and make a correction to her announcement.

   D. Examine the project plan to see whether there are any phases that can be fast tracked, and then revise the project plan to reflect the compression of the schedule.

2. These types of dependencies can create arbitrary total float values and limit your scheduling options.

   A. Discretionary

   B. External

   C. Mandatory

   D. Hard logic

3. Project managers spend what percentage of their time communicating?

   A. 90

   B. 85

   C. 75

   D. 50

4. Inspections are also called each of the following except for which one?

   A. Reviews

   B. Assessment

   C. Walk-throughs

   D. Audits

5. The primary function of the Closing processes is to perform which of the following?

   A. Formalize lessons learned and distribute this information to project participants.

   B. Perform audits to verify the project results against the project requirements.

   C. Formalize project completion and disseminate this information to project participants.

   D. Perform post-implementation audits to document project successes and failures.

6. During your project meeting, a problem was discussed, and a resolution to the problem was reached. During the meeting, the participants started wondering why they thought the problem was such a big issue. Sometime after the meeting, you received an email from one of the meeting participants saying they've changed their mind about the solution reached in the meeting and need to resurface the problem. The solution reached during the initial project meeting is a result of which of the following conflict resolution techniques?

   A. Confrontation

   B. Forcing

   C. Smoothing

   D. Storming

7. What are decision models?

   A. Project selection criteria

   B. Project selection methods

   C. Project selection committees

   D. Project resource and budget selection methods

8. You've been assigned as a project manager on a research and development project for a new dental procedure. You're working in the Scope Management Knowledge Area. What is the purpose of the project scope management plan?

   A. The project scope management plan describes and documents a scope baseline to help make future project decisions.

   B. The project scope management plan decomposes project deliverables into smaller units of work.

   C. The project scope management plan describes how project scope will be developed and how changes will be managed.

   D. The project scope management plan describes how cost and time estimates will be developed for project scope changes.

9. All of the following statements are true regarding Ishikawa diagrams in the Identify Risks process except which one?

   A. Ishikawa diagrams are also called *cause-and-effect diagrams.*

   B. Ishikawa diagrams are also called *fishbone diagrams.*

   C. Ishikawa diagrams are part of the diagramming tool and technique of this process.

   D. Ishikawa diagrams show the steps needed to identify the risk.

10. All of the following are outputs of the Perform Integrated Change Control process except for which one?

   A. Change request status updates

   B. Project management plan updates

   C. Organizational process assets updates

   D. Project document updates

11. What is one of the most important skills a project manager can have?
   A. Negotiation skills
   B. Influencing skills
   C. Communication skills
   D. Problem-solving skills

12. All of the following are a type of project ending except for which one?
   A. Extinction
   B. Starvation
   C. Desertion
   D. Addition

13. You are the project manager for a construction company that is building a new city and county office building in your city. Your CCB recently approved a scope change. You know that scope change might come about as a result of all of the following except which one?
   A. Schedule revisions
   B. Product scope change
   C. Changes to the agreed-upon WBS
   D. Changes to the project requirements

14. You are the project manger for Xylophone Phonics. It produces children's software programs that teach basic reading and math skills. You're performing cost estimates for your project and don't have a lot of details yet. Which of the following techniques should you use?
   A. Analogous estimating techniques, because this is a form of expert judgment that uses historical information from similar projects
   B. Bottom-up estimating techniques, because this is a form of expert judgment that uses historical information from similar projects
   C. Monte Carlo analysis, because this is a modeling technique that uses simulation to determine estimates
   D. Parametric modeling, because this is a form of simulation used to determine estimates

15. Project managers have the highest level of authority and the most power in which type of organizational structure?
   A. Projectized
   B. Strong matrix
   C. Functional
   D. Balanced matrix

16. This process is concerned with determining the information stakeholders will need throughout the project and the methods of communication.

    A. Distribute Information

    B. Report Performance

    C. Plan Communications

    D. Identify Stakeholder Needs

17. All of the following statements are true regarding risk events except which one? Choose the least correct answer.

    A. Project risks are uncertain events.

    B. If risks occur, they can have a positive or negative effect on project objectives.

    C. Unknown risks are threats to the project objectives, and nothing can be done to plan for them.

    D. Risks that have more perceived rewards to the organization than consequences should be accepted.

18. This process applies evaluation criteria to the bids and proposals received from potential vendors.

    A. Plan Procurements

    B. Administer Procurements

    C. Conduct Procurements

    D. Perform Quality Assurance

19. You are the project manger for Xylophone Phonics. This company produces children's software programs that teach basic reading and math skills. You are ready to assign project roles, responsibilities, and reporting relationships. Which project Planning process are you working on?

    A. Estimate Activity Resources

    B. Develop Human Resource Plan

    C. Acquire Project Team

    D. Plan Organizational Resources

20. You know that PV = 470, AC = 430, EV = 480, EAC = 500, and BAC = 525. What is VAC?

    A. 70

    B. 20

    C. 25

    D. 30

21. You are a project manager who has recently held a project team kickoff meeting where all the team members were formally introduced to each other. Some of the team members know each other from other projects and have been working with you for the past three weeks. Which of the following statements is true?

   A. Team building improves the knowledge and skills of team members.

   B. Team building builds feelings of trust and agreement among team members, which can improve morale.

   C. Team building can create a dynamic environment and cohesive culture to improve productivity of both the team and the project.

   D. Team building occurs throughout the life of the project and can establish clear expectations and behaviors for project team members, leading to increased productivity.

22. You are a project manager for the Swirling Seas Cruises food division. You're considering two different projects regarding food services on the cruise lines. The initial cost of Project Fish'n for Chips will be $800,000, with expected cash inflows of $300,000 per quarter. Project Picnic's payback period is six months. Which project should you recommend?

   A. Project Fish'n for Chips, because its payback period is two months shorter than Project Picnic's

   B. Project Fish'n for Chips, because the costs on Project Picnic are unknown

   C. Project Picnic, because Project Fish'n for Chips's payback period is four months longer than Project Picnic's.

   D. Project Picnic, because Project Fish'n for Chips's payback period is two months longer than Project Picnic's.

23. Which of the following compression techniques increases risk?

   A. Crashing

   B. Resource leveling

   C. Fast tracking

   D. Lead and lag

24. Name the ethical code you'll be required to adhere to as a PMP.

   A. *Project Management Policy and Ethics Code*

   B. *PMI Standards and Ethics Code of Conduct*

   C. *Project Management Code of Professional Ethics*

   D. *PMI Code of Ethics and Professional Conduct*

25. You have been assigned to a project that will allow job seekers to fill out applications and submit them via the company website. You report to the VP of human resources. You are also responsible for screening applications for the information technology division and setting up interviews. The project coordinator has asked for the latest version of your changes to the online application page for his review. Which organizational structure do you work in?

    A. Functional organization

    B. Weak matrix organization

    C. Projectized organization

    D. Balanced matrix organization

26. You are the project manager for Lucky Stars Candies. You've identified the requirements for the project and documented them where?

    A. In the requirements document, which will be used as an input to the Create WBS process

    B. In the project scope statement, which is used as an input to the Create WBS process

    C. In the product requirements document, which is an output of the Define Scope process

    D. In the project specifications document, which is an output of the Define Scope process

27. What is the purpose of the project charter?

    A. To recognize and acknowledge the project sponsor

    B. To recognize and acknowledge the existence of the project and commit organizational resources to the project

    C. To acknowledge the existence of the project team, project manager, and project sponsor

    D. To describe the selection methods used to choose this project over its competitors

28. Which of the following are tools and techniques of the Identify Stakeholder process?

    A. Stakeholder analysis and expert judgment

    B. Stakeholder analysis, expert judgment, and stakeholder register

    C. Stakeholder analysis

    D. Stakeholder analysis, stakeholder management strategy, and expert judgment

29. You are a project manager working on a software development project. You've developed the risk management plan, identified risks, and determined risk responses for the risks. A risk event occurs, and you implement the response. Then, another risk event occurs as a result of the response you implemented. What type of risk is this called?

    A. Trigger risk

    B. Residual risk

    C. Secondary risk

    D. Mitigated risk

30. You are working on a project that will upgrade the phone system in your customer service center. You have used analogous estimating, parametric estimating, bottom-up estimating, and three-point estimates to determine activity costs. Which process does this describe?

 A. Estimating Activity Resources

 B. Estimate Costs

 C. Determine Budget

 D. Estimating Activity Costs

31. Failure costs are also known as which of the following?

 A. Internal costs

 B. Cost of poor quality

 C. Cost of keeping defects out of the hands of customers

 D. Prevention costs

32. Feeding buffers and the project buffer are part of which of the following Develop Schedule tool and technique?

 A. Critical path method

 B. Schedule network analysis

 C. Applying leads and lags

 D. Critical chain method

33. You are working on a project that will upgrade the phone system in your customer service center. You have used bottom-up estimating techniques to assign costs to the project activities and have determined the cost performance baseline. Which of the following statements is true?

 A. You have completed the Estimate Cost process and now need to complete the Determine Budget process to develop the project's cost performance baseline.

 B. You have completed the Estimate Cost process and established a cost performance baseline to measure future project performance against.

 C. You have completed the Determine Budget process and now need to complete the Schedule Development process to establish a project baseline to measure future project performance against.

 D. You have completed the Determine Budget process, and the cost performance baseline will be used to measure future project performance.

34. Each of the following statements describes an element of the Develop Project Management Plan process except for which one?

 A. Project charter

 B. Outputs from other planning processes

 C. Configuration management system

 D. Organizational process assets

35. There are likely to be team loyalty issues in a matrixed environment. All of the following are true regarding this situation as it pertains to the Manage Project Team process except for which one?

   A. Two of the tools and techniques you might use to manage these relationships effectively are communications methods and conflict management.

   B. In this type of structure, team members report to both a functional manager and a project manager. Both managers should have input to the project performance appraisal for this team member, which is a tool and technique of this process.

   C. The project manager is generally responsible for managing this relationship.

   D. The effective management of these reporting relationships is often a critical success factor for the project.

36. Monte Carlo analysis can help predict the impact of risks on project deliverables. This is an element of one of the tools and techniques of which of the following processes?

   A. Plan Risk Responses

   B. Perform Quantitative Risk Analysis

   C. Identify Risks

   D. Perform Qualitative Risk Analysis

37. All of the following statements are true regarding configuration management except which one?

   A. Configuration management requires acceptance decisions for all change requests to be made through the CCB.

   B. Change control systems are a subset of the configuration management system.

   C. Configuration management focuses on the specifications of the deliverables of the project.

   D. Configuration management validates and improves the project by evaluating the impact of each change.

38. Which performance measurement tells you what the projected total cost of the project will be at completion?

   A. ETC

   B. EV

   C. AC

   D. EAC

39. Which of the following contracts should you use for projects that have a degree of uncertainty and require a large investment early in the project life cycle?

   A. Fixed price

   B. Cost reimbursable

   C. Lump sum

   D. T&M

40. According to the *PMBOK® Guide*, the project manager is identified and assigned during which process?
   A. During the Develop Project Charter process
   B. At the conclusion of the Develop Project Charter process
   C. Prior to beginning the Planning processes
   D. Prior to beginning the Define Scope process

41. All of the following are tools and techniques of the Close Procurements process except for which one?
   A. Expert judgment
   B. Procurement audits
   C. Negotiated settlements
   D. Records management system

42. The inputs of the Report Performance process include all of the following except for which one?
   A. Work performance information
   B. Work performance measurements
   C. Budget forecasts
   D. Performance reviews

43. All of the following statements are true regarding risks except for which one?
   A. Risks might be threats to the objectives of the project.
   B. Risks are certain events that may be threats or opportunities to the objectives of the project.
   C. Risks might be opportunities to the objectives of the project.
   D. Risks have causes and consequences.

44. Which performance measurement tells you the cost of the work that has been authorized and budgeted for a WBS component?
   A. PV
   B. EV
   C. AC
   D. BCWP

45. Which of the following statements is true regarding the Project Management Knowledge Areas?
   A. They include Initiation, Planning, Executing, Monitoring and Controlling, and Closing.
   B. They consist of nine areas that bring together processes that have things in common.
   C. They consist of five processes that bring together phases of projects that have things in common.
   D. They include Planning, Executing, and Monitoring and Controlling processes because these three processes are commonly interlinked.

46. You have just prepared an RFP for release. Your project involves a substantial amount of contract work detailed in the RFP. Your favorite vendor drops by and offers to give you and your spouse the use of their company condo for your upcoming vacation. It's located in a beautiful resort community that happens to be one of your favorite places to go for a get-away. What is the most appropriate response?

  A. Thank the vendor, but decline the offer because you know this could be considered a conflict of interest.

  B. Thank the vendor, and accept. This vendor is always offering you incentives like this, so this offer does not likely have anything to do with the recent RFP release.

  C. Thank the vendor, accept the offer, and immediately tell your project sponsor so they're aware of what you're doing.

  D. Thank the vendor, but decline the offer because you've already made another arrangement for this vacation. Ask them whether you can take a rain check and arrange another time to use the condo.

47. What are the Define Scope process tools and techniques?

  A. Cost benefit analysis, scope baseline, expert judgment, and facilitated workshops

  B. Product analysis, alternatives identification, and expert judgment

  C. Product analysis, alternatives identification, expert judgment, and facilitated workshops

  D. Alternatives identification, stakeholder analysis, and expert judgment

48. You are the project manager for Heartthrobs by the Numbers Dating Services. You're working on an updated Internet site that will display pictures as well as short bios of prospective heartbreakers. You have your activity list and resource requirements in hand and are planning to use parametric estimates and reserve analysis to determine activity durations. Which of the following statements is true?

  A. You are using inputs from the Estimate Activity Duration process.

  B. You are using tools and techniques of the Estimate Cost process.

  C. You are using tools and techniques of the Estimate Activity Durations process.

  D. You are using inputs of the Estimate Costs process.

49. Your team is developing the risk management plan. Which tool and technique of this process is used to develop risk cost elements and schedule activities that will be included in the project budget and schedule?

  A. Planning meetings and analysis

  B. Strategies for both threats and opportunities

  C. Information gathering techniques

  D. Risk data quality assessment

50. What type of organization experiences the least amount of stress during project closeout?

  A. Projectized

  B. Functional

  C. Weak matrix

  D. Strong matrix

51. You are the project manager for Xylophone Phonics. It produces children's software programs that teach basic reading and math skills. You are performing the Plan Quality process and are identifying nonproductive activities. Part of this involves capturing information such as process boundaries, process configurations, and process metrics. Which of the following does this describe?

   A. The process improvement plan

   B. The quality management plan

   C. The quality metrics

   D. The cost of quality

52. You need to convey some very complex, detailed information to the project stakeholders. What is the best method for communicating this kind of information?

   A. Verbal

   B. Vertical

   C. Horizontal

   D. Written

53. You are the project manager for Heartthrobs by the Numbers Dating Services. You're working on an updated Internet site that will display pictures as well as short bios of prospective heartbreakers. You've just completed your project staff assignments and published the project team directory. Which process are you in?

   A. Develop Human Resource Plan

   B. Manage Project Team

   C. Develop Project Team

   D. Acquire Project Team

54. You are a project manager for Waterways Houseboats, Inc. You've been asked to perform a cost-benefit analysis for two proposed projects. Project A costs $2.4 million, with potential benefits of $12 million and future operating costs of $3 million. Project B costs $2.8 million, with potential benefits of $14 million and future operating costs of $2 million. Which project should you recommend?

   A. Project A, because the cost to implement is cheaper than Project B

   B. Project A, because the potential benefits plus the future operating costs are less in value than the same calculation for Project B

   C. Project B, because the potential benefits minus the implementation and future operating costs are greater in value than the same calculation for Project A

   D. Project B, because the potential benefits minus the costs to implement are greater in value than the same calculation for Project A

55. These diagrams rank-order factors for corrective action by frequency of occurrence. They are also a type of histogram.

A. Control charts

B. Process flowcharts

C. Scatter diagrams

D. Pareto charts

56. You are a project manager working in a foreign country. You observe that some of your project team members are having a difficult time adjusting to the new culture. You provided them with training on cultural differences and the customs of this country before arriving, but they still seem uncomfortable and disoriented. Which of the following statements is true?

A. This is the result of working with teams of people from two different countries.

B. This condition is known as *culture shock*.

C. This is the result of jet lag and travel fatigue.

D. This condition is known as *global culturalism*.

57. Your project involves the research and development of a new food additive. You're ready to release the product to your customer when you discover that a minor reaction might occur in people with certain conditions. The reactions to date have been very minor, and no known long-lasting side effects have been noted. As project manager, what should you do?

A. Do nothing because the reactions are so minor that very few people will be affected.

B. Inform the customer that you've discovered this condition and tell them you'll research it further to determine its impacts.

C. Inform your customer that there is no problem with the additive except for an extremely small percentage of the population and release the product to them.

D. Tell the customer you'll correct the reaction problems in the next batch, but you'll release the first batch of product to them now to begin using.

58. The project manager has the greatest influence over quality during which process?

A. Plan Quality

B. Perform Quality Assurance

C. Perform Quality Control

D. Perform Quality Change Control

59. You are the project manager for a construction company that is building a new city and county office building in your city. You recently looked over the construction site to determine whether the work to date was conforming to the requirements and quality standards. Which tool and technique of the Perform Quality Control process are you using?

A. Defect repair review

B. Inspection

C. Sampling

D. Quality audit

60. All of the following statements are true of the project Closing processes except for which one?

 A. Probability for success is greatest in the project Closing processes.

 B. The project manager's influence is greatest in the project Closing processes.

 C. The stakeholders' influence is least in the project Closing processes.

 D. Risk is greatest in the project Closing processes.

61. You are refining the product description for your company's new line of ski boots. Which of the following statements is true?

 A. You are in the Initiating processes of your project and know that the product description will contain more detail in this stage and that a decreasing amount of detail will be added to it as the project progresses.

 B. You are in the Planning processes of your project and know that the product description will contain less detail in this stage and greater detail as the project progresses.

 C. You are in the Planning processes of your project and know that the product description should contain the most detail possible at this stage because this is critical information for the Planning process.

 D. You are in the Initiating process of your project and know that the product description will contain less detail in this stage and greater detail as the project progresses.

62. Every status meeting should have time allotted for Risk Monitoring and Control. Which of the following sentences is not true?

 A. Risk identification and monitoring should occur throughout the life of the project.

 B. Risk audits should occur throughout the life of the project and are specifically interested in measuring the team's performance in the Identify Risk and Monitor and Control Risk processes.

 C. Risks should be monitored for their status and to determine whether the impacts to the objectives have changed.

 D. Technical performance measurement variances may indicate that a risk is looming and should be reviewed at status meetings.

63. The business need, product scope description, and strategic plan together describe elements of which of the following?

 A. Organizational process assets

 B. Tools and techniques of the Initiating processes

 C. The project statement of work

 D. The project charter

64. Which of the following statements is true regarding constraints and assumptions?

A. Constraints restrict the actions of the project team, and assumptions are considered true for planning purposes.

B. Constraints are considered true for planning purposes, and assumptions limit the options of the project team.

C. Constraints consider vendor availability and resource availability to be true for planning purposes. Assumptions limit the project team to work within predefined budgets or timelines.

D. Constraints and assumptions are inputs to the Initiation process. They should be documented because they will be used throughout the project Planning process.

65. People are motivated by the need for achievement, power, or affiliation according to which theory?

A. Expectancy Theory

B. Achievement Theory

C. Contingency Theory

D. Theory X

66. As a result of a face-to-face meeting you recently had to discuss the items in your issue log, you have resolved issues and come away with an approved corrective action and an update to the project management plan. Which process does this describe?

A. Manage Stakeholder Expectations

B. Report Performance

C. Distribute Information

D. Manage Project Team

67. You've just completed the WBS. Which of the following statements is true?

A. The WBS breaks the project deliverables down to a level where alternatives identification can be used to determine how level-two assignments should be made.

B. The WBS breaks the project deliverables down to a level where project constraints and assumptions can be easily identified.

C. The WBS breaks the project deliverables down to the work package level, where product analysis can be documented.

D. The WBS breaks the project deliverables down to the work package level, where cost and time estimates can be easily determined.

68. As a PMP, one of your responsibilities is to ensure integrity on the project. When your personal interests are put above the interests of the project or when you use your influence to cause others to make decisions in your favor without regard for the project outcome, this is considered which of the following?

A. Conflict of interest

B. Using professional knowledge inappropriately

C. Culturally unacceptable

D. Personal conflict issue

69. Which of the following describes the Executing process group?
   A. Project plans are put into action.
   B. Project performance measurements are taken and analyzed.
   C. Project plans are developed.
   D. Project plans are published.

70. All of the following statements are true regarding the ADM method except which one?
   A. The ADM method is a tool and technique of Sequence Activities.
   B. The ADM method uses one time estimate to determine durations.
   C. The ADM method is also called AOA.
   D. The ADM method is rarely used today.

Answers to Assessment Test

1. D. Fast tracking is the best answer in this scenario. Budget was the original constraint on this project, so it's unlikely the project manager would get more resources to assist with the project. The next best thing is to compress phases to shorten the project duration. For more information, please see Chapter 1 and Chapter 7.

2. A. Discretionary dependencies can create arbitrary total float values and they can also limit scheduling options. For more information, please see Chapter 4.

3. A. Project managers spend about 90 percent of their time communicating through status meetings, team meetings, email, verbal communications, and so on. For more information, please see Chapter 9.

4. B. Inspections are also called reviews, peer reviews, walk-throughs, and audits. For more information, please see Chapter 11.

5. C. The primary function of the Closing processes is to formalize project completion and disseminate this information to the project participants. For more information, please see Chapter 12.

6. C. The smoothing technique does not usually result in a permanent solution. The problem is downplayed to make it seem less important than it is, which makes the problem tend to resurface later. For more information, please see Chapter 8.

7. B. Decision models are project selection methods used as tools and techniques in the Develop Project Charter process. Decision models include benefit measurement methods and mathematical models. For more information, please see Chapter 2.

8. C. The scope management plan outlines how project scope will be managed and how changes will be incorporated into the project. For more information, please see Chapter 3.

9. D. Cause-and-effect diagrams—also called *Ishikawa* or *fishbone diagrams*—show the relationship between the effects of problems and their causes. Kaoru Ishikawa developed cause-and-effect diagrams. For more information, please see Chapter 6.

10. C. The outputs of this process are change request status updates, project management plan updates, and project document updates. For more information, please see Chapter 10.

11. C. Negotiation, influencing, and problem-solving skills are all important for a project manager to possess. However, good communication skills are the most important skills a project manager can have. For more information, please see Chapter 1.

12. C. The four types of project endings are addition, integration, starvation, and extinction. For more information, please see Chapter 12.

13. A. Scope changes will cause schedule revisions, but schedule revisions do not change the project scope. Project requirements are part of the project scope statement, and therefore D is one of the correct responses. For more information, please see Chapter 11.

14. A. Analogous estimating—also called *top-down estimating*—is a form of expert judgment. Analogous estimating can be used to estimate cost or time and considers historical information from previous, similar projects. For more information, please see Chapter 4.

15. A. Project managers have the highest level of power and authority in a projectized organization. They also have high levels of power and authority in a strong matrix organization but a matrix organization is a blend of functional and projectized organizations. Therefore, the project manager has the most authority and power in a projectized organization. For more information, please see Chapter 1.

16. C. Plan Communications is concerned with determining stakeholder information needs and defining the technology, methods, and models you'll use to transfer the information. For more information, please see Chapter 5.

17. C. Unknown risks might be threats or opportunities to the project, and the project manager should set aside contingency reserves to deal with them. For more information, please see Chapter 6.

18. C. The Plan Procurements process is where bids and proposals are received from potential vendors and source selection criteria are applied to them to make a selection. For more information, please see Chapter 9.

19. B. The Develop Human Resource Plan process identifies project resources, documents roles and responsibilities of project team members, and documents reporting relationships. For more information, please see Chapter 7.

20. C. VAC is calculated this way: VAC = BAC – EAC. Therefore, 525 – 500 = 25. For more information, please see Chapter 11.

21. D. Team building does occur throughout the life of the project, but it's ground rules that establish clear expectations and behaviors for project team members. For more information, please see Chapter 8.

22. D. The payback period for Project Fish'n for Chips is eight months. This project will receive $300,000 every three months, or $100,000 per month. The $800,000 will be paid back in eight months. For more information, please see Chapter 2.

23. C. Fast tracking is a compression technique that increases risk and potentially causes rework. Fast tracking is starting two activities previously scheduled to start one after the other at the same time. For more information, please see Chapter 4.

24. D. The *PMI Code of Ethics and Professional Conduct* is published by PMI, and all PMPs are expected to adhere to its standards. For more information, please see Chapter 12.

25. B. Functional managers who have a lot of authority and power working with project coordinators who have minimal authority and power characterizes a weak matrix organization. Project managers in weak matrix organizations are sometimes called *project coordinators*, *project leaders*, or *project expeditors*. For more information, please see Chapter 1.

26. A. The requirements document contains a list of requirements for the project along with other important information regarding the requirements. For more information, please see Chapter 3.

27. B. The purpose of a project charter is to recognize and acknowledge the existence of a project and commit resources to the project. The charter names the project manager and project sponsor, but that's not its primary purpose. For more information, please see Chapter 2.

28. A. Identify Stakeholders tools and techniques are stakeholder analysis and expert judgment. For more information, please see Chapter 2.

29. C. Secondary risk events occur as a result of the implementation of a response to another risk. For more information, please see Chapter 6.

30. B. Estimate Costs is where activity costs are estimated using some of the tools and techniques listed in the question. The remaining tools and techniques of this process are expert judgment, reserve analysis, cost of quality, project management estimating software, and vendor bid analysis. For more information, please see Chapter 5.

31. B. Failure costs are associated with the cost of quality and are also known as cost of poor quality. For more information, please see Chapter 7.

32. D. The critical chain is a resource-constrained critical path that adds duration buffers to help protect schedule slippage. For more information, please see Chapter 4.

33. D. The Determine Budget process establishes the cost baseline, which is used to measure and track the project throughout the remaining process groups. For more information, please see Chapter 5.

34. C. The inputs to Develop Project Management Plan include project charter, outputs from planning processes, enterprise environmental factors, and organizational process assets. The only tool and technique of this process is expert judgment. For more information, please see Chapter 3.

35. A. Communications methods are a tool and technique of the Manage Stakeholders process. The tools and techniques of the Manage Project Team process are observation and conversation, project performance appraisals, conflict management, issue log, and interpersonal skills. For more information, please see Chapter 8.

36. B. Monte Carlo analysis is a modeling and simulation technique that is a tool and technique of the Perform Quantitative Risk Analysis process. For more information, please see Chapter 6.

37. A. Change control systems are a subset of the configuration management system. Change requests should be approved by the CCB, but in the case of an emergency, change requests may be approved by the project manager in accordance with the process outlined in the configuration management system. The project team might have discretion to approve changes within certain parameters without CCB approval. For more information, please see Chapter 10.

38. D. Estimate at completion (EAC) estimates the total cost of the project at completion based on the performance of the project to date. For more information, please see Chapter 11.

39. B. Cost-reimbursable contracts are used when the degree of uncertainty is high and when the project requires a large investment prior to completion. For more information, please see Chapter 7.

40. A. According to the *PMBOK® Guide*, the project manager should be assigned during the development of the project charter, which occurs in the Develop Project Charter process. For more information, please see Chapter 2.

41. A. The tools and techniques of Close Procurements are procurement audits, negotiated settlements, and records management systems. For more information, please see Chapter 12.

42. D. Performance reviews are not an input of the Report Performance process. The remaining inputs of this process are project management plan and organizational process assets. For more information, please see Chapter 10.

43. B. Risks are uncertain events that may be threats or opportunities to the objectives of the project. For more information, please see Chapter 6.

44. A. Planned value is the cost of work that has been authorized and budgeted for a schedule activity or WBS component. For more information, please see Chapter 11.

45. B. The project management Knowledge Areas bring processes together that have commonalities. For example, the Project Quality Management Knowledge Area includes the Quality Planning, Perform Quality Assurance, and Perform Quality Control processes. For more information, please see Chapter 2.

46. A. The best response is to decline the offer. This is a conflict of interest, and accepting the offer puts your own integrity and the contract award process in jeopardy. For more information, please see Chapter 12.

47. C. The tools and techniques of the Define Scope process include product analysis, alternatives identification, expert judgment, and facilitated workshops. For more information, please see Chapter 3.

48. C. Parametric estimates and reserve analysis are two of the tools and techniques of the Estimate Activity Duration process. The other tools are analogous estimating and three-point estimates. For more information, please see Chapter 4.

49. A. Planning meetings and analysis is the only tool and technique of the Project Risk Management Process. For more information, please see Chapter 6.

50. C. Weak matrix organizational structures tend to experience the least amount of stress during the project closeout processes. For more information, please see Chapter 12.

51. A. This describes the process improvement plan, which is a subsidiary of the project management plan and an output of the Plan Quality process. For more information, please see Chapter 7.

52. D. Information that is complex and detailed is best conveyed in writing. A verbal follow-up would be good to answer questions and clarify information. Vertical and horizontal are ways of communicating within the organization. For more information, please see Chapter 9.

53. D. Project staff assignments are an output of the Acquire Project Team process and it includes a team directory. For more information, please see Chapter 8.

54. C. Project B's cost-benefit analysis is a $9.2 million benefit to the company, compared to $6.6 million for Project A. Cost-benefit analysis takes into consideration the initial costs to implement and future operating costs. For more information, please see Chapter 2.

55. D. Pareto charts rank-order important factors for corrective action by frequency of occurrence. For more information, please see Chapter 11.

56. B. When people work in unfamiliar environments, culture shock can occur. Training and researching information about the country you'll be working in can help counteract this. For more information, please see Chapter 12.

57. B. Honesty and truthful reporting are required of PMPs. In this situation, you would inform the customer of everything you know regarding the problem and work to find alternative solutions. For more information, please see Chapter 12.

58. B. Perform Quality Assurance is the process where project managers have the greatest amount of influence over quality. For more information, please see Chapter 9.

59. B. Inspection involves physically looking at, measuring, or testing results to determine whether they conform to your quality standards. For more information, please see Chapter 11.

60. D. Risk is lowest during the Closing processes because you've completed the work of the project at this point. For more information, please see Chapter 12.

61. D. Product descriptions are used during the Initiating process group and contain less detail now and more detail as the project progresses. For more information, please see Chapter 2.

62. B. Risk audits should be performed throughout the life of the project and are specifically interested in looking at the implementation and effectiveness of risk strategies. For more information, please see Chapter 11.

63. C. These elements are part of the project statement of work used as an input to both of the Initiating processes. For more information, please see Chapter 2.

64. A. Constraints limit the options of the project team by restricting action or dictating action. Scope, time, and cost are the three most common constraints, and each of these has an effect on quality. Assumptions are presumed to be true for planning purposes. Always validate your assumptions. For more information, please see Chapter 3.

65. B. Achievement Theory conjectures that people are motivated by the need for achievement, power, or affiliation. For more information, please see Chapter 8.

66. A. The two clues in this question are the face-to-face meetings (a communication method) and the resolved issues, which is a primary purpose of the Manage Stakeholder Expectations process. For more information, please see Chapter 9.

67. D. The work package level is the lowest level in the work breakdown structure. Schedule and cost estimates are easily determined at this level. For more information, please see Chapter 3.

68. A. A conflict of interest is any situation that compromises the outcome of the project or ignores the impact to the project to benefit yourself or others. For more information, please see Chapter 12.

69. A. The Executing process group takes published project plans and turns them into actions to accomplish the goals of the project. For more information, please see Chapter 1.

70. B. The arrow diagramming method (ADM)—also called activity on arrow (AOA)—uses more than one time estimate to determine project duration. For more information, please see Chapter 4.

Chapter

1

What Is a Project?

Congratulations on your decision to study for and take the Project Management Institute (PMI®) Project Management Professional (PMP) certification exam (PMP® Exam). This book was written with you in mind. The focus and content of this book revolve heavily around the information contained in *A Guide to the Project Management Body of Knowledge (PMBOK® Guide), Fourth Edition*, published by PMI. I will refer to this guide throughout this book and elaborate on those areas that appear on the test. Keep in mind that the test covers all the project management processes, so don't skip anything in your study time.

When possible, I'll pass on hints and study tips that I collected while studying for the exam. My first tip is to familiarize yourself with the terminology used in *PMBOK® Guide*. Volunteers from differing industries from around the globe worked together to come up with the standards and terms used in the guide. These folks worked hard to develop and define project management terms, and these terms are used interchangeably among industries. For example, *resource planning* means the same thing to someone working in construction, information technology, or telecommunications. You'll find many of the *PMBOK® Guide* terms explained throughout this book. Even if you are an experienced project manager, you might find you use specific terms for processes or actions you regularly perform but the *PMBOK® Guide* calls them by another name. So, the first step is to get familiar with the terminology.

The next step is to become familiar with the processes as defined in the *PMBOK® Guide*. The process names are unique to PMI, but the general principles and guidelines underlying the processes are used for most projects across industry areas.

This chapter lays the foundation for building and managing your project. I'll address project and project management definitions as well as organizational structures. Good luck!

Is It a Project?

Let's start with an example of how projects come about, and later in this section, we'll look at a definition of a project. Consider the following scenario: You work for a wireless phone provider, and the VP of marketing approaches you with a fabulous idea—"fabulous" because he's the big boss and because he thought it up. He wants to set up kiosks in local grocery and big-box stores as mini-offices. These offices will offer customers the ability to sign up for new wireless phone services, make their wireless phone bill payments, and purchase equipment and accessories. He believes that the exposure in grocery stores will increase awareness of the company's offerings. After all, everyone has to eat, right? He told you that the board of directors has already cleared the project, and he'll dedicate as many resources to this as he can. He wants the new kiosks in place in 12 stores by the end of this year. The best news is he has assigned you to head up this project.

Your first question should be "Is it a project?" This might seem elementary, but confusing projects with ongoing operations happens often. Projects are temporary in nature; have definite start and end dates; produce a unique product, service, or result; and are completed when their goals and objectives have been met and signed off by the stakeholders.

When considering whether you have a project on your hands, you need to keep some issues in mind. First, is it a project or an ongoing operation? Next, if it is a project, who are the stakeholders? And third, what characteristics distinguish this endeavor as a project? We'll look at each of these next.

Projects versus Operations

Projects are temporary in nature and have definitive start dates and definitive end dates. The project is completed when its goals and objectives are accomplished to the satisfaction of the stakeholders. Sometimes projects end when it's determined that the goals and objectives cannot be accomplished or when the product, service, or result of the project is no longer needed and the project is canceled. Projects exist to bring about a product, service, or result that didn't exist before. This might include tangible products, services such as consulting or project management, and business functions that support the organization. Projects might also produce a result or an outcome, such as a document that details the findings of a research study. In this sense, a project is unique. However, don't get confused by the term *unique*. For example, Ford Motor Company is in the business of designing and assembling cars. Each model that Ford designs and produces can be considered a project. The models differ from each other in their features and are marketed to people with various needs. An SUV serves a different purpose and clientele than a luxury sedan or a hybrid. The initial design and marketing of these three models are unique projects. However, the actual assembly of the cars is considered an operation—a repetitive process that is followed for most makes and models.

Determining the characteristics and features of the different car models is carried out through what the *PMBOK® Guide* terms *progressive elaboration*. This means the characteristics of the product, service, or result of the project (the hybrid, for example) are determined incrementally and are continually refined and worked out in detail as the project progresses. More information and better estimates become available the further you progress in the project. Progressive elaboration improves the project team's ability to manage greater levels of detail and allows for the inevitable change that occurs throughout a project's life cycle. This concept goes along with the temporary and unique aspects of a project because when you first start the project, you don't know all the minute details of the end product. Product characteristics typically start out broad-based at the beginning of the project and are progressively elaborated into more and more detail over time until they are complete and finalized.

Exam Spotlight

Progressive elaboration is most often used when creating the project or product scope, developing requirements, determining human resources, scheduling, and defining risks and their mitigation plans.

Real World Scenario

The New Website Project

You've just been charged with creating a new intranet site for your organization. At the beginning of the project, you don't know a lot of detail other than the high-level purpose of the project. One of the next steps is to discover the elements that should be included on the website. For example, you might need to make available human resources policies and procedures, travel request forms, expense reimbursement forms, and so on. At this point, you are progressively elaborating the scope of the project. Each of these elements will need its own progressive elaboration process to further define its requirements and develop estimates. For example, as you interview stakeholders, you discover that travel request forms require two electronic signatures, one from the employee's supervisor and one from the section manager. Progressive elaboration continues throughout the project life cycle, including defining the requirements and scope, delivering the end product or result, and obtaining acceptance from the stakeholders.

Operations are ongoing and repetitive. They involve work that is continuous without an ending date, and you often repeat the same processes and produce the same results. The purpose of operations is to keep the organization functioning, while the purpose of a project is to meet its goals and to conclude. At the completion of a project, the end product (or result) may get turned over to the organization's operational areas for ongoing care and maintenance. For example, let's say your company implements a new human resources software package that tracks employees' time, expense reports, benefits, and so on, like the example described in the sidebar, "The New Website Project." Defining the requirements and implementing the software is a project. The ongoing maintenance of the site, updating content, and so on are ongoing operations.

It's a good idea to include some members of the operational area on the project team when certain deliverables or the end product of the project will be incorporated into their future work processes. They can assist the project team in defining requirements, developing scope, creating estimates, and so on, helping to assure that the project will meet their needs. This isn't a bad strategy in helping to gain buy-in from the end users of the product or service either. Often, business units are resistant to new systems or services, but getting them involved early in the project rather than simply throwing the end product over the fence when it's completed may help gain their acceptance.

According to the *PMBOK® Guide*, there are several examples where the deliverables from a project may integrate with business processes:

- Developing new products or services that the organization will market
- Implementing products or services that the organization will have to support as part of their ongoing operations

- Implementing projects that impact the culture, organizational structure, or staffing levels of the organization
- Implementing or enhancing an information system

The preceding list isn't all inclusive. Whenever you find yourself working on a project that ultimately impacts your organization's business processes, I recommend you get people from the business units to participate on the project.

Stakeholders

A project is successful when it achieves its objectives and meets or exceeds the expectations of the stakeholders. *Stakeholders* are those folks (or organizations) with a vested interest in your project. They are the people who are actively involved with the work of the project or have something to either gain or lose as a result of the project. Stakeholder identification is not a one-time process. You should continue to ask fellow team members and stakeholders if there are other stakeholders who should be a part of the project.

NOTE Key stakeholders can make or break the success of a project. Even if all the deliverables are met and the objectives are satisfied, if your key stakeholders aren't happy, nobody is happy.

The *project sponsor*, generally an executive in the organization with the authority to assign resources and enforce decisions regarding the project, is a stakeholder. The project sponsor generally serves as the tie-breaker decision maker and is one of the people on your escalation path. The customer is a stakeholder, as are contractors and suppliers. The project manager, the project team members, and the managers from other departments in the organization are stakeholders as well. It's important to identify all the stakeholders in your project up front. If you leave out an important stakeholder or their department's function and don't discover the error until well into the project, it could be a project killer.

Figure 1.1 shows a sample listing of the kinds of stakeholders involved in a typical project.

Many times, stakeholders have conflicting interests. It's the project manager's responsibility to understand these conflicts and try to resolve them. It's also the project manager's responsibility to manage stakeholder expectations. Be certain to identify and meet with all key stakeholders early in the project to understand their needs and constraints. And when in doubt, you should always resolve stakeholder conflicts in favor of the customer.

NOTE I'll talk more about identifying key stakeholders and their needs in Chapter 2, "Creating the Project Charter." I'll discuss managing stakeholder expectations in Chapter 9, "Conducting Procurements and Sharing Information."

FIGURE 1.1 Project stakeholders

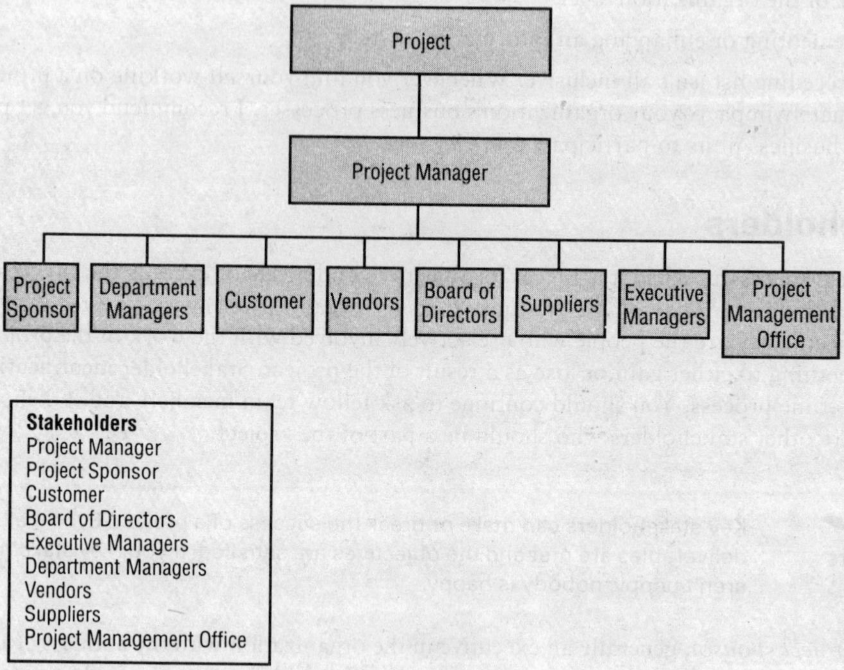

Project Characteristics

You've just learned that a project has several characteristics:

- Projects are unique.
- Projects are temporary in nature and have a definite beginning and ending date.
- Projects are completed when the project goals are achieved or it's determined the project is no longer viable.
- A successful project is one that meets or exceeds the expectations of your stakeholders.

Using these criteria, let's examine the assignment from the VP of marketing to determine whether it is a project:

Is it unique? Yes, because the kiosks don't exist now in the local grocery stores. This is a new way of offering the company's services to its customer base. Although the service the company is offering isn't new, the way it is presenting its services is.

Does the project have a limited time frame? Yes, the start date of this project is today, and the end date is the end of this year. It is a temporary endeavor.

Is there a way to determine when the project is completed? Yes, the kiosks will be installed, and services will be offered from them. Once all the kiosks are intact and operating, the project will come to a close.

Is there a way to determine stakeholder satisfaction? Yes, the expectations of the stakeholders will be documented in the form of deliverables and requirements during the planning processes. Some of the requirements the VP noted are that customers can sign up for new services, pay their bills, and purchase equipment and accessories. These deliverables and requirements will be compared to the finished product to determine whether it meets the expectations of the stakeholder.

Houston, we have a project.

What Is Project Management?

You've determined that you indeed have a project. What now? The notes you scratched on the back of a napkin during your coffee break might get you started, but that's not exactly good project management practice.

We have all witnessed this scenario—an assignment is made, and the project team members jump directly into the project, busying themselves with building the product, service, or result requested. Often, careful thought is not given to the project-planning process. I'm sure you've heard co-workers toss around statements like "That would be a waste of valuable time" or "Why plan when you can just start building?" Project progress in this circumstance is rarely measured against the customer requirements. In the end, the delivered product, service, or result doesn't meet the expectations of the customer! This is a frustrating experience for all those involved. Unfortunately, many projects follow this poorly constructed path.

Project management brings together a set of tools and techniques—performed by people—to describe, organize, and monitor the work of project activities. *Project managers* are the people responsible for managing the project processes and applying the tools and techniques used to carry out the project activities. All projects are composed of processes, even if they employ a haphazard approach. There are many advantages to organizing projects and teams around the project management processes endorsed by PMI. We'll be examining those processes and their advantages in depth throughout the remainder of this book.

According to the *PMBOK® Guide*, project management involves applying knowledge, skills, tools, and techniques during the course of the project to accomplish the project's objective. It is the responsibility of the project manager to ensure that project management techniques are applied and followed.

Exam Spotlight

Remember that according to the *PMBOK® Guide,* the definition of project management is applying tools, techniques, skills, and knowledge to project activities to bring about successful results and meet the project requirements.

Project management is a process that includes initiating a new project, planning, putting the project plan into action, and measuring progress and performance. It involves identifying the project requirements, establishing project objectives, balancing constraints, and taking the needs and expectations of the key stakeholders into consideration. Planning is one of the most important functions you'll perform during the course of a project. It sets the standard for the remainder of the project's life and is used to track future project performance. Before we begin the planning process, let's look at some of the ways the work of project management is organized.

Programs

Programs are groups of related projects that are managed using the same techniques in a coordinated fashion. When projects are managed collectively as programs, it's possible to capitalize on benefits that wouldn't be achievable if the projects were managed separately. This would be the case where a very large program exists with many subprojects under it—for example, building a new shopping mall. Many subprojects exist underneath this program, such as excavation, construction, interior design, store placement, marketing, facilities management, and so on. Each of the subprojects is really a project unto itself. Each subproject has its own project manager, who reports to a project manager with responsibility over several of the areas, who in turn reports to the head project manager who is responsible for the entire program. All the projects are related and are managed together so that collective benefits are realized and controls are implemented and managed in a coordinated fashion. Sometimes programs involve aspects of ongoing operations as well. After the shopping mall in our example is built, the management of the facility becomes an ongoing operation. The management of this collection of projects—determining their interdependencies, managing among their constraints, and resolving issues among them—is called *program management*. Program management also involves centrally managing and coordinating groups of related projects to meet the objectives of the program.

Portfolios

Portfolios are collections of programs and projects that support a specific business goal or objective. Let's say our company is in the construction business. Our organization has several business units: retail, single-family residential, and multifamily residential. Collectively, the projects within all of these business units make up the portfolio. The program I talked about in the preceding section (the collection of projects associated with building the new shopping mall) is a program within our portfolio. Other programs and projects could be within this portfolio as well. Programs and projects within a portfolio are not necessarily related to one another in a direct way. However, the overall objective of any program or project in this portfolio is to meet the strategic objectives of the portfolio, which in turn should meet the objectives of the department and ultimately the business unit or corporation.

Portfolio management encompasses managing the collections of programs, projects, other work, and sometimes other portfolios. This includes weighing the value of each project, or potential project, against the business's strategic objectives. It also concerns monitoring active projects for adherence to objectives, balancing the portfolio among the other investments of the organization, and assuring the efficient use of resources. Portfolio management is generally performed by a senior manager who has significant experience in both project and program management.

Exam Spotlight

Programs are collections of related projects. Portfolios consist of programs, projects, and other portfolios that meet a business objective. Projects or programs within a portfolio are not necessarily related or dependent on each other.

Project Management Offices

The *project management office (PMO)* is usually a centralized organizational unit that oversees the management of projects and programs throughout the organization. The most common reason a company starts a project management office is to establish and maintain procedures and standards for project management methodologies and to manage resources assigned to the projects in the PMO. In some organizations, project managers and team members might report directly to the PMO and are assigned to projects as they are initiated. In other organizations, the PMO may provide support functions for projects and train employees in project management procedures and techniques. Still others, depending on their size and function, have experts available that assist project managers in project planning, estimating, and business assumption verification tasks. They serve as mentors to junior-level project managers and act as consultants to the senior project managers.

NOTE

A PMO can exist in all organizational structures—functional, projectized, or matrix. (These structures will be discussed later in this chapter.) It might have full authority to oversee projects, including the authority to cancel projects, or it might serve only in an advisory role. PMOs might also be called *project offices* or *program management offices* or *Centers of Excellence*.

The PMO usually has responsibility for maintaining and archiving project documentation for future reference. This office compares project goals with project progress and gives feedback to the project teams. It also measures the project performance of active projects and suggests corrective actions. The PMO evaluates completed projects for their adherence to the project plan and asks questions like, "Did the project meet the time frames established?" and "Did it stay within budget?" and "Was the quality acceptable?"

NOTE Project managers are typically responsible for meeting the objectives of the project they are managing, controlling the resources within the project, and managing the individual project constraints. The PMO is responsible for managing the objectives of a collective set of projects, managing resources across the projects, and managing the interdependencies of all the projects within the PMOs authority.

Project management offices are common in organizations today, if for no other reason than to serve as a collection point for project documentation. Some PMOs are fairly sophisticated and prescribe the standards and methodologies to be used in all project phases across the enterprise. Still others provide all these functions and also offer project management consulting services. However, the establishment of a PMO is not required in order for you to apply good project management practices to your next project.

There Ought to Be a Law

The importance of practicing sound project management techniques has grown significantly over the past several years. The state of Colorado recently passed legislation requiring project managers on large projects conducted by state employees or vendors working on behalf of the state to be certified in project management best practices. This was an attempt to increase the probability of project success and reduce risk. We all know that certified project managers are not a guarantee of project success. But the state of Colorado will likely see more projects delivered on time, on budget, and within scope because of the application of best practices in this area and because their project managers are highly trained and have a great deal of experience at managing projects.

Skills Every Good Project Manager Needs

Many times, organizations will knight their technical experts as project managers. The skill and expertise that made them stars in their technical fields are mistakenly thought to translate into project management skills. This is not necessarily so.

Project managers are generalists with many skills in their repertoires. They are also problem solvers who wear many hats. Project managers might indeed possess technical skills, but technical skills are not a prerequisite for sound project management skills. Your project team should include a few technical experts, and these are the people on whom the project manager will rely for technical details. Understanding and applying good project management techniques, along with a solid understanding of general management skills, are career builders for all aspiring project managers.

Project managers have been likened to small-business owners. They need to know a little bit about every aspect of management. General management skills include every area of management, from accounting to strategic planning, supervision, personnel administration, and more. General management skills are called into play on every project. But some projects require specific skills in certain application areas. Application areas consist of categories of projects that have common elements. These elements, or application areas, can be defined several ways: by industry group (automotive, pharmaceutical), by department (accounting, marketing), and by technical (software development, engineering) or management (procurement, research and development) specialties. These application areas are usually concerned with disciplines, regulations, and the specific needs of the project, the customer, or the industry. For example, most governments have specific procurement rules that apply to their projects that wouldn't be applicable in the construction industry. The pharmaceutical industry is acutely interested in regulations set forth by the Food and Drug Administration. The automotive industry has little or no concern for either of these types of regulations. Having experience in the application area you're working in will give you a leg up when it comes to project management. Although you can call in the experts who have application area knowledge, it doesn't hurt for you to understand the specific aspects of the application areas of your project.

The general management skills listed in the following sections are the foundation of good project management practices. Your mastery of them (or lack thereof) will likely affect project outcomes. The various skills of a project manager can be broken out in a more or less declining scale of importance. We'll look at an overview of these skills now, and I'll discuss each in more detail in subsequent chapters.

Communication Skills

One of the single most important characteristics of a first-rate project manager is excellent communication skills. Written and oral communications are the backbone of all successful projects. Many forms of communication will exist during the life of your project. As the creator or manager of most of the project communication (project documents, meeting updates, status reports, and so on), it's your job to ensure that the information is explicit, clear, and complete so that your audience will have no trouble understanding what has been communicated. Once the information has been distributed, it is the responsibility of the person receiving the information to make sure they understand it.

> **NOTE** Many forms of communication and communication styles exist. I'll discuss them more in depth in Chapter 8, "Acquiring the Project Team."

Organizational and Planning Skills

Organizational and planning skills are closely related and probably the most important skills, after communication skills, a project manager can possess. Organization takes on many forms. As project manager, you'll have project documentation, requirements information, memos, project reports, personnel records, vendor quotes, contracts, and much more to track and be able to locate at a moment's notice. You will also have to organize meetings, put together teams, and perhaps manage and organize media-release schedules, depending on your project.

Time management skills are closely related to organizational skills. It's difficult to stay organized without an understanding of how you're managing your time. I recommend you attend a time management class if you've never been to one. They have some great tips and techniques to help you prioritize problems and interruptions, prioritize your day, and manage your time.

I discuss planning extensively throughout the course of this book. There isn't any aspect of project management that doesn't first involve planning. Planning skills go hand in hand with organizational skills. Combining these two with excellent communication skills is almost a sure guarantee of your success in the project management field.

Budgeting Skills

Project managers establish and manage budgets and therefore need some knowledge of finance and accounting principles. Especially important in this skill area is the ability to perform cost estimates for project budgeting. Different methods are available to determine the project costs. They range from estimating individual activities and rolling the estimates up to estimating the project's cost in one big chunk. I'll discuss these methods more fully in later chapters.

After a budget is determined, you can start spending. This sounds more exciting than it actually is. Reading and understanding vendor quotes, preparing or overseeing purchase orders, and reconciling invoices are budgeting skills that the project manager will use on most projects. These costs will be linked back to project activities and expense items in the project's budget.

Conflict Management Skills

Show me a project, and I'll show you problems. All projects have some problems, as does, in fact, much of everyday life. Isn't that what they say builds character? But I digress.

Conflict management involves solving problems. Problem solving is really a twofold process. First, you must define the problem by separating the causes from the symptoms. Often when defining problems, you end up just describing the symptoms instead of really getting to the heart of what's causing the problem. To avoid that, ask yourself questions like "Is it an internal or external problem? Is it a technical problem? Are there interpersonal problems between team members? Is it managerial? What are the potential impacts or consequences?" These kinds of questions will help you get to the cause of the problem.

Next, after you have defined the problem, you have some decisions to make. It will take a little time to examine and analyze the problem, the situation causing it, and the alternatives available. After this analysis, the project manager will determine the best course of action to take and implement the decision. The timing of the decision is often as important as the decision itself. If you make a good decision but implement it too late, it might turn into a bad decision.

Negotiation and Influencing Skills

Effective problem solving requires negotiation and influencing skills. We all utilize negotiation skills in one form or another every day. For example, on a nightly basis I am asked, "Honey, what do you want for dinner?" Then the negotiations begin, and the fried chicken versus swordfish discussion commences. Simply put, negotiating is working with others to come to an agreement.

Negotiation on projects is necessary in almost every area of the project, from scope definition to budgets, contracts, resource assignments, and more. This might involve one-on-one negotiation or with teams of people, and it can occur many times throughout the project.

Influencing is convincing the other party that swordfish is a better choice than fried chicken, even if fried chicken is what they want. It's also the ability to get things done through others. Influencing requires an understanding of the formal and informal structure of all the organizations involved in the project.

Power and politics are techniques used to influence people to perform. *Power* is the ability to get people to do things they wouldn't do otherwise. It's also the ability to change minds and the course of events and to influence outcomes.

> NOTE: I'll discuss power further in Chapter 8.

Politics involve getting groups of people with different interests to cooperate creatively even in the midst of conflict and disorder.

These skills will be utilized in all areas of project management. Start practicing now because, guaranteed, you'll need these skills on your next project.

Leadership Skills

Leaders and *managers* are not synonymous terms. Leaders impart vision, gain consensus for strategic goals, establish direction, and inspire and motivate others. Managers focus on results and are concerned with getting the job done according to the requirements. Even though leaders and managers are not the same, project managers must exhibit the characteristics of both during different times on the project. Understanding when to switch from leadership to management and then back again is a finely tuned and necessary talent.

Team-Building and Motivating Skills

Project managers will rely heavily on team-building and motivational skills. Teams are often formed with people from different parts of the organization. These people might or might not have worked together before, so some component of team-building groundwork might involve the project manager. The project manager will set the tone for the project team and will help the team members work through the various stages of team development to become fully functional. Motivating the team, especially during long projects or when experiencing a lot of bumps along the way, is another important role the project manager fulfills during the course of the project.

An interesting caveat to the team-building role is that project managers many times are responsible for motivating team members who are not their direct reports. This has its own set of challenges and dilemmas. One way to help this situation is to ask the functional manager to allow you to participate in your project team members' performance reviews. Use the negotiation and influencing skills I talked about earlier to make sure you're part of this process.

Multiple Dimensions

Project managers are an interesting bunch. They know a little bit about a lot of topics and are excellent communicators. They have the ability to motivate people, even those who have no reason to be loyal to the project, and they can make the hard-line calls when necessary. Project managers can get caught in sticky situations that occasionally require making decisions that are good for the company (or the customer) but aren't good for certain stakeholders. These offended stakeholders will then drag their feet, and the project manager has to play the heavy in order to motivate and gain their cooperation again. Some organizations hire contract project managers to run their large, company-altering projects just because they don't want to burn out a key employee in this role. Fortunately, that doesn't happen often.

Now that you've been properly introduced to some of the skills you need in your tool kit, you'll know to be prepared to communicate, solve problems, lead, and negotiate your way through your next project.

Understanding Organizational Structures

Just as projects are unique, so are the organizations in which they're carried out. Organizations have their own styles and cultures that influence how project work is performed. One of the keys to determining the type of organization you work in is measuring how much authority senior management is willing to delegate to project managers. Although uniqueness abounds in business cultures, all organizations are structured in one of three ways: functional, projectized, or matrix. It's helpful to know and understand the organizational structure and the culture of the entity in which you're working. Companies with aggressive cultures that are comfortable in a leading-edge position within their industries are highly likely to take on risky projects. Project managers who are willing to suggest new ideas and projects that have never been undertaken before are likely to receive a warm reception in this kind of environment. Conversely, organizational cultures that are risk averse and prefer the follow-the-leader position within their industries are highly unlikely to take on risky endeavors. Project managers with risk-seeking, aggressive styles are likely to receive a cool reception in a culture like this.

The level of authority the project manager enjoys is denoted by the organizational structure. For example, a project manager within a functional organization has little to no formal authority. And their title might not be project manager; instead, they might be called a *project leader*, a *project coordinator*, or perhaps a *project expeditor*.

We'll now take a look at each of these types of organizations individually to better understand how the project management role works in each one.

Functional Organizations

One common type of organization is the *functional organization*. Chances are you have worked in this type of organization. This is probably the oldest style of organization and is therefore known as the traditional approach to organizing businesses.

Functional organizations are centered on specialties and grouped by function, which is why it's called *functional organization*. As an example, the organization might have a human resources department, finance department, marketing department, and so on. The work in these departments is specialized and requires people who have the skill sets and experiences in these specialized functions to perform specific duties for the department. Figure 1.2 shows a typical organizational chart for a functional organization.

You can see that this type of organization is set up to be a hierarchy. Staff personnel report to managers who report to department heads who report to vice presidents who report to the CEO. In other words, each employee reports to only one manager; ultimately, one person at the top is in charge. Many companies today, as well as governmental agencies, are structured in a hierarchical fashion. In organizations like this, be aware of the chain of command. A strict chain of command might exist, and the corporate culture might dictate that you follow it. Roughly translated: *Don't talk to the big boss without first talking to your boss who talks to their boss who talks to the big boss*. Wise project managers should determine whether there is a chain of command, how strictly it's enforced, and how the chain is linked before venturing outside it.

FIGURE 1.2 Functional organizational chart

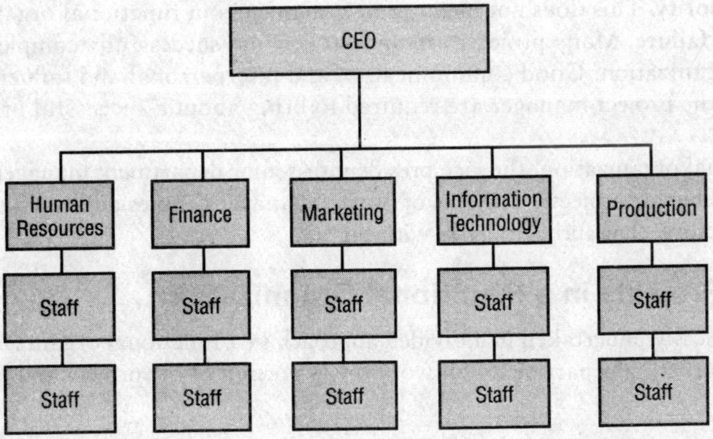

Each department or group in a functional organization is managed independently and has a limited span of control. Marketing doesn't run the finance department or its projects, for example. The marketing department is concerned with its own functions and projects. If it were necessary for the marketing department to get input from the finance department on a project, the marketing team members would follow the chain of command. A marketing manager would speak to a manager in finance to get the needed information and then pass it back down to the project team.

Human Resources in a Functional Organization

Commonalities exist among the personnel assigned to the various departments in a functional organization. In theory, people with similar skills and experiences are easier to manage as a group. Instead of scattering them throughout the organization, it is more efficient to keep them functioning together. Work assignments are easily distributed to those who are best suited for the task when everyone with the same skill works together. Usually, the supervisors and managers of these workers are experienced in the area they supervise and are able to recommend training and career enrichment activities for their employees.

NOTE Workers in functional organizations specialize in an area of expertise—finance or personnel administration, for instance—and then become very good at their specialty.

People in a functional organization can see a clear upward career path. An assistant budget analyst might be promoted to a budget analyst and then eventually to a department manager over many budget analysts.

The Downside of Functional Organizations

Functional organizations have their disadvantages. If this is the kind of organization you work in, you probably have experienced some of them.

One of the greatest disadvantages for the project manager is that they have little to no formal authority. This does not mean project managers in functional organizations are doomed to failure. Many projects are undertaken and successfully completed within this type of organization. Good communication and interpersonal and influencing skills on the part of the project manager are required to bring about a successful project under this structure.

In a functional organization, the vice president or senior department manager is usually the one responsible for projects. The title of project manager denotes authority, and in a functional structure, that authority rests with the VP.

Managing Projects in a Functional Organization

Projects are typically undertaken in a divided approach in a functional organization. For example, the marketing department will work on its portion of the project and then hand it off to the manufacturing department to complete its part, and so on. The work the marketing department does is considered a marketing project, while the work the manufacturing department does is considered a manufacturing project.

Some projects require project team members from different departments to work together at the same time on various aspects of the project. Project team members in this structure will more than likely remain loyal to their functional managers. The functional manager is responsible for their performance reviews, and their career opportunities lie within the functional department—not within the project team. Exhibiting leadership skills by forming a common vision regarding the project and the ability to motivate people to work toward that vision are great skills to exercise in this situation. As previously mentioned, it also doesn't hurt to have the project manager work with the functional manager in contributing to the employee's performance review.

Resource Pressures in a Functional Organization

Competition for resources and project priorities can become fierce when multiple projects are undertaken within a functional organization. For example, in my organization, it's common to have competing project requests from three or more departments all vying for the same resources. Thrown into the heap is the requirement to make, for example, mandated tax law changes, which automatically usurps all other priorities. This sometimes causes frustration and political infighting. One department thinks their project is more important than another and will do anything to get that project pushed ahead of the others. Again, it takes great skill and diplomatic abilities to keep projects on track and functioning smoothly. In Chapter 2, "Creating the Project Charter," I'll discuss the importance of gaining stakeholder buy-in, and in Chapter 5, "Developing the Project Budget," I'll talk about the importance of communication to avert some of these problems.

Project managers have little authority in functional organizations, but with the right skills, they can successfully accomplish many projects. Table 1.1 highlights the advantages and disadvantages of this type of organization.

TABLE 1.1 Functional Organizations

Advantages	Disadvantages
There is an enduring organizational structure.	Project managers have little to no formal authority.
There is a clear career path with separation of functions, allowing specialty skills to flourish.	Multiple projects compete for limited resources and priority.
Employees have one supervisor with a clear chain of command.	Project team members are loyal to the functional manager.

Projectized Organizations

Projectized organizations are nearly the opposite of functional organizations. The focus of this type of organization is the project itself. The idea behind a projectized organization is to develop loyalty to the project, not to a functional manager.

Figure 1.3 shows a typical organizational chart for a projectized organization.

FIGURE 1.3 Projectized organizational chart

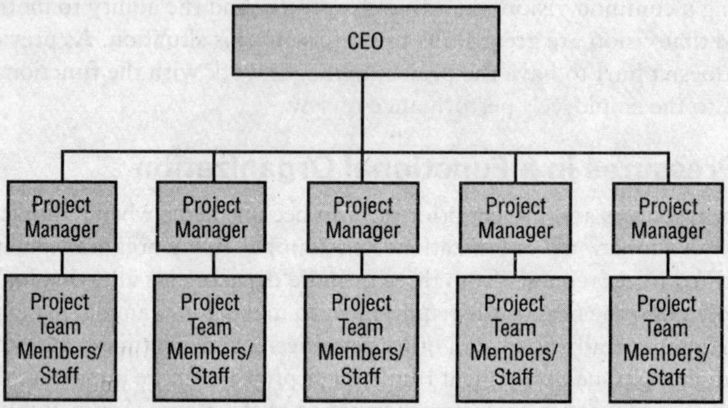

Organizational resources are dedicated to projects and project work in purely projectized organizations. Project managers almost always have ultimate authority over the project in this structure and report directly to the CEO. In a purely projectized organization, supporting functions such as human resources and accounting might report directly to the project manager as well. Project managers are responsible for making decisions regarding the project and acquiring and assigning resources. They have the authority to choose and assign resources from other areas in the organization or to hire them from outside if needed. For example, if there isn't enough money in the budget to hire additional resources, the project manager will have to come up with alternatives to solve this problem. This is known as a *constraint*. Project managers in all organizational structures are limited by constraints such as scope, schedule, and cost (or budget). Quality is sometimes considered a constraint, and it's generally affected by scope, schedule, and/or cost. We'll talk more about constraints in Chapter 2, "Creating the Project Charter."

NOTE You may come across the term *triple constraints* in your studies. The term refers to scope, schedule, and cost, and there is a potential you may see a question regarding the triple constraints on the exam. However, please note that the *PMBOK® Guide* lists the constraints of a project as scope, schedule, cost, and quality.

Teams are formed and often *co-located*, which means team members physically work at the same location. Project team members report to the project manager, not to a functional or departmental manager. One obvious drawback to a projectized organization is that project team members might find themselves out of work at the end of the project. An example of this might be a consultant who works on a project until completion and then is put on the bench or let go at the end of the project. Some inefficiency exists in this kind of organization when it comes to resource utilization. If you have a situation where you need a highly specialized skill at certain times throughout the project, the resource you're using to perform this function might be idle during other times in the project.

In summary, you can identify projectized organizations in several ways:

- Project managers have ultimate authority over the project.
- The focus of the organization is the project.
- The organization's resources are focused on projects and project work.
- Team members are co-located.
- Loyalties are formed to the project, not to a functional manager.
- Project teams are dissolved at the conclusion of the project.

The Projectized Graphic Artist

You've been appointed project manager for your company's website design and implementation. You're working in a projectized organization, so you have the authority to acquire and assign resources. You put together your team, including programmers, technical writers, testers, and business analysts. Julianne, a highly qualified graphic arts designer, is also part of your team. Julianne's specialized graphic arts skills are needed only at certain times throughout the project. When she has completed the graphic design portion of the screen she's working on, she doesn't have anything else to do until the next page is ready. Depending on how involved the project is and how the work is structured, days or weeks might pass before Julianne's skills are needed. This is where the inefficiency occurs in a purely projectized organization. The project manager will have to find other duties that Julianne can perform during these down times. It's not practical to let her go and then hire her back when she's needed again.

In this situation, you might assign Julianne to other project duties when she's not working on graphic design. Perhaps she can edit the text for the web pages or assist with the design of the upcoming marketing campaign. You might also share her time with another project manager in the organization.

During the planning process, you will discover the skills and abilities of all your team members so that you can plan their schedules accordingly and eliminate idle time.

Matrix Organizations

Matrix organizations came about to minimize the differences between, and take advantage of, the strengths and weaknesses of functional and projectized organizations. The idea at play here is that the best of both organizational structures can be realized by combining them into one. The project objectives are fulfilled and good project management techniques are utilized while still maintaining a hierarchical structure in the organization.

Employees in a matrix organization report to one functional manager and to at least one project manager. It's possible that employees could report to multiple project managers if they are working on multiple projects at one time. Functional managers pick up the administrative portion of the duties and assign employees to projects. They also monitor the work of their employees on the various projects. Project managers are responsible for executing the project and giving out work assignments based on project activities. Project managers and functional managers share the responsibility of performance reviews for the employee.

NOTE In a nutshell, in a matrix organization, functional managers assign employees to projects, while project managers assign tasks associated with the project.

Matrix organizations have unique characteristics. We'll look at how projects are conducted and managed and how project and functional managers share the work in this organizational structure next.

Project Focus in a Matrix Organization

Matrix organizations allow project managers to focus on the project and project work just as in a projectized organization. The project team is free to focus on the project objectives with minimal distractions from the functional department.

Project managers should take care when working up activity and project estimates for the project in a matrix organization. The estimates should be given to the functional managers for input before publishing. The functional manager is the one in charge of assigning or freeing up resources to work on projects. If the project manager is counting on a certain employee to work on the project at a certain time, the project manager should determine their availability up front with the functional manager. Project estimates might have to be modified if it's discovered that the employee they were counting on is not available when needed.

Balance of Power in a Matrix Organization

As we've discussed, a lot of communication and negotiation takes place between the project manager and the functional manager. This calls for a balance of power between the two, or one will dominate the other.

In a strong matrix organization, the balance of power rests with the project manager. They have the ability to strong-arm the functional managers into giving up their best resources for projects. Sometimes, more resources than necessary are assembled for the project, and then project managers negotiate these resources among themselves, cutting out the functional manager altogether, as you can see in Figure 1.4.

FIGURE 1.4 Strong matrix organizational chart

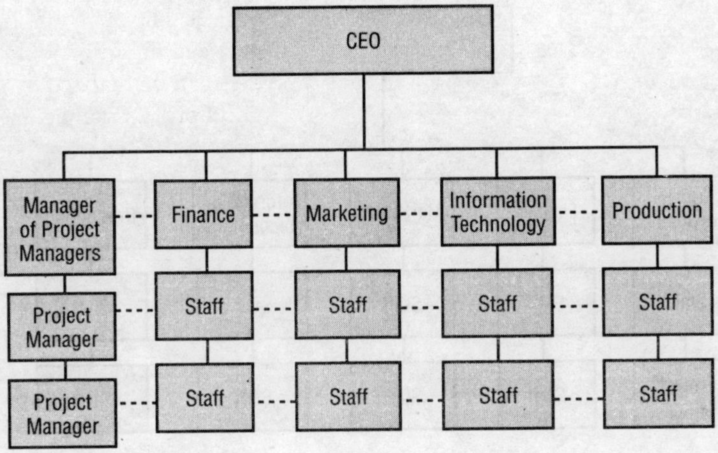

On the other end of the spectrum is the weak matrix (see Figure 1.5). As you would suspect, the functional managers have all the power in this structure. Project managers are really project coordinators or expeditors with part-time responsibilities on projects in a weak matrix organization. Project managers have little to no authority, just as in the functional organization. On the other hand, the functional managers have a lot of authority and make all the work assignments. The project manager simply expedites the project.

In between the weak matrix and the strong matrix is an organizational structure called the *balanced matrix* (see Figure 1.6). The features of the balanced matrix are what I've been discussing throughout this section. The power is balanced between project managers and functional managers. Each manager has responsibility for their parts of the project or organization, and employees get assigned to projects based on the needs of the project, not the strength or weakness of the manager's position.

FIGURE 1.5 Weak matrix organizational chart

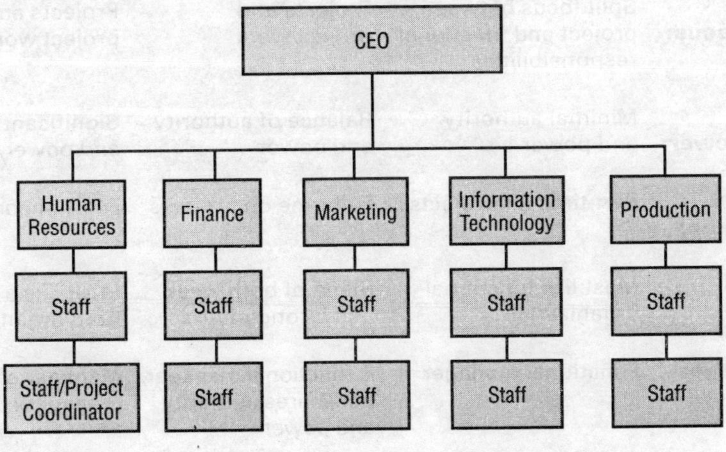

FIGURE 1.6 Balanced matrix organizational chart

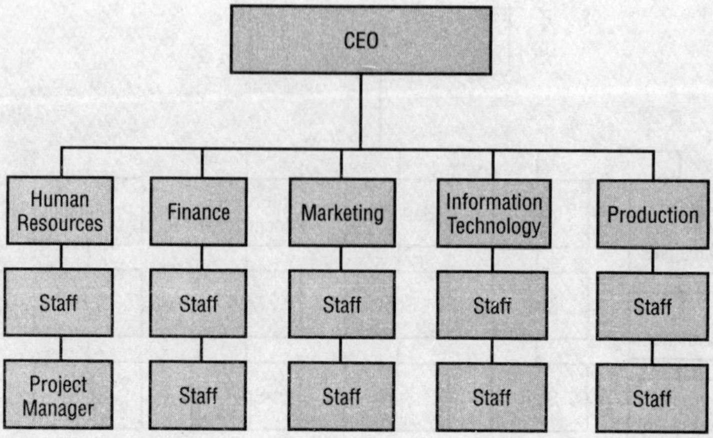

Matrix organizations have subtle differences, and it's important to understand their differences for the PMP exam. The easiest way to remember them is that the weak matrix has many of the same characteristics as the functional organization, while the strong matrix has many of the same characteristics as the projectized organization. The balanced matrix is exactly that—a balance between weak and strong, where the project manager shares authority and responsibility with the functional manager. Table 1.2 compares all three structures.

TABLE 1.2 Comparing Matrix Structures

	Weak Matrix	Balanced Matrix	Strong Matrix
Project Manager's Title:	Project coordinator, project leader, or project expeditor	Project manager	Project manager
Project Manager's Focus:	Split focus between project and functional responsibilities	Projects and project work	Projects and project work
Project Manager's Power:	Minimal authority and power	Balance of authority and power	Significant authority and power
Project Manager's Time:	Part-time on projects	Full-time on projects	Full-time on projects
Organization Style:	Most like functional organization	Blend of both weak and strong matrix	Most like a projectized organization
Project Manager Reports To:	Functional manager	A functional manager, but shares authority and power	Manager of project managers

Most organizations today use some combination of the organizational structures described here. They're a composite of functional, projectized, and matrix structures. It's rare that an organization would be purely functional or purely projectized. For example, projectized structures can coexist within functional organizations.

In the case of a high-profile, critical project, the functional organization might appoint a special project team to work only on that project. The team is structured outside the bounds of the functional organization, and the project manager has ultimate authority for the project. This is a workable project management approach and ensures open communication between the project manager and team members. At the end of the project, the project team is dissolved, and the project members return to their functional areas to resume their usual duties.

Exam Spotlight

Understand the characteristics of each organizational structure and their strengths and weaknesses for the exam.

Organizations are unique, as are the projects they undertake. Understanding the organizational structure will help you, as a project manager, with the cultural influences and communication avenues that exist in the organization to gain cooperation and successfully bring your projects to a close.

Understanding Project Life Cycles and Project Management Processes

Project life cycles are similar to the life cycle that parents experience raising their children to adulthood. Children start out as infants and generate lots of excitement wherever they go. However, not much is known about them at first. So, you study them as they grow, and you assess their needs. Over time, they mature and grow (and cost a lot of money in the process), until one day the parents' job is done.

Projects start out just like this and progress along a similar path. Someone comes up with a great idea for a project and actively solicits support for it. The project, after being approved, progresses through the intermediate phases to the ending phase, where it is completed and closed out.

Project Phases and Project Life Cycles

Most projects are divided into phases, and all projects, large or small, have a similar project life cycle structure. Project phases generally consist of segments of work that allow for easier management, planning, and control of the work. The work and the deliverables produced during the phase are typically unique to that phase. Some projects may consist of one phase and others may have many phases.

The number of phases depends on the project complexity and the industry. For example, information technology projects might progress through phases such as requirements, design, program, test, and implement. All the collective phases the project progresses through in concert are called the *project life cycle*. Project life cycles are similar for all projects regardless of their size or complexity. The phases that occur within the project life cycle are sequential and sometimes overlap each other. Most projects include at least the following four project life cycles (not to be confused with the project process groups that we'll discuss in the section titled "Project Management Process Groups"):

- Beginning the project
- Planning and organizing the work of the project
- Performing the work of the project
- Closing out the project

The end of each phase within the life cycle structure allows the project manager, stakeholders, and project sponsor the opportunity to determine whether the project should continue to the next phase. In order to progress to the next phase, the deliverable from the phase before it must be reviewed for accuracy and approved. As each phase is completed, it's handed off to the next phase. We'll look at handoffs and progressions through these phases next.

Handoffs

Project phases evolve through the life cycle in a series of phase sequences called *handoffs*, or technical transfers. For projects that consist of sequential phases, the end of one phase typically marks the beginning of the next. For example, in the construction industry, feasibility studies often take place in the beginning phase of a project and are completed prior to the beginning of the next phase.

The purpose of the *feasibility study* is to determine whether the project is worth undertaking and whether the project will be profitable to the organization. A feasibility study is a preliminary assessment of the viability of the project; the viability or perhaps marketability of the product, service, or result of the project; and the project's value to the organization. It might also determine whether the product, service, or result of the project is safe and meets industry or governmental standards and regulations. The completion and approval of the feasibility study triggers the beginning of the requirements phase, where requirements are documented and then handed off to the design phase, where blueprints are produced. The feasibility might also show that the project is not worth pursuing and the project is then terminated; thus, the next phase never begins.

Phase Completion

You will recognize phase completion because each phase has a specific deliverable, or multiple deliverables, that marks the end of the phase. A *deliverable* is an output that must be produced, reviewed, and approved to bring the phase or project to completion. Deliverables are tangible and can be measured and easily proved. For instance, a deliverable produced in the beginning phase of a construction industry project might be the feasibility study. Deliverables might also include things such as design documents, project budgets, blueprints, project schedules, prototypes, and so on.

A phase-end review allows those involved with the work to determine whether the project should continue to the next phase. The successful conclusion of one phase does not guarantee authorization to begin the next phase. The feasibility study mentioned earlier might show that environmental impacts of an enormous nature would result if the construction project were undertaken at the proposed location. Based on this information, a go or no-go decision can be made at the end of the phase. Phase-end reviews give the project manager the ability to discover, address, and take corrective action against errors discovered during the phase.

NOTE

The *PMBOK® Guide* states that phase-ending reviews are also known by a few other names: *phase exits, phase gates, milestones, stage gates, decision gates,* and *kill points.*

Multi-Phased Projects

Projects may consist of one or more phases. The phases of a project are often performed sequentially, but there are situations where performing phases concurrently, or overlapping the start date of a sequential phase, can benefit the project. According to the *PMBOK® Guide* there are three types of phase-to-phase relationships:

Sequential relationships One phase must finish before the next phase can begin.

Overlapping relationships One phase starts before the prior phase completes.

Iterative relationships Work for subsequent phases are planned as the work of the previous phase is performed.

Sometimes phases are overlapped to shorten or compress the project schedule. This is called *fast tracking*. Fast tracking means that a later phase is started prior to completing and approving the phase, or phases, that come before it. This technique is used to shorten the overall duration of the project.

Project phases are performed within a project life cycle as I mentioned earlier in this section. Project life cycles typically consist of initiating the project, performing the work of the project, and so on. As a result, most projects have the following characteristics in common:

- In the beginning of the project life cycle, when the project is initiated, costs are low, and few team members are assigned to the project.
- As the project progresses, costs and staffing increase and then taper off at closing.
- The potential that the project will come to a successful ending is lowest at the beginning of the project; its chance for success increases as the project progresses through its phases and life cycle stages.
- Risk is highest at the beginning of the project and gradually decreases the closer the project comes to completion.

- Stakeholders have the greatest chance of influencing the project and the characteristics of the product, service, or result of the project in the beginning phases and have less and less influence as the project progresses.

This same phenomenon exists within the project management processes as well. We'll look at those next.

Project Management Process Groups

Project management processes organize and describe the work of the project. The *PMBOK® Guide* describes five process groups used to accomplish this end. These processes are performed by people and, much like project phases, are interrelated and dependent on one another.

These are the five project management process groups that the *PMBOK® Guide* documents:

- Initiating
- Planning
- Executing
- Monitoring and Controlling
- Closing

All these process groups have individual processes that collectively make up the group. For example, the Initiating process group has two processes called Develop Project Charter and Identify Stakeholders. Collectively, these process groups—including all their individual processes—make up the project management process. Projects start with the Initiating process and progress through all the processes in the Planning process group, the Executing process group, and so on, until the project is successfully completed or it's canceled. All projects must complete the Closing processes, even if a project is killed.

NOTE

Don't confuse project phases and life cycles with the project management process groups. Project phases and life cycles describe how the work associated with the product of the project will be completed. For example, a construction project might have phases such as feasibility study, design, build, inspection, and turnover. The five project management process groups (Initiating, Planning, Executing, Monitoring and Controlling, and Closing) organize and describe how the project activities will be conducted in order to meet the project requirements. These processes are generally performed for each phase of a large project. The five process groups are the heart of the *PMBOK® Guide* and the exam. As you progress through this book, be certain you understand each of these processes as they're described in the *PMBOK® Guide*.

Let's start with a high-level overview of each process group. The remainder of this book will cover each of these processes in detail. If you want to peek ahead, Appendix A lists each of the process groups, the individual processes that make up each process group, and the Knowledge Areas in which they belong. (I'll introduce Knowledge Areas in the section "Exploring the Project Management Knowledge Areas" in Chapter 2.)

Initiating The *Initiating* process group, as its name implies, occurs at the beginning of the project and at the beginning of each project phase for large projects. Initiating acknowledges that a project, or the next project phase, should begin. This process group grants the approval to commit the organization's resources to working on the project or phase and authorizes the project manager to begin working on the project. The outputs of the Initiating process group, including the project charter and identification of the stakeholders, become inputs into the Planning process group.

Planning The *Planning* process is the process group of formulating and revising project goals and objectives and creating the project management plan that will be used to achieve the goals the project was undertaken to address. The Planning process group also involves determining alternative courses of action and selecting from among the best of those to produce the project's goals. This process group is where the project requirements are fleshed out and stakeholders are identified. Planning has more processes than any of the other project management process groups. In order to carry out their functions, the Executing, Monitoring and Controlling, and Closing process groups all rely on the Planning processes and the documentation produced during the Planning processes. Project managers will perform frequent iterations of the Planning processes prior to project completion. Projects are unique and, as such, have never been done before. Therefore, Planning must encompass all areas of project management and consider budgets, activity definition, scope planning, schedule development, risk identification, staff acquisition, procurement planning, and more. The greatest conflicts a project manager will encounter in this process group are project prioritization issues.

Executing The *Executing* process group involves putting the project management plan into action. It's here that the project manager will coordinate and direct project resources to meet the objectives of the project plan. The Executing processes keeps the project plan on track and ensures that future execution of project plans stays in line with project objectives. This process group is typically where approved changes are implemented. The Executing process group will utilize the most project time and resources, and as a result, costs are usually highest during the Executing processes. Project managers will experience the greatest conflicts over schedules in this cycle.

Monitoring and Controlling The *Monitoring and Controlling* process group is where project performance measurements are taken and analyzed to determine whether the project is staying true to the project plan. The idea is to identify problems as soon as possible and apply corrective action to control the work of the project and assure successful outcomes. For example, if you discover that variances exist, you'll apply corrective action to get the project activities realigned with the project plan. This might require additional passes through the Planning processes to adjust project activities, resources, schedules, budgets, and so on.

NOTE

Monitoring and Controlling is used to track the progress of work being performed and identify problems and variances within a process group as well as the project as a whole.

Closing The *Closing* process group is probably the most often skipped process group in project management. Closing brings a formal, orderly end to the activities of a project phase or to the project itself. Once the project objectives have been met, most of us are ready to move on to the next project. However, Closing is important because all the project information is gathered and stored for future reference. The documentation collected during the Closing process group can be reviewed and utilized to avert potential problems on future projects. Contract closeout occurs here, and formal acceptance and approval are obtained from project stakeholders.

Exam Spotlight

The project manager and project team are responsible for determining which processes within each process group are appropriate for the project on which you're working. This is called *tailoring*. You should consider the size and complexity of the project and the various inputs and outputs of each of the processes when determining which processes to implement and perform. Small, independent projects might not require the rigor of each of the processes within a process group, but every process should be addressed and its level of implementation determined. Use your judgment when deciding which processes to follow, particularly for small projects.

Characteristics of the Process Groups

The progression through the project management process groups exhibits the same characteristics as progression through the project phases. That is, costs are lowest during the Initiating processes, and few team members are involved. Costs and staffing increase in the Executing process group and then decrease as you approach the Closing process group. The chances for success are lowest during Initiating and highest during Closing. The chances for risks occurring are higher during Initiating, Planning, and Executing, but the impacts of risks are greater during the later processes. Stakeholders have the greatest influence during the Initiating and Planning processes and less and less influence as you progress through Executing, Monitoring and Controlling, and Closing. To give you a better idea of when certain characteristics influence a project, refer to Table 1.3.

TABLE 1.3 Characteristics of the Project Process Groups

	Initiating	Planning	Executing	Monitoring and Controlling	Closing
Costs	Low	Low	Highest	Lower	Lowest
Staffing Levels	Low	Lower	High	High	Low

TABLE 1.3 Characteristics of the Project Process Groups *(continued)*

	Initiating	Planning	Executing	Monitoring and Controlling	Closing
Chance for Successful Completion	Lowest	Low	Medium	High	Highest
Stakeholder Influence	Highest	High	Medium	Low	Lowest
Risk Probability of Occurrence	Lowest	Low	High	High	Lower

The Process Flow

You should not think of the five process groups as one-time processes that are performed as discrete elements. Rather, these processes interact and overlap with each other. They are *iterative* and might be revisited and revised throughout the project's life several times as the project is refined. The *PMBOK® Guide* calls this process of going back through the process groups an *iterative process*. The conclusion of each process group allows the project manager and stakeholders to reexamine the business needs of the project and determine whether the project is satisfying those needs. And it is another opportunity to make a go or no-go decision.

Figure 1.7 shows the five process groups in a typical project. Keep in mind that during phases of a project, the Closing process group can provide input to the Initiating process group. For example, once the feasibility study discussed earlier is accepted or closed, it becomes an input to the Initiating process group of the design phase.

It's important to understand the flow of these processes for the exam. If you remember the processes and their inputs and outputs, it will help you when you're trying to decipher an exam question. The outputs of one process group may in some cases become the inputs into the next process group (or the outputs might be a deliverable of the project). Sometimes just understanding which process the question is asking about will help you determine the answer. One trick you can use to memorize these processes is to remember syrup of ipecac. You probably have some of this poison antidote in your medicine cabinet at home. If you think of the Monitoring and Controlling process group as simply "Controlling," when you sound out the first initial of each of the processes, it sounds like "ipecac"—IPECC (Initiating, Planning, Executing, *Monitoring and* Controlling, and Closing).

As I stated earlier, individual processes make up each of the process groups. For example, the Closing life cycle process group consists of two processes: Close Project and Phase and Close Procurements. Each process takes inputs and uses them in conjunction with various tools and techniques to produce outputs.

FIGURE 1.7 Project management process groups

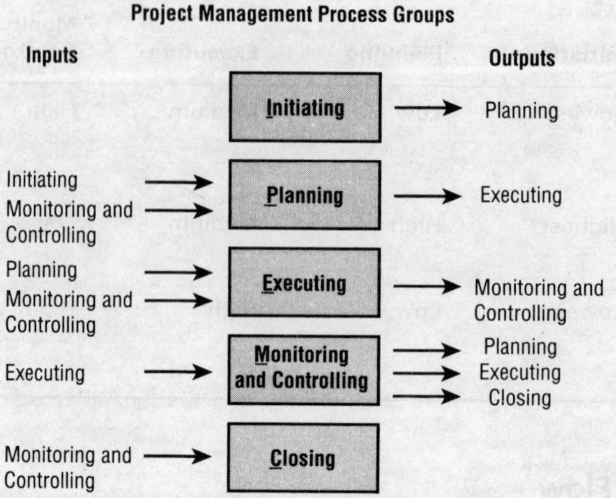

NOTE It's outside the scope of this book to explain all the inputs, tools and techniques, and outputs for each process in each process group (although each is listed in Appendix A). You'll find all the inputs, tools and techniques, and outputs detailed in the *PMBOK® Guide*, and I highly recommend you get familiar with them.

Exam Spotlight

Understand each project management process group and all the processes that make up these groups. Appendix A contains a table of all the processes, their inputs, their tools and techniques, their outputs, and the Knowledge Area in which they each belong. (I'll introduce Knowledge Areas in the section "The Project Management Knowledge Areas" in Chapter 2.)

You'll see test questions regarding inputs, tools and techniques, and outputs of many of the processes within each process group. One way to keep them all straight is to remember that tools and techniques usually require action of some sort, be it measuring, applying some skill or technique, planning, or using expert judgment. Outputs are usually in the form of a deliverable. Remember that a deliverable is characterized with results or outcomes that can be measured, are tangible, and are provable. Last but not least, outputs from one process sometimes serve as inputs to another process.

Process Interactions

We've covered a lot of material, but I'll explain one more concept before concluding. As stated earlier, project managers must determine the processes that are appropriate for effectively managing a project based on the complexity and scope of the project, available resources, budget, and so on. As the project progresses, the project management processes might be revisited and revised to update the project management plan as more information becomes known. Underlying the concept that process groups are iterative is a cycle the *PMBOK® Guide* describes as the Plan-Do-Check-Act cycle, which was originally defined by Walter Shewhart and later modified by Edward Deming. The idea behind this concept is that each element in the cycle is results oriented. The results from the Plan cycle become inputs into the Do cycle, and so on, much like the way the project management process groups interact. The cycle interactions can be mapped to work in conjunction with the five project management process groups. For example, the Plan cycle maps to the Planning process group. Before going any further, here's a brief refresher:

- Project phases describe how the work required to produce the product of the project will be completed.
- Project management process groups organize and describe how the project activities will be completed in order to meet the goals of the project.
- The Plan-Do-Check-Act cycle is an underlying concept that shows the integrative nature of the process groups.

Figure 1.8 shows the relationships and interactions of the concepts you've learned so far. Please bear in mind that a simple figure can't convey all the interactions and iterative nature of these interactions; however, I think you'll see that the figure ties the basic elements of these concepts together.

Understanding How This Applies to Your Next Project

As you can tell from this first chapter, managing projects is not for the faint of heart. You must master multiple skills and techniques in order to complete projects successfully. In your day-to-day work environment, it probably doesn't matter much if you're working in a functional or strong matrix organization. More important are your communication, conflict management, and negotiation and influencing skills. And good communications are the hallmark of successful projects. (We'll talk more about communication and give you some communication tips in the coming chapters.)

In any organizational structure, you'll find leaders, and you'll find people who have the title of leader. Again, the organizational structure itself probably isn't as important as knowing who the real leaders and influencers are in the organization. These are the people you'll lean on to help with difficult project decisions and hurdles.

FIGURE 1.8 Project management process groups

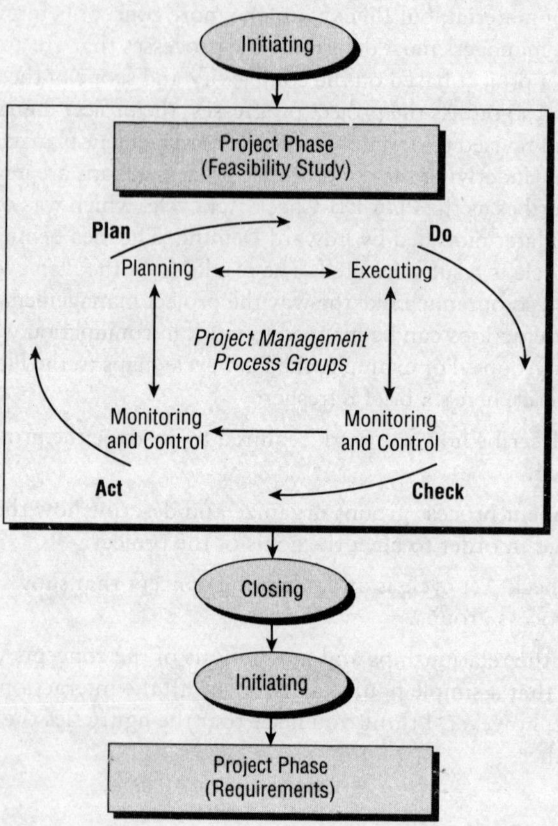

I talked about the definition of a project in this chapter. You'd be surprised how many people think ongoing operations are projects. Here's a tip to help you explain the definition to your stakeholders: projects involve the five project process groups (Initiating through Closing). Ongoing operations typically involve the Planning, Executing, and Monitoring and Controlling processes. But here's the differentiator—ongoing operations don't include Initiating or Closing process groups because ongoing operations don't have a beginning or an end.

Most projects I've ever worked on involved more than one stakeholder. And stakeholders often have conflicting interests. On your next project, make certain to find out what those stakeholder interests are. It's easier to resolve conflicts at the beginning of the project than it is at the end. Resolving conflicts will likely involve negotiating and influencing skills.

I've made the mistake of thinking the project process groups are overkill for a small project. My team once embarked on a small project and thought that within a matter of weeks we'd have it wrapped up and delivered. We neglected to get signatures from the project requestor on the agreed-upon scope, and you guessed it, the scope grew and grew and changed several times before we were able to get the project back under control. If you're reading between the lines here, you can also tell we didn't have adequate change control in place. As you progress through the book, I'll highlight the important processes you'll want to include on all projects, large and small, so you don't get caught in this trap.

Summary

Phew! I covered a lot of ground in this chapter. You learned that projects exist to bring about a unique product, service, or result. Projects are temporary in nature and have definite beginning and ending dates.

Stakeholders are those people or organizations that have a vested interest in the outcome of the project. Stakeholders include people such as the project sponsor, the customer, key management personnel, the project manager, contractors, suppliers, and more. Projects are considered complete when the project meets or exceeds the expectations of the stakeholders.

Project management is a discipline that brings together a set of tools and techniques to describe, organize, and monitor the work of project activities. Project managers are the ones responsible for carrying out these activities. Projects might be organized into programs or portfolios and might be managed centrally by a PMO.

Project managers have a wide variety of skills. They should they be versed not only in the field they're working in but in general management skills as well. Communication is the most important skill a project manager will use in the course of a project.

Organizational structures come in variations of three forms: functional, projectized, and matrix. Functional organizations are traditional with hierarchical reporting structures. Project managers have little to no authority in this kind of organization. Projectized organizations are structured around project work, and staff personnel report to project managers. Project managers have full authority in this organizational structure. Matrix organizations are a combination of the functional and projectized. A project manager's authority varies depending on the structure of the matrix, be it a weak matrix, a balanced matrix, or a strong matrix.

Projects progress through phases along a life cycle path to complete the product of the project. The project management process groups are performed throughout the project's life cycle. The process groups described in the *PMBOK® Guide* are Initiating, Planning, Executing, Monitoring and Controlling, and Closing.

Exam Essentials

Be able to describe the difference between projects and operations. A project is temporary in nature with a definite beginning and ending date. Projects produce unique products, services, or results. Operations are ongoing and use repetitive processes that typically produce the same result over and over.

Be able to denote some of the skills every good project manager should possess. Communication, budgeting, organizational, problem solving, negotiation and influencing, leading, and team building are skills a project manager should possess.

Be able to differentiate the different organizational structures and the project manager's authority in each. Organizations are usually structured in some combination of the following: functional, projcctized, and matrix (including weak matrix, balanced matrix, and strong matrix). Project managers have the most authority in a projectized organization and the least amount of authority in a functional organization.

Be able to name the five project management process groups. The five project management process groups are Initiating, Planning, Executing, Monitoring and Controlling, and Closing.

Key Terms

I've introduced the processes you'll use while managing projects. You need to understand each of these processes to be an effective project manager and know them by the names used in the *PMBOK® Guide* to be successful on the exam. I will discuss each in greater detail in the chapters to come.

Closing

Executing

Initiating

Monitoring and Controlling

Planning

You've learned many new key words in this chapter. PMI has worked hard to develop and define standard project management terms that apply across industries. Here is a list of some of the terms you came across in this chapter:

balanced matrix

co-located

deliverable

fast tracking

feasibility study

functional organization

handoffs

iterative

leaders

managers

matrix organizations

operations

politics

portfolio management

portfolios

power

product scope

program management

programs

progressive elaboration

project life cycle

project management

project management office

project managers

project scope

project sponsor

projectized organizations

projects

stakeholders

tailoring

Review Questions

1. Which organization has set the de facto standards for project management techniques?
   - A. PMBOK
   - B. PMO
   - C. PMI
   - D. PMA
2. The VP of marketing approaches you and requests that you change the visitor logon screen on the company's website to include a username with at least six characters. This is considered which of the following?
   - A. Project initiation
   - B. Ongoing operations
   - C. A project
   - D. Project execution
3. Your company manufactures small kitchen appliances. It is introducing a new product line of appliances in designer colors with distinctive features for kitchens in small spaces. These new products will be offered indefinitely starting with the spring catalog release. Which of the following is true?
   - A. This is a project because this new product line has never been manufactured and sold by this company before.
   - B. This is an ongoing operation because the company is in the business of manufacturing kitchen appliances. Introducing designer colors and features is simply a new twist on an existing process.
   - C. This is an ongoing operation because the new product line will be sold indefinitely. It's not temporary.
   - D. This is not a project or an ongoing operation. This is a new product introduction not affecting ongoing operations.
4. Your company manufactures small kitchen appliances. It is introducing a new product line of appliances in designer colors with distinctive features for kitchens in small spaces. These new products will be offered indefinitely starting with the spring catalog release. To determine the characteristics and features of the new product line, you will have to perform which of the following?
   - A. Fast tracking
   - B. Consulting with the stakeholders
   - C. Planning the project life cycle
   - D. Progressive elaboration

5. A project is considered successful when ______________.

   A. the product of the project has been manufactured

   B. the project sponsor announces the completion of the project

   C. the product of the project is turned over to the operations area to handle the ongoing aspects of the project

   ✓ D. the project meets or exceeds the expectations of the stakeholders

6. The VP of customer service has expressed concern over a project in which you're involved. His specific concern is that if the project is implemented as planned, he'll have to purchase additional equipment to staff his customer service center. The cost was not taken into consideration in the project budget. The project sponsor insists that the project must go forward as originally planned or the customer will suffer. Which of the following is true?

   ✗ A. The VP of customer service is correct. Since the cost was not taken into account at the beginning of the project, the project should not go forward as planned. Project initiation should be revisited to examine the project plan and determine how changes can be made to accommodate customer service.

   ✓ B. The conflict should be resolved in favor of the customer.

   C. The conflict should be resolved in favor of the project sponsor.

   D. The conflict should be resolved in favor of the VP of customer service.

7. Which of the following applies a set of tools and techniques used to describe, organize, and monitor the work of project activities to meet the project requirements?

   A. Project managers

   B. The *PMBOK® Guide*

   ✓ C. Project management

   D. Stakeholders

8. All of the following are true regarding phase-to-phase relationships except for which one?

   A. Planning for an iterative phase begins when the work of the previous phase is progressing.

   ✗ ✓ B. Handoffs occur after a phase-end review in an overlapping phased project.

   C. During sequentially phased projects, the previous phase must finish before the next phase can begin.

   D. Fast tracking is a compression technique that can be applied as a phase-to-phase relationship.

9. All of the following statements are true except for which one?

   A. Programs are groups of related projects.

   B. Project life cycles are collections of sequential and occasionally overlapping project phases.

   ✗ C. A project may or may not be part of a program.

   ✓ D. Portfolios are collections of interdependent projects or programs.

10. You are the project manager for a large construction project. The project objective is to construct a set of outbuildings to house the Olympic support team that will be arriving in your city 18 months from the project start date. Resources are not readily available because they are currently assigned to other projects. Jack, an expert crane operator, is needed for this project two months from today. Which of the following skills will you use to get Jack assigned to your project?

A. Negotiation and influencing skills

B. Communication and organizational skills

C. Communication skills

D. Problem-solving skills

11. You've decided to try your hand at project management in the entertainment industry. You're working on a movie production and the phases are performed sequentially. The team has just completed the storyboard phase of the project. Which of the following is true?

A. The storyboard is a deliverable that marks the end of the phase.

B. The storyboard phase marks the end of the Initiating process group, and the next phase of the project should begin.

C. The writing phase can begin once the majority of the storyboard phase is complete.

D. The division of phases and determining which processes to use in each phase is called *tailoring.*

12. You are managing a project to install a new postage software system that will automatically print labels and administer postage for certified mailings, overnight packages, and other special mailing needs. You've attempted to gain the cooperation of the business analyst working on this project, and you need some answers. She is elusive and tells you that this project is not her top priority. What should you do to avoid situations like this in the future?

A. Establish the business analyst's duties well ahead of due dates, and tell her you'll be reporting on her performance to her functional manager.

B. Establish the business analyst's duties well ahead of due dates, and tell her you are expecting her to meet these expectations because the customer is counting on the project meeting due dates to save significant costs on their annual mailings.

C. Negotiate with the business analyst's functional manager during the planning process to establish expectations and request to participate in the business analyst's annual performance review.

D. Negotiate with the business analyst's functional manager during the planning process to establish expectations, and inform the functional manager of the requirements of the project. Agreement from the functional manager will assure the cooperation of the business analyst.

13. The amount of authority a project manager possesses can be related to which of the following?

A. The project manager's communication skills

B. The organizational structure

C. The amount of authority the manager of the project manager possesses

D. The key stakeholder's influence on the project

14. What is one of the advantages of a functional organization?

✓ • **A.** All employees report to one manager and have a clear chain of command.

B. All employees report to two or more managers, but project team members show loyalty to functional managers.

C. The organization is focused on projects and project work.

D. Teams are co-located.

15. You have been assigned to a project in which the objectives are to direct customer calls to an interactive voice response system before being connected to a live agent. You are in charge of the media communications for this project. You report to the project manager in charge of this project and the VP of marketing, who share responsibility for this project. Which organizational structure do you work in?

A. Functional organization

B. Weak matrix organization

C. Projectized organization

✓ • **D.** Balanced matrix organization

16. You have been assigned to a project in which the objectives are to expand three miles of the north-to-south highway through your city by two lanes in each direction. You are in charge of the demolition phase of this project, and you report to the project manager in charge of this project. You have been hired on contract and will be released at the completion of the demolition phase. What type of organizational structure does this represent?

A. Functional organization

B. Weak matrix organization

✓ **C.** Projectized organization

D. Balanced matrix organization

17. What are the five project management process groups, in order?

A. Initiating, Executing, Planning, Monitoring and Controlling, and Closing

B. Initiating, Monitoring and Controlling, Planning, Executing, and Closing

C. Initiating, Planning, Monitoring and Controlling, Executing, and Closing

✓ • **D.** Initiating, Planning, Executing, Monitoring and Controlling, and Closing

18. You have been assigned to a project in which the objectives are to expand three miles of the north-to-south highway through your city by two lanes in each direction. You are interested in implementing a new project process called Design-Build in order to speed up the project schedule. The idea is that the construction team will work on the first mile of the highway reconstruction at the same time the design team is coming up with plans for the third mile of the reconstruction rather than completing all design before any construction begins. This is an example of which of the following?

A. Managing the projects as a program

✓ • **B.** An iterative phase-to-phase relationship

C. Progressive elaboration

D. Fast tracking

19. During which project management process group are risk and stakeholder's ability to influence project outcomes the highest at the beginning of the process?

- **A.** Planning
- **B.** Executing
- **C.** Initiating
- **D.** Monitoring and Controlling

20. You are a project manager working on gathering requirements and establishing estimates for the project. Which process group are you in?

- **A.** Planning
- **B.** Executing
- **C.** Initiating
- **D.** Monitoring and Controlling

Answers to Review Questions

1. C. The Project Management Institute (PMI) is the industry-recognized standard for project management practices.

2. B. Projects exist to create a unique product, service, or result. The logon screen in this question is not a unique product. A minor change has been requested, indicating that this is an ongoing operations function. Some of the criteria for projects are that they are unique, temporary with definitive start and end dates, and considered complete when the project goals are achieved.

3. A. This is a project. The product line is new, which implies that this is a unique product—it hasn't been done before. You can discern a definite start and end date by the fact that the new appliances must be ready by the spring catalog release.

4. D. Progressive elaboration is the process of determining the characteristics and features of the product of the project. Progressive elaboration is carried out via steps in detailed fashion.

5. D. A project is considered successful when stakeholder needs and expectations are met or exceeded.

6. B. Conflicts between stakeholders should always be resolved in favor of the customer. This question emphasizes the importance of identifying your stakeholders and their needs as early as possible in the project.

7. C. Project management brings together a set of tools and techniques to organize project activities. Project managers are the ones responsible for managing the project processes.

8. B. Phase-end reviews can occur for all phase-to-phase relationships. Handoffs are typical of a sequentially phased project, not an overlapping phased project. Fast tracking occurs in an overlapping relationship.

9. D. Portfolios are collections of projects or programs. The projects or programs do not have to be directly related or interdependent on each other to reside within the portfolio.

10. A. Negotiation and influencing skills are needed to convince Jack's boss and come to agreement concerning his assignment.

11. A. The storyboard is a deliverable. Since the phases are performed sequentially, the deliverable must be approved before the next phase of the project can begin.

12. C. The best answer to this question according to the *PMBOK® Guide* is to negotiate with the functional manager to participate in the business analyst's annual performance review. D is an appropriate response but doesn't include the direction that the project manager should participate in the performance review.

13. B. The level of authority the project manager has is determined by the organizational structure. For instance, in a functional organization, the project manager has little to no authority, but in a projectized structure, the project manager has full authority.

14. A. Advantages for employees in a functional organization are that they have only one supervisor and a clear chain of command exists.

15. D. Employees in a balanced matrix often report to two or more managers. Functional managers and project managers share authority and responsibility for projects. There is a balance of power between the functional managers and project managers.

16. C. Projectized organizations are focused on the project itself. One issue with this type of structure is determining what to do with project team members when they are not actively involved in the project. One alternative is to release them when they are no longer needed.

17. D. Remember the acronym that sounds like syrup of ipecac: IPECC (Initiating, Planning, Executing, *Monitoring and* Controlling, and Closing).

18. B. An iterative phase-to-phase relationship allows you to begin planning for the next phase before the phase you're working on is completed. Fast tracking is where the work of the next phase begins during the current phase. This question describes planning for the next phase, not performing the work of the phase.

19. C. The Initiating process group is where stakeholders have the greatest ability to influence outcomes of the project. Risk is highest during this stage because of the high degree of unknown factors.

20. A. The Planning process is where requirements are fleshed out, stakeholders are identified, and estimates on project costs and time are made.

Chapter 2

Creating the Project Charter

THE PMP® EXAM CONTENT FROM THE INITIATING THE PROJECT PERFORMANCE DOMAIN COVERED IN THIS CHAPTER INCLUDES THE FOLLOWING:

- ✓ **Conduct Project Selection Methods**
- ✓ **Define Scope**
- ✓ **Document Project Risks, Assumptions, and Constraints**
- ✓ **Develop Project Charter**
- ✓ **Obtain Project Charter Approval**
- ✓ **Identify and Perform Stakeholder Analysis**

Now that you're armed with a detailed overview of project management, you can easily determine whether your next assignment really is a project or an ongoing operation. You've also learned some of the basics of good project management techniques. You'll now start putting those techniques into practice during the Initiating process group, which is where all projects start. And, as you've probably already guessed, you'll be using some of the general management skills outlined in Chapter 1, "What Is a Project?"

One of the first skills you will put to use will be your communication skills. Are you surprised? Of course you're not. It all starts with communication. You can't start defining the project until you've first talked to the project sponsor, key stakeholders, and management personnel. All good project managers have honed their communication skills to a nice sharp edge.

You'll remember from Chapter 1 that *Initiating* is the first process group in the five project management process groups. You can think of it as the official project kickoff. Initiating acknowledges that the project, or the next phase in an active project, should begin. This process group culminates in the publication of a project charter and a stakeholder register. I'll cover each in this chapter. But before we dive into the Initiating processes, we have one more preliminary topic to cover regarding the nine Knowledge Areas.

At the end of this chapter, I'll introduce a case study that will illustrate the main points of the chapter. I'll expand on this case study from chapter to chapter, and you'll begin building a project using each of the skills you learn.

Exploring the Project Management Knowledge Areas

We talked about the five process groups in Chapter 1. They are Initiating, Planning, Executing, Monitoring and Controlling, and Closing. Each process group is made up of a collection of processes used throughout the project life cycle The *PMBOK® Guide* groups these processes into nine categories that it calls The *Project Management Knowledge Areas*. These groupings, or Knowledge Areas, bring together processes that have characteristics in common. For example, the *Project Cost Management Knowledge Area* involves all aspects of the budgeting process, as you would suspect. Therefore, processes such as Estimate Costs, Determine Budget, and Control Costs belong to this Knowledge Area. Here's the tricky part—these processes don't belong to the same project management process groups (Estimate Costs and Determine Budget are part of the Planning process group, and Control Costs is part of the Monitoring and Controlling process group). Think of it this way: Knowledge Areas bring together processes by commonalities, whereas project management process groups are more or less the order in which you perform the project management processes (although remember that you can come back through these processes more than once). The nine Knowledge Areas are as follows:

- Project Integration Management
- Project Scope Management
- Project Time Management
- Project Cost Management
- Project Quality Management
- Project Human Resource Management
- Project Communications Management
- Project Risk Management
- Project Procurement Management

Let's take a closer look at each Knowledge Area so you understand how they relate to the process groups. Included in each of the following sections are tables that illustrate the processes that make up the Knowledge Area and the project management process group to which each process belongs. This will help you see the big picture in terms of process groups compared to Knowledge Areas. I'll discuss each of the processes in the various Knowledge Areas throughout the book, but for now, you'll take a high-level look at each of them.

Exam Spotlight

The PMP exam may have a question or two regarding the processes that make up a Knowledge Area. Remember that Knowledge Areas bring together processes by commonalities, so thinking about the Knowledge Area itself should tip you off to the processes that belong to it. Projects are executed in process group order, but the Knowledge Areas allow a project manager to think about groups of processes that require specific skills. This makes the job of assigning resources easier because team members with specific skills might be able to work on and complete several processes at once. To broaden your understanding of the Knowledge Areas, cross-reference the purposes and the processes that make up each Knowledge Area with the *PMBOK® Guide*.

Project Integration Management

The *Project Integration Management Knowledge Area* comprises six processes, as shown in Table 2.1.

TABLE 2.1 Project Integration Management

Process Name	Project Management Process Group
Develop Project Charter	Initiating
Develop Project Management Plan	Planning
Direct and Manage Project Execution	Executing
Monitor and Control Project Work	Monitoring and Controlling
Perform Integrated Change Control	Monitoring and Controlling
Close Project or Phase	Closing

The *Project Integration Management Knowledge Area* is concerned with coordinating all aspects of the project plan and is highly interactive. This Knowledge Area involves identifying and defining the work of the project and combining, unifying, and integrating the appropriate processes. This Knowledge Area also takes into account satisfactorily meeting the requirements of the customer and stakeholder and managing their expectations.

Project planning, project execution, project work monitoring, and change control occur throughout the project and are repeated continuously while you're working on the project. Project planning and execution involve weighing the objectives of the project against the alternatives to bring the project to a successful completion. This includes making choices about how to effectively use resources and coordinating the work of the project on a continuous basis. Monitoring the work of the project involves anticipating potential problems and issues and dealing with them before they reach the critical point. Change control impacts the project plan, which in turn impacts the work of the project, which in turn can impact the project management plan, so you can see that these processes are tightly linked. The processes in this area, as with all the Knowledge Areas, also interact with other processes in the remaining Knowledge Areas. For example, the Identify Stakeholders process uses an output from the Develop Project charter process as an input.

The *Project Integration Management Knowledge Area* has two tools for assisting with process integration: earned value management (EVM) and project management software. EVM is a project-integrating methodology used in this Knowledge Area to integrate the processes and measure project performance through a project's life cycle. I'll further define EVM and talk more about project management software tools in Chapter 4, "Creating the Project Schedule."

Project Scope Management

The *Project Scope Management Knowledge Area* has five processes, as shown in Table 2.2.

TABLE 2.2 Project Scope Management

Process Name	Project Management Process Group
Collect Requirements	Planning
Define Scope	Planning
Create WBS	Planning
Verify Scope	Monitoring and Controlling
Control Scope	Monitoring and Controlling

Project Scope Management is concerned with defining all the work of the project and only the work needed to successfully produce the project goals. These processes are highly interactive. They define and control what is and what is not part of the project. Each process occurs at least once—and often many times—throughout the project's life.

Project Scope Management encompasses both product scope and project scope. *Product scope* concerns the characteristics of the product, service, or result of the project. It's measured against the product requirements to determine successful completion or fulfillment. The application area usually dictates the process tools and techniques you'll use to define and manage product scope. *Project scope* involves managing the work of the project and only the work of the project. Project scope is measured against the project management plan, the project scope statement, the work breakdown structure (WBS), and the WBS dictionary.

NOTE

To ensure a successful project, both product and project scope must be well integrated. This implies that Project Scope Management is well integrated with the other Knowledge Area processes.

Define Scope, Create WBS, Verify Scope, and Control Scope involve the following:

- Defining and detailing the deliverables and requirements of the product of the project
- Creating a project scope management plan
- Creating a WBS
- Verifying deliverables using measurement techniques
- Controlling changes to these processes

Project Time Management

The *Project Time Management Knowledge Area* has six processes, as shown in Table 2.3.

TABLE 2.3 Project Time Management

Process Name	Project Management Process Group
Define Activities	Planning
Sequence Activities	Planning
Estimate Activity Resources	Planning
Estimate Activity Durations	Planning
Develop Schedule	Planning
Control Schedule	Monitoring and Controlling

This Knowledge Area is concerned with estimating the duration of the project plan activities, devising a project schedule, and monitoring and controlling deviations from the schedule. Collectively, this Knowledge Area deals with completing the project in a timely manner. Time management is an important aspect of project management because it concerns keeping the project activities on track and monitoring those activities against the project plan to ensure that the project is completed on time.

Although each process in this Knowledge Area occurs at least once in every project (and sometimes more), in many cases, particularly on small projects, Sequence Activities, Estimate Activity Durations, and Develop Schedule are completed as one activity. Only one person is needed to complete these processes for small projects, and they're all worked on at the same time.

Project Cost Management

As its name implies, the *Project Cost Management Knowledge Area* centers around costs and budgets. Table 2.4 shows the processes that make up this Knowledge Area.

TABLE 2.4 Project Cost Management

Process Name	Project Management Process Group
Estimate Costs	Planning
Determine Budget	Planning
Control Costs	Monitoring and Controlling

The activities in The *Project Cost Management Knowledge Area* establish cost estimates for resources, establish budgets, and keep watch over those costs to ensure that the project stays within the approved budget. This Knowledge Area is primarily concerned with the costs of resources, but you should think about other costs as well. For example, make certain to examine ongoing maintenance and support costs for software you're considering for the project.

Depending on the complexity of the project, these processes might need the involvement of more than one person. For example, the finance person might not have expertise about the resources documented in the staffing management plan, so the project manager will need to bring in a staff member with those skills to assist with the activities in this process.

Two techniques are used in this Knowledge Area to decide among alternatives and improve the project process: life cycle costing and value engineering. The *life cycle costing* technique considers a group of costs collectively (such as acquisition, operations, disposal, and so on) when deciding among or comparing alternatives. The *value engineering* technique helps improve project schedules, profits, quality, and resource usage and optimizes life cycle costs, among others. Value engineering, in a nutshell, involves optimizing project performance and cost and is primarily concerned with eliminating unnecessary costs. By examining the project processes, performance, or even specific activities, the project manager can identify those elements that are not adding value and could be eliminated, modified, or reduced to realize cost savings. These techniques can improve decision making, reduce costs, reduce activity durations, and improve the quality of the deliverables. Some application areas require additional financial analysis to help predict project performance. Techniques such as payback analysis, return on investment, and discounted cash flows are a few of the tools used to accomplish this.

Project Quality Management

The *Project Quality Management Knowledge Area* is composed of three processes, as shown in Table 2.5.

TABLE 2.5 Project Quality Management

Process Name	Project Management Process Group
Plan Quality	Planning
Perform Quality Assurance	Executing
Perform Quality Control	Monitoring and Controlling

The *Project Quality Management Knowledge Area* assures that the project meets the requirements that it was undertaken to produce. This Knowledge Area focuses on product quality as well as on the quality of the project management process used during the project.

These processes measure overall performance and monitor project results and compare them to the quality standards set out in the project-planning process to ensure that the customers will receive the product, service, or result they commissioned.

Project Human Resource Management

The *Project Human Resource Management Knowledge Area* consists of four processes, as shown in Table 2.6.

TABLE 2.6 Project Human Resource Management

Process Name	Project Management Process Group
Develop Human Resource Plan	Planning
Acquire Project Team	Executing
Develop Project Team	Executing
Manage Project Team	Executing

Project Human Resource Management involves all aspects of people management and personal interaction, including leading, coaching, dealing with conflict, conducting performance appraisals, and more. These processes ensure that the human resources assigned to the project are used in the most effective way possible. Some of the project participants whom you'll get to practice these skills on are stakeholders, team members, and customers. Each requires the use of different communication styles, leadership skills, and team-building skills. A good project manager knows when to enact certain skills and communication styles based on the situation.

Projects are unique and temporary and so usually are project teams. Teams are put together based on the skills and resources needed to complete the activities of the project, and many times project team members might not know one another. Because the makeup of each team is different and the stakeholders involved in the various stages of the project might change, you'll use different techniques at different times throughout the project to manage the processes in this Knowledge Area.

Project Communications Management

The processes in The *Project Communications Management Knowledge Area* are related to general communication skills, but they encompass much more than an exchange of information. Communication skills are considered general management skills that the project manager utilizes on a daily basis. The processes in the Process Communications Management Knowledge Area seek to ensure that all project information—including project plans, risk assessments, meeting notes, and more—is collected, documented, archived, and disposed of at the proper time. These processes also ensure that information is distributed and shared with stakeholders, management, and project members at appropriate times. When the project is closed, the information is archived and used as a reference for future projects. This is referred to as *historical information* in several project processes.

Everyone on the project has some involvement with this Knowledge Area because all project members will send and/or receive project communication throughout the life of the project. It is important that all team members and stakeholders understand how communication affects the project.

Five processes make up The *Project Communications Management Knowledge Area*, as shown in Table 2.7.

TABLE 2.7 Project Communication Management

Process Name	Project Management Process Group
Identify Stakeholders	Initiating
Plan Communications	Planning
Distribute Information	Executing
Manage Stakeholder Expectations	Executing
Report Performance	Monitoring and Controlling

Time to Communicate

Project Communication Management is probably the most important Knowledge Area on any project. And most project managers understand the importance of good communication skills and making sure stakeholders are informed of project status. I know a project manager who had difficulties getting time with the project sponsor. The project sponsor agreed to meet with the project manager, even set up the meetings himself, and then canceled or simply didn't show up. The poor project manager was at wits end about how to communicate with the sponsor and get some answers to the questions she had. Her desk was not far outside the project sponsor's office. One day as she peeked around the corner of her cube, she decided if the sponsor wouldn't come to her, she would go to him. From then on, every time the sponsor left his office, she would jump up from her chair and ride with him on the elevator. He was a captive audience. She was able to get some easy questions answered and finally convince him, after the fourth or fifth elevator ride, that they needed regular face-to-face meetings. She understood the importance of communication and went to great lengths to make certain the sponsor did too.

Project Risk Management

Project Risk Management, as shown in Table 2.8, contains six processes.

TABLE 2.8 Project Risk Management

Process Name	Project Management Process Group
Plan Risk Management	Planning
Identify Risks	Planning
Perform Qualitative Risk Analysis	Planning
Perform Quantitative Risk Analysis	Planning
Plan Risk Responses	Planning
Monitor and Control Risk	Monitoring and Controlling

Risks include both threats to and opportunities within the project. The processes in this Knowledge Area are concerned with identifying, analyzing, and planning for potential risks, both positive and negative, that might impact the project. This means minimizing the probability and impact of negative risks while maximizing the probability and impact of positive risks. These processes are also used to identify the positive consequences of risks and exploit them to improve project objectives or discover efficiencies that might improve project performance.

Organizations will often combine several of these processes into one step. For example, Identify Risks and Perform Qualitative Risk Analysis might be performed at the same time. The important factor of The *Project Risk Management Knowledge Area* is that you should strive to identify all the risks and develop responses for those with the greatest consequences to the project objectives.

Project Procurement Management

Four processes are in The *Project Procurement Management Knowledge Area*, as shown in Table 2.9.

TABLE 2.9 Project Procurement Management

Process Name	Project Management Process Group
Plan Procurements	Planning
Conduct Procurements	Executing

TABLE 2.9 Project Procurement Management *(continued)*

Process Name	Project Management Process Group
Administer Procurements	Monitoring and Controlling
Close Procurements	Closing

The *Project Procurement Management Knowledge Area* includes the processes involved with purchasing goods or services from vendors, contractors, suppliers, and others outside the project team. When discussing the Project Procurement Management processes, it's assumed that the discussion is taking place from your perspective as a buyer, while sellers are external to the project team. Interestingly, the seller might manage their work as a project, particularly when the work is performed on contract, and you as the buyer become a key stakeholder in their project.

The remainder of this book will deal with processes and process groups as they occur in order (that is, Initiating, Planning, Executing, Monitoring and Controlling, and Closing), because this is the way you will encounter and manage them during a project.

Understanding How Projects Come About

Your company's quarterly meeting is scheduled for today. You take your seat, and each of the department heads gets up and gives their usual "We can do it" rah-rah speech, one after the other. You sit up a little straighter when the CEO takes the stage. He starts his part of the program pretty much the same way the other department heads did, and before long, you find yourself drifting off. You are mentally reviewing the status of your current project when suddenly your daydreaming trance is shattered. You perk up as you hear the CEO say, "And the new phone system will be installed by Thanksgiving."

Wait a minute. You work in the telecom department and haven't heard a word about this project until today. You also have a funny feeling that you've been elected to manage this project. It's amazing how good communication skills are so important for project managers but not for, well, we won't go there.

Project *initiation* is the formal recognition that a project, or the next phase in an existing project, should begin and resources should be committed to the project. Unfortunately, many projects are initiated the way the CEO did in this example. Each of us, at one time or another, has experienced being handed a project with little to no information and told to "make it happen." The new phone system scenario is an excellent example of how *not* to initiate a project.

Taking one step back leads you to ask, "How do projects come about in the first place? Do CEOs just make them up like in this example?" Even though your CEO announced this new project at the company meeting with no forewarning, no doubt it came about as a result of a legitimate need. Believe it or not, CEOs don't just dream up projects just to give you something to do. They're concerned about the future of the company and the needs of the business and its customers.

The business might drive the need for a project, customers might demand changes to products, or legal requirements might create the need for a new project. According to the *PMBOK® Guide*, projects come about as a result of one of seven needs or demands. Once those needs and demands are identified, the next logical step might include performing a feasibility study to determine the viability of the project. I'll cover these topics next.

Needs and Demands

Organizations exist to generate profits or serve the public. To stay competitive, organizations are always examining new ways of creating business, new ways of gaining efficiencies, or new ways of serving their customers. Sometimes laws are passed to force organizations to make their products safer or to make them less harmful to the environment. Projects might result from any of these needs as well as from business requirements, opportunities, or problems. Most projects will fit one of the seven needs and demands described next. Let's take a closer look at each of these areas:

Market demand The demands of the marketplace can drive the need for a project. For example, a bank initiates a project to offer customers the ability to apply for mortgage loans over the Internet because of a drop in interest rates and an increase in demand for refinancing and new home loans.

Strategic opportunity/business need The new phone system talked about earlier that was announced at the quarterly meeting came about as a result of a business need. The CEO, on advice from his staff, was advised that call volumes were maxed on the existing system. Without a new system, customer service response times would suffer, and that would eventually affect the bottom line.

Customer request Customer requests run the gamut. Generally speaking, most companies have customers, and their requests can drive new projects. Customers can be internal or external to the organization. Government agencies don't have external customers per se (we're captive customers at any rate), but there are internal customers within departments and across agencies.

Perhaps you work for a company that sells remittance-processing equipment and you've just landed a contract with a local utility company. This project is driven by the need of the utility company to automate its process or upgrade its existing process. The utility company's request to purchase your equipment and consulting services is the project driver.

Technological advance Many of us own a multifunctioning cell phone that keeps names and addresses handy along with a calendar and a to-do list of some kind. I couldn't live without mine. However, a newer, better version is always coming to market. Satellite communications now allows these devices to also act as GPS units. The introduction of satellite communications is an example of a technological advance. Because of this introduction, electronics manufacturers revamped their products to take advantage of this new technology.

Legal requirement Private industry and government agencies both generate new projects as a result of laws passed during every legislative season. For example, new sales tax laws might require new programming to the existing sales tax system. The requirement that food labels appear on every package describing the ingredients and the recommended daily allowances is another example of legal requirements that drive a project.

Ecological impacts Many organizations today are undergoing a "greening" effort to reduce energy consumption, save fuel, reduce their carbon footprint, and so on. These are examples of ecological impacts that result in projects.

Social need The last need is a result of social demands. For example, perhaps a developing country is experiencing a fast-spreading disease that's infecting large portions of the population. Medical supplies and facilities are needed to vaccinate and treat those infected with the disease. Another example might include manufacturing or processing plants that voluntarily remove their waste products from water prior to putting the water back into a local river or stream to prevent contamination.

Exam Spotlight

Understand the needs and demands that bring about a project for the exam.

All of these needs and demands represent opportunities, business requirements, or problems that need to be solved. Management must decide how to respond to these needs and demands, which will more often than not initiate new projects.

Real World Scenario

Project Initiation

Corey is an information technology manager who works for the National Park Service. One warm spring Sunday morning he was leafing through the newspaper and came across an article about new services being offered at some of the national parks. He really perked up when he saw his boss's name describing the changing nature of technology and how it impacted the types of services the public would like to see at the parks. Corey knew that the public had been asking when wireless Internet services would be available in some of the larger parks. He had also been involved in the discussions about the resources needed to make this happen. But the project never seemed to get off the ground. A higher-priority project always took precedence. However, all that changed when Corey saw the next sentence in the paper, which was his boss promising wireless access in two of the largest parks in their region by July 4. It looks like the customer requests finally won out, and Corey just learned he has a new project on his hands.

Feasibility Studies

After the opportunity for a project becomes evident, the next step might be to initiate it, which means you're ready to jump right into creating a project charter for the project. But before you take that plunge, you should know that some organizations will require a feasibility study prior to making a final decision about starting the project.

Feasibility studies are undertaken for several reasons. One is to determine whether the project is a viable project. A second reason is to determine the probability of the project succeeding. Feasibility studies can also examine the viability of the product, service, or result of the project. For example, the study might ask, "Will the new lemon-flavored soda be a hit? Is it marketable?" The study might also look at the technical issues related to the project and determine whether the technology proposed is feasible, reliable, and easily assimilated into the organization's existing technology structure.

Feasibility studies might be conducted as separate projects, as subprojects, or as the first phase of a project. When you don't know the outcome of the study, it's best to treat it as a separate project. The group of people conducting the feasibility study should not be the same people who will work on the project. Project team members might have built-in biases toward the project and will tend to influence the feasibility outcome toward those biases.

Real World Scenario

The Interactive Voice Response (IVR) Tax-Filing System

Jason, Sam, and Kate are web programmers working for the Department of Revenue in the State of Bliss. Ron, their manager, approaches them one day with an idea.

"Team, business unit managers are thinking it would be a great idea to offer taxpayers the ability to file their income tax returns over the telephone. We already offer them the ability to file on the Internet, thanks to all your efforts on that project last year. It has been a fabulous success. No other state has had the success that Bliss has had with our Internet system.

"Kate, I know you've had previous experience with IVR technology, but I'm not sure about you guys, so this is new territory for us. I'd like to hear what each of you thinks about this project."

Jason speaks up first. "I think it's a great idea. You know me, I'm always up for learning new things, especially when it comes to programming. When can we start?"

Sam echoes Jason's comments.

"This technology is pretty sophisticated," Kate says. "Jason and Sam are excellent coders and could work on the programming side of things, but I would have to pick up the telephony piece on my own. After we're up and running, we could go over the telephony portions step by step, so Jason and Sam could help me support it going forward. I'd really like to take on this project. It would be good for the team and good for the department."

Ron thinks for a minute. "Let's not jump right into this. I know you're anxious to get started, but I think a feasibility study is in order. The senior director of the tax business unit doesn't know whether this project is cost justified and has some concerns about its life span. A feasibility study will tell us the answers to those questions. It should also help us determine whether we're using the right technology to accomplish our goals, and it will outline alternative ways of performing the project that we haven't considered. I don't want Kate going it alone without first examining all the issues and potential impacts to the organization."

Selecting and Prioritizing Projects

Most organizations don't have the luxury of performing every project that's proposed. Even consulting organizations that sell their project management services must pick and choose the projects on which they want to work. Selection methods help organizations decide among alternative projects and determine the tangible benefits to the company of choosing or not choosing the project.

Project selection methods will vary depending on the company, the people serving on the selection committee, the criteria used, and the project. Sometimes the criteria for selection methods will be purely financial, sometimes purely marketing, and sometimes they'll be based on public perception or political perception. In most cases, the decision is based on a combination of all these and more.

Most organizations have a formal, or at least semiformal, process for selecting and prioritizing projects. In my organization, a steering committee is responsible for project review, selection, and prioritization. A *steering committee* is a group of folks comprising senior managers and sometimes midlevel managers who represent each of the functional areas in the organization.

Here's how our process works: The steering committee requests project ideas from the business staff prior to the beginning of the fiscal year. These project ideas are submitted in writing and contain a high-level overview of the project goals, a description of the deliverables, the business justification for the project, a desired implementation date, what the organization stands to gain from implementing the project, a list of the functional business areas affected by the project, and (if applicable) a cost-benefit analysis (I'll talk about that in a bit).

A meeting is called to review the projects, and a determination is made on each project about whether it will be included on the upcoming list of projects for the new year. Once the no-go projects have been weeded out, the remaining projects are prioritized according to their importance and benefit to the organization. The projects are documented on an official project list, and progress is reported on the active projects at the regular monthly steering committee meetings.

In theory, it's a great idea. In practice, it works only moderately well. Priorities can and do change throughout the year. New projects come up that weren't originally submitted during the call for projects, and they must be added to the list. Reprioritization begins anew, and resource alignment and assignments are shuffled. But again, I'm getting ahead of myself. Just be aware that organizations usually have a process to recognize and screen project requests, accept or reject those requests based on some selection criteria, and prioritize the projects based on some criteria.

The project selection methods I'll talk about next are ones you should know and understand for the exam. However, keep in mind they are only one aspect of project selection in the real world. The individual opinion, and power, of selection committee members also plays a part in the projects the organization chooses to perform. Don't underestimate the importance of the authority, political standing, and individual aspirations of selection committee members. Those committee members who happen to carry a lot of weight in company circles, so to speak, are likely to get their projects approved just because they are who they are. This is sometimes how project selection works in my organization. How about yours?

Using Project Selection Methods

Project selection methods are concerned with the advantages or merits of the product of the project. In other words, selection methods measure the value of what the product, service, or result of the project will produce and how it will benefit the organization. Selection methods involve the types of concerns executive managers are typically thinking about. This includes factors such as market share, financial benefits, return on investment, customer retention and loyalty, and public perceptions. Most of these are reflected in the organization's strategic goals. Projects, whether large or small, should always be weighed against the strategic plan. If the project doesn't help the organization reach its goals (increased market share, for example), then the project probably shouldn't be undertaken.

There are generally two categories of selection methods: *mathematical models* (also known as *calculation methods*) and *benefit measurement methods* (also known as *decision models*). Decision models examine different criteria used in making decisions regarding project selection, while calculation methods provide a way to calculate the value of the project, which is then used in project selection decision making.

Mathematical Models

For the exam, all you need to understand about mathematical models is that they use linear, dynamic, integer, nonlinear, and/or multi-objective programming in the form of algorithms—or in other words, a specific set of steps to solve a particular problem. These are complicated mathematical formulas and algorithms that are beyond the scope of this book and require an engineering, statistical, or mathematical background to fully understand. Organizations considering undertaking projects of enormous complexity might use mathematical modeling techniques to make decisions regarding these projects. Mathematical models are also known as *constrained optimization methods*. The vast majority of project selection techniques will use the benefit measurement methods to make project selection decisions.

Exam Spotlight

Project selection methods are also used to evaluate and choose between alternative ways of performing the project.

Benefit Measurement Methods

Benefit measurement methods employ various forms of analysis and comparative approaches to make project decisions. These methods include comparative approaches such as cost-benefit analysis, scoring models, and benefit contribution methods that include various cash flow techniques and economic models. You'll examine several of these methods, starting with cost-benefit analysis.

Cost-Benefit Analysis

One common benefit measurement method is the *cost-benefit* analysis. The name of this method implies what it does—it compares the cost to produce the product, service, or result of the project to the benefit (usually financial in the form of savings or revenue generation) that the organization will receive as a result of executing the project. Obviously, a sound project choice is one where the costs to implement or produce the product of the project are less than the financial benefits. How much less is the organization's decision. Some companies are comfortable with a small margin, while others are comfortable with a much larger margin between the two figures.

NOTE Cost-benefit analysis is also known as *benefit/cost analysis*. The techniques are the same. *Benefit/cost* has a more positive connotation because it shows the benefit, or the good stuff, before the cost, which is the not-so-good stuff.

When examining costs for a cost-benefit analysis, include the costs to produce the product or service, the costs to take the product to market, and the ongoing operational support costs. For example, let's say your company is considering writing and marketing a database software product that will allow banks to dissect their customer base, determine which types of customers buy which types of products, and then market more effectively to those customers. You will take into account some of the following costs:

- The costs to develop the software, such as programmer costs, hardware costs, and testing costs
- Marketing costs such as advertising, traveling costs to perform demos at potential customer sites, and so on
- Ongoing costs such as having a customer support staff available during business hours to assist customers with product questions and problems

Let's say the cost to produce this software plus the ongoing support costs total $5 million. Initial projections look like the demand for this product is high. Over a three-year period, which is the potential life of the software in its proposed form, projected revenues are $12 million. Taking only the financial information into account, the benefits outweigh the costs of this project. This project should receive a go recommendation.

NOTE

Projects of significant cost or complexity usually involve more than one benefit measurement method when go or no-go decisions are being made or one project is being chosen over another. Keep in mind that selection methods can take subjective considerations into account as well—the project is a go because it's the new CEO's pet project; nothing else needs to be said.

Scoring Models

Another project selection technique in the benefit measurement category is a *scoring model*, or *weighted scoring model*. My organization uses weighted scoring models not only to choose between projects but also as a method to choose between competing bids on outsourced projects.

Weighted scoring models are quite simple. The project selection committee decides on the criteria that will be used on the scoring model—for example, profit potential, marketability of the product or service, ability of the company to quickly and easily produce the product or service, and so on. Each of these criteria is assigned a weight depending on its importance to the project committee. More important criteria should carry a higher weight than less important criteria.

Then each project is rated on a scale from 1 to 5 (or some such assignment), with the higher number being the more desirable outcome to the company and the lower number having the opposite effect. This rating is then multiplied by the weight of the criteria factor and added to other weighted criteria scores for a total weighted score. Table 2.10 shows an example that brings this together.

TABLE 2.10 Weighted Scoring Model

Criteria	Weight	Project A Score*	Project A Totals	Project B Score*	Project B Totals	Project C Score*	Project C Totals
Profit potential	5	5	25	5	25	3	15
Marketability	3	4	12	3	9	4	12
Ease to produce/ support	1	4	4	3	3	2	2
Weighted score	—	—	41	—	37	—	29

*5 = highest

In this example, Project A is the obvious choice.

Cash Flow Analysis Techniques

The remaining benefit measurement methods involve a variety of cash flow analysis techniques, including payback period, discounted cash flows, net present value, and internal rate of return. We'll look at each of these techniques individually, and I'll provide you with a crash course on their meanings and calculations.

PAYBACK PERIOD

The *payback period* is the length of time it takes the company to recoup the initial costs of producing the product, service, or result of the project. This method compares the initial investment to the cash inflows expected over the life of the product, service, or result. For example, say the initial investment on a project is $200,000, with expected cash inflows of $25,000 per quarter every quarter for the first two years and $50,000 per quarter from then on. The payback period is two years and can be calculated as follows:

Initial investment = $200,000

Cash inflows = $25,000 * 4 (quarters in a year) = $100,000 per year total inflow

Initial investment ($200,000) – year 1 inflows ($100,000) = $100,000 remaining balance

Year 1 inflows remaining balance – year 2 inflows = $0

Total cash flow year 1 and year 2 = $200,000

The payback is reached in two years.

The fact that inflows are $50,000 per quarter starting in year 3 makes no difference because payback is reached in two years.

The payback period is the least precise of all the cash flow calculations. That's because the payback period does not consider the value of the cash inflows made in later years, commonly called the *time value of money*. For example, if you have a project with a five-year payback period, the cash inflows in year 5 are worth less than they are if you received them today. The next section will explain this idea more fully.

DISCOUNTED CASH FLOWS

As I just stated, money received in the future is worth less than money received today. The reason for that is the time value of money. If I borrowed $2,000 from you today and promised to pay it back in three years, you would expect me to pay interest in addition to the original amount borrowed. OK, if you were a family member or a really close friend, maybe you wouldn't, but ordinarily this is the way it works. You would have had the use of the $2,000 had you not lent it to me. If you had invested the money (does this bring back memories of your mom telling you to save your money?), you'd receive a return on it. Therefore, the future value of the $2,000 you lent me today is $2,315.25 in three years from now at 5 percent interest per year. Here's the formula for future value calculations:

$$FV = PV(1 + i)^n$$

In English, this formula says the future value (FV) of the investment equals the present value (PV) times (1 plus the interest rate) raised to the value of the number of time periods (n) the interest is paid. Let's plug in the numbers:

$FV = 2{,}000(1.05)^3$

$FV = 2{,}000(1.157625)$

FV = $2,315.25

The *discounted cash flow* technique compares the value of the future cash flows of the project to today's dollars. In order to calculate discounted cash flows, you need to know the value of the investment in today's terms, or the PV. PV is calculated as follows:

$PV = FV / (1 + i)^n$

This is the reverse of the FV formula talked about earlier. So, if you ask the question, "What is $2,315.25 in three years from now worth today given a 5 percent interest rate?" you'd use the preceding formula. Let's try it:

$PV = \$2{,}315.25 / (1 + .05)^3$

PV = $2,315.25 / 1.157625

PV = $2,000

$2,315.25 in three years from now is worth $2,000 today.

Discounted cash flow is calculated just like this for the projects you're comparing for selection purposes or when considering alternative ways of doing the project. Apply the PV formula to the projects you're considering, and then compare the discounted cash flows of all the projects against each other to make a selection. Here is an example comparison of two projects using this technique:

Project A is expected to make $100,000 in two years.

Project B is expected to make $120,000 in three years.

If the cost of capital is 12 percent, which project should you choose?

Using the PV formula used previously, calculate each project's worth:

The PV of Project A = $79,719.

The PV of Project B = $85,414.

Project B is the project that will return the highest investment to the company and should be chosen over Project A.

NET PRESENT VALUE

Projects might begin with a company investing some amount of money into the project to complete and accomplish its goals. In return, the company expects to receive revenues, or cash inflows, from the resulting project. *Net present value (NPV)* allows you to calculate an accurate value for the project in today's dollars. The mathematical formula for NPV is complicated, and you do not need to memorize it in that form for the test. However, you do need to know how to calculate NPV for the exam, so I've given you some examples of a less complicated way to perform this calculation in Table 2.11 and Table 2.12 using the formulas you've already seen.

TABLE 2.11 Project A

Year	Inflows	PV
1	10,000	8,929
2	15,000	11,958
3	5,000	3,559
Total	30,000	24,446
Less investment	—	24,000
NPV	—	**446**

TABLE 2.12 Project B

Year	Inflows	PV
1	7,000	6,250
2	13,000	10,364
3	10,000	7,118
Total	30,000	23,732
Less investment	—	24,000
NPV	—	**(268)**

Net present value works like discounted cash flows in that you bring the value of future monies received into today's dollars. With NPV, you evaluate the cash inflows using the discounted cash flow technique applied to each period the inflows are expected instead of in one sum. The total present value of the cash flows is then deducted from your initial investment to determine NPV. NPV assumes that cash inflows are reinvested at the cost of capital.

Here's the rule: If the NPV calculation is greater than zero, accept the project. If the NPV calculation is less than zero, reject the project.

Look at the two project examples in Tables 2.11 and 2.12. Project A and Project B have total cash inflows that are the same at the end of the project, but the amount of inflows at each period differs for each project. We'll stick with a 12 percent cost of capital. Note that the PV calculations were rounded to two decimal places.

Project A has an NPV greater than zero and should be accepted. Project B has a NPV less than zero and should be rejected. When you get a positive value for NPV, it means that the project will earn a return at least equal to or greater than the cost of capital.

Another note on NPV calculations: projects with high returns early in the project are better projects than projects with lower returns early in the project. In the preceding examples, Project A fits this criterion also.

INTERNAL RATE OF RETURN

The *internal rate of return (IRR)* is the most difficult equation to calculate of all the cash flow techniques we've discussed. It is a complicated formula and should be performed on a financial calculator or computer. IRR can be figured manually, but it's a trial-and-error approach to get to the answer.

Technically speaking, IRR is the discount rate when the present value of the cash inflows equals the original investment. When choosing between projects or when choosing alternative methods of doing the project, projects with higher IRR values are generally considered better than projects with low IRR values.

Exam Spotlight

For the exam, you need to know three facts concerning IRR:

- IRR is the discount rate when NPV equals zero.
- IRR assumes that cash inflows are reinvested at the IRR value.
- You should choose projects with the highest IRR value.

Exam Spotlight

Although the *PMBOK® Guide* doesn't specifically address project selection methods or cash flow techniques, you may see exam questions on these topics.

Applying Project Selection Methods

Now that we've discussed some of the project selection techniques, let's look at how to apply them when choosing projects or project alternatives. You can use one, two, or several of the benefit measurement methods alone or in combination to come up with a selection decision. Remember that payback period is the least precise of all the cash flow techniques, NPV is the most conservative cash flow technique, and NPV and IRR will generally bring you to the same accept/reject conclusion.

You can use project selection methods, and particularly the benefit measurement methods, to evaluate multiple projects or a single project. You might be weighing one project against another or simply considering whether the project you're proposing is worth performing.

Real World Scenario

Fun Days Vacation Resorts

Jerry is a project manager for Fun Days Vacation Resorts. He is working on three different project proposals to present to the executive steering committee for review. As part of the information-gathering process, Jerry visits the various resorts pretending to be a guest. This gives him a feel for what Fun Days guests experience on their vacations, and it better prepares him to present project particulars and alternatives.

Jerry has prepared the project overviews for three projects and called upon the experts in marketing to help him out with the projected revenue figures. He works up the numbers and finds the following:

- Project A: payback period = 5 years; IRR = 8 percent
- Project B: payback period = 3.5 years; IRR = 3 percent
- Project C: payback period = 2 years; IRR = 3 percent

Funding exists for only one of the projects. Jerry recommends Project A and predicts this is the project the steering committee will choose since the projects are mutually exclusive.

Jerry's turn to present comes up at the steering committee. Let's listen in on the action:

"And, on top of all the benefits I've just described, Project A provides an IRR of 8 percent, a full 5 percent higher than the other two projects we discussed. I recommend the committee choose Project A."

"Thank you Jerry," Colleen says. "Good presentation." Colleen is the executive chairperson of the steering committee and has the authority to break ties or make final decisions when the committee can't seem to agree.

"However, here at Fun Days we like to have our fun sooner rather than later." Chuckles ensue from the steering committee. They've all heard this before. "I do agree that an 8 percent IRR is a terrific return, but the payback is just too far out into the future. There are too many risks and unknowns for us to take on a project with a payback period this long. As you know, our industry is directly impacted by the health of the economy. Anything can happen in five years' time. I think we're much better off going with Project C. I recommend we accept Project C. Committee members, do you have anything to add?"

Kicking Off the Project Charter

Your first stop in the Initiating group is a process called Develop the Project Charter. As the name of the process suggests, your purpose is to create a project charter. As I talked about in Chapter 1, the purpose for the Initiating group is to authorize a project, or the next phase of a project, to begin. It also gives the project manager the authority to apply resources to the project. These are also the purposes of a project charter: formally authorizing the project to begin and committing resources.

NOTE The charter contains several elements that I'll discuss in the section "Formalizing and Publishing the Project Charter" later in this chapter.

Exam Spotlight

The *project charter* (which is an output of the Develop the Project Charter process) is the written acknowledgment that the project exists. The project charter documents the name of the project manager and gives that person the authority to assign organizational resources to the project. The project is officially authorized when the project charter is signed.

As you'll discover, every process has inputs, tools and techniques, and outputs, and this one is no exception. You'll start with the inputs. Let's get to it.

Inputs to the project processes are typically informational in nature, or they are outputs from previously completed processes. Inputs are used in combination with the tools and techniques to produce the outputs of each process. Process outputs are usually tangible, such as a report or an update or a list, for example. To get to the output, you have to start with the inputs. Let's take a look at the *Develop Project Charter* process inputs:

- Project statement of work
- Business case
- Contract
- Enterprise environmental factors
- Organizational process assets

The contract input is applicable only when the organization you are working for is performing a project for a customer external to the organization. The contract is used as an input to this process because it typically documents the conditions under which the project will be executed, the time frame, and a description of the work.

Project Statement of Work

The *project statement of work (SOW)* describes the product, service, or result the project was undertaken to complete. When the project is internal, this document is usually written by either the project sponsor or the initiator of the project. When the project is external to the organization, the buyer typically writes the SOW. For example, suppose you work for a consulting firm and have been assigned as the project manager for a project your company is performing on contract. The customer, the organization you'll be performing the project for, is the one who writes the SOW.

According to the *PMBOK® Guide*, a project SOW should contain or consider the following elements:

Business need The business need for the project here relates to the needs of the organization itself. The need might be based on governmental regulation, technological advances, market demands, or a legal requirement.

Product scope description The product scope description describes the characteristics of the product, service, or result of the project. The product scope description should be documented and should also include a description of the relationship between the business need or demand that's driving the project and the products being created.

Product descriptions contain less detail in the early phases of a project and more detail as the project progresses. Product scope descriptions, like the work of the project, are progressively elaborated. They will contain the greatest amount of detail in the project Executing processes.

When a project is performed under contract, typically the buyer of the product or service will provide the product description to the vendor or contractor. The product description can serve as a statement of work when the project is contracted to a vendor. A statement of work describes the product, service, or result in enough detail so that the vendor can accurately price the contract and satisfactorily fulfill the requirements of the project.

Strategic plan Part of the responsibility of a project manager during the Initiating processes is to take into consideration the company's strategic plan. Perhaps the strategic plan states that one of the company goals is to build 15 new stores by the end of the next fiscal year. If your project entails installing a new human resources software system, it makes sense to write the requirements for your project with the 15 new stores in mind. Your management team will refer to the strategic plan when choosing which new projects to initiate and which ones to drop, depending on their relationship to the strategic vision of the company.

Business Case

The purpose of a business case is to understand the business need for the project and determine whether the investment in the project is worthwhile. The business case often describes the cost-benefit analysis as well. The project comes about and the business case is written as a result of one of the needs or demands listed in the section "Needs and Demands."

Enterprise Environmental Factors

The enterprise environmental factors input shows up as an input to many of the other processes we'll discuss throughout the book. This input refers to the factors outside the project that have (or might have) significant influence on the success of the project. According to the *PMBOK® Guide*, the environmental factors include the following:

Organizational culture, structure, and processes I talked about organizational structures and their influence on the organization in Chapter 1.

Governmental or industry standards These include elements such as regulatory standards and regulations (for instance, doctors must be licensed to practice medicine on people or pets), quality standards (International Standards Organization standards, for example), product standards, and workmanship standards.

Infrastructure This refers to the organization's facilities and capital equipment. I'll also include information technology in this category.

Human resources This refers to the existing staff's skills and knowledge.

Personnel administration These are guidelines for hiring and firing, training, and employee performance reviews.

Organization's work authorization system This defines how the work of the project is authorized.

Marketplace conditions The old supply-and-demand theory applies here along with economic and financial factors.

Stakeholder risk tolerances This is the level of risk stakeholders are willing to take on. I'll talk more about this in Chapter 6, "Risk Planning."

Political climate This concerns both the internal and external political climate or influences on the project or organization.

Organization's established communications channels These are the mechanisms the organization uses to communicate both internally and externally

Commercial databases These refer to industry-specific information, risk databases, and so on.

These factors can influence the way you manage the project and, in some cases, the outcomes of the project. For example, perhaps the folks assigned to your project are junior level and don't have the skills, experience, or knowledge needed to complete the work of the project. It's up to the project manager to understand the organization's environmental factors and account for and consider how they can influence the management and outcomes of the project.

Organizational Process Assets

Organizational process assets are the organization's policies, guidelines, procedures, plans, approaches, and standards for conducting work, including project work. This includes a wide range of elements that might affect several aspects of the project, such as project management policies, safety policies, performance measurement criteria, templates, financial controls, communication requirements, issue and defect management procedures, change control procedures, risk control procedures, and the procedures used for authorizing work. Organizational process assets are divided into two categories: processes and procedures and corporate knowledge base.

Organizational process assets also include the information the organization has learned on previous projects (including how to store and retrieve that information). For example, previous project risks, performance measurements, earned value data, and schedules for past projects are valuable resources of knowledge for the current project. This information is also known as *historical information* and it falls into the corporate knowledge base category. If you don't capture and store this information, however, it won't be available when you're starting a new project. You'll want to capture and store information such as project financial data (budgets, costs, overruns), historical information, lessons learned, project files, issues and defects, process measurements, and configuration management knowledge.

NOTE

There are too many organizational process assets to cover in this chapter. I'll discuss many of them throughout the Planning chapters when a certain organizational process asset pertains to a specific process.

Organizational process assets and historical information should be reviewed and examined when a new project is starting. Historical information can be very useful to project managers and to stakeholders. When you're evaluating new projects, historical information about previous projects of a similar nature can be handy in determining whether the new project should be accepted and initiated. Historical information gathered and documented during an active project is used to assist in determining whether the project should proceed to the next phase. Historical information will help you with the project charter, project scope statement, development of the project management plan, the process of defining and estimating activities, and more during the project-planning processes.

Understanding previous projects of a similar nature—their problems, successes, issues, and outcomes—will help you avoid repeating mistakes while reusing successful techniques to accomplish the goals of this project to the satisfaction of the stakeholders. Many of the processes in the project management process groups have organizational process assets as an input, implying that you should review the pertinent organizational assets that apply for the process you're about to start. For example, when performing the Estimating Costs process, you might find it helpful to review the activity estimates and budgets on past projects of similar size and scope before estimating the costs for the activities on the new project.

Exam Spotlight

Remember that organizational process assets encompass many elements, including policies, guidelines, standards, historical information, and so on, and that they're divided into two categories: processes and procedures and corporate knowledge base. Make certain you understand what the organizational process assets entail for the exam and that you can differentiate them from the enterprise environmental factors input.

Expert Judgment Tool and Technique

Expert judgment is the only tool and technique in this process. The concept behind expert judgment is to rely on individuals, or groups of people, who have training, specialized knowledge, or skills in the areas you're assessing. These folks might be stakeholders, consultants, other experts in the organization, subject matter experts, the PMO, industry experts, or technical or professional organizations. Expert judgment is a tool and technique used in other planning processes as well.

In the case of developing a project charter, expert judgment would be helpful in assessing the inputs of this process, the environmental factors, organizational assets, and historical information. For example, as the project manager, you might rely on the expertise of your executive committee to help you understand how the proposed project gels with the strategic plan. Or you might rely on team members who have participated on similar projects in the past to make recommendations regarding the proposed project.

Formalizing and Publishing the Project Charter

The *project charter* is the official, written acknowledgment and recognition that a project exists. It ties the work of the project with the ongoing operations of the organization. It's usually signed by a senior manager or project sponsor, and it gives the project manager the authority to assign organizational resources to the project.

The charter documents the business need or demand that the project was initiated to address, and it includes a description of the product, service, or result of the project. It is usually the first official document of the project once acceptance of the project has been granted. Project charters are often used as a means to introduce a project to the organization. Since this document outlines the high-level project description, the business opportunity or need, and the project's purpose, executive managers can get a "first-glance" look at the benefits of the project. Good project charters that are well documented will address many of the questions your stakeholders are likely to have up front.

Let's take a brief look at the key stakeholders who might be involved with the project charter and the role they'll play in its development and on the project in the future.

Key Stakeholders

The *PMBOK® Guide* states that the project charter forms a partnership between the organization requesting the project and the one performing the project. The project charter should always be written before beginning the Planning process group. The signature of the project initiator signifies the formal authorization of the project. In practice, my experience has been that the project charter requires input from the key stakeholders and is published under the name of the project sponsor. Let's take a look at the roles of some of the key stakeholders in the project process next.

Project Manager

The project manager is the person who assumes responsibility for the success of the project. The project manager should be identified as early as possible in the project and ideally should participate in writing the project charter.

The project charter identifies the project manager and describes the authority the project manager has in carrying out the project. The project manager's primary responsibilities are project planning and then executing and managing the work of the project. By overseeing the project charter and the project planning documents created later in the project, the project manager is assured that everyone knows and understands what's expected of them and what constitutes a successful project.

Project managers are responsible for setting the standards and policies for the projects on which they work. As a project manager, it is your job to establish and communicate the project procedures to the project team and stakeholders.

Project managers will identify activities and tasks, resource requirements, project costs, project requirements, performance measures, and more. Communication and documentation must become the project manager's best friends. Keeping stakeholders, the project sponsor, the project team, and all other interested parties informed is "job one," as the famous car manufacturer's ads say.

Project Sponsor

Have you ever attended a conference or event that was put on by a sponsor? In the information technology field, software development companies often sponsor conferences and seminars. The sponsor pays for the event, the facilities, and the goodies and provides an opportunity for vendors to display their wares. In return, the sponsor comes out looking like a winner. Because it is footing the bill for all this fun, the sponsor gets to call the shots on conference content, and it gets the prime spots for discussing its particular solutions. And last but not least, it usually provides the keynote speaker and gets to present its information to a captive audience.

Project sponsors are similar to this in that they rally support from stakeholders and the executive management team for the project. The project sponsor is usually an executive in the organization who has the power and authority to make decisions and settle disputes or conflicts regarding the project. The sponsor takes the project into the limelight, so to speak, and gets to call the shots regarding project outcomes. The project sponsor is also the one with the big bucks who provides funds for your project. The project sponsor should be named in the project charter and identified as the final authority and decision maker for project issues.

Sponsors are actively involved in the Initiating and Planning phases of the project and tend to have less involvement during the Execution and Monitoring and Controlling phases. It's up to the project manager to keep the project sponsor informed of all project activities, project progress, and any conflicts or issues that arise. The sponsor is the one with the authority to resolve conflicts and set priorities when these things can't be dealt with any other way.

Project Champion

The project champion is another strong project supporter. Unlike the sponsor, the project champion doesn't necessarily have a lot of authority or executive powers. The champion helps focus attention on the project from a technical perspective. The project champion is usually someone with a great deal of technical expertise or industry knowledge regarding the project. They can lend credibility to the viability of the project and to the skills and abilities of the key project team members to carry out project activities. Sometimes, the project manager might act as project champion.

The project champion isn't necessarily identified in the project charter. But as a project manager, you'll want to know who this person is because the person is a strong project advocate, and because you might need them later to help rally support for project decisions.

Functional Managers

I covered functional managers briefly in Chapter 1. Project managers must work with and gain the support of functional managers in order to complete the project. Functional managers fulfill the administrative duties of the organization, provide and assign staff members to projects, and conduct performance reviews for their staff. It's a good idea to identify the functional managers who will be working on project tasks or assigned project responsibilities in the charter.

It's also a good idea to identify the key project stakeholders in the project charter. Although this isn't explicitly stated as part of this process, you'll see in the next section that stakeholder influences make up one of the components of the project charter. To identify stakeholder influences, it's also necessary to identify the stakeholders and describe their roles in high-level terms as I've done here.

Pulling the Project Charter Together

According to the *PMBOK® Guide*, to create a useful and well-documented project charter, you should include at least these elements:

- Purpose or justification for the project
- Project objectives that are measurable

- High-level list of requirements
- High-level description of the project
- High-level list of risks
- Summary milestone schedule
- Summary budget
- Criteria for project approval
- Name of the project manager and their authority levels
- Name of the sponsor (or authorizer of the project) and their authority levels

The important factors to remember for the exam about the project charter are that it authorizes the project to begin, it authorizes the project manager to assign resources to the project, it documents the business need and justification, it describes the customer's requirements, and it ties the project to the ongoing work of the organization.

Exam Spotlight

In some organizations, the project manager might write the project charter. However, if you (as the project manager) are asked to write the charter, remember that your name should not appear as the author. Since the project charter authorizes the project and authorizes you as the project manager, it doesn't make sense for you to write a document authorizing yourself to manage the project. The author of the charter should be an executive manager in your organization (external to the project) with the power and authority to assign resources to this project. This is usually the project sponsor or initiator. Remember for the exam that the charter is authorized by someone external to the project.

Project Charter Sign-Off

The project charter isn't complete until you've received sign-off from the project sponsor, senior management, and key stakeholders. Sign-off indicates that the document has been read by those signing it (let's hope so, anyway), and that they agree with its contents and are on board with the project. It also involves the major stakeholders right from the beginning and should win their continued participation in the project going forward. If someone has a problem with any of the elements in the charter, now is the time to raise the red flag.

Prior to publishing the charter, I like to hold a kickoff meeting with the key stakeholders to discuss the charter and then obtain their sign-off. I think it's imperative you identify your key stakeholders as soon as possible and involve them in the creation of the project charter. Remember that stakeholder identification is an ongoing activity.

NOTE

I'll talk more about key stakeholder roles in Chapter 3.

Signing the project charter document is the equivalent of agreeing to and endorsing the project. This doesn't mean the project charter is set in stone, however. Project charters will change throughout the course of the project. As more details are uncovered and outlined and as the Planning processes begin, more project issues will come to light. This is part of the iterative process of project management and is to be expected. The charter will occasionally be revised to reflect these new details, project plans will be revised, and project execution will change to incorporate the new information or direction.

The last step in this process is publishing the charter. Publishing, in this case, simply means distributing a copy of the project charter to the key stakeholders, the customer, the management team, and others who might be involved with the project. Publication can take several forms, including printed format or electronic format distributed via the company email system or on the company's intranet.

Next, we'll look at the Identify Stakeholders process.

Identifying Stakeholders

Think of stakeholders and project participants as a highly polished orchestra. Each participant has a part to play. Some play more parts than others, and, alas, some don't play their parts as well as others. An integral part of project management is getting to know your stakeholders and the parts they play. You'll remember from Chapter 1 that stakeholders are those people or organizations who have a vested interest in the outcome of the project. They have something to either gain or lose as a result of the project, and they have the ability to influence project results.

Identify Stakeholders Inputs

The Identify Stakeholders process involves identifying and documenting all the stakeholders on the project, including their interests and potential positive or negative impacts on the project.

Identifying key stakeholders seems like it should be fairly easy, but once you get beyond the obvious stakeholders, the process can get difficult. Sometimes stakeholders, even key stakeholders, will change throughout the project's life. The key stakeholders on a project might include the project sponsor, the customer (who might also be the project sponsor), the project manager, project team members, management personnel, contractors, suppliers, and so on. The stakeholders involved in the project charter and the contract are obvious picks to be included in the stakeholder register, one output of this process.

The inputs of this process are as follows:

- Project charter
- Procurement documents

- Enterprise environmental factors
- Organizational process assets

According to the *PMBOK® Guide*, the environmental factors you'll want to pay particular attention to during this process are company culture, organizational structure, and governmental or industry standards. The organization structure will help you understand who has influence and power based on position and where they reside in the organization. The organizational process assets you should be concerned about include stakeholder register templates, lessons learned, and the stakeholder registers from previous projects. We'll talk more about stakeholder register templates later in this chapter.

Don't forget important stakeholders. That could be a project killer. Leaving out an important stakeholder, or one whose business processes weren't considered particularly during the Initiating and Planning processes, could spell disaster for your project.

Exam Spotlight

Stakeholder identification should occur as early as possible in the project and continue throughout its life. Likewise, the stakeholder analysis and strategy should be reviewed periodically throughout the project and updated as needed.

Stakeholder Analysis

The tools and techniques of Identify Stakeholders are stakeholder analysis and expert judgment.

During stakeholder analysis, you'll want to identify the influences stakeholders have in regard to the project and understand their expectations, needs, and desires. From there, you'll derive more specifics regarding the project goals and deliverables. Be warned that stakeholders are mostly concerned about their own interests and what they (or their organizations) have to gain or lose from the project. In all fairness, we all fall into the stakeholder category, so we're all guilty of focusing on those issues that impact us most.

According to the *PMBOK® Guide*, there are three steps involved in stakeholder analysis: identifying stakeholders, identifying potential impact, and assessing how stakeholders are likely to react to given situations. Let's look at each step independently.

The first step is identifying all potential stakeholders and capturing general information about them such as the department they work in, contact information, knowledge levels, and influence levels. Since the output of this process is the stakeholder register, I would devise a stakeholder register template now and capture all information about the stakeholders in one place. Table 2.13 is an example of a stakeholder register template.

TABLE 2.13 Stakeholder Register Template

Name	Department	Knowledge Level	Expectations	Influence Levels	Phone	Email

When we discuss the stakeholder register output later in this section, I'll tell you what additional elements you need to add to your chart.

Stakeholders can be internal or external to the organization. One way to uncover stakeholders whom you might not have thought about at the start is to ask known stakeholders if they're aware of anyone else who might be impacted by this project. Ask team members whether they're aware of stakeholders who haven't been identified. Stakeholders might also come to the forefront once you start uncovering some of the goals and deliverables of the project.

Understanding Stakeholder Roles

The second step in identifying stakeholders is identifying the potential impact on or support for the project each may have and then classifying them according to impact so that you can devise a strategy to deal with those impacts should they arise.

In order to determine potential impact, it's important for the project manager to understand each stakeholder's role in the project and in the organization. Get to know them and their interests. Determine the relationship structure among the various stakeholders. Start cultivating partnerships with these stakeholders now, because it's going to get pretty cozy during the course of your project. If you establish good working relationships up front and learn a little about their business concerns and needs, it might be easier to negotiate or motivate them later when you have a pressing issue that needs action. Knowing which stakeholders work well together and which don't can also help you in the future. One stakeholder might have the authority or influence to twist the arm of another, figuratively speaking, of course. Or, conversely, you might know of two stakeholders who are like oil and water when put into the same room together. This can be valuable information to keep under your hat for future reference.

Some stakeholders may have a significant amount of influence over the project and its outcomes. Understanding the organizational structure, and where the stakeholders fit in that structure, should be your first step in determining the level of influence they have. For example, if Melanie in accounting wields a significant amount of power and influence over the organization, when you need input or decisions from her regarding costs or budgets for the project, you better believe that those decisions are not likely to be overridden. Conversely, if stakeholders with little influence provide direction that you don't verify, that input could be overridden at a later date by a more powerful stakeholder, causing changes to the project.

You can essentially classify the power and influence of each stakeholder on a simple four-square grid. The *PMBOK® Guide* lists four classification models for this task:

- Power/Interest grid
- Power/Influence grid
- Influence/Impact grid
- Salience model

The first three grids are self-explanatory. The Salience model is more complicated than a four-square grid because it charts three factors: stakeholder power, urgency, and legitimacy. Urgency refers to a stakeholders level of need for attention as immediate, occasional, or rarely. Legitimacy concerns the appropriateness of the stakeholder's participation at given times during the project.

Assessing Stakeholders

The third step in stakeholder analysis is assessing the influence and potential negative impacts key stakeholders may have on the project. As I said earlier, some stakeholders may have a significant amount of influence over the project and its outcomes. And as with assessing a stakeholder's role, your first step in determining the level of influence they have should be to understand the organizational structure and where they fit in. Once the stakeholder assessment is complete, you should devise a plan to deal with any potential impacts like the case mentioned earlier where a stakeholder with little influence makes a decision that could later be overturned.

NOTE

Remember that the definition of a successful project is one that accomplishes the goals of the project and meets or exceeds stakeholders' expectations. Understand and document those expectations, and you're off to a good start.

Stakeholder Register and Strategy

Stakeholder register and stakeholder management strategy are the two outputs of this process. The stakeholder register contains the information we discussed earlier in this section in the stakeholder register template. In addition to the elements we already discussed, the stakeholder register should also contain at least the following details according to the *PMBOK® Guide*:

Identifying information This includes items like contact information, department, role in the project, and so on.

Assessment information This includes elements regarding influence, expectations, key requirements, and when the stakeholder involvement is most critical.

Stakeholder classification Stakeholders can be classified according to their relationship to the organization (internal or external for example) and, more importantly, whether they support the project, are resistant to the project, or have no opinion.

The stakeholder management strategy is the documented approach you'll use to minimize negative impacts or influences that stakeholders may have throughout the life of the project. You could use a spreadsheet approach similar to the stakeholder register template to document this information. I would most likely combine the stakeholder register information with the stakeholder management strategy so all the information is contained in one place.

According to the *PMBOK® Guide*, you'll want to include the following elements in the stakeholder management strategy:

- Name of key stakeholders who could have a significant impact on the project
- Stakeholders' anticipated level of participation
- Stakeholder groups
- Assessment of impact
- Potential strategies for gaining support

> **NOTE** Remember that project documents are usually easily accessible by the project team and stakeholders. Use caution when documenting sensitive information regarding a stakeholder and your strategy for dealing with that stakeholder because it could become public knowledge.

Introducing the Kitchen Heaven Project Case Study

This chapter introduces a case study that we'll follow throughout the remainder of the book. The case study is updated at the end of every chapter. It's designed to show you how a project manager might apply the material covered in the chapter to a real-life project. As happens in real life, not every detail of every process is followed during all projects. Remember that the processes from the *PMBOK® Guide* that I'll cover in the remaining chapters are project management guidelines. You will often combine processes during your projects, which will allow you to perform several steps at once. The case studies will present situations or processes that you might find during your projects and describe how one project manager resolves them.

Real World Scenario

Project Case Study: New Kitchen Heaven Retail Store

You are a project manager for Kitchen Heaven, a chain of retail stores specializing in kitchen utensils, cookware, dishes, small appliances, and some gourmet foodstuffs, such as bottled sauces and spices. You're fairly new to the position, having been hired to replace a project manager who recently retired.

Kitchen Heaven currently owns 49 stores in 34 states and Canada. The world headquarters for Kitchen Heaven is in Denver, Colorado. Counting full-time and part-time employees, the company employs 1,500 people, 200 of whom work at headquarters.

The company's mission statement reads, "Great gadgets for people interested in great food."

Recently, the vice president of marketing paid you a visit. Dirk Perrier is a very nice, well-dressed man with the formal air you would expect a person in his capacity might have. He shakes your hand and gives you a broad, friendly smile.

"We've decided to go forward with our 50th store opening! Sales are up, and our new line of ceramic cookware is a hot seller, no pun intended. I don't know if you're familiar with our store philosophy, so let me take a moment to explain it. We like to place our stores in neighborhoods that are somewhat affluent. The plain fact is that most of our shoppers have incomes of more than $150,000 a year. So, we make an effort to place our stores in areas where those folks usually shop.

"We're targeting the type of customer who watches the Food Network channel and must have all the gadgets and tools they see the famous chefs using. So, the stores are upbeat and convey a fun, energetic feel, if you will.

"Our next store is going to be right here in our home area—Colorado Springs. Because this is going to be our 50th store, we plan on having a 50th grand-opening celebration, with the kind of surprises and activities you might expect for such a notable opening.

"Our stores generally occupy from 1,500 to 2,500 square feet of retail space, and we typically use local contractors for the build-out. A store build-out usually takes 120 days from the date the property has been procured until the doors open to the public. I can give you our last opening's project plan so you have a feel for what happens. Your job will be to procure the property, negotiate the lease, procure the shelving and associated store furnishings, get a contractor on the job, and prepare the 50th store festivities. My marketing folks will assist you with that last part.

"You have six months to complete the project. Any questions?"

You take in a deep breath and collect your thoughts. Dirk has just given you a lot of information with hardly a pause in between thoughts. A few initial ideas drift through your head while you're reaching for your notebook.

You work in a functional organization with a separate projectized department responsible for carrying out projects of this nature. You've been with the company long enough to know that Dirk is high up there in the executive ranks and carries the authority and power to make things happen. Therefore, Dirk is the perfect candidate for project sponsor.

You grab your notebook and start documenting some of the things Dirk talked about, clarifying with him as you write:

- The project objective is to open a new store in Colorado Springs six months from today.
- The store should be located in an affluent area.
- The store will carry the full line of products from utensils to gourmet food items.
- The grand opening will be accompanied by lots of fanfare because this is the 50th store opening.

You have a question or two for Dirk.

"Is there a special reason we have to open, let's see, six months from now, which is February 1?"

He responds, "Yes, we want the store open the first week in February. Early February is when the Garden and Home Show conference hits the Springs area. We'll have a trade show booth there. We know from experience in other areas that our stores generally see a surge in sales during this month as a result of the trade show. It's a great way to get a lot of advertising out there and let folks know where we're located."

"Another question, Dirk. Is there a budget set for this project yet?"

"We haven't set a hard figure," Dirk replies. "But again, from past experience we know it takes anywhere from $1.5 to $2 million to open a new store. And we don't want to forget the big bash for the grand opening."

"Thanks, Dirk. I'll get started writing the project charter right away. I'll be putting your name on the document since you're the project sponsor."

Dirk concludes with, "Feel free to come to me with questions or concerns at any time."

One week later.

You review your notes and reread the project charter you've prepared for the Kitchen Heaven retail store one last time before looking for Dirk. You finally run across Dirk in a hallway near the executive washroom.

"Dirk, I'm glad I caught you. I'd like to go over the project charter with you before the kick-off meeting tomorrow. Do you have a few minutes?"

"Sure," Dirk says to you. "Let's have it."

"The project charter states the purpose of the project, which of course is to open the 50th Kitchen Heaven store in Colorado Springs. I also documented some of the high-level requirements, many of which we talked about last time we met. I documented the assumptions and constraints you gave me with the understanding that we'll define these much more closely when I create the scope statement. I've included a section that outlines a preliminary milestone schedule, and I've included some preliminary return on investment calculations. Using your estimate of $2 million as our initial budget request and based on the projected inflows you gave me last week, I've calculated a payback period of 19 months, with an IRR of 6 percent."

"That's impressive," replies Dirk. "That's even better than our Phoenix store. If I recall, the payback period there was just over two years. Let's hope those numbers hold true."

"I think they're reliable figures," you say. "I researched our data based on recent store openings in similar-sized cities and factored in the economic conditions of the Colorado Springs area. Since they're on a growth pattern, we think the timing is perfect.

"As you know, the project kickoff is scheduled for tomorrow. What I'll need, then, is for you to talk about the project and the goals, talk about the commitment you'll need from the management team to support this project, and introduce me as the project manager. I've already forwarded a copy of the project charter to the meeting attendees so that they can review it before the meeting. And I included a list of the assumptions we've made so far as an appendix to the charter. Lastly, I'll need you to ask everyone present to sign a copy of the project charter."

"Sounds like you've covered everything," Dirk says. "I don't anticipate any problems tomorrow, because everyone is looking forward to this store opening."

Project Case Study Checklist

- **Project objective**: To open a new store in Colorado Springs six months from today.
- **Business need or demand for project**: Company data concludes that the Kitchen Heaven consumers have incomes of more than $150,000 a year. The Colorado Springs area is home to a large number of people with that income. Currently, there is not a Kitchen Heaven there, but there appears to be a demand for one.
- **Project sponsor**: Dirk Perrier, VP of marketing.
- **Organizational structure**: Functional organization with a separate projectized department.

- **Project selection methods**: Payback period calculated at 19 months and IRR calculated at 6 percent.
- **Created project charter**: Project charter contains the following:
  - High-level overview of project
  - List of measurable project objectives
  - High-level risks
  - Summary milestone schedule with initial completion date of February 1
  - Summary budget of $2 million
  - Project manager authority levels
  - Definition of roles of project sponsor and project manager

Next steps: Kickoff meeting set up to discuss charter and obtain sign-off.

Understanding How This Applies to Your Next Project

There are as many ways to select and prioritize projects as there are organizations. You might be profit driven, so money will be king. You might have a stakeholder committee that weighs the pros and cons, or you might have an executive director who determines which project is up next. Scoring models and cash flow analysis techniques are useful on the job. Whether you use these methods or others, you'll need an organized, consistent way to select and prioritize projects. I know I could work the next 100 years straight and probably still not get all the projects completed my organization would like to see implemented. What I've found is that the selection method must be fair and reasonable. If you have an arbitrary method—say you like Tara better than Joe, so Tara's projects always end up on the "yes" list—it won't be long before your stakeholders demand that you devise a way to select projects that everyone can understand. Whatever method you're using, stick to it consistently.

If you're like me, when I'm faced with a new project, I want to get right to the heart of the matter and understand the purpose of the project. Projects come about for many reasons. Most of the time, understanding the reason it came about will give you some insight into its purpose. For example, if a new law is passed that requires anyone applying for a driver's license to show two forms of identification but the existing system has the space to record verification of only one document, you immediately have a firm grasp on the purpose of the project—you'll have to update the system to include additional space for recording the second document.

It has been my experience in working with project teams that when the team understands the reason or the need that brought about the project and it understands the goal of the project, the project is more successful. Now I don't have any scientific evidence for this, but when the teams have a clear understanding of what they're working on and why, they tend to stay more focused and fewer unplanned changes make their way into the project. Don't assume everyone on the project team understands the goal of the project. It's good practice to review the project goal early in the project and again once the work of the project is underway. Reminding the team of the goal helps keep the work on track.

I usually write a project charter for all but the smallest of projects. I believe the most important sections of the charter are the objectives of the project, the summary milestone schedule, and the summary budget. If the project is so small that a charter seems like too much, I'll write a statement of work. It's important that the goal or objective of the project is written down, no matter how small the project is, so that the team and the stakeholders know what they're working toward.

Identifying the stakeholders early in the project is imperative to project success. You won't really want to write the charter without their involvement. The two processes described in this chapter are almost performed simultaneously when you're conducting a project. I won't begin writing the charter without stakeholder input first. And it's just as important to understand the role stakeholders will play in the project as well as their influence. If the CFO has ultimate influence over which projects proceed and what they'll include, you'll want the CFO's buy-in as soon as possible. Involvement in writing the charter and developing the future Planning process outputs helps to assure their buy-in. At a minimum, it helps reduce surprises midway through the project.

Always, and I mean *always*, get approval and signatures on the project charter. You will use this document as your basis for project planning, so you want to make certain the sponsor, key stakeholders, and the project manager understand the goals of the project the same way.

Summary

This chapter started with a discussion of the nine Knowledge Areas. The Knowledge Areas bring together processes that have characteristics in common. And they help you understand what types of skills and resources are needed to complete the processes within them.

Next I detailed how projects are initiated. Projects come about as a result of one of seven needs or demands: market demands, organizational needs, customer requests, technological advances, legal requirements, ecological impacts, or social needs.

Project selection methods include decision models in the form of benefit measurement methods and mathematical models (also called *constrained optimization methods*). The mathematical methods utilize mathematical models. Benefit measurement methods come in the form of cost-benefit analyses, scoring models, and economic analyses. These are primarily comparative approaches. Besides cost-benefit analysis, the most commonly used form of benefit measurement methods is cash flow analysis.

Analysis of cash flows includes payback period, discounted cash flows, net present value (NPV), and internal rate of return (IRR). These last three methods are concerned with the time value of money—or, in other words, converting future dollars into today's value. Generally, projects with a shorter payback period are desired over those with longer payback periods. Projects that have an NPV greater than zero should be accepted. Projects with the highest IRR value are considered a better benefit to the organization than projects with lower IRR values.

The Develop the Project Charter process is the first process within the Initiating process group. The project statement of work is an input to this process that describes the product, service, or result the project was undertaken to complete. The SOW should include the business needs of the organization and a product scope description and should map to the organization's strategic plan.

Enterprise environmental factors are factors outside the project that might have significant influence on the success of the project. Organizational process assets refer to policies, guidelines, and procedures for conducting the project work.

Expert judgment is the only tool and technique of this process. Experts usually have specialized knowledge or skills and can include staff from other departments in the company, external or internal consultants, and members of professional and technical associations or industry groups.

The output of this process is the project charter, which is the formal recognition that a project, or the next project phase, should begin. The charter authorizes the project to begin, it authorizes the project manager to assign resources to the project, it documents the business need and justification, it describes the customer's requirements, and it ties the project to the ongoing work of the organization.

The Identify Stakeholders process concerns identifying, assessing, and classifying stakeholders in a stakeholder register and developing a stakeholder management strategy. Stakeholder involvement is critical to the success of the project. The more the project manager understands stakeholder influences, expectations, and impacts, the easier it is to prepare a strategy plan to deal with the impacts or issues, sometimes before they occur.

Exam Essentials

Be able to name the nine Project Management Knowledge Areas. The nine Project Management Knowledge Areas are Project Integration Management, Project Scope Management, Project Time Management, Project Cost Management, Project Quality Management, Project Human Resource Management, Project Communications Management, Project Risk Management, and Project Procurement Management.

Be able to distinguish between the seven needs or demands that bring about project creation. The seven needs or demands that bring about project creation are market demand, organizational need, customer requests, technological advances, legal requirements, ecological impacts, and social needs.

Be able to define decision models. Decision models are project selection methods that are used prior to the Develop Project Charter process to determine the viability of the project. Decision models include benefit measurement methods and mathematical models.

Be able to describe and calculate payback period. Payback period is the amount of time it will take the company to recoup its initial investment in the product of the project. It's calculated by adding up the expected cash inflows and comparing them to the initial investment to determine how many periods it takes for the cash inflows to equal the initial investment.

Be able to denote the decision criteria for NPV and IRR. Projects with an NPV greater than zero should be accepted, and those with an NPV less than zero should be rejected. Projects with high IRR values should be accepted over projects with lower IRR values. IRR is the discount rate when NPV is equal to zero, and IRR assumes reinvestment at the IRR rate.

Be able to denote the Develop Project Charter inputs. The inputs for Develop the Project Charter are project statement of work, business case, contract, enterprise environmental factors, and organizational process assets.

Be able to describe the importance of the project charter. The project charter is the document that officially recognizes and acknowledges that a project exists. The charter authorizes the project to begin, it authorizes the project manager to assign resources to the project, it documents the business need and justification, it describes the customer's requirements, and it ties the project to the ongoing work of the organization.

Understand the Identify Stakeholders process. The purpose of this process is to identify the project stakeholders, assess their influence and level of involvement, devise a plan to deal with potential negative impacts, and record stakeholder information in the stakeholder register.

Key Terms

You've learned just how important a charter is to every project. Be sure you understand the elements essential to the document and the processes used to ensure that your charter is complete. Skimping on the planning steps is almost certain to spell disaster down the road. Know these processes, and know them by the names used in the *PMBOK®* Guide:

Develop Project Charter

Identify Stakeholders

You've also learned a lot of new key words in this chapter. PMI has worked hard to develop and define standard project management terms that apply across industries. Here is a list of some of the terms you came across in this chapter:

benefit measurement methods	internal rate of return (IRR)
calculation methods	mathematical models
constrained optimization methods	net present value (NPV)
cost-benefit	payback period
decision models	project charter
discounted cash flow	project statement of work (SOW)
expert judgment	scoring model
historical information	steering committee
Initiating	weighted scoring model

Review Questions

1. When a project is being performed under contract, the SOW is provided by which of the following?
   - **A.** The buyer
   - **B.** The project sponsor
   - **C.** The project manager
   - **D.** The contractor

2. You've been hired as a manager for the adjustments department of a nationwide bank based in your city. The adjustments department is responsible for making corrections to customer accounts. This is a large department, with several smaller sections that deal with specific accounts, such as personal checking or commercial checking. You've received your first set of management reports and can't make heads or tails of the information. Each section appears to use a different methodology to audit their work and record the data for the management report. You request that a project manager from the PMO comes down and get started right away on a project to streamline this process and make the data and reports consistent. This project came about as a result of which of the following?
   - **A.** Technological advance
   - **B.** Organizational need
   - **C.** Customer request
   - **D.** Legal requirement

3. What are the inputs to the Develop Project Charter process?
   - **A.** Contract, project SOW, business case, enterprise environmental factors, and organizational process assets
   - **B.** Project SOW, business case, and organizational process assets
   - **C.** Contract, enterprise environmental factors, and organizational process assets
   - **D.** Project SOW, enterprise environmental factors, and organizational process assets

4. You work for a large manufacturing plant. Your firm is thinking of initiating a new project to release an overseas product line. This is the company's first experience in the overseas market, and it wants to make a big splash with the introduction of this product. The project entails producing your product in a concentrated formula and packaging it in smaller containers than the U.S. product uses. A new machine is needed in order to mix the first set of ingredients in the concentrated formula. Which of the following actions is the next best step the project manager should take?
   - **A.** The project manager should document the project's high-level requirements in a project charter document and recommend that the project proceed.
   - **B.** The project manager knows the project is a go and should document the description of the product in the statement of work.

C. The project manager should document the business need for the project and recommend that a feasibility study be performed to determine the viability of the project.

D. The project manager should document the key stakeholders and their potential impacts in the stakeholder register.

5. You are the project manager for Fun Days Vacation Resorts. Your new project assignment is to head up the Fun Days resort opening in Austin, Texas. You are estimating the duration of the project plan activities, devising the project schedule, and monitoring and controlling deviations from the schedule. Which of the Project Management Knowledge Areas are you working in?

   A. Project Scope Management

   B. Project Quality Management

   C. Project Integration Management

   D. Project Time Management

6. According to the *PMBOK® Guide*, the project statement of work should contain or reference which of the following elements?

   A. Strategic plan, product scope description, measurable project objectives, and business need

   B. Business need, strategic plan, product scope description

   C. Project purpose, measurable project objectives, business case, and product scope description

   D. Product scope description, project purpose, and business need

7. Your nonprofit organization is preparing to host its first annual 5K run/walk in City Park. You worked on a similar project for the organization two years ago when it cohosted the 10K run through Overland Pass. Which of the organizational process assets might be most helpful to you on your new project?

   A. The organization's marketing plans

   B. Historical information from a pervious 10K run or similar project

   C. The marketplace and political conditions

   D. The organization's project management information systems

8. Which of the following lists of processes belong to The *Project Integration Management Knowledge Area*?

   A. Define Scope, Close Procurements, and Perform Integrated Change Control

   B. Develop Project Management Plan, Direct and Manage Project Execution, and Perform Integrated Change Control

   C. Define Scope, Direct and Manage Project Execution, and Manage Stakeholders Expectations

   D. Define Scope, Collect Requirements, and Close Project or Phase

9. Comparative methods, scoring methods, and economic and cash flow analysis are all part of which of the following?

A. Benefit measurement methods

B. Constrained optimization methods

C. Benefit measurement methods, which are a component of a tool and technique of the Develop Project Charter process

D. Constrained optimization methods, which are a component of a tool and technique of the Develop Project Charter process

10. You are the project manager for the Late Night Smooth Jazz Club chain, with stores in 12 states. Smooth Jazz is considering opening a new club in Arizona or Nevada. You have derived the following information:

Project Arizona: The payback period is 18 months, and the NPV is (250).

Project Nevada: The payback period is 24 months, and the NPV is 300.

Which project would you recommend to the selection committee?

A. Project Arizona, because the payback period is shorter than the payback period for Project Nevada

B. Project Nevada, because its NPV is a positive number

C. Project Arizona, because its NPV is a negative number

D. Project Nevada, because its NPV is a higher number than Project Arizona's NPV

11. You are the project manager for the Late Night Smooth Jazz Club chain, with stores in 12 states. Smooth Jazz is considering opening a new club in Kansas City or Spokane. You have derived the following information:

Project Kansas City: The payback period is 27 months, and the IRR is 6 percent.

Project Spokane: The payback period is 25 months, and the IRR is 5 percent.

Which project should you recommend to the selection committee?

A. Project Spokane, because the payback period is the shortest

B. Project Kansas City, because the IRR is the highest

C. Project Spokane, because the IRR is the lowest

D. Project Kansas City, because the payback period is the longest

12. Which of the following is true regarding NPV?

A. NPV assumes reinvestment at the cost of capital.

B. NPV decisions should be made based on the highest value for all the selections.

C. NPV assumes reinvestment at the prevailing rate.

D. NPV assumes reinvestment at the NPV rate.

13. You are the project manager for Insomniacs International. Since you don't sleep much, you get a lot of project work done. You're considering recommending a project that costs $575,000; expected inflows are $25,000 per quarter for the first two years and then $75,000 per quarter thereafter. What is the payback period?

    A. 40 months
    B. 38 months
    C. 39 months
    D. 41 months

14. Which of the following is true regarding IRR?

    A. IRR assumes reinvestment at the cost of capital.
    B. IRR is not difficult to calculate.
    C. IRR is a constrained optimization method.
    D. IRR is the discount rate when NPV is equal to zero.

15. Mathematical models using linear, dynamic, integer, or algorithm models are considered ________.

    A. project selection criteria
    B. a form of expert judgment
    C. project selection methods
    D. a form of historical information

16. Your project selection committee used a weighted scoring model and found that Project B, with a score of 54, should be chosen over the other competing projects. Which of the following is true?

    A. Weighted scoring models are benefit measurement methods.
    B. Weighted scoring models are constrained optimization methods.
    C. Weighted scoring models are benefit measurement methods and are the least efficient method of project selection.
    D. Weighted scoring models are a type of mathematical model that can be used for both project selection and vendor selection.

17. Your selection committee is debating between two projects. Project A has a payback period of 18 months. Project B has a cost of $125,000, with expected cash inflows of $50,000 the first year and $25,000 per quarter after that. Which project should you recommend?

    A. Either Project A or Project B, because the payback periods are equal
    B. Project A, because Project B's payback period is 21 months
    C. Project A, because Project B's payback period is 24 months
    D. Project A, because Project B's payback period is 20 months

18. Which of the following is true?

A. Discounted cash flow analysis is the least precise of the cash flow techniques because it does not consider the time value of money.

B. NPV is the least precise of the cash flow analysis techniques because it assumes reinvestment at the discount rate.

C. Payback period is the least precise of the cash flow analysis techniques because it does not consider the time value of money.

D. IRR is the least precise of the cash flow analysis techniques because it assumes reinvestment at the cost of capital.

19. You are a project manager for Zippy Tees. Your selection committee has just chosen a project you recommended for implementation. Your project is to manufacture a line of miniature stuffed bears that will be attached to your company's trendy T-shirts. The bears will be wearing the same T-shirt design as the shirt to which they're attached. Your project sponsor thinks you've really impressed the big boss and wants you to skip to the manufacturing process right away. What is your response?

A. Agree with the project sponsor because that person is your boss and has a lot of authority and power in the company.

B. Require that a preliminary budget be established and a resource list be put together to alert other managers of the requirements of this project. This should be published and signed by the other managers who are impacted by this project.

C. Require that a project charter be written and signed off on by all stakeholders before proceeding.

D. Suggest that a preliminary statement of work be written to outline the objectives of the project.

20. Which of the following is true regarding the project charter?

A. The project charter should be published under the name of a manager external to the project.

B. The project charter should be published under a key stakeholder's name.

C. The project charter should be published under the name of the project manager.

D. The project charter should be published under the name of the project champion.

Answers to Review Questions

1. A. The buyer provides the SOW when projects are performed under contract.
2. B. This came about because of an organizational need. Staff members were spending unproductive hours producing information for the management report that wasn't consistent or meaningful.
3. A. Develop Project Charter has five inputs, and they are project SOW, business case, contract, enterprise environmental factors, and organizational process assets.
4. C. The most correct answer is to perform a feasibility study. Since this project is taking the company into a new, unknown market, there's lots of potential for error and failure. A feasibility study would help the stakeholders determine whether the project is viable and cost effective and whether it has a high potential for success.
5. D. Project Time Management involves the following processes: Define Activities, Sequence Activities, Estimate Activity Resources, Estimate Activity Durations, Develop Schedule, and Control Schedule.
6. B. The project SOW should contain the business need for the project and the product scope description and should support the organization's strategic plan.
7. B. Historical information on projects of a similar nature can be helpful when initiating new projects. They can help in formulating project deliverables and identifying constraints and assumptions and will be helpful later in the project Planning processes as well.
8. B. The *Project Integration Management Knowledge Area* consists of the following processes: Develop Project Charter, Develop Project Management Plan, Direct and Manage Project Execution, Monitor and Control Project Work, Perform Integrated Change Control, and Close Project or Phase.
9. A. Benefit measurement methods include comparative methods, scoring models, and cash flow analysis. They are used as project selection tools to determine which project to proceed with or to determine which project among a list of projects should be undertaken.
10. B. Projects with NPV greater than zero should be given an accept recommendation.
11. B. Projects with the highest IRR value are favored over projects with lower IRR values.
12. A. Net present value (NPV) assumes reinvestment is made at the cost of capital.
13. C. Year 1 and 2 inflows are each $100,000 for a total of $200,000. Year 3 inflows are an additional $300,000. Add one more quarter to this total, and the $575,000 is reached in three years and three months, or 39 months.
14. D. IRR assumes reinvestment at the IRR rate and is the discount rate when NPV is equal to zero.
15. C. Mathematical models can be used to determine which projects are worth undertaking.

16. A. Benefit measurement methods include comparative methods and scoring models, among others, to make project selections.

17. B. Project B has a payback period of 21 months; $50,000 is received in the first 12 months, with another $75,000 coming in over each of the next three quarters, or nine months.

18. C. Payback period does not consider the time value of money and is therefore the least precise of all the cash flow analysis techniques.

19. C. The project should be kicked off with a project charter that authorizes the project to begin, assigns the project manager, and describes the project objectives and purpose for the project. This ensures that everyone is working with the same purposes in mind.

20. A. According to the *PMBOK® Guide*, the project charter should be published by a manager external to the project (usually the project sponsor) but with sufficient power and authority to carry it off.

Chapter

3

Developing the Project Scope Statement

THE PMP EXAM CONTENT FROM THE PLANNING THE PROJECT PERFORMANCE DOMAIN COVERED IN THIS CHAPTER INCLUDES THE FOLLOWING:

- ✓ **Define and Record Requirements, Constraints, and Assumptions**
- ✓ **Develop Change Management Plan**
- ✓ **Create the WBS**

Great job! You've successfully completed the project Initiating processes and published the project charter, the stakeholder register, and stakeholder management strategy. The project is officially underway. Stakeholders have been identified and informed of the project, you have management buy-in on the project, the project manager has been assigned, and the project objectives and description have been identified. A solid foundation for the planning process is in place.

In this chapter, we will begin the Planning processes for the project. In fact, I will continue discussing the Planning processes through Chapter 7, "Planning Project Resources." Planning is a significant activity in any project and, if done correctly, will go a long way toward ensuring project success.

This chapter begins with the Develop Project Management Plan process. This process will describe the overall approach you'll use to manage the project. The result of this process is the project management plan document that describes how you'll execute, monitor, and control the project outcomes as the project progresses and how you'll close out the project once it concludes.

Then you'll move on to the Collect Requirements process. It's during this process that quantified requirements are gathered and documented to assure stakeholder needs are met and expectations are managed.

During the Define Scope process, you'll use the project charter and the requirements documentation—plus some other inputs—and then apply the tools and techniques of this process to come up with the project scope statement. I'll talk in depth about project objectives, requirements, constraints, assumptions, and other elements of writing the project scope statement, which is an output of this process.

Once you have the deliverables and requirements well defined, you'll begin the process of breaking down the work of the project via a work breakdown structure (WBS). You'll accomplish this task in the Create WBS process. The WBS defines the scope of the project and breaks the work down into components that can be scheduled and estimated as well as easily monitored and controlled.

We have a lot to cover in this chapter so let's get started.

Developing the Project Management Plan

The first process in the Planning process group is the *Develop Project Management Plan* process. It's first for good reason. This process is part of the Integration Management Knowledge Area and is concerned with defining, coordinating, and integrating all the various subsidiary project plans.

This process involves defining and documenting the processes you're going to use to manage this project. For example, let's say you and the project team have determined you will use project management processes involving costs, human resources, risks, and a project schedule. (Warning: This is a demonstration only—don't try this at home. In reality, professionals perform many more processes than this on a typical project.) Each particular process might have a management plan that describes it. For instance, a cost management plan (an example of a subsidiary plan) would describe how costs will be managed and controlled and how changes to costs will be approved and managed throughout the project. The Develop Project Management Plan process brings all these subsidiary plans together, along with the outputs of the Planning group processes, into one document called the *project management plan.*

NOTE

In Chapter 1, "What Is a Project?", I talked about *tailoring*—determining which processes within each process group are appropriate for the project on which you're working. Tailoring is used in the Develop Project Management Plan process because it's here you'll determine what processes to use to best manage the project.

To create and document the plan, you need to gather some inputs and build on the information you've already collected.

Developing Inputs

The Develop Project Management Plan has four inputs:

- Project charter
- Outputs from planning processes
- Enterprise environmental factors
- Organizational process assets

Let's take a look at each next.

Project charter You'll recall that the project charter describes the objectives of the project and the high-level requirements needed to satisfy stakeholder expectations. The reason it's an input into this process is because the content of the project charter—including project objectives, project description, high-level requirements, summary milestone schedule, summary budget, and so on—will help you and the team determine exactly which project management processes to use on the project.

Outputs from Planning processes The project management processes include all the individual processes that make up the process groups we're talking about throughout this book. The Initiating group, for example, has two processes, Planning has a zillion (OK, not that many, but it seems like it), and so on. The outputs from the Planning processes you use on the project become inputs to the Develop Management Plan. For example, the cost management plan we talked about in the introduction is an input. Any processes you use that produce a baseline (such as schedule or cost) or a subsidiary management plan (such as a risk management plan, communication management plan, and so on) are included as inputs to this process.

> **NOTE** I'll talk more about baselines and the makeup of individual subsidiary management plans as we discuss the various Planning processes from now throughout Chapter 7 of this book.

Enterprise environmental factors You've seen enterprise environmental factors before. Some of the key elements of the environmental factors you should consider when choosing the processes to perform for this project include company culture and organizational structure, personnel administration, and the *project management information system (PMIS)*.

Organizational process assets Some of the key elements of the organizational process assets input you should consider when choosing the processes to perform for this project include standards and regulations (both industry and governmental), project management plan template, change control procedures, historical information, and the configuration management knowledge database that contains the official company policies, standards, procedures, and other project documents.

The PMIS is an automated (or manual) system used to document the project management plan and subsidiary plans, to facilitate the feedback process, and to revise the documents. It incorporates the configuration management system and the change control system, both of which I'll cover in Chapter 10, "Measuring and Controlling Project Performance." Later in the project, the PMIS can be used to control changes to any of the plans. When you're thinking about the PMIS as an input (that is, as part of the enterprise environmental factors), think of it as a collection and distribution point for information as well as an easy way to revise and update documents. When you're thinking about the PMIS as a tool and technique, think of it just that way—as a tool to facilitate the automation, collection, and distribution of data and to help monitor processes such as scheduling, resource leveling, budgeting, and web interfaces.

Exam Spotlight

Be aware that the *PMBOK® Guide* describes the PMIS as a tool in the glossary but in this process it's listed as an organizational process assets input. The PMIS in the Develop Project Management Plan process includes a subsystem called the *configuration management system* (I'll cover this topic in Chapter 10) and the change control system, which is a subsystem of the configuration management system.

As I talked about in Chapter 1, the processes you choose to perform for the project will be based on the complexity of the project, the project scope, and the type of industry in which you work. Your organization's standards, guidelines, and policies or the project management office (PMO) might also dictate the types of processes you'll use for the project. You should also consider whether your organization has existing change control processes in place, templates that you're required to use, or financial controls and processes.

Historical information and past project files are useful in helping you decide which processes to use for this project.

The only tool and technique of this project is expert judgment. According to the *PMBOK® Guide*, the types of expert judgment you'll need to complete this process include the following:

- Tailoring techniques
- Understanding technical and management details that need included in the project management plan
- Determining resources and assessing skill levels needed for project work
- Determining and defining the amount of configuration management to apply on the project
- Determining which project documents require formal change control processes

Documenting the Project Management Plan

The purpose of most processes is, of course, to produce an output. Outputs are usually a report or document of some type or a deliverable. In this case, you end up with a document—the project management plan—that describes, integrates, and coordinates baselines and subsidiary plans for the processes you've determined to use for the project. The project management plan can be detailed or it can be a high-level summary based on the needs of the project.

According to the *PMBOK® Guide*, the project management plan defines how the project is executed, how it's monitored and controlled, and how it's closed. It also documents the outputs of the Planning group processes, which I'll cover over the next several chapters. The project management plan should include or discuss the following elements:

- Processes you'll use to perform each phase of the project
- The life cycle you'll use for the project and for each phase of the project if applicable
- The tailoring results the project team defines
- Methods for executing the work of the project to fulfill the objectives
- Change management plan describing methods for monitoring and controlling change
- Configuration management
- Methods for determining and maintaining the validity of performance baselines
- Communication needs of the stakeholders and techniques to fulfill those needs
- Management reviews of content, issues, and pending decisions

In addition to the elements just listed, the subsidiary plans that are associated with the processes you'll be using for this project should be documented in the project management plan. Each of these subsidiary management plans might contain the same elements as the overall project management plan does, but they're specifically related to the topic at hand. For example, the cost management plan should define how changes to cost estimates will be reflected in the project budget and how changes or variances with a significant impact should be communicated to the project sponsor and stakeholders. The schedule management plan describes how changes to the schedule will be managed, and so on.

The subsidiary plans might be detailed or simply a synopsis, depending on the needs of the project. I've listed the subsidiary plans along with a brief description next. I will cover each of these plans in more detail throughout the remainder of this book. According to the *PMBOK® Guide*, the subsidiary plans are as follows:

Scope management plan Describes the process for determining project scope, facilitates creating the work breakdown structure (WBS), describes how the product or service of the project is verified and accepted, and documents how changes to scope will be handled.

Requirements management plan Describes how requirements will be analyzed, documented, traced, reported, and managed throughout the project.

Schedule management plan Describes how the project schedule will be developed and controlled and how changes will be incorporated into the project schedule.

Cost management plan Describes how costs will be managed and controlled and how changes to costs will be approved and managed.

Quality management plan Describes how the organization's quality policy will be implemented. It should address and describe quality control procedures and measures, quality assurance procedures and measures, and continuous process improvement.

Communications management plan Describes the communication needs of the stakeholders, including timing, frequency, and methods of communications.

Risk management plan Describes how risks will be managed and controlled during the project. This should include risk management methodology; roles and responsibilities; definitions of probability and impact; when project management will be performed; and the categories of risk, risk tolerances, and reporting and tracking formats.

Procurement management plan Describes how the procurement processes will be managed throughout the project. This might include elements such as type of contract, procurement documents, and lead times for purchases.

The project management plan is not limited to the subsidiary plans listed here. You might include other plans and documentation that help describe how the project will be executed or monitored and controlled. Perhaps you're working on a project that requires precise calculations and exact adherence to requirements. You could include a plan that describes these calculations, how they'll be monitored and measured, and the processes you'll use to make changes or corrections.

The project management plan also includes other project planning documents, such as these:

- Milestone list
- Resource calendar
- Schedule baseline

- Cost baseline
- Quality baseline
- Risk register
- Scope baseline

I'll talk about each of these documents in the remaining chapters as well.

Exam Spotlight

Understand that the purpose of the project management plan is to define how the project is executed, monitored and controlled, and closed as well as to document the processes you'll use during the project.

As the project progresses and more and more processes are performed, the subsidiary plans and the project management plan itself might change. These changes should be reviewed, and the project management plan should be updated to reflect the approved changes. Depending on the nature of the changes, the project manager, stakeholders, or sponsor (or some combination) should review and approve the changes.

Exam Spotlight

In practice, you'll find that you'll prepare the project management plan after you've progressed through several of the other Planning processes. It's difficult to create some of these subsidiary plans without performing the process they're associated with first. However, for the exam, remember that Develop Project Management Plan is the first process in the Planning group, and it should be performed first. Updates can and should occur to the Project Management Plan as subsidiary plans are created or changed.

Collecting Requirements

Collect Requirements is the first process in the Project Scope Management Knowledge Area and the second process in the Planning process group. You might recall from Chapter 1 that the purpose of the Project Scope Management Knowledge Area is to describe and control what is and what is *not* work of the project. This is the first process where we get into the meat of the Planning processes and get down to defining what the final product or service of the project looks like—thus we're starting off defining what *is* included in the work of the project.

> **NOTE** In practice, you will likely perform the Define Scope process before the Collect Requirements process. Deliverables must be identified before you can document their detailed requirements. The project charter, an input to this process, does capture some of the high-level requirements of the project, but they are not usually sufficient enough to jump into requirements gathering. For the exam, remember that Collect Requirements comes before Define Scope. We'll discuss Define Scope in the section "Defining Scope" later in this chapter.

Requirements describe the characteristics of the deliverables. They might also describe functionality that a deliverable must have or specific conditions a deliverable must meet in order to satisfy the objective of the project. Requirements are typically conditions that must be met or criteria that the product or service of the project must possess in order to satisfy the objectives of the project. Requirements quantify and prioritize the wants, needs, and expectations of the project sponsor and stakeholders. According to the *PMBOK® Guide* and lots of personal experience, you must be able to measure, trace, and test requirements. It's important that they're complete and accepted by your project sponsor and key stakeholders.

The primary purpose of the Collect Requirements process is to define and document the project sponsor, the customer, and the stakeholder's expectations and needs for meeting the project objective. In my experience, understanding, documenting, and agreeing upon requirements is a critical factor to project success. Recording the requirements and attaining stakeholder approval of the requirements will help you define and manage their expectations throughout the project.

> **Exam Spotlight**
>
> Requirements must be documented, analyzed, and quantified in enough detail that they can be measured once the work of the project begins. Requirements become the basis for developing the WBS and are essential in estimating costs, developing the project schedule, and quality planning.

You've already learned about the two inputs to this process, the project charter and stakeholder register, so we'll move on to tools and techniques.

Using the Tools and Techniques of Collect Requirements

Your communication skills are about to come in handy. Gathering and documenting requirements is not a task for the faint of heart. Since defining and producing requirements are so critical to the success of the project, I recommend using team members with excellent communication skills to perform this task. If they have the ability to read minds, all the better. Stakeholders almost always know what they want the end product to look like but often have difficulty articulating their needs. An expert communicator can read between the lines and ask the probing questions that will draw the information out of the stakeholder.

Business process owners are those people who are experts in their particular area of the business. They are invaluable resources to the project manager and in gathering requirements for the project. They are usually the midlevel managers and line managers who still have their fingers in the day-to-day portion of the business. For example, it takes many experts in various areas to produce and market a great bottle of beer. Machinists regulate and keep the stainless steel and copper drums in top working order. Chemists check and adjust the secret formulas brewing in the vats daily. Graphic artists must develop colorful and interesting labels and ads to attract the attention of those thirsty patrons. And of course, those great TV commercials advertising the tasty brew are produced by yet another set of business experts. These are the kinds of people you'll interview and ask to assist you in identifying requirements.

There are several tools and techniques in this process you can use to help identify the requirements of the project. Some of these tools and techniques can also be used during the Identify Risk process and the Plan Quality Process. We'll cover those processes in Chapter 6 and Chapter 7, respectively. The following tools and techniques are used for Collect Requirements:

Interviews Interviews are typically one-on-one conversations with stakeholders. Interviews can be formal or informal and generally consist of questions prepared ahead of time. The advantages to this tool are that subject matter experts and experienced project participants can impart a lot of information in a short amount of time and typically have a good understanding of the features and functions needed from the project deliverables. You should record the responses during the interviews and don't be afraid to ask spontaneous questions as they occur to you during the interview.

Focus groups Focus groups are usually conducted by a trained moderator. The key to this tool lies in picking the subject matter experts and stakeholders to participate in the focus group.

Facilitated workshops Cross-functional stakeholders come together in a facilitated workshop to discuss and define requirements that affect more than one department. For example, if you're implementing a software package that impacts several business units, you'll need representatives from each unit together in a workshop so that each of their needs are represented and prioritized. This way, all the participants understand the various needs and have a facilitated forum to discuss and resolve their issues.

Exam Spotlight

The primary difference between focus groups and facilitated workshops are that focus groups are gatherings of prequalified subject matter experts and stakeholders and facilitated workshops consist of cross-functional stakeholders who can define cross-functional requirements. Differences among stakeholders can be resolved more quickly and consensus is more easily attained in a facilitated workshop environment.

Group creativity techniques Group creativity involves several techniques, like brainstorming, Nominal group technique, the Delphi technique, and affinity diagrams. We will cover each of these techniques in either the Risk Planning process (Chapter 6) or the Plan Quality process (Chapter 7).

Idea/mind mapping is a group creativity technique where participants first use brainstorming techniques to record their ideas. White boards or flip charts are a great tool to use with this process. The facilitator uses the white board to map ideas and, using a mind-mapping layout, group similar topics together. There are a few mind-mapping software packages available on the market that can greatly assist with this process. Mind mapping allows the participants to get an understanding of common ideas and themes, create new ideas, and understand differences.

Group decision making techniques According to the *PMBOK® Guide*, there are many methods groups can use to reach decisions. These methods can also be used with the group creativity techniques. The four methods mentioned include unanimity, where everyone agrees on the resolution or course of action; majority, where more than 50 percent of the members support the resolution; plurality, where the largest subgroup within the group makes the decision if majority is not reached; and dictatorship, where one person makes the decision on behalf of the group.

Questionnaires and surveys This technique involves querying a large group of participants via questionnaires or surveys. These tools allow you to gather information quickly and apply statistical analysis, if needed, to the results.

Observations This technique is typically a one-on-one experience where an observer sits side by side with the participant to observe how the participant interacts with the product or service. This technique is also known as job shadowing. For example, you may use this technique to determine requirements for an upgrade to a software product. Sitting with the user and watching their interactions with the product enables the observer to uncover requirements they would not have ordinarily discovered. This technique can also involve participant observers who perform the job themselves in order to ascertain requirements.

Prototypes Prototyping is a technique involving constructing a working model or mock-up of the final product for participants to experiment with. The prototype does not usually contain all the functionality the end product does, but it gives participants enough information that they can provide feedback regarding the mock-up. This is an iterative process where participants experiment and provide feedback and the prototype is revised and the cycle starts again.

Documenting Requirements

Now that you've employed the tools and techniques of this process to gather requirements, you'll want to record them in a requirements document. Stakeholders sometimes have short memories, particularly on long-term projects, so documenting requirements and obtaining their approval is essential for project success. And you will use the requirements documentation throughout the project to manage stakeholder and customer expectations. This is a lot easier to accomplish when they've agreed to the requirements ahead of time and you have their approval documented.

I've already mentioned the first output of this process, which is requirements documentation. The remaining two outputs are the requirements management plan (this could be a subsidiary plan to the project management plan) and the requirements traceability matrix. I'll describe each in detail next.

Requirements Documentation

As I mentioned in the opening to this section, requirements quantify and prioritize the wants, needs, and expectations of the project sponsor and stakeholders. Requirements typically start out high-level and are progressively elaborated as the project progresses. You must be able to track, measure, test, and trace the requirements of the project. If you can't measure or test whether the requirement satisfies the business need of the project, the definition of success is left to the subjective opinions of the stakeholders and team members.

You're worked hard to gather and define requirements and you don't want all that effort going to waste. This output involves recording the requirements in a requirements document. The *PMBOK® Guide* does not dictate the format of this document and acknowledges it can be formal with lots of detail or a simple list categorized by stakeholder and priority. However, it does state that the requirements document may include at least the following elements:

- Business need for the project and why it was undertaken
- Objectives of the project and the business objectives the project hopes to fulfill
- Functional requirements
- Nonfunctional requirements
- Quality requirements
- Acceptance criteria
- Business rules
- Organizational areas and outside entities impacted
- Support and training requirements
- Assumptions and constraints

NOTE

Functional requirements is a term used often in software development. It typically describes a behavior, such as calculations or processes that should occur once data is entered. In non-software terms, functional requirements might describe specifications, quantities, colors, and more. *Nonfunctional requirements* refer to elements that are related to the product but don't describe the product directly. In the case of a software product, this could be a security requirement or performance criteria.

One of the most important elements of the requirements document that isn't in the preceding list is the signatures of the key stakeholders indicating their acceptance of the requirements. They will also sign the scope statement, which we'll talk about in the section "Defining Scope" later in this chapter.

Creating the Requirements Management Plan

The requirements management plan defines how the requirements will be analyzed, documented, and managed throughout all phases of the project. The type of phase relationship you choose to manage the project will determine how requirements are managed throughout the project. For example, in a sequentially phased project, it's possible to define requirements in later phases of the project after some work has been completed. In an overlapping phased relationship, you'll need to define and document most all the requirements early in the life cycle.

NOTE We talked about phase-to-phase relationships in Chapter 2. There are three types: sequential, overlapping, and iterative.

Exam Spotlight

Make certain you document the phase-to-phase relationship you'll use during the project life cycle in the requirements management plan.

There are several components of a sound requirements management plan. According to the *PMBOK® Guide*, you should include the following factors in the plan:

- How planning, tracking, and reporting of requirements activities will occur
- How changes to the requirements will be requested, tracked, and analyzed along with other configuration management activities
- How requirements will be prioritized
- What metrics will be used to trace product requirements
- What requirements attributes will be documented in the traceability matrix (the last output of this process)

Remember that the requirements management plan can be considered a subsidiary management plan and be included in the project management plan.

Documenting the Requirements Traceability Matrix

The last output of the Collect Requirements process is the requirements traceability matrix. The idea behind the traceability matrix is to document where the requirement originated, document what the requirement will be traced to, and then follow it through to delivery or completion. Table 3.1 shows a sample traceability matrix with several attributes that identify the requirement.

TABLE 3.1 Requirements Traceability Matrix

Unique ID	Description of Requirement	Source	Priority	Test Scenario	Test Verification	Status
001	Requirement one	Project objective	B	User acceptance		Approved

Each requirement should have its own unique identifier. You could devise a numbering system that defines both the category of the requirement and a unique, ascending number—for example, HR (for human resources) 001. Or, a simple numbering system as shown in this example may suffice.

The description should be brief but have enough information to easily identify the requirement.

The source column refers to where the requirement originated. Requirements may come from many sources, including project objectives, business needs, product design, the work breakdown structure, deliverables, and so on.

Priority refers to the priority of the requirement. You can use any prioritization process like a simple numbering system or an alpha system as the example shows here. The definition of a "B" priority should be included in the requirements management plan. Perhaps an "A" is essential to project success and a "B" is highly desirable.

The test scenario in this example is where you record how the requirement will be tested or during which project phase, and test verification indicates if it passes or fails the test.

Status may capture information about the requirement that refers to whether the requirement has been approved to be included in the project; if it was added, deferred, canceled; and so on.

Exam Spotlight

According to the *PMBOK® Guide*, the requirements traceability matrix helps assure that business value is realized when the project is complete because each requirement is linked to a business and project objective.

The next process in the Planning process group is the Define Scope process. Before we jump into that process, I want to talk a little about the scope management plan. We'll look at that next.

Documenting the Scope Management Plan

The *scope management plan* describes how the project team will go about defining project scope, verifying the work of the project, and managing and controlling scope. The *PMBOK® Guide* does not go into detail regarding this plan, but there are some things you may need to know about this plan for the exam.

The project scope management plan should contain the following:

- The process you'll use to prepare the project scope statement. The project scope statement (which I'll define later in this chapter) contains a detailed description of the project deliverables.
- A process for creating the work breakdown structure (WBS). The WBS further defines the work of the project (as defined in the scope statement) by breaking down the deliverables into smaller pieces of work. We'll talk about the WBS at the end of this chapter.
- A definition of how the deliverables will be verified for accuracy and the process used for accepting deliverables.
- A description of the process for controlling scope change requests, including the procedure for requesting changes and how to obtain a change request form.

Exam Spotlight

The project scope management plan is a planning tool that documents how the project team will go about defining project scope, how the work breakdown structure will be developed, how changes to scope will be controlled, and how the work of the project will be verified and accepted. And don't forget, the scope management plan is a subsidiary of the project management plan.

Defining Scope

Scope is collectively the product, service, or result of the project. Scope can refer to product scope (the features and characteristics that describe the product, service, or result of the project) or project scope (the project management work). We'll look at both product and project scope in this section.

Now that you've documented the project requirements, you're ready to further define the needs of the project in the *Define Scope* process. The project scope statement (an output of this process) is what you'll use to develop and document a detailed description of the deliverables of the project and the work needed to produce them. This process is progressively elaborated as more detail becomes known.

Real World Scenario

Scope Management Plan Requirements

Phil Reid is a gifted engineer. He works as an accident reconstructionist and has a 90 percent success rate at assisting his clients (who are attorneys) at winning court cases. Phil can intuitively and scientifically determine whether the scene of an accident is real or is insurance fraud. Most cases Phil works on are managed as projects because each accident is unique, the cause of each accident is unique, and each investigation has a definite beginning and ending. The attorneys that Phil's organization works with want the final results of the investigation delivered in different formats. Although Phil is exceptionally good at determining the forensic evidence needed to prove or disprove how the accident occurred, he is not at all gifted in oral communication skills. As a result, the scope management plan requires the client to define how the outcome of the investigation should be presented and whether the engineer might be required to testify regarding the results of the investigation. That way, Phil's organization can plan in advance how to use his talents on the project and assign a resource to work with him who has the communication skills and ability to testify if that's required.

Exam Spotlight

You'll want to pay particular attention to the accuracy and completeness of this process. Defining project scope is critical to the success of the project since it spells out exactly what the product or service of the project looks like. Conversely, poor scope definition might lead to cost increases, rework, schedule delays, and poor morale.

First you'll examine the inputs and tools and techniques of this process.

The inputs to the Define Scope process are as follows:

- Project charter
- Requirements documentation
- Organizational process assets

One of the important elements from the project charter that you'll want to consider when writing the project scope statement (we'll cover this output later) is the project objectives.

Objectives are quantifiable criteria used to measure project success. They describe the "what" you're trying to do, accomplish, or produce. Quantifiable criteria should at least include schedule, cost, and quality measures. You might use business measures or quality targets as well. These objectives will be broken down shortly into deliverables that will describe the objectives outlined in the charter.

Some of the other important information you'll want to key in on from these inputs are historical information; the product description; and the project objectives, assumptions, and constraints. (I'll cover each of these in the section "Writing the Project Scope Statement" later in this chapter.)

Exam Spotlight

If the project charter is missing or was not created, you'll need to develop the information normally found in the charter (or obtain it from other sources) to use as the foundation for creating the project scope statement .

You'll see some new tools and techniques in this process:

- Expert judgment
- Product analysis
- Alternatives identification
- Facilitated workshops

I covered expert judgment and facilitated workshops in Chapter 2. I'll discuss product analysis and alternatives identification in the following sections.

Product Analysis

Product analysis goes hand in hand with the product scope description and therefore is most useful when the project's end result is a product. Product analysis is a method for converting the product description and project objectives into deliverables and requirements. According to the *PMBOK® Guide*, product analysis might include performing value analysis, functional analysis, requirements analysis, systems-engineering techniques, systems analysis, product breakdown, or value-engineering techniques to further define the product or service.

Exam Spotlight

It's beyond the scope of this book to go into the various analysis techniques used in product analysis. For exam purposes, remember that product analysis is a tool and technique of the Define Scope process, and memorize the list of analysis techniques that might be performed in this process.

Alternatives Identification

Alternatives identification is a technique used for discovering different methods or ways of accomplishing the work of the project. For example, brainstorming might be used to discover alternative ways of achieving one of the project objectives. Perhaps the project's budget doesn't allow for a portion of the project that the stakeholders really think needs to be included. Brainstorming might uncover an alternative that would allow the needed portion to be accomplished.

Lateral thinking is a form of alternatives identification that can be used to help define scope. Edward de Bono created this term and has done extensive research and writing on the topic of lateral thinking. The simplest definition is that it's thinking outside the box. Lateral thinking is a process of separating the problem—or in our case the components of project scope (the deliverables and requirements)—looking at them from angles other than their obvious presentation and encouraging team members to come up with ways to solve problems or look at scope that are not apparently obvious.

Outside the Box

Lateral thinking is a way of reasoning and thinking about problems from perspectives other than the obvious. It challenges our perceptions and assumptions. Consider these two examples of lateral thinking that I crafted based on some puzzles I found at this website: `www.folj.com/lateral/`. Use your favorite search engine and run a query on "lateral thinking puzzles" to find many more examples.

Question: How could your pet Yorkie fall from the window of an 18-story building and live?

Answer: The question asks how your pet could fall from an 18-story building and live; however, the question doesn't state your pet fell from the 18th floor. So, your pet Yorkie fell from the basement-level window.

Question: Eight chocolates are arranged in an antique candy dish. Eight people each take one chocolate. There is one chocolate remaining in the dish. How can that be?

Answer: If there are eight chocolates in an antique dish, how can the last person take the last chocolate yet one remains in the dish? Well, the last person to take a chocolate took the dish as well—therefore, the last chocolate remained in the dish.

Remember these examples the next time you're defining scope or looking for alternative answers to a problem.

Writing the Project Scope Statement

The purpose of the *project scope statement* is to document the project objectives, deliverables, and the work required to produce the deliverables so that it can be used to direct the project team's work and as a basis for future project decisions. The scope statement is an agreement between the project and the project customer that states precisely what the work of the project will produce. Simply put, the scope statement tells everyone concerned with the project exactly what they're going to get when the work is finished.

Exam Spotlight

Understand that the purpose of the scope statement, according to the *PMBOK® Guide*, is to provide all the stakeholders with a foundational understanding of the project scope. Also remember that the scope statement defines and progressively elaborates the work of the project. It guides the work of the project team during the Executing process, and all change requests will be evaluated against the scope statement. If the change request is outside the bounds of the project scope as documented in the project scope statement, it should be denied.

Since the scope statement serves as a baseline for the project, if questions arise or changes are proposed later in the project, they can be compared to what's documented in the scope statement. Making change decisions is easier when the original deliverables and requirements are well documented. You'll also know what is out of scope for the project simply because the work isn't documented in the scope statement (or conversely, deliverables or other elements are documented and noted as being specifically out of scope). The criteria outlined in the scope statement will also be used to determine whether the project was completed successfully. I hope you're already seeing the importance of documenting project scope.

Understanding the Scope Statement Components

According to the *PMBOK® Guide*, the project scope statement should include all of the following:

- Product scope description
- Product acceptance criteria
- Project deliverables
- Project exclusions
- Project constraints
- Project assumptions

If the details surrounding these are spelled out in other documents, you don't have to reenter all the information in the scope statement. Simply reference the other document in the scope statement so that readers know where to find it.

Product Scope Description

The *product scope description* describes the characteristics of the product, service, or result of the project. I talked about this in Chapter 2. If the product scope description is contained in the project charter, you can reference the project charter in the project scope statement or you can copy and paste the information from the project charter into the scope statement. It won't hurt anything to have it in both places and will make reading the scope statement easier.

Exam Spotlight

You'll use the project management plan as your measurement of project scope completion, and product scope completion will be measured against product requirements.

Product Acceptance Criteria

Product *acceptance criteria* include the process and criteria that will be used to determine whether the deliverables and the final product, service, or results of the project are acceptable and satisfactory. Product acceptance criteria help you describe project success because it defines the specifications the deliverables must meet in order to be acceptable to the stakeholder. Acceptance criteria might include any number of elements, such as quality criteria, fitness for use, and performance criteria. This component should also describe the process stakeholders will use to indicate their acceptance of the deliverables.

Project Deliverables

Deliverables are measurable outcomes, measurable results, or specific items that must be produced to consider the project or project phase completed. Deliverables should be specific and verifiable. For example, one of your deliverables might include widgets with a three-inch diameter that will in turn be assembled into the final product. This deliverable, a three-inch-diameter widget, is specific and measurable. However, if the deliverable was not documented or not communicated to the manager or vendor responsible for manufacturing the widgets, there could be a disaster waiting to happen. If they deliver two-inch widgets instead of the required three-inch version, it would throw the entire project off schedule or perhaps cause the project to fail. This could be a career-limiting move for the project manager because it's the project manager's responsibility to document deliverables and monitor the progress of those deliverables throughout the project. Most projects have multiple deliverables. As in this example, if you are assembling a new product with many parts, each of the parts might be considered independent deliverables.

A project deliverable is typically a unique and verifiable product or result or a service that's performed. The product or service must be produced or performed in order to consider the project complete. The deliverables might also include supplementary outcomes such as documentation or project management reports.

The bottom line is this: no matter how well you apply your project skills, if the wrong deliverables are produced or the project is managed to the wrong objectives, you will have an unsuccessful project on your hands.

Documenting *All* the Deliverables and Requirements

One of the project manager's primary functions is to accurately document the deliverables and requirements of the project and then manage the project so that they are produced according to the agreed-upon criteria. Deliverables describe the components of the goals and objectives in a quantifiable way. Requirements are the specifications of the deliverables. (Remember for the exam that requirements are documented in the Collect Requirements process that occurs before the Define Scope process.)

The project manager should use the project charter as a starting point for identifying and progressively elaborating project deliverables, but it's possible that only some of the deliverables will be documented there. Remember that the charter was signed by a manager external to the project, and it was the first take at defining the project objectives and deliverables. As the project manager, it's your job to make certain *all* the deliverables are identified and documented in the project scope statement. That's because the scope statement (not the project charter) serves as the agreement among stakeholders—including the customer of the project—regarding what deliverables will be produced in order to meet and satisfy the business needs of the project.

Interview the stakeholders, other project managers, project team members, customers, management staff, industry experts, and any other experts who can help you identify all the deliverables of the project. Depending on the size of the project, you might be able to accomplish this in a group setting using simple brainstorming techniques, but large complex projects might have scope statements for each deliverable of the project. Remember that the project scope statement is progressively elaborated into finer detail and is used later to help decompose the work of the project into smaller tasks and activities.

Project Exclusions

Project exclusions are, as you'd guess, anything that isn't included as a deliverable or work of the project. You'll want to note the project exclusions in the project scope statement so that you can continue to manage stakeholder expectations throughout the project.

Technology constraints Technology is marvelous. In fact, how did humans survive prior to the invention of computers and cell phones? However, it can also be a project constraint. For example, your project might require the use of new technology that is still so new it hasn't been released on a wide-scale basis or hasn't been adequately tested to determine stability in production. One impact might be that the project will take an additional six months until the new technology is ready and tested.

Directive constraints Directives from management can be constraints as well. Your department might have specific policies that management requires for the type of work you're about to undertake. This might add time to the project, so you must consider those policies when identifying project constraints. And when you're performing work on contract, the provisions of the contract can be constraints

Constraints, particularly the classic triple constraints, can be used to help drive out the objectives and requirements of the project. If it's difficult to discern which constraint is the primary constraint, ask the project sponsor something like this, "Ms. Sponsor, if you could have only one of these two alternatives, which would you choose? The project is delivered on the date you've stated, or we don't spend one penny more than the approved budget." If Ms. Sponsor replies with the date response, you know your primary constraint is time. If push comes to shove during the project Planning processes for this project, the budget might have to give because time cannot.

You'll want to understand what the primary constraint is on the project. If you assume the primary constraint is budget when in actuality the primary constraint is time, in the immortal words of two-year-olds worldwide, uh-oh. Understanding the constraints and which one carries the most importance will help you later in the project Planning process group with details such as scope planning, scheduling, estimating, and project plan development. That's assuming your project gets to the project Planning processes, which brings me to the next topic: project assumptions.

Project Assumptions

You've probably heard the old saying about the word *assume*, something about what it makes out of "u" and "me." In the case of project management, however, throw this old saying out the window, because it's not true.

Assumptions, for the purposes of project management, are things you believe to be true. For example, if you're working on a large construction project, you might make assumptions about the availability of materials. You might assume that concrete, lumber, drywall, and so on are widely available and reasonably priced. You might also assume that finding contract labor is either easy or difficult, depending on the economic times and the availability of labor in your locale. Each project will have its own set of assumptions, and the assumptions should be identified, documented, and updated throughout the project.

It's essential to understand and document the assumptions you're making, and the assumptions your stakeholders are making, about the project. It's also important to find out as many of the assumptions as you can up front. Projects can fail, sometimes after lots of progress has been made, because an important assumption was forgotten or the assumption was incorrect. Defining new assumptions and refining old ones are forms of progressive elaboration.

Let's say you make plans to meet your buddy for lunch at 11:30 on Friday at your favorite spot. When Friday rolls around, you assume he's going to show up, barring any catastrophes between the office and the restaurant. Project assumptions work the same way. For planning purposes, you presume the event or thing you've made the assumptions about is true, real, or certain. You might assume that key resources will be available when needed on the project. Document that assumption. If Dara is the one and only resource who can perform a specific task at a certain point in the project, document your assumption that Dara will be available and run it by her manager. If Dara happens to be on a plane for Helsinki at the time you thought she was going to be working on the project, you could have a real problem on your hands.

Other assumptions could be factors, such as vendor delivery times, product availability, contractor availability, the accuracy of the project plan, the assumption that key project members will perform adequately, contract signing dates, project start dates, and project phase start dates. This is not an exhaustive list, but it should get you thinking in the right direction. As you interview your stakeholders, ask them about their assumptions, and add them to your list. Use brainstorming exercises with your team and other project participants to come up with additional assumptions.

NOTE

Think about some of the factors you usually take for granted when you're trying to identify assumptions. Many times they're the elements everyone expects will be available or will behave in a specific way. Think about factors such as key team members' availability, access to information, access to equipment, management support, and vendor reliability.

Try to validate your assumptions whenever possible. When discussing assumptions with vendors, make them put them in writing. In fact, if the services or goods you're expecting to be delivered by your suppliers are critical to the project, include a clause in the contract to assure a contingency plan in case your suppliers fail to perform. For example, if you're expecting 200 computers to be delivered, configured, and installed by a certain date, require the vendor to pay the cost of rental equipment in the event the vendor can't deliver on the promised due date.

Remember, when assumptions are incorrect or not documented, it could cause problems partway through the project and might even be a project killer.

Approval Requirements

Approval requirements are not an official component of the scope statement according to the *PMBOK® Guide*, but I recommend that you know something about them. *Approval requirements* refer to how the objectives, deliverables, project management documents, and other outcomes and results of the project will be approved. This is different from product acceptance criteria—that element describes how the product itself will be approved, whereas this element describes the requirements that must be met in order to approve the deliverables. An example product acceptance criteria might be "All widgets must measure three inches." A deliverable approval requirement might be that the director of sales must approve a prototype before the project can proceed. This section might also contain the process and approval requirements of the project scope statement.

Approving and Publishing the Project Scope Statement

Just like the project charter, the project scope statement should be approved, agreed upon, published, and distributed to the stakeholders, key management personnel, and project team members. This isn't an official output of this process, nor is it noted in the *PMBOK® Guide*. You can accomplish this with a formal sign-off procedure that's documented as part of the approval requirements section of the scope statement. When stakeholders sign off and agree to the scope statement, they're agreeing to the deliverables and requirements of the project. And, as with the project charter, their agreement and endorsement of the project requirements and deliverables will likely sustain their participation and cooperation throughout the rest of the project. That doesn't mean they'll agree to everything as the project progresses, but it does mean the stakeholders are informed and will likely remain active project participants.

NOTE

Remember that the definition of a successful project is one that accomplishes the goals of the project and meets or exceeds stakeholders' expectations. Understand and document those expectations and you're off to a good start.

Updating the Project Documents

The last output of this process is project document updates. When you're in the midst of defining deliverables, you'll often find that changes to the original project objectives, requirements, or stakeholder register will occur. This may require updates to the stakeholder register, the requirements documentation, and requirements traceability matrix. Changes to scope may occur later in the project. When the changes are approved, you'll need to update the scope statement and notify stakeholders that changes have been made.

Real World Scenario

Mountain Streams Services

Maria Sanchez is the CEO of Mountain Streams Services. She recently accepted a prestigious industry award on behalf of the company. Maria knows that without the dedication and support of her employees, Mountain Streams Services wouldn't have achieved this great milestone.

Maria wants to host a reception for the employees and their guests in recognition of all their hard work and contributions to the company. Maria has appointed you to arrange the reception.

The reception is scheduled for April 12, and Maria has given you a budget of $125 per person. The company employs 200 people. The reception should be semiformal.

You've documented the deliverables as follows:

- Location selection
- Food and beverage menu
- Invitations
- Entertainment
- Insurance coverage
- Decorations
- Photographer
- Agenda

In addition to the deliverables, you want to go over the following requirements with Maria to be certain you both are in agreement:

- The location should be somewhere in the downtown area.
- Employees are encouraged to bring one guest but no children.
- There will be an open bar paid for by Maria.
- The agenda will include a speech by Maria, followed by the distribution of bonus checks to every employee. This is to be kept secret until the reception.
- The decorations should include gold-trimmed fountain pens with the company logo at every place setting for the attendees to keep.

Once you've documented all the particulars, you ask to speak with Maria to go over this project scope statement and get her approval before proceeding with the project.

Creating the Work Breakdown Structure

Have you ever mapped out a family tree? In the *Create WBS* process, you'll construct something like it called a *work breakdown structure (WBS)*. It maps the deliverables of the project with subdeliverables and other components stemming from each major deliverable in a tree or chart format. The *PMBOK® Guide* describes a WBS as "a deliverable-oriented hierarchical decomposition of the work to be executed by the project team, to accomplish the project objectives and create the required deliverables…the WBS defines the total scope of the project." Simply put, a WBS is a deliverable-oriented hierarchy that defines and organizes the work of the project and only the work of the project. Like the scope statement, the WBS serves as a foundational agreement among the stakeholders and project team members regarding project scope.

Exam Spotlight

Subdividing deliverables into smaller components is the purpose of the Create WBS process. The *PMBOK® Guide* calls this *decomposition*, which is also a tool and technique of this process.

The WBS will be used throughout many of the remaining Planning processes and is an important part of project planning. As you probably have concluded, everything you've done so far builds on the previous step. The project charter, requirements document, and project scope statement outline the project objectives, requirements, and deliverables. Now you'll use that comprehensive list of requirements and deliverables to build the framework of the WBS.

NOTE I can't stress enough the importance of the work you've done up to this point. Your WBS will be only as accurate as your list of requirements and deliverables. The deliverables will become the groupings that will form the higher levels of the WBS from which activities will be derived later in the Planning processes.

The WBS should detail the full scope of work needed to complete the project. This breakdown will smooth the way for estimating project cost and time, scheduling resources, and determining quality controls later in the Planning processes. Project progress will be based on the estimates and measurements assigned to the WBS segments. So, again, accuracy and completeness are required when composing your WBS.

Before you begin constructing the WBS, you'll need to gather and review some important project documents. You'll look at those next.

Gathering the WBS Inputs

The inputs to the Create WBS process aren't new. They are as follows:

- Project scope statement
- Requirements documentation
- Organizational process assets

The important aspect to note about the inputs to this process is that the approved project scope statement is the document you will use to define and organize the work of the project in the WBS. Make certain you're using the most current version of the scope statement. And note also that the WBS, just like the project scope statement, contains the work of the project and only the work of the project.

Decomposing the Deliverables

The Create WBS process consists of one tool and technique called *decomposition*. This technique involves breaking down the deliverables into smaller, more manageable components of work. The idea here is to break down the deliverables to a point where you can easily plan, execute, monitor and control, and close out the project deliverables. Decomposition typically pertains to breaking deliverables down into smaller deliverables, or component deliverables, where each level of the WBS (or each level of decomposition) is a more detailed definition of the level above it.

This breaking-down or decomposing process will accomplish several tasks for you, one of which is improving estimates. It's easier to estimate the costs, time, and resources needed for individual work components than it is to estimate them for a whole body of work or deliverable. Using smaller components also makes it easier to assign performance measures and controls. These give you a baseline to compare against throughout the project or phase. And finally, assigning resources and responsibility for the components of work makes better sense because several resources with different skills might be needed to complete one deliverable. Breaking them down assures that an assignment, and the responsibility for that assignment, goes to the proper parties.

According to the *PMBOK® Guide*, decomposition is a five-step process:

1. Identify the deliverables and work. This step involves identifying all the major project deliverables and related work. The *PMBOK® Guide* makes a point of noting that you can use the expert judgment technique to analyze the project scope statement and identify the major deliverables.
2. Organize the WBS. This step involves organizing the work of the project and determining the WBS structure. (I'll talk more about constructing the WBS in the next section).
3. Decompose the WBS components into lower-level components. WBS components, like the deliverables and requirements, should be defined in tangible, verifiable terms so that performance and successful completion (or delivery) are easily measured and verified. Each component must clearly describe the product, service, or result in verifiable terms, and it must be assigned to a unit in the organization that will take responsibility for completing the work and making certain of its accuracy.
4. Assign identification codes. This step is a process where you assign identification codes or numbers to each of the WBS components.
5. Verify the WBS. This step is a verification step. Examine the decomposition to determine whether all the components are clear and complete. Determine whether each component listed is absolutely necessary to fulfill the requirements of the deliverable, and verify that the decomposition is sufficient to describe the work.

NOTE

I'll talk more about the process in step 4 in the section "Understanding the Unique WBS Identifiers" later in this chapter.

You can now plug the components you've identified into the WBS. This all sounds like a lot of work. I won't kid you—it is, but it's essential to project success. If you don't perform the WBS process adequately and accurately, you might end up setting yourself up for a failed project at worst or for lots of project changes, delayed schedules, and increased costs at best, not to mention all those team members who'll throw up their hands when you return to them for the third or fourth time to ask that they redo work they've already completed. I know you won't let this happen, so let's move on to constructing the WBS.

The Create WBS process has several outputs, one of which is the WBS. You'll look at the specifics of how to create the WBS next.

Constructing the WBS

There is no "right" way to construct a WBS. In practice, the chart structure is used quite often. (This structure resembles an organization chart with different levels of detail.) But a WBS could be composed in outline form as well. The choice is yours. You'll look at both ways shortly, along with some figures that depict the different levels of a WBS.

According to the *PMBOK® Guide*, you can organize the WBS in several ways:

Major deliverables and subprojects The major deliverables of the project are used as the first level of decomposition in this structure. If you're opening a new store, for example, the deliverables might include determining location, store build-out, furnishings, product, and so on. I'll talk about subprojects in the next section.

Subproject that may be executed outside the project team Another way to organize the work is by subprojects. Perhaps you're expanding an existing highway and several subprojects are involved. Some of your first level of decomposition might include these subprojects: demolition, design, bridgework, and paving. Each of the subproject managers will develop a WBS for their subproject that details the work required for that deliverable. When subproject work is involved, often times the subproject work is contracted out. In this example, if you contracted out the bridgework deliverable, this subproject requires its own WBS, which the seller (the bridgework subcontractor) is responsible for creating as part of the contract and contract work.

Project phases Many projects are structured or organized by project phases. For example, let's say you work in the construction industry. The project phases used in your industry might include project initiation, planning, design, build, inspection, and turnover. A feasibility study might be a deliverable under the project initiation phase, blueprints might be a deliverable under the planning phase, and so on. Each phase listed here would be the first level of decomposition (that is, the first level of the WBS), their deliverables would be the next level, and so on.

We'll take a look at some example WBS structures next.

Understanding the Various WBS Levels

Although the project manager is free to determine the number of levels in the WBS based on the complexity of the project, all WBS structures start with the project itself. Some WBS structures show the project as level one. Others show the level under the project, or the first level of decomposition, as level one. The *PMBOK® Guide* notes that level one is the project level, so I'll follow that example here.

The first level of decomposition might be the deliverables, phases, or subprojects, as I talked about earlier. (Remember that the first level of decomposition is actually the second level of the WBS because the project level is the first level.) The levels that follow show more and more detail and might include more deliverables followed by requirements. Each of these breakouts is called a *level* in the WBS. The lowest level of any WBS is called the *work package level*. (I'll talk more about this in "Defining Work Packages" later in this chapter.) The goal is to construct the WBS to the work package level where you can easily and reliably estimate cost and schedule dates. Keep in mind that some projects or deliverables may need only one or two levels of decomposition.

Exam Spotlight

Remember that each descending level of the WBS is a more detailed description of the project deliverables than the level above it. Each component of the WBS should be defined clearly and completely and should describe how the work of the project will be performed and controlled. Collectively, all the levels of the WBS roll up to the top so that all the work of the project is captured (and no additional work is added). According to the *PMBOK® Guide*, this is known as the 100% rule.

NOTE

There is some controversy among project managers over whether activities should be listed on the WBS. In practice, I often include activities on my work breakdown structure for small projects only because it facilitates other Planning processes later. In this case, the activities are the work package level. However, you should realize that large, complex projects do not include activities on the WBS. For the exam, remember that you will decompose activities during the Activity Definition process that I'll talk about in Chapter 4, "Creating the Project Schedule," and that activities are *not* part of the WBS.

The easiest way to describe the steps for creating a WBS is with an example. Let's suppose you work for a software company that publishes children's games. You're the project manager for the new Billy Bob's Bassoon game, which teaches children about music, musical rhythm, and beginning sight reading. The first box on the WBS is the project name; it appears at the top of the WBS, as shown in Figure 3.1, and is defined as WBS Level One.

The next level is the first level of decomposition and should describe the major deliverables for the project. In this example, some of the deliverables might be requirements definition, design specifications, and programming. This isn't an exhaustive list of deliverables; in practice, you would go on to place all of your major deliverables into the WBS as level-one content. For illustration purposes, just look at a slice of the WBS for this project. Refer to Figure 3.1 to see the WBS with level-one and level-two detail added.

FIGURE 3.1 WBS level one and two

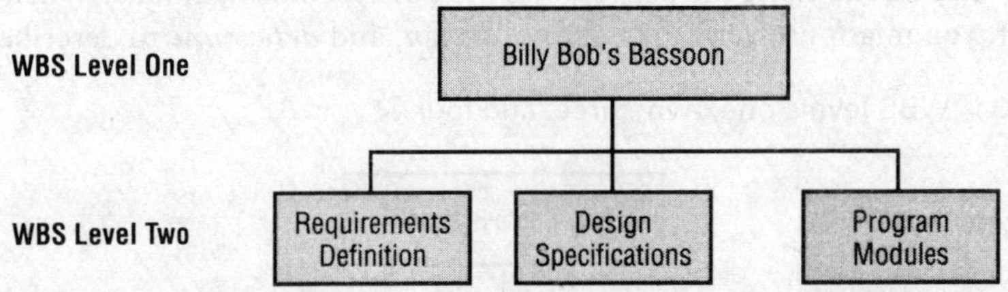

Level-three content might be the component deliverables that are further broken out from the major deliverables of level two, or it might be products or results that contribute to the deliverable. The Billy Bob's Bassoon example shows further deliverables as level-three content. See Figure 3.2 for an illustration of the WBS so far.

FIGURE 3.2 WBS levels one, two, and three

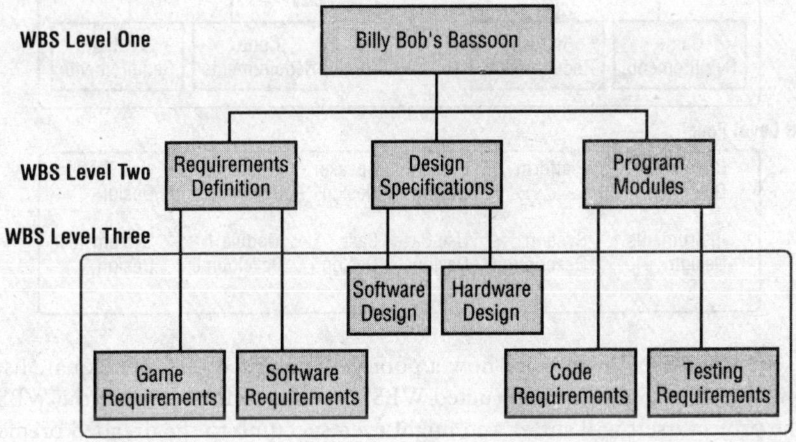

NOTE Large, complex projects are often composed of several subprojects that collectively make up the main project. The WBS for a project such as the Billy Bob's Bassoon game would show the subprojects as level-one detail. These subprojects' major deliverables would then be listed as level-two content, perhaps more deliverables as level three, and so on.

The goal here is to eventually break the work out to the point where the responsibility and accountability for each work package can be assigned to an organizational unit or a team of people. In Figure 3.3, I've decomposed this WBS to the fourth level to show an even finer level of deliverable detail. Remember that activities are not usually included in the WBS. An easy way to differentiate between deliverables and activities is to use nouns as the deliverable descriptors and verbs as activity descriptors (we'll talk about activities in

Chapter 4). Reaching way back to my grade-school English, I recall that a noun is a person, place, or thing. In this example, the deliverables are described using nouns. When we get to the activity list, you might use verbs like *define*, *design*, and *determine* to describe them.

FIGURE 3.3 WBS levels one, two, three, and four

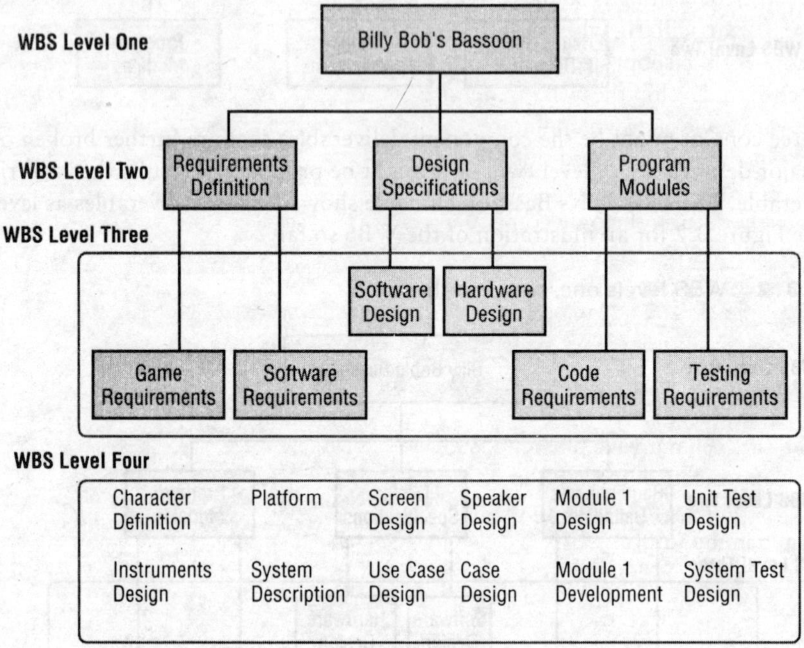

You can see from these illustrations how a poorly defined scope or inadequate list of deliverables will lead to a poorly constructed WBS. Not only will this make the WBS look sickly, but the project itself will suffer and might even succumb to the dreaded premature project demise. The final cost of the project will be higher than estimated, and lots of rework (translation: late nights and weekends) will be needed to account for the missing work not listed on the WBS. You can construct a good WBS and maintain a healthy project by taking the time to document all the deliverables during the Define Scope process.

WBS Templates

Work breakdown structures can be constructed using WBS templates or the WBS from a similar completed project. Although every project is unique, many companies and industries perform the same kind of projects repeatedly. The deliverables are similar from project to project, and they generally follow a consistent path. WBS templates can be used in a case like this as a tool to simplify the WBS process, saving the project manager time.

Don't get too carried away when creating a WBS. The object is to define the work of the project so you can easily plan, manage, monitor, and control the work. But, you don't want to take this too far. If you decompose the work to the point that you're showing every minute detail, you've ventured into inefficiency and will find it more difficult to plan and manage. In addition, you're potentially stifling the creativity of the people working on the project because everything is so narrowly defined.

Sometimes, particularly when working on large projects that consist of several subprojects, some of the subprojects might not be scheduled until a future date. Obviously, it makes sense to develop the WBS in detail at that future date when the deliverables and subprojects are better known and more details are available. This technique is called *rolling wave planning*. The idea behind this technique is that you elaborate the work of the project to the level of detail you know about at the time. If a subproject or deliverable is scheduled sometime in the future, the only component that might appear on the WBS today is the subproject itself. As you get closer to the subproject, you'll elaborate the details of the subproject and record them on the WBS.

Exam Spotlight

Understand that rolling wave planning is a process of elaborating deliverables, project phases, or subprojects in the WBS to differing levels of decomposition depending on the expected date of the work. Work in the near term is described in more detail than work to be performed in the future.

Understanding the Unique WBS Identifiers

Each element at each level of the WBS is generally assigned a unique identifier according to the *PMBOK® Guide*. This unique identifier is typically a number, and it's used to sum and track the costs, schedule, and resources associated with the WBS elements. These numbers are usually associated with the corporation's chart of accounts, which is used to track costs by category. Collectively, these numeric identifiers are known as the *code of accounts*. The unique identifiers for the requirements definition branch of the WBS might look something like this:

10-1 Billy Bob's Bassoon

10-2 Requirements Definition

10-3 Game Requirements

    10-3-1 Character Definition

    10-3-2 Instruments Design

    10-4 Software Requirements

    10-4-1 Platform

    10-4-2 System Description

Defining Work Packages

NOTE As mentioned earlier, the project manager is free to determine the number of levels in the WBS based on the complexity of the project. You need to include enough levels to accurately estimate project time and costs but not so many levels that it's difficult to distinguish between the components. Regardless of the number of levels in a WBS, the lowest level in a WBS is called the *work package level*.

Work packages are the components that can be easily assigned to one person, or a team of people, with clear accountability and responsibility for completing the assignment. Assignments are easily made at the work package level; however, assignments can be made at any level in the WBS. The work package level is where time estimates, cost estimates, and resource estimates are determined.

Work package levels on large projects can represent subprojects that are further decomposed into their own work breakdown structures. They might also consist of project work that will be completed by a vendor, another organization, or another department in your organization. If you're giving project work to another department in your organization, you'll assign the work packages to individual managers, who will in turn break them down into activities during the Activity Definition process later in the Planning process group.

Work packages might be assigned to vendors or others external to the organization. For example, perhaps one of the deliverables in your project is special packaging and a vendor is responsible for completing this work. The vendor will likely treat this deliverable as a project within its own organization and construct its own WBS with several levels of decomposition. However, for your project, it's a deliverable listed at the work package level of the WBS.

Real World Scenario

The Lincoln Street Office Building

Flagship International has just purchased a new building to house its growing staff. The folks at Flagship consider themselves very lucky to have won the bid on the property located in a prime section of the downtown area. The building is a historic building and is in need of some repairs and upgrades to make it suitable for office space. Constructing the renovations will require special handling and care, as outlined in the *Historical Society Building Revisions Guide*.

Alfredo Martini is the project manager assigned to the renovation project. Alfredo has already determined the deliverables for this project. In so doing, he has discovered that he will not be able to manage all the work himself. He will need several subproject managers working on individual deliverables, all reporting to him. Alfredo calls a meeting with the other project managers to develop the WBS. Let's eavesdrop on the meeting.

"As you all know, we're planning to move into the Lincoln Street building by November 1. There is quite a bit of work to do between now and then, and I'm enlisting each of you to manage a segment of this project. Take a look at this WBS."

Here's how a portion of the WBS Alfredo constructed looks.

Lincoln Street Building Renovation

- 2.0 Facility Safety
  - 2.1 Sprinkler System
  - 2.2 Elevators
  - 2.3 Emergency Evacuation Plans
- 3.0 Asbestos Abatement
  - 3.1 Inspection and Identification
  - 3.2 Plans for Removal
- 4.0 Office Space
  - 4.1 Building Floor Plans
  - 4.2 Plans for Office Space Allocation
  - 4.3 Plans for Break Room Facilities
  - 4.4 Plans for Employee Workout Room

Alfredo continues, "I'm going to manage the Facility Safety project. Adrian, I'd like you to take the Asbestos Abatement project, and Orlando, you're responsible for the Office Space project."

"Alfredo," Adrian says, "asbestos abatement is going to take contractors and specialized equipment. We don't have staff to do these tasks."

"I understand. You'll need to take charge of securing the contractor to handle this. Your responsibility will be to manage the contractor and keep them on schedule," Alfredo answers.

Orlando reminds Alfredo that he has missed a deliverable on the WBS. "Part of the Office Space project needs to include the network communications and telecommunications equipment rooms. I don't see that on here."

"Good point, Orlando," Alfredo says. "The level-two and level-three elements of this WBS are not complete. Each of you has been assigned to the subproject level, level one. Your first assignment is to meet back here in two weeks with a WBS for your subproject. And I'd like to see some ideas about the staff assignments you'd make at the work package level and how long you think these components will take. We'll refine those after we meet next."

NOTE This might seem self-evident, but work packages not shown on the WBS are not included in the project. The same holds true for the project scope statement—if the deliverable isn't noted there, it isn't part of the project.

Creating WBS Process Outputs

The Create WBS process has four outputs:

- Work breakdown structure
- WBS dictionary
- Scope baseline
- Project document updates

I've covered the WBS in detail already. Updates to the scope statement and project document updates might come about as a result of changes that occur when you're creating the WBS. You can see from the examples you've walked through in this chapter how new deliverables or requirements might surface as a result of working on the WBS. These requested changes should be reviewed and either approved or denied using your change control processes. (I'll talk about that in Chapter 10.) The approved changes should be noted in the project scope statement, and the project management plan and other project documents should be updated to reflect the new approved project scope statement.

WBS Dictionary

The *WBS dictionary* is where work component descriptions are documented. According to the *PMBOK® Guide*, the WBS dictionary should include the following elements for each component of the WBS:

- Code of accounts identifier
- Description of the work of the component
- Organization responsible for completing the component
- List of schedule milestones
- Schedule activities associated with the schedule milestones
- Required resources
- Cost estimates
- Quality requirements
- Criteria for acceptance
- Technical references
- Contract information

Let's look at an example of what some of the elements of a WBS dictionary entry might look like. You'll use the work package level called Inspection and Identification defined in the sidebar "The Lincoln Street Office Building" earlier. The WBS dictionary entry for this might look like the following:

3.1 Inspection and Identification

Description of work: Inspect the building for asbestos, and identify all areas where it's found. Update the plan for removal (WBS 2.2) with each location identified.

Responsible organization: Adrian in Facilities will hire and oversee a contractor to perform this work.

Schedule milestones: Inspection and identification to start after contractor is identified and hired (no later than July 1). Work should be completed no later than September 15.

Contract information: Two contractors have been identified as qualified and experienced in this type of work. Contract process should close no later than June 12.

Scope Baseline

Remember how I said that everything you've done so far has built upon itself? This is an important concept you should know for this output. The *scope baseline* for the project is the approved project scope statement, the WBS, and the WBS dictionary. (You'll recall from Chapter 2 that the project scope statement serves as a baseline for future project decisions because it helps the team determine whether requested changes are inside or outside of scope.) In other words, these documents together describe in detail all the work of the project. From these documents, you'll document schedules, assign resources, and monitor and control the work of the project according to what's described here.

Exam Spotlight

The scope baseline is defined as the detailed project scope statement, the WBS, and the WBS dictionary. Understand this concept for the exam.

If the WBS is constructed well, you've given yourself a huge helping hand with the remaining Planning processes. The completion of many of the remaining processes depends on the project scope statement and WBS being accurate and complete. In Chapter 4, for example, you'll use the work packages created here to further elaborate the work into activities. From there, you can estimate costs, develop schedules, and so on. The WBS is an essential tool for project planning, so keep it handy.

Project Case Study: New Kitchen Heaven Retail Store

The project charter kickoff meeting was held and well attended. You're ready to start gathering requirements and writing the project scope statement and have a question or two for Dirk. You knock on his door, and he invites you in.

"Shoot," he says.

"I'm ready to define the deliverables and requirements for this project. I want to make sure I get the right folks involved in the meeting. Who are key stakeholders you recommend I speak with?"

"I can think of a few people right off that you don't want to miss. There's Jake Peterson over in Facilities. He's in charge of store furnishings, shelving, things like that—any supplies for the stores that aren't retail products. He can help out with store build-outs too. He supervised our last eight stores and did a terrific job."

"Anyone else?" you ask.

"You should also talk to Jill Overstreet, the director in charge of retail products. She can help with the initial store stocking, and once the store is open, her group will take over the ongoing operations. All the district managers report to Jill."

You thank Dirk and tell him you're going to contact Jake and Jill and set up a brainstorming session to determine requirements.

A few days later.

You review your notes and reread the first draft of the project scope statement you've prepared for the Kitchen Heaven retail store before looking for Dirk. After your meetings with the stakeholders, you were better able to refine the project objectives and deliverables.

"Dirk, I'm glad I caught you. I'd like to go over the project scope statement with you before I give it to the stakeholders. Do you have a few minutes?"

"Sure," Dirk says to you. "Let's have it."

"The project objective is to open the 50th Kitchen Heaven store in Colorado Springs by February 1. When I met with Jake, he confirmed it takes 120 days to do the store build-out. That includes having the shelves set up and in place, ready to stock with inventory."

Dirk asks whether Jake told you about his store location idea.

"Yes, Jake gave me a contact name of the leasing agent, and I've left her a voicemail. The sooner we can get that lease signed, the better. It takes Jake 120 days to do the build-out, and Jill said she needs two weeks lead time to order the initial inventory and stock the shelves. That puts us pretty close to our February 1 deadline, counting the time to get the lease papers signed."

"Sounds good so far," Dirk replies. "What else?"

You continue, "I've included an updated description of the products and services the new store will offer, based on the documentation that was written from the last store opening. Jill reviewed the updates to the description, so we should be in the clear there. The store will include some new lines that we've decided to take on—cookware from famous chefs, that kind of thing.

"Jake has already made contact with a general contractor in Colorado Springs, and he is ready to roll once we've signed the lease.

"One more thing, Dirk. Since we're including the big bash at grand opening as part of the deliverables, I talked to some of your folks in marketing to get some ideas. They are thinking we should have some great giveaways as door prizes and that we will want the food catered. They also thought having some live cooking demonstrations with some local chefs would be a good attraction."

"Sounds like you're on the right track. So, what's next?" Dirk asks.

"Once you approve the scope statement, I'd like to send a copy to the stakeholders. My next step is to break down the deliverables and requirements I've documented here into the WBS so we can get rolling on the work of the project."

Project Case Study Checklist

The main topics discussed in the case study are as follows:

Stakeholder analysis for requirements gathering: Jake Peterson and Jill Overstreet interviewed. Needs, wants, and expectations recorded and requirements prioritized.

Organizational structure: Functional organization with a separate projectized department.

Constraints: February 1 date to coincide with home and garden show.

Assumptions: These are the assumptions:

- A store build-out usually takes 120 days.
- Jill Overstreet will help with the initial store stocking.
- Jake Peterson will provide supplies for the stores that aren't retail products, such as store furnishings, shelving, and so on, and can help with the store build-out as well.
- The budget for the project will be between $1.5 and $2 million.

The project scope statement includes the following:

Project objectives: Open 50th store by February 1 in Colorado Springs.

Project deliverables: These are the project deliverables:

- Build out storefront, including shelving.
- Retail product line will be delivered two weeks prior to grand opening.
- Have grand-opening party with cooking demos.

Project requirements: These are the project requirements:

- Sign lease within 14 days.
- Offer new line of gourmet food products.
- Have classroom space in back of store for cooking demos and classes.

Constraints: February 1 date will coincide with home and garden show.

Fund limitations: Spend no more than $2 million for the project.

Assumptions: (These are the same as listed earlier.) Decomposed deliverables into a WBS.

The WBS includes the following:

- Level one is the project.
- Level two is subprojects or deliverables.
- Level three is deliverables.
- Last level of WBS is the work package level, where time and cost estimates can be defined in the next process.

NOTE

I'll talk more about change control and change request processes in Chapter 9.

Approved changes might also impact the project scope management plan or some of the subsidiary plans that make up this plan. Make certain you update this plan as a result of the changes made during the Define Scope process.

Understanding How This Applies to our Next Project

In this chapter, you dealt with the realities of life on the job. The reality is, many project managers I know are managing several projects at once as opposed to one large project. Although every concept presented in this chapter is a sound one, it's important to note that you have to balance the amount of effort you'll put into project management processes against the size and complexity of the project.

As a manager who prides herself and my team on excellent customer service, I have once or twice gotten my team into precarious situations because I was so focused on helping the customer that I hurt them and our department in the process. If you're wondering how that happened, it's because we didn't take the time to document the scope of the project and the final acceptance criteria. In one case, in the interest of getting the project completed quickly because of our customer's own internal deadlines, we decided the project was straightforward enough that we didn't need to document deliverables. The customer promised to work side by side with us as we produced the work of the project. Unfortunately, that wasn't the case, and we didn't meet the expectations of our customer. Further, after we did implement the project (two months behind schedule), we went through another six weeks of "fixes" because of the miscommunication between the customer and the project team on what constituted some of the features of the final product. There's always a great reason for cutting corners—but they almost always come back to haunt you. My advice is to always create a scope statement and a requirements list and get stakeholder signatures on both. (In practice, small projects can include both the deliverables and requirements within the scope statement.)

Decomposing the deliverables is the first step toward determining resource requirements and estimates. A WBS is always a good idea, no matter the size of the project. I have to admit I have cheated a time or two on small projects and used the project schedule as the WBS. And in all fairness that's worked out fine when the team is small and there aren't more than three or four people working on the project. If you get many more than four people on the project team, it can be a little cumbersome to track deliverables with a schedule only. The WBS is the perfect tool to use to assign names to work packages, and it's the foundation for determining estimates for the work of the project.

The five-step process outlined by the *PMBOK® Guide* works very well. Starting with the 50,000-foot view, the team determines the major deliverables of the project. From there, the deliverables are decomposed into ever smaller units of work. The trick here is to break the work down into measurable units so that you can verify the status of the work and the completion and acceptance of the work when you're finished. If you have "fuzzy" WBS levels or work packages, you won't be able to determine status accurately. In the information technology field, we have a saying about the status of projects: "It's 90 percent complete." The problem is it always seems that the last 10 percent takes twice as long to complete as the first 90 did. If you've taken the time to document a WBS, you'll have a much better idea of what that 90 percent constitutes. The last step is the verification step where you determine whether everything you've identified in the WBS is absolutely necessary to fulfill the work of the project and whether it's decomposed enough to adequately describe the work. It has been my experience that documenting the WBS will save you time later in the Planning processes, particularly developing the project schedule and determining the project budget.

I believe the most important idea to take from this chapter is a simple one: always use a scope statement and requirements list, and always get them signed.

Summary

This chapter started you on the road to project planning via the Develop Project Management Plan process, the Collect Requirements process, the Define Scope process, and the Create WBS process. We covered a lot of material in this chapter. Everything you've learned so far becomes the foundation for further project planning.

The output of the Develop Project Management Plan process is the project management plan, which is concerned with defining, coordinating, and integrating all the ancillary project plans. The purpose of this plan is to define how the project is executed, how it's monitored and controlled, and how it's closed.

The Collect Requirements process involves gathering and documenting the requirements of the project. It's important that requirements be measurable, traceable, testable and so on. Measurement criteria for project requirements are agreed upon by the stakeholders and project manager. Additionally, requirements should be tracked in a traceability matrix that documents where they originated, the results of the tests, the priority of the requirement and more.

The scope statement is produced during the Define Scope process. It describes the project deliverables. The scope statement forms a baseline you'll use to weigh future project decisions, most particularly change requests. The scope statement contains a list of project deliverables that will be used in future Planning processes.

The project scope statement contains many elements, including product scope description, product acceptance criteria, deliverables, exclusions from scope, constraints, and assumptions.

Constraints restrict or dictate the actions of the project team. Constraints usually involve time, cost, and scope but can also include schedules, technology, quality, resources, risk, and more.

Assumptions are things believed to be true. You'll want to document project assumptions and validate them as the project progresses.

A WBS is a deliverable-oriented group of project essentials. The highest levels of the WBS are described using nouns, and the lowest levels are described with verbs. Each element in the WBS has its own set of objectives and deliverables that must be met in order to fulfill the deliverables of the next highest level and ultimately the project itself. In this way, the WBS validates the completeness of the work.

The lowest level of the WBS is known as the work package level. This breakdown allows the project manager to determine cost estimates, time estimates, resource assignments, and quality controls.

Exam Essentials

Be able to state the purpose of the Develop Project Management Plan process. It defines, coordinates, and integrates all subsidiary project plans.

Understand the purpose of the project scope statement. The scope statement serves as a common understanding of project scope among the stakeholders. The project objectives and deliverables and their quantifiable criteria are documented in the scope statement and are used by the project manager and the stakeholders to determine whether the project was completed successfully. It also serves as a basis for future project decisions.

Be able to define project constraints and assumptions. Project constraints limit the options of the project team and restrict their actions. Sometimes constraints dictate actions. Time, budget, and cost are the most common constraints Assumptions are conditions that are presumed to be true or real.

Be able to describe the purpose of the scope management plan. The scope management plan has a direct influence on the project's success and describes the process for determining project scope, facilitates creating the WBS, describes how the product or service of the project is verified and accepted, and documents how changes to scope will be handled. The scope management plan is a subsidiary plan of the project management plan.

Be able to define a WBS and its components. The WBS is a deliverable-oriented hierarchy. It uses the deliverables from the project scope statement or similar documents and decomposes them into logical, manageable units of work. Level one is the major deliverable level or subproject level, level two is a further elaboration of the deliverables, and so on. The lowest level of any WBS is called a work package.

Key Terms

Planning, planning, planning…I can't stress enough how important the planning processes are to a successful project. In this chapter, you learned about the processes involved in developing your project scope statement. Understand these processes well, and know them by the name used in the *PMBOK® Guide*:

Develop Project Management Plan

Collect Requirements

Define Scope

Create WBS

Before you take the exam, also be certain you are familiar with the following terms:

acceptance criteria

alternatives identification

approval requirements

assumptions

code of accounts

constraints

critical success factors

deliverables

product analysis

project boundaries

project management information system (PMIS)

project management plan

project scope management plan

project scope statement

requirements

rolling wave planning

scope

WBS dictionary

work package

Review Questions

1. You are a project manager for Laredo Pioneer's Traveling Rodeo Show. You're heading up a project to promote a new line of souvenirs to be sold at the shows. You are getting ready to write the project management plan and know that all the following are true regarding the PMIS except for one. Which of the following is not true?
   - **A.** The PMIS is a tool and technique of this process.
   - **B.** The configuration management system is a subsystem of the PMIS.
   - **C.** The PMIS includes a change control system.
   - **D.** The PMIS is an automated system.

2. Which of the following is true?
   - **A.** You are a project manager for Laredo Pioneer's Traveling Rodeo Show. You're heading up a project to promote a new line of souvenirs to be sold at the shows. You're ready to document the processes you'll use to perform the project as well as define how the project will be executed, controlled, and closed. You are working on the project scope management plan.
   - **B.** You are a project manager for Laredo Pioneer's Traveling Rodeo Show. You're heading up a project to promote a new line of souvenirs to be sold at the shows. You're ready to document the processes you'll use to perform the project as well as define how the project will be executed, controlled, and closed. You are working on the product scope statement.
   - **C.** You are a project manager for Laredo Pioneer's Traveling Rodeo Show. You're heading up a project to promote a new line of souvenirs to be sold at the shows. You're ready to document the processes you'll use to perform the project as well as define how the project will be executed and controlled and how changes will be monitored and controlled. You are working on the project management plan.
   - **D.** You are a project manager for Laredo Pioneer's Traveling Rodeo Show. You're heading up a project to promote a new line of souvenirs to be sold at the shows. You're ready to document the processes you'll use to perform the project as well as define how the project will be executed, controlled, and closed. You are working on the project scope statement.

3. You are a project manager responsible for the construction of a new office complex. You are taking over for a project manager who recently left the company. The prior project manager completed the scope statement and scope management plan for this project. In your interviews with some key team members, you conclude which of the following?

   A. They understand that the scope statement assesses the stability of the project scope and outlines how scope will be verified and used to control changes. They also know that project scope is measured against the product requirements.

   B. They understand that the scope management plan describes how project scope will be managed and controlled and how the WBS will be created and defined. They also know that product scope is measured against the product requirements.

   C. They understand that the scope management plan is deliverables oriented and includes cost estimates and stakeholder needs and expectations. They understand that project scope is measured against the project management plan.

   D. They understand that the scope statement describes how the high-level deliverables and requirements will be defined and verified. They understand that product scope is measured against the project management plan.

4. Unanimity, majority, plurality, and dictatorship are four examples of which of the following techniques?

   A. Group creativity techniques, which is a tool and technique of the Collect Requirements process

   B. Interviews, which is a tool and technique of the Define Scope process

   C. Facilitated workshops technique, which is a tool and technique of the Define Scope process

   D. Group decision making techniques, which is a tool and technique of the Collect Requirements process

5. Which of the following is true regarding the project scope statement?

   A. The project scope statement includes a change control system that describes how to make changes to the project scope.

   B. The project scope statement further elaborates the details from the Initiating and Planning processes and serves as a basis for future project decisions.

   C. The project scope statement describes how the team will define and develop the work breakdown structure.

   D. The project scope statement assesses the reliability of the project scope and describes the process for verifying and accepting completed deliverables.

6. You are a project manager for an agricultural supply company. You have interviewed stakeholders and gathered requirements. Which of the following is true regarding the process this question refers to?

   A. The requirements document lists the requirements and describes how they will be analyzed, documented, and managed throughout the project.

   B. Requirements documentation consist of formal, complex documents that include elements such as the business need of the project, functional requirements, nonfunctional requirements, impacts to others inside and outside the organization, and requirements assumptions and constraints.

   C. The requirements documentation details the work required to create the deliverables of the project, including deliverables description, product acceptance criteria, exclusions from requirements, and requirements assumptions and constraints.

   D. The requirements traceability matrix ties requirements to project objectives, business needs, WBS deliverables, product design, test strategies, and high-level requirements and traces them through to project completion.

7. Which of the following makes up the project scope baseline?

   A. The approved project scope statement

   B. The approved scope management plan and WBS

   C. The WBS, approved project scope statement, and WBS dictionary

   D. The approved scope management plan, the WBS, and the WBS dictionary

8. Which of the following statements is true regarding brainstorming and lateral thinking?

   A. They are forms of expert judgment used to help define and develop requirements and develop the project scope statement.

   B. They are tools and techniques used to elaborate the product scope description.

   C. They are group decision making techniques, which are a tool and technique of the Collect Requirements process.

   D. They are alternatives identification techniques, which are a tool and technique of the Define Scope process.

9. Your company, Kick That Ball Sports, has appointed you project manager for its new Cricket product line introduction. This is a national effort, and all the retail stores across the country need to have the new products on the shelves before the media advertising blitz begins. The product line involves three new products, two of which will be introduced together and a third one that will follow within two years. You are ready to create the WBS. All of the following are true except for which one?

   A. The WBS can be structured using each product as a level-one entry.

   B. The WBS should be elaborated to a level where costs and schedule are easily estimated. This is known as the work package level.

   C. *Rolling wave* refers to how all levels of the WBS collectively roll up to reflect the work of the project and only the work of the project.

   D. Each level of the WBS represents verifiable products or results.

10. You are a project manager for Giraffe Enterprises. You've recently taken over for a project manager who lied about his PMI certification and was subsequently fired. Unfortunately, he did a poor job of defining the scope. Which of the following could happen if you don't correct this?

    A. The stakeholders will require overtime from the project team to keep the project on schedule.

    B. The poor scope definition will adversely affect the creation of the work breakdown structure, and costs will increase.

    C. The project management plan's process for verification and acceptance of the deliverables needs to be updated as a result of the poor scope definition.

    D. The project costs could increase, there might be rework, and schedule delays might result.

11. You are the project manager for Lucky Stars nightclubs. They specialize in live country and western band performances. Your newest project is in the Planning processes group. You are working on the WBS. The finance manager has given you a numbering system to assign to the WBS. Which of the following is true?

    A. The numbering system is a unique identifier known as the WBS dictionary, which is used to assign quality control codes to the individual work elements.

    B. The numbering system is a unique identifier known as the WBS dictionary, which is used to track the descriptions of individual work elements.

    C. The numbering system is a unique identifier known as the code of accounts, which is used to track time and resource assignments for individual work elements.

    D. The numbering system is a unique identifier known as the code of accounts, which is used to track the costs of the WBS elements.

12. You've constructed the WBS for your recent project. You've requested that the subproject managers report to you in three weeks with each of their individual WBSs constructed. Which statement is not true regarding the subproject managers' WBS?

    A. The work package level is decomposed to create the activity list.

    B. The work package level is the lowest level in the WBS.

    C. The work package level facilitates resource assignments.

    D. The work package level facilitates cost and time estimates.

13. You are a project manager working on a new software product your company plans to market to businesses. The project sponsor told you that the project must be completed by September 1. The company plans to demo the new software product at a trade show in late September and therefore needs the project completed in time for the trade show. However, the sponsor has also told you that the budget is fixed at $85,000, and it would take an act of Congress to get it increased. You must complete the project within the given time frame and budget. Which of the following is the primary constraint for this project?

    A. Budget

    B. Scope

    C. Time

    D. Quality

14. Which of the following statements about decomposition is the least true?

A. Decomposition involves structuring and organizing the WBS so that deliverables are always listed at level one.

B. Decomposition requires a degree of expert judgment and also requires close analysis of the project scope statement.

C. Decomposition is a tool and technique used to create a WBS.

D. Decomposition subdivides the major deliverables into smaller components until the work package level is reached.

15. You are in the process of translating project objectives into tangible deliverables and requirements. All the following are techniques used in the product analysis tool and technique of the Define Scope process except for which one?

A. Value engineering and value analysis

B. Product configuration and specification analysis

C. Systems analysis and systems engineering

D. Product breakdown and functional analysis

16. You are a project manager for a documentary film company. In light of a recent regional tragedy, the company president wants to get a new documentary on the efforts of the heroic rescue teams to air as soon as possible. She's looking to you to make this documentary the best that has ever been produced in the history of this company. She guarantees you free rein to use whatever resources you need to get this project done quickly. However, the best photographer in the company is currently working on another assignment. Which of the following is true?

A. The primary constraint is time because the president wants the film done quickly. She told you to get it to air as soon as possible.

B. Resources are the primary constraint. Even though the president has given you free rein on resource use, you assume she didn't mean those actively assigned to projects.

C. The schedule is the primary constraint. Even though the president has given you free rein on resource use, you assume she didn't mean those actively assigned to projects. The photographer won't be finished for another three weeks on his current assignment, so schedule adjustments will have to be made.

D. The primary constraint is quality because the president wants this to be the best film ever produced by this company. She's given you free rein to use whatever resources needed to get the job done.

17. Your project depends on a key deliverable from a vendor you've used several times before with great success. You're counting on the delivery to arrive on June 1. This is an example of a/an ________________.

A. constraint

B. objective

C. assumption

D. requirement

18. What limits the options of the project team?

A. Technology

B. Constraints

C. Deliverables

D. Assumptions

19. Your company provides answering services for several major catalog retailers. The number of calls coming into the service center per month has continued to increase over the past 18 months. The phone system is approaching the maximum load limits and needs to be upgraded. You've been assigned to head up the upgrade project. Based on the company's experience with the vendor who worked on the last phone upgrade project, you're confident they'll be able to assist you with this project as well. Which of the following is true?

A. You've made an assumption about vendor availability and expertise. The project came about because of a business need.

B. Vendor availability and expertise are constraints. The project came about because of a business need.

C. You've made an assumption about vendor availability and expertise. The project came about because of a market demand.

D. Vendor availability and expertise are constraints. The project came about because of a market demand.

20. Which of the following is not a major step of decomposition?

A. Identify major deliverables.

B. Identify resources.

C. Identify components.

D. Verify correctness of decomposition.

Answers to Review Questions

1. A. The PMIS is one of the elements of the enterprise environmental factors, which is an input to the Develop Project Management Plan process.

2. C. The project management plan describes the processes you'll use to perform the project and describes how the project will be executed, monitored, controlled and how the work of the project will be executed to meet the objectives.

3. B. The scope management plan describes how project scope will be defined and verified, how the scope statement will be developed, how the WBS will be created and defined, and how project scope will be managed and controlled. Project scope is measured against the project management plan, whereas product scope is measured against the product requirements.

4. D. These four decision making techniques belong to the Collect Requirements process and are part of the group decision making tool and technique in this process.

5. B. The scope statement further elaborates the project deliverables and documents the constraints and assumptions for the project. It serves as a basis for future project decisions.

6. D. The traceability matrix links requirements to their origin and traces them throughout the project. Option A describes the requirements management plan, not the requirements document. Option B is partially true with the exception of the first statement. Requirements documents do not have to be formal or complex. Option C refers to the project scope statement, not the requirements.

7. C. The scope baseline consists of the approved project scope statement, the WBS, and the WBS dictionary.

8. D. Alternatives identification are a tool and technique of the Define Scope process that includes brainstorming and lateral thinking techniques.

9. C. Each of the three products might have different amounts of elaboration and levels. The question said the third product would not be introduced until two years after the first two. This WBS entry might contain only one level stating the product name.

10. D. Option A might seem like a correct answer, but option D is more correct. There isn't enough information to determine whether stakeholders will require overtime. We do know that poor scope definition might lead to cost increases, rework, schedule delays, and poor morale.

11. D. Each element in the WBS is assigned a unique identifier. These are collectively known as the *code of accounts*. Typically, these codes are associated with a corporate chart of accounts and are used to track the costs of the individual work elements in the WBS.

12. A. The work package level is the lowest level in the WBS and facilitates resource assignment and cost and time estimates. The agreed-upon deliverables in C would appear in the higher levels in the WBS.

13. C. The primary constraint is time. Since the trade show demos depend on project completion and the trade show is in late September, the date cannot be moved. The budget is the secondary constraint in this example.

14. A. Decomposition subdivides the major deliverables into smaller components. It is a tool and technique of the Create WBS process and is used to create a WBS. Level-two components might be deliverables, phases, subprojects, or some combination.

15. B. Product analysis includes techniques such as value engineering, value analysis, systems analysis, systems engineering, product breakdown, and functional analysis.

16. D. The primary constraint is quality. If you made the assumption as stated in B, you assumed incorrectly. Clarify these assumptions with your stakeholders and project sponsors. This applies to C as well.

17. C. This is an example of an assumption. You've used this vendor before and not had any problems. You're assuming there will be no problems with this delivery based on your past experience.

18. B. Constraints restrict the actions of the project team.

19. A. The project came about because of a business need. The phones have to be answered because that's the core business. Upgrading the system to handle more volume is a business need. An assumption has been made regarding vendor availability. Always validate your assumptions.

20. B. The steps of decomposition include identify major deliverables, organize and determine the structure, identify lower-level components, assign identification codes, and verify correctness of decomposition.

Chapter 4

Creating the Project Schedule

THE PMP EXAM CONTENT FROM THE PLANNING THE PROJECT PERFORMANCE DOMAIN COVERED IN THIS CHAPTER INCLUDES THE FOLLOWING:

✓ **Obtain Plan Approval**

The Planning process group has more processes than any other process group. As a result, a lot of time and effort goes into the Planning processes of any project. You'll find on some projects that you might spend almost as much time planning the project as you do executing and controlling it. This isn't a bad thing. The better planning you do up front, the more likely you'll have a successful project. Speaking of planning, together the Planning, Executing, and Monitoring and Controlling process groups account for almost 70 percent of the PMP exam questions, so *plan* on spending about the same percentage of your study time on these areas.

This is another fun-filled, action-packed chapter. We'll start off by defining the activities that become the work of the project. The WBS will come in handy here, so keep it close by. Then we'll sequence the activities in their proper order, estimate the resources we'll need to complete the work, and estimate how long each activity will take. Last but not least, we'll develop the project schedule.

Everything you've done up to this point and the processes we'll discuss in this chapter will help you create an accurate project schedule. You'll use these documents (along with several other documents you've created along the way) throughout the Executing and Monitoring and Controlling processes to help measure the progress of the project. Let's get going.

Defining Activities

Now you're off and running toward the development of your project schedule. To develop the schedule, you first need to define the activities, sequence them in the right order, estimate resources, and estimate the time it will take to complete the tasks. I'll cover the Define Activities process here, the Sequence Activities process next, and pick up with the estimating processes in the next chapter.

NOTE Define Activities and Sequence Activities are separate processes, each with their own inputs, tools and techniques, and outputs. In practice, especially for small to medium-sized projects, you can combine these processes into one process or step.

The *Define Activities* process is a further breakdown of the work package elements of the WBS. It documents the specific activities needed to fulfill the deliverables detailed on the WBS. This process might be performed by the project manager, or when the WBS is broken down to the subproject level, this process (and all the activity-related processes that follow) might be assigned to a subproject manager.

Define Activities Process Inputs

The following are inputs to the Define Activities process:

- Scope baseline (deliverables, constraints, and assumptions)
- Enterprise environmental factors (project management information systems)
- Organizational process assets (existing guidelines and policies, lessons learned knowledge base)

Tools and Techniques for Defining Activities

The tools and techniques of the Define Activities process are as follows:

- Decomposition
- Rolling wave planning
- Templates
- Expert judgment

We've covered most of these topics in the previous chapter. Decomposition in this process involves breaking the work packages into smaller, more manageable units of work called *activities*. These are not deliverables but the individual units of work that must be completed to fulfill the deliverables listed in the WBS. Activities will help in later Planning processes to define estimates and create the project schedule. Activity lists (which are one of the outputs of this process) from prior projects can be used as templates in this process. Rolling wave planning involves planning near-term work in more detail than future-term work. As we discussed in Chapter 3, this is a form of progressive elaboration. Expert judgment, in the form of project team members with prior experience developing project scope statements and WBSs, can help you define activities.

Exam Spotlight

The purpose of the Define Activities process is to decompose the work packages into schedule activities where the basis for estimating, scheduling, executing, and monitoring and controlling the work of the project is easily supported and accomplished.

Define Activities Outputs

Define Activities has three outputs:

- Activity list
- Activity attributes
- Milestone list

We'll look at each of these outputs next.

Activity List

One primary output of the Define Activities process is an *activity list*. The activity list should contain all the schedule activities that will be performed for the project, with a scope of work description of each activity and an identifier (such as a code or number) so that team members understand what the work is and how it is to be completed. The schedule activities are individual elements of the project schedule, and the activity list is a subsidiary of the project management plan.

Activity Attributes

Activity attributes describe the characteristics of the activities and are an extension of the activity list. Activity attributes will change over the life of the project as more information is known. In the early stages of the project, activity attributes might include the activity ID, the WBS identification code it's associated with, and the activity name. As you progress through the project and complete other Planning processes, you might add predecessor and successor activities, logical relationships, leads and lags, resource requirements, and constraints and assumptions associated with the activity. We'll cover these topics throughout the remainder of this chapter.

The activity attributes are used as in input to the Develop Schedule process that we'll talk about in the section "Developing the Project Schedule" later in this chapter.

NOTE In practice, I like to tie the activity list to the WBS. Remember from Chapter 2 that each WBS element has a unique identifier, just like the activities in the activity list. When recording the identifier code for the activity list, I'll use a system whereby the first three or four digits represent the WBS element the activity is tied to and the remaining digits will refer to the activity itself.

Milestone Lists

Milestones are typically major accomplishments of the project and mark the completion of major deliverables or some other key event in the project. For example, approval and sign-off on project deliverables might be considered milestones. Other examples might be the completion of a prototype, system testing, contract approval, and so on. The milestone list records these accomplishments and documents whether the milestone is mandatory or optional. The milestone list is part of the project management plan and is also used to help develop the project schedule.

Understanding the Sequence Activities Process

Now that you've identified the schedule activities, you need to sequence them in a logical order and find out whether dependencies exist among the activities. The interactivity of logical relationships must be sequenced correctly in order to facilitate the development of a realistic, achievable project schedule in a later process.

Consider a classic example. Let's say you're going to paint your house, but unfortunately, it's fallen into a little disrepair. The old paint is peeling and chipping and will need to be scraped before a coat of primer can be sprayed on the house. After the primer dries, the painting can commence. In this example, the primer activity depends on the scraping. You can't—OK, you *shouldn't*—prime the house before scraping off the peeling paint. The painting activity depends on the primer activity in the same way. You really shouldn't start painting until the primer has dried.

During *Sequence Activities*, you will use a host of inputs and tools and techniques to produce the primary output, project schedule network diagrams. You've already seen all the inputs to this process. They are activity list, activity attributes, milestone list, project scope statement, and organizational process assets. We'll look at several new tools and techniques next.

Sequence Activities Tools and Techniques

Sequence Activities has four tools and techniques, all of which are new to you:

- Precedence diagramming method (PDM)
- Dependency determination
- Applying leads and lags
- Schedule network templates

I'll switch the order of these and cover dependency determination first. In practice, you'll define dependencies either before or while you're using the PDM to draw your schedule network templates, so to make sure you're on the same page with the *PMBOK® Guide* terminology regarding dependencies, I'll cover them first and then move on to the other tools and techniques.

Dependency Determination

Dependencies are relationships between the activities in which one activity is dependent on another to complete an action, or perhaps an activity is dependent on another to start an action before it can proceed. Dependency determination is a matter of determining where those dependencies exist. Thinking back to the house-painting example, you couldn't paint until the scraping and priming activities were completed. You'll want to know about three types of dependencies for the exam:

- Mandatory dependencies
- Discretionary dependencies
- External dependencies

As you've probably guessed, the *PMBOK® Guide* defines dependencies differently depending on their characteristics:

Mandatory dependencies *Mandatory dependencies*, also known as *hard logic* or *hard dependencies*, are defined by the type of work being performed. The scraping, primer, and painting sequence is an example of mandatory dependencies. The nature of the work itself dictates the order in which the activities should be performed. Activities with physical limitations are a telltale sign that you have a mandatory dependency on your hands.

Discretionary dependencies *Discretionary dependencies* are defined by the project team. Discretionary dependencies are also known as *preferred logic*, *soft logic*, or *preferential logic*. These are usually process- or procedure-driven or "best-practice" techniques based on past experience. For example, both past experience and best practices on house-painting projects have shown that all trim work should be hand-painted while the bulk of the main painting work should be done with a sprayer.

Exam Spotlight

Discretionary dependencies have a tendency to create arbitrary total float values that will limit your options when scheduling activities that have this type of dependency. If you are using fast tracking to compress your schedule, you should consider changing or removing these dependencies.

External dependencies *External dependencies* are, well, external to the project. This might seem obvious, but the *PMBOK® Guide* points out that even though the dependency is external to the project (and therefore a nonproject activity), it impacts project activities. For example, perhaps your project is researching and marketing a new drug. The FDA must approve the drug before your company can market it. This is not a project activity, but the project cannot move forward until approval occurs. That means FDA approval is an external dependency.

Once you've identified the dependencies and assembled all the other inputs for the Sequence Activities process, you'll take this information and produce a diagram—or schematic display—of the project activities. The project schedule network diagram shows the dependencies—or logical relationships—that exist among the activities. You can use one of the other tools and techniques of this process to produce this output. You'll now examine each in detail.

Precedence Diagramming Method (PDM)

The *precedence diagramming method (PDM)* is what most project management software programs use to sequence activities. Precedence diagrams use boxes or rectangles to represent the activities (called *nodes*). The nodes are connected with arrows showing the dependencies between the activities. This method is also called *activity on node (AON)*.

The minimum information that should be displayed on the node is the activity name, but you might put as much information about the activity on the node as you'd like. Sometimes the nodes are displayed with activity name, activity number, start and stop dates, due dates, slack time, and so on. (I'll cover slack time in the section "Develop Schedule Tools and Techniques" later in this chapter.)

Exam Spotlight

For the exam, remember that the PDM uses only one time estimate to determine duration.

The following graphic shows a PDM—or AON—of the house-painting example.

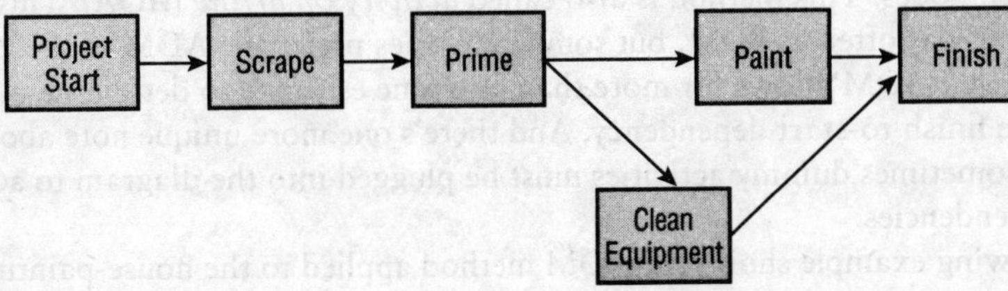

The PDM is further defined by four types of *logical relationships*. The terms *dependencies* and *precedence relationships* also are used to describe these relationships. You might already be familiar with these if you've used Microsoft Project or similar project management software program. The four dependencies, or logical relationships, are as follows:

Finish-to-start (FS) The finish-to-start relationship is the most frequently used relationship. This relationship says that the predecessor—or *from* activity—must finish before the successor—or *to* activity—can start. In PDM diagrams, this is the most often used logical relationship.

Start-to-finish (SF) The start-to-finish relationship says that the predecessor activity must start before the successor activity can finish. This logical relationship is seldom used.

Finish-to-finish (FF) The finish-to-finish relationship says that the predecessor activity must finish before the successor activity finishes.

Start-to-start (SS) I think you're getting the hang of this. The start-to-start relationship says that the predecessor activity depends on starting before the successive activity can start.

Exam Spotlight

For the exam, know that finish-to-start is the most commonly used dependency in the PDM method and that start-to-finish is rarely used.

Keep these logical relationships (or dependencies) in mind when constructing your project schedule network diagram.

Arrow Diagramming Method (ADM)

This is not a listed tool and technique of the Sequence Activities process, but there is a possibility you could see a question on the exam regarding this diagramming method. It's a very old technique that's rarely used anymore, but nonetheless you should have some familiarity with it.

The *arrow diagramming method (ADM)* is visually the opposite of the PDM. The arrow diagramming method places activities on the arrows, which are connected to dependent activities with nodes. This method is also called *activity on arrow (AOA)*. This technique isn't used nearly as often as PDM, but some industries prefer the ADM to the PDM. For the record, note that ADM allows for more than one time estimate to determine duration and uses only the finish-to-start dependency. And there's one more unique note about ADM to tuck away: sometimes dummy activities must be plugged into the diagram to accurately display the dependencies.

The following example shows the ADM method applied to the house-painting example.

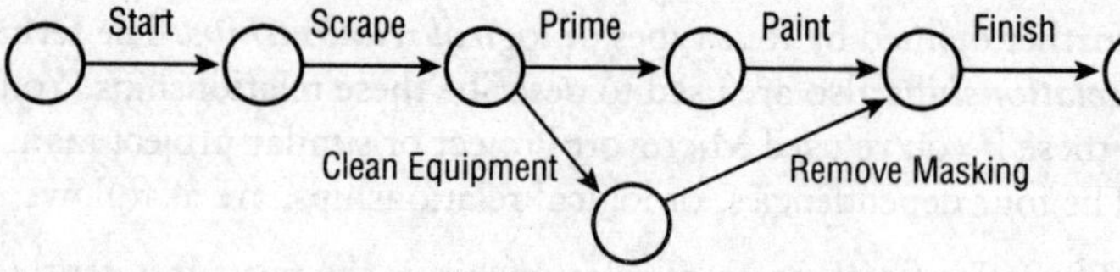

Exam Spotlight

I recommend that you memorize the following graphic to help you remember the tools and techniques of the Sequence Activities process and their characteristics for the exam. This might look a little strange, but I think it will work for you now that you understand what each of these diagramming methods is. This is information you need to know for the exam. If this graphic isn't useful for you, come up with your own mnemonic or sample that will help you remember which of these is which. Don't say I didn't warn you.

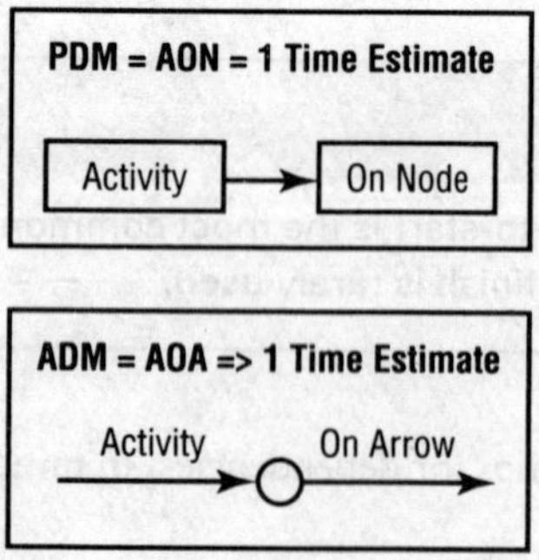

There is one other diagramming method you could potentially see a question about on the exam. It's called GERT, which stands for Graphical Evaluation and Review Technique. What you should know for the exam is that this diagramming method allows for conditions, branches, and loops.

Applying Leads and Lags

Leads and lags should be considered when determining dependencies. *Lags* occur when time elapses between two activities, which delays *successor activities* (those that follow a predecessor activity)from starting, and as a result, time is added either to the start date or to the finish date of the activity you're scheduling. *Leads*, conversely, speed up the successor activities, and as a result, time needs to be subtracted from the start date or the finish date of the activity you're scheduling.

Exam Spotlight

Leads and lags speed up or delay successor activities but should not replace schedule logic.

Let's revisit the house-painting example to put all this in perspective. In order to paint, you first need to scrape the peeling paint and then prime. However, you can't begin painting until the primer has dried, so you shouldn't schedule priming for Monday and painting for Tuesday if you need the primer to dry on Tuesday. Therefore, the priming activity generates the need for lag time at the end of the activity to account for the drying time needed before you can start painting.

Lead time works just the opposite. Suppose, for this example, you could start priming before the scraping is finished. Maybe certain areas on the house don't require scraping, so you don't really need to wait until the scraping activity finishes to begin the priming activity. In this example, lead time is subtracted from the beginning of the priming activity so that this activity begins prior to the previous activity finishing.

Schedule Network Templates

Schedule network templates are like the templates I've talked about in other processes. Perhaps the project you're working on is similar to a project that has been completed in the past. You can use a previous project schedule network diagram as a template for the current project. Or you might be working on a project with several deliverables that are fairly identical to projects you've performed in the past and can use the old schedule network diagrams as templates for this project.

Sequence Activities Outputs

There are only two outputs of the Sequence Activities process. They are project schedule network diagrams and project document updates.

I've just spent a good deal of time describing the different types of project schedule network diagrams you can construct using PDM or ADM techniques. You can generate project schedule network diagrams on a computer, or you can draw them out by hand. Like the WBS, these diagrams might contain all the project details or might contain only summary-level details, depending on the complexity of the project. Summary-level activities are a collection of related activities also known as *hammocks*. Think of hammocks as a group of related activities rolled up into a summary heading that describes the activities likely to be contained in that grouping.

Keep in mind that the construction of these project schedule network diagrams might bring activities to light that you missed when defining your activity list, or it might make you break an activity down into two activities in places where you thought one activity might work. If this is the case, you will need to update the activity list and the activity attributes. The other project document update that may be required as a result of this process is an update to the risk register. (We'll talk about the risk register in Chapter 6, "Risk Planning.")

After the activities are sequenced, the next steps involve estimating the resources and estimating the durations of the activities so that they can be plugged into the project schedule. We'll look at these topics in the next sections of this chapter.

Estimating Activity Resources

All projects, from the smallest to the largest, require resources. The term *resources,* in this case, does not mean just people; it means all the physical resources required to complete the project. The *PMBOK® Guide* defines resources as people, equipment, and materials. In reality, this includes people, equipment, supplies, materials, software, hardware—the list goes on depending on the project on which you're working. *Estimate Activity Resources* is concerned with determining the types of resources needed (both human and materials) and in what quantities for each schedule activity within a work package.

NOTE

Remember, the activity resource requirements output from the Estimate Activity Resources process is an input to the Develop Human Resource Plan process.

The *PMBOK® Guide* notes that Estimate Activity Resources should be closely coordinated with the Estimate Costs process (I'll talk about Estimate Costs in Chapter 5, "Developing the Project Budget"). That's because resources—whether people or material or both—are typically the largest expense you'll have on any project. Identifying the resources becomes a critical component of the project planning process so estimates—and ultimately the project budget—can be accurately derived. You'll look at the inputs and tools and techniques that will help you document these requirements next.

Estimate Activity Resources Inputs

The Estimate Activity Resources process has several inputs, most of which you already know:

- Activity list
- Activity attributes
- Resource calendars
- Enterprise environmental factors
- Organizational process assets

The only input you haven't seen before is resource calendars.

NOTE Resource calendars is an output of the Acquire Project Team and Conduct Procurements processes. Both of these processes are performed during the Executing process group, so you may find this input perplexing here. However, you may have some resource availability information (resource calendars) on a preliminary basis during this process and you'll further define it when resources are actually assigned to the project later in the Executing processes. In practice, you may find that you perform the Acquire Project Team process during the later stages of the Planning portion of the project rather than in the Executing process.

The *resource calendars* input describes the time frames in which resources (both human and material) are available. They look at a particular resource or groups of resources and their skills, abilities, quantity, and availability. Perhaps your project calls for a marketing resource and the person assigned to the marketing activities is on an extended vacation in October. The resource calendar would show this person's vacation schedule. (The overall project calendar shows the holidays the company recognizes.)

Resource calendars also examine the quantity, capability, and availability of equipment and material resources that have a potential to impact the project schedule. For example, suppose your project calls for a hydraulic drill and your organization owns only one. The resource calendar will tell you whether it's scheduled for another job at the same time it's needed for your project.

Estimating Activity Resources Tools and Techniques

Your goal with the Estimate Activity Resources process is to determine the activity resource requirements, including quantity and availability. This process has five tools and techniques to help accomplish this output: expert judgment, alternatives analysis, published estimating data, bottom-up estimating, and project management software. You already know what expert judgment entails, so take a look at the remaining tools:

Alternatives analysis Alternatives analysis is used when thinking about the methods you might use to accomplish the activities your resources have been assigned. Many times, you can accomplish an activity in more than one way, and alternatives analysis helps decide among the possibilities. For example, a subcompact car drives on the same roads a six-figure sports car travels. The sports car has a lot more features than the subcompact, it's faster, it's probably more comfortable, and it has a visual appeal that the subcompact doesn't. The sports car might be the valid resource choice for the project, but you should consider all the alternatives. The same idea applies to human resources in that you might apply senior-level resources versus junior-level resources, or you could add resources to speed up the schedule. You may also use make-or-buy analysis when determining alternative resources.

Published estimating data Estimating data might include organizational guidelines, industry rates or estimates, production rates, and so on. For example, your organization might have established price agreements with vendors that outline rates by resource types, or there might be industry estimates for production rates for your particular activity.

Bottom-up estimating Bottom-up estimating is a process of estimating individual schedule activities or costs and then adding these together to come up with a total estimate for the work package. Here you estimate every schedule activity individually and then roll up that estimate, or add them all together, to come up with a total. This is an accurate means of estimating provided the estimates at the schedule activity level are accurate. However, it takes a considerable amount of time to perform bottom-up estimating because every activity must be assessed and estimated accurately to be included in the bottom-up calculation. The smaller and more detailed the activity, the greater the accuracy and cost of this technique.

Project management software Project management software can help plan, organize, and estimate resource needs and document their availability. It might also help you to produce resource breakdown structures, resource rates, resource calendars, and availability.

Estimate Activity Resources Outputs

The purpose of the Estimate Activity Resources process is to develop the activity resource requirements output. This output describes the types of resources and the quantity needed for each activity associated with a work package. You should prepare a narrative description for this output that describes how you determined the estimate, including the information you used to form your estimate and the assumptions you made about the resources and their availability.

NOTE Work package estimates are derived by taking a cumulative total of all the schedule activities within the work package.

You'll use the information from this output in the next process (Estimate Activity Durations) to determine the length of time each activity will take to complete. That, of course, depends on the quantity and skill level of the resources assigned, which is the reason you estimate resources before you try to determine duration.

The two other outputs of this process are resource breakdown structure and project document updates.

The resource breakdown structure (RBS) is much like an organizational breakdown structure only the RBS lists the resources by category and type. You may several categories of resources, including labor, hardware, equipment, supplies, and so on. Type describes the types of resources needed, such as skill levels or quality grades of the material and so on.

The project document updates portion of this output refers to updating the activity list, activity attributes, and the resource calendars with changes to any of the elements you've recorded here.

You can see how these "Activity" processes have built upon each other. First you defined the activities, then you determined dependencies and sequenced them in the correct order, and next you determined what types and quantities of resources are required to complete the activities. Now you're ready to begin estimating the duration of these activities so you can plug them into the project schedule.

Estimating Activity Durations

The *Estimate Activity Durations* process attempts to estimate the work effort, resources, and number of work periods needed to complete each activity. The *activity duration estimates* are the primary output of this process. These are quantifiable estimates expressed as the number of work periods needed to complete a schedule activity. Work periods are usually expressed in hours or days. However, larger projects might express duration in weeks or months. Work periods are the activity duration estimates, and they become inputs to the Develop Schedule process.

When estimating activity duration, make certain to include all the time that will elapse from the beginning of the activity until the work is completed. For example, consider the earlier example of the house-painting project. You estimate that it will take three days, including drying time, to prime the house. Now, let's say priming is scheduled to begin on Saturday, but your crew doesn't work on Sunday. The activity duration in this case is four days, which includes the three days to prime and dry plus the Sunday the crew doesn't work. Most project management software programs will handle this kind of situation automatically once you've keyed in the project calendar and work periods.

Progressive elaboration comes into play during this process also. Estimates typically start at a fairly high level, and as more and more details are known about the deliverables and their associated activities, the estimates become more accurate. You should rely on those folks who have the most knowledge of the activities you're trying to estimate to help you with this process.

Estimate Activity Durations Inputs

The inputs to this process include activity list, activity attributes, activity resource requirements, resource calendars, project scope statement, enterprise environmental factors, and organization process assets.

A few of the important elements regarding these inputs apply here as you've seen in past processes: databases, productivity metrics, historical information regarding durations on similar projects, project calendars, scheduling methodology, and lessons learned. The project calendars (considered a part of the organizational process assets) and activity resource requirements are especially useful during this process.

Estimate Activity Durations Tools and Techniques

The Estimate Activity Durations process has several new tools and techniques:

- Expert judgment
- Analogous estimating
- Parametric estimating
- Three-point estimates
- Reserve analysis

You'll take a look at each of these tools and techniques next.

Expert Judgment

The staff members who will perform activities will most accurately estimate them. In this case, team members use expert judgment because of their experience with similar activities in the past. You should be careful with these estimates, though, because they are subject to bias and aren't based on any scientific means. Your experts should consider that resource levels, resource productivity, resource capability, risks, and other factors can impact estimates. It's good practice to combine expert judgment with historical information and use as many experts as you can.

Analogous Estimating

Analogous estimating, also called *top-down estimating*, is a form of expert judgment. With this technique, you will use the actual duration of a similar activity completed on a previous project to determine the duration of the current activity—provided the information was documented and stored with the project information on the previous project. This technique is most useful when the previous activities you're comparing are similar to the activity you're estimating and don't just appear to be similar. And you want the folks who are working on the estimate to have experience with these activities so they can provide reasonable estimates. This technique is especially helpful when detailed information about the project is not available, such as in the early phases of the project.

Top-down estimating techniques are also used to estimate total project duration, particularly when you have a limited amount of information about the project. The best way to think about top-down techniques is to look at the estimate as a whole. Think about being on a mountaintop where you can see the whole picture as one rather than all the individual items that make up the picture.

For instance, let's return to the house-painting example. You would compare a previous house-painting project to the current house-painting project, where the houses are of similar size and the paint you're using is the same quality. You can use the first house-painting project to estimate the project duration for the second house-painting project because of the similarities in the project.

Top-down techniques are useful when you're early in the project Planning processes and are just beginning to flesh out all the details of the project. Sometimes during the project selection process, the selection committee might want an idea of the project's duration. You can derive a project estimate at this stage by using top-down techniques.

Exam Spotlight

The *PMBOK® Guide* states that you can also use analogous estimating to determine overall project duration and cost estimates for the entire project (or phases of the project). For the exam, remember that the analogous technique is typically less time consuming and less costly than other estimating techniques, but it's also less accurate.

Parametric Estimating

Parametric estimating is a quantitatively based estimating method that multiplies the quantity of work by the rate. The best way to describe it is with an example. Suppose you are working on a companywide network upgrade project. This requires you to run new cable to the switches on every floor in the building. You can use parametric estimates to determine activity duration estimates by taking a known element—in this case, the amount of cable needed—and multiplying it by the amount of time it takes to install a unit of cable to come up with an estimate. In other words, suppose you have 10,000 meters of new cable to run. You know from past experience it takes 1 hour to install 100 meters. Using this measurement, you can determine an estimate for this activity of 100 hours to run the new cable. Therefore, the cable activity duration estimate is 100 hours.

Exam Spotlight

The *PMBOK® Guide* states that you can also use parametric estimating to determine time estimates for the entire project or portions of the project. For the exam, remember that there is a statistical relationship between historical data and other variables (as explained in the cable example earlier) when using parametric estimates and that this technique can be highly accurate if the data you are using is reliable.

Three-Point Estimates

Three-point estimates, as you can probably guess, use three estimates that when averaged, come up with a final estimate. The three estimates you'll use in this technique are the most likely estimate, an optimistic estimate, and a pessimistic estimate. The most likely estimate assumes there are no disasters and the activity can be completed as planned. The optimistic estimate is the fastest time frame in which your resource can complete the activity. And the pessimistic estimate assumes the worst happens and it takes much longer than planned to get the activity completed. You'll want to rely on experienced folks to give you these estimates.

Reserve Analysis

Reserve time—also called *buffers*, *time reserves*, or *contingency reserve* in the *PMBOK® Guide* —means a portion of time that is added to the activity to account for schedule risk or uncertainty. You might choose to add a percentage of time or a set number of work periods to the activity or the overall schedule. For example, you know it will take 100 hours to run new cable based on the quantitative estimate you came up with earlier. You also know that sometimes you hit problem areas when running the cable. To make sure you don't impact the project schedule, you build in a reserve time of 10 percent of your original estimate to account for the problems you might encounter. This brings your activity duration estimate to 110 hours for this activity.

Estimate Activity Durations Outputs

Everything I've discussed to this point has brought you to the primary output of this process: the activity duration estimates. You use the inputs and tools and techniques to establish these estimates. As mentioned earlier, activity duration estimates are an estimate of the required work periods needed to complete the activity. This is a quantitative measure usually expressed in hours, weeks, days, or months.

One factor to note about your final estimates as an output to this process is that they should contain a range of possible results. In the cable-running example, you would state the activity duration estimates as "100 hours ±10 hours" to show that the actual duration will take at least 90 hours and might go as long as 110 hours. Or you could use percentages to express this range.

The other output of Estimate Activity Durations is project document updates. Some of the information that may need revisited and updated as a result of this process are the activity attributes and the assumptions you made regarding resource availability and skill levels.

Now that you have all the activity information in hand, along with a host of other inputs, you're ready to develop the project schedule.

Exam Spotlight

Remember that you perform the "Activity" processes in this order: Define Activities, Sequence Activities, Estimate Activity Resources, and Estimate Activity Durations. Develop Schedule comes after you've completed all of these processes.

Real World Scenario

Desert State University (DSU)

DSU has hired a contract agency to create its new registration website. The website will allow students in good academic standing to register for classes over the Internet. You have been appointed the project manager for the DSU side of this project. You'll be working with Henry Lu from Websites International to complete this project.

Henry has given you an activity list and asked for time estimates that he can plug into the project plan.

Your first stop is Mike Walter's desk. He's the expert on the mainframe registration system and will be writing the interface programs to accept registration data from the new website. Mike will also create the download that the Internet program will use to verify students' academic standing. Mike has created other programs just like this in the past. His expertise and judgment are very reliable.

The next stop is Kate Langdon. She's the new team leader over the testing group. Kate has been with DSU for only one month. Since she has no experience working with DSU data and staff members, she tells you she'll get back to you within a week with estimates for the testing activities. She plans to read through the project binders of some similar projects and base her estimates against the historical information on similar projects. She'll run the estimates by her lead tester before giving them to you.

You've asked both of your resources to provide you with three-point estimates. Mike Walter's estimates are an example of using the tool and technique of expert judgment to derive activity duration estimates. The estimates expected from Kate Langdon will be derived using historical information (implied by the research she's going to do into past similar projects) and expert judgment because she's involving her lead tester to verify the estimates.

Developing the Project Schedule

The *Develop Schedule* process is the heart of the Planning process group. This is where you lay out the schedule for your project activities, determine their start and finish dates, and finalize activity sequences and durations. Develop Schedule, along with Estimate Activity Resources and Estimate Activity Durations, is repeated several times before you actually come up with the project schedule. Most project management software programs today can automatically build a schedule for you once you've entered the needed information for the activities. The project schedule, once it's approved, serves as the *schedule baseline* for the project that you can track against in later processes.

NOTE: Remember that you cannot perform Develop Schedule until you have completed at least the following processes of the Planning process group: Collect Requirements, Define Scope, Create WBS, Define Activities, Sequence Activities, Estimate Activity Durations, and Develop Human Resource Plan. In practice, it's also beneficial to perform Identify Risks, Perform Qualitative Risk Analysis, Perform Quantitative Risk Analysis, Plan Risk Responses, and Plan Procurements prior to developing the schedule.

There is a lot of material to cover in this process, so grab a cup of coffee or a soda now. I'll start with the inputs to the Develop Schedule process and then follow up with an in-depth discussion of the tools and techniques of the process. These techniques will help you get to the primary output of this process, which is the project schedule.

Develop Schedule Inputs

Develop Schedule has nine inputs, seven of which are outputs from other Planning processes. The inputs are as follows:

- Activity list
- Activity attributes
- Project schedule network diagrams
- Activity resource requirements
- Resource calendars
- Activity duration estimates
- Project scope statement
- Enterprise environmental factors
- Organizational process assets

You can see how important it is to perform all the Planning processes accurately because the information you derive from almost every process in the Planning group is used somewhere else in Planning, many of them here. Your project schedule will reflect the information you know at this point in time. If you have incorrectly estimated activity durations or didn't identify the right dependencies, for example, the inputs to this process will be distorted and your project schedule will not be correct. It's definitely worth the investment of time to correctly plan your project and come up with accurate outputs for each of the Planning processes.

As with several other processes, you should pay particular attention to constraints and assumptions when performing Develop Schedule. Constraints are with you throughout the life of the project. The most important constraints to consider in the Develop Schedule process are time constraints, and they fall into two categories, imposed dates and key events/major milestones.

Imposed dates restrict the start or finish date of activities. The two most common constraints, *start no earlier than* and *finish no later than*, are used by most computerized project management software programs. Let's look once again at the house-painting example. The painting activity cannot start until the primer has dried. If the primer takes 24 hours to dry and is scheduled to be completed on Wednesday, this implies the painting activity can *start no earlier than* Thursday. This is an example of an imposed date.

Key events or milestones refer to the completion of specific deliverables by a specific date. Stakeholders, customers, or management staff might request that certain deliverables be completed or delivered by specific dates. Once you've agreed to those dates (even if the agreement is only verbal), it's often cast in stone and difficult to change. These dates, therefore, become constraints.

NOTE

Be careful of the delivery dates you commit to your stakeholders or customers. You might think you're simply discussing the matter or throwing out ideas, while the stakeholder might take what you've said as fact. Once the stakeholder believes the deliverable or activity will be completed by a specific date, there's almost no convincing them that the date needs changing.

Develop Schedule Tools and Techniques

The primary output of Develop Schedule is the project schedule. You can employ several tools and techniques in order to produce this output. The tools and techniques you choose will depend on the complexity of the project. For the exam, however, you'll need to know them all.

Develop Schedule has eight tools and techniques:

- Schedule network analysis
- Critical path method
- Critical chain method
- Resource leveling
- What-if scenario analysis
- Applying leads and lags
- Schedule compression
- Scheduling tool

A lot of information is packed into some of these tools and techniques, and you should dedicate study time to each of them for the exam. We'll look at each one next.

Schedule Network Analysis

Schedule network analysis produces the project schedule. It involves calculating early and late start dates and early and late finish dates for project activities (as does the critical path method). It uses a schedule model and other analytical techniques such as critical path and critical chain method, what-if analysis, and resource leveling (all of which are other tools and techniques in this process) to help calculate these dates and create the schedule. These calculations are performed without taking resource limitations into consideration, so the dates you end up with are theoretical. What you're attempting to establish at this point is the time periods within which the activities can be scheduled. Resource limitations and other constraints will be taken into consideration when you get to the outputs of this process.

Critical Path Method

Critical path method (CPM) is a schedule network analysis technique. It determines the amount of float, or schedule flexibility, for each of the network paths by calculating the earliest start date, earliest finish date, latest start date, and latest finish date for each activity. This is a schedule network analysis technique that relies on sequential networks (one activity occurs before the next, a series of activities occurring concurrently is completed before the next series of activities begins, and so on) and on a single duration estimate for each activity. The precedence diagramming method (PDM) can be used to perform CPM. Keep in mind that CPM is a method to determine schedule durations without regard to resource availability.

The *critical path (CP)* is generally the longest full path on the project. Any project activity with a float time that equals zero is considered a critical path task. The critical path can change under a few conditions. When activities with float time use up all their float, they can become critical path tasks. Or you might have a milestone midway through the project with a *finish no later than* constraint that can change the critical path if it isn't met.

Float time is also called *slack time*, and you'll see these terms used interchangeably. There are two types of float: total float and free float. *Total float (TF)* is the amount of time you can delay the earliest start of a task without delaying the ending of the project. *Free float (FF)* is the amount of time you can delay the start of a task without delaying the earliest start of a successor task.

In the following section, you'll calculate the CP for a sample project, and I'll illustrate how you derive all the dates, the CP, and the float times.

Gathering Activity and Dependency Information

Let's say you are the project manager for a new software project. The company you are working for is venturing into the movie rental business over the Web. You need to devise a software system that tracks all the information related to rentals and also supplies the management team with reports that will help them make good business decisions. For purposes of illustration, I'm showing only a limited portion of the tasks that you would have on a project like this.

You'll start this example by plugging information from the processes you've already completed into a table (a complete example is shown later in Table 4.1 in the section "Calculating the Critical Path"). The list of activities comes from the Define Activities process. The durations for each activity are listed in the Duration column and were derived during the Estimate Activity Durations process. The duration times are listed in days.

The Dependency column lists the activities that require a previous activity to finish before the current activity can start. You're using only finish-to-start relationships. For example, you'll see that activity 2 and activity 4 each depend on activity 1 to finish before they can begin. The dependency information came from the Sequence Activities process. Now, you'll proceed to calculating the dates.

Calculating the Forward and Backward Pass

Project Deliverables is the first activity and, obviously, where the project starts. This activity begins on April 1. Project Deliverables has a 12-day duration. So, take April 1 and add 12 days to this to come up with an early finish date of April 12. Watch out, because you need to count day one, or April 1, as a full workday. The simplest way to do this calculation is to take the early start date, add the duration, and subtract one. Therefore, the early finish date for the first activity is April 12. By the way, we are ignoring weekends and holidays for this example. Activity 2 depends on activity 1, so it cannot start until activity 1 has finished. Its earliest start date is April 13 because activity 1 finished at the end of the previous day. Add the duration to this date minus one to come up with the finish date.

You'll notice that, since activity 4 depends on activity 1 finishing, its earliest start date is also April 13. Continue to calculate the remaining early start and early finish dates in the same manner. This calculation is called a *forward pass.*

To calculate the latest start and latest finish dates, you begin with the last activity. The latest finish for activity 9 is July 10. Since the duration is only one day, July 10 is also the latest start date. You know that activity 8 must finish before activity 9 can begin, so activity 8's latest finish date, July 9, is one day prior to activity 9's latest start date, July 10. Subtract the duration of activity 8 (three days) from July 9 and add one day to get the latest start date of July 7. You're performing the opposite calculation that you did for the forward pass. This calculation is called a *backward pass*, as you might have guessed. Continue calculating the latest start and latest finish through activity 4.

Activity 3 adds a new twist. Here's how it works: activity 7 cannot begin until activity 3 and activity 6 are completed. No other activity depends on the completion of activity 3. If activity 7's latest start date is June 29, activity 3's latest finish date must be June 28. June 28 minus eight days plus one gives you a latest start date of June 21. Activity 3 depends on activity 2, so activity 2 must be completed prior to beginning activity 3. Calculate these dates just as you did for activities 9 through 4.

Activity 1 still remains. Activity 4 cannot start until activity 1 is completed. If activity 4's latest start date is April 13, the latest finish date for activity 1 must be April 12. Subtract the duration of activity 1, and add one to come up with a latest start date of April 1. Alternatively, you can calculate the forward pass and backward pass by saying the first task starts on day zero and then adding the duration to this. For example, activity number 1's earliest start date is April 1, which is day zero. Add 12 days to day zero, and you come up with an earliest finish date of April 12.

You determine the calculation for float/slack time by subtracting the earliest start date from the latest start date. If the float time equals zero, the activity is on the critical path.

Calculating the Critical Path

To determine the CP duration of the project, add the duration of every activity with zero float. You should come up with 101 days because you're adding the duration for all activities except for activity 2 and activity 3. A critical path task is any task that cannot be changed without impacting the project end date. By definition, these are all tasks with zero float.

Another way to determine the critical path is by looking at the network diagram. If the duration is included with the information on the node or if start and end dates are given, you simply calculate the duration and then add the duration of the longest path in the diagram to determine the CP. However, this method is not as accurate as what's shown in Table 4.1. Figure 4.1 shows the same project in diagram form. The duration is printed in the top-right corner of each node. Add the duration of each path to determine which one is the critical path.

Remember that CP is usually the path with the longest duration. In Figure 4.1, path 1-2-3-7-8-9 equals 34 days. Path 1-4-5-6-7-8-9 equals 101 days; therefore, this path is the critical path.

TABLE 4.1 CPM Calculation

Activity Number	Activity Description	Dependency	Duration	Early Start	Early Finish	Late Start	Late Finish	Float/ Slack
1	Project Deliverables	—	12	4/1	4/12	4/1	4/12	0
2	Procure Hardware	1	2	4/13	4/14	6/19	6/20	67
3	Test Hardware	2	8	4/15	4/22	6/21	6/28	67
4	Procure Software Tools	1	10	4/13	4/22	4/13	4/22	0
5	Write Programs	4	45	4/23	6/6	4/23	6/6	0
6	Test and Debug	5	22	6/7	6/28	6/7	6/28	0
7	Install	3, 6	8	6/29	7/6	6/29	7/6	0
8	Training	7	3	7/7	7/9	7/7	7/9	0
9	Acceptance	8	1	7/10	7/10	7/10	7/10	0

Calculating Expected Value Using PERT

Program Evaluation and Review Technique (PERT) is a method that the United States Navy developed in the 1950s. The Navy was working on one of the most complex engineering projects in history at the time—the Polaris Missile Program—and needed a way to manage the project and forecast the project schedule with a high degree of reliability. PERT was developed to do just that.

FIGURE 4.1 Critical path diagram

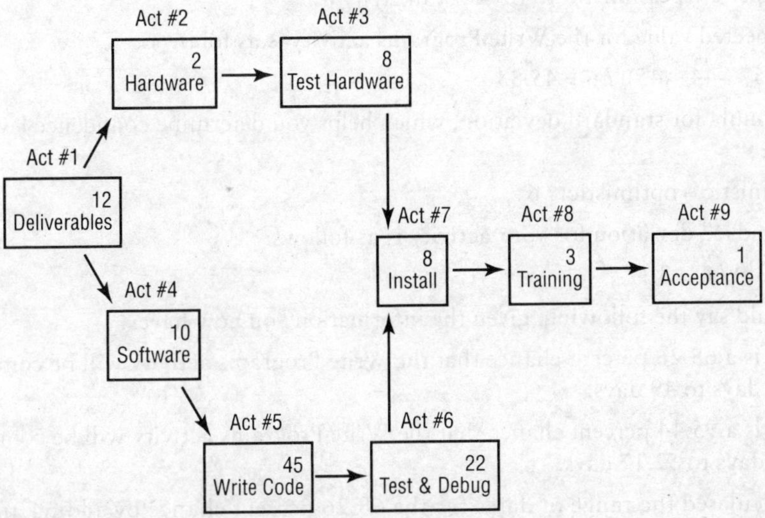

PERT and CPM are similar techniques. The difference is that CPM uses the most likely duration to determine project duration, while PERT uses what's called *expected value* (or the weighted average). *Expected value* is calculated using the three-point estimates for activity duration (I talked about three-point estimates earlier in this chapter) and then finding the weighted average of those estimates (I'll talk about weighted average in the next section "Calculating Expected Value.") If you take this one step further and determine the standard deviation of each activity, you can assign a confidence factor to your project estimates. Without getting too heavily involved in the mathematics of probability, understand that for data that fits a bell curve, which is what you're about to calculate with the PERT technique, the following is true:

- Work will finish within plus or minus three standard deviations 99.73 percent of the time.
- Work will finish within plus or minus two standard deviations 95.44 percent of the time.
- Work will finish within plus or minus one standard deviation 68.26 percent of the time.

Calculating Expected Value

The three-point estimates used to calculate expected value are the optimistic estimate, the pessimistic estimate, and the most likely estimate. Going back to the software example, let's find out what these three time estimates might look like for the activity called Write Programs. You get these estimates by asking the lead programmer, or key team member, to estimate the optimistic, pessimistic, and most likely duration for the activity based on past experience. Other historical information could be used to determine these estimates as well. Say in this case that you're given 38 days for the optimistic time, 57 days for the pessimistic, and 45 days for the most likely. (Forty-five days was derived from the Estimate Activity Durations process and is the estimate you used to calculate CPM.)

The formula to calculate expected value is as follows:

(optimistic + pessimistic + (4 * most likely)) / 6

The expected value for the Write Programs activity is as follows:

(38 + 57 + (4 * 45)) / 6 = 45.83

The formula for standard deviation, which helps you determine confidence level, is as follows:

(pessimistic – optimistic) / 6

The standard deviation for your activity is as follows:

(57 – 38) / 6 = 3.17

You could say the following, given the information you now have:

- There is a 68.26 percent chance that the Write Programs activity will be completed in 42.66 days to 49 days.
- There is a 95.44 percent chance that the Write Programs activity will be completed in 39.49 days to 52.17 days.

You calculated the range of dates for the 68.26 percent chance by adding and subtracting one standard deviation, 3.17, from the expected value, 45.83. You calculated the 95.44 percent chance by multiplying the standard deviation times 2, which equals 6.34, and adding and subtracting that result from the expected value to come up with the least number of days and the most number of days it will take to finish the activity. Generally speaking, two standard deviations, or 95.44 percent, is a close enough estimate for most purposes.

NOTE The higher the standard deviation is for an activity, the higher the risk. Since standard deviation measures the difference between the pessimistic and the optimistic times, a greater spread between the two, which results in a higher number, indicates a greater risk. Conversely, a low standard deviation means less risk.

Determining Date Ranges for Project Duration

Let's bring your table of activities back and plug in the expected values and the standard deviation for each (please see Table 4.2).

Now let's look at the total project duration using PERT and the standard deviation to determine a range of dates for project duration. You should add only the tasks that are on the critical path. Remember from the CPM example that activities 2 and 3 are not on the critical path, so their expected value and standard deviation calculations have been left blank in this table. When you add all the remaining tasks, the total expected value duration is 102.99 days, or 103 days rounded to the nearest day.

TABLE 4.2 PERT Calculation

Activity Number	Activity Description	Optimistic	Pessimistic	Most Likely	Expected Value	Standard Deviation	SD Squared
1	Project Deliverables	10	14	12	12.00	0.67	0.45
2	Procure Hardware	—	—	—	—	—	—
3	Test Hardware	—	—	—	—	—	—
4	Procure Software Tools	8	14	10	10.33	1.00	1.0
5	Write Programs	38	57	45	45.83	3.17	10.05
6	Test and Debug	20	30	22	23.00	1.67	2.79
7	Install	5	10	8	7.83	0.83	0.69
8	Training	3	3	3	3.00	0	0
9	Acceptance	1	1	1	1.00	0	0
Totals for CP Tasks					**102.99**		**14.98**

Your next logical conclusion might be to add the Standard Deviation column to get the standard deviation for the project. Unfortunately, you cannot add the standard deviations because you will come out with a number that is much too high. Totaling the standard deviations assumes that all the tasks will run over schedule, and that's not likely. It is likely that a few tasks will run over but not every one of them. So now you're probably wondering how to calculate the magic number.

You might have noticed an extra column at the right called SD Squared. This is the standard deviation squared—or for those of you with math phobias out there, the standard deviation multiplied by itself.

Once you have calculated the standard deviation squared for each activity, add the squares, for a total of 14.98. There's one more step, and you're done. Take the square root of 14.98 (you'll need a calculator) to come up with 3.87. This is the standard deviation you will use to determine your range of projected completion dates. Here's a recap of these last few calculations:

Total expected value = 103.00
Sum of SD Squared = 14.98
Square root of SD Squared = 3.87

You can now make the following predictions regarding your project:

- There is a 68.26 percent chance that the project will be completed in 99.13 days to 106.87 days.
- There is a 95.44 percent chance that the project will be completed in 95.26 days to 110.74 days.

Exam Spotlight

For the exam, I recommend that you know that one standard deviation gives you a 68 percent (rounded) probability and two standard deviations gives you a 95 percent (rounded) probability. Also, know how to calculate the range of project duration dates based on the expected value and standard deviation calculation. You probably don't need to memorize how to calculate the standard deviation because most of the questions give you this information. You should, however, memorize the PERT formula and know how it works. It wouldn't hurt to memorize the standard deviation formula as well—you never know what might show up on the exam.

PERT is not used often today. When it is, it's used for very large, highly complex projects. However, PERT is a useful technique to determine project duration when your activity durations are uncertain. It's also useful for calculating the duration for individual tasks in your schedule that might be complex or risky. You might decide to use PERT for a handful of the activities (those with the highest amount of risk, for example) and use other techniques to determine duration for the remaining activities.

Critical Chain Method

Critical chain method is a schedule network analysis technique that will modify the project schedule by accounting for limited or restricted resources. After the project schedule network diagram is constructed using duration estimates, dependencies, and constraints, resource availability is entered into the scheduling tool. The modified schedule is calculated and you'll find that it often changes the critical path. The new critical path showing the resource restrictions is called the *critical chain*.

Critical chain uses both deterministic (step-by-step) and probabilistic approaches. A few steps are involved in the critical chain process:

- Construct the schedule network diagram using activity duration estimates (you'll use nonconservative estimates in this method).

- Define dependencies.
- Define constraints.
- Calculate critical path.
- Enter resource availability into the schedule.
- Recalculate for the critical chain.

As I stated earlier, the critical path will often change once you've entered the resource availability. That's because the critical chain method adds nonwork activities where needed as duration buffers to help manage the planned activity durations. These buffers are known as feeding buffers and they protect the critical chain schedule from slipping. A project buffer is placed at the end of the critical chain to help keep the finish date from slipping. After the buffers are added, the planned activities are then scheduled at their latest start and finish dates.

This method typically schedules high-risk tasks early in the project so that problems can be identified and addressed right away. It allows for combining several tasks into one task when one resource is assigned to all the tasks.

Exam Spotlight

CPM manages the total float of schedule network paths, whereas critical chain manages buffer activity durations.

Resource Leveling

Earlier, I said that CPM and PERT do not consider resource availability. Now that you have a schedule of activities and have determined the critical path, it's time to plug in resources for those activities and adjust the schedule according to any resource constraints you discover. You should use this technique with CPM-based schedules.

Resource leveling—also called the *resource-based method*—is used when resources are overallocated. You'll also use this technique when they are time constrained (especially those assigned to critical path activities) or when you need to meet specific schedule dates and are concerned about resource availability.

Remember that you identified resource estimates during the Estimate Activity Resources processes. Now during Develop Schedule, resources are assigned to specific activities. Usually, you'll find that your initial schedule has periods of time with more activities than you have resources to work on them. You will also find that it isn't always possible to assign 100 percent of your team members' time to tasks. Sometimes your schedule will show a team member who is overallocated, meaning they're assigned to more work than they can physically perform in the given time period. Other times, they might not be assigned enough work to keep them busy during the time period. This problem is easy to fix. You can assign underallocated resources to multiple tasks to keep them busy.

Overallocated Resources

Having overallocated resources is a little more difficult problem to resolve than having underallocated resources. Resource leveling attempts to smooth out the resource assignments to get tasks completed without overloading the individual while trying to keep the project on schedule. This typically takes the form of allocating resources to critical path tasks first.

The project manager can accomplish resource leveling in several ways. You might delay the start of a task to match the availability of a key team member. Or you might adjust the resource assignments so that more tasks are given to team members who are underallocated. You could also require the resources to work mandatory overtime—that one always goes over well! Perhaps you can split some tasks so that the team member with the pertinent knowledge or skill performs the critical part of the task and the noncritical part of the task is given to a less-skilled team member. All these methods are forms of resource leveling.

Generally speaking, resource leveling of overallocated team members extends the project end date. If you're under a date constraint, you'll have to rework the schedule after assigning resources to keep the project on track with the committed completion date. This might include moving key resources from noncritical tasks and assigning them to critical path tasks or adjusting assignments as previously mentioned. Reallocating those team members with slack time to critical path tasks to keep them on schedule is another option. Don't forget, fast tracking is an option to keep the project on schedule also.

Reverse Resource Allocation Scheduling

Reverse resource allocation scheduling is a technique used when key resources—like a thermodynamic expert, for example—are required at a specific point in the project and they are the only resource, or resources, available to perform these activities. This technique requires the resources to be scheduled in reverse order (that is, from the end date of the project rather than the beginning) in order to assign this key resource at the correct time.

Exam Spotlight

Resource leveling can cause the original critical path to change.

What-If Scenario Analysis

What-if scenario analysis uses different sets of activity assumptions to produce multiple project durations. For example, what would happen if a major deliverable was delayed or the weather prevents you from completing a deliverable on time? What-if analysis weighs these questions and their assumptions and determines the feasibility of the project schedule under these conditions. Simulation techniques such as Monte Carlo analysis use a range of probable activity durations for each activity, and those ranges are then used to calculate a range of probable duration results for the project itself. Monte Carlo runs the possible activity durations and schedule projections many, many times to come up with the schedule projections and their probability, critical path duration estimates, and float time.

Exam Spotlight

For the exam, remember that Monte Carlo is a simulation technique that shows the probability of all the possible project completion dates.

Applying Leads and Lags

I talked about leads and lags earlier in this chapter. You'll recall that lags delay successor activities and require time added either to the start date or to the finish date of the activity you're scheduling. Leads require time to be subtracted from the start date or the finish date of the activity. Keep in mind that as you go about creating your project schedule, you might need to adjust lead and lag time to come up with a workable schedule.

Schedule Compression

Schedule compression is a form of mathematical analysis that's used to shorten the project schedule without changing the project scope. Compression is simply shortening the project schedule to accomplish all the activities sooner than estimated.

Schedule compression might happen when the project end date has been predetermined or if, after performing the CPM or PERT techniques, you discover that the project is going to take longer than the original promised date. In the CPM example, you calculated the end date to be July 10. What if the project was undertaken and a July 2 date was promised? That's when you'll need to employ one or both of the duration compression techniques: crashing and fast tracking.

Crashing

Crashing is a compression technique that looks at cost and schedule trade-offs. One of the things you might do to crash the schedule is add resources—from either inside or outside the organization—to the critical path tasks. It wouldn't help you to add resources to noncritical path tasks; these tasks don't impact the schedule end date anyway because they have float time. Crashing could be accomplished by requiring mandatory overtime for critical path tasks or requiring overnight deliveries of materials rather than relying on standard shipping times. You may find that crashing the schedule can lead to increased risk and or increased costs.

NOTE

Be certain to check the critical path when you've used the crashing technique because crashing might have changed the critical path. Also consider that crashing doesn't always come up with a reasonable result. It often increases the costs of the project as well. The idea with crashing is to try to gain the greatest amount of schedule compression with the least amount of cost.

Fast Tracking

I talked about fast tracking in Chapter 1, "What Is a Project?" *Fast tracking* is performing two tasks in parallel that were previously scheduled to start sequentially. Fast tracking can increase project risk and might cause the project team to have to rework tasks. Fast tracking will only work for activities that can be overlapped. For example, fast tracking is often performed in object-oriented programming. The programmers might begin writing code on several modules at once, out of sequential order and prior to the completion of the design phase. However, if you remember way back to our house-painting example, you couldn't start priming and painting at the same time, so fast tracking isn't a possibility for those activities.

Scheduling Tool

Given the examples you've worked through on Develop Schedule and resource leveling, you probably already have concluded how much a scheduling tool might help you with these processes. The scheduling tools I've used are in the form of project management software programs. They will automate the mathematical calculations (such as forward and backward pass) and perform resource-leveling functions for you. Obviously, you can then print the schedule that has been produced for final approval and ongoing updates. It's common practice to email updated schedules with project notes so that stakeholders know what activities are completed and which ones remain to be done.

It's beyond the scope of this book to go into all the various software programs available to project managers. Suffice it to say that scheduling tools and project management software range from the simple to the complex. The level of sophistication and the types of project management techniques that you're involved with will determine which software product you should choose. Many project managers that I know have had great success with Microsoft Project software and use it exclusively. It contains a robust set of features and reporting tools that will serve most projects well.

Don't forget that you are the project manager, and your good judgment should never be usurped by the recommendation of a software product. Your finely tuned skills and experience will tell you whether relationship issues between team members might cause bigger problems than what the resource-leveling function indicates. Constraints and stakeholder expectations are difficult for a software package to factor in. Rely on your expertise when in doubt. If you don't have the experience yet to make knowledge-based decisions, seek out another project manager or a senior stakeholder, manager, or team member and ask them to confirm whether you're on the right track. And a word of caution: don't become so involved with the software that you're managing the software instead of managing the project. Project management software is a wonderful tool, but it is not a substitute for sound project management practices or experience.

Scheduling Process Outputs

The Develop Schedule process has four outputs:

- Project schedule
- Schedule baseline

- Schedule data
- Project document updates

We'll take a look at all of the outputs of this process next. Take note that the two primary outputs from this process that will carry forward throughout the rest of the project are the project schedule and the schedule baseline.

Real World Scenario

Sunny Surgeons, Inc.

Kate Newman is a project manager for Sunny Surgeons, Inc. Sunny Surgeons, Inc. is a software company that produces software for handheld devices for the medical profession. The software allows surgeons to keep notes regarding patients, upcoming surgeries, and ideas about new medicines and techniques to research. Kate's latest project is to write an enhanced version of the patient-tracking program with system integration capabilities to a well-known desktop software product used by the medical industry.

The programming department has had some recent turnover. Fortunately, Stephen, the senior programmer who led the development effort on the original version of the patient tracker, still works for Sunny. His expertise with handheld technologies, as well as his knowledge of the desktop software product, makes him an invaluable resource for this project.

Kate discovered a problem during the development of the project schedule. Stephen is overallocated for three key activities. Kate decides to see what his take is on the situation before deciding what to do.

Stephen, the eternal optimist programmer who loves his job and does all but sleep in his office at night, says he can easily complete all the activities and that Kate shouldn't give it a second thought. He also suggests to Kate that Karen Wong, a junior programmer on his team who worked on the last project with him, might be able to handle the noncritical path task on her own, with a little direction from Stephen.

Kate thinks better of the idea of overallocating her key project resource, even if he does think he can do the entire thing single-handedly. She decides to try some resource leveling to see what that turns up.

Kate discovers that rearranging the order of activities, along with assigning Karen to handle the noncritical path activity, might be a possible solution. However, this scenario lengthens the project by a total of eight days. Since Kate knows the primary constraint on this project is quality, she's fairly sure she can get buy-off from the project sponsor and stakeholders on the later schedule date. She can also sell the resource-leveled schedule as a low-risk option as opposed to assigning Stephen to all the activities and keeping the project end date the same. Overallocating resources can cause burnout and stress-related illnesses, which will ultimately have a negative impact on the project schedule.

Project Schedule

The purpose of the Develop Schedule process is to determine the start and finish dates for each of the project activities. One of the primary outputs of this process is the *project schedule*, which details this information as well as the resource assignments. However, depending on the size and complexity of your project or your organization's culture, the resource assignments and determining the start and finish dates might not be completed yet. If that's the case, the project schedule is considered preliminary until the resources are assigned to the activities.

WARNING In *PMBOK® Guide* terms, the project schedule is considered preliminary until resources are assigned. In reality, beware that once you've published the project schedule (even though it's in a preliminary state), some stakeholders might regard this as the actual schedule and expect you to keep to the dates shown. Use caution when publishing a schedule in its preliminary form.

The project schedule should be approved and signed off by stakeholders and functional managers. This assures you that they have read the schedule, understand the dates and resource commitments, and will likely cooperate. You'll also need to obtain confirmation that resources will be available as outlined in the schedule when you're working in a functional organization. The schedule cannot be finalized until you receive approval and commitment for the resource assignments outlined in it.

Once the schedule is approved, it will become your baseline for the remainder of the project. Project progress and task completion will be monitored and tracked against the project schedule to determine whether the project is on course as planned.

You can create the schedule in a variety of ways, some of which are variations on what you've already seen. Project schedule network diagrams, like the ones discussed earlier, will work as schedule diagrams when you add the start and finish dates to each activity. These diagrams usually show the activity dependencies and critical path. Figure 4.2 shows a sample portion of a project schedule network diagram highlighting the programming activities.

Gantt charts are easy to read and commonly used to display schedule activities. Depending on the software you're using to produce the Gantt chart, it might also show activity sequences, activity start and end dates, resource assignments, activity dependencies, and the critical path. Figure 4.3 is a simple example that plots various activities against time. These activities do not relate to the activities in the tables or other figures shown so far. Gantt charts are also known as *bar charts*.

Milestone charts are another way to depict schedule information. Milestones mark the completion of major deliverables or some other key event in the project. For example, approval and sign-off on project deliverables might be considered a milestone. Other examples might be completion of a prototype, system testing, contract approval, and so on.

Milestone charts might show the key events and their start or completion dates in a bar chart form similar to a Gantt chart. Or they can be written in a simple table format with milestones listed in the rows and expected schedule dates in one column and actual completion dates in another, as shown in Table 4.3. As the milestones are met, the Actual Date column is filled in. This information can be included with the project status reports.

FIGURE 4.2 Project schedule network diagram with activity dates

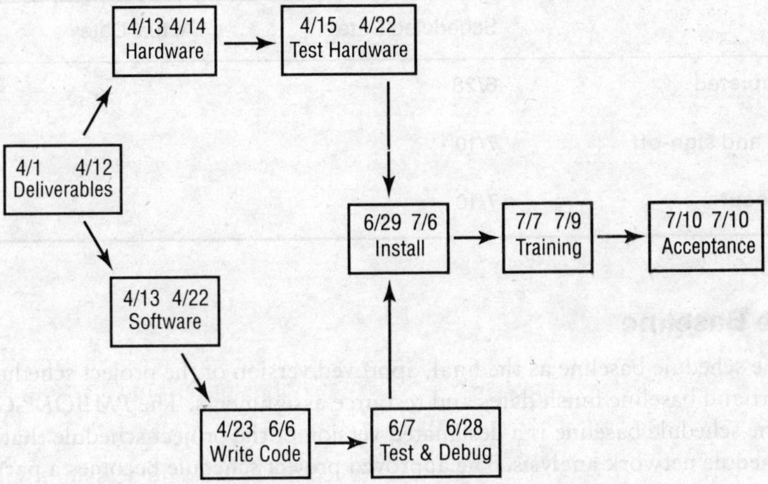

FIGURE 4.3 Gantt chart

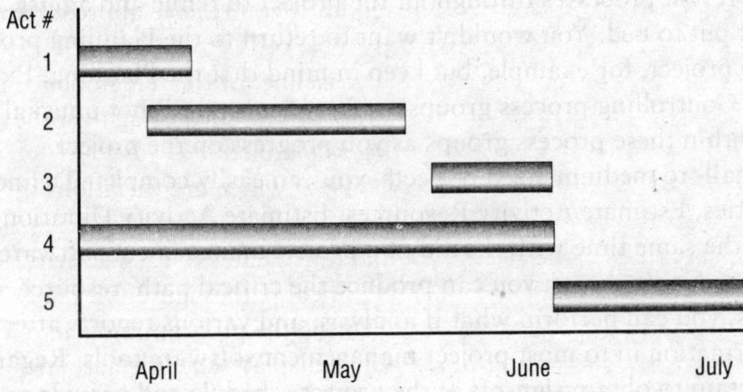

TABLE 4.3 Milestone Chart

Milestone	Scheduled Date	Actual Date
Sign-off on deliverables	4/12	4/12
Sign-off on hardware test	4/22	4/25
Programming completed	6/06	

TABLE 4.3 Milestone Chart *(continued)*

Milestone	Scheduled Date	Actual Date
Testing completed	6/28	
Acceptance and sign-off	7/10	
Project closeout	7/10	

Schedule Baseline

I think of the schedule baseline as the final, approved version of the project schedule with baseline start and baseline finish dates and resource assignments. The *PMBOK® Guide* notes that the schedule baseline is a designated version of the project schedule that's derived from the schedule network analysis. The approved project schedule becomes a part of the project management plan we talked about in Chapter 3.

As I've noted during discussions of some of the other Planning processes, project planning and project management are iterative processes. Rarely is anything cast in cement. You will continue to revisit processes throughout the project to refine and adjust. Eventually, processes do get put to bed. You wouldn't want to return to the Planning process at the conclusion of the project, for example, but keep in mind that the Planning, Executing, and Monitoring and Controlling process groups are iterative, and it's not unusual to have to revise processes within these process groups as you progress on the project.

In practice, for small- to medium-sized projects, you can easily complete Define Activities, Sequence Activities, Estimate Activity Resources, Estimate Activity Durations, and Develop Schedule at the same time with the aid of a project management software tool. You can easily produce Gantt charts, you can produce the critical path, resource allocation, activity dependencies, you can perform what-if analysis, and various reports after plugging your scheduling information in to most project management software tools. Regardless of your methods, be certain to obtain sign-off of the project schedule and provide your stakeholders and project sponsor with regular updates. And keep your schedule handy—there will likely be changes and modifications as you go. While you're at it, make certain to save a schedule baseline for comparative purposes. Once you get into the Executing and Monitoring and Controlling processes, you'll be able to compare what you planned to do against what actually happened.

Schedule Data

The schedule data refers to documenting the supporting data for the schedule. The minimum amount of information in this output includes the milestones, schedule activities and activity attributes, and the assumptions and constraints regarding the schedule. You should document any other information that doesn't necessarily fit into the other categories. Always err on the side of too much documentation rather than not enough.

You will have to be the judge of what other information to include here because it will depend on the nature of the project. The *PMBOK® Guide* suggests that you might include resource histograms. Chapter 7, "Planning Project Resources," contains an example resource histogram if you want to peek ahead. Resource histograms typically display hours needed on one axis and period of time (days, weeks, months, years) on the other axis. You might also include alternative schedules or contingency schedule reserves in the schedule data section.

Project Document Updates

Like many of the other processes we've seen in this chapter, creating the project schedule may require updates to the activity resource requirements document, activity attributes, calendars, and the risk register.

Real World Scenario

Project Case Study: New Kitchen Heaven Retail Store

You worked with the stakeholders to document the activity list last week. After creating the first draft of the project schedule network diagram, you went back to each of them to ask for time estimates for each of the activities. Ricardo's estimates are shown here:

1. Procure the T1 connection. This takes 30 to 45 days. This activity can be done concurrently with the other activities listed here. Ricardo will perform this activity.
2. Run Ethernet cable throughout the building. This activity depends on the lease being signed and must finish before the build-out can start. The estimated time to complete is 16 hours, which was figured using parametric estimating techniques. Ricardo has one person on staff who can complete this specialized activity. His first available date is October 5.
3. Purchase the router, switch, server, and rack for the equipment room and the four point-of-service terminals. Delivery time is two weeks. Ricardo will perform this activity.
4. Install the router and test the connection. Testing depends on the T1 installation at demarcation. The time estimate to install is eight hours. Ricardo's staff will perform this activity.
5. Install the switch. Based on past experience, the time estimate to install is two hours. Ricardo's staff will do this activity.
6. Install the server and test. The testing depends on the T1 connection installation. Based on past experience, the time estimate to install is six hours. Ricardo's staff will do this activity.
7. The web team will add the new store location and phone number to the lookup function on the Internet site. The time estimate is two hours. Ricardo will assign his applications programming manager to this activity. This activity depends on the lease being signed.

Jake and Jill have each written similar lists with estimates and potential resource assignments. You begin to align all the activities in sequential order and discover a problem. Jill needs 14 days to hire personnel and stock shelves, meaning that the build-out must be finished by January 16. Build-out takes approximately 120 days and can't start before September 20 because of the contractor's availability. This is a problem because Ricardo's Ethernet cable expert isn't available until October 5, and he needs 2 days to complete the cabling. This pushes out the build-out start date by almost 2 weeks, which means the project completion date, or store-opening date, is delayed by 2 weeks.

After gathering more information from Ricardo, you head to Dirk's office.

"So, Dirk," you conclude after filling him in on all the details, "we have two options. Hire a contractor to perform the cable run since Ricardo's person isn't available or push the store opening out by two weeks."

Dirk asks, "How much will the contractor charge to run the cable, and are they available within the time frame you need?"

"Yes, they are available, and I've already requested that Ricardo book the week of September 18 to hold this option open for us. They've quoted a price of $10,000."

"OK, let's bring in the contractor. At this point, $10,000 isn't going to break the budget. How is that planning coming anyway? Signed a lease yet?"

"Yes, we've signed the lease. Jake has been meeting with Gomez construction on the build-out. We've used Gomez on three out of the last five new stores and have had good luck with them."

You spend the next couple of days working on the project schedule in Microsoft Project, clarifying tasks and activities with Jake, Ricardo, and Jill. You decide that a Gantt chart will work excellently for reporting status for this project. You stare intensely at the problem you see on the screen. The Grand Opening task is scheduled to occur 13 days later than when you need it! Grand opening must happen February 1 and 2, not February 14 and 15 as the schedule shows. You trace the problem back and see that Grand Opening task depends on Train Store Personnel, which itself depends on several other tasks, including Hire Store Personnel and Install and Test Hardware. Digging deeper, build-out can't begin until the Ethernet cable is run throughout the building. Ricardo already set up the time with the contractor to run the cable on September 18. This date cannot move, which means build-out cannot start any sooner than September 20, which works with Gomez's availability.

You pick up the phone and dial Jake's number. "Jake," you say into the receiver, "I'm working on the project schedule, and I have some issues with the Gomez activity."

"Shoot," Jake says.

"Gomez Construction can't start work until the Ethernet cable is run. I've already confirmed with Ricardo that there is no negotiation on this. Ricardo is hiring a contractor for this activity, and the earliest they can start is September 18. It takes them two days to run the cable, which puts the start date for build-out at September 20."

"What's the problem with the September 20 date?" Jake asks.

"Jill wants to have the build-out finished prior to hiring the store personnel. During the last store opening, those activities overlapped, and she said it was unmanageable. She wants to hire folks and have them stock the shelves in preparation for store opening but doesn't want contractors in there while they're doing it. A September 20 start date for Gomez puts us at a finish date of January 26, which is too late to give Jill time to hire and stock shelves. My question is this: is 120 days to finish a build-out a firm estimate?"

"Always—I've got this down to a science. Gomez has worked with me on enough of these build-outs that we can come within just a couple of days of this estimate either way," Jake says.

You pick up your schedule detail and continue, "I've scheduled Gomez's resource calendar as you told me originally. Gomez doesn't work Sundays, and neither do we. Their holidays are Labor Day, a couple of days at Thanksgiving, Christmas, and New Year's, but this puts us too far out on the schedule. We must have our February 1 opening coincide with the Garden and Home Show dates."

"I can't change the 120 days. Sounds like you have a problem."

"I need to crash the schedule," you say. "What would the chances be of Gomez agreeing to split the build-out tasks? We could hire a second contractor to come in and work alongside Gomez's crew to speed up this task. That would shorten the duration to 100 days, which means we could meet the February 1 date."

"Won't happen. I know Gomez. They're a big outfit and have all their own crews. We typically work with them exclusively. If I brought another contractor into the picture, I might have a hard time negotiating any kind of favors with them later if we get into a bind."

"All right," you say. "How about this? I'm making some changes to the resource calendar while we're talking. What if we authorize Gomez's crew to work six 10-hour days, which still leaves them with Sundays off, and we ask them to work on Labor Day and take only one day at Thanksgiving instead of two?"

"I think Gomez would go for that. You realize it's going to cost you?"

"Project management is all about trade-offs. We can't move the start date, so chances are the budget might take a hit to accommodate schedule changes or risk. Fortunately, I'm just now wrapping up the final funding requirements, or the cost budget, so if you can get me the increased cost from Gomez soon, I'd appreciate it. This change will keep us on track and resolve Jill's issues too."

"I don't think Gomez's crew will mind the overtime during the holiday season. Everyone can use a little extra cash at that time of year, it seems. I'll have the figures for you in a day or two."

Project Case Study Checklist

The main topics discussed in the case study are as follows:

- Estimate Activity Durations
- Estimate Activity Resources
- Developing project schedule
  - Calendars
  - Lead and lag time
  - Critical path
- Duration compression
  - Crashing
  - Fast tracking
- Utilizing project management software
- Producing project schedule
  - Milestones
  - Gantt chart
  - Resource leveling

Understanding How This Applies to Your Next Project

Define Activities and Sequence Activities are the first two processes in the "Activity" sequence you'll complete on the road to Develop Schedule. You perform Estimate Activity Resources to determine the resource requirements and quantity of resources needed for each schedule activity. I've found for small- to medium-sized projects, you can perform this process at the same time as the Estimate Activity Durations process. And, if you work in an organization where the same resource pool is used for project after project, you already know the people's skills sets and availability, so you can perform this process at the same time you're creating the project schedule. The same logic holds for projects where the material resources are similar for every project you conduct. If you don't have the need to perform this process, I do recommend that you create a resource calendar at a minimum so that you can note whether team members have extended vacations or family issues that could impact the project schedule. Needless to say, if you're working on a large project or your project teams are new for every project, you should perform the Estimate Activity Resources process rather than combining it with Develop Schedule. It will come in handy later when you're ready to plug names into the activities listed on the project schedule.

Estimate Activity Durations is a process you'll perform for most projects you work on. For larger projects, I'm a big fan of PERT estimates. PERT gives you estimates with a high degree of reliability, which are needed for projects that are critical to the organization, projects that haven't been undertaken before, or projects that involve complex processes or scope. It's easy to create a spreadsheet template to automatically calculate these estimates for you. List your schedule activities in each row, and in the individual columns to the right, record the most likely, pessimistic, and optimistic estimates. The final column can hold the calculation to perform the weighted average of these three estimates, and you can transfer the estimates to your schedule. You can easily add columns to calculate standard deviation as well.

In theory, if you've performed all the "Activity" processes, the schedule should almost be a no-brainer. You can plug the activity list, resources, estimates, and successor and predecessor tasks into the schedule. From there, you will want to take the next step and determine the critical path. The critical path is, well, critical to your project's success. If you don't know which activities are on the critical path, you won't know what the impacts that delays or risk events will have on the project. No matter how big or small the project, be sure you know and understand the critical path activities.

Summary

Great job, you've made it through the Planning activities associated with the Project Time Management Knowledge Area. I covered several processes in this chapter, including Define Activities, Sequence Activities, Estimate Activity Resources, Estimate Activity Durations, and Develop Schedule.

Define Activities uses the scope baseline (which includes the scope statement, WBS, and WBS dictionary) to help derive activities. Activities are used to help derive a basis for estimating and scheduling project work during the Planning processes and for executing and monitoring and controlling the work of the project in later processes.

The Sequence Activities process takes the activities and puts them in a logical, sequential order based on dependencies. Dependencies exist when the current activity relies on some action from a predecessor activity or it impacts a successor activity. Three types of dependencies exist: mandatory, discretionary, and external. PDM (also known as AON) and ADM (also known as AOA) are two methods for displaying project schedule network diagrams. PDM has four logical relationships, or dependencies: finish-to-start, start-to-finish, finish-to-finish, and start-to-start.

The Estimate Activity Resources process considers all the resources needed and the quantity of resources needed to perform project activities. This information is determined for each activity and is documented in the activity resource requirements output.

Duration estimates are produced as a result of the Estimate Activity Durations process. Activity duration estimates document the number of work periods needed for each activity, including their elapsed time. Analogous estimating—also called *top-down estimating*—is one way to determine activity duration estimates. You can also use top-down techniques to estimate project durations and total project costs. Parametric estimating techniques multiply a known element—such as the quantity of materials needed—by the time it takes to install or complete one unit of materials. The result is a total estimate for the activity. Three-point estimates calculate an average estimate based on the most likely estimate, a pessimistic estimate, and an optimistic estimate. Reserve analysis takes schedule risk into consideration by adding a percentage of time or another work period to the estimate just in case you run into trouble.

PERT calculates a weighted average estimate for each activity by using the optimistic, pessimistic, and most likely times. It then determines variances, or standard deviations, to come up with a total project duration within a given confidence range. Work will finish within plus or minus one standard deviation 68.26 percent of the time. Work will finish within plus or minus two standard deviations 95.44 percent of the time.

Develop Schedule is the process in which you assign beginning and ending dates to activities and determine their duration. You might use CPM to accomplish this. CPM calculates early start, early finish, late start, and late finish dates. It also determines float time. All tasks with zero float are critical path tasks. The critical path is the longest path of tasks in the project.

Schedules sometimes need to be compressed to meet promised dates or to shorten the schedule times. Crashing looks at cost and schedule trade-offs. Adding resources to critical path tasks and limiting or reducing the project requirements or scope are ways to crash the schedule. Fast tracking involves performing tasks in parallel that were originally scheduled to start one after the other. Fast tracking usually increases project risk. You can use Monte Carlo analysis in the Develop Schedule process to determine multiple, probable project durations.

Resource leveling attempts to smooth out the schedule and properly allocate resources to critical path tasks. This might require updates to the resource management plan.

The project schedule details the activities in graphical form through the use of project schedule network diagrams with dates, Gantt charts, milestone charts, and project schedule network diagrams.

Exam Essentials

Be able to name the purpose of the Estimate Activity Resources process. The purpose of Estimate Activity Resources is to determine the types of resources needed (human, equipment, and materials) and in what quantities for each schedule activity within a work package.

Be able to name the tools and techniques of Estimate Activity Durations. The tools and techniques of Estimate Activity Durations are expert judgment, analogous estimating, parametric estimating, and reserve analysis.

Be able to define the difference between analogous estimating and bottom-up estimating. Analogous estimating is a top-down technique that uses expert judgment and historical information. Bottom-up estimating performs estimates for each work item and rolls them up to a total.

Be able to calculate the critical path. The critical path includes the activities whose durations add up to the longest path of the project schedule network diagram. Critical path is calculated using the forward pass, backward pass, and float calculations.

Be able to define a critical path task. A critical path task is a project activity with zero float.

Be able to describe and calculate PERT duration estimates. This is a weighted average technique that uses three estimates: optimistic, pessimistic, and most likely. The formula is as follows: (optimistic + pessimistic + (4 * most likely)) / 6.

Be able to name the duration compression techniques. The duration compression techniques are crashing and fast tracking.

Be able to describe a critical chain. The critical chain is the new critical path in a modified schedule that accounts for limited resources.

Be able to name the outputs of the Develop Schedule process. The outputs are project schedule, schedule baseline, schedule data, and project document updates.

Key Terms

Accurately planning a project budget and schedule is one of the most difficult tasks you'll face as a project manager. Know the processes I've discussed and the terms used to identify them in the *PMBOK® Guide*. Here's a list of the schedule planning processes you'll need to be successful.

Define Activities

Sequence Activities

Estimate Activity Resources

Estimate Activity Durations

Develop Schedule

You've also learned a lot of new key words in this chapter. PMI has worked hard to develop and define standard project management terms that apply across industries. Here is a list of some of the terms you came across in this chapter:

activity duration estimates

analogous estimating

backward pass

bar charts

buffer

contingency time

crashing

critical chain

critical chain method

critical path (CP)

critical path method (CPM)

fast tracking

float time

forward pass

Gantt charts

milestone charts

parametric estimating

Program Evaluation and Review Technique (PERT)

project calendars

project plan

project schedule

reserve time

resource calendars

resource leveling

resource-based method

resources

reverse resource allocation scheduling

schedule baseline

schedule compression

schedule network analysis

slack time

three-point estimates

top-down estimating

Review Questions

1. You are the project manager for Changing Tides video games. You have gathered the inputs for the Estimate Activity Durations process. Which of the following tools and techniques will you employ to produce the outputs for this process?
   - **A.** Activity list, expert judgment, alternatives analysis, analogous estimating, parametric estimating, three-point estimates, and reserve analysis
   - **B.** Activity list, expert judgment, analogous estimating, parametric estimating, and three-point estimates
   - **C.** Expert judgment, analogous estimating, parametric estimating, three-point estimates, and reserve analysis
   - **D.** Expert judgment, alternatives analysis, analogous estimating, parametric estimating, and three-point estimates

2. You are the project manager for Changing Tides video games. You have produced a project schedule network diagram and have updated the activity list. Which process have you just finished?
   - **A.** The Define Activities process, which identifies all the specific activities of the project
   - **B.** The Sequence Activities process, which identifies all the activity dependencies
   - **C.** The Develop Schedule process, which diagrams project network time estimates
   - **D.** The Estimate Activity Durations process, which estimates activity durations

3. Your project's primary constraint is quality. To make certain the project team members don't feel too pressed for time and to avoid schedule risk, you decide to use which of the following activity estimating tools?
   - **A.** Three-point estimates
   - **B.** Analogous estimating
   - **C.** Reserve analysis
   - **D.** Parametric estimating

4. You have been hired as a contract project manger for Grapevine Vineyards. Grapevine wants you to design an Internet wine club for its customers. One of the activities for this project is the installation and testing of several new servers. You know from past experience it takes about 16 hours per server to accomplish this task. Since you're installing 10 new servers, you estimate this activity to take 160 hours. Which of the estimating techniques have you used?
   - **A.** Parametric estimating
   - **B.** Analogous estimating
   - **C.** Bottom-up estimating
   - **D.** Reserve analysis

5. All of the following statements describe the activity list except which one?
   - **A.** The activity list is an output of the Define Activities process.
   - **B.** The activity list includes all activities of the project.
   - **C.** The activity list is an extension of and a component of the WBS.
   - **D.** The activity list includes an identifier and description of the activity.

6. You have been hired as a contract project manager for Grapevine Vineyards. Grapevine wants you to design an Internet wine club for its customers. Customers must register before being allowed to order wine over the Internet so that legal age can be established. You know that the module to verify registration must be written and tested using data from Grapevine's existing database. This new module cannot be tested until the data from the existing system is loaded. This is an example of which of the following?
   - **A.** Preferential logic
   - **B.** Soft logic
   - **C.** Discretionary dependency
   - **D.** Hard logic

7. You are the project manager for Design Your Web Site, Inc. Your company is designing the website for a national grocery store chain. You have your activity list in hand and are ready to diagram the activity dependencies using the PDM technique. Which of the following statements is true?
   - **A.** PDM is also the AON diagramming method and it uses one time estimate.
   - **B.** PDM is also the AOA diagramming method and uses logical relationships.
   - **C.** PDM is also the ADM diagramming method and its most common logical relationship is finish-to-start.
   - **D.** PDM is also the GERT method, which allows for conditions, branches, and loops.

8. You are working on a project that requires resources with expertise in the areas of hospitality management and entertainment. You are preparing your project schedule network diagram and know that you will use only finish-to-start dependencies. Which of the following diagramming methods does this describe?
   - **A.** PDM
   - **B.** ADM
   - **C.** AON
   - **D.** Network template

9. Which logical relationship does the PDM use most often?
   - **A.** Start-to-finish
   - **B.** Start-to-start
   - **C.** Finish-to-finish
   - **D.** Finish-to-start

10. You are a project manager for Picture Shades, Inc. It manufactures window shades that have replicas of Renaissance-era paintings for hotel chains. Picture Shades is taking its product to the home market, and you're managing the new project. It will offer its products at retail stores as well as on its website. You're developing the project schedule for this undertaking and have determined the critical path. Which of the following statements is true?

A. You calculated the most likely start date and most likely finish dates, float time, and weighted average estimates.

B. You calculated the activity dependency and the optimistic and pessimistic activity duration estimates.

C. You calculated the early and late start dates, the early and late finish dates, and float times for all activities.

D. You calculated the optimistic, pessimistic, and most likely duration times and the float times for all activities.

11. You are a project manager for Picture Shades, Inc. It manufactures window shades that have replicas of Renaissance-era paintings for hotel chains. Picture Shades is taking its product to the home market, and you're managing the new project. It will offer its products at retail stores as well as on its website. You're developing the project schedule for this undertaking. Looking at the following graph, which path is the critical path?

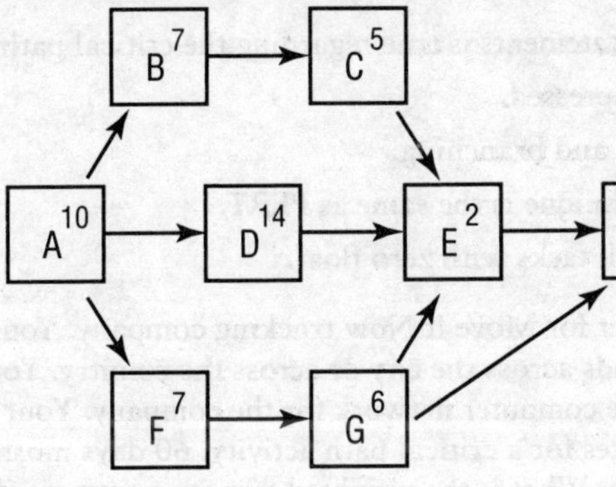

A. A-B-C-E-H

B. A-D-E-H

C. A-F-G-H

D. A-F-G-E-H

12. Use the following graphic to answer this question. If the duration of activity B was changed to 10 days and the duration of activity G was changed to 9 days, which path is the critical path?

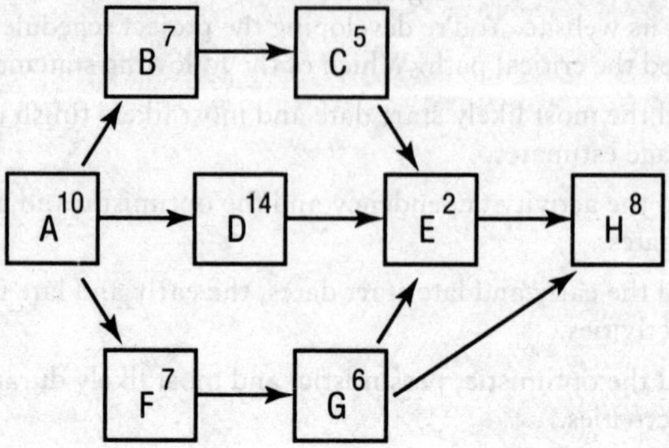

A. A-B-C-E-H

B. A-D-E-H

C. A-F-G-H

D. A-F-G-E-H

13. Which of the following statements is true regarding the critical path?

A. It should not be compressed.

B. It allows for looping and branching.

C. The critical path technique is the same as PERT.

D. It's the duration of all tasks with zero float.

14. You are a project manager for Move It Now trucking company. Your company specializes in moving household goods across the city or across the country. Your project involves upgrading the nationwide computer network for the company. Your lead engineer has given you the following estimates for a critical path activity: 60 days most likely, 72 days pessimistic, 48 days optimistic. What is the weighted average or expected value?

A. 54

B. 66

C. 60

D. 30

15. You are a project manager for Move It Now trucking company. Your company specializes in moving household goods across the city or across the country. Your project involves upgrading the nationwide computer network for the company. Your lead engineer has given you the following estimates for a critical path activity: 60 days most likely, 72 days pessimistic, 48 days optimistic. What is the standard deviation?

A. 22

B. 20

C. 2

D. 4

16. If you know the expected value is 500 and the standard deviation is 12, you can say with approximately a 95 percent confidence rating which of the following?
    - **A.** The activity will take from 488 to 512 days.
    - **B.** The activity will take from 464 to 536 days.
    - **C.** The activity will take from 494 to 506 days.
    - **D.** The activity will take from 476 to 524 days.

17. If your expected value is 110 and the standard deviation is 12, which of the following is true?
    - **A.** There is approximately a 99 percent chance of completing this activity in 86 to 134 days.
    - **B.** There is approximately a 68 percent chance of completing this activity in 98 to 122 days.
    - **C.** There is approximately a 95 percent chance of completing this activity in 98 to 122 days.
    - **D.** There is approximately a 75 percent chance of completing this activity in 86 to 134 days.

18. You are the project manager working on a research project for a new drug treatment. Your preliminary project schedule runs past the due date for a federal grant application. The manager of the R&D department has agreed to release two resources to work on your project in order to meet the federal grant application date. This is an example of ____________________.
    - **A.** crashing
    - **B.** fast tracking
    - **C.** resource leveling
    - **D.** adjusting the resource calendar

19. You are the project manager for Rivera Gourmet Adventure Vacations. Rivera combines the wonderful tastes of great gourmet food with outdoor adventure activities. Your project involves installing a new human resources software system. Jason, the database analyst working on this project, is overallocated. Which of the following statements is true?
    - **A.** You should use resource requirements updates to determine availability and smooth out resource overallocation.
    - **B.** You should use crashing to resource level the critical path tasks.
    - **C.** You should use resource leveling to smooth out resource assignments.
    - **D.** You should use fast tracking to resource level the critical path tasks.

20. What is one of the problems with project management software?
    - **A.** The project manager manages the software instead of the project.
    - **B.** Project duration calculations are sometimes approximate.
    - **C.** You cannot override the project management software decisions regarding schedules.
    - **D.** It's expensive and difficult to use.

Answers to Review Questions

1. C. The tools and techniques for Estimate Activity Durations are expert judgment, analogous estimating, parametric estimating, three-point estimates, and reserve analysis.

2. B. The Sequence Activities process produces project schedule network diagrams and project document updates, which may include activity attributes. The purpose of this process is to identify all activity dependencies.

3. C. Reserve analysis takes schedule risk into consideration and adds a percentage of time or additional work periods to the estimate to prevent schedule delays.

4. A. Parametric estimating multiplies a known element—such as the quantity of materials needed—by the time it takes to install or complete one unit of materials. The result is a total estimate for the activity. In this case, 10 servers multiplied by 16 hours per server gives you a 160-hour total duration estimate.

5. C. The activity list is a component of the project schedule, not the WBS. The activity list includes all the project activities, an identifier, and a description of the activity. The activity list is an output of the Define Activities process.

6. D. This is an example of a mandatory dependency, also known as *hard logic*. Mandatory dependencies are inherent in the nature of the work. Discretionary dependencies, also called *preferred logic*, *preferential logic*, and *soft logic*, are defined by the project management team.

7. A. The precedence diagramming method is also known as the activity on node (AON) diagramming method. GERT stands for Graphical Evaluation and Review Technique, a diagramming method that allows for conditions, branches, and loops.

8. B. The arrow diagramming method uses only finish-to-start dependencies.

9. D. Finish-to-start (FS) is the most commonly used logical relationship in PDM and the default relationship in most project management software packages.

10. C. The CPM calculates a single early and late start date and a single early and late finish date for each activity. Once these dates are known, float time is calculated for each activity to determine the critical path. The other answers contain elements of PERT calculations.

11. B. The only information you have for this example is activity duration; therefore, the critical path is the path with the longest duration. Path A-D-E-H with a duration of 34 days is the critical path.

12. D. The only information you have for this example is activity duration, so you must calculate the critical path based on the durations given. The duration of A-B-C-E-H increased by 3 days for a total of 35 days. The duration of A-F-G-H and A-F-G-E-H each increased by 3 days. A-F-G-E-H totals 36 days and becomes the new critical path.

13. D. You calculate the critical path by adding together the durations of all the tasks with zero float. The critical path can be compressed using crashing techniques.

14. C. The calculation for PERT is the sum of optimistic time plus pessimistic time plus four times the most likely time divided by 6. The calculation for this example is as follows: (48 + 72 + (4 * 60)) / 6 = 60.

15. D. You calculate the standard deviation by subtracting the optimistic time from the pessimistic time and dividing the result by 6. The calculation for this example is as follows: (72 – 48) / 6 = 4.

16. D. There is a 95 percent probability that the work will finish within plus or minus two standard deviations. The expected value is 500, and the standard deviation times 2 is 24, so the activity will take from 476 to 524 days.

17. B. A 68 percent probability is calculated using plus or minus one standard deviation, a 95 percent probability uses plus or minus two standard deviations, and a 99 percent probability uses plus or minus three standard deviations.

18. A. Crashing the schedule includes tasks such as adding resources to the critical path tasks or speeding up deliveries of materials and resources.

19. C. Resource leveling attempts to smooth out resource assignments by splitting tasks, assigning underallocated team members to more tasks, or delaying the start of tasks to match team members' availability.

20. A. Project management software is a useful tool for the project manager, and it automates project scheduling, allowing for what-if analysis and easy changes. But if you focus too much on the tool and ignore the project, the tool becomes a hindrance.

Chapter 5

Developing the Project Budget

THE PMP® EXAM CONTENT FROM THE PLANNING THE PROJECT PERFORMANCE DOMAIN COVERED IN THIS CHAPTER INCLUDES THE FOLLOWING:

- ✓ **Obtain Plan Approval**

Two of the most important documents you'll prepare for any project are the project schedule and the project budget. You'll use the schedule and budget documents throughout the Executing and Monitoring and Controlling processes to measure progress and determine if the project is on track. I believe the budget is easier to prepare after the activities have been defined and the resource estimates calculated. So now that we have the schedule in hand, we're going to spend our time in this chapter developing the budget.

There are two processes in the Planning group we'll perform that will lead us to the cost performance baseline output that is the authorized budget. They are Estimate Costs and Determine Budget. There are several tools and techniques to cover in these processes that you'll want to understand for the exam. Before we get into the details of these two processes, we'll talk about the cost management plan and its importance in guiding the development of the budget.

Next we'll talk about how project information is documented and communicated. I've talked a lot about documentation so far, and I will discuss it more in this chapter. Documentation is something you will do throughout the remainder of the project, and the Plan Communications process details how to collect information, how to store it, and when and how to distribute it to stakeholders.

Creating the Project Cost Management Plan

You now have an exhaustive breakdown of project activities, and you have some pretty good duration estimates. Now the question that's forever on the mind of the executive management staff: How much is it going to cost? The purpose of the Estimate Costs process is to answer that question.

Every project has a budget, and part of completing a project successfully is completing it within the approved budget. Sometimes project managers are not responsible for the budget portion of the project. This function is assigned instead to a functional manager who is responsible for tracking and reporting all the project costs. I believe project mangers will have more and more responsibility in this area as the project management discipline evolves. Keep in mind that if you, as the project manager, don't have responsibility for the project budget, your performance evaluation for the project should not include budget or cost measurements.

Before diving into the Estimate Costs and Determine Budget process particulars, you should know that these processes are governed by a cost management plan that is created when you perform the Develop Project Management Plan process (we talked about that in Chapter 3, "Developing the Project Scope Statement"). You should know a couple of facts about this plan for the exam.

The cost management plan establishes the format and conditions you'll use to plan for project costs. It also outlines how you will estimate, budget, and control project costs. Like all the other management plans, the cost management plan is a subsidiary of the project management plan.

According to the *PMBOK® Guide*, some of the elements of this plan includes, but is not limited to, the following elements:

Level of accuracy This refers to the precision level you'll use to round activity estimates—for example, hundreds, thousands, and so on. Level of accuracy is based on the scope and complexity of the activities and the project itself.

Units of measure This refers to the unit of measure you'll use to estimate resources—for example, hours, days, weeks, or a lump sum amount.

Organizational procedures links In Chapter 3, we talked about the WBS and the identifiers associated with each component of the WBS. These identifiers are called the code of accounts. A *control account (CA)* is a point where several factors such as actual cost, schedule, and scope can be used to determine earned value performance measures. (We'll talk more about earned value in Chapter 10, "Measuring and Controlling Project Performance"). The control account is what's used in the Project Cost Management Knowledge Area to monitor and control project costs. The control account is typically associated with the work package level of the WBS, but there could be control accounts established at any level of the WBS. The control account also has a unique identifier that's linked to the organization's accounting system, sometimes known as a *chart of accounts*.

Exam Spotlight

The project cost management plan is established using the WBS and its associated control accounts.

Control thresholds Most actual project costs do not match the estimate exactly. The control threshold refers to the amount of variance the sponsor or stakeholders are willing to allow before action is required. Document the threshold amount as a percentage of deviation allowed from the cost performance baseline.

Rules of performance measurement This component of the cost management plan refers to how you will set the earned value management measurements. It's here you'll document where the control accounts exist within the WBS, the earned value management (EVM) techniques you'll use to measure performance, and the equations you'll use for calculating estimate at completion forecasts and other measurements. We'll talk about EVM and estimate at completion forecasts in detail in Chapter 10.

Reporting formats This refers to the types of cost reports you'll produce for this project and how often they'll be created.

Process descriptions This describes the Estimate Cost, Determine Budget, and Control Costs processes and how you'll use these processes to manage project cost.

The key to determining accurate cost estimates (and as we discovered in Chapter 4, accurate time estimates) is the work breakdown structure (WBS). Next we'll look at how to determine cost estimates for the WBS components.

Estimating Costs

The *Estimate Costs* process develops a cost estimate for the resources (human and material) required for each schedule activity. This includes weighing alternative options and examining risks and trade-offs. Some alternatives you may consider are make-versus-buy, buy-versus-lease, and sharing resources across either projects or departments.

Let's look at an example of trade-offs. Many times software development projects take on a life of their own. The requested project completion dates are unrealistic; however, the project team commits to completing the project on time and on budget anyway. How do they do this? They do this by cutting things such as design, analysis, and documentation. In the end, the project might get completed on time and on budget, but was it really? The costs associated with the extended support period because of a lack of design and documentation and the hours needed by the software programmers to fix the reported bugs weren't included in the original cost of the project (but they should have been). Therefore, the costs actually exceed what was budgeted. You should examine trade-offs such as these when determining cost estimates.

When you are determining cost estimates, be certain to include all the costs of the project over its entire life cycle. As in the preceding example, software projects often have warranty periods that guarantee bug fixes or problem resolution within a certain time frame. This is a legitimate cost that should be included in your estimates.

NOTE Don't confuse pricing with Estimate Costs. If you are working for a company that performs consulting services on contract, for example, the price you will charge for your services is not the same as the costs to perform the project. The costs are centered on the resources needed to produce the product, service, or result of the project. The price your company might charge for the service includes not only these costs but a profit margin as well.

Estimate Costs Inputs

Many of the inputs of the Estimate Costs process are already familiar to you. However, we'll look briefly at each one so you can see the key elements that should be considered when creating the project budget. The inputs to this process are as follows:

- Scope baseline
- Project schedule
- Human resource plan
- Risk register
- Enterprise environmental factors
- Organizational process assets

Scope Baseline

Pop quiz time. Do you remember the elements of the scope baseline? They are the project scope statement, the WBS, and the WBS dictionary. You'll want to consider a few key elements from the project scope statement in this process, including key deliverables, constraints, and assumptions. I can safely say that every project I've ever worked on had a limited budget, which is a classic example of a project constraint. You should also understand other constraints that have the potential to impact costs, such as required delivery dates or availability of resources.

The WBS, as we've discussed, serves as the basis for estimating costs. It contains all the project deliverables and the control accounts are typically established at the work package level. When considering deliverables, think about those that may have contractual obligations that should be considered when determining cost estimates. Or, perhaps you have deliverables that have legal or governmental regulations that will require additional expense to fulfill. Health, safety, security, licenses, and environmental factors are some of the other elements of the scope baseline you should consider when estimating costs, according to the *PMBOK® Guide*.

Exam Spotlight

Scope definition is a key component of determining the estimated costs and should be completed as early in the project as possible because it's easier to influence costs in the beginning phases of the project. But you can't influence costs if you don't understand the project scope.

Project Schedule

We determined the types and quantities of resources we needed in Chapter 4, "Creating the Project Schedule," using the Estimate Activity Resources (this process is closely associated with the Estimate Cost process according to the *PMBOK® Guide*) and Estimate Activity

Durations processes. Activity resource requirements and activity duration estimates are the key outputs you should consider when estimating costs.

Be aware that duration estimates can affect costs. For example, make certain you account for costs like interest charges when you're financing the work of the project. Also watch for duration estimates that are calculated for resources who are scheduled to work for a per unit period of time. Duration estimates can be incorrect (hopefully not wildly incorrect) and can end up costing you more. For example, I recently bought a new home requiring a move of about eight miles. The moving company told me that the work was performed on a per-hour basis. The person providing the estimate assured me he had been doing this for over 25 years and his estimates were typically right on the money. Unfortunately, I swallowed that line and the estimate I was given was wildly incorrect. It took them almost twice the amount of time I was quoted, and you guessed it, the total ended up being almost twice the original estimate.

Human Resource Plan

We will look more closely at the human resource plan (an output of the Develop Human Resource Plan process) in Chapter 7, "Planning Project Resources." For the purposes of the Estimate Costs process, understand that the human resources plan includes elements such as personnel rates, project staffing attributes, and employee recognition or rewards programs. All of these elements should be considered when determining cost estimates.

Risk Register

The risk register is an output of the Identify Risks process that we'll discuss in Chapter 6, "Risk Planning." You should consider the cost of mitigating risks (identified in the risk register), particularly those with negative impacts to the project, when developing project cost estimates.

Enterprise Environmental Factors

According to the *PMBOK® Guide*, the enterprise environmental factors you should consider in this process are market conditions and published commercial information. Market conditions help you understand the materials, goods, and services available in the market and what terms and conditions exist to procure those resources. Published commercial information refers to resource cost rates. You can obtain these from commercial databases or published seller price lists.

Organizational Process Assets

The organization process assets considered in the process are similar to those we've seen before. Historical information and lessons learned on previous projects of similar scope and complexity can be very useful in determining estimates for the current project—particularly if the past projects occurred recently. Your organization's business office or PMO may also have cost estimating templates you can use to help with this process. You could use cost-estimating worksheets from past projects as templates for the current project as well.

Tools and Techniques to Estimate Costs

Estimate Costs has nine tools and techniques used to derive estimates:

- Expert judgment
- Analogous estimating
- Parametric estimating
- Bottom-up estimating
- Three-point estimate
- Reserve analysis
- Cost of quality
- Project management estimating software
- Vendor bid analysis

I covered analogous estimating, parametric estimating, three-point estimate, and reserve analysis techniques in Chapter 4. These are also tools and techniques of the Estimate Activity Durations process to help determine schedule estimates. All of the information we discussed in Chapter 4 applies here as well, except you're using the tools and techniques to derive cost estimates. Three-point estimates are used in this process when you want to improve your estimates and account for risk and estimation uncertainty. And, in the case of reserve analysis, you're adding cost reserves (or contingencies) during this process, not schedule reserves. You could aggregate these cost contingencies and assign them to a schedule activity or a WBS work package level.

The project management estimating software tool can help you quickly determine estimates given different variables and alternatives. Some systems are quite sophisticated and use simulation and statistical techniques to determine estimates, while others are less complex. A simple spreadsheet program can do the trick much of the time. We'll look at the remaining tools and techniques next.

Exam Spotlight

According to the *PMBOK® Guide*, if the Project Cost Management Knowledge Area includes predicting the potential financial performance of the product of the project, or if the project is a capital facilities project, you may also use additional tools and techniques in the process, such as return on investment, discounted cash flow, and payback analysis. We talked about these techniques in Chapter 2, "Creating the Project Charter."

Bottom-Up Estimating

I discussed this technique in Chapter 4, but there are a few pointers to consider for this process. This technique estimates costs associated with every activity individually and then rolls them up to derive a total project cost estimate. You wouldn't choose this technique to provide a cost estimate for the project during Initiating if one were requested because you don't have enough information at that stage to use it. Instead, use the top-down estimating technique (analogous estimating) when a project cost estimate is needed early in the project selection stage. Bottom-up estimating will generally provide you with the most accurate cost estimates, but it is the most time-consuming estimating technique of all those mentioned here. However, the size and complexity of the project impact the accuracy you can achieve using this technique.

Cost of Quality

The *cost of quality (COQ)* is the total cost to produce the product or service of the project according to the quality standards. We will talk more in depth about cost of quality in Chapter 7, "Planning Project Resources."

Vendor Bid Analysis

As the name implies, this is a process of gathering information from vendors to help you establish cost estimates. You can accomplish this by requesting bids or quotes or working with some of your trusted vendor sources for estimates. You should compare vendor bids when using this tool and technique and not rely solely on one vendor to provide you with estimates.

Exam Spotlight

For the exam, make sure you're familiar with all the Estimate Costs tools and techniques, their benefits, and under what conditions you use them.

Estimate Costs Process Outputs

One of the outputs of the Estimate Costs process is activity cost estimates. These are quantitative amounts—usually stated in monetary units—that reflect the cost of the resources needed to complete the project activities. The tools and techniques I just described help you derive these estimates. Resources in this case include human resources, material, equipment, information technology needs, and so on, as well as any contingency reserve amounts and inflation factors (if you're using them).

The remaining outputs of the Estimate Costs process are basis of estimates and project document updates. Basis of estimates is the supporting detail for the activity cost estimates and includes any information that describes how the estimates were developed, what assumptions were made during the Estimate Costs process, and any other details you think are needed. According to the *PMBOK® Guide*, the basis of estimates should include at least the following:

- A description of how the estimate was developed or the basis for the estimate.
- A description of the assumptions made about the estimates or the method used to determine them.

- A description of the constraints.
- A range of possible results. You should state the cost estimates within ranges such as $5000 ± 10%.
- The confidence level regarding the final estimates.

Real World Scenario

This Older House

Janie is an accomplished project manager. She and her husband recently purchased an 80-year-old home in need of several repairs and modern updates. She decided to put her project management skills to work on the house project. First, they hired a general contractor to oversee all the individual projects needed to bring the house up-to-date. Janie worked with the general contractor to construct a WBS, and she ended up with 23 work packages. With each work package (or multiple work packages in some cases) assigned to a subcontractor, it was easy to track who was responsible for completing the work and for determining duration estimates. Janie and the general contractor worked together to determine schedule dependencies and make certain the work was performed in the correct order and that each subcontractor knew when their activity was to begin and end.

Some of the cost estimates for certain work packages were easy to determine using the parametric estimating method. Others required expert judgment and the experience of the general contractor (analogous techniques) to determine a cost estimate. Resource rates for laborers for some of the work packages were agreed to when the subcontractors bid on the work. Once Janie had all the cost estimates, she used the bottom-up estimating technique to come up with an overall cost estimate for the project. She added a contingency reserve in addition to the overall estimate for unforeseen risk events.

The last output of this process is project document updates. Cost variances will occur and estimates will be refined as you get further into your project. As a result, you'll update cost estimates and ultimately the project budget to reflect these changes. The risk register may also require an update after cost estimates are complete.

Estimate Costs uses several techniques to make an accurate assessment of the project costs. In practice, using a combination of techniques is your best bet to come up with the most reliable cost estimates. The activity cost estimates will become an input to the Determine Budget process, which allows you to establish a baseline for project costs to track against.

Establishing the Cost Budget Baseline

The next process concerns determining the cost performance baseline, which is the primary output of the Determine Budget process. The *Determine Budget* process aggregates the cost estimates of activities and establishes a cost performance baseline for the project that is used to measure performance of the project throughout the remaining process groups. Only the costs associated with the project become part of the authorized project budget. For example, future period operating costs are not project costs and therefore aren't included in the project budget.

The *cost performance baseline* is the total expected cost for the project when using a budget at completion calculation, an earned value management technique. When you're using earned value management techniques, the cost performance baseline is also known as the performance measurement baseline (PMB). We'll talk about budget at completion and earned value management techniques in detail in Chapter 10, "Measuring and Controlling Project Performance." Remember that costs are tied to the financial system through the chart of accounts—or code of accounts—and are assigned to project activities at the work package level or to control accounts at various points in the WBS. The budget will be used as a plan for allocating costs to project activities.

NOTE As we've discussed with several other processes, in practice you can sometimes perform the Estimate Costs and Determine Budget processes at the same time.

Determine Budget Inputs

Outputs from other Planning processes, including the Create WBS, Schedule Development, and Estimate Costs processes, must be completed prior to working on Determine Budget because some of their outputs become the inputs to this process. The inputs for Determine Budget are as follows:

Activity cost estimates These are an output of the Estimate Costs process. Activity cost estimates are determined for each activity within a work package and then summed to determine the total estimate for a work package.

Basis of estimates This is also an output of the Estimate Costs process and contains all the supporting detail regarding the estimates. You should consider assumptions regarding indirect costs and whether they will be included in the project budget. Indirect costs cannot be directly linked to any one project. They are allocated among several projects, usually within the department or division in which the project is being performed. Indirect costs can include items like building leases, management and administrative salaries (those not directly assigned full time to a specific project), and so on.

Scope baseline Scope baseline includes the scope statement, WBS, and WBS dictionary. The scope statement describes the constraints of the project you should consider when developing the budget. The WBS shows how the project deliverables are related to their components, and the work package level typically contains control account information (although control accounts can be assigned at any level of the WBS).

Project schedule The schedule contains information that is helpful in developing the budget, such as start and end dates for activities, milestones, and so on. Based on the information in the schedule, you can determine budget expenditures for calendar periods.

Resource calendars Resource calendars help you determine costs in calendar periods and over the length of the project because they describe what resources are needed when on the project.

Contracts Contracts include cost information you should include in the overall project budget. We'll talk more about contracts in Chapter 7.

Organizational process assets The organization process assets that will assist you with the work of this process include cost budgeting tools, the policies and procedures your organization (or PMO) may have regarding budgeting exercises, and reporting methods.

Determine Budget Tools and Techniques

The Determine Budget process has five tools and techniques, including two you haven't seen before:

- Cost aggregation
- Reserve analysis
- Expert judgment
- Historical relationships
- Funding limit reconciliation

I've covered expert judgment previously. Let's look at the remaining tools and techniques.

Cost aggregation Cost aggregation is the process of tallying the schedule activity cost estimates at the work package level and then totaling the work package levels to higher-level WBS component levels (such as the control accounts). Then all of the costs can be aggregated to obtain a total project cost.

Reserve analysis We talked about reserve analysis in Chapter 4 as it pertains to the project schedule. Reserve analysis works the same for the Determine Budget process, only you're planning contingency reserves for unplanned project scope and project costs. Reserves are not included as part of the cost performance baseline (an output of this process) but should be included in the project budget. Reserves are also not considered when calculating earned value measurements.

NOTE Reserve analysis should also contain appropriations for risk responses. I'll talk about several categories and tools of Risk Response Planning in Chapter 6. Additionally, you'll want to set aside money for contingency reserves for unknown risks. This is for the unforeseen, unplanned risks that might occur. Even with all the time and effort you spend on planning, unexpected issues do crop up. It's better to have the money set aside and not need it than to need it and not have it.

Historical relationships Analogous estimates and parametric estimates can be used to help determine total project costs. Remember from Chapter 4 that analogous estimates are a form of expert judgment. Actual costs from previous projects of similar size, scope, and complexity are used to estimate the costs for the current project. This is helpful when detailed information about the project is not available or it's early in the project phases and not much information is known.

Parametric estimates are quantitatively based and, for example, multiply the amount of time needed to perform an activity by the resource rate to determine total cost. This technique can be very accurate when the data you're using is reliable.

Funding limit reconciliation Funding limit reconciliation involves reconciling the amount of funds to be spent with the amount of funds budgeted for the project. The organization or the customer sets these limits. Reconciling the project expenses will require adjusting the schedule so that the expenses can be smoothed. You do this by placing imposed date constraints (I talked about these in the Schedule Development process in Chapter 4) on work packages or other WBS components in the project schedule.

Determine Budget Process Outputs

The goal of Determine Budget is to develop a cost performance baseline (an output of this process) for the project that you can use in the Executing and Monitoring and Controlling processes to measure performance. You now have all the information you need to create the cost performance baseline. In addition, you'll establish the project funding requirements.

The following are the outputs of the Determine Budget process:

- Cost performance baseline
- Project funding requirements
- Project document updates

We've covered the project document updates in other processes. For Determine Budget, you may need to update the risk register, cost estimates, and/or the project schedule. Let's look at the other two outputs next.

Documenting the Cost Performance Baseline

You develop the cost performance baseline, the first output of Determine Budget, by adding the costs of the WBS elements (remember, these costs were aggregated with the cost aggregation tool and technique) by time periods. This is also known as the project's *time-phased budget*. Most projects span some length of time, and most organizations time the funding with the project. In other words, you won't get all the funds for the project at the beginning of the project; they'll likely be disbursed over time. The cost performance baseline provides the basis for measurement, over time, of the expected cash flows (or funding disbursements) against the requirements.

Cost performance baselines can be displayed graphically, with time increments on one axis and dollars expended on the other axis, as shown in Figure 5.1. The costs shown on this graph are cumulative costs, meaning that what you spent this period is added to what was spent last period and then charted. Many variations of this graph exist showing dollars budgeted against dollars expended to date and so on. Cost budgets can be displayed using this type of graph as well, by plotting the sum of the estimated costs excepted per period.

FIGURE 5.1 Cost performance baseline

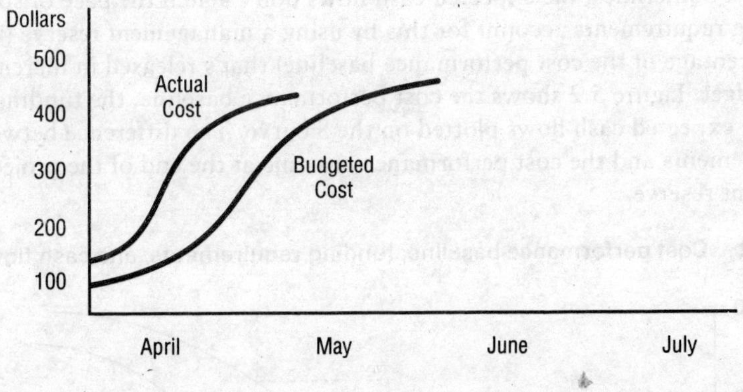

The cost performance baseline should contain the costs for all of the expected work on the project. You would have identified these costs in the Estimate Costs process. You'll find most projects' largest expense is resource costs (as in labor costs). In the case of projects where you're purchasing the final product, the purchase price is the largest cost.

Exam Spotlight

For the exam, remember that cost performance baselines are displayed as an S curve. The reason for this is that project spending starts out slowly, gradually increases over the project's life until it reaches a peak, and then tapers off again as the project wraps up. Large projects are difficult to graph in this manner because the timescale isn't wide enough to accurately show fluctuations in spending. There are other methods that more accurately graph costs that you'll look at in the Cost Control process.

NOTE Large projects might have more than one cost performance baseline. For example, you might be required to track human resources costs, material costs, and contractor costs separately.

You'll revisit the cost performance baseline when you learn about the Cost Control process and examine different ways to measure costs in Chapter 10.

Gathering the Project Funding Requirements

Project funding requirements describe the need for funding over the course of the project and are derived from the cost performance baseline. Funding requirements can be expressed in monthly, quarterly, or annual increments or other increments that are appropriate for your project.

As I said earlier, spending usually starts out slowly on the project and picks up speed as you progress. Sometimes, the expected cash flows don't match the pace of spending. Project funding requirements account for this by using a management reserve (usually a margin or percentage of the cost performance baseline) that's released in increments with the project budget. Figure 5.2 shows the cost performance baseline, the funding requirements, and the expected cash flows plotted on the S curve. The difference between the funding requirements and the cost performance baseline at the end of the project is the management reserve.

FIGURE 5.2 Cost performance baseline, funding requirements, and cash flow

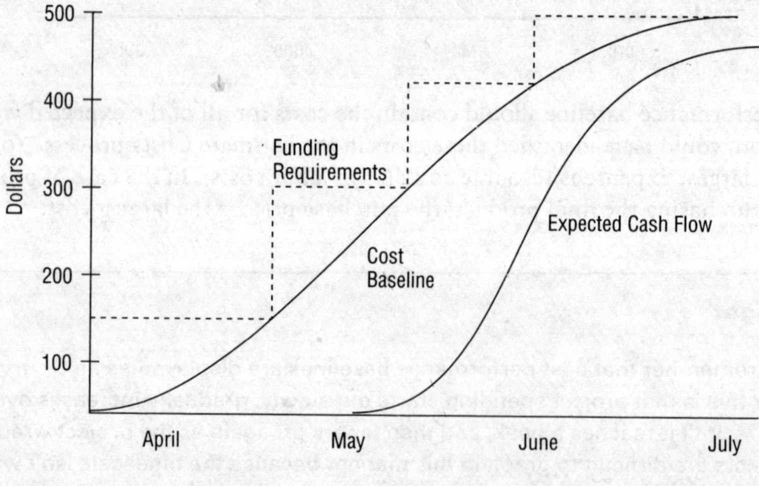

We've now completed two critical components of the project plan, the project schedule and the project budget. I've mentioned several times throughout the book about the need for documenting, publishing, and communicating project information. As you can imagine, the *PMBOK® Guide* has a process for communications. We'll discuss it next.

Communicating the Plan

I've talked a good deal about documentation so far, and this topic will continue to come up throughout the remainder of the book. "Is that documented?" should be an ever-present question on the mind of the project manager. Documentation can save your bacon, so to speak, later in the project. Documentation is only one side of the equation, though—communication is the other. You and your stakeholders need to know who gets what information and when.

The *Plan Communications* process involves determining the communication needs of the stakeholders by defining the types of information needed, the format for communicating the information, how often it's distributed, and who prepares it. All of this is documented in the communications management plan, which is an output of this process.

NOTE

Pop quiz: Do you remember where else the communications management plan belongs? I'll give you the answer later in the section "Communications Management Plan."

Plan Communications Inputs

The inputs to the Plan Communications process will look familiar to you. They are as follows:

- Stakeholder register
- Stakeholder management strategy
- Enterprise environmental factors
- Organizational process assets

The stakeholder register and stakeholder management strategy should give you a lot of insight into the communication needs of the stakeholders. The stakeholder register is a list of all the project stakeholders and includes additional information including their potential influence on the project and their classification. The stakeholder management strategy defines the level of participation needed for each stakeholder and potential strategies you can use to gain their support or reduce the negative impacts or obstacles they could present to the project.

The *PMBOK® Guide* notes that all the elements described in the enterprise environmental factors and in the organizational process assets are inputs to this process. However, special note is made of the lessons learned and historical information elements of the organizational process assets input. Information you learn as you're progressing through the project is documented as lessons learned. This information is helpful for future projects of similar scope and complexity. Historical information is also useful to review when starting the Plan Communications process. Either of these documents might contain information about communication decisions on past projects and their results. Why reinvent the wheel? If something didn't work well on a past project, you'd want to know that before implementing that procedure on this project, so review past project documentation.

The project management plan is not an input to this process, but you'll recall that it defines how the subsidiary plans will be defined and integrated into the overall project management plan. As such, it's rich with constraints and assumptions that you should review as they pertain to stakeholder communication needs.

Exam Spotlight

The *PMBOK® Guide* notes that there is a difference between effective and efficient communication. Effective communication refers to providing the information in the right format for the intended audience at the right time. Efficient communication refers to providing the appropriate information at the right time, that is, only the information that's needed at the time.

Tools and Techniques for Plan Communications

The Plan Communications process concerns defining and documenting the types of information you're going to deliver, the format it will take, to whom it will be delivered, and when. The process consists of two tools and techniques to help determine these elements. They are communications requirements analysis and communications technology. You'll look at both of these next.

Communications Requirements Analysis

Communications requirements analysis involves analyzing and determining the communication needs of the project stakeholders. According to the *PMBOK® Guide*, there are several sources of information you can examine to help determine these needs, including the following:

- Company and departmental organizational charts
- Stakeholder responsibility relationships
- Other departments and business units involved on the project
- The number of resources involved on the project and where they're located in relation to project activities

- Internal needs that the organization may need to know about the project
- External needs that organizations such as the media, government, or industry groups might have that require communication updates
- Stakeholder information (This was documented in the stakeholder register and stakeholder management strategy outputs of Identify Stakeholders.)

This tool and technique requires an analysis of the items in the preceding list to make certain you're communicating information that's valuable to the stakeholders. Communicating valuable information doesn't mean you always paint a rosy picture. Communications to stakeholders might consist of either good or bad news—the point is that you don't want to bury stakeholders in too much information but you want to give them enough so that they're informed and can make appropriate decisions.

Project communication will always involve more than one person, even on the tiniest of projects. As such, communication network models have been devised to try to explain the relationships between people and the number or type of interactions needed between project participants. What you need to remember for the exam is that network models consist of nodes with lines connecting the nodes that indicate the number of communication channels, also known as *lines of communication*. Figure 5.3 shows an example of a network communication model with six channels of communication.

FIGURE 5.3 Network communication model

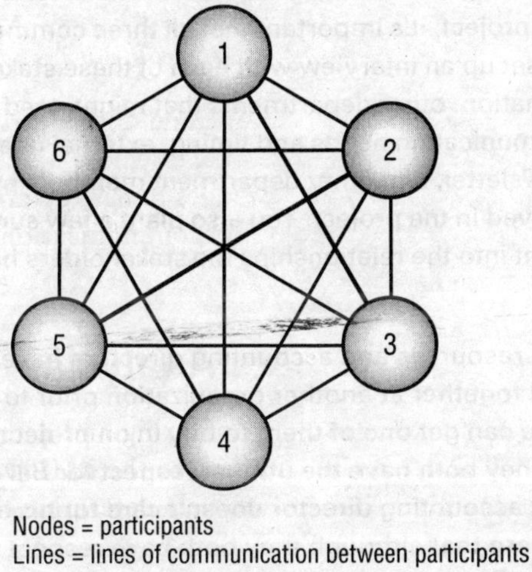

The nodes are the participants, and the lines show the connection between them all. You'll need to know how to calculate the number of communication channels when you take the exam. You could draw them out as in this example and count up the lines, but there's an easier way. The formula for calculating the lines of communication is as follows:

(number of participants * (number of participants less 1)) divided by 2

Here's the calculation in mathematical terms:

$$n (n - 1) / 2$$

Figure 5.3 shows six participants, so let's plug that into the formula to determine the lines of communication:

$$6 (6 - 1) / 2 = 15$$

Real World Scenario

Stakeholder Relationships

Bill is an information technology manager working on an enterprise resource planning project. He's one of the key stakeholders on this project. Bill reports to the CIO, who in turn reports to the executive vice president, who also happens to be the project sponsor. Bill is close friends with the human resources director but doesn't get along so well with the accounting department director. This project requires heavy involvement from the accounting department and medium-level involvement from the human resources department.

You are the project manager for this project and are new to the organization. You know Bill's relationship with both the accounting and human resources directors. What you don't know is the relationship the two directors have with each other. Since all three stakeholders are key to the success of this project, it's important that all three communicate with you as well as with each other. You set up an interview with each of these stakeholders to determine several pieces of information: other departments that might need to be involved on the project, stakeholder communication needs and timing, external needs, timing of status updates for the company newsletter, and other department members aside from the stakeholders who need to be involved in the project. You also plant a few surreptitious questions that will give you some insight into the relationships the stakeholders have with each other and with the project sponsor.

You discover that the human resources and accounting directors have known each other for several years and worked together at another organization prior to coming to work here. This tells you that if you can get one of them to buy in on project decisions, the other will likely follow suit. They both have the utmost respect for Bill and his technical capabilities, even though the accounting director doesn't care for his abrupt, direct communication style. You also learn that although they both have respect for the position of the executive vice president, they don't believe the person filling that role is competent to do the job. They question his decision-making ability—or lack thereof—and warn you that you need to write down his answers and direction so that he doesn't change his story halfway through the project. Although you won't formally document this valuable piece of information, you'll definitely put it into action right away.

Exam Spotlight

I recommend you memorize the communications channel formula before taking the exam.

Communications Technology

The second tool and technique of this process is communications technology. This examines the methods (or technology) used to communicate the information to, from, and among the stakeholders. Methods of communicating can take many forms, such as written, spoken, email, formal status reports, meetings, online databases, online schedules, and so on. This tool and technique examines the technology elements that might affect project communications. You should consider several factors before deciding what methods you'll choose to transfer information. The timing of the information exchange or need for updates is the first factor. The availability of the technology you're planning on using to communicate project information is important as well. Do you need to procure new technology or systems, or are there systems already in place that will work? Staff experience with the technology is another factor. Are the project team members and stakeholders experienced at using this technology, or will you need to train them? Consider the duration of the project and the project environment. Will the technology you're choosing work throughout the life of the project, or will it have to be upgraded or updated at some point? And how does the project team function? Are they all located together or spread out across several campuses or locations?

The answers to these questions should be documented in the communications management plan output. I'll cover that in the next section.

Communications Models

Communication models depict how information is transmitted from the sender and how it's received by the receiver. According to the *PMBOK® Guide*, a communications model includes the following key components:

- Encode
- Message and feedback message
- Medium
- Noise
- Decode

Encoding the message simply means putting the information or your thoughts or ideas into a language that the receiver will understand. The message is the result or output of the encoding.

The medium is the method you'll use to communicate. This could be written, oral, email, and so on.

Noise refers to anything that keeps the message from either being transmitted or understood. And decode refers to translating the information that was sent.

The sender is responsible for the encoding of the message, the medium, and decoding the feedback message. The receiver is responsible for decoding the original message from the sender and encoding and sending the feedback message.

Communications Methods

Communication methods refer to how the project information is shared among the stakeholders. According to the *PMBOK® Guide*, there are three classifications of communication methods. We'll briefly look at each of them.

Interactive communication Interactive communication involves multidirectional communication where two or more parties must exchange thoughts or ideas. This method includes videoconferencing, phone or conference calls, and meetings.

Push communications Push communications is one way and refers to sending information to intended receivers. It includes methods such as letters, memos, reports, emails, voicemails, and so on. This method assures the communication was sent but is not concerned with whether it was actually received or understood by the intended receivers.

Pull communications This is the opposite of push communications. The likely recipients of the information access the information themselves using methods such as web sites, e-learning sites, knowledge repositories, shared network drives, and so on.

NOTE

We'll discuss communication models and communication methods in more detail in Chapter 9, "Conducting Procurements and Sharing Information."

Communications Management Plan

There are two outputs to the Plan Communications process. They are communications management plan and product document updates. The updates that may be required as a result of performing this process are the project schedule, the stakeholder register, and the stakeholder management strategy. Let's take a closer look at the details of the communications management plan.

All projects require sound communication plans, but not all projects will have the same types of communication or the same methods for distributing the information. The *communications management plan* documents the types of information needs the stakeholders have, when the information should be distributed, and how the information will be delivered. The answer to the pop quiz posed earlier in this chapter is the communications management plan is a subsidiary plan of the project management plan I talked about in Chapter 3.

The type of information you will typically communicate includes project status, project scope statements and scope statement updates, project baseline information, risks, action items, performance measures, deliverable acceptance, and so on. What's important to know for this process is that the information needs of the stakeholders should be determined as early in the Planning process group as possible so that as you and your team develop project planning documents, you already know who should receive copies of them and how they should be delivered.

According to the *PMBOK® Guide*, the communications management plan typically describes the following elements:

- The communication requirements of each stakeholder or stakeholder group
- Purpose for communication
- Frequency of communications, including time frames for distribution
- Name of the person responsible for communicating information
- Format of the communication and method of transmission
- Method for updating the communications management plan
- Glossary of common terms

NOTE

I've included only some of the most important elements of the communications management plan in the list of elements for the communications management plan. I recommend you review the entire list in the *PMBOK® Guide*.

The information that will be shared with stakeholders and the distribution methods are based on the needs of the stakeholders, the project complexity, and the organizational policies. Some communications might be informal—a chat by the coffeemaker, for instance—while other communications are more formal and are kept with the project files for later reference. The communications management plan may also include guidelines for conducting status meetings, team meetings, and so on.

You might consider setting up an intranet site for your project and posting the appropriate project documentation there for the stakeholders to access anytime they want. If you use this method, make sure to document it in the communications management plan and notify your stakeholders when updates or new communication is posted.

Exam Spotlight

For the exam, know that the communications management plan documents how the communication needs of the stakeholders will be met, including the types of information that will be communicated, who will communicate it, who receives the communication, the methods used to communicate, the timing and frequency, the method for updating this plan as the project progresses, the escalation process, and a glossary of common terms.

Real World Scenario

Project Case Study: New Kitchen Heaven Retail Store

After creating the first draft of the project schedule network diagram, you went back to each stakeholder to ask for cost estimates for each of the activities. Ricardo's estimates are shown here with the activities he gave you last time:

1. Procure the T1 connection. This takes 30 to 45 days and will have ongoing costs of $3,000 per month. Procurement costs are covered in the monthly expense.
2. Run Ethernet cable throughout the building. The estimated time to complete is 16 hours at $100 per hour, which was figured using parametric estimating techniques.
3. Purchase the router, switch, server, and rack for the equipment room and four point-of-service terminals. The estimated costs are $17,000.
4. Install the router and test the connection. Testing depends on the T1 installation at demarcation. The time estimate to install is eight hours. Ricardo's staff will perform this activity at an average estimated cost of $78 per hour.
5. Install the switch. Based on past experience, the time estimate to install is two hours. Ricardo's staff will perform this activity at an average estimated cost of $78 per hour.
6. Install the server and test. Based on past experience, the estimate to install is six hours at $84 per hour.
7. The web team will add the new store location and phone number to the lookup function on the Internet site. The time estimate is two hours at $96 per hour.

Jake and Jill have each written similar lists with time and cost estimates. Using this information, you create the activity cost estimates and are careful to document the basis of estimates. The following list includes some of the information you document in the basis of estimates:

- Ricardo's use of parametric estimates for his cost estimates.
- Jake's use of both analogous and parametric estimating techniques.
- Jill's use of reserve analysis to include contingencies for unplanned changes involving vendor deliveries.
- Assumptions made about vendor deliveries and availability of the T1 and assumptions made regarding when lease payments begin.
- The range of possible estimates is stated as plus or minus 10%.

You also document the cost performance baseline and project funding requirements. Since this project will occur fairly quickly, there are only two funding requirement periods needed.

The communications management plan is also complete, and you've asked the key stakeholder to review it before posting it to the intranet site for the project. You want to make certain you've identified stakeholder communication needs, the method of communication, and the frequency with which they will occur.

Project Case Study Checklist

The main topics discussed in the case study are as follows:

- Estimate Costs
- Determine Budget
  - Cost aggregation
  - Reserve analysis
  - Expert judgment
  - Parametric estimates
  - Cost performance baseline
  - Project funding requirements
- Plan Communications
  - Determine effective and efficient communications
  - Review stakeholder register and stakeholder management strategy
  - Communications requirements analysis
  - Communication technology
  - Communication models
  - Communication methods
- Communications management plan
  - Stakeholder needs
  - Format and language for information
  - Time frame and frequency of communication
  - Person responsible for communication
  - Methods for communicating
  - Glossary of terms

Understanding How This Applies to Your Next Project

Estimate Costs is something I have to do rather early in the project because of our long procurement cycle. The way our process works, I must have an estimated cost for the project before I can request funding. If funding is approved, the project is approved. If I'm not awarded funding, the project dies and we move on to the next one.

I rely on expert judgment and parametric estimating techniques to determine activity and total project costs. I often engage vendors and my own project team to help determine the costs. When I have a large project that must go out for bid, I have a well-defined scope and some idea of schedule dates and overall costs, but I won't complete the schedule until after the contract is awarded. In an ideal world, I would prefer to create the schedule prior to determining cost estimates and budgets…but we don't live in an ideal world and sometimes Planning processes have to be performed out of order.

The authorized project budget becomes one of the key measurements of project success. In a later chapter we'll talk about monitoring the budget to determine whether we're tracking to our estimates.

The communications management plan is a must-have for every project. I can't stress enough how often I've seen the root cause of project issues end up being communication problems. Never assume keeping the stakeholders informed is an easy job. Even if you know the stakeholders well, always create a communication plan. Document how you'll communicate status, baseline information, risks, and deliverables acceptance. That way there's no question as to how information will be relayed, who's going to receive it, or when it will be delivered.

Summary

The Estimate Costs process determines how much the project resources will cost, and these costs are usually stated in monetary amounts. Some of the techniques used specifically for estimating costs are analogous estimating, parametric estimating, bottom-up estimating, three-point estimates, and reserve analysis. You can also use bottom-up estimating for total project cost estimates. This involves estimating the cost of each activity and then rolling these up to come up with a total work package cost. The output of this process is the activity cost estimates and the basis of estimates that details all the support information related to the estimates.

The tools and techniques of the Determine Budget process include cost aggregation, reserve analysis, expert judgment, historical relationships, and funding limit reconciliation. These tools together help you produce the final, authorized project budget known as the cost performance baseline, which is an output of this process. You will use the cost performance baseline throughout the remainder of the project to measure project expenditures, variances, and project performance. The cost performance baseline is graphically displayed as an S curve.

The cost performance baseline is also known as a performance measurement baseline (PMB) when you're calculating earned value management formulas. PMBs are management controls that should change only infrequently. Examples of the performance measurement baselines you've looked at so far are the scope, schedule, and cost baselines. The completed project plan itself also becomes a baseline. If changes in scope or schedule do occur after Planning is complete, you should go through a formalized process (which I'll cover in Chapter 10, "Measuring and Controlling Project Performance") to implement the changes.

The purpose of the communications management plan is to determine and document the communication needs of the stakeholders by defining the types of information needed, the format for communicating the information, how often it's distributed, and who prepares it. This plan is a subsidiary plan of the project management plan.

Exam Essentials

Be able to identify and describe the primary output of the Estimate Costs process. The primary output of Estimate Costs is activity cost estimates. These estimates are quantitative amounts—usually stated in monetary units—that reflect the cost of the resources needed to complete the project activities.

Be able to identify the tools and techniques of the Estimate Costs process. The tools and techniques of Estimate Costs are expert judgment, analogous estimating, parametric estimating, bottom-up estimating, three-point estimates, reserve analysis, cost of quality, project management estimating software, and vendor bid analysis.

Be able to identify additional general management techniques that can be used in the Project Cost Management Knowledge Area. Some of the general management techniques that can be used in this Knowledge Area are return on investment, discounted cash flow, and payback analysis.

Be able to identify the tools and techniques of the Determine Budget process. The tools and techniques of Determine Budget are cost aggregation, reserve analysis, expert judgment, historical relationships, and funding limit reconciliation.

Be able to describe the cost performance baseline. The cost performance baseline is the authorized, time-phased cost of the project when using budget-at-completion calculations. The cost performance baseline is displayed as an S curve.

Be able to describe project funding requirements. Project funding requirements are an output of the Determine Budget process. They detail the funding requirements needed on the project by time period (monthly, quarterly, annually).

Be able to describe the purpose of the communications management plan. The communications management plan determines the communication needs of the stakeholders. It documents what information will be distributed, how it will be distributed, to whom, and the timing of the distribution.

Key Terms

Here's a list of the processes from the Planning process group we talked about in this chapter that you'll need to help bring about a successful project:

Estimate Costs

Determine Budget

Plan Communications

Here is a list of some of the terms you came across in this chapter:

chart of accounts

communications management plan

control account

cost of quality

cost performance baseline

lines of communication

time-phased budget

Review Questions

1. All of the following are true regarding the Project Cost Management Knowledge Area processes except for which one? (Choose the least correct answer.)

   A. The primary concern of the Project Cost Management Knowledge Area is determining the amount of resources needed to complete project activities.

   B. The Estimate Costs and Determine Budget processes can be combined into one process for small projects.

   C. The Estimate Cost process is closely linked with the Estimate Activity Resources process.

   D. General management techniques such as ROI, discounted cash flow, and payback analysis can be used to help derive cost estimates.

2. This document is used to establish the criteria for planning, estimating, budgeting, and controlling costs.

   A. Cost performance baseline

   B. Performance management baseline

   C. Project funding requirements

   D. Cost management plan

3. You are a project manager working for iTrim Central and you're preparing your cost management plan. You know that all of the following are true regarding this plan except for which one?

   A. The WBS provides the framework for this plan.

   B. Units of measure should be described in the plan usually as hours, days, weeks, or lump sum.

   C. This plan is a subsidiary of the project management plan.

   D. Control thresholds should be described in the plan as to how estimates will adhere to rounding ($100 or $1000 and so on).

4. You are a project manager working for iTrim Central. Your organization has developed a new dieting technique that is sure to be the next craze. One of the deliverables of your feasibility study was an analysis of the potential financial performance of this new product and your executives are very pleased with the numbers. You will be working with several vendors to produce products, marketing campaigns, and software that will track customers' progress with the new techniques. For purposes of performing earned value measurements for project costs, you are going to place which of the following in the WBS?

   A. Chart of accounts

   B. Code of accounts

   C. Control account

   D. Reserve account

5. All of the following are inputs of the Estimate Costs process except for which one?

   A. Resource calendars

   B. Scope baseline

   C. Project schedule

   D. Human resource plan

6. You want to improve your activity cost estimates by taking into account estimation uncertainty and risk. Which of the following tools and techniques will you use?

   A. Analogous estimates

   B. Three-point estimates

   C. Parametric estimates

   D. Bottom-up estimates

7. You have received estimates for activity costs associated with one work package of the WBS. Additional contingencies have been added to the estimates to account for cost uncertainty. Which of the following tools and techniques of Estimate Costs does this describe?

   A. Reserve analysis

   B. Three-point estimates

   C. Vendor bid analysis

   D. Analogous estimates

8. You have received the following estimates for a complex activity that is critical to the success of your project. The most likely estimate is $42, the optimistic estimate is $35, and the pessimistic estimate is $54. What is the expected activity cost of this activity (rounded to the nearest dollar)?

   A. 49

   B. 39

   C. 43

   D. 41

9. You are the project manager for a custom home-building construction company. You are working on the model home project for the upcoming Show Homes Tour. The model home includes Internet connections in every room, talking appliances, and wiring for home theaters. You are working on the cost performance baseline for this project. All of the following statements are true except which one?

   A. This process aggregates the estimated costs of project activities, including risks and contingency reserves.

   B. The cost performance baseline will be used to measure variances and future project performance.

   C. This process assigns cost estimates for expected future period operating costs.

   D. The cost performance baseline is the time-phased budget at completion for the project.

10. Your project sponsor has requested a cost estimate for the project. She would like the cost estimate to be as accurate as possible because this might be her one and only chance to secure the budget for this project because of recent cuts in special projects. You decide to use ____________.

    A. analogous estimating techniques

    B. bottom-up estimating techniques

    C. top-down estimating techniques

    D. expert judgment techniques

11. You are the project manager for a custom home-building construction company. You are working on the model home project for the upcoming Show Homes Tour. The model home includes Internet connections in every room, talking appliances, and wiring for home theaters. You are working on the Determine Budget process. All of the following statements are true except which one?

    A. You document the funding limit reconciliation to include a contingency for unplanned risks.

    B. You discover that updates are needed to the risk register as a result of performing this process.

    C. You document that funding requirements are based on a quarterly basis and are derived from the cost baseline.

    D. The performance measurement baseline will be used to perform earned value management calculations.

12. Which of the following is displayed as an S curve?

    A. Funding requirements

    B. Cost performance baseline

    C. Cost estimates

    D. Expenditures to date

13. All of the following are tools and techniques of the Determine Budget process except for which one?

    A. Reserve analysis

    B. Expert judgment

    C. Historical relationships

    D. Cost of quality

14. Your project sponsor has requested a cost estimate for the project on which you're working. This project is similar in scope to a project you worked on last year. She would like to get the cost estimates as soon as possible. Accuracy is not her primary concern right now. She needs a ballpark figure by tomorrow. You decide to use ________.

A. analogous estimating techniques

B. bottom-up estimating techniques

C. parametric estimating techniques

D. three-point estimating techniques

15. You have eight key stakeholders to communicate with on your project. Which of the following is true?

A. There are 36 channels of communication, and this should be a consideration when using the communications technology tool and technique.

B. There are 28 channels of communication, and this should be a consideration when using the communications requirements analysis tool and technique.

C. There are 28 channels of communication, and this should be a consideration when using the communications technology tool and technique.

D. There are 36 channels of communication, and this should be a consideration when using the communications requirements analysis tool and technique.

16. All of the following are true regarding Plan Communications except for which one?

A. The communications management plan is a subsidiary plan of the project management plan.

B. This process should be completed as early in the project as possible.

C. It's tightly linked with enterprise environmental factors and all organization process assets are used as inputs for this process.

D. Communications requirements analysis, communication technology, communication methods, and expert judgment are tools and techniques of this process.

17. You are preparing your communications management plan and know that all of the following are true except for which one? (Choose the least correct response.)

A. Encode means to translate thoughts or ideas so they can be understood by others.

B. The medium is how the message will be conveyed.

C. Acknowledgment means the receiver has received and agrees with the message.

D. Encoding and decoding are the responsibility of both the sender and receiver.

18. This ensures that information is distributed but does not acknowledge or certify that it was understood by intended receiver(s).

A. Push communication

B. Interactive communication

C. Medium

D. Message and feedback message

19. You need to communicate information in a multidirectional fashion with several stakeholders. Which of the following is true?

A. This describes push communication, which is a communication model.

B. This describes interactive communication, which is a communication method.

C. This describes communication requirements analysis, which is a communication model.

D. This describes pull communication, which is a communication method.

20. Communication technology takes into account all of the following factors that can affect the project except for which one?

A. Urgency of the need for information

B. Project environment

C. Reasons for the distribution of information

D. Duration of the project

Answers to Review Questions

1. A. Determining the cost of resources (not the amount) to complete all the activities for the project is the primary concern of the Project Cost Management Knowledge Area.

2. D. The cost management plan is used to establish the criteria for planning, estimating, budgeting, and controlling costs.

3. D. Control thresholds are variance thresholds (typically stated as a percentage of deviation from the baseline) used for monitoring cost performance.

4. C. A control account can be placed at any level of the WBS and is used for earned value measurement calculations regarding project costs.

5. A. The inputs of Estimate Costs are scope baseline, project schedule, human resource plan, risk register, enterprise environmental factors, and organizational process assets.

6. B. Three-point estimates can improve activity cost estimates because they factor in estimation uncertainty and risk.

7. A. Reserve analysis accounts for cost uncertainty by including a contingency reserve, usually expressed as a percentage of the estimated cost.

8. C. The expected activity cost is calculated this way: (4 * most likely + optimistic + pessimistic) / 6. Therefore, the answer is (4 * 42 + 35 + 54) / 6 = 43.

9. C. Future period operating costs are considered ongoing costs and are not part of project costs.

10. B. Bottom-up techniques are the most time consuming and generally the most accurate estimates you can use. With bottom-up estimating, each work item is estimated and rolled up to a project total.

11. A. Funding limit reconciliation concerns reconciling the funds to be spent on the project with funding limits placed on the funding commitments for the project.

12. B. The cost performance baseline is displayed as an S curve because of the way project spending occurs. Spending begins slowly, picks up speed until the spending peak is reached, and then tapers off as the project winds down.

13. D. Cost of quality is a tool and technique of Estimate Costs. The tools and techniques of Determine Budget are cost aggregation, reserve analysis, expert judgment, historical relationships, and funding limit reconciliation.

14. A. Analogous—or top-down—estimating techniques are a form of expert judgment. Since this project is similar to another recent project, you can use the cost estimates from the previous project to help you quickly determine estimates for the current project.

15. B. There are 28 channels of communication, which is considered when using the communications requirements analysis tool and technique.

16. D. Communications requirements analysis, communication technology, communication models, and communication methods are the tools and techniques of the Plan Communications process.

17. C. Acknowledgment means the receiver has received the message but does not mean they agree with the message.

18. A. Push communication assures that information is distributed to specific recipients but does not certify that it was understood by the intended recipients.

19. B. This describes interactive communication. It is a communication method, which is a tool and technique of Plan Communications.

20. C. Reasons for the distribution of information belong in the communications management plan.

Chapter 6

Risk Planning

THE PMP® EXAM CONTENT FROM THE PLANNING THE PROJECT PERFORMANCE DOMAIN COVERED IN THIS CHAPTER INCLUDES THE FOLLOWING:

- ✓ **Identify Risks and Define Risk Strategies**

Risk is evident in everything we do. When it comes to project management, understanding risk and knowing how to minimize its impacts (or take full advantage of its opportunities) on your project are essential for success. This entire chapter is dedicated to project risk. Five of the six risk processes, all contained in the Risk Management Knowledge Area, fall in the Planning process group. I'll cover Plan Risk Management, Identify Risks, Perform Qualitative Risk Analysis, Perform Quantitative Risk Analysis, and Plan Risk Responses in this chapter. I'll follow up with the last risk process, Monitor and Control Risks, in Chapter 10, "Measuring and Controlling Project Performance."

Hold on to your hats! I'm going to cover a lot of material in this chapter, but it will go fast, I promise.

Planning for Risks

Every one of us takes risks on a daily basis. Just getting out of bed in the morning is a risk. You might stub your toe in the dark on the way to the light switch or trip over the dog and break a leg. These events don't usually happen, but the possibility exists. The same is true for your project. Risk exists on all projects, and the potential that a particular risk will occur depends on the nature of the risk.

Risk, like most of the elements of the other Planning processes, changes as the project progresses and should be monitored throughout the project. As you get close to a risk event, that's the time to reassess your original assumptions about the risk and your plans to deal with the risk and to make any adjustments as required.

Not all risks are bad. Risks can present future opportunities as well as future threats to a project. They may occur due to one reason or several reasons, and they may have multiple impacts. All risks have causes, and if the risk event occurs during a project, there are consequences. Those consequences will likely impact one or more of the project objectives, and you'll need to know whether the consequences have positive or negative impacts.

Risk is, after all, uncertainty. The more you know about risks and their impacts beforehand, the better equipped you are to handle a risk when it occurs. The processes that involve risk, probably more than any other project Planning process, concern balance. You want to find that point where you and the stakeholders are comfortable with the risk based on the benefits you can potentially gain. In a nutshell, you're balancing the action of taking a risk against avoiding the consequences or impacts of a risk. The rest of this chapter will deal with finding out what risk events might occur (and how to deal with those risks that are unknown), determining an organization's tolerance for risk taking, and developing action plans for those risks you've determined have hefty impacts. The first step is performing the Plan Risk Management process. Here, you determine the approach you'll use for risk management activities and document your plans for them in a risk management plan. You'll look at that process now.

Planning Your Risk Management

Risks come about for many reasons. Some are internal to the project, and some are external. The project environment, the planning process, the project management process, inadequate resources, and so on can all contribute to risk. Some risks you'll know about in advance and plan for during this process; others risk events will occur unannounced during the project. The *Plan Risk Management* process determines how you'll plan for risks on your project.

> **Exam Spotlight**
>
> The *PMBOK® Guide* states that the Plan Risk Management process is the foundation for all the Risk processes that follow. The risk management plan assures that the appropriate amount of resources and the appropriate time are dedicated to risk management. "Appropriate" is determined based on the levels, the importance, and the types of risks. The most important function the risk management plan serves is that it's an agreed-upon baseline for evaluating project risk.

To document the risk management plan, you need to gather some inputs that will help you determine your organization's risk policies and tolerance for risk. You'll look at those inputs next.

Plan Risk Management Inputs

Risks associated with a project generally concern four project objectives—time, cost, scope, and quality—or any combination of the four. As you might have guessed, the project scope statement is an input to this process since it describes your project deliverables. The inputs of this process are as follows:

- Project scope statement
- Cost management plan
- Schedule management plan
- Communications management plan
- Enterprise environmental factors
- Organizational process assets

One of the key elements of the enterprise environmental factors to consider as in input in this process is the *risk tolerance* levels of the organization and the stakeholders. Risk tolerance is that balance I talked about earlier where stakeholders are comfortable taking a risk because the benefits to be gained outweigh what could be lost—or just the opposite. They will avoid taking a risk because the cost or impact is too great given the amount of benefit that can be derived. Here's an example to describe risk tolerance: Suppose you're a 275-pound brute who's surrounded by three bodyguards of equal proportion everywhere you go. Chances are, walking down a dark alley in the middle of the night doesn't faze you in the least. That means your risk tolerance for this activity is high. However, if you're a petite 90-pounder without benefit of bodyguards or karate lessons, performing this same activity might give you cause for concern. Your risk tolerance is low, meaning you wouldn't likely do this activity. The higher your tolerance for risk, the more you're willing to take on risk and its consequences.

NOTE

Organizations and stakeholders, as well as individuals, all have different tolerances for risk. One organization might believe that the risk of a potential 7 percent cost overrun is high, while another might think it's low. However, either one of these organizations might decide to accept the risk if it believes the risk is in balance with the potential rewards. It's important for the project manager to understand the tolerance level that the organization and the stakeholders have for risk before evaluating and ranking risk.

Remember that organizational process assets include policies and guidelines that might already exist in the organization. Your organization's risk categories, risk statement formats, and risk templates should be considered when planning for risks. Defined roles and responsibilities and the authority levels the stakeholders and project manager have for making decisions regarding risk planning should also be considered when developing the risk management plan.

The project scope statement, as mentioned earlier, contains the project deliverables. This is the first place you'll start looking when identifying risks and it should be considered when determining the process you'll use to evaluate risks. The risk management plan (the only output of this process) will become part of the project management plan; therefore, other project management processes and guidelines should be considered when performing this process so that the risk management plan is in line with the overall direction and management of the project.

Tools and Techniques for Plan Risk Management

The Plan Risk Management process has only one tool and technique: planning meetings and analysis. The purpose of these meetings, which are held with project team members, stakeholders, functional managers, and others who might have involvement in the risk management process, is to contribute to the risk management plan. During these meetings, the fundamental plans for performing risk management activities will be discussed and determined and then documented in the risk management plan.

The key outcomes of performing these planning meetings are as follows:

- Risk cost elements are developed for inclusion in the project budget.
- Schedule activities associated with risk are developed for inclusion in the project schedule.
- Risk responsibilities are assigned.
- The risk contingency reserve process is established or reviewed.
- Templates for risk categories are defined or modified for this project.
- Definitions of terms (*probability*, *impact*, *risk types*, *risk levels*, and so on) are developed and documented.
- The probability and impact matrix is defined or modified for this project.

NOTE

I'll discuss risk responsibilities, define the terms associated with risk management, and help you construct your own probability and impact matrix in the remaining sections of this chapter.

Real World Scenario

Do We Need a Risk Management Plan?

Julia is the project manager for a small project her department is undertaking. The project objective is to give customers the ability to download videos of the properties her organization has listed for lease. Two programmers from the information technology department will be working on the updates to the website, programming the links, and so on. The project sponsor wants to fast track this project. She'd like to skip most of the Planning processes, and she sees no need for a risk management plan. Julia explains to the sponsor that the risk management plan for a project this size might be only a paragraph or two long. She emphasizes the importance of documenting how they'll identify risks, how they'll quantify them, and how they'll monitor the risks as the project progresses. Julia has project management experience on projects of all sizes and knows first-hand that ignoring this step could bring some unexpected surprises to the sponsor later in the project. She explains a bad past experience where this step was ignored and then assures the sponsor they can probably agree to the plan, identify and quantify the risks, and determine response plans in an hour and a half or less. The sponsor now understands the issues and agrees to the meeting.

Ultimately, your goal for this process concerns documenting the risk management plan (the output of this process). This document is the basis for understanding the remaining risk processes. Since the risk management plan encompasses a wealth of information, I've given this topic its own section. Let's get to it.

Creating the Risk Management Plan

The purpose of the Plan Risk Management process is to create a *risk management plan*, which describes how you will define, monitor, and control risks throughout the project. The risk management plan is a subsidiary of the project management plan, and it's the only output of this process.

The risk management plan details how risk management processes (including Identify Risks, Perform Qualitative Risk Analysis, Perform Quantitative Risk Analysis, Plan Risk Responses, and Monitor and Control Risks) will be implemented, monitored, and controlled throughout the life of the project. It details how you will manage risks but does not attempt to define responses to individual risks.

NOTE I'll talk about how to develop the risk response plans in the section "Developing a Risk Response Plan" later in this chapter.

According to the *PMBOK® Guide*, the risk management plan should include the following elements:

- Methodology
- Roles and responsibilities
- Budgeting
- Timing
- Risk categories
- Definitions of risk probability and impact
- Probability and impact matrix
- Revised stakeholder tolerances
- Reporting formats
- Tracking

Exam Spotlight

It's important to spend time developing the risk management plan because it's an input to every other risk-planning process and enhances the probability of risk management success.

You'll take a look at most of these elements next. However, risk categories, probability and impact, and probability and impact matrix are pretty meaty topics, so I'll cover those in their own sections following this one.

Methodology Methodology is a description of how you'll perform risk management, including elements such as methods, tools, and where you might find risk data that you can use in the later processes.

Roles and responsibilities Roles and responsibilities describe the people who are responsible for managing the identified risks and their responses and for each type of activity identified in the risk management plan. These risk teams might not be the same as the project team. Risk analysis should be unbiased, which might not be possible when project team members are involved.

Budgeting The budget for risk management is included in the plan as well. In this section, you'll assign resources and estimate the costs of risk management and its methods. These costs are then included in the project cost baseline.

Timing Timing documents the timing of the risk management processes (including when and how often they'll be performed on the project) and includes the activities associated with risk management in the project schedule.

Revised stakeholder tolerances This is just as it implies. As you proceed through the risk management processes, you might find that risk tolerances will change. Document those new tolerance levels in the risk management plan.

Reporting formats Reporting formats describe the content of the risk register and the format of this document. (I'll talk more about the risk register later in this chapter.) Reporting formats also detail how risk management information will be maintained, updated, analyzed, and reported to project participants.

Tracking This includes a description of how you'll document the history of the risk activities for the current project and how the risk processes will be audited. You can reference this information when you're performing risk-planning processes later in the current project or on future projects. This information is also helpful for lessons learned, which I'll cover in Chapter 11, "Controlling Work Results."

Risk Categories

Risk categories are a way to systematically identify risks and provide a foundation for understanding. When determining and identifying risks, the use of risk categories helps improve the process by giving everyone involved a common language or basis for describing risk.

Risk categories should be identified during this process and documented in the risk management plan. These categories will assist you in making sure the next process, Identify Risks, is performed effectively and produces a quality output. The following list includes some examples of the categories you might consider during this process (or modify based on previous project information):

- Technical, quality, or performance risks
- Project management risks
- Organizational risks
- External risks

You can go about describing categories of risk in a couple of ways. One way is simply listing them. You could, and should, review prior projects for risk categories and then tailor them for this project.

You could also construct a *risk breakdown structure (RBS)*, which lists the categories and subcategories. Figure 6.1 shows a sample of an RBS.

FIGURE 6.1 Risk breakdown structure

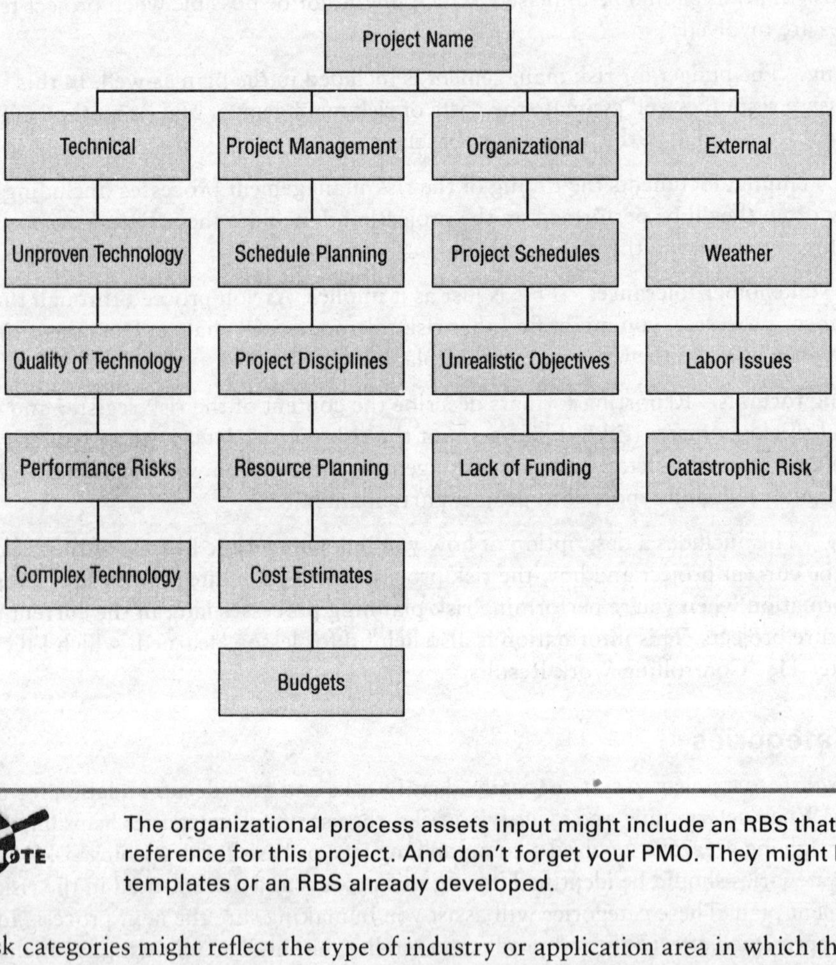

NOTE The organizational process assets input might include an RBS that you can reference for this project. And don't forget your PMO. They might have templates or an RBS already developed.

Risk categories might reflect the type of industry or application area in which the project exists. For example, information technology projects will likely have many risks that fall into the technical category, whereas construction projects might be more subject to risks that fall into the external risks category. The categories do not have to be industry specific, however. Keep in mind that project management, for example, is a risk for every project in every industry. You can find a description of each of the categories next:

Technical/quality/performance risks Technical, quality, or performance risks include risks associated with unproven technology, complex technology, or changes to technology anticipated during the course of the project. Performance risks might include unrealistic performance goals. Perhaps one of the project deliverables concerns a component manufactured to specific performance standards that have never been achieved. That's a performance risk.

Project management risks The project management risk category includes improper schedule and resource planning, poor project planning, and improper or poor project management disciplines or methodologies.

Organizational risks The organizational risk category can include resource conflicts because of multiple projects occurring at the same time in the organization; scope, time, and cost objectives that are unrealistic given the organization's resources or structure; and lack of funding for the project or diverting funds from this project to other projects.

External risks The external risk category includes those aspects that are external to the project, such as new laws or regulations, labor issues, weather, changes in ownership, and foreign policy for projects performed in other countries. Catastrophic risks—known as *force majeure*—are usually outside the scope of Plan Risk Management and instead require disaster recovery techniques. Force majeure includes events such as earthquakes, meteorites, volcanoes, floods, civil unrest, terrorism, and so on.

Defining Probability and Impact

When you're writing the risk management plan, you'll want to document the definitions for probability and impact as they relate to potential negative risk events and their impacts on the four project objectives. Probability describes the potential for the risk event occurring, while impact describes the effects or consequences the project will experience if the risk event occurs. This definition can be sophisticated or simple. For example, you might use numeric values to define probability and impact or simply assign a high-medium-low rating to each risk. What's important to note now is that you don't use these probability and impact definitions here. You use these definitions later in the Perform Qualitative Risk Analysis process. (I'll talk in depth about probability and impact in the section "Analyzing Risks Using Qualitative Techniques" later in this chapter.) But you should define and document them here in the risk management plan.

Probability and Impact Matrix

A *probability and impact matrix* prioritizes the combination of probability and impact scores and helps you determine which risks need detailed risk response plans. For example, a risk event with a high probability of occurring and a high impact will likely need a response plan. This matrix is typically defined by the organization, but if you don't have one, you'll need to develop this now—during your planning meeting and analysis (the tool and technique of this process). You'll use this matrix in the Perform Qualitative Risk Analysis process, and I'll talk more in depth about it in the section "Analyzing Risks Using Qualitative Techniques" later in this chapter. Again, you want to define (or modify) and document the probability and impact matrix in the risk management plan.

NOTE The key point about this process is that you'll define what the probability and impact tools look like now during Plan Risk Management so that the team has an agreed-upon basis for evaluating the identified risks later during the Perform Qualitative Risk Analysis process.

To recap, the steps associated with these last few elements of the risk management plan are as follows:

1. Define the risk categories (these will assist the risk team in the Identify Risks process).
2. Determine how probability and impact will be defined (to be used in the Perform Qualitative Risk Analysis process).
3. Develop or modify the probability and impact matrix (to be used in the Perform Qualitative Risk Analysis process).

Doing all these steps, together with the other elements of the risk management plan, gives you and the risk management team a common understanding for evaluating risks throughout the remainder of the project.

Identifying Potential Risk

The *Identify Risks* process involves identifying all the risks that might impact the project, documenting them, and documenting their characteristics. Identify Risks is an iterative process that continually builds on itself. As you progress through the project, more risks might present themselves. Once you've identified or discovered a potential new risk, you should analyze it to determine whether a response plan is needed. You can see that the risk management cycle starts again with Identify Risks and progresses through the remaining risk processes to determine what to do about them.

You can include several groups of folks to help identify risks, including project team members, risk team members, stakeholders, subject matter experts, users of the final product or service, and anyone else who you think might help in the process. Perhaps in the first round of Identify Risks you could include just the project team and subject matter experts and then bring in the stakeholders or risk management team to further flesh out risks during the second round of identification. Risk events can occur at any time during the project, and all project participants should be encouraged to continually watch for and report potential risk events.

NOTE I'll talk more about the techniques you can use to identify risks in the section "Tools and Techniques for Identify Risk."

Risks might or might not adversely affect the project. Some risks have positive consequences, while others have negative consequences. However, you should identify all risk events and their consequences. Here's a partial list to get you thinking about where risk might be found:

- Budgets/funding
- Schedules
- Scope or requirements changes
- Project plan
- Project management processes
- Technical issues
- Personnel issues
- Hardware
- Contracts
- Political concerns
- Business risk
- Legal risk
- Environmental risk
- Management risk

This is by no means an exhaustive list. Remember that risk is uncertainty, and realize that risk (uncertainty) is lurking almost anywhere on your project. It's your job to discover as many of the potential risks as possible using the tools and techniques of this process and to document these risks.

Identify Risks Inputs

The inputs to the Identify Risks process are as follows:

- Risk management plan
- Activity cost estimates
- Activity duration estimates
- Scope baseline
- Stakeholder register
- Cost management plan
- Schedule management plan
- Quality management plan
- Project documents
- Enterprise environmental factors
- Organizational process assets

We have covered each of these inputs previously, with the exception of the quality management plan. We'll talk about that in Chapter 7, "Planning Project Resources." For purposes of the Identify Risk process, understand that the quality management process, identified in the quality management plan, has the potential to produce or prevent risks itself. We'll touch on a few of the key elements of some of these other inputs also.

You should pay particular attention to the roles and responsibilities section of the risk management plan and the budget and schedule for risk activities. Don't forget to examine the categories of risks as well. This is a great place to start when you get the team together and begin brainstorming your list of risks.

The project scope statement, part of the scope baseline, contains a list of project assumptions. You'll recall that assumptions are things believed to be true. It's imperative during the risk-planning stages of your project and throughout the work of the project to revisit and revalidate your project assumptions. At the time you recorded an assumption about vendor deliveries, for example, the vendor had a great track record and never missed a date. Months later on the project, that vendor merges with one of its competitors. Now you'll need to reexamine your assumptions about delivery times and determine whether the assumption is still valid or whether you have a risk on your hands.

The project management plan contains several other management plans (such as schedule, quality, and cost) that can be helpful sources also when identifying risks. You should also consider network diagrams, baselines, work performance reports, and other project information during this process.

The enterprise environmental factors input concerns aspects from outside the project that might help you determine or influence project outcomes. Be certain to check for industry information (commercial databases, checklists, benchmarking studies, and so on) or academic research that might exist for your application areas regarding risk information.

As always, don't forget about historical information such as previous project experiences via the project files. Project team knowledge is another form of historical information.

NOTE

Although the *PMBOK® Guide* doesn't mention it, I've found that other elements of your project are helpful when identifying risk, such as the work breakdown structure (WBS), the staffing management plan, project staff assignments, and resource availability. In practice, you should examine the outputs of most of the Planning processes when attempting to identify risks.

Tools and Techniques for Identify Risks

The Identify Risks process is undertaken using seven tools and techniques:

- Documentation reviews
- Information-gathering techniques
- Checklist analysis

- Assumptions analysis
- Diagramming techniques
- SWOT analysis
- Expert judgment

You'll learn more about each of these in the following sections.

Documentation Reviews

Documentation reviews involve reviewing project plans, assumptions, and historical information from previous projects from both a total project perspective and an individual deliverables and activities level. This review helps the project team identify risks associated with the project objectives. Pay attention to the quality of the plans (is the content complete, or does it seem to be lacking detail?) and the consistency between plans. An exceptionally documented schedule is great, but if the budget isn't as well documented, you might have some potential risks.

Information Gathering

Information gathering encompasses several techniques, including brainstorming, the Delphi technique, interviewing, and root cause identification. The goal of these techniques is to end up with a comprehensive list of risks at the end of the meeting. Let's take a quick look at each of these techniques.

Brainstorming

Brainstorming is probably the most often used technique of the Identify Risks process. You've probably used this technique many times for many purposes. Brainstorming involves getting subject matter experts, team members, risk management team members, and anyone else who might benefit the process in a room and asking them to start identifying possible risk events. The trick here is that one person's idea might spawn another idea, and so on so that by the end of the session you've identified all the possible risks. The facilitator could start the group off by going through the categories of risks to get everyone thinking in the right direction.

Nominal Group Technique

This technique is mentioned in the brainstorming tool and technique in the *PMBOK® Guide*. The *Nominal Group Technique* is a type of brainstorming or can be conducted as a mass interview technique.

This technique requires the participants to be together in the same room. Each participant has paper and pencil in front of them, and they are asked to write down what risks they think the project faces. Using sticky-backed notes is a good way to do this. Each piece of paper should contain only one risk. The papers are given to the facilitator, who sticks them up to the wall or a white board. The panel is then asked to review all the risks posted on the board; rank them and prioritize them, in writing; and submit the ranking to the facilitator. Once this is done, you should have a complete list of risks.

Delphi Technique

The *Delphi technique* is a lot like brainstorming, only the people participating in the meeting don't necessarily know each other. In fact, the people participating in this technique don't all have to be located in the same place and usually participate anonymously. You can use email to facilitate the Delphi technique easily.

What you do is assemble your experts, from both inside and outside the company, and provide them with a questionnaire to identify potential risks. They in turn send their responses back to you (or to the facilitator of this process). All the responses are organized by content and sent back to the Delphi members for further input, additions, or comments. The participants then send their comments back one more time, and the facilitator compiles a final list of risks.

The Delphi technique is a great tool that allows consensus to be reached quickly. It also helps prevent one person from unduly influencing the others in the group and thus prevents bias in the outcome because the participants are usually anonymous and don't necessarily know how others in the group responded.

Interviewing

Interviews are question-and-answer sessions held with others, including other project managers, subject matter experts, stakeholders, customers, the management team, project team members, and users. These folks provide you with possible risks based on their past experiences with similar projects.

This technique involves interviewing those folks with previous experience on projects similar to yours or those with specialized knowledge or industry expertise. Ask them to tell you about any risks that they've experienced or that they think might happen on your project. Show them the WBS and your list of assumptions to help get them started thinking in the right direction.

Root Cause Identification

Did you ever hear someone say you're looking at the symptoms and not at the problem? That's the idea here. Root cause identification involves digging deeper than the risk itself and looking at the cause of the risk. This helps define the risk more clearly, and it also helps you later when it's time to develop the response plan for the risk.

Exam Spotlight

Not all the techniques listed here are detailed in the *PMBOK® Guide*. Be aware that there might be questions about any of the techniques I've shown here. Understand the difference between the various information-gathering techniques for the exam.

Checklist Analysis

Checklists used during the Identify Risks process are usually developed based on historical information and previous project team experience. If you typically work on projects that are similar in nature, begin to compile a list of risks. You can then convert this to a checklist that will allow you to identify risks on future projects quickly and easily. You can also use the lowest level of the RBS as a checklist. However, don't rely solely on checklists for Identify Risks because you might miss important risks. It isn't possible for a single checklist to be an exhaustive source for all projects. You can improve your checklists at the end of the project by adding the new risks that were identified.

Assumptions Analysis

Assumptions analysis is a matter of validating the assumptions you identified and documented during the course of the project-planning processes. Assumptions should be accurate, complete, and consistent. Examine all your assumptions for these qualities. Assumptions are also used as a jumping-off point to further identify risks.

The important point to note about the project assumptions is that all assumptions are tested against two factors:

- The strength of the assumption or the validity of the assumption
- The consequences that might impact the project if the assumption turns out to be false

All assumptions that turn out to be false should be evaluated and scored just as risks.

Diagramming Techniques

Three types of diagramming techniques are used in Identify Risks: cause-and-effect, system or process flowcharts, and influence diagrams. *Cause-and-effect diagrams* show the relationship between the effects of problems and their causes. This diagram depicts every potential cause and subcause of a problem and the effect that each proposed solution will have on the problem. This diagram is also called a *fishbone diagram* or *Ishikawa diagram* after its developer, Kaoru Ishikawa. Figure 6.2 shows an example cause-and-effect diagram.

FIGURE 6.2 Cause-and-effect diagram

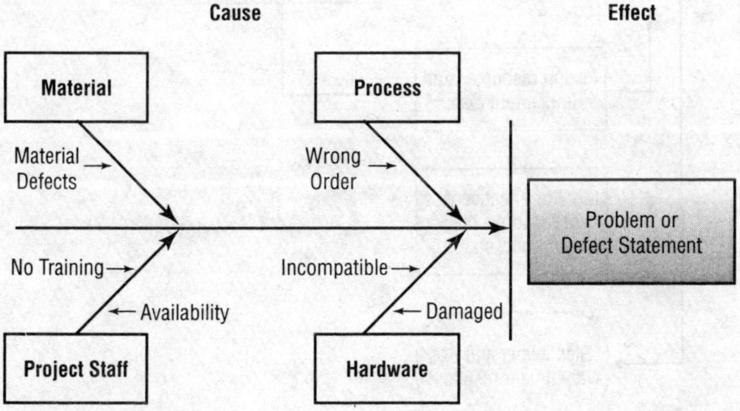

The *system or process flowchart* shows the logical steps needed to accomplish an objective, how the elements of a system relate to each other, and what actions cause what responses. This flowchart is probably the one with which you're most familiar. It's usually constructed with rectangles and parallelograms that step through a logical sequence and allow for "yes" and "no" branches (or some similar type of decision). Figure 6.3 shows a flowchart to help determine whether risk response plans should be developed for the risk (I'll talk about response plans in the section "Developing a Risk Response Plan" later in this chapter).

FIGURE 6.3 Flowchart diagram

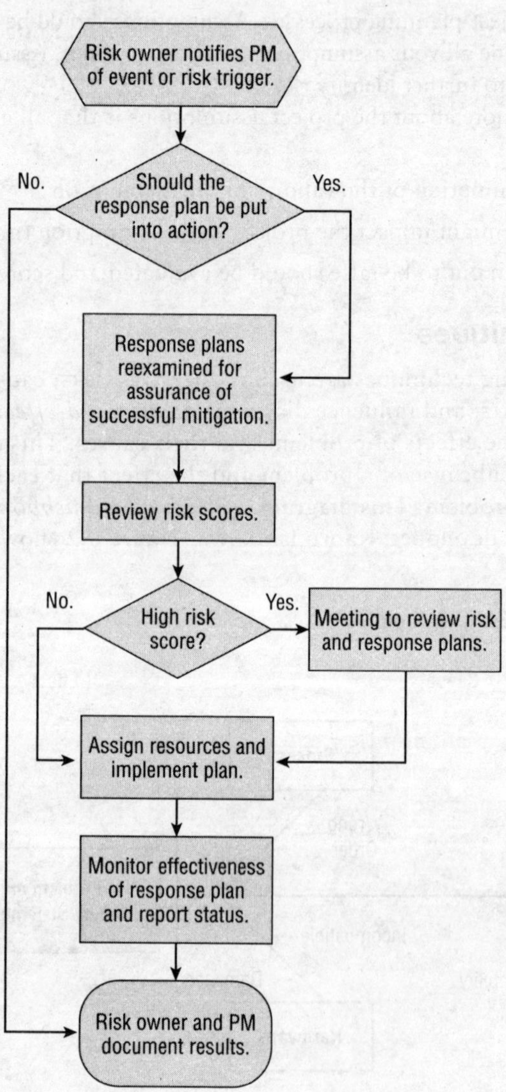

NOTE Cause-and-effect diagrams and system or process flowcharts are used in the Identify Risks process as well as in the Perform Quality Control process.

A third diagramming technique used during Identify Risks is called *influence diagramming.* According to the *PMBOK® Guide*, influence diagrams typically show the causal influences among project variables, the timing or time ordering of events, and the relationships among other project variables and their outcomes. Simply put, they visually depict risks (or decisions), uncertainties or impacts, and how they influence each other. Figure 6.4 shows an influence diagram for a product introduction decision. The weather is a variable that could impact delivery time, and delivery time is a variable that can impact when revenues will occur.

FIGURE 6.4 Influence diagram

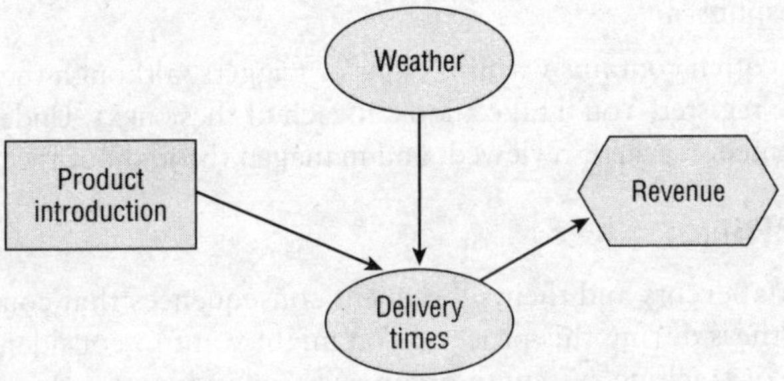

Each of these techniques provides a way for you to help identify project risks. It's important that you identify all the risks early in the process. The better job you do of identifying the project's risks at the Planning stage, the more comprehensive the risk response plan will be. Identify Risks is not an area of project planning that you should skip.

Strengths, Weaknesses, Opportunities, and Threats (SWOT)

Strengths, weaknesses, opportunities, and threats (also known as SWOT analysis) is a technique that examines the project from each of these viewpoints. It also requires examing the project from the viewpoint of the project itself and from project management processes, resources, the organization, and so on to identify risks, including those that are generated internally to the project. Strengths and weaknesses are generally related to issues that are internal to the organization. Strengths examine what your organization does well and what your customers, or the marketplace, view as your strengths. Weaknesses are areas the organization could improve upon. Typically negative risks are associated with the organization's weaknesses and positive risks are associated with its strengths. Opportunities and threats are usually external to the organization. SWOT analysis is sometimes known as internal-external analysis and can be used in combination with brainstorming techniques to help discover and document potential risks.

Expert Judgment

Experts for risk identification purposes can include anyone who has experience working on similar projects, experience working in the business area for which the project was undertaken, or specific industry experience. You should consider any bias your experts may have regarding the project or potential risk events when using this technique.

Identify Risks Outputs

The output of the Identify Risks process is the *risk register*. Everything you've done in this process up to this point will get documented here. The risk register contains the following elements:

- List of identified risks
- List of potential responses

The risk register also often contains warning signs or triggers, although these aren't listed as an official part of the register. You'll take a look at each of these next. Understand that all risks should be documented, tracked, reviewed, and managed throughout the project.

List of Identified Risks

Risks are all the potential events and their subsequent consequences that could occur as identified by you and others during this process. You might want to consider logging your risks in a risk database or tracking system to organize them and keep a close eye on their status. This can easily be done in spreadsheet format or whatever method you choose. List the risks, assign each risk a tracking number, and note the potential cause or event and the potential impact. This list gives you a means to track the risks, their occurrence, and the responses implemented.

List of Potential Responses

You might identify potential responses to risk at the same time you're identifying the risks. Sometimes just identifying the risk will tell you the appropriate response. Document those responses here. You'll refer to them again in the Plan Risk Responses process a little later in this chapter.

A sample risk register is shown in Table 6.1. As you progress through the risk, planning processes and through the project itself, more risks may be identified and more information will become know about the risks. You should update the risk register with new information as it becomes known.

TABLE 6.1 Risk Register

ID	Risk	Trigger	Event	Cause	Impact	Owner	Response Plan

Triggers

Triggers are warning signs or symptoms that a risk event is about to occur. For example, if you've ever suffered from a hay fever attack, you can't mistake the itchy, runny nose and scratchy throat that can come on suddenly and send you into a sneezing frenzy. Signals like this are known as *triggers* and work the same way when determining whether a risk event is about to occur. For example, if you're planning an outdoor gathering and rain clouds start rolling in from the north on the morning of the activity, you probably have a risk event waiting to happen. A key team member hinting about job hunting is a warning sign that the person might be thinking of leaving, which in turn can cause schedule delays, increased costs, and so on. This is another example of a trigger.

Triggers are *not* listed as one of the risk register elements, but in practice this is an appropriate place to list them. You will likely encounter questions on the exam about triggers, so don't say I didn't warn you. Also, throughout the remainder of the project, be on the alert for triggers that might signal that a risk event is about to occur.

Analyzing Risks Using Qualitative Techniques

The *Perform Qualitative Risk Analysis* process involves determining what impact the identified risks will have on the project objectives and the probability they'll occur. It also ranks the risks in priority order according to their effect on the project objectives. This helps the team determine whether Perform Quantitative Risk Analysis should be performed or whether you can skip right to developing response plans. The Perform Qualitative Risk Analysis process also considers risk tolerance levels, especially as they relate to the project constraints (scope, time, cost, and quality) and the time frames of the potential risk events.

The Perform Qualitative Risk Analysis process should be performed throughout the project. This process is the one you'll find you'll use most often when prioritizing project risks because it's fast, relatively easy to perform, and cost effective. The *PMBOK® Guide* notes that you should identify and manage the risk attitudes of those assisting with this process, and if bias is introduced, you should evaluate it and correct it if necessary.

Perform Qualitative Risk Analysis Inputs

The Perform Qualitative Risk Analysis process has four inputs:

- Risk register
- Risk management plan
- Project scope statement
- Organizational process assets

The critical element in this process, as with most of the processes where the risk register is an input, is the list of risks. The risk management plan documented the roles and responsibilities of risk team members, budget and schedule factors for risk activities, the stakeholder risk tolerances, the definitions for probability and impact, and the probability and impact matrix, all of which should be utilized when prioritizing risks. You'll examine probability and impact more closely in the next section, "Tools and Techniques for Perform Qualitative Risk Analysis."

The project scope statement describes the deliverables of the project, and from there you should be able to determine whether you're dealing with a high level of uncertainty or a project that's similar in size and scope to one you've performed before. Projects with high levels of uncertainty or that are more complex than what the team has undertaken before require more diligence during the Perform Qualitative Risk Analysis process.

As with the Identify Risks process, you should examine historical information and lessons learned from past projects as a guide for prioritizing the risks for this project. Risk databases from your industry or application area can be used here as well. These are part of the organizational process assets input.

The real key to this process lies in the tools and techniques you'll use to prioritize risks. Hold on tight because you're going in the deep end.

Tools and Techniques for Perform Qualitative Risk Analysis

The Perform Qualitative Risk Analysis process's tools and techniques are primarily concerned with discovering the probability of a risk event and determining the impact (or consequences) the risk will have if it does occur. The output of this process is a risk register update where you'll document the prioritized risks you've scored using these tools and techniques. All the information you gather regarding risks and probability needs to be as accurate as possible. It's also important that you gather unbiased information so that you don't unintentionally overlook risks with great potential or consequences.

The purpose of this process is to determine risk event probability and risk impact. You'll use the tools and techniques of this process to establish risk scores, which is a way of categorizing the probability and risk impact. The Perform Qualitative Risk Analysis process includes the following tools and techniques:

- Risk probability and impact assessment
- Probability and impact matrix
- Risk data quality assessment
- Risk categorization
- Risk urgency assessment
- Expert judgment

We'll look at each of these tools and techniques next.

Risk Probability and Impact Assessment

This tool and technique assesses the probability that the risk events you've identified will occur, and it determines the effect their impacts have on the project objectives, including time, scope, quality, and cost. Analyzing risks in this way allows you to determine which risks require the most aggressive management. When determining probabilities and impacts, you'll refer to the risk management plan element called "definitions of risk probability and impact."

Probability

Probability is the likelihood that an event will occur. The classic example is flipping a coin. There is a .50 probability of getting heads and a .50 probability of getting tails on the flip. Note that the probability that an event will occur plus the probability that the event will not occur always equals 1.0. In this coin-flipping example, you have a .50 chance that you'll get heads on the flip. Therefore, you have a .50 chance you will not get heads on the flip. The two responses added together equal 1.0. Probability is expressed as a number from 0.0—which means there is no probability of the event occurring—to 1.0—which means there is 100% certainty the risk will occur.

Determining risk probability can be difficult because it's most commonly accomplished using expert judgment. In non-PMP terms, this means you're guessing (or asking other experts to guess) at the probability a risk event will occur. Granted, you're basing your guess on past experiences with similar projects or risk events, but no two risk events (or projects) are ever the same. It's best to fully develop the criteria for determining probability and get as many experts involved as you can. Carefully weigh their responses to come up with the best probability values possible.

Impact

Impact is the amount of pain (or the amount of gain) the risk event poses to the project. The risk *impact scale* can be a relative scale (also known as an ordinal scale) that assigns values such as high-medium-low (or some combination of these) or a numeric scale known as a *cardinal scale*. Cardinal scale values are actual numeric values assigned to the risk impact. Cardinal scales are expressed as values from 0.0 to 1.0 and can be stated in equal (linear) or unequal (nonlinear) increments.

Table 6.2 shows a typical risk impact scale for cost, time, and quality objectives based on a high-high to low-low scale. You'll notice that each of the high-medium-low value combinations on this impact scale have been assigned a cardinal value. I'll use these in the next section when I talk about the probability and impact matrix.

When you're using a high-medium-low scale, it's important that your risk team understands what criteria was used to determine a high score versus a medium or low score and how these should be applied to the project objectives.

TABLE 6.2 Risk Impact Scale

Objectives	Low-Low	Low	Medium	High	High-High
	0.05	0.20	0.40	0.60	0.80

TABLE 6.2 Risk Impact Scale *(continued)*

Objectives	Low-Low	Low	Medium	High	High-High
Cost	No significant impact	Less than 6% increase	7–12% increase	13–18% increase	More than 18% increase
Time	No significant impact	Less than 6% increase	7–12% increase	13–18% increase	More than 18% increase
Quality	No significant impact	Few components impacted	Significant impact requiring customer approval to proceed	Unacceptable quality	Product not usable

Assessing Probability and Impact

The idea behind both probability and impact values is to develop predefined measurements that describe what value to place on a risk event.

Exam Spotlight

For the exam, don't forget that you define probability and impact values during the Plan Risk Management process.

If the risk impact scale has not been previously defined, develop one for the project as early in the Planning processes as possible. You can use any of the techniques I talked about earlier in the section "Tools and Techniques for Identify Risk," such as brainstorming or the Delphi technique, to come up with the values for probability and impact.

During the Perform Qualitative Risk Analysis process, you'll determine and assess probability and impact for every risk identified during the Identify Risks process. You could interview or hold meetings with project team members, subject matter experts, stakeholders, or others to help assess these factors. During this process, you should document not only the probability and impact but also the assumptions your team members used to arrive at these determinations. The next technique—probability and impact matrix—takes the probability and impact values one step further by assigning an overall risk score.

Probability and Impact Matrix

The outcome of a probability and impact matrix is an overall risk rating for each of the project's identified risks. The combination of probability and impact results in a classification usually expressed as high, medium, or low. According to the *PMBOK® Guide*, high risks are considered a red condition, medium risks are considered a yellow condition, and low risks are considered a green condition. This type of ranking is known as an *ordinal scale* because the values are ordered by rank from high to low. (In practice, ordinal values might also include ranking by position. In other words, the risks are listed in order by rank as the first, the second, the third, and so on.)

Exam Spotlight

The *PMBOK® Guide* notes that the probability and impact matrix values are usually set by the organization and are part of the organizational process assets.

Now let's look at an example. You have identified a risk event that could impact project costs, and your experts believe costs could increase by as much as 9 percent. According to the risk impact rating matrix in Table 6.2, this risk carries a medium impact, with a value of 0.40. Hold on to that number because you're going to plug it into the probability impact matrix—along with the probability value—to determine an overall risk value next.

You'll remember from the discussion previously that probability values should be assigned numbers from 0.0 to 1.0. In this example, the team has determined that there is a 0.2 probability of this risk event occurring. The risk impact scale shows a medium or 0.4 impact should the event occur.

Now, to determine whether the combination of the probability and impact of this risk is high, medium, or low, you'll need to check the probability impact matrix. Table 6.3 shows a sample probability and impact matrix.

TABLE 6.3 Sample Probability and Impact Matrix

Probability	Impact Values* Low-Low.05	Low .20	Medium .40	High .60	High-high .80
.8	**.04**	**.16**	***.32***	***.48***	***.64***
.6	**.03**	**.12**	**.24**	***.36***	***.48***
.4	.02	**.08**	**.16**	**.24**	***.32***
.2	.01	.04	.08	**.12**	**.16**

*No formatting = low assignment or green condition; **bold** = medium assignment or yellow condition; ***bold italic*** = high assignment or red condition.

First look at the probability column. Your risk event has a probability of .2. Now follow that row across until you find the column that shows the impact score of .40 (it's the Medium column). According to your probability and impact matrix values, this risk carries an overall score of .08 and falls in the low threshold, so this risk is assigned a low (or green condition) value.

The values assigned to the risks determine how Plan Risk Responses is carried out for the risks later during the risk-planning processes. Obviously, risks with high probability and high impact are going to need further analysis and formal responses. Remember that the values for this matrix (and the probability and impact scales discussed earlier) are determined prior to the start of this process and documented in the risk management plan. Also keep in mind that probability and impact do not have to be assigned the same values as I've done here. You might use 0.8, 0.6, 0.4, and 0.2 for probability, for example, and assign .05, 0.1, .03, 0.5, and 0.7 for impact scales.

Real World Scenario

Screen Scrapers, Inc.

Screen Scrapers is a software-manufacturing company that produces a software product that looks at your mainframe screens, commonly called *green screens*, and converts them to browser-based screens. The browser-based screens look like any other Windows-compatible screens with buttons, scroll bars, and drop-down lists.

Screen Scrapers devised this product for companies that use mainframe programs to update and store data because many of the entry-level workers beginning their careers today are not familiar with green screens. They're cumbersome and difficult to learn, and no consistency exists from screen to screen or from program to program. An F5 key in one program might mean go back one page, while an F5 key in another program might mean clear the screen. New users are easily confused, make a lot of mistakes, and have to write tablets full of notes on how to navigate all the screens.

Your company has purchased the Screen Scraper product and has appointed you the project manager over the installation. This project consists of a lot of issues to address, and you've made great headway. You're now at the Identify Risks and Perform Qualitative Risk Analysis stage. You decide to use the Delphi technique to assist you in identifying risk and assigning probability and impact rankings. Some experts are available in your company to serve on the Delphi panel, as well as some folks in industry organizations you belong to outside the company.

You assemble the group, set up a summary of the project, and send it out via email, requesting responses to your questions about risk. After the first pass, you compile the list of risks as follows (this list is an example and isn't exhaustive because your list will be project specific):

- Vendor viability (will the software company stay in business?)
- Vendor responsiveness with problems after implementation

- Software compatibility risks with existing systems
- Hardware compatibility risk
- Connection to the mainframe risk
- Training IT staff members to maintain the product

You send this list back to the Delphi members and ask them to assign a probability of 0.0 to 1.0 and an impact of high-high, high, medium, low, or low-low to each risk. The Delphi members assign probability and impact based on a probability scale and an impact scale designed by the risk management team. The values of the impact scale are as follows:

- High-high = 0.8
- High = 0.6
- Medium = 0.4
- Low = 0.2
- Low-low = 0.05

The results are compiled to determine the following probability and impact values:

- Vendor viability = .6 probability, high impact
- Vendor responsiveness = .4 probability, medium impact
- Software compatibility = .4 probability, medium impact
- Hardware compatibility = .6 probability, high-high impact
- Mainframe connection = .2 probability, high-high impact
- Training = .2 probability, low-low impact

The probability and impact matrix you used to assign the overall risk scores were derived from the probability and impact matrix shown in the following table.

Based on the probability and impact matrix thresholds, the project risks are assigned the following overall probabilities:

- Vendor viability = high
- Vendor responsiveness = medium
- Software compatibility = medium
- Hardware compatibility = high
- Mainframe connection = medium
- Training = low

TABLE: PI Matrix for Screen Scrapers, Inc.

Probability	Impact Scores*.05	.20	.40	.60	.80
.8	**.04**	**.16**	***.32***	***.48***	***.64***
.6	**.03**	**.12**	**.24**	***.36***	***.48***
.4	.02	**.08**	**.16**	**.24**	***.32***
.2	.01	.04	.08	**.12**	**.16**

*No formatting = low assignment or green condition; **bold** = medium assignment or yellow condition; ***bold italic*** = high assignment or red condition.

Risk Data Quality Assessment

The data quality assessment involves determining the usefulness of the data gathered to evaluate risk. Most important, the data must be unbiased and accurate. You will want to examine elements such as the following when using this tool and technique:

- The quality of the data used
- The availability of data regarding the risks
- How well the risk is understood
- The reliability and integrity of the data
- The accuracy of the data

Low-quality data will render the results from the Perform Qualitative Risk Analysis process almost useless. Spend the time to validate and verify the information you've collected about risks so that your prioritization and analysis is as accurate as it can be. If you find that the quality of the data is questionable, you guessed it—go back and get better data.

Risk Categorizations

This tool and technique is used to determine the effects risk has on the project. You can examine not only the categories of risk determined during the Plan Risk Management process (and described in the RBS) but also the project phase and the WBS to determine the elements of the project that are affected by risk.

Risk Urgency Assessment

Using this tool you'll determine how soon the potential risk events might occur and quickly determine responses for those risk events that could occur soon. You should consider the risk triggers, the time to develop and implement a response, and the overall risk rating when determining how quickly responses are needed.

Expert Judgment

Because this process determines qualitative values, by its very nature you must rely on expert judgment to determine the probability, impact, and other information we've derived so far. The more knowledge and similar experience your experts have, the better your assessments will be. Interviews and facilitated workshops are two techniques you can use in conjunction with expert judgment to perform this process. As with the Identify Risks process, make certain to take into account any bias your experts have and to correct it when necessary.

Ranking Risks in the Risk Register

The goal of the Perform Qualitative Risk Analysis process is to rank the risks and determine which ones need further analysis and, eventually, risk response plans. The output of this process is risk register updates. According to the *PMBOK® Guide*, you'll update the register with the following information:

- Risk ranking (or priority) for the identified risks
- Risks grouped by categories
- Causes of risk
- List of risks requiring near-term responses
- List of risks that need additional analysis and response
- Watch list of low-priority risks
- Trends in qualitative risk analysis results

Each element becomes a new entry in the risk register. For example, risk ranking assigns the risk score or priority you determined using the probability and impact matrix to the list of identified risks previously recorded in the risk register. I discussed the categories and the list of risks requiring near-term responses earlier. Note these in the risk register.

You'll also note those risks that require further analysis (including using the Perform Quantitative Risk Analysis process), you'll create a list of risks that have low risk scores to review periodically, and you should note any trends in Perform Qualitative Risk Analysis that become evident as you perform this process.

Quantifying Risk

The *Perform Quantitative Risk Analysis* process evaluates the impacts of risk prioritized during the Perform Qualitative Risk Analysis process and quantifies risk exposure for the project by assigning numeric probabilities to each risk and their impacts on project objectives. This quantitative approach is accomplished using techniques such as Monte Carlo simulation and decision tree analysis. To paraphrase the *PMBOK® Guide*, the purpose of this process is to perform the following:

- Quantify the project's possible outcomes and probabilities.
- Determine the probability of achieving the project objectives.

- Identify risks that need the most attention by quantifying their contribution to overall project risk.
- Identify realistic and achievable schedule, cost, or scope targets.
- Determine the best project management decisions possible when outcomes are uncertain.

Perform Quantitative Risk Analysis—like Perform Qualitative Risk Analysis—examines each risk and its potential impact on the project objectives. You might choose to use both of these processes to assess all risks or only one of them, depending on the complexity of the project and the organizational policy regarding risk planning. The Perform Quantitative Risk Analysis process can follow either the Identify Risks process or the Perform Qualitative Risk Analysis process. If you do use this process, be certain to repeat it every time the Plan Risk Responses process is performed and as part of the Monitor and Control Risks process so that you can determine if overall project risk has decreased.

I've already covered many of the inputs to the Perform Quantitative Risk Analysis process in previous sections of this chapter. They are as follows:

- Risk register
- Risk management plan
- Cost management plan
- Schedule management plan
- Organizational process assets

The elements of the organizational process assets you'll want to pay close attention to as an input to this process are the historical information from previous projects, risk databases, and risk specialists studies performed on similar projects.

Tools and Techniques for Perform Quantitative Risk Analysis

The Perform Quantitative Risk Analysis process includes three tools and techniques: data gathering and representation techniques, Quantitative Risk Analysis and modeling techniques, and expert judgment.

Data Gathering and Representation Techniques

The data gathering techniques include interviewing techniques and probability distributions.

Interviewing

This technique is like the interviewing technique discussed earlier in the section "Identifying Potential Risk." Project team members, stakeholders, and subject-matter experts are prime candidates for risk interviews. Ask them about their experiences on past projects and about working with the types of technology or processes you'll use during this project.

NOTE

For the exam, remember that interviewing is a tool and technique of the Perform Quantitative Risk Analysis process. Although you can use this technique in the Identify Risks process, remember that it's part of the data gathering and representation technique and not a named tool and technique itself.

When using this technique, you should first determine what methods of probability distribution (described next) you'll use to analyze your information. The technique you choose will dictate the type of information you need to gather. For example, you might use a three-point scale that assesses the low, high, and most likely risk scenarios or take it a step further and use standard deviations calculations.

Make certain you document how the interviewees decided upon the risk ranges, the criteria they used to place risks in certain categories, and the results of the interview. This will help you later in developing risk responses as well.

Exam Spotlight

For the exam, you should know that several types of probability distributions exist that are useful in determining and displaying risk information. The type of distribution you use determines the type of information you should gather during the interviewing process.

Probability Distributions

It's beyond the scope of this book to delve into probability distributions and calculations, so I'll point out a few aspects of them that you should remember for the exam.

Continuous probability distributions (particularly beta and triangular distributions) are commonly used in Perform Quantitative Risk Analysis. According to the *PMBOK® Guide*, continuous probability distributions include normal, lognormal, triangular, beta, and uniform distributions. Distributions are graphically displayed and represent both the probability and time or cost elements.

Triangular distributions use estimates based on the three-point estimate (the pessimistic, most likely, and optimistic values). This means that during your interviews, you'll gather these pieces of information from your experts. Then you'll use them to quantify risk for each WBS element.

Normal and lognormal distributions use mean and standard deviations to quantify risk, which also require gathering the optimistic, most likely, and pessimistic estimates.

Discrete distributions represent possible scenarios in a decision tree (we'll discuss this in the next section), outcomes of a test, results of a prototype, and other uncertain events.

Quantitative Risk Analysis and Modeling Techniques

There are four analysis and modeling techniques within the Quantitative Risk Analysis tool and technique you should know for the exam: sensitivity analysis, expected monetary value analysis, decision tree analysis, and modeling and simulation. Let's take a brief look at each of them.

Sensitivity Analysis

Sensitivity analysis is a quantitative method of analyzing the potential impact of risk events on the project and determining which risk event (or events) has the greatest potential for impact by examining all the uncertain elements at their baseline values. One of the ways sensitivity analysis data is displayed is a *tornado diagram*. Figure 6.5 shows a sample tornado diagram.

FIGURE 6.5 Tornado diagram

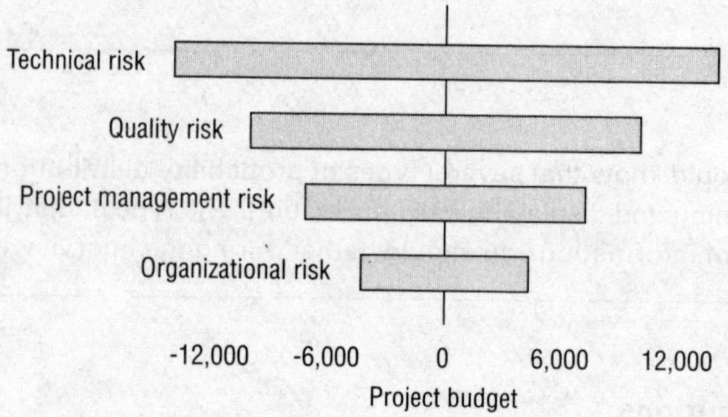

You can see by the arrangement of horizontal bars (each representing a sensitivity variable) how the diagram gets its name. The idea is that each sensitivity bar displays the low and high value possible for the element the bar represents. It's beyond the scope of this book to explain how these values are determined. The questions you might encounter on the exam are focused on the context of this type of analysis. The variables with the greatest effect on the project appear at the top of the graph and decrease in impact as you progress down through the graph. This gives you a quick overview of how much the project can be affected by uncertainty in the various elements. It also allows you to see at a glance which risks might have the biggest impacts on the project and will require carefully crafted, detailed response plans. You can use tornado diagrams to determine sensitivity in cost, time, and quality objectives or for risks you've identified during this process. Sensitivity analysis can also be used to determine stakeholder risk tolerance levels.

Expected Monetary Value (EMV) Analysis

Expected monetary value (EMV) analysis is a statistical technique that calculates the average, anticipated future impact of the decision. EMV is calculated by multiplying the probability of the risk by its impact for two or more potential outcomes (for example, a good outcome and a poor outcome) and then adding the results of the potential outcomes together. EMV is used in conjunction with the decision tree analysis technique, which is covered next. I'll give you an example of the EMV formula in the next section. Positive results generally mean the risks you're assessing pose opportunities to the project, while negative results generally indicate a threat to the project.

Decision Tree Analysis

Unfortunately, this isn't a tree outside your office door that produces "yes" and "no" leaves that you can pick to help you make a decision. *Decision trees* are diagrams that show the sequence of interrelated decisions and the expected results of choosing one alternative over the other. Typically, more than one choice or option is available when you're faced with a decision or, in this case, potential outcomes from a risk event. The available choices are depicted in tree form starting at the left with the risk decision branching out to the right with possible outcomes. Decision trees are usually used for risk events associated with time or cost.

Figure 6.6 shows a sample decision tree using expected monetary value (EMV) as one of its inputs.

FIGURE 6.6 Decision tree

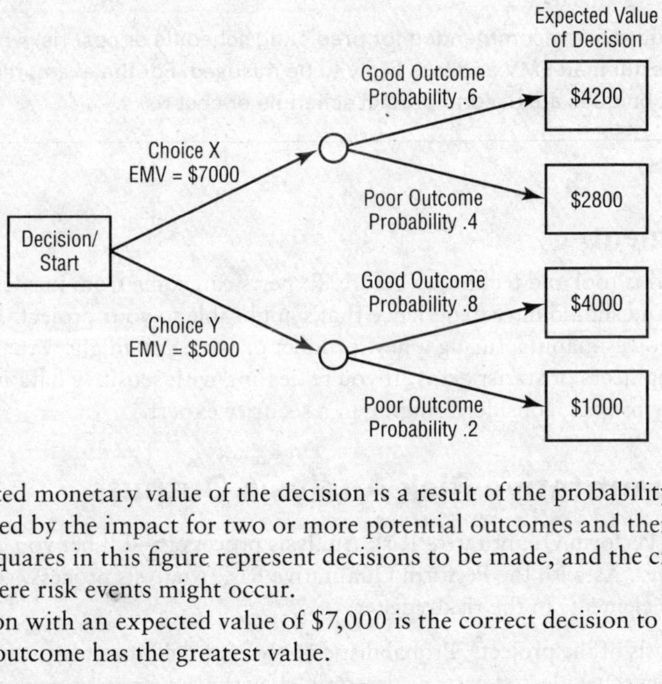

The expected monetary value of the decision is a result of the probability of the risk event multiplied by the impact for two or more potential outcomes and then summing their results. The squares in this figure represent decisions to be made, and the circles represent the points where risk events might occur.

The decision with an expected value of $7,000 is the correct decision to make because the resulting outcome has the greatest value.

Modeling and Simulation

Modeling and simulation techniques are often used for schedule risk analysis and cost analysis. For example, modeling allows you to translate the potential risks at specific points in the project into their impacts so you can determine how the project objectives are affected. Simulation techniques compute the project model using various inputs, such as cost or schedule duration, to determine a probability distribution for the variable chosen. (Cost risks typically use either a work breakdown structure or a cost breakdown structure as the input variable. Schedule risks always use the precedence diagramming method as the input variable. I'll cover schedule diagramming methods in Chapter 7.) If you used simulation techniques to determine project cost and use the cost of the project elements as the input variable, a probability distribution for the total cost of the project would be produced after running the simulation numerous times. Modeling and simulation techniques examine the identified risks and their potential impacts to the project objectives from the perspective of the whole project.

Monte Carlo analysis is an example of a simulation technique. Monte Carlo analysis is replicated many times, typically using cost or schedule variables. Every time the analysis is performed, the values for the variable are changed using a probability distribution for each variable. Monte Carlo analysis can also be used during the Schedule Development process.

Exam Spotlight

Simulation techniques are recommended for predicting schedule or cost risks because they're more powerful than EMV and less likely to be misused. For the exam, remember that simulation techniques are used to predict schedule or cost risks.

Expert Judgment

I've talked about this tool and technique before. Experts can come from inside or outside the organization and should have experience that's applicable to your project. For example, if your project involves manufacturing a new product or part, you might want to consider experts such as engineers or statisticians. If you're dealing with sensitive data in an information technology project, consider bringing in a security expert.

Perform Quantitative Risk Analysis Outputs

The output of the Perform Quantitative Risk Analysis process is—I'll bet you can guess—risk register updates. As with the Perform Qualitative Risk Analysis process, you'll record the following new elements in the risk register:

Probabilistic analysis of the project Probabilistic analysis of the project is the forecasted results of the project schedule and costs as determined by the outcomes of risk analysis. These results include projected completion dates and costs, along with a confidence level associated with each. According to the *PMBOK® Guide*, this output is often expressed as a cumulative distribution, and you'll use these results along with stakeholder risk tolerances to quantify the time and cost contingency reserves. (I'll talk about contingency reserves in the next section, "Developing a Risk Response Plan.")

Confidence levels can also be used to describe the level of confidence placed on the outcome of the forecasted results. For example, suppose the projected schedule completion date is July 12 and the confidence level is .85. This says you believe the project will finish on or before July 12 and that you have an 85 percent level of confidence that this date is accurate.

Probability of achieving the cost and time objectives Using the tools and techniques of Perform Quantitative Risk Analysis allows you to assign a probability of achieving the cost and time objectives of the project. This output documents those probabilities and as such requires a thorough understanding of the current project objectives and knowledge of the risks.

Prioritized list of quantified risks The prioritized list in this process is similar to the list produced during the Perform Qualitative Risk Analysis process. The list of risks includes those that present the greatest risk or threat to the project and their impacts. It also lists those risks that present the greatest opportunities to the project. This list should also indicate which risks are most likely to impact the critical path and those that have the largest cost contingency.

Trends in Perform Quantitative Risk Analysis results Trends in Perform Quantitative Risk Analysis will likely appear as you repeat the risk analysis processes. This information is useful as you progress, making those risks with the greatest threat to the project more evident, which gives you the opportunity to perform further analysis or go on to develop risk response plans.

Exam Spotlight

Understand the differences between the Perform Qualitative Risk Analysis and Perform Quantitative Risk Analysis processes for the exam.

Developing a Risk Response Plan

The *Plan Risk Responses* process is the last process covered in this chapter. (I hear you cheering out there!) Plan Risk Responses is a process of deciding what actions to take to reduce threats and take advantage of the opportunities discovered during the risk analysis processes. This process also includes assigning departments or individual staff members the responsibility of carrying out the risk response plans you'll outline in this process. These folks are known as *risk owners*.

NOTE

The more effective your risk response plans are, the better your chances for a successful project. Well-developed and well-written risk response plans will likely decrease overall project risk.

Generally, you'll want to develop risk response plans for those risks with a combination of high probability of occurrence and significant impact to the project, those ranked high (or red) on the probability/impact matrix, or those ranked high as a result of Perform Quantitative Risk Analysis. Developing risk response plans for risks of low severity or insignificant impact is not an efficient or good use of the project team's time. Spend your time planning responses that are appropriate given the impact the risk itself poses (or the opportunity the risk presents), and don't spend more time, money, or energy to produce a response than the risk event itself would produce if it occurred.

The inputs you'll use to assist you in this process are the risk register and the risk management plan. Several strategies are used in this process to reduce or control risk. It's important that you choose the right strategy for each risk so that the risk and its impacts are dealt with effectively. After deciding on which strategy to use, you'll develop an action plan to put this strategy into play should the risk event occur. You might also choose to designate a secondary or backup strategy.

Exam Spotlight

The rank of the risk will dictate the level of Plan Risk Responses that should be performed. For example, a risk with low severity wouldn't warrant the time it takes to develop a detailed risk response plan. Risk responses should be cost effective—if the cost of the response is more than the consequences of the risk, you might want to examine a different risk response. Risk responses should also be timely, agreed to by all the project stakeholders, and assigned to an individual (risk owner) who is responsible for monitoring and carrying out the risk response plan if needed.

Tools and Techniques for Plan Risk Responses

The Plan Risk Responses process consists of four tools and techniques, and each one of them involves a strategy. The tools and techniques are as follows:

- Strategies for negative risks or threats
- Strategies for positive risks or opportunities
- Contingent response strategy
- Expert judgment

You'll take a look at the first three next.

Strategies for Negative Risks or Threats

Four strategies exist to deal with negative risks or threats to the project objectives. They are avoid, transfer, mitigate, and accept.

Avoid

To *avoid* a risk means you'll evade it altogether, eliminate the cause of the risk event, or change the project plan to protect the project objectives from the risk event. Let's say you're going to take a car trip from your home to a point 800 miles away. You know—because your friends who just took the same trip told you—that there is a long stretch of construction on one of the highways you're planning on using. To avoid the risk of delay, you plan the trip around the construction work and use another highway for that stretch of driving. In this way, you change your plans, avoid the risk of getting held up in construction traffic, and arrive at your destination on time.

With risk avoidance, you essentially eradicate the risk by eliminating its cause. Here's another example: Suppose your project was kicked off without adequate scope definition and requirements gathering. You run a high probability of experiencing *scope creep*—ever-changing requirements—as the project progresses, thus impacting the project schedule. You can avoid this risk by adequately documenting the project scope and requirements during the Planning processes and taking steps to monitor and control changes to scope so it doesn't get out of hand.

Risks that occur early in the project might easily be avoided by improving communications, refining requirements, assigning additional resources to project activities, refining the project scope to avoid risk events, and so on.

Transfer

The idea behind a risk *transfer* is to transfer the risk and the consequences of that risk to a third party. The risk hasn't gone away, but the responsibility for the management of that risk now rests with another party. Most companies aren't willing to take on someone else's risk without a little cash thrown in for good measure. This strategy will impact the project budget and should be included in the cost estimate exercises if you know you're going to use it.

Transfer of risk can occur in many forms but is most effective when dealing with financial risks. Insurance is one form of risk transfer. You are probably familiar with how insurance works. Car insurance is a good example. You purchase car insurance so that if you come upon an obstacle in the road and there is no way to avoid hitting it, the cost to repair the damage to the car is paid by the insurance company...OK, minus the deductible and all the calculations for the age of the car, the mileage, the color and make of the car, the weather conditions the day you were driving—but I digress.

Another method of risk transfer is contracting. Contracting transfers specific risks to the vendor, depending on the work required by the contract. The vendor accepts the responsibility for the cost of failure. Again, this doesn't come without a price. Contractors charge for their services, and depending on the type of contract you negotiate, the cost might be quite high. For example, in a fixed-price contract, which I'll talk more about in Chapter 7, the vendor (or seller) increases the cost of the contract to compensate for the level of risk they're accepting. A cost reimbursable contract, however, leaves the majority of the risk with you, the buyer. This type of contract might reduce costs if there are project changes midway through the project.

Keep in mind that contracting isn't a cure-all. You might just be swapping one risk for another. For example, say you hire a driver to go with you on your road trip, and that person's job is to do all the driving. If the driver becomes ill or in some way can't fulfill their obligation, you aren't going to get to your destination on time. You've placed the risks associated with the trip on the contract driver; however, you've taken on a risk of delay because of nonperformance, which means you've just swapped one risk for another. You'll have to weigh your options in cases like this and determine which side of the risk coin your organization can more readily accept.

Other forms of transference include warranties, guarantees, and performance bonds.

Mitigate

When you *mitigate* a risk, you attempt to reduce the probability of a risk event and its impacts to an acceptable level. This strategy is a lot like defensive driving. You see an obstacle in the road ahead, survey your options, and take the necessary steps to avoid the obstacle and proceed safely on your journey. Seeing the obstacle ahead (identifying risk) allows you to reduce the threat by planning ways around it or planning ways to reduce its impact if the risk does occur (mitigation strategies).

According to the *PMBOK® Guide*, the purpose of mitigation is to reduce the probability that a risk will occur and reduce the impact of the risk to a level where you can accept the risk and its outcomes. It's easier to take actions early on that will reduce the probability of a risk or its consequences than it is to fix the damage once it has occurred. Some examples of risk mitigation include performing more tests, using less complicated processes, creating prototypes, and choosing more reliable vendors.

Accept

The acceptance strategy is used when you aren't able to eliminate all the threats on the project. *Acceptance* of a risk event is a strategy that can be used for risks that pose either threats or opportunities to the project. *Passive acceptance* is a strategy that means you won't make any plans to try to avoid or mitigate the risk. You're willing to accept the consequences of the risk should it occur. Acceptance might also mean the project team was unable to come up with an adequate response strategy and must accept the risk and its consequences. *Active acceptance* might include developing contingency reserves to deal with risks should they occur. (You'll look at contingency reserves in the next section.)

Let's revisit the road trip example. You could plan the trip using the original route and just accept the risk of running into construction. If you get to that point and you're delayed, you'll just accept it. This is passive acceptance. You could also go ahead and make plans to take an alternate route but not enact those plans until you actually reach the construction and know for certain that it is going to impede your progress. This is active acceptance and might involve developing a contingency plan.

Exam Spotlight

Understand all the strategies and their characteristics in each Plan Risk Response tool and technique for the exam.

Real World Scenario

New Convention Center Wing

You work for a small hotel and resort in western Colorado. Your company has taken on a project to expand the convention center by adding another wing. This wing will add six more meeting rooms (four of which can be combined into a large room by folding back the movable walls to accommodate large groups). This is a popular resort, and one of the risks identified with this project was an increase in demand for conference reservations after the construction finishes. The marketing team members decide they'll mitigate this risk by contacting the organizations who've consistently reserved space with them over the past three years and offer them incentives on their next reservation if they book their convention before the construction is completed. That way, their most important customers won't be turned away when the new reservations start pouring in.

Strategies for Positive Risk or Opportunities

Four strategies exist to deal with opportunities or positive risks that might present themselves on the project: exploit, share, enhance and accept. We already covered accept, so we'll look at the remaining strategies next.

Exploit

When you *exploit* a risk event, you're looking for opportunities for positive impacts. This is the strategy of choice when you've identified positive risks that you want to make certain will occur on the project. Examples of exploiting a risk include reducing the amount of time to complete the project by bringing on more qualified resources or by providing even better quality than originally planned.

Share

The *share* strategy is similar to transferring because you'll assign the risk to a third-party owner who is best able to bring about the opportunity the risk event presents. For example, perhaps what your organization does best is investing. However, it isn't so good at marketing. Forming a joint venture with a marketing firm to capitalize on a positive risk will make the most of the opportunities.

Enhance

The *enhance* strategy closely watches the probability or impact of the risk event to assure that the organization realizes the benefits. This entails watching for and emphasizing risk triggers and identifying the root causes of the risk to help enhance impacts or probability.

Contingency Planning

The last tool and technique of the Plan Risk Responses process is called the *contingent response strategy*, better known as *contingency planning*. Contingency planning involves planning alternatives to deal with the risks should they occur. This is different from mitigation planning in that mitigation looks to reduce the probability of the risk and its impact, whereas contingency planning doesn't necessarily attempt to reduce the probability of a risk event or its impacts. Contingency planning says the risk might very well occur, and you better have plans in place to deal with it when it does.

Contingency comes into play when the risk event occurs. This implies you need to plan for your contingencies well in advance of the threat occurring. After the risks have been identified and quantified, contingency plans should be developed and kept at the ready.

Contingency allowances or reserves are a common contingency response. *Contingency reserves* include project funds that are held in reserve to offset any unavoidable threats to project scope, schedule, cost, or quality. It also includes reserving time and resources to account for risks. You should consider stakeholder risk tolerances when determining the amount of contingency reserves.

Fallback plans should be developed for risks with high impact or for risks with identified strategies that might not be the most effective at dealing with the risk.

In practice, you'll find that identifying, prioritizing, quantifying, and developing responses for potential threats might happen simultaneously. In any case, you don't want to be taken by surprise, and that's the point of the risk processes. If you know about potential risks early, you can often mitigate them or prepare appropriate response plans or contingency plans to deal with them.

Plan Risk Responses Outputs

As you've no doubt concluded, the purpose of the Plan Risk Responses process is to develop risk responses for those risks with the highest threat to or best opportunity for the project objectives. The Plan Risk Responses process has four outputs: risk register updates, risk-related contract decisions, project management plan updates, and project document updates.

NOTE Remember that you might need to revisit other Planning processes after performing Plan Risk Responses to modify project plans as a result of risk responses.

Risk Register Updates

Again, the risk register is updated at the end of this process with the information you've discovered during this process. The response plans are recorded in the risk register. You'll recall that the risk register lists the risk in order of priority (those with the highest potential for threat or opportunity first), so it makes sense that the response plans you have for these risks will be more detailed than the remaining lists. Some risks might not require response plans at all, but you should put them on a watch list and monitor them throughout the project.

Let's take a look at what the risk register should contain at this point. According to the *PMBOK® Guide*, after Identify Risks, Perform Qualitative Risk Analysis, and Perform Quantitative Risk Analysis are preformed, the following elements should appear in the risk register:

- Prioritized list of identified risks, including their descriptions, what WBS element they impact (or area of the project), categories (RBS), root causes, and how the risk impacts the project objectives
- Risk ranking
- Risk owners and their responsibility
- Outputs from the Perform Qualitative Analysis
- Agreed-upon response strategies
- Actions needed to implement response plans
- Cost and schedule activities needed to implement risk responses
- Contingency plans
- Fallback plans
- List of residual and secondary risks
- Contingency reserves

The only elements in the preceding list I haven't talked about so far are residual and secondary risks. A *residual risk* is a leftover risk, so to speak. After you've implemented a risk response strategy—say mitigation, for example—some minor risk might still remain. The contingency reserve is set up to handle situations like this.

Secondary risks are risks that come about as a result of implementing a risk response. The example given previously where you transferred risk by hiring a driver to take you to your destination but the person became ill along the way is an example of a secondary risk. The driver's illness delayed your arrival time, which is a risk directly caused by hiring the driver or implementing a risk response. When planning for risk, identify and plan responses for secondary risks.

Risk-Related Contractual Agreements

If you're planning on using strategies such as transference or sharing, for example, you might need to purchase services or items from third parties. You can prepare the contracts for those services now and discuss them with the appropriate parties.

Risks exist on all projects, and risk planning is an important part of the project Planning processes. Just the act of identifying risks and planning responses can decrease their impact if they occur. Don't take the "What I don't know won't hurt me" approach to risk planning. This is definitely a case where not knowing something can be devastating. Risks that are easily identified and have planned responses aren't likely to kill projects or your career. Risks that you should have known about but ignored could end up costing the organization thousands or millions of dollars, causing schedule delays, causing loss of competitive advantage, or ultimately killing the project. There could be a personal cost as well, because cost and schedule overruns due to poor planning on your part are not easily explained.

Project Management Plan and Project Document Updates

As we've discussed throughout the book, the management plans created that document how the schedule, budget, quality, procurement, and human resources will be defined, managed, and controlled on the project become subsidiary plans to the project management plan. Any and all of these management plans may require updates after you perform the risk processes. In addition, the WBS, the schedule baseline, and cost performance baseline may require updates as well.

Other project documents, such as technical documentation and the assumptions documented in project scope statement, could need an update after performing these processes as well.

Real World Scenario

Project Case Study: New Kitchen Heaven Retail Store

Ricardo knocks on your office door and asks whether you have a few minutes to talk. "Of course," you reply, and he takes a seat on one of the comfy chairs at the conference table. You have a feeling this might take a while.

"I think you should know that I'm concerned about the availability of the T1 line. I've already put in the call to get us on the list because, as I said last week, there's a 30- to 45-day lead time on these orders."

"We're only part way through the Planning processes. Do you need to order the T1 so soon? We don't even know the store location yet," you say.

"Even though they say lead time is 30 to 45 days, I've waited as long as five or six months to get a T1 installed in the past. I know we're really pushing for the early February store opening, so I thought I'd get the ball rolling now. What I need from you is the location address, and I'll need that pretty quick."

"We're narrowing down the choices between a couple of properties, so I should have that for you within the next couple of weeks. Is that soon enough?"

"The sooner, the better," Ricardo replies.

"Great. I'm glad you stopped by, Ricardo. I wanted to talk with you about risk anyway, and you led us right into the discussion. Let me ask you, what probability would you assign to the T1 line installation happening six months from now?"

"I'd say the probability for six months is low. It's more likely that if there is a delay, it would be within a three- to four-month time frame."

"If they didn't get to it for six months, would it be a showstopper? In other words, is there some other way we could transfer Jill's data until the T1 did get installed?"

"Sure, we could use other methods. Jill won't want to do that for very long, but work-arounds are available."

"Good. Now, what about the risk for contractor availability and hardware availability and delivery schedules?" you ask.

You and Ricardo go on to discuss the risks associated with the IT tasks. Later, you ask Jill and Jake the same kinds of questions and compile a list of risks. In addition, you review the project information for the Atlanta store opening because it's similar in size and scope to this store. You add the risks from that store opening to your list as well. You divide some of the risks into the following categories: IT, Facilities, and Retail. A sample portion of your list appears as follows, with overall assignments made based on Perform Qualitative Risk Analysis and the probability and impact matrix:

- **Category: IT**
  - T1 line availability and installation. Risk score: Low
  - Contractor availability for Ethernet installation. Risk score: Medium
  - POS and server hardware availability. Risk score: Medium
- **Category: Facilities**
  - Desirable location in the right price range. Risk score: High
  - Contractor availability for build-out. Risk score: Low
  - Availability of fixtures and shelving. Risk score: Low
- **Category: Retail**
  - Product availability. Risk score: Medium
  - Shipment dates for product. Risk score: Medium

After examining the risks, you decide that response plans should be developed for the last two items listed under the IT source, the first item under Facilities, and both of the risks listed under Retail.

Ricardo has already mitigated the T1 connection and installation risk by signing up several months ahead of the date when the installation is needed. The contractor availability can be handled with a contingency plan that specifies a backup contractor should the first choice not be available. For the POS terminals and hardware, you decide to use the transfer strategy. As part of the contract, you'll require these vendors to deliver on time, and if they cannot, they'll be required to provide and pay for rental equipment until they can get your gear delivered.

The Facilities risk and Retail risks will be handled with a combination of acceptance, contingency plans, and mitigation.

You've calculated the expected monetary value for several potential risk events. Two of them are detailed here.

Desirable location has an expected monetary value of $780,000. The probability of choosing an incorrect or less than desirable location is 60 percent. The potential loss in sales is the difference between $2.5 million in sales per year that a high-producing store generates versus $1.2 million in sales per year that an average store generates.

The expected monetary value of the product availability event is $50,000. The probability of the event occurring is 40 percent. The potential loss in sales is $125,000 for not opening the store in conjunction with the Garden and Home Show.

Project Case Study Checklist

- Plan Risk Management
- Identify Risks
    - Documentation reviews
    - Information-gathering techniques
- Perform Qualitative Risk Analysis
    - Risk probability and impact
    - Probability and impact rating
    - List of prioritized risks
- Perform Quantitative Risk Analysis
    - Interviewing
    - Expected monetary value
- Plan Risk Responses
    - Avoidance, transference, mitigation, and acceptance strategies
    - Risk response plans documented

Understanding How This Applies to Your Next Project

Risk management and all the processes it involves is not a process I recommend you skip on any size of project. This is where the Boy Scouts of America motto, "Be Prepared" is wise advice. If you haven't examined what could be lurking around the corner on your project and come up with a plan to deal with it, then you can be assured you're in for some surprises. Then again, if you like living on the edge, never knowing what might occur next, you'll probably find yourself back on the job-hunting scene sooner than you planned (oh, wait, you didn't plan because you're living on the edge).

In all seriousness, as with most of the Planning processes I've discussed so far, risk management should be scaled to match the complexity and size of your project. If you're working on a small project with a handful of team members and a short timeline, it doesn't make sense to spend a lot of time on risk planning. However, it does warrant spending *some* time identifying project risk, determining impact and probability, and documenting a plan to deal with the risk.

My two favorite Identify Risks techniques are brainstorming and the Nominal Group Technique. Both techniques help you quickly get to the risks with the greatest probability and impact because, more than likely, these are the first risks that come to mind. Identify Risks can also help the project team find alternative ways of completing the work of the project. Further digging and the ideas generated from initial identification might reveal opportunities or alternatives you wouldn't have thought about during the regular Planning processes.

After you've identified the risks with the greatest impact to the project, document response plans that are appropriate for the risk. Small projects might have only one or two risks that need a response plan. The plans might consist of only a sentence or two, depending on the size of the project. I would question a project where no risks require a response plan. If it seems too good to be true, it probably is.

The avoid, transfer, and mitigate strategies are the most often used strategies to deal with risk, along with contingency planning. Of these, mitigation and contingency planning are probably the most common. Mitigation generally recognizes that the risk will likely occur and attempts to reduce the impact.

I have used brainstorming and the Nominal Group Technique to strategize response plans for risks on small projects. When you're working on a small project, you can typically identify, quantify, and create response plans for risks at one meeting.

Identifying positive risk, in my experience, is fairly rare. Typically, when my teams perform Identify Risks, it's to determine what can go wrong and how bad the impact will be if it does. The two most important concepts from this chapter that you should apply to your next project are that you and your team should identify risks and create response plans to deal with the most significant ones.

Summary

Congratulations! You've completed another fun-filled, action-packed chapter, and all of it on a single topic—risk. Risk is inherent in all projects, and risks pose both threats and opportunities to the project. Understanding the risks facing the project better equips you to determine the appropriate strategies to deal with those risks and helps you determine the response plans for the risks (and the level of effort you should put into preparing those plans).

The Plan Risk Management process determines how you will plan for risks on your project. Its only output is the risk management plan, which details how you'll define, monitor, and control risks throughout the project. The risk management plan is a subsidiary of the project management plan.

The Identify Risks process seeks to identify and document the project risks using information-gathering techniques like brainstorming, the Nominal Group technique the Delphi technique, interviewing, and root cause identification. This list of risks gets recorded in the risk register, the only output of this process.

Perform Qualitative Risk Analysis and Perform Quantitative Risk Analysis involve evaluating risks and assigning probability and impact values to the risks. Many tools and techniques are used during these processes, including risk probability and impact, probability and impact matrix, interviewing, probability distributions, expert judgment, sensitivity analysis, decision tree analysis, and simulation.

A probability and impact matrix uses the probability multiplied by the impact value to determine the risk score. The threshold of risk based on high, medium, and low tolerances is determined by comparing the risk score based on the probability level to the probability and impact matrix.

Monte Carlo simulation is a technique used to quantify schedule or cost risks. Decision trees graphically display decisions and their various choices and outcomes and is typically used in combination with earned monetary value.

The Plan Risk Responses process is the last Planning process and culminates with an update to the risk register documenting the risk response plans. The risk response plans detail the strategies you'll use to respond to risk and assign individuals to manage each risk response. Risk response strategies for negative risks include avoidance, mitigation, and transference. Risk strategies for positive risks include exploit, share, and enhance. Acceptance is a strategy for both negative and positive risks.

Contingency planning involves planning alternatives to deal with risk events should they occur. Contingency reserves are set aside to deal with risks associated with cost and time according to the stakeholder tolerance levels.

Exam Essentials

Be able to define the purpose of the risk management plan. The risk management plan describes how you will define, monitor, and control risks throughout the project. It details how risk management processes (including Identify Risks, Perform Qualitative Risk Analysis, Perform Quantitative Risk Analysis, Plan Risk Responses, and Monitor and Control Risks) will be implemented, monitored, and controlled throughout the life of the project. It describes how you will manage risks but does not attempt to define responses to individual risks. The risk management plan is a subsidiary of the project management plan, and it's the only output of the Plan Risk Management process.

Be able to name the purpose of Identify Risks. The purpose of the Identify Risks process is to identify all risks that might impact the project, document them, and identify their characteristics.

Be able to define the purpose of Perform Qualitative Risk Analysis. Perform Qualitative Risk Analysis determines the impact the identified risks will have on the project and the probability they'll occur, and it puts the risks in priority order according to their effects on the project objectives.

Be able to define the purpose of Perform Quantitative Risk Analysis. Perform Quantitative Risk Analysis evaluates the impacts of risk prioritized during the Perform Qualitative Risk Analysis process and quantifies risk exposure for the project by assigning numeric probabilities to each risk and their impacts on project objectives.

Be able to define the purpose of the Plan Risk Responses process. Plan Risk Responses is the process where risk response plans are developed using strategies such as avoid, transfer, mitigate, accept, exploit, share, enhance, develop contingent response strategies, and apply expert judgment. The risk response plan describes the actions to take should the identified risks occur. It should include all the identified risks, a description of the risks, how they'll impact the project objectives, and the people assigned to manage the risk responses.

Be able to define the risk register and some of its primary elements. The risk register is an output of the Identify Risks process, and updates to the risk register occur as an output of every risk process that follows this one. By the end of the Plan Risk Responses process, the risk register contains these primary elements: identified list of risks, risk owners, risk triggers, risk strategies, contingency plans, and contingency reserves.

Key Terms

Life is a risky business, but with proper planning, your project doesn't have to be. Using processes I've discussed in this chapter, you'll be prepared for the foreseeable and the not so foreseeable. Understand them well, and know each process by the name used in the *PMBOK® Guide*:

Perform Qualitative Risk Analysis

Perform Quantitative Risk Analysis

Identify Risks

Plan Risk Management

Plan Risk Responses

Before you take the exam, also be certain you are familiar with the following terms:

acceptance

avoid

brainstorming

cardinal scale

cause-and-effect diagrams

contingency planning

contingency reserves

decision trees

Delphi technique

Enhance

expected monetary value (EMV)

exploit

force majeure

impact

impact scale

influence diagramming

interviews

mitigate

Monte Carlo analysis

Nominal Group Technique

ordinal scale

passive acceptance

probability

probability and impact matrix

residual risk

risk breakdown structure (RBS)

risk categories

risk management plan

risk register

risk tolerance

secondary risks

sensitivity analysis

share

tornado diagram

transfer

triggers

Review Questions

1. You are a project manager for Fountain of Youth Spring Water bottlers. Your project involves installing a new accounting system, and you're performing the risk-planning processes. You have identified several problems along with the causes of those problems. Which of the following diagrams will you use to show the problem and its causes and effects?

   A. Decision tree diagram

   B. Fishbone diagram

   C. Benchmark diagram

   D. Simulation tree diagram

2. Assessing the probability and consequences of identified risks to the project objectives, assigning a risk score to each risk, and creating a list of prioritized risks describes which of the following processes?

   A. Perform Quantitative Risk Analysis

   B. Identify Risks

   C. Perform Qualitative Risk Analysis

   D. Plan Risk Management

3. Each of the following statements is true regarding the risk management plan except for which one?

   A. The risk management plan is an output of the Plan Risk Management process.

   B. The risk management plan includes a description of the responses to risks and triggers.

   C. The risk management plan includes thresholds, scoring and interpretation methods, responsible parties, and budgets.

   D. The risk management plan is an input to all the remaining risk-planning processes.

4. You are using the interviewing technique of the Perform Quantitative Risk Analysis process. You intend to use normal and lognormal distributions. All of the following statements are true regarding this question except which one?

   A. Interviewing techniques are used to quantify the probability and impact of the risks on project objectives.

   B. Normal and lognormal distributions use mean and standard deviation to quantify risks.

   C. Distributions graphically display the impacts of risk to the project objectives.

   D. Triangular distributions rely on optimistic, pessimistic, and most likely estimates to quantify risks.

5. The information-gathering techniques used in the Identify Risks process include all of the following except ________________.

   A. toot cause analysis

   B. the Delphi technique

   C. brainstorming

   D. checklist analysis

6. Which of the following processes assesses the likelihood of risk occurrences and their consequences using a numerical rating?

   A. Perform Qualitative Risk Analysis

   B. Identify Risks

   C. Perform Quantitative Risk Analysis

   D. Plan Risk Responses

7. You are the project manager for a new website for the local zoo. You need to perform the Perform Qualitative Risk Analysis process. When you've completed this process, you'll produce all of the following as part of the risk register update output except which one?

   A. Priority list of risks

   B. Watch list of low-priority risks

   C. Probability of achieving time and cost estimates

   D. Risks grouped by categories

8. You've identified a risk event on your current project that could save $100,000 in project costs if it occurs. Which of the following is true based on this statement? (Choose the best answer.)

   A. This is a risk event that should be accepted because the rewards outweigh the threat to the project.

   B. This risk event is an opportunity to the project and should be exploited.

   C. This risk event should be mitigated to take advantage of the savings.

   D. This a risk event that should be avoided to take full advantage of the potential savings.

9. You've identified a risk event on your current project that could save $500,000 in project costs if it occurs. Your organization is considering hiring a consulting firm to help establish proper project management techniques in order to assure it realizes these savings. Which of the following is true based on this statement? (Choose the best answer.)

   A. This is a risk event that should be accepted because the rewards outweigh the threat to the project.

   B. This risk event is an opportunity to the project and should be exploited.

   C. This risk event should be mitigated to take advantage of the savings.

   D. This a risk event that should be shared to take full advantage of the potential savings.

10. Your hardware vendor left you a voicemail saying that a snowstorm in the Midwest might prevent your equipment from arriving on time. She wanted to give you a heads-up and asked that you return the call. Which of the following statements is true? (Choose the best answer.)

A. This is a trigger.

B. This is a contingency plan.

C. This is a residual risk.

D. This is a secondary risk.

11. You are constructing a probability and impact matrix for your project. Which of the following statements is true?

A. The probability and impact matrix multiplies the risk's probability by the cost of the impact to determine an expected value of the risk event.

B. The probability and impact matrix multiplies the risk's probability—which fall from 0.0 to 1.0—and the risk's impact for each potential outcome and then adds the result of the potential outcomes together to determine a risk score.

C. The probability and impact matrix are predetermined thresholds that use the risk's probability multiplied by the impact of the risk event to determine an overall risk score.

D. The probability and impact matrix multiplies the risk's probability by the risk impact—which both fall from 0.0 to 1.0—to determine a risk score.

12. Your stakeholders have asked for an analysis of the cost risk. All of the following are true except for which one?

A. Monte Carlo analysis is the preferred method to use to determine the cost risk.

B. Monte Carlo analysis is a modeling technique that computes project costs one time.

C. A traditional work breakdown structure can be used as an input variable for the cost analysis.

D. Monte Carlo usually expresses its results as probability distributions of possible costs.

13. Your hardware vendor left you a voicemail saying that a snowstorm in the Midwest will prevent your equipment from arriving on time. You identified a risk response strategy for this risk and have arranged for a local company to lease you the needed equipment until yours arrives. This is an example of which risk response strategy?

A. Transfer

B. Acceptance

C. Mitigate

D. Avoid

14. All of the following are elements of the enterprise environmental factors input of the Identify Risks process that you should evaluate except for which one?

A. Assumptions analysis

B. Industry studies

C. Benchmarking

D. Risk attitudes

15. You work for a large manufacturing plant. You are working on a new project to release an overseas product line. This is the company's first experience in the overseas market, and it wants to make a big splash with the introduction of this product. The stakeholders are a bit nervous about the project and historically proceed cautiously and take a considerable amount of time to examine information before making a final decision. The project entails producing your product in a concentrated formula and packaging it in smaller containers than the U.S. product uses. A new machine is needed in order to mix the ingredients into a concentrated formula. After speaking with one of your stakeholders, you discover this will be the first machine your organization has purchased from your new supplier. Which of the following statements is true given the information in this question?

A. The question describes risk tolerance levels of the stakeholders, which should be considered when performing the Plan Risk Management process.

B. This question describes the interviewing tool and technique used during the Identify Risks process.

C. This question describes risk triggers that are derived using interviewing techniques and recorded in the risk register during the Perform Qualitative Risk Analysis process.

D. This question describes a risk that requires a response strategy from the positive risk category.

16. Your project team has identified several potential risks on your current project that could have a significant impact if they occurred. The team examined the impact of the risks by keeping all the uncertain elements at their baseline values. What type of diagram will the team use to display this information?

A. Fishbone diagram

B. Tornado diagram

C. Influence diagram

D. Process flowchart

17. Your project team is in the process of identifying project risks on your current project. The team has the option to use all of the following tools and techniques to diagram some of these potential risks except for which one?

A. Ishikawa diagram

B. Decision tree diagram

C. Process flowchart

D. Influence diagram

18. All of the following statements are true regarding the RBS except for which one?

A. The RBS is contained in the risk management plan.

B. It describes risk categories, which are a systematic way to identify risks and provide a foundation for understanding for everyone involved on the project.

C. The lowest level of the RBS can be used as a checklist, which is a tool and technique of the Identify Risks process.

D. The RBS is similar to the WBS in that the lowest levels of both are easily assigned to a responsible party or owner.

19. Your team has identified the risks on the project and determined their risk score. The team is in the midst of determining what strategies to put in place should the risks occur. After some discussion, the team members have determined that the risk of losing their network administrator is a risk they'll just deal with if and when it occurs. Although they think it's a possibility and the impact would be significant, they've decided to simply deal with it after the fact. Which of the following is true regarding this question?

A. This is a negative response strategy.

B. This is a positive response strategy.

C. This is a response strategy for either positive or negative risk known as *contingency planning.*

D. This is a response strategy for either positive or negative risks known as *passive acceptance.*

20. All of the following are true regarding the Perform Qualitative Risk Analysis process except which one?

A. Probability and impact and expert interviews are used to help correct biases that occur in the data you've gathered during this process.

B. The probability and impact matrix is used during this process to assign red, yellow, and green conditions to risks.

C. Perform Qualitative Risk Analysis is an easy method of determining risk probability and impact that usually takes a good deal of time to perform.

D. Risk urgency assessment is a tool and technique of this process used to determine which risks need near-term response plans.

Answers to Review Questions

1. B. The cause-and-effect flowcharts—also called *fishbone diagrams* or *Ishikawa diagrams*—show the relationship between the causes and effects of problems.

2. C. The purpose of Perform Qualitative Risk Analysis is to determine what impact the identified risk events will have on the project and the probability they'll occur. It also puts risks in priority order according to their effects on the project objectives and assigns a risk score for the project.

3. B. The risk management plan details how risk management processes will be implemented, monitored, and controlled throughout the life of the project. The risk management plan does not include responses to risks or triggers. Responses to risks are documented in the risk register as part of the Plan Risk Responses process.

4. C. Distributions graphically display the probability of risk to the project objectives as well as the time or cost elements.

5. D. The information-gathering techniques in the Identify Risks process are brainstorming, the Delphi technique, interviewing, and root cause analysis.

6. C. Perform Quantitative Risk Analysis analyzes the probability of risks and their consequences using a numerical rating. Perform Qualitative Risk Analysis might use numeric ratings but can use a high-medium-low scale as well.

7. C. Probability of achieving time and cost estimates is an update that is produced from the Perform Quantitative Risk Analysis process.

8. B. This risk event has the potential to save money on project costs, so it's an opportunity, and the appropriate strategy to use in this case is the exploit strategy.

9. D. This risk event has the potential to save money on project costs. Sharing involves using a third party to help assure that the opportunity take place.

10. A. The best answer is A. Triggers are warning signs of an impending risk event.

11. C. The probability and impact matrix multiplies the probability and impact to determine a risk score. Using this score and a predetermined matrix, you determine if the scores is a high, medium, or low designation.

12. B. Monte Carlo analysis is a simulation technique that computes project costs many times in an iterative fashion.

13. C. Mitigation attempts to reduce the impact of a risk event should it occur. Making plans to arrange for the leased equipment reduces the consequences of the risk.

14. A. Assumptions analysis is a tool and technique of the Identify Risks process.

15. A. This question describes risk tolerance levels of the stakeholders. Risk triggers are recorded in the risk register during the Plan Risk Responses process. The risk of buying a machine from a new supplier would pose a threat to the project, not an opportunity. Interviewing might have been used, but this question wasn't describing the Identify Risks process.

16. B. The question describes sensitivity analysis, which is a tool and technique of the Perform Quantitative Risk Analysis process. Tornado diagrams are often used to display sensitivity analysis data.

17. B. Decision tree diagrams are used during the Perform Quantitative Risk Analysis process. All the other options are diagramming techniques used in the Identify Risks process.

18. D. The RBS describes risk categories, and the lowest level can be used as a checklist to help identify risks. Risk owners are not assigned from the RBS but typically are assigned as soon as the risk is identified.

19. D. This is a response strategy known as *passive acceptance* because the team has decided to take no action and make no plans for the risk. This is a strategy that can be used for either positive or negative risks.

20. C. Perform Qualitative Risk Analysis is a fast and easy method of determining probability and impact.

Chapter 7

Planning Project Resources

THE PMP EXAM CONTENT FROM THE PLANNING THE PROJECT PERFORMANCE DOMAIN COVERED IN THIS CHAPTER INCLUDES THE FOLLOWING:

- ✓ **Identify Project Team and Define Roles and Responsibilities**
- ✓ **Obtain Plan Approval**

We're closing in on finishing up the Planning group processes. We're at a place where we need to talk about some processes that aren't necessarily related to each other but need to be completed before you can construct the project schedule and budget. So, we'll start out this chapter by discussing resources.

All projects require resources. Some may require materials or goods, but all projects require human resources to perform the activities to bring them to completion. We'll discuss the Plan Procurements process, which deals with the goods and services procurements and then move on to Develop Human Resource Plan, where you will develop the staffing management plan. This plan will help guide you later on in acquiring your project team members in the Executing process.

We'll wrap up the chapter with the Plan Quality process. This process focuses on determining the quality standards that are necessary for the project and on documenting how you'll go about meeting them. Let's get going.

Procurement Planning

Plan Procurements is a process of identifying what goods or services you're going to purchase from outside the organization and which needs the project team can meet. Part of what you'll accomplish in this process is determining whether you should purchase the goods or services and, if so, how much and when. Keep in mind that I'm discussing the procurement from the buyer's perspective, because this is the approach used in the *PMBOK® Guide.*

The Plan Procurements process can influence the project schedule, and the project schedule can influence this process. For example, the availability of a contractor or special-order materials might have a significant impact on the schedule. And conversely, your organization's business cycle might have an impact on the Plan Procurements process if the organization is dependent on seasonal activity. The Estimate Activity Resources process can also be influenced by this process, as will make-or-buy decisions (I'll get to those shortly).

NOTE You need to perform each process in the Project Procurement Management Knowledge Area (beginning with Plan Procurements and ending with Close Procurements) for each product or service that you're buying outside the organization. If you're procuring all your resources from within the organization, the only process you'll perform in this Knowledge Area is the Plan Procurements process.

Sometimes, you'll procure all the materials and resources for your project from a vendor. In cases like these, the vendor will have a project manager assigned to the project. Your organization might choose to have an internal project manager assigned as well to act as the conduit between your company and the vendor and to provide information and monitor your organization's deliverables. When this happens, the vendor or contracting company is responsible for fulfilling all the project management processes as part of the contract. In the case of an outsourced project, the seller—also known as the *vendor*, *supplier*, or *contractor*—manages the project and the buyer becomes the stakeholder. If you're hiring a vendor, don't forget to consider permits or professional licenses that might be required for the type of work you need them to perform.

Several inputs are needed when planning for purchases. You'll look at them next.

Plan Procurements Inputs

The Plan Procurements process has eleven inputs:

- Scope baseline
- Requirements documentation
- Teaming agreements
- Risk register
- Risk-related contract decisions
- Activity resource requirements
- Project schedule
- Activity cost estimates
- Cost performance baseline
- Enterprise environmental factors
- Organizational process assets

The scope baseline includes the project scope statement that describes the need for the project and lists the deliverables and the acceptance criteria for the product or service of the project. Obviously, you'll want to consider these when thinking about procuring goods and services. You'll also want to consider the constraints (issues such as availability and timing of funds, availability of resources, delivery dates, and vendor availability) and assumptions (issues such as reliability of the vendor, assuming availability of key resources, and adequate stakeholder involvement). The product scope description is included in the project scope statement as well and might alert you to special considerations (services, technical requirements, and skills) needed to produce the product of the project.

As part of the scope baseline, the WBS and WBS dictionary identify the deliverables and describe the work required for each element of the WBS.

Teaming agreements are contractual agreements between multiple parties that are forming a partnership or joint venture to work on the project. Teaming agreements are often used when two or more vendors form a partnership to work together on a particular project. If teaming agreements are used on the project, typically the scope of work, requirements for competition, buyer and seller roles, and other important project concerns should be predefined.

Exam Spotlight

According to the *PMBOK® Guide*, when teaming agreements are in force on a project, the planning processes are significantly impacted. For example, the teaming agreement predefines the scope of work, and that means that elements like the requirements and the deliverables may change the completion dates, thus impacting the project schedule, or they may impact the project budget, quality, human resources availability, procurement decisions, and so on.

The risk register and risk-related contract decisions will guide you in determining the types of services or goods needed for risk management. For example, the transference strategy might require the purchase of insurance. You should review each of these elements when determining which goods and services will be performed within the project and which will be purchased.

Marketplace conditions are the key element of enterprise environmental factors you should consider for this process. The organization's guidelines and organizational policies (including any procurement policies) are the elements of the organizational process assets you should pay attention to here.

NOTE

Many organizations have procurement departments that are responsible for procuring goods and services and writing and managing contracts. Some organizations also require that all contracts be reviewed by their legal department prior to signing. These are organizational process assets that you should consider when you need to procure goods and services.

It's important for the project manager to understand organizational policies because they might impact many of the Planning processes, including the Procurement Planning processes. For example, the organization might have purchasing approval processes that must be followed. Perhaps orders for goods or services that exceed certain dollar amounts need different levels of approval. As the project manager, you need to be aware of policies like this so you're certain you can execute the project smoothly. It's frustrating to find out later that you should have followed a certain process or policy and now, because you didn't, you've got schedule delays or worse. You could consider using the "Sin now, ask forgiveness later" technique in extreme emergencies, but you didn't hear that from me. (By the way, that's not a technique that's authorized by the *PMBOK® Guide*.)

The project manager and the project team will be responsible for coordinating all the organizational interfaces for the project, including technical, human resources, purchasing, and finance. It will serve you well to understand the policies and politics involved in each of these areas in your organization.

NOTE

My organization is steeped in policy. (A government organization steeped in policy? Go figure!) It's so steeped in policy that we have to request the funds for large projects at least two years in advance. There are mounds and mounds of request forms, justification forms, approval forms, routing forms—you get the idea. But my point is if you miss one of the forms or don't fill out the information correctly, you can set your project back by a minimum of a year, if not two. Then once the money is awarded, there are more forms to fill out and policies to follow. Again, if you don't follow the policies correctly, you can jeopardize future project funds. Many organizations have a practice of not giving you all the project money up front in one lump sum. In other words, you must meet major milestones or complete a project phase before they'll fund your next phase. Know what your organizational policies are well ahead of time. Talk to the people who can walk you through the process and ask them to check your work to avoid surprises.

Tools and Techniques for Plan Procurements

The Plan Procurements process consists of three tools and techniques. They are make-or-buy analysis, expert judgment, and contract types. I've already covered expert judgment, so you'll look at make-or-buy analysis next, and then I'll cover contract types.

Make-or-Buy Analysis

The main decision you're trying to get to in *make-or-buy analysis* is whether it's more cost effective to buy the products and services or more cost effective for the organization to produce the goods and services needed for the project. Costs should include both direct costs (in other words, the actual cost to purchase the product or service) and indirect costs, such as the salary of the manager overseeing the purchase process or ongoing maintenance costs. Costs don't necessarily mean the cost to purchase. In make-or-buy analysis, you might weigh the cost of leasing items versus the cost of buying them. For example, perhaps your project requires using a specialized piece of hardware that you know will be outdated by the end of the project. In a case like this, leasing might be a better option so that when the project is ready to be implemented, a newer version of the hardware can be tested and put into production during rollout.

Other considerations in make-or-buy analysis might include elements such as capacity issues, skills, availability, and trade secrets. Strict control might be needed for a certain process and thus the process cannot be outsourced. Perhaps your organization has the skills in-house to complete the project but your current project list is so backlogged that you can't get to the new project for months, so you need to bring in a vendor.

Make-or-buy analysis is considered a general management technique and concludes with the decision to do one or the other.

Contract Types

A *contract* is a compulsory agreement between two or more parties and is used to acquire products or services from outside the organization. Typically, money is exchanged for the goods or services. Contracts are enforceable by law and require an offer and an acceptance.

There are different types of contracts for different purposes. The *PMBOK® Guide* divides contracts into three categories:

- Fixed price or lump sum
- Cost reimbursable
- Time and materials (T&M)

Within the fixed-price and cost-reimbursable categories are different types of contracts. You'll look at each in the following sections. Keep in mind that several factors will impact the type of contract you should use. The product requirements (or service criteria) might drive the contract type. The market conditions might drive availability and price—remember back in the dot-com era when trying to hire anyone with programming skills was next to impossible? And the amount of risk—for the seller, the buyer, and the project itself—will help determine contract type.

Exam Spotlight

There could always be an exam question or two regarding contract types, so spend some time getting familiar with them.

Fixed-Price or Lump-Sum Contracts

Fixed-price contracts (also referred to as *lump-sum contracts*) can either set a specific, firm price for the goods or services rendered (known as a *firm fixed-price contract*, or *FFP*) or include incentives for meeting or exceeding certain contract deliverables.

Fixed-price contracts can be disastrous for both the buyer and the seller if the scope of the project is not well defined or the scope changes dramatically. It's important to have accurate, well-defined deliverables when you're using this type of contract. Conversely, fixed-price contracts are relatively safe for both buyer and seller when the original scope is well defined and remains unchanged. They typically reap only small profits for the seller and force the contractor to work productively and efficiently. This type of contract also minimizes cost and quality uncertainty. There are three types of fixed-price contracts you should know for the exam:

Firm Fixed-Price (FFP) In the *FFP contract*, the buyer and seller agree on a well-defined deliverable for a set price. In this kind of contract, the biggest risk is borne by the seller.

The seller—or contractor—must take great strides to assure they've covered their costs and will make a comfortable profit on the transaction. The seller assumes the risks of increasing costs, nonperformance, or other problems. However, to counter these unforeseen risks, the seller builds in the cost of the risk to the contract price.

Fixed-Price Plus Incentive (FPIF) *Fixed-price plus incentive (FPIF) contracts* are another type of fixed-price contract. The difference here is that the contract includes an incentive—or bonus—for early completion or for some other agreed-upon performance criterion that meets or exceeds contract specifications. The criteria for early completion, or other performance enhancements, are typically related to cost, schedule, or technical performance and must be spelled out in the contract so both parties understand the terms and conditions.

Another aspect of fixed-price plus incentive contracts to consider is that some of the risk is borne by the buyer, unlike the firm fixed-price contract where most of the risk is borne by the seller. The buyer takes some risk, albeit minimal, by offering the incentive to, for example, get the work done earlier. Suppose the buyer really would like the product delivered 30 days prior to when the seller thinks they can deliver. In this case, the buyer assumes the risk for the early delivery via the incentive.

Fixed-Price with Economic Price Adjustment (FP-EPA) There's one more type of fixed-price contract, known as a *fixed-price with economic price adjustment contract (FP-EPA)*. This contract allows for adjustments due to changes in economic conditions like cost increases or decreases, inflation, and so on. These contracts are typically used when the project spans many years. This type of contract protects both the buyer and seller from economic conditions that are outside of their control.

Exam Spotlight

The economic adjustment section of an FP-EPA contract should be tied to a known financial index.

Cost-Reimbursable Contracts

Cost-reimbursable contracts are as the name implies. The allowable costs—allowable is defined by the contract—associated with producing the goods or services are charged to the buyer. All the costs the seller takes on during the project are charged back to the buyer; thus, the seller is reimbursed.

Cost-reimbursable contracts carry the highest risk to the buyer because the total costs are uncertain. As problems arise, the buyer has to shell out even more money to correct the problems. However, the advantage to the buyer with this type of contract is that scope changes are easy to make and can be made as often as you want—but it will cost you.

Cost-reimbursable contracts have a lot of uncertainty associated with them. The contractor has little incentive to work efficiently or be productive. This type of contract protects the contractor's profit because increasing costs are passed to the buyer rather than taken out of profits, as would be the case with a fixed-price contract. Be certain to audit your statements when using a contract like this so that charges from some other project the vendor is working on don't accidentally end up on your bill.

Cost-reimbursable contracts are used most often when the project scope contains a lot of uncertainty, such as for cutting-edge projects and research and development. They are also used for projects that have large investments early in the project life. We'll look at four types of cost-reimbursable contracts:

Cost plus fixed fee (CPFF) *Cost plus fixed fee (CPFF) contracts* charge back all allowable project costs to the seller and include a fixed fee upon completion of the contract. This is how the seller makes money on the deal; the fixed fee portion is the seller's profit. The fee is always firm in this kind of contract, but the costs are variable. The seller doesn't necessarily have a lot of motivation to control costs with this type of contract, as you can imagine. And one of the strongest motivators for completing the project is driven by the fixed fee portion of the contract.

Cost plus incentive fee (CPIF) The next category of cost-reimbursable contract is *cost plus incentive fee (CPIF)*. This is the type of contract in which the buyer reimburses the seller for the seller's allowable costs and includes an incentive for meeting or exceeding the performance criteria laid out in the contract. An incentive fee actually encourages better cost performance by the seller, and there is a possibility of shared savings between the seller and buyer if performance criteria are exceeded. The qualification for exceeded performance must be written into the contract and agreed to by both parties, as should the definition of allowable costs; the seller can possibly lose the incentive fee if agreed-upon targets are not reached.

There is moderate risk for the buyer under the cost plus incentive fee contract, and if well written, it can be more beneficial for both the seller and then buyer than a cost-reimbursable contract.

Cost plus percentage of cost (CPPC) In the *cost plus percentage of cost (CPPC)*, the seller is reimbursed for allowable costs plus a fee that's calculated as a percentage of the costs. The percentage is agreed upon beforehand and documented in the contract. Since the fee is based on costs, the fee is variable. The lower the costs, the lower the fee, so the seller doesn't have a lot of motivation to keep costs low.

Cost plus award fee (CPAF) This is the riskiest of the cost plus contracts for the seller. In this contract, the seller will recoup all the costs expended during the project but the award fee portion is subject to the sole discretion of the buyer. The performance criteria for earning the award is spelled out in the contract, but these criteria can be subjective and the awards are not usually contestable.

Time and Materials (T&M) Contracts

Time and materials (T&M) contracts are a cross between fixed-price and cost-reimbursable contracts. The full amount of the material costs is not known at the time the contract is awarded. This resembles a cost-reimbursable contract because the costs will continue to grow during the contract's life and are reimbursable to the contractor. The buyer bears the biggest risk in this type of contract.

T&M contracts can resemble fixed-price contracts when unit rates are used, for example. Unit rates might be used to preset the rates of certain elements or portions of the project. For example, a contracting agency might charge you $135 per hour for a .NET programmer, or a leasing company might charge you $2,000 per month for the hardware you're leasing during the testing phase of your project. These rates are preset and agreed upon by the buyer and seller ahead of time. T&M contracts are most often used when you need human resources with specific skills and when you can quickly and precisely define the scope of work needed for the project.

Exam Spotlight

Understand the difference between fixed-price, cost-reimbursable, and time and materials contracts for the exam. Also know when each type of contract should be used, and know which party bears the most risk under each type of contract.

Plan Procurements Outputs

The Plan Procurements process consists of six outputs. The first is the *procurement management plan*. You've seen a few of the other management plan outputs, so you're probably already ahead of me on this one. But hold the phone—I'll make sure to touch on the important points. The other outputs are the procurement statements of work, make-or-buy decisions, procurement documents, source selection criteria, and change requests.

Procurement Management Plan

The procurement management plan details how the procurement process will be managed. According to the *PMBOK® Guide,* it includes the following information:

- The types of contract to use
- The authority of the project team
- How the procurement process will be integrated with other project processes
- Where to find standard procurement documents (provided your organization uses standard documents)
- How many vendors or contractors are involved and how they'll be managed
- How the procurement process will be coordinated with other project processes, such as performance reporting and scheduling
- How the constraints and assumptions might be impacted by purchasing
- How multiple vendors or contractors will be managed
- The coordination of purchasing lead times with the development of the project schedule

- The schedule dates that are determined in each contract
- Identification of prequalified sellers (if known)
- Risk management issues
- Procurement metrics for managing contracts and for evaluating sellers

The procurement management plan, like all the other management plans, becomes a subsidiary of the project management plan.

Real World Scenario

Streamlining Purchases

Russ is a project manager for a real estate development company in Hometown, USA. Recently he transferred to the office headquarters to develop a process for streamlining purchases and purchase requests for the construction teams in the field. His first step was to develop a procurement management plan for the construction managers to use when ordering materials and equipment. Russ decided the procurement management plan could be used as a template for all new projects. That meant the project managers in the field didn't have to write their own procurement management plan when starting a new construction project. They could use the template, which had many of the fields prepopulated with corporate headquarters processes, and then they could fill in the information specific to their project. For example, the Types of Contracts section states that all equipment and materials purchases require fixed-price contracts. When human resources are needed for the project on a contract basis, a T&M contract should be used with the unit rates stated in the contract. A "not to exceed" amount should also be written into the contract so that there are no surprises as to the total amount of dollars the company will be charged for the resources.

Procurement Statements of Work

A *procurement statement of work (SOW)* contains the details of the procurement item in clear, concise terms. It includes the following elements:

- The project objectives
- A description of the work of the project and any postproject operational support needed
- Concise specifications of the product or services required
- The project schedule, time period of services, and work location

The procurement SOW might be prepared by either the buyer or the seller. Buyers might prepare the SOW and give it to the sellers, who in turn rewrite it so that they can price the work properly. If the buyer does not know how to prepare a SOW or the seller would be better at creating the SOW because of their expertise about the product or service, the seller might prepare it and then give it to the buyer to review. In either case, the procurement statement of work is developed from the project scope statement and the WBS and WBS dictionary.

The seller uses the SOW to determine whether they are able to produce the goods or services as specified. In addition, it wouldn't hurt to include a copy of the WBS with the SOW. Any information the seller can use to properly price the goods or services helps both sides understand what's needed and how it will be provided.

Projects might require some or all of the work of the project to be provided by a vendor. The Plan Procurements process determines whether goods or services should be produced within the organization or procured from outside, and if goods or services are procured from outside, it describes what will be outsourced and what kind of contract to use and then documents the information in the SOW and procurement management plan. The SOW will undergo progressive elaboration as you proceed through the procurement processes. There will likely be several iterations of the SOW before you get to the actual contract award.

NOTE

You prepared a SOW during the Develop Project Charter process. You can use that SOW as the procurement SOW during this process if you're contracting out the entire project. Otherwise, you can use just those portions of the SOW that describe the work you've contracted.

Make-or-Buy Decisions

The *make-or-buy decision* is a document that outlines the decisions made during the process regarding which goods and/or services will be produced by the organization and which will be purchased. This can include any number of items, including services, products, insurance policies, performance, and performance bonds.

Procurement Documents

Procurement documents are used to solicit vendors and suppliers to bid on your procurement needs. You're probably familiar with some of the titles of procurement documents. They might be called request for proposal (RFP), request for information (RFI), invitation for bid (IFB), request for quotation (RFQ), and so on.

Procurement documents should clearly state the description of the work requested, they should include the contract SOW, and they should explain how sellers should format and submit their responses. These documents are prepared by the buyer to assure as accurate and complete a response as possible from all potential bidders. Any special provisions or contractual needs should be spelled out as well. For example, many organizations have data concerning their marketing policies, new product introductions planned for the next few years, trade secrets, and so on. The vendor will have access to this private information, and in order to ensure that they maintain confidentiality, you should require that they sign a nondisclosure agreement.

A few terms that you should understand are used during this process; they are usually used interchangeably even though they have distinct definitions. When your decision is going to be made primarily on price, the terms *bid* and *quotation* are used, as in IFB or RFQ.

When considerations other than price (such as technology or specific approaches to the project) are the deciding factor, the term *proposal* is used, as in RFP. These terms are used interchangeably in practice, even though they have specific meanings in the *PMBOK® Guide*.

NOTE In my organization, all solicitation requests are submitted as RFPs, even though our primary decision factor is price.

Exam Spotlight

Understand the difference between *bid* and/or *quotation* and *proposal* for the exam. Bids or quotations are used when price is the only deciding factor among bidders. Proposals are used when there are considerations other than price.

Procurement documents are posted or advertised according to your organizational policies. This might include ads in newspapers and magazines or ads/posts on the Internet.

Source Selection Criteria

The term *source selection criteria* refers to the method your organization will use to choose a vendor from among the proposals you receive. The criteria might be subjective or objective. In some cases, price might be the only criteria, and that means the vendor that submits the lowest bid will win the contract. You should use purchase price (which should include costs associated with purchase price, such as delivery and setup charges) as the sole criteria only when you have multiple qualified sellers from which to choose.

Other projects might require more extensive criteria than price alone. In this case, you might use scoring models as well as rating models, or you might utilize purely subjective methods of selection. I described an example weighted-scoring method in Chapter 2, "Creating the Project Charter." You can use this method to score vendor proposals.

Sometimes, the source selection criteria are made public in the procurement process so that vendors know exactly what you want in a vendor. This approach has pros and cons. If the organization typically makes known the source selection criteria, you'll find that almost all the vendors that bid on the project meet every criteria you've outlined (in writing, that is). When it comes time to perform the contract, however, you might encounter some surprises. The vendor might have done a great job of writing the bid based on your criteria, but in reality they don't know how to put the criteria into practice. On the other hand, having all the criteria publicly known beforehand gives ground to great discussion points and discovery later in the procurement processes.

The following list includes some of the criteria you can consider using for evaluating proposals and bids:

- Comprehension and understanding of the needs of the project as documented in the contract SOW
- Cost

- Technical ability of vendor and its proposed team
- Technical approach
- Risk
- Experience on projects of similar size and scope, including references
- Project management approach
- Management approach
- Financial stability and capacity
- Production capacity
- Reputation, references, and past performance
- Intellectual and proprietary rights

You could include many of these in a weighted scoring model and rate each vendor on how well they responded to these issues.

Real World Scenario

The Customer Relationship Management System Response

Ryan Hunter is preparing the source selection criteria for an RFP for a customer relationship management (CRM) software system. After meeting with key stakeholders and other project managers in the company who've had experience working on projects of this size and scope, he devised the first draft of the source selection criteria. A partial list is as follows:

- Successful bidder's response must detail how business processes (as documented in the RFP page 24) will be addressed with their solution.
- Successful bidder must document their project management approach, which must follow the *PMBOK® Guide* project practices. They must provide an example project management plan based on a previous project experience of similar size and scope to the one documented in the RFP.
- Successful bidder must document previous successful implementations, including integration with existing organization's PBX and network operating system, and must provide references.
- Successful bidder must provide financial statements for the previous three years.

Change Requests

As you perform the Plan Procurements process, the project management plan, including its subsidiary plans, may require changes due to vendor availability, vendor capability, or the vendor's proposed solution as well as cost and quality considerations. Change requests must be processed through the Perform Integrated Change Control process that we'll discuss in Chapter 10, "Measuring and Controlling Project Performance."

Now we'll switch our focus to the human resource needs for the project and discuss the Develop Human Resource Plan process next.

Developing the Human Resource Plan

All projects require human resources, from the smallest project to the largest. The *Develop Human Resource Plan* process documents the roles and responsibilities of individuals or groups for various project elements and then documents the reporting relationships for each. Reporting relationships can be assigned to groups as well as to individuals, and the groups or individuals might be internal or external to the organization or a combination of both. Plan Communications goes hand in hand with Develop Human Resource Plan because the organizational structure affects the way communications are carried out among project participants and the project interfaces.

When developing the human resource plan, the only output of this process, you'll have to consider factors such as the availability of resources, skill levels, training needs, and more. Each of these factors can have an impact on the project cost, schedule, and quality and may introduce risks not previously considered.

Develop Human Resource Plan Inputs

Develop Human Resource Plan has three inputs: activity resource requirements, enterprise environmental factors, and organizational process assets. We'll look at the key elements of each of these next.

Activity Resource Requirements

Human resources are needed to perform and complete the activities outlined in the activity resource requirement output of the Estimate Activity Resources process. During the Develop Human Resource Plan process, you'll define those resource needs in further detail.

Key Environmental Factors

Enterprise environmental factors play a key role in determining human resource roles and responsibilities. The type of organization you work in, the reporting relationships, and the technical skills needed to complete the project work are a few of the factors you should consider when developing the staffing management plan. Here is a list of some of the factors you should consider during this process:

Organizational factors Consider what departments or organization units will have a role in the project, the interactions between and among departments, organizational culture, and the level of formality among these working relationships.

Existing human resources and marketplace conditions The existing base of human resources that are employed, or available to, the organization should be considered when developing the human resource plan. Marketplace conditions will dictate the availability of resources you're acquiring outside the organization and their going rate.

Personnel policies Make certain you have an understanding of the personnel policies in the organization regarding hiring, firing, and tasking employees. Other considerations include holiday schedules, leave time policies, and so on.

Technical factors Consider the types of specialized skills needed to complete the work of the project (for example, programming languages, engineering skills, knowledge of pharmaceuticals) and any technical considerations during handoff from phase to phase or from project completion to production.

Interpersonal factors Interpersonal factors have to do with potential project team members. You should consider their experience, skills, current reporting relationships, cultural considerations, and perceptions regarding their levels of trust and respect for co-workers and superiors.

Location and logistics Consider where the project team is physically located and whether they are all located together or at separate facilities (or cities or countries).

Political factors Political factors involve your stakeholders. Consider the amount of influence the stakeholders have, their interactions and influence with each other, and the power they can exert over the project.

In addition to these factors, you should also consider constraints that pertain to project teams, including the following:

Organizational structures Organizational structures can be constraints. For example, a strong matrix organization provides the project manager with much more authority and power than the weak matrix organization does. Functional organizations typically do not empower their project managers with the proper authority to carry out a project. If you work in a functional organization as I do, it's important to be aware that you'll likely face power struggles with other managers and, in some cases, a flat-out lack of cooperation. Don't tell them I said this, but functional managers tend to be territorial and aren't likely to give up control easily. The best advice I have for you in this case is as follows:

- Establish open communications early in the project.
- Include all the functional managers with key roles in important decisions.
- Get the support of your project sponsor to empower you (as the project manager) with as much authority as possible. It's important that the sponsor makes it clear to the other managers that their cooperation on project activities is expected.

Collective bargaining agreements Collective bargaining agreements are actually contractual obligations of the organization to the employees. Collective bargaining is typically associated with unions and organized employee associations. Other organized employee associations or groups might require specialized reporting relationships as well—especially if they involve contractual obligations. You will not likely be involved in the negotiations of collective bargaining agreements, but if you have an opportunity to voice opinions regarding employee duties or agreements that would be helpful to your project or future projects, by all means take it.

Economic conditions These conditions refer to the availability of funds for the project team to perform training, hire staff, and travel. If funds are severely limited and your project requires frequent trips to other locations, you have an economic constraint on your hands.

Exam Spotlight

For the exam, understand the key environmental factors (organizational factors, existing human resources and market conditions, personnel policies, technical factors, interpersonal, location and logistics, and political factors) and the three constraints (organizational structures, collective bargaining agreements, and economic conditions) that can impact the Develop Human Resource Plan process.

Organizational Process Assets

You should consider three primary elements of the organizational process assets input during this process. They are organizational processes and standardized role descriptions, templates and checklists, and historical information.

The term *templates*, in this case, refers to documentation such as project descriptions, organizational charts, performance appraisals, and the organization's conflict management process. Checklists might include elements such as training requirements, project roles and responsibilities, skills and competency levels, and safety issues.

Exam Spotlight

Using templates and checklists is one way to ensure that you don't miss any key responsibilities when planning the project and will help reduce the amount of time spent on project planning.

Develop Human Resource Plan Tools and Techniques

The Develop Human Resource Plan process consists of three tools and techniques. Remember that your goal is to produce the human resource plan output of this process that includes a description of the team's roles and responsibilities, organizational charts, and a staffing management plan. You'll see that the tools and techniques of this process directly contribute to the components of the human resource plan. They are organization charts and position descriptions, networking, and organizational theory. We'll look at each of these in the following sections.

Organization Charts and Position Descriptions

We've all seen an organization chart. It usually documents your name, your position, your boss, your boss's boss, your boss's boss's boss, and so on. The important point to note about this tool and technique is that this information might be presented in one of four ways:

Hierarchical charts Hierarchical charts, like a WBS, are designed in a top-down format. For example, the organization or department head is at the top, the management employees who report to the organization head are next, and so on, descending down the structure. An *organization breakdown structure (OBS)* is a form of organization chart that shows the departments, work units, or teams within an organization (rather than individuals) and their respective work packages.

A *resource breakdown structure (RBS)* is another type of hierarchical chart that breaks down the work of the project according to the types of resources needed. (RBS also stands for *risk breakdown structure*, as you learned in the previous chapter.) For example, you might have programmers, database analysts, and network analysts as resource types on the RBS. However, they won't all necessarily work on the project team. You might have programmers reporting to the project team, the finance department, and the customer service department, for example. An RBS can help track project costs because it ties to the organization's accounting system. Let's suppose you have programming resources in the RBS at the junior, advanced, and senior levels. Each of these levels of programmer has an average hourly salary recorded in the accounting system that makes it easy for you to track project costs. Ten senior programmers, 14 advanced, and 25 junior-level programmers are easy to calculate and track.

Matrix-based charts Matrix-based charts are used to show the type of resources and the responsibility they have on the project. Many times a project manager will use a *responsibility assignment matrix (RAM)* to graphically display this information. A RAM is usually depicted as a chart with resource names listed in each row (for example, programmers, testers, and trainers) and project phases or WBS elements listed as the columns. (It can also be constructed using team member names.) Indicators in the intersections show where the resources are needed. However, the level of detail is up to you. One RAM might be developed showing only project phases. Another RAM might show level-two WBS elements for a complex project, with more RAMs subsequently produced for the additional WBS levels. Or a RAM might be constructed with level-three elements only.

Exam Spotlight

The RAM relates the OBS to the WBS to assure that every component of the work of the project is assigned to an individual.

Table 7.1 shows a sample portion of a type of RAM called a *RACI chart* for a software development team. In this example, the RACI chart shows the level of accountability each of the participants has on the project. The letters in the acronym RACI are the designations shown in the chart:

R = Responsible for performing the work

A = Accountable, the one who is responsible for producing the deliverable or work package and approves or signs off on the work

C = Consult, someone who has input to the work or decisions

I = Inform, someone who must be informed of the decisions or results

TABLE 7.1 Sample RAM

	Olga	Rae	Jantira	Nirmit
Design	R	A	C	C
Test	I	R	C	A
Implement	C	I	R	A

R = Responsible, A = Accountable, C = Consult, I = Inform

In this example, Olga is responsible for design, meaning she creates the software programming design document, but Rae is accountable and is the one who must make certain the work of the project is completed and approved. This is a great tool because it shows at a glance not only where a resource is working but what that resource's responsibility level is on the project.

Text-oriented formats Text-oriented formats are used when you have a significant amount of detail to record. These are also called *position descriptions* or *role-responsibility-authority forms*. These forms detail (as the name implies) the role, responsibility, and authority of the resource, and they make great templates to use for future projects.

Other sections of the project management plan Don't forget that other subsidiary plans of the project management plan might also describe roles and responsibilities. For example, you'll recall from Chapter 6, "Risk Planning," that the risk register lists the risk owners and their responsibility, so be certain to check these documents when outlining roles and responsibilities as well.

Networking

Networking in this process doesn't refer to the technical kind of networking with servers, switches, and fiber. It means human resource networking; that is, you know someone who knows someone and you can share information, learn new techniques, and interact with each other. According to the *PMBOK® Guide*, several types of networking activities exist including: proactive communication, lunch meetings (my personal favorite), informal conversations (ah, the information you learn by hanging out at the espresso machine), and trade conferences (another favorite because they get you out of the office). Networking might help when you have a specific resource need on the project but can't seem to locate someone with that set of skills.

Organizational Theory

Organizational theory refers to all the theories that attempt to explain what makes people, teams, and work units perform the way they do. I'll talk more about motivation techniques (which are a type of organizational theory) in Chapter 8, "Developing the Project Team." Organizational theory improves the probability that planning will be effective and helps shorten the amount of time it takes to produce the Develop Human Resource Plan outputs.

Develop Human Resource Plan Outputs

The Develop Human Resource Plan process has one output, the human resource plan. According to the *PMBOK® Guide*, the human resource plan, a subsidiary of the project management plan, documents how human resources should be defined, staffed, managed and controlled, and released from the project when their activities are complete.

This output has three components that we'll look at:

- Roles and responsibilities
- Project organizational charts
- Staffing management plan

I've already covered organizational charts in detail, so we'll look at the other two components of the human resource plan now.

Roles and Responsibilities

This output is the list of roles and responsibilities for the project team. It can take the form of the RAM or RACI chart I talked about earlier, or the roles and responsibilities can be recorded in text format. The following are the key elements you should include in the roles and responsibilities documentation:

Role Describes what part of the project the individuals or teams are accountable for. This should also include a description of authority levels, responsibilities, and what work is not included as part of the role.

Authority Describes the amount of authority the resource has to make decisions, dictate direction, and approve the work.

Responsibility Describes the work required to complete the project activities.

Competency Describes the skills and ability needed to perform the project activities.

Staffing Management Plan

The staffing management plan documents how and when human resources are introduced to the project and the criteria for releasing them. As with the other management plans I've discussed, the level and amount of detail contained in this plan are up to you. It can be formal or informal, and it can contain lots of detail or only high-level detail.

The staffing management plan should be updated throughout the project. According to the *PMBOK® Guide,* you should consider several elements for inclusion in the staffing management plan, including the following:

Staff acquisition This describes how team members are acquired (from inside or outside the organization), where they're located, and the costs for specific skills and expertise. I'll talk more about staff acquisition in Chapter 8.

Resource calendars This describes the time frames in which the resources will be needed on the project and when the recruitment process should begin. The resources can be described individually, by teams, or by function (programmers, testers, and so on). Many staffing management plans use a resource histogram. This is usually drawn in chart form, with project time along the horizontal axis and hours needed along the vertical axis. The following example histogram shows the hours needed for an asphalt crew on a construction project.

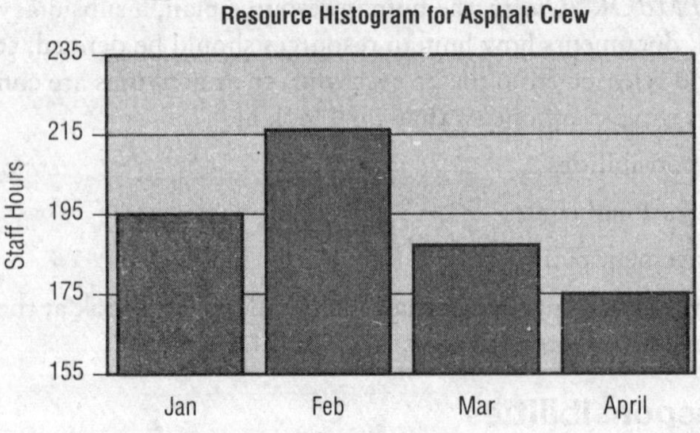

Exam Spotlight

Project calendars are used in the Develop Schedule process we talked about in Chapter 4. They describe the working and nonworking days (or shifts) for the entire project, including company holidays and weekends. Resource calendars describe availability for individuals or for categories or groups of resources. For example, a resource calendar shows planned vacation time for an individual or nonworking time for a category of resources.

Staff release plan Attention should be given to how you'll release project team members at the end of their assignment. You should have reassignment procedures in place to move folks on to other projects or back to assignments they had before the project. This reduces overall project costs because you pay them only for the time they work and then release them. You won't have a tendency to simply keep them busy between assignments or until the end of their scheduled end date if they complete their activities early. Having these procedures in place will also improve morale because everyone will be clear about how reassignment will occur. This should reduce anxiety about their opportunity for employment at the conclusion of the project or their assignment.

Training needs This describes any training plans needed for team members who don't have the required skills or abilities to perform project tasks.

Recognition and rewards This describes the systems you'll use to reward and reinforce desired behavior. I'll talk more about recognition and rewards in Chapter 8.

Compliance If your project involves regulations that must be met or contractual obligations (such as union contracts), the staffing management plan should detail these and any human resource policies the organization has in place that deal with compliance issues.

Safety Any safety policies and procedures that are applicable to the project or industry you work in should be included in the staffing management plan.

Exam Spotlight

Make certain you understand the roles and responsibilities and the staffing management elements of the human resource plan for the exam.

In the next section, we'll shift our focus once again but to a completely new topic. We'll look at quality and its effect on the project planning processes.

Quality Planning

Quality is affected by the triple constraints (project scope, schedule, and cost), and quality concerns are found in all projects. Quality typically defines whether stakeholder expectations were met. Being on time and on budget is one thing; if you deliver the wrong product or an inferior product, on time and on budget suddenly don't mean much.

The *Plan Quality* process is concerned with targeting quality standards that are relevant to the project at hand and devising a plan to meet and satisfy those standards. The quality management plan is an output of this process that describes how the quality policy will be implemented by the project management team during the course of the project. Another key output of this process is the process improvement plan, which documents the actions for analyzing processes to ultimately increase customer value. Everything discussed in this section, including the inputs and tools and techniques of this process, will be used to help develop these two primary outputs.

Exam Spotlight

Plan Quality is a key process performed during the Planning processes and when developing the project management plan. It should be performed in conjunction with other Planning processes. According to the *PMBOK® Guide*, "quality is planned, designed, and built in—not inspected in."

Plan Quality Inputs

The Plan Quality process has several inputs:

- Scope baseline
- Stakeholder register
- Cost performance baseline
- Schedule baseline
- Risk register
- Enterprise environmental factors
- Organizational process assets

The two key elements I'll cover regarding inputs are standards and regulations, which are part of the enterprise environmental factors input, and the quality policy, which is part of the organizational process assets input.

Standards and Regulations

The project manager should consider any standards, regulations, guidelines, or rules that exist concerning the work of the project when writing the quality plan. A *standard* is something that's approved by a recognized body and that employs rules, guidelines, or characteristics that should be followed. For example, the Americans with Disabilities Act (ADA) has established standards for web page designers that outline alternative viewing options of web pages for people with disabilities. PMI guidelines regarding project management are another example of standards.

Standards aren't legally mandatory, but it's a good idea to follow them. Many organizations (or industries) have standards in place that are proven best practice techniques. Disregarding accepted standards can have significant consequences. For example, if you're creating a new software product that ignores standard protocols, your customers won't be able to use it. Standards can be set by the organization, independent bodies, organizations such as the International Organization for Standardization (ISO), and so on. In fact, according to the *PMBOK® Guide,* the Project Quality Management Knowledge Area is designed to be in alignment with the ISO.

A *regulation* is mandatory. Regulations are almost always imposed by governments or institutions like the American Medical Association. However, organizations might have their own self-imposed regulations that you should be aware of as well. Regulations require strict adherence, particularly in the case of government-imposed regulations, or stiff penalties and fines could result—maybe even jail time if the offense is serious enough. Hmm, it might be tough to practice project management from behind bars—not a recommended career move.

If possible, it's a good idea to include information from the quality policy (I'll cover this in the next section) and any standards, regulations, or guidelines that affect the project in the quality management plan. If it's not possible to include this information in the quality management plan, then at least make reference to the information and where it can be found. It's the project management team's responsibility to be certain all stakeholders are aware of and understand the policy issues and standards or regulations that might impact the project.

NOTE Contracts might have certain provisions for quality requirements that you should account for in the quality management plan. If the quality management plan was written prior to the Plan Procurements process, you should update the quality plan to reflect it.

Quality Policy

The quality policy is part of the organizational process assets input. It's a guideline published by executive management that describes what quality policies should be adopted for projects the company undertakes. It's up to the project manager to understand this policy and incorporate any predetermined company guidelines into the quality plan. If a quality policy does not exist, it's up to the project management team to create one for the project.

Exam Spotlight

It is the responsibility of the project management team to assure that all key project stakeholders are aware of and have received copies of the quality policy.

Tools and Techniques for Plan Quality

The Plan Quality process has nine tools and techniques used to help construct the quality management plan:

- Cost-benefit analysis
- Cost of quality
- Control charts

- Benchmarking
- Design of experiments
- Statistical sampling
- Flowcharting
- Proprietary quality management methodologies
- Additional quality planning tools

Make sure you understand each of these tools and techniques and its purpose for the exam. We'll take a look at them now with the exception of flowcharting. We discussed that tool and technique in Chapter 6.

Cost-Benefit Analysis

You've seen the cost-benefit analysis technique before in the Initiating process group. In the case of quality management, you'll want to consider the trade-offs of the cost of quality. It's cheaper and more efficient to prevent defects in the first place than to spend time and money fixing them later. The benefits of meeting quality requirements are as follows:

- Stakeholder satisfaction is increased.
- Costs are lower.
- Productivity is higher.
- There is less rework.

The *PMBOK® Guide* notes that the primary cost of meeting quality requirements for a project is the expense incurred while performing project quality management activities.

Cost of Quality

The *cost of quality (COQ)* is the total cost to produce the product or service of the project according to the quality standards. These costs include all the work necessary to meet the product requirements whether the work was planned or unplanned. It also includes the costs of work performed due to nonconforming quality requirements, assessing whether the product or service meets requirements, and rework.

Three costs are associated with the cost of quality:

Prevention costs Prevention means keeping defects out of the hands of customers. *Prevention costs* are the costs associated with satisfying customer requirements by producing a product without defects. These costs are manifested early in the process and include aspects such as Plan Quality, training, design review, and contractor and supplier costs.

Appraisal costs *Appraisal costs* are the costs expended to examine the product or process and make certain the requirements are being met. Appraisal costs might include costs associated with aspects such as inspections and testing. Prevention and appraisal costs are often passed on to the acquiring organization because of the limited duration of the project.

Failure costs *Failure costs* are what it costs when things don't go according to plan. Failure costs are also known as cost of poor quality. Two types of failure costs exist:

Internal failure costs These result when customer requirements are not satisfied while the product is still in the control of the organization. Internal failure costs might include corrective action, rework, scrapping, and downtime.

External failure costs These occur when the product has reached the customer who determines that the requirements have not been met. Costs associated with external failure costs might include inspections at the customer site, returns, and customer service costs.

There are two categories of costs within COQ, the cost of conformance and the cost of nonconformance. Conformance costs are associated with activities undertaken to avoid failures, while nonconformance costs are those undertaken because a failure has occurred. All of the types of costs of quality we just covered fall into one of these categories. Table 7.2 is a quick reference.

TABLE 7.2 Cost of Conformance and Nonconformance

Conformance Costs	Nonconformance Costs
Prevention costs	Internal failure costs
Appraisal costs	External failure costs

NOTE

The cost of quality can be affected by project decisions. Let's say you're producing a new product. Unfortunately, the product scope description or project scope statement was inadequate in describing the functionality of the product. And, the project team produced the product exactly as specified in the project scope statement, the WBS, and other planning documents. Once the product hit the store shelves, the organization was bombarded with returns and warranty claims because of the poor quality. Therefore, your project decisions impacted the cost of quality. Recalls of products can also impact the cost of quality.

Cost of quality is a topic you'll likely encounter on the exam. The following sections will discuss some of the pioneers in this field. Quality must be planned into the project, not inspected in after the fact to make certain the product or service meets stakeholders' expectations.

Four people in particular are responsible for the rise of the quality management movement and the theories behind the cost of quality: Philip B. Crosby, Joseph M. Juran, W. Edwards Deming, and Walter Shewhart. Each of these men developed steps or points that led to commonly accepted quality processes that we use today and either developed or were the foundation for the development of quality theories such as Total Quality Management, Six Sigma, cost of quality, and continuous improvement. I'll also cover a quality technique called the Kaizen approach that originated in Japan.

Philip B. Crosby

Philip B. Crosby devised the *zero defects* practice, which means, basically, do it right the first time. (Didn't your dad use to tell you this?) Crosby says that costs will increase when quality planning isn't performed up front, which means you'll have to engage in rework, thus affecting productivity. Prevention is the key to Crosby's theory. If you prevent the defect from occurring in the first place, costs are lower, conformance to requirements is easily met, and the cost measurement for quality becomes the cost of nonconformance rather than the cost of rework.

Joseph M. Juran

Joseph M. Juran is noted for his *fitness for use* premise. Simply put, this means the stakeholders' and customers' expectations are met or exceeded. This says that conformance to specifications—meaning the product of the project that was produced is what the project set out to produce—is met or exceeded. Fitness for use specifically reflects the customers' or stakeholders' view of quality and answers the following questions:

Did the product or service produced meet the quality expectation?

Did it satisfy a real need?

Is it reliable and safe?

Juran also proposed that there could be grades of quality. However, you should not confuse grade with quality. *Grade* is a category for products or services that are of the same type but have differing technical characteristics. *Quality* describes how well the product or service (or characteristics of the product or service) fulfills the requirements. Low quality is usually not an acceptable condition; however, low grade might be. For example, your new Dad's Dollars Credit Card software tracking system might be of high quality, meaning it has no bugs and the product performs as advertised, but of low grade, meaning it has few features. You'll almost always want to strive for high quality, regardless of the acceptable grade level.

Exam Spotlight

Understand the difference between quality and grade for the exam.

W. Edwards Deming

W. Edwards Deming suggested that as much as 85 percent of the cost of quality is a management problem. Once the quality issue has hit the floor, or the worker level, the workers have little control. For example, if you're constructing a new highway and the management team that bid on the project proposed using inferior-grade asphalt, the workers laying the asphalt have little control over its quality. They're at the mercy of the management team responsible for purchasing the supplies.

Deming also proposed that workers cannot figure out quality on their own and thus cannot perform at their best. He believed that workers need to be shown what acceptable quality is and that they need to be made to understand that quality and continuous improvement are necessary elements of any organization—or project, in your case.

Many consider Deming to be a major contributor to the *Total Quality Management (TQM)* theory. TQM, like Deming, says that the process is the problem, not people. Every person and all activities the company undertakes are involved with quality. TQM stipulates that quality must be managed in and that quality improvement should be a continuous way of doing business, not a one-time performance of a specific task or process.

Exam Spotlight

There is some controversy surrounding who is the actual founder of TQM. Some say Deming, but others say Armand V. Feigenbaum. For the exam, I recommend knowing that Feigenbaum is the founder of TQM and Deming believes quality is a management issue. *Six Sigma* is a quality management approach that is similar to TQM and is typically used in manufacturing and service-related industries. Six Sigma is a measurement-based strategy that focuses on process improvement and variation reduction, which you can achieve by applying Six Sigma methodologies to the project. There are two Six Sigma methodologies. The first is known as DMADV (define, measure, analyze, design, and verify) and is used to develop new processes or products at the Six Sigma level. The second is called DMAIC (define, measure, analyze, improve, and control) and is used to improve existing processes or products. Another tidbit you should understand about Six Sigma is that it aims to eliminate defects and stipulates that no more than 3.4 defects per million are produced.

Walter Shewhart

Some sources say that Walter Shewhart is considered the grandfather of TQM, which was further popularized by Feigenbaum and Deming. Shewhart developed statistical tools to examine when a corrective action must be applied to a process. He invented control chart techniques (control charts are a tool and technique of the Perform Quality Control process) and was also the inventor of the Plan-Do-Check-Act cycle that I talked about in Chapter 1.

Kaizen Approach

The Kaizen approach is a quality technique from Japan. In fact, *Kaizen* means *continuous improvement* in Japanese. With this technique, all project team members and managers should be constantly watching for quality improvement opportunities. The Kaizen approach states that you should improve the quality of the people first and then the quality of the products or service.

Continuous improvement involves everyone in the organization watching for ways to improve quality, whether incrementally or by incorporating new ideas into the process. This involves taking measurements, improving processes by making them repeatable and systemized, reducing variations in production or performance, reducing defects, and improving cycle times. TQM and Six Sigma are examples of continuous improvement.

Exam Spotlight

Understand each of these theories on the cost of quality for the exam. Here's a key to help you remember:

- Crosby = Zero defects and prevention or rework results.
- Juran = Fitness for use, conformance. Quality by design.
- Deming = Quality is a management problem.
- Feigenbaum = Founder of TQM.
- Shewhart = Plan-Do-Check-Act cycle.
- TQM = Quality must be managed in and must be a continuous process.
- Six Sigma = Six Sigma is a measurement-based strategy; no more than 3.4 defects per million opportunities.
- Kaizen = Continuous improvement; improve quality of people first.
- Continuous improvement = Watch continuously for ways to improve quality.

Control Charts

Control charts help you determine if a process is stable and whether process variances are in control or out of control. We will discuss control charts in more depth in Chapter 9, "Conducting Procurements and Sharing Information."

Benchmarking

Benchmarking is a process of comparing previous similar activities to the current project activities to provide a standard to measure performance against. This comparison will also help you derive ideas for quality improvements on the current project. For example, if your current printer can produce 8 pages per minute and you're considering a new printer that produces 14 pages per minute, the benchmark is 8 pages per minute.

Design of Experiments

Design of experiments (DOE) is a statistical technique that identifies the elements—or variables—that will have the greatest effect on overall project outcomes. It is used most often concerning the product of the project but can also be applied to project management processes to examine trade-offs. DOE designs and sets up experiments to determine the ideal solution for a problem using a limited number of sample cases. It analyzes several variables at once, allowing you to change all (or some of) the variables at the same time and determine which combination will produce the best result at a reasonable cost.

Exam Spotlight

For the exam, remember that the key to DOE is that it equips you with a statistical framework that allows you to change the variables that have the greatest effect on overall project outcomes at once instead of changing one variable at a time.

Statistical Sampling

Statistical sampling involves taking a sample number of parts from the whole population and inspecting them to determine whether they fall within acceptable variances. We will discuss statistical sampling in more detail in Chapter 9.

Flowcharting

A flowchart graphically depicts the relationships between and among steps. They typically show activities, decision points, and the flow or order of steps in a process.

Proprietary Quality Management Methodologies

We've covered most of these during our discussion of cost of quality. Proprietary quality management methodologies include Six Sigma, Lean Six Sigma, Total Quality Management, Quality Function Deployment, and others.

Additional Quality Planning Tools

The last tool and technique of the Plan Quality process is additional quality-planning tools. The *PMBOK® Guide* lists these additional tools as follows:

- Brainstorming
- Affinity diagrams
- Force field analysis
- Nominal Group technique
- Matrix diagrams
- Prioritization matrices

We've already covered brainstorming and the Nominal Group technique. Let's briefly look at the remaining tools next.

Affinity diagrams are used to group and organize thoughts and facts and can be used in conjunction with brainstorming. After you've gathered all ideas possible with brainstorming, you group similar ideas together on an affinity diagram.

Force field analysis is a method of examining the drivers and resistors of a decision. You could use the old T-square approach and list all the drivers down the left column and all the resistors in the right. Determine which of these elements in the list are barriers and which are enablers to the project. Assign a priority or rank to each, and develop strategies for leveraging the strengths of the high-priority enablers while minimizing the highest-ranked barriers.

Matrix diagrams are also used as a decision-making tool, particularly when several options or alternatives are available. Using a spreadsheet format, you list common elements down the rows in the first column and then list each alternative in its own column to the right of this one. Then rank each alternative in the corresponding cell where the common element and the alternative intersect.

Prioritization matrices are useful when you need to prioritize complex issues that have numerous criteria for decision making. They're best used in situations where you can use data or inputs to score the criteria. They work similarly to a weighted scoring model (I talked about those in Chapter 2) in that the most important criteria carries the greatest weight.

You should memorize the names of these additional Plan Quality tools for the exam, but more important, you should understand both the names and concepts of the other tools and techniques I talked about earlier in this chapter.

Plan Quality Outputs

Plan Quality uses many techniques to determine the areas of quality improvement that can be implemented, controlled, and measured throughout the rest of the project, as you've seen. These are recorded in the primary output of this process, which is called the *quality management plan*. The following list includes all the outputs of this process:

- Quality management plan
- Quality metrics
- Quality checklists
- Process improvement plan
- Project document updates

Project document updates include updates to the stakeholder register and the RAM and may also involve updates to the quality management plan and process improvement plan as a result of changes or corrections that result from the Perform Quality Assurance process. We'll talk about the Perform Quality Assurance process in Chapter 9. We'll look at the remaining outputs of Plan Quality next.

Quality Management Plan

The *quality management plan* describes how the project management team will carry out the quality policy. It should document the resources needed to carry out the quality plan, the responsibilities of the project team in implementing quality, and all the processes and procedures the project team and organization should use to satisfy quality requirements, including quality control, quality assurance techniques, and continuous improvement processes.

The project manager, in cooperation with the project staff, writes the quality management plan. You can assign quality actions to the activities listed on the WBS based on the quality plan requirements. Isn't that WBS a handy thing? Later in the Perform Quality Control process, measurements will be taken to determine whether the quality to date is on track with the quality standards outlined in the quality management plan.

Exam Spotlight

The Project Quality Management Knowledge Area, which includes the Plan Quality, Perform Quality Assurance, and Perform Quality Control processes, involves the quality management of the project as well as the quality aspects of the product or service the project was undertaken to produce. We'll discuss Quality Assurance and Quality Control in later chapters.

Quality Metrics

A *quality metric*, also known as *operational definition*, describes what is being measured and how it will be measured during the Perform Quality Control process. For example, let's say you're managing the opening of a new restaurant in July of next year. Perhaps one of the deliverables is the procurement of flatware for 500 place settings. The operational definition in this case might include the date the flatware must be delivered and a counting or inventory process to ensure you received the number of place settings you ordered. Measurements of this variable consist of actual values, not "yes" or "no" results. In our example, receiving the flatware is a "yes" or "no" attribute result (you have it or you don't), but the date it was delivered and the number of pieces delivered are actual values. Failure rates are another type of quality metric that is measurable, as are reliability, availability, test coverage, and defect density measurements.

Quality Checklists

If you're like me, you start your day at the office with a big to-do list that has so many items on it you won't be able to finish them all. Nevertheless, you faithfully write the list every day and check off the items that you accomplish throughout the day. *Checklists* are like this in that they provide a means to determine whether the required steps in a process have been followed. As each step is completed, it's checked off the list. Checklists can be activity specific or industry specific and might be very complex or easy to follow. Sometimes, organizations might have standard checklists they use for projects. You might also be able to obtain checklists from professional associations.

Real World Scenario

Candy Works

Juliette Walters is a contract project manager for Candy Works. She is leading a project that will introduce a new line of hard candy drops in various exotic flavors: café latte, hot buttered popcorn, and jalapeño spice, just to name a few.

Juliette is writing the quality management plan for this project. After interviewing stakeholders and key team members, she has found several quality factors of importance to the organization. Quality will be measured by the following criteria:

Candy size Each piece should measure 3 mm.

Appearance No visible cracks or breaks should appear in the candy.

Flavor Flavor must be distinguishable when taste tested.

Number produced The production target is 9,000 pieces per week. The current machine has been benchmarked at 9,200 candies per week.

Intensity of color There should be no opaqueness in the darker colors.

Wrappers Properly fitting wrappers cover the candies, folding over twice in back and twisted on each side. There is a different wrapper for each flavor of candy, and they must match exactly.

The candy is cooked and then pulled into a long cylinder shape roughly 6 feet long and 2 feet in diameter. This cylinder is fed into the machine that molds and cuts the candy into drops. The cylinders vary a little in size because they're hand-stretched by expert candy makers prior to feeding them into the drop maker machine. As a result, the end of one flavor batch—the café latte flavor—and the beginning of the next batch—the hot buttered popcorn flavor—merge. This means the drops that fall into the collection bins are intermingled during the last run of the first flavor batch. In other words, the last bin of the café latte flavor run has some hot buttered popcorn drops mixed in. And, there isn't a way to separate the drops once they've hit the bin. From here, the drops go on to the candy-wrapping machine, where brightly colored wrappers are matched to the candy flavor. According to the quality plan, hot buttered popcorn drops cannot be wrapped as café latte drops. Juliette ponders what to do.

As she tosses and turns that night thinking about the problem, it occurs to her to present this problem to the company as an opportunity rather than as a problem. To keep production in the 9,000 candies per week category, the machines can't be stopped every time a new batch is introduced. So, Juliette comes up with the idea to wrap candies from the intermixed bins with wrappers that say "Mystery Flavor." This way, production keeps pace with the plan, and the wrapper/flavor quality problem is mitigated.

Exam Spotlight

Be aware that a checklist shows up as an input, an output, and a tool and technique. Quality checklists are an output of the Plan Quality process and an input to the Perform Quality Control process, and checklist analysis is a tool and technique of the Identify Risk process.

Process Improvement Plan

The *process improvement plan* focuses on finding inefficiencies in a process or activity and eliminating them. The idea here is that if you're doing activities or performing processes that don't add any value, you'll want to either stop doing what you're doing or modify the process so that you are adding value. You should note that the process improvement plan is a subsidiary plan of the project management plan. Some of the elements you should consider when thinking about process improvement are the process boundaries, which describes the purpose for the process and its expected start and end dates; the process configuration so that you know what processes are performed when and how they interact; the process metrics; and any specific elements you want to target for improvement.

Quality Baseline

The quality baseline is not a listed output of this process. But almost everything you've done throughout the Plan Quality process culminates in the quality baseline. The *quality baseline* is the quality objective of the project. It's what you'll use to measure and report quality against as you perform the remaining Quality processes. You should understand the definition of the quality baseline for the exam.

NOTE

One of the results of the Plan Quality process is that your product or process might require adjustments to conform to the quality policy and standards. These changes might result in cost changes and schedule changes. You might also discover that you'll need to perform risk analysis techniques for problems you uncover or when making adjustments as a result of this process.

Bringing It All Together

Believe it or not, you have officially completed the Planning process group. Along the way, I've mentioned gaining approvals for portions of the project plan such as the schedule and budget.

The *project plan* is the approved, formal, documented plan that's used to guide you throughout the project Executing process group. The plan consists of all the outputs of the

Planning process groups, including the project management plan. It's the map that tells you where you're going and how to perform the activities of the project plan during the Project Plan Execution process. It serves several purposes, the most important of which is tracking and measuring project performance through the Executing and Monitoring and Controlling processes and making future project decisions. The project plan is critical in all communications you'll have from here forward with the stakeholders, management, and customers. The project plan also documents all project planning assumptions, all project planning decisions, and important management reviews needed.

The project plan encompasses everything I've talked about up to now and is represented in a formal document, or collection of documents. This document contains the project scope statement, deliverables, assumptions, risks, WBS, milestones, project schedule, resources, and more. It becomes the baseline you'll use to measure and track progress against. It's also used to help you control the components that tend to stray from the original plan so you can get them back in line.

The project plan is used as a communication and information tool for stakeholders, team members, and the management team. They will use the project plan to review and gauge progress as well.

Exam Spotlight

Performance measurement baselines are management controls that should change only infrequently. Examples of the performance measurement baselines you've looked at so far are budget, quality, and schedule baselines. However, the project plan itself also becomes a baseline. If changes in scope or schedule do occur after Planning is complete, you should go through a formalized process (which I'll cover in Chapter 10) to implement the changes.

Don't forget that sign-off of the project plan is important to the project's success. Your last step in the Planning process group is obtaining sign-off of the project plan from stakeholders, the sponsor, and the management team. If they've been an integral part of the Planning processes all along (and I know you know how important this is), obtaining sign-off of the project plan should simply be a formality.

Note that you will use all the management plans I discussed during the Planning processes—the project management plan and its subsidiary plans, including the scope management plan, the schedule management plan, and so on, plus the cost budgeting baseline, the schedule baseline, and the quality baseline—throughout the Executing process group to manage the project and keep the performance of the project on track with the project objectives. If you don't have a project plan, you'll have no way of managing the process. You'll find that even with a project plan, project scope has a way of changing. Stakeholders and others tend to sneak in a few of the "Oh, I didn't understand that before" statements and hope that they slide right by you. With that signed, approved project plan in your files, you are allowed to gently remind them that they read and agreed to the project plan and you're sticking to it.

Real World Scenario

Project Case Study: New Kitchen Heaven Retail Store

You're just finishing a phone conversation with Jill, and you see Dirk headed toward your office.

Dirk walks in, crosses his arms over his chest, and stands next to your desk with an "I'm here for answers" look.

"I thought I'd drop by and see whether you have signed a lease and gotten Jake started on that build-out yet," says Dirk.

"I just got off the phone with Jill," you reply. "The Realtor found a great location, and we've set up a tour for tomorrow."

"What has been the holdup?" Dirk asks. "I thought we'd be ready to start the build-out about now."

"I've been working on the project plans."

"Project plans," Dirk interrupts. "We already have a plan. That schedule thing and risk stuff and the budget you drew up over the last couple of weeks spelled things out pretty clearly."

"I'm almost finished with the project plans. I'd like you to take a look at the human resource plan after I review with you what we've done to date."

"I don't understand why you're wasting all this time planning. We all know what the objectives are."

"Dirk," you reply, "if we put the right amount of effort and time into planning, the actual work of the project should go pretty smoothly. Planning is probably one of the most important things we can do on this project. If we don't plan correctly, we might miss something very important that could delay the store opening. That date is pretty firm, I thought."

"Yes, the date is firm. But I don't see how we could miss anything. You and I have met several times, and I know you've met with Jill and Jake. They're the other key players on this."

"Let me finish," you reply. "I have met with all the key stakeholders and after you review these last few documents I have for you, we're finished with the planning phase of this project. Ricardo drafted a procurement statement of work. He needs to hire some external resources—and I noted that in the human resource management plan by the way—to help run Ethernet cable, procure a T1 line, and purchase some routers and switches. The purchase of the routers and switches will be accomplished using a fixed-price contract and the human resources he needs will be procured using a time and materials contract. Jill also drew up a procurement statement of work for the gourmet and cookware lines purchase. I documented a lot of the human resource plan when we worked through the activity estimating and duration exercise and put some finishing touches on it yesterday. It includes a RACI chart for all our project key deliverables." You sneak in a quick breath because you don't want Dirk to interrupt. "And the quality management plan is complete. After your review, I'll distribute it to the key stakeholders. The quality management plan describes how we'll implement our quality policy. You know the old saying, 'Do it right the first time.' I took the time to write down the specific quality metrics we're looking for, including the lease signing date (this one must start and finish on time) and the IT equipment specifications, and Jill has documented the gourmet products and the cookware line specifications."

Dirk looks impressed but you can't tell for sure.

"After I look at the last of these planning documents, are we ready to actually start working?"

"Yes, as soon as the lease is signed. I anticipate that happening by the end of this week. Tomorrow's tour is the fifth location Jill will look at. She's very happy with the third property she saw but wants to look at this last property before she makes her final decision."

"Great. Let's take a look at that human plan or whatever it is."

After reviewing the last of the planning documents, Dirk signs off on the project plan.

- Procurement
  - Fixed-price contract
  - Time and materials contract
  - Procurement documents prepared
  - Procurement statement of work prepared
- Develop Human Resource Plan
  - Roles and responsibilities documented
  - RACI chart developed
  - Organizational chart developed
- Quality Management Plan and Quality Metrics
  - Lease signing start and end dates
  - IT equipment specifications
  - Gourmet products—availability rates and defects
  - Cookware products—availability rates
  - Organizational chart developed
- Obtain approval and sign-off on project plan

Understanding How This Applies to Your Next Project

In my organization, the Plan Procurements process comes right after finalizing project scope because it takes a great deal of time and effort to procure goods and services. That means we have to start procuring resources as early in the project as possible in order to meet the project deadlines.

In all the organizations I've worked in, someone has always been responsible for procurement—whether it was a single person or an entire department. Typically, the procurement department defines many elements of the procurement management plan. Sure, the project team determines how many vendors need to be involved and how they'll be managed along with the schedule dates, but many other elements are predetermined, such as the type of contract to use, the authority of the project team regarding the contract, how multiple vendors will be managed, and the identification of prequalified sellers.

The procurement department also determines what type of procurement document you should use depending on the types of resources you're acquiring and the amount of money you're spending. Typically, they'll have a template for you to use with all the legalese sections pre-populated, and you'll work on the sections that describe the work or resources you need for the project, milestones or schedule dates, and evaluation criteria.

Don't make the mistake of thinking your procurement department will take care of all the paperwork for you. At a minimum, you will likely be responsible for writing the statement of work, writing the RFP, writing the contract requirements (as they pertain to the work of the project), creating the vendor selection criteria, and determining the schedule dates for contract work.

Develop Human Resource Plan is a process you might not need to complete, depending on the size and complexity of the project. I typically work with the same team members over and over again, so I know their skills, capabilities, and availability. However, if you're hiring contract resources for the project or you typically work with new team members on each project, I recommend creating a staffing management plan.

The quality management plan is another important element of your project plan. You should take into consideration the final result or product of the project and the complexity of the project to determine if you need a multipage document with detailed specifications or if the plan can be more informal and broad in nature. Again, depending on the project complexity, the measurements or criteria you'll use to determine the quality objective could be a few simple sentences or bullet items or a more formal, detailed document. The quality baseline should be documented during this process as well.

Summary

This chapter's focus was on planning for project resources. Several aspects are involved in these planning activities, including procuring goods and services, planning human resources, and defining the activities in which human resources will be involved.

This chapter started with the Plan Procurements process. This process identifies the goods or services you're going to purchase from outside the organization and determines which project the project team needs can meet. This involves tools and techniques such as make-or-buy decisions, expert judgment, and contract types. The procurement management plan is one of the outputs of this process and describes how procurement services will be managed throughout the project. The procurement SOW (another output of this process) describes the work that will be contracted.

In our discussion of contract types, we covered fixed-price, cost plus, and time and materials contracts and the benefits and risks of using them.

The Develop Human Resource Plan process identifies and assigns roles and responsibilities and reporting relationships. Many times the roles and responsibilities assignments are depicted in a responsibility assignment matrix (RAM) or a RACI chart. The staffing management plan describes how and when project team members will be acquired and is part of the human resource plan output of this process.

Plan Quality targets the quality standards that are relevant to your project. The quality management plan outlines how the project team will enact the quality policy.

You need to consider the cost of quality when considering stakeholder needs. Four men led to the rise of the cost of quality theories. Crosby is known for his zero defects theory, Juran for the fitness for use theory, Deming for attributing 85 percent of cost of quality to the management team, and Shewhart for the Plan-Do-Check-Act cycle. The Kaizen approach says that the project team should continuously be on the lookout for ways to improve the process and that people should be improved first and then the quality of the products or services. TQM and Six Sigma are examples of continuous improvement techniques.

Cost-benefit analysis considers trade-offs in the Plan Quality process. Benchmarking compares previous similar activities to the current project activities to provide a standard to measure performance against. Design of experiments is an analytical technique that determines what variables have the greatest effect on the project outcomes. This technique equips you with a statistical framework, allowing you to change all the important variables at once instead of changing one variable at a time.

Cost of quality involves three types of costs: prevention, appraisal, and failure costs; the latter is also known as the cost of poor quality. Failure costs include the costs of both internal and external failures.

The process improvement plan is a subsidiary plan of the project management plan and targets inefficiencies in a process or activity. The quality baseline is used to document the quality objectives of the project and is used as a basis for future Quality processes.

Exam Essentials

Be able to name the purpose for the Plan Procurements process. The purpose of the Plan Procurements process is to identify which project needs should be obtained from outside the organization. Make-or-buy analysis is used as a tool and technique to help determine this.

Be able to identify the contract types and their usage. Contract types are a tool and technique of the Plan Procurements process and include fixed-price and cost-reimbursable contracts. Use fixed-price contracts for well-defined projects with a high value to the company, and use cost-reimbursable contracts for projects with uncertainty and large investments early in the project life. The three types of fixed-price contracts are FFP, FPIF, and FP-EPA. The four types of cost-reimbursable contracts are CPFF, CPIF, CPF (or CPPC), and CPAF. Time and materials contracts are a cross between fixed-price and cost-reimbursable contracts.

Be able to name the outputs of the Plan Procurements process. The outputs of Plan Procurements are procurement management plan, procurement statements of work, make-or-buy decisions, procurement documents, source selection criteria, and change requests.

Be able to name the purpose of the Develop Human Resource Plan process. Develop Human Resource Plan involves determining roles and responsibilities, reporting relationships for the project, and creating the staffing management plan, which describes how team members are acquired and the criteria for their release.

Be able to identify the benefits of meeting quality requirements. The benefits of meeting quality requirements include increased stakeholder satisfaction, lower costs, higher productivity, and less rework and are discovered during the Plan Quality process.

Be able to define the cost of quality. The COQ is the total cost to produce the product or service of the project according to the quality standards. These costs include all the work necessary to meet the product requirements for quality. The three costs associated with cost of quality are prevention, appraisal, and failure costs (also known as cost of poor quality).

Be able to name four people associated with COQ and some of the techniques they helped establish. They are Crosby, Juran, Deming, and Shewhart. Some of the techniques they helped to establish are TQM, Six Sigma, cost of quality, and continuous improvement. The Kaizen approach concerns continuous improvement and says people should be improved first.

Be able to name the tools and techniques of the Plan Quality process. The Plan Quality process consists of cost-benefit analysis, cost of quality, control charts, benchmarking, design of experiments, statistical sampling, flowcharting, proprietary quality management methodologies, and additional quality planning tools.

Key Terms

In this chapter, you began to see just how important communication is to every successful project. You learned about planning what work needs to be done, how you will communicate during the project, and how you will judge whether the project is successful. The processes that follow allow you to accomplish those portions of project planning. Understand them well, and know each process by the name used in the *PMBOK® Guide:*

Plan Quality

Develop Human Resource Plan

Plan Procurements

Before you take the exam, also be certain you are familiar with the following terms:

appraisal costs

benchmarking

checklists

continuous improvement

cost of quality (COQ)

cost plus fee (CPF)

cost plus fixed fee (CPFF)

cost plus incentive fee (CPIF)

cost plus percentage of cost (CPCC)

cost-reimbursable contract

design of experiments (DOE)

failure costs

firm fixed-price contracts (FFP)

fitness for use

fixed-price plus incentive contract (FPIF)

fixed-price with economic price adjustment (FP-EPA)

Kaizen approach

lump-sum contract

make-or-buy analysis

operational definition

organization breakdown structure (OBS)

prevention

process improvement plan

procurement documents

procurement management plan

procurement statement of work (SOW)

quality baseline

quality management plan

quality metric

RACI chart

regulation

resource breakdown structure (RBS)

responsibility assignment matrix (RAM)

Six Sigma

standard

time and materials (T&M) contract

Total Quality Management (TQM)

zero defects

Review Questions

1. You are the project manager for an upcoming outdoor concert event. You're working on the procurement plan for the computer software program that will control the lighting and screen projections during the concert. You're comparing the cost of purchasing a software product to the cost of your company programmers writing a custom software program. You are engaged in which of the following?

   A. Procurement planning

   B. Using expert judgment

   C. Creating the procurement management plan

   D. Make-or-buy analysis

2. You are the project manager for an outdoor concert event scheduled for one year from today. You're working on the procurement documents for the computer software program that will control the lighting and screen projections during the concert. You've decided to contract with a professional services company that specializes in writing custom software programs. You want to minimize the risk to the organization, so you'll opt for which contract type?

   A. FPIF

   B. CPFF

   C. FFP

   D. CPIF

3. You are the project manager for the Heart of Texas casual clothing company. It's introducing a new line of clothing called Black Sheep Ranch Wear. You will outsource the production of this clothing line to a vendor. The vendor has requested a procurement SOW. All of the following statements are true except for which one?

   A. The procurement SOW contains a description of the new clothing line.

   B. As the purchaser, you are required to write the procurement SOW.

   C. The procurement SOW contains the objectives of the project.

   D. The vendor requires a procurement SOW to determine whether it can produce the clothing line given the detailed specifications of this product.

4. You are the project manager for the Heart of Texas casual clothing company. It's introducing a new line of clothing called Black Sheep Ranch Wear. You will outsource the production of this clothing line to a vendor. Your legal department has recommended you use a contract that reimburses the seller's allowable costs and builds in a bonus based on the vendor achieving the performance criteria they've outlined in their memo. Which of the following contract types will you use?

   A. CPIF

   B. CPFF

   C. CPF

   D. FPIF

5. All of the following statements are true regarding the Develop Human Resource Plan process except for which one?

   A. The Develop Human Resource Plan involves determining roles and responsibilities.

   B. Included in the Develop Human Resource Plan output are project organization charts that show the project's reporting relationships.

   C. The staffing management plan created in this process describes how and when resources will be acquired and released.

   D. A RAM (or RACI chart) is an output of this process that allows you to see all the people assigned to an activity.

6. Sally is a project manager working on a project that will require a specially engineered machine. Only three manufacturers can make the machine to the specifications Sally needs. The price of this machine is particularly critical to this project. The budget is limited, and there's no chance of securing additional funds if the bids for the machine come in higher than budgeted. She's developing the source selection criteria for the bidders' responses and knows all of the following are true except for which one?

   A. Sally will use understanding of need and warranties as two of the criteria for evaluation.

   B. Sally will review the scope baseline, teaming agreements, and risk register as some of the inputs to this process.

   C. Sally will base the source selection criteria on price alone since the budget is a constraint.

   D. Sally will document a SOW, the desired form of response, and any required contractual provisions in the RFP.

7. Which of the following are constraints that you might find during the Develop Human Resource Plan process?

   A. Organizational structures, collective bargaining agreements, and economic conditions

   B. Organizational structures, technical interfaces, and interpersonal interfaces

   C. Organizational interfaces, collective bargaining agreements, and economic conditions

   D. Organizational interfaces, technical interfaces, and interpersonal interfaces

8. You have been hired as a contract project manager for Grapevine Vineyards. Grapevine wants you to design an Internet wine club for its customers. Customers must register before being allowed to order wine over the Internet so that legal age can be established. You know this project will require new hardware and an update to some existing infrastructure. You will have to hire an expert to help with the infrastructure assessment and upgrades. You also know that the module to verify registration must be written and tested using data from Grapevine's existing database. This new module cannot be tested until the data from the existing system is loaded. You are going to hire a vendor to perform the programming and testing tasks for this module to help speed up the project schedule. The vendor will be reimbursed for all their costs and you want to use a contract type that will allow you to give the vendor a little something extra if you are satisfied with the work they do. You know all of the following apply in this situation except for which one? Choose the least correct response.

A. Contract type is determined by the risk shared between the buyer and seller.

B. You'll use a CPAF contract for the programming vendor.

C. Fixed-price contracts can include incentives for meeting or exceeding performance criteria.

D. Each procurement item needs a SOW.

9. You are the project manager for BB Tops, a nationwide toy store chain. Your new project involves creating a prototype display at several stores across the country. You are using a RACI chart to display individuals and activities. What does RACI stand for?

A. Responsible, accountable, consult, inform

B. Responsible, assignment, control, inform

C. Resource, activity, control, identify

D. Resource, accountable, consult, identify

10. This process has the greatest ability to directly influence the project schedule.

A. Develop Human Resource Plan

B. Plan Procurements

C. Plan Communications

D. Plan Quality

11. You are the project manager for BB Tops, a nationwide toy store chain. Your new project involves creating a prototype display at several stores across the country. You are hiring a contractor for portions of the project. The contract stipulates that you'll pay all allowable costs and a 6 percent fee over and above the allowable costs at the end of the contract. Which of the following describes this contract type?

A. CPPF

B. CPPC

C. CPF

D. CPIF

12. All of the following are true regarding the Plan Quality process except for which one?

A. DOE is a tool and technique of this process that provides statistical analysis for changing product or process elements one at a time to optimize the process.

B. This is one of the key processes performed during the Planning process group and during the development of the project management plan.

C. Changes to the product as a result of meeting quality standards might require cost or schedule adjustments.

D. The tools and techniques of this process are cost-benefit analysis, COQ, control charts, benchmarking, DOE, statistical sampling, flowcharting, proprietary quality management methodologies, and additional quality planning tools.

13. Four people are responsible for establishing cost of quality theories. Crosby and Juran are two them, and their theories are ________________, respectively.

A. grades of quality, fitness for use

B. fitness for use, zero defects

C. zero defects, fitness for use

D. cost of quality, zero defects

14. The theory that 85 percent of the cost of quality is a management problem is attributed to ________________?

A. Deming

B. Shewhart

C. Juran

D. Crosby

15. All of the following are benefits of meeting quality requirements except which one?

A. An increase in stakeholder satisfaction

B. Less rework

C. Lower risk

D. Higher productivity

16. Which of the following describes the cost of quality associated with scrapping, rework, and downtime?

A. Internal failure costs

B. External failure costs

C. Prevention costs

D. Appraisal costs

17. The quality management plan documents how the project team will implement the quality policy. It must address at least all of the following except which one?

A. Quality control

B. Quality metrics

C. Quality assurance

D. Continuous process improvement

18. You work for a furniture manufacturer. Your project is going to design and produce a new office chair. The chair will have the ability to function as a regular chair and also the ability to transform its occupant into an upright, kneeling position. The design team is trying to determine the combination of comfort and ease of transformation to the new position that will give the chair the best characteristics while keeping the costs reasonable. Several different combinations have been tested. This is an example of which of the following tools and techniques of Plan Quality?

A. Benchmarking

B. Quality metrics

C. COQ

D. DOE

19. Which of the following best characterizes Six Sigma?

A. Stipulates that quality must be managed in

B. Focuses on process improvement and variation reduction by using a measurement-based strategy

C. Asserts that quality must be a continuous way of doing business

D. Focuses on improving the quality of the people first, then improving the quality of the process or project

20. Your organization is embarking on a long-term project that will require additional human resources on a contract basis to complete the work of the project. Since the project will span several years, you know one vendor probably can't supply all the resources you'll need over the course of the contract. However, you only want to work with one vendor throughout the project to minimize the amount of procurement documents you'll have to produce. So you'll specify in your procurement documents that contractors will have to form partnerships to work on this project. You know all of the following are true regarding this question except for which one?

A. You will use an RFP, which is an output of the Plan Procurements process, as your procurement document for this project.

B. You'll use an FP-EPA contract, which is described in the contract types tool and technique of the Plan Procurements process.

C. You should consider teaming agreements, which are an input to the Develop Human Resource Plan process.

D. Some of the quality metrics you'll use for this project include on-time performance, failure rates, budget control, and test coverage. Quality metrics are an output of the Plan Quality process.

Answers to Review Questions

1. D. Make-or-buy analysis is determining whether it's more cost effective to purchase the goods or services needed for the project or more cost effective for the organization to produce them internally.

2. C. Firm fixed-price contracts have the highest risk to the seller and the least amount of risk to the buyer. However, the price the vendor charges for the product or service will compensate for the amount of risk they're taking on.

3. B. Either the buyer or the seller can write the SOW. Sometimes the buyer will write the SOW and the seller might modify it and send it back to the buyer for verification and approval.

4. A. The cost plus incentive fee contract reimburses the seller for the seller's allowable costs and includes an incentive or bonus for exceeding the performance criteria laid out in the contract.

5. D. The RAM and RACI charts are tools and techniques of this process.

6. C. Source selection criteria can be based on price alone when there are many vendors who can readily supply the goods or services. The question states that only three vendors make the machine, which means source selection criteria should be based on more than price.

7. A. Constraints can be anything that limits the option of the project team. Organizational structures, collective bargaining agreements, and economic conditions are all constraints that you might encounter during this process.

8. C. Fixed-price contracts can include incentives for meeting performance criteria, but the questions states the vendor helping with the programming task will be reimbursed for their costs and, depending on your satisfaction with their results, may receive an additional award. This describes a cost plus award fee contract.

9. A. RACI stands for responsible, accountable, consult, and inform.

10. B. Plan Procurements can directly influence the project schedule, and the project schedule can directly influence this process.

11. B. This is a cost-reimbursable contract that includes a fee as a percentage of allowable costs. This type of contract is known as a cost plus percentage of cost (CPPC) contract.

12. A. Design of experiments is a tool and technique of the Plan Quality process that provides statistical analysis for changing key product or process elements all at once (not one at a time) to optimize the process.

13. C. Philip Crosby devised the zero defects theory, meaning do it right the first time. Proper Plan Quality leads to less rework and higher productivity. Joseph Juran's fitness for use says that stakeholders' and customers' expectations are met or exceeded.

14. A. W. Edwards Deming conjectured that the cost of quality is a management problem 85 percent of the time and that once the problem trickles down to the workers, it is outside their control.

15. C. The benefits of meeting quality requirements are increased stakeholder satisfaction, lower costs, higher productivity, and less rework.

16. A. Internal failure costs are costs associated with not meeting the customer's expectations while you still had control over the product. This results in rework, scrapping, and downtime.

17. B. Quality metrics are an output of the Plan Quality process.

18. D. This is an example of design of experiments.

19. B. Six Sigma is a measurement-based strategy that focuses on process improvement and variation reduction by applying Six Sigma methodologies to the project.

20. C. Teaming agreements are an input of the Plan Procurements process.

Chapter

8

Developing the Project Team

THE PMP EXAM CONTENT FROM THE EXECUTING THE PROJECT PERFORMANCE DOMAIN COVERED IN THIS CHAPTER INCLUDES THE FOLLOWING:

- ✓ **Execute Tasks Defined in Project Plan**
- ✓ **Implement Approved Changes**
- ✓ **Ensure Common Understanding and Set Expectations**
- ✓ **Implement the Procurement of Project Resources**
- ✓ **Manage Resource Allocation**
- ✓ **Improve Team Performance**

This chapter begins the project Executing process group. I'll cover four of the processes in this chapter: Direct and Manage Project Execution, Acquire Project Team, Develop Project Team, and Manage Project Team. I'll cover the remaining four Executing processes in the next chapter.

Direct and Manage Project Execution is the action process. This is where you'll put the plans into action and begin working on the project activities. Execution also involves keeping the project in line with the original project plan and bringing wayward activities back into alignment.

The Acquire, Develop, and Manage Project Team processes are all interrelated, as you can imagine, and work together to help obtain the best project team available.

Several things happen during the Executing processes. The majority of the project budget will be spent during this process group, and often the majority of the project time is expended here as well. The greatest conflicts you'll see during the project Executing processes are schedule conflicts. In addition, the product description will be finalized here and contain more detail than it did in the Planning processes.

There might be several exam questions from every process within the Executing process group. Don't skip studying these processes and the ones in Chapter 9 because roughly one quarter of the exam questions concern the Executing process group. Are you ready to dive into Executing? Let's go.

Executing the Project Plan

The purpose of the *Direct and Manage Project Execution* process is to carry out the project plan. This is where your project comes to life and the work of the project happens. The work is authorized to begin and activities are performed. Resources are committed and carry out their assigned activities to create the product, result, or service of the project. Funds are spent to accomplish project objectives. Performing project activities, training, selecting sellers, collecting project data, utilizing resources, and so on are all integrated with or are part of this process.

Direct and Manage Project Execution is where the rubber meets the road. If you've done a good job planning the project, things should go relatively smoothly for you during this process. The deliverables and requirements are agreed upon, the resources have been identified and are ready to go, and the stakeholders know exactly where you're headed because you had them review, agree to, and approve the project plan.

Some project managers think this is the time for them to kick back and put their feet up. After all, the project plan is done, everyone knows what to do and what's expected of them, and the work of the project should almost carry itself out because your project plan is a work of genius, right? Wrong! You must stay involved. Your job now is a matter of overseeing the actual work, staying on top of issues and problems, and keeping the work lined up with the project plan.

Exam Spotlight

The project plan serves as the project baseline. During the Executing processes, you should continually compare and monitor project performance against the baseline so that corrective actions can be taken and implemented at the right time to prevent disaster. This information will also be fed into the Monitoring and Controlling processes for further analysis.

One of the most difficult aspects of this process is coordinating and integrating all the elements of the project. Although you do have the project plan as your guide, you still have a lot of balls in the air. You'll find yourself coordinating and monitoring many project elements—occasionally all at the same time—during the course of the Direct and Manage Project Execution process. You might be negotiating for team members at the same time you're negotiating with vendors at the same time you're working with another manager to get a project component completed so your deliverables stay on schedule. You should monitor risks and risk triggers closely. The Plan Procurements process might need intervention or cause you delays. The organizational, technical, and interpersonal interfaces might require intense coordination and oversight. And of course, you should always be concerned about the pulse of your stakeholders. Are they actively involved in the project? Are they throwing up roadblocks now that the work has started?

According to the *PMBOK® Guide*, this process also requires implementing corrective actions to bring the work of the project back into alignment with the project plan, preventive actions to reduce the probability of negative consequences, and defect repairs to correct product defects discovered during the quality processes.

As you can see, your work as project manager is not done yet. Many elements of the project require your attention, so let's get to work.

NOTE

Later in this chapter I'll also talk about Develop Project Team because this is an integral part of the Direct and Manage Project Execution process as well. You'll want to monitor the team's performance, the status of their work, and their interactions with you and other team members as you execute the project plan.

Executing Inputs

Direct and Manage Project Execution has four inputs:

- Project management plan
- Approved change requests
- Enterprise environmental factors
- Organization process assets

The project management plan documents the collection of outputs of the Planning processes and describes and defines how the project should be executed, monitored, controlled, and closed. You'll take a brief look at each of the other inputs next.

Approved Change Requests

Approved change requests come about as a result of the change request status updates output of the Perform Integrated Change Control process. (We'll cover this process in Chapter 10, "Measuring and Controlling Project Performance"). Change requests are approved or denied during this process, and once the decision has been made, approved changes come back through the Direct and Manage Project Execution process for the project team to implement.

Approved changes might either expand or reduce project scope and may also cause revisions to project budgets, schedules, procedures, project management plans, and so on. Change requests can be internal or external to the project or organization. For example, you may need to make changes because of a new law that affects your project.

Enterprise Environmental Factors

There are several enterprise environmental factors to consider when performing this process, including the company culture and organizational structure, the facilities available to the project team, personnel guidelines and hiring practices, risk tolerance levels, and project management information systems.

Organizational Process Assets

Like many of the other processes we've covered, historical information from past projects, organizational guidelines, and work processes are some of the organizational process assets you should consider when performing this process. In addition, measurement databases and issue and defect databases can be used in this process to compare past projects to the current project and to capture information about the current project for future reference.

Tools and Techniques of Direct and Manage Project Execution

The tools and techniques of the Direct and Manage Project Execution process are expert judgment and project management information system. You've looked at both of these before. Remember that in the Executing processes, you'll be actively using both of these tools, consulting with stakeholders, professionals, and others and employing the project management methodology you've developed in the Planning process and using the project management information system to update and track progress.

Some of the outputs of this process are going to look familiar and some are new. We'll examine them next.

Outputs of Direct and Manage Project Execution

The outputs of the Direct and Manage Project Execution process are as follows:

- Deliverables
- Work performance information
- Change requests
- Project management plan updates
- Project document updates

The three most important outputs of this process are deliverables (meaning actually accomplishing the activities leading to the completion of the product, result, or service you set out to produce), work performance information, and change requests. Almost every process you've performed up to this point has defined and outlined what the work of the project entails and what the final results should look like. Now you're ready to begin performing the work. Let's look at these three outputs that will help us document our progress.

Deliverables

During Direct and Manage Project Execution, you'll gather and record information regarding the outcomes of the work, including activity completion dates, milestone completions, the status of the deliverables, the quality of the deliverables, costs, schedule progress and updates, and so on. Deliverables aren't always tangible. For example, perhaps your team members require training on a piece of specialized equipment. Completion of the training is recorded as a work result. Capabilities required to perform a service that's described in the project management plan are also considered a deliverable. All of this information gets used during the Performance Reporting process, which I'll discuss during the Monitoring and Controlling processes.

Executing and Monitoring and Controlling are two process groups that work hand in hand. As you gather the information from work results, you'll measure the outputs and take corrective actions where necessary. This means you'll loop back through the Executing processes to put the corrections into place. The *PMBOK® Guide* breaks these processes up for ease of explanation, but in practice, you'll work through several of the Executing and Monitoring and Controlling processes together.

Work Performance Information

Work performance information concerns gathering, documenting, and recording the status of project activities. The types of information you might gather during this process include some of the following:

- Schedule status and progress

- Status of deliverable completion
- Progress and status of schedule activities
- Adherence to quality standards
- Status of costs (those authorized and costs incurred to date)
- Schedule activity completion estimates for those activities started
- Schedule activities percent complete
- Lessons learned
- Resource consumption and utilization

Work performance information becomes an input to a few of the Monitoring and Controlling processes where you'll perform further analysis on the data. It's important that you document this information so that when you get to the Monitoring and Controlling processes, you don't have to backtrack.

Change Requests

As a result of working through activities and producing your product, service, or result, you will inevitably come upon things that need to be changed. Changes can also come about from stakeholder requests, external sources, technological advances, and so on. These change requests might encompass schedule, scope, requirement, or resource changes. The list really could go on. Your job as project manager, if you choose to accept it, is to collect the change requests and make determinations about their impact on the project.

Implementation of change requests may incorporate two types of actions: corrective actions or preventive actions. They may also require defect repairs. Each of these topics are described next.

Corrective actions In my organization, a corrective action means an employee is in big trouble. Fortunately, this isn't what's meant here. *Corrective actions* are taken to get the anticipated future project outcomes to align with the project plan. Maybe you've discovered that one of your programmers is adding an unplanned feature to the software project because he's friends with the user. You'll have to redirect him to the activities assigned to him originally to avoid schedule delays. Perhaps your vendor isn't able to deliver the laboratory equipment needed for the next project phase. You'll want to exercise your contract options (let's hope there's a clause in the contract that says the vendor must provide rental equipment until they can deliver your order), put your contingency plan into place, and get the lab the equipment that's needed to keep the project on schedule.

Preventive action *Preventive action* involves anything that will reduce the potential impacts of risk events should they occur. Contingency plans and risk responses are examples of preventive action. I described these and other risk responses while talking about the Plan Risk Response process in Chapter 6. You should be aware of contingency plans and risk responses so that you're ready to implement them at the first sign of trouble.

Defect repairs A defect occurs when a project component does not meet the requirements or specifications. Defects might be discovered when conducting quality audits in the

Perform Quality Assurance process or when performing inspections during the Perform Quality Control process.

You should understand the difference between a validated defect repair and a defect repair for the exam. A validated defect repair is the result of a reinspection of the original defect repair. In other words, you found a problem with the product during the Quality processes, you corrected the problem (defect repair), and now you're reinspecting that repair (validated defect repair) to make certain the fix is accurate, correct, and fixed the problem.

I'll discuss change requests more in the coming chapters as well. Change requests are an output of several processes, including the Direct and Manage Project Execution process and the Report Performance process in the Monitoring and Controlling process group. Remember that Executing and Monitoring and Controlling outputs feed each other as inputs. And in this particular case, approved change requests are an input, and change requests are an output of the same process.

Real World Scenario

We All Scream for Ice Cream

Heather is a pharmaceutical sales person who is fed up with the rat race. She ran the numbers, decided to quit her day job, and bought an ice cream shop in a quaint tourist town. Having been involved in a few research and development projects, she understands the value of project management planning and using that plan as her guide to perform the work of the project.

Heather documented the deliverables needed to prepare for opening day in her scope statement. Some of those deliverables are as follows: remodel, develop staffing plan, procure equipment, and procure materials. Confident in her planning, Heather hired a contractor and began remodeling the shop. And then real life happened. The contractors discovered a water problem in the storage room. They installed a sump pump, which took care of the water, but discovered an even bigger problem when they moved the storage shelves. There was mold growing up the drywall. The drywall had to be removed, as did the insulation behind it, and the mold remaining on permanent fixtures had to be eliminated. Then new insulation and drywall had to be installed. The drywall had to be primed and painted, and Heather decided since that portion of the storage room was getting a fresh coat of paint, the contractors might as well paint the entire room.

All of these actions required another pass through the Planning processes. The schedule didn't require much modification because other work could be started at the same time the water problem was being addressed, but the budget needed to be modified as a result of the additional work. To avoid more surprises, Heather requested that the contractor perform a thorough inspection of the property and determine whether there were any other hidden issues. Armed with the inspection report, Heather could knowledgeably plan corrective action for other items that needed to be addressed.

Exam Spotlight

Direct and Manage Project Execution is where the work of the project is performed and the project plan is put into action and carried out. In this process, the project manager is like an orchestra conductor signaling the instruments to begin their activities, monitoring what should be winding down, and keeping that smile going to remind everyone that they should be enjoying themselves. I recommend that you know the outputs of the Direct and Manage Project Execution process for the exam.

I told you the Executing process group is about performing the work of the project, and in order to do that, you need resources. You'll look at two processes, Acquire the Project Team and Develop the Project Team, in the next few sections.

Acquiring the Project Team

The *Acquire Project Team* process involves attaining and assigning human resources to the project. Project staff might come from inside the company or from outside the company in the form of employees hired specifically for the project or as contract help. In any case, it's your job as the project manager to ensure that resources are available and skilled in the project activities to which they're assigned. However, in practice, you might find that you don't always have control over the selection of team members. Someone else, the big boss for example, might handpick the folks they want working on the project, and it's up to you to assess their skills and decide where they best fit on the project.

The Acquire Project Team process inputs are as follows:

- Project management plan
- Enterprise environmental factors
- Organizational process assets

The project management plan describes the roles and responsibilities, project organization charts, and staffing management plan by way of subsidiary plans.

Enterprise environmental factors in this process account for project activities that might require special skills or knowledge in order to be completed. They may also consider personal interests, cost rates, prior experience, and availability of potential team members before making assignments. For example, consider the previous experience of the staff member you're thinking of assigning to a specific activity. Have they performed this function before? Do they have the experience necessary for the level of complexity this project activity calls for? Are they competent and proficient at these skills?

Personal interests and personal characteristics play a big role as well. If the person you're thinking of just isn't interested in the project, they aren't likely to perform at their best. If you can, think about assigning someone else in a case like this. Unfortunately, some people just don't play well with others. When you're assigning staff, if at all possible, don't put the only two people in the whole company who can't get along together on the same project. If a staff member you need has a skill no one else has or they can perform a function like no one else can, you might not have a choice. In this case, you'll have to employ other techniques to keep the team cohesive and working well together despite the not-so-friendly relationship between the two staff members.

One final consideration: Check on the availability of key team members. If the team member you must have for the activity scheduled in February is on their honeymoon, you probably aren't going to win the toss.

Exam Spotlight

Remember that the availability, experience levels, interests, cost, and abilities of your resources are considered part of the enterprise environmental factors input. You should understand these inputs and their importance to the Acquire Project Team process for the exam.

The organizational process assets input refers to standard processes, policies, and procedures the organization has in place. Recruitment practices are one example to watch for in this process. You'll want to make certain you're following the organization's recruitment procedures and processes when hiring and assigning staff. You should also note that organizational policies that dictate recruitment practices are constraints.

We've looked at the other inputs in previous processes, so we'll move on to the tools and techniques of this process.

Tools and Techniques of Acquire Project Team

The tools and techniques of the Acquire Project Team process are as follows:

- Pre-assignment negotiation
- Acquisitions
- Virtual teams

Pre-Assignment *Pre-assignment* can happen when the project is put out for bid and specific team members are promised as part of the proposal or when internal project team members are promised and assigned as a condition of the project. When staff members are promised as part of the project proposal—particularly on internal projects—they should be identified in the project charter.

Negotiation As the project manager, you will use the negotiation technique a lot, so brush up on those skills every chance you get. You'll have to negotiate with functional managers and other organizational department managers—and sometimes with the vendor to get some of their best people—for resources for your project and for the timing of those resources.

Availability is one part of the negotiating equation. You'll have to work with the functional manager or other project managers to ensure that the staff member you're requesting is available when the schedule says they're needed.

The second part of the equation is the competency level of the staff member they're assigning to your project. I remember hearing someone say once that availability is not a skill set. Be wary of functional managers who are willing to offer up certain individuals "anytime" while others are "never available." Be certain your negotiations include discussions about the skills and personal characteristics of the team members you want on your project.

Acquisition Acquisition involves hiring individuals or teams of people for certain project activities, either as employees or as contract help during the course of the project or project phase or for specific project activities. Procurement is usually required when the organization does not have employees with the required skills and competencies available to work on the project.

NOTE We talked about Plan Procurements in Chapter 7, "Planning Project Resources."

Virtual teams *Virtual teams* are the last tool and technique of this process. Virtual teams don't necessarily work in the same location, but their members all share the goals of the project and have a role to fulfill. This type of team allows you to include folks from different geographic locations, those who work different hours or shifts than the other team members, those with mobility limitations, and so on. According to the *PMBOK® Guide*, "Virtual teams can be defined as groups of people with a shared goal, who fulfill their roles with little or no time spent meeting face to face." In today's wonderful world of technology, team members can use the Internet, email, videoconferencing, teleconferencing, and more to meet and communicate on a regular basis. This of course brings to light the importance of communication. Make certain all team members are aware of the protocols for communicating in a virtual team environment, understand the expectations, and are clear regarding decision making processes.

It's vital in this type of team structure that you, as the project manager, give credit to the appropriate team members for their performance and actions on the project. You might be the only one who fully understands the contributions individual team members have made. When teams are co-located, members have the opportunity to see for themselves the extraordinary efforts others are making on the project. Virtual team members don't necessarily know what their teammates have contributed to the project (or the level of effort they've exerted), so it's up to you to let everyone know about outstanding performance.

Outputs of Acquire Project Team

The resulting outputs of the Acquire Project Team process are as follows:

- Project staff assignment
- Resource calendars
- Project management plan updates

Project staff assignment Your ability to influence the selection of resources (using the negotiating technique) will impact the project staff assignment output. After determining elements such as the roles and responsibilities, reviewing recruitment practices, and negotiating for staff, you assign project team members to project activities. Along with this output, a project team directory is published listing the names of all project team members and stakeholders. Don't forget to also include team member names in project organization charts, RAM charts, and other planning documents if their assignments or names weren't known when you created those documents.

Resource calendars Resource calendars show the team members' availability and the times they are scheduled to work on the project. A composite resource calendar includes availability information for potential resources as well as their capabilities and skills. (Resource calendars are an input to the Estimate Activity Resources process). This comes in handy when you're creating the final schedule and assigning resources to activities.

Real World Scenario

The Only Candidate

"Hey, did you hear?" your friend Story asks. "Roger has been assigned to the project team."

"Over my dead body," you reply, pushing away from your computer screen. You head straight for the project manager's office and don't wait for a response from Story.

Ann sets the phone into the cradle just as you walk through the door. Fortunately for you, Ann's door is always open, and she welcomes drop-ins.

"Seems like something is on your mind," Ann says. "What can I help with?"

"Story just told me that Roger has been assigned to the project team. I can't work with Roger. He's arrogant and doesn't respect anyone's work but his own. He belittles me in front of others, and I don't deserve that. I write good code, and I don't need Roger looking over my shoulder. I want to be on this team, but not if Roger is part of it."

Ann thinks for a minute and replies, "I want you to work on this project; it's a great opportunity for you. But there isn't anyone else who can work on the analysis phase of this project except Roger. He's the only one left who has a solid understanding of the mainframe legacy code. Unfortunately, those old programs were never documented well, and they've evolved over the years into programs on top of programs. Without Roger's knowledge of the existing system, we'd blow the budget and time estimates already established for this project. Since I need both of you on this project, here's what I propose. I will clearly outline the roles and responsibilities for all the key team members at the kickoff meeting. I'll also make it clear that negative team interactions won't be allowed. And if you have a problem with Roger that you can't resolve on your own, you should get me involved right away."

Project management plan updates The time periods your project staff are available are documented in the resource calendars output. The human resource plan and staffing management plan might require updates to document the project roles and responsibilities of the staff assigned to the project. These documents might require updates throughout the project if you have staff members leave because of a promotion or, heaven forbid, if they leave for employment in another company (unless you want them to leave—that's another story).

Now that you have the team, what do you do with them? You'll look at topics such as motivation, rewards, and recognition in the next process, Develop Project Team.

Developing the Project Team

Projects exist to create a unique product, result, or service within a limited time frame. Projects are performed by people, and most projects require more than one person to perform all of the activities. If you've got more than one person working on your project, you've got a team. And if you've got a team, you've got a wide assortment of personalities, skills, needs, and issues in the mix. Couple this with part-time team members, teams based in functional organizations whose loyalty lies with the functional manager, or teams based in matrix organizations that report to you for project-related activities and another manager for their functional duties, and you could have some real challenges on your hands. Good luck—OK, I won't leave you hanging like that.

The *Develop Project Team* process is about creating an open, encouraging environment for your team and developing it into an effective, functioning, coordinated group. Projects are performed by individuals, and the better they work together, the smoother and the more efficient the execution of the project will be. I'm sure you all have had the experience of working with a team that pitched in and shared workloads when the work became unbalanced. I'm also sure you all have worked with teams that didn't do this—teams whose members took on a "me first" attitude and couldn't care less about the plight of their fellow team members. I'd much rather work with a team like the first example.

NOTE

The proper development of the team is critical to a successful project. Since teams are made up of individuals, individual development becomes a critical factor to project success. Individual team members need the proper development and training to perform the activities of the project or to enhance their existing knowledge and skills. The development needed will depend on the project. Perhaps you have a team member who's ready to make the jump into a lead role but they don't have any experience at lead work. Give them some exposure by assigning them a limited amount of activities in a lead capacity, provide them with some training if needed, and be available to coach and mentor where needed. The best option is to work with the management team to provide this person with the development they need prior to the start of the project (if you're lucky enough to know early on who your resources might be and what their existing skills are).

Develop Project Team inputs include project staff assignments, project management plan, and resource calendars. Funny thing, these inputs are all outputs that I discussed in the Acquire Project Team process, so we'll move on.

Tools and Techniques of Develop Project Team

The tools and techniques of Develop Project Team are as follows:

- Interpersonal skills
- Training
- Team-building activities
- Ground rules
- Co-location
- Recognition and rewards

I'll cover all these tools and techniques next.

Interpersonal Skills

Interpersonal skills are often referred to as soft skills. Soft skills include such things as leadership, influence, negotiation, communications, empathy, and creativity. For example, it's important for you as the project manager to have an understanding of your project team members' attitudes and opinions about their work. Bad attitudes, like the saying goes, are contagious. It doesn't mean the person who has the attitude is bad, but if you're paying attention to your team members and taking the appropriate amount of time to listen to their legitimate concerns and issues, and taking action on them, you can go a long way toward stemming bad attitudes.

Soft skills can be learned but in my experience are more often inherent in project managers' personalities. But just because certain soft skills may not be in your nature, it doesn't mean you can't observe this behavior in others and incorporate them into your management techniques.

One other issue to consider regarding this tool and technique is that you'll have resources from other departments who have assignments on the project that you're responsible for overseeing. For example, the finance department and the marketing department might have assigned project activities, and as the project manager, you'll manage their progress. This implies that you'll need general knowledge management skills to understand what the assignments entail and strong leadership and negotiation skills to influence the departments to stay on schedule.

Training

Training is a matter of assessing your team members' skills and abilities, assessing the project needs, and providing the training necessary for the team members to carry out their assigned activities. Training can sometimes be a reward as well. In the software industry, programmers seek out positions that offer training on the latest and greatest technologies, and they consider it a benefit or bonus to attend training on the company dollar and time. If you know early in the Planning processes that training is necessary, include the details of this in the staffing management plan. During the course of the project, you might observe team members who need training, or they might ask for training. Update the staffing management plan with this information.

Team-Building Activities

Many times, project teams consist of folks who don't know each other. They aren't necessarily aware of the project objectives and might not even want to be a part of the team. The project manager might not have worked with the people assigned to the project team before either. Sound like a recipe for disaster? It's not. Thousands of projects are started with team members and project managers who don't know each other, and those projects come to a successful completion. How is that done? It's a result of the project manager's team-building and communication skills.

The project manager's job is to bring the team together, get its members all headed in the right direction, and provide motivation, reward, and recognition to keep the team in tip-top shape. This is done using a variety of team-building techniques and exercises. *Team building* is simply getting a diverse group of people to work together in the most efficient and effective manner possible. This might involve events organized by the management team or individual actions designed to improve team performance. There are entire volumes on this subject, and it's beyond the scope of this book to go into all the team-building possibilities. The exam tends to focus more on the theories behind team building and the characteristics of effective teams, so that's what you'll spend your time exploring.

Dr. Bruce Tuckman developed a model that describes how teams develop and mature. According to Tuckman, all newly formed teams go through five stages of development:

1. Forming
2. Storming
3. Norming
4. Performing
5. Adjourning

Tuckman originally devised this theory using the first four stages of development. Based on later research by Tuckman and Mary Ann Jensen, a fifth stage of development was added called adjourning. You may see this model referred to as the Tuckman-Jensen model in other literature, and you might want to tuck that piece of information away for the exam. You've probably seen this model elsewhere, but since these stages might show up on the exam, you'll want to memorize them. Take a brief look at each of them:

Forming This one is easy. Forming is the beginning stage of team formation, when all the members are brought together, introduced, and told the objectives of the project. This is where team members learn why they're working together. During this stage, team members tend to be formal and reserved and take on an "all-business" approach.

Storming Storming is where the action begins. Team members become confrontational with each other as they're vying for position and control during this stage. They're working through who is going to be the top dog and jockeying for status.

Norming Now things begin to calm down. Team members know each other fairly well by now. They're comfortable with their positions in the team, and they begin to deal with project problems instead of people problems. In the norming stage, they confront the project concerns and problems instead of each other. Decisions are made jointly at this stage, and team members exhibit mutual respect and familiarity with one another.

Performing Ahh, perfection. Well, almost, anyway. This is where great teams end up. This stage is where the team is productive and effective. The level of trust among team members is high, and great things are achieved. This is the mature development stage.

Adjourning As the name implies, this phase refers to the breakup of the team after the work is completed.

Exam Spotlight

Different teams progress through the stages of development at different rates. When new team members are brought onto the team, the development stages start all over again. It doesn't matter where the team is in the first four phases of the development process—a new member will start the cycle all over again.

According to Tuckman, leaders adapt their leadership styles as the teams develop maturity and progress through the development stages. For example, early in the forming stage, leaders take on a direct style of leadership. As the team progresses, their leaders will employ a coaching, participating, and then delegating style of leadership to match the level of development the team has achieved.

You'll now take a closer look at focusing your team members throughout these stages of development, along with some of the characteristics of effective teams.

Team Focus

Have you ever watched any of those old pirate movies on late-night TV? Remember the scenes where the captain goes down into the bowels of the ship to check on the teams of rowers? He scrutinizes the crew and literally whips the rowers who aren't pulling their weight into shape. I don't recommend this as a team-building technique, but imagine for a minute that your project team members are like those rowing teams. If the members on the left are rowing one way and the members on the right are rowing another, you're creating a lot of energy and looking busy, but in the end you aren't making any progress.

It's paramount that the team members know and understand the goals and objectives of the project. They should all understand the direction you're headed and work toward that end. After all, that's the reason they've been brought together in the first place. Keep in mind that people see and hear things from their own perspective. A room full of people attending a speech will each come away with something a little different because what was said speaks to their particular situation in life at the time. In other words, their own perceptions filter what they hear. It's your job as project manager to make certain the team members understand the project goals and their own assignments correctly. I suggest you use solid communication skills to get your point across. Ask your team members to tell you in their own words what they believe the project goals are. This is a great way to know whether you've got everyone on board and a great opportunity for you to clarify any misunderstandings regarding the project goals.

Effective Team Characteristics

Effective teams are typically very energetic teams. They often are characterized as high-performance teams and are motivated by results and the successful completion of tasks. Their enthusiasm is contagious, and it feeds on itself. They generate a lot of creativity and become good problem solvers. Teams like this are every project manager's dream. Investing yourself in team building as well as relationship building—especially when you don't think you have the time to do so—will bring many benefits. Here's a sample of the benefits:

- Better conflict resolution
- Commitment to the project
- Commitment to the project team members and project manager
- High job satisfaction
- Enhanced communication
- A sense of belonging and purpose
- A successful project

Dysfunctional teams will typically produce the opposite results of the benefits just listed. Dysfunctional teams don't just happen by themselves any more than great teams do. Sure, sometimes you're lucky enough to get the right combination of folks together right off the bat. But usually, team building takes work and dedication on the part of the project manager. Even in the situations where you do get that dynamite combination of people, they will benefit from team-building exercises and feedback.

Unfortunately, sour attitudes are just as contagious as enthusiasm. Watch for these symptoms among your team members, and take action to correct the situation before the entire team is affected:

- Lack of motivation or "don't care" attitudes
- Project work that isn't satisfying
- Status meetings that turn into whining sessions
- Poor communication
- Lack of respect and lack of trust for the project manager

NOTE No amount of team building will make up for poor project planning or ineffective project management techniques. Neglecting these things and fooling yourself into thinking that your project team is good enough to make up for the poor planning or poor techniques could spell doom for your project. And besides that, it's not fair to your project team to put them in that position.

Ground Rules

Ground rules are expectations set by the project manager and project team that describe acceptable team behavior. For example, one of my pet peeves is team members who interrupt each other. In this case, one of the ground rules is one person speaks at a time during a meeting. Another ground rule might be reporting potential issues as soon as the team member becomes aware of them. Outlining ground rules like this helps the team understand expectations regarding acceptable behavior and increases productivity.

Co-location

Team members are often in the same physical location—for example, the same office building or meeting space. This tool and technique is called co-location. *Co-location* enables teams to function more effectively than if they're spread out among different localities. Many times on large projects, the project manager will make provisions in the project budget to bring the team together at the same location. (It's difficult, but not impossible, to manage project team members who are not physically located together.) One way to achieve co-location might be to set aside a common meeting room, sometimes called a *war room*, for team members who are located in different buildings or across town to meet and exchange information.

Multiple locations can also be a big time waster for you as the project manager and for your team members. If some team members are located in one part of town and another set of team members are located across town, you'll find yourself in the car (or the bus) driving back and forth to make face-to-face contact and get status updates. Conducting team meetings also becomes a hassle as one set of team members or the other must drive to another location (or both to a central location) to have a meeting.

Our busy, conflicting schedules and differences in location don't always allow for face-to-face communication, so email is the next best thing. I'm a huge email fan—it's one of my favorite forms of communication. Email can keep the information flowing when you aren't able to meet in person, and it can even help take the heat out of conflicts that might escalate if you were meeting one on one. However, email cannot reveal tone of voice, facial expressions, or body language. Sometimes those nonverbal cues are more important than what's being said. If you don't know your team members or stakeholders well, I recommend meeting with them personally whenever you can. Once you've established good relationships with them, you should be able to balance the use of email and personal interactions and know when it's time to call a face-to-face meeting. In reality, it's often difficult to get your team together physically. A good solution in lieu of having people relocate is videoconferencing or conference calling. Team members scattered across the country all have access to the telephone, and it's relatively easy to find a time everyone can meet over the phone. Videoconferencing is the best option if it's available because it allows intonation and nonverbal behaviors to be part of the communication process.

Recognition and Rewards

I have quite a bit of ground to cover with recognition and rewards. As I said earlier, you could see several exam questions regarding team building, so dig out all your favorite memorization techniques and put them to use.

Team building starts with project planning and doesn't stop until the project is completed. It involves employing techniques to improve your team's performance and in keeping team members motivated. Motivation helps people work more efficiently and produce better results. If clear expectations, clear procedures, and the right motivational tools are used, project teams will excel.

Motivation can be extrinsic or intrinsic. Extrinsic motivators are material rewards and might include bonuses, the use of a company car, stock options, gift certificates, training opportunities, extra time off, and so on.

Intrinsic motivators are specific to the individual. Some people are just naturally driven to achieve—it's part of their nature. (I suspect this is a motivator for you since you're reading this book.) Cultural and religious influences are forms of intrinsic motivators as well. Reward and recognition—a tool and technique of the Develop Project Team process—are examples of extrinsic motivators. We'll look at them next.

Recognition and rewards are an important part of team motivation. They are formal ways of recognizing and promoting desirable behavior and are most effective when carried out by the management team and the project manager. You should develop and document the criteria for rewards, especially monetary awards. Although rewards and recognition help build a team, they can also kill morale if you don't have an established method or criteria for handing them out. Track who is receiving awards throughout the project. For example, if you have consistent overachievers on the team, you could kill morale by consistently rewarding the same one or two people repeatedly. It could also be perceived that you're playing favorites. If team members believe the rewards are win-lose (also known as *zero-sum*) and that only certain team members will be rewarded, you might end up hurting morale more than helping. If you find yourself in this position, consider team awards. This is a win-win because all team members are recognized for their contributions. Recognition and rewards should be proportional to the achievement. In other words, appropriately link the reward to the performance. For example, a project manager who has responsibility for the project budget and the procurement process and keeps the costs substantially under budget without sacrificing the results of the project should be rewarded for this achievement. However, if these responsibilities are assigned to a functional manager in the organization, it wouldn't be appropriate to reward a project manager who was not the one responsible for keeping the costs in line.

Team members should be rewarded for going above and beyond the call of duty. Perhaps they put in a significant amount of overtime to meet a project goal or spent nights round-the-clock babysitting ill-performing equipment. These types of behaviors should be rewarded and formally recognized by the project manager and the management team. On the other hand, if the ill-performing equipment was a direct result of mistakes made or if it happened because of poor planning, rewards would not be appropriate, obviously.

Consider individual preferences and cultural differences when using rewards and recognitions. Some people don't like to be recognized in front of a group; others thrive on it. Some people appreciate an honest thank-you with minimal fanfare, and others just won't accept individual rewards as their culture doesn't allow it. Keep this in mind when devising your reward system.

There are many theories on motivation. As a project manager, it's important to understand them so that you can tailor your recognition and rewards programs to take into account the reasons people do what they do. You might encounter questions on these theories on the exam, so we'll discuss their primary points in the following sections.

Real World Scenario

Baker's Gift Baskets

You're a contract project manager for Baker's Gift Baskets. This company assembles gift baskets of all styles and shapes with every edible treat imaginable. The company has recently experienced explosive growth, and you've been brought on board to manage its new project. The owners of the company want to offer "pick-your-own" baskets that allow customers to pick the individual items they want included in the basket. In addition, they're introducing a new line of containers to choose from, including items such as miniature golf bags, flowerpots, serving bowls, and the like. This means changes to the catalog and the website to accommodate the new offerings.

The deadline for this project is the driving constraint. The website changes won't cause any problems with the deadline. However, the catalog must go to press quickly to meet holiday mailing deadlines, which in turn are driving the project deadline.

Your team members put their heads together and came up with an ingenious plan to meet the catalog deadline. It required lots of overtime and some weekend work on their part to pull it off, but they met the date.

You decide this is a perfect opportunity to recognize and reward the team for their outstanding efforts. You've arranged a slot on the agenda at the next all-company meeting to bring your team up front and praise them for their cooperation and efforts to get the catalog to the printers on time. You'll also present each of them with two days of paid time off and a gift certificate for a dinner with their family at an exclusive restaurant in the city.

Motivational Theories

Motivational theories came about during the modern age. Prior to today's information- and service-type jobs and yesterday's factory work, the majority of people worked the land and barely kept enough food on the table to feed their family. No one was concerned about motivation at work. You worked because you wouldn't have anything to eat if you didn't. Fortunately, that isn't the only reason most people work today.

Today we have a new set of problems in the workplace. Workers in the service- and knowledge-based industries aren't concerned with starvation—that need has been replaced with other needs such as job satisfaction, a sense of belonging and commitment to the project, good working conditions, and so on. Motivational theories present ideas on why people act the way they do and how you can influence them to act in certain ways to get the results you want. Again, there are libraries full of books on this topic. I'll cover four of them here.

MASLOW'S HIERARCHY OF NEEDS

You have probably seen this classic example of motivational theory. Abraham Maslow theorized that humans have five basic needs arranged in hierarchical order. The first needs are physical needs, such as the need for food, clothing, and shelter. The idea is that these needs must be met before the person can move to the next level of needs in the hierarchy, which includes safety and security needs. Here, the concern is for the person's physical welfare and the security of their belongings. Once that need is met, they progress to the next level, and so on.

Maslow's hierarchy of needs theory suggests that once a lower-level need has been met, it no longer serves as a motivator and the next higher level becomes the driving motivator in a person's life. Maslow conjectures that humans are always in one state of need or another. Here is a recap of each of the needs, starting with the highest level and ending with the lowest:

Self-actualization Performing at your peak potential

Self-esteem needs Accomplishment, respect for self, capability

Social needs A sense of belonging, love, acceptance, friendship

Safety and security needs Your physical welfare and the security of your belongings

Basic physical needs Food, clothing, shelter

The highest level of motivation in this theory is the state of self-actualization. The United States Army had a slogan a few years ago that I think encapsulates self-actualization very well: "Be all that you can be." When all the physical, safety, social, and self-esteem needs have been met, a person reaches a state of independence where they're able to express themselves and perform at their peak. They'll do good work just for the sake of doing good work. Recognition and self-esteem are the motivators at lower levels; now the need for being the best they can be is reached.

NOTE In Maslow's later work, he discussed three additional aspects of motivation: cognitive, aesthetic, and transcendence. The five key needs are the ones you'll most likely need to know for the exam, but it wouldn't hurt to be familiar with the names of the three additional motivational levels.

HYGIENE THEORY

Frederick Herzberg came up with the *Hygiene Theory*, also known as the *Motivation-Hygiene Theory*. He postulates that two factors contribute to motivation: hygiene factors and motivators. Hygiene factors deal with work environment issues. The thing to remember about hygiene factors is that they prevent dissatisfaction. Examples of hygiene factors are pay, benefits, the conditions of the work environment, and relationships with peers and managers. Pay is considered a hygiene factor because Herzberg believed that over the long term, pay is not a motivator. Being paid for the work prevents dissatisfaction but doesn't necessarily bring satisfaction in and of itself. He believed this to be true as long as the pay system is equitable. If two workers performing the same functions have large disparities in pay, then pay can become a motivator.

Motivators deal with the substance of the work itself and the satisfaction one derives from performing the functions of the job. Motivators lead to satisfaction. The ability to advance, the opportunity to learn new skills, and the challenges involved in the work are all motivators according to Herzberg.

Exam Spotlight

For the exam, remember that Herzberg was the inventor of the Hygiene Theory and that this theory claims that hygiene factors (pay, benefits, and working conditions) prevent dissatisfaction while motivators (challenging work, opportunities to learn, and advancement) lead to satisfaction.

EXPECTANCY THEORY

The *Expectancy Theory,* first proposed by Victor Vroom, says that the expectation of a positive outcome drives motivation. People will behave in certain ways if they think there will be good rewards for doing so. Also note that this theory says the strength of the expectancy drives the behavior. This means the expectation or likelihood of the reward is linked to the behavior. For example, if you tell your two-year-old to put the toys back in the toy box and you'll give her a cookie to do so, chances are she'll put the toys away. This is a reasonable reward for a reasonable action. However, if you promise your project team members vacations in Hawaii if they get the project done early and they know there is no way you can deliver that reward, there is little motivation to work toward it.

This theory also says that people become what you expect of them. If you openly praise your project team members and treat them like valuable contributors, you'll likely have a high-performing team on your hands. Conversely, when you publicly criticize people or let them know that you have low expectations regarding their performance, they'll likely live up (or down as the case might be) to that expectation as well.

ACHIEVEMENT THEORY

Achievement Theory, attributed to David McClelland, says that people are motivated by the need for three things: achievement, power, and affiliation. The achievement motivation is obviously the need to achieve or succeed. The power motivation involves a desire for influencing the behavior of others. And the need for affiliation is relationship oriented. Workers want to have friendships with their co-workers and a sense of camaraderie with their fellow team members. The strength of your team members' desire for each of these will drive their performance on various activities.

Exam Spotlight

Make certain you understand the theories of motivation and their premises for the exam. Here's a summary to help you memorize them.

Maslow's hierarchy of needs Abraham Maslow. Needs must be satisfied in a hierarchical order.

Hygiene Theory Frederick Herzberg. Work environment (pay, benefits, and working conditions) prevents dissatisfaction.

Expectancy Theory Victor Vroom. Expectation of positive outcomes drives motivation.

Achievement Theory David McClelland. People are motivated by achievement, power, and affiliation.

I'll cover two more theories in the leadership section, which is next. These deal specifically with how leaders interact with their project team members.

Leadership versus Management

Chapter 1 introduced the differences between leaders and managers. I'll add a bit more information here regarding leadership theories and the types of power leaders possess, but first I'll recap leadership and management.

Recall that leadership is about imparting vision and rallying people around that vision. Leaders motivate and inspire and are concerned with strategic vision. Leaders have a knack for getting others to do what needs to be done.

Two of the techniques they use to do this are power and politics. *Power* is the ability to get people to do what they wouldn't do ordinarily. It's also the ability to influence behavior. *Politics* imparts pressure to conform regardless of whether people agree with the decision. Leaders understand the difference between power and politics and when to employ each technique. I'll talk more about power shortly.

Good leaders have committed team members who believe in the vision of the leader. Leaders set direction and time frames and have the ability to attract good talent to work for them. Leaders inspire a vision and get things done through others by earning loyalty, respect, and cooperation from team members. They set the course and lead the way. Good leaders are directive in their approach but allow for plenty of feedback and input. Good leaders commonly have strong interpersonal skills and are well respected.

Managers are generally task oriented and concerned with issues such as plans, controls, budgets, policies, and procedures. They're generalists with a broad base of planning and organizational skills, and their primary goal is satisfying stakeholder needs. They also possess motivational skills and the ability to recognize and reward behavior.

NOTE Project managers need to use the traits of both leaders and managers at different times during a project. On large projects, a project manager will act more like a leader inspiring the subproject managers to get on board with the objectives. On small projects, project managers will act more like managers because they're responsible for all the planning and coordinating functions.

I'll discuss four theories regarding leadership and management. They are Douglas McGregor's Theory X and Theory Y, Dr. William Ouchi's Theory Z, and the Contingency Theory. Then I'll discuss the types of power leaders use and the outputs of Develop Project Team.

THEORY X, THEORY Y, AND THEORY Z

Douglas McGregor defined two models of worker behavior, Theory X and Theory Y, that attempt to explain how different managers deal with their team members. *Theory X* managers believe most people do not like work and will try to steer clear of it; they believe people have little to no ambition, need constant supervision, and won't actually perform the duties of their job unless threatened. As a result, Theory X managers are like dictators and impose very rigid controls over their people. They believe people are motivated only by punishment, money, or position. Unfortunately for the team members, Theory X managers unknowingly also subscribe to the Expectancy Theory. If they expect people to be lazy and unproductive and treat them as such, their team members probably will be lazy and unproductive.

Theory Y managers believe people are interested in performing their best given the right motivation and proper expectations. These managers provide support to their teams, are concerned about their team members, and are good listeners. Theory Y managers believe people are creative and committed to the project goals, that they like responsibility and seek it out, and that they are able to perform the functions of their positions with limited supervision.

Theory Z was developed by Dr. William Ouchi. This theory is concerned with increasing employee loyalty to their organizations. It came about in Japan in the 1980s when jobs were often offered for life. This theory results in increased productivity, it puts an emphasis on the well-being of the employees both at work and outside of work, it encourages steady employment, and it leads to high employee satisfaction and morale.

CONTINGENCY THEORY

The Contingency Theory builds on a combination of Theory Y behaviors and the Hygiene Theory. The Contingency Theory, in a nutshell, says that people are motivated to achieve levels of competency and will continue to be motivated by this need even after competency is reached.

The Power of Leaders

As stated earlier, power is the ability to influence others to do what you want them to do. This can be used in a positive manner or a negative one. But that old saying of your grandmother's about attracting more flies with honey than vinegar still holds true today.

Leaders, managers, and project managers use power to convince others to do tasks a specific way. The kind of power they use to accomplish this depends on their personality, their personal values, and the company culture.

A project manager might use several forms of power. I've already talked about reward power, which is the ability to grant bonuses or incentive awards for a job well done. Here are a few more:

Punishment power Punishment, also known as *coercive* or *penalty power*, is just the opposite of reward power. The employee is threatened with consequences if expectations are not met.

Expert power Expert power occurs when the person being influenced believes the manager, or the person doing the influencing, is knowledgeable about the subject or has special abilities that make them an expert. The person goes along just because they think the influencer knows what they're doing and it's the best thing for the situation.

Legitimate power Legitimate, or formal, power comes about as a result of the influencer's position. Because that person is the project manager, executive vice president, or CEO, they have the power to call the shots and make decisions.

Referent power Referent power is inferred to the influencer by their subordinates. Project team members who have a great deal of respect and high regard for their project managers willingly go along with decisions made by the project manager because of referent power.

Punishment power should be used as a last resort and only after all other forms have been exhausted. Sometimes you'll have to use this method, but I hope much less often than the other three forms of power. Sometimes, you'll have team members who won't live up to expectations and their performance suffers as a result. This is a case where punishment power is enacted to get the employee to correct their behavior.

Exam Spotlight

Know the difference between leaders and managers, Theory X and Theory Y, the Contingency Theory, and the types of power for the PMP exam. Here's a summary to help you memorize them:

Leaders Leaders motivate, inspire, and create buy-in for the organization's strategic vision. Leaders use power and politics to accomplish the vision.

Managers Managers are task oriented and concerned with satisfying stakeholder needs.

Theory X Most people don't like work.

Theory Y: People are motivated to perform their best given proper expectations and motivation.

Theory Z The implementation of this theory increases employee loyalty and leads to high satisfaction and morale.

Contingency Theory People are motivated to achieve levels of competency and will continue to be motivated after competency is reached.

Reward power You reward desirable behavior with incentives or bonuses.

Punishment power You threaten team members with consequences if expectations are not met (also known as *penalty power*).

Expert power The person doing the influencing has significant knowledge or skills regarding the subject.

Legitimate power This is the power of the position held by the influencer (the president or vice president, for example).

Referent power This is power that's inferred to the influencer.

Outputs of Develop Project Team

You're now ready to close out the Develop Project Team process. This process has only two outputs, team performance assessment and enterprise environmental factors updates. Team performance assessments involves determining a team's effectiveness. As a result of positive team-building experiences, you'll see individuals improving their skills, team behaviors and relationships improving, conflict resolutions going smoothly, and team members recommending ways to improve the work of the project. I talked about effective team characteristics earlier in this chapter. Assessing these characteristics will help you determine where (or whether) the project team needs improvements.

NOTE

Project managers wear a lot of hats. This is one of the things that make this job so interesting. You need organization and planning skills to plan the project. You need motivation and sometimes disciplinary skills to execute the project plans. You need to exercise leadership and power where appropriate. And all the while, you have a host of relationships to manage, involving team members, stakeholders, managers, and customers. It's a great job and brings terrific satisfaction.

Managing Project Teams

The *Manage Project Team* process is concerned with tracking and reporting on the performance of individual team members. During this process, performance appraisals are prepared and conducted, issues are identified and resolved, and feedback is given to the team members. Some team behavior is also observed during this process, but the main focus here is on individuals and their performance.

Exam Spotlight

Take note that the *PMBOK® Guide* states that one of the outcomes or results of the Manage Project Team process is an update to the human resource plan, which is part of the project management plan updates output of this process.

You've seen all the inputs to this process before with the exception of performance reports:

- Project staff assignments
- Project management plan
- Team performance assessments
- Performance reports
- Organizational process assets

Performance reports document the status of the project compared to the forecasts. We'll talk more at length about performance reports in Chapter 10. Keep in mind that this is another example of an input to an Executing process coming from an output of a Monitoring and Controlling process.

Tools and Techniques for Managing Teams

Most of the tools and techniques for this process are new. Don't skip studying any of them because you'll likely see exam questions regarding them. The tools and techniques of the Manage Project Team process are as follows:

- Observation and conversation
- Project performance appraisals
- Conflict management
- Issue log
- Interpersonal skills

We'll take a closer look at each of these tools in the following sections.

Observation and Conversation

Observation and conversation is another one of those tools and techniques that is self-evident. To assess team member performance, you have to observe it. I hope you've also learned how important communication is to the success of the project. This includes communicating with your team members. I know project managers who are reticent to engage their teams in conversation unless it's official project business. I've even known project managers who instructed their administrative assistant to give a specific direction to another team member. It's difficult to understand a team member's attitude or viewpoint toward the project if you're communicating through someone else. Establish an open door policy with your team members and live up to it. The benefits are so great that it's worth a few minutes a day of chitchat to establish that feeling of trust and camaraderie. If your team perceives you as open, honest, and willing to listen, you'll be the first person they come to when issues arise.

Real World Scenario

What Not to Do

Tina is a newly minted project manager. She has worked on many projects as the assistant project manager, but this is the first time she has led the charge. Tina is so shy she finds it difficult to give team members any kind of direction or to assign tasks, so she has her administrative assistant do it for her. Tina tells her administrative assistant what needs to be done and who needs to do it and leaves it to the assistant to inform the appropriate team members.

As the project progresses, schedule milestone dates are missed, and Tina discovers tasks that haven't started that were scheduled to start two weeks ago. Coming in from lunch one day she saw several project team members huddled around her administrative assistant's desk. From what she overheard, they were discussing a risk event that occurred on the project.

Fortunately for Tina, one of the project managers she has worked for in the past saw what was happening. Because the administrative assistant was the one who had established relationships with the team and was in effect giving the orders, the team began treating her as the project manager instead of Tina. Tina's friend had a one-on-one coaching session with Tina about her management style and the importance of conversation and observation. Together they were able to get the project back on track.

Project Performance Appraisal

Project performance appraisals are typically annual or semiannual affairs where managers let their employees know what they think of their performance over the past year and rate them accordingly. These are usually manager-to-employee exchanges but can incorporate a *360-degree review*, which takes in feedback from just about everyone the team member interacts with, including stakeholders, customers, project manager, peers, subordinates, and the delivery person if they have a significant amount of project interaction. I'm not a fan of 360-degree reviews because it makes most nonmanager types uncomfortable. "I don't want to rate my peer" is a typical response. I also find 360-degree reviews are biased. At best you'll get a response like this: "Oh, Ken is great, just great. No problems—a good guy." Or you'll get exactly the opposite if the person you're speaking with doesn't like the team member you're reviewing. Performance appraisal should be a bit more constructive than this. Nonetheless, understand the 360-degree concept for the exam.

No matter what type of appraisal is conducted, project managers should contribute to the performance appraisals of all project team members. You should be aware of potential loyalty issues when you're working in a matrix organizational structure. The team member in this structure reports to both you (as the project manager) and a functional manager. If the project manager does not have an equal say, or at least some say about the employee's performance, it will cause the team member to be loyal to the functional manager and show little loyalty to the project or project manager. Managing these dual reporting relationships is often a critical success factor for the project, and it is the project manager's responsibility to assure that these relationships are managed effectively.

Performance appraisal time is also a good time to explore training needs, to clarify roles and responsibilities, to set goals for the future, and so on.

Conflict Management

I said earlier in this chapter that if you have more than one person working on your project, you have a team. Here's another fact: if you have more than one person working on your project, you'll have conflict.

Everyone has desires, needs, and goals. Conflict comes into the picture when the desires, needs, or goals of one party are incompatible with the desires, needs, or goals of another party (or parties). *Conflict*, simply put, is the incompatibility of goals, which often leads to one party resisting or blocking the other party from attaining their goals. Wait—this doesn't sound like a party!

There are six ways of resolving conflict that might show up on the exam:

Forcing *Forcing* is just as it sounds. One person forces a solution on the other parties. This is where the boss puts on the "Because I'm the boss and I said so" hat. Although this is a permanent solution, it isn't necessarily the best solution. People will go along with it because, well, they're forced to go along with it. It doesn't mean they agree with the solution. This isn't the best technique to use when you're trying to build a team. This is an example of a win-lose conflict resolution technique. The forcing party wins, and the losers are those who are forced to go along with the decision.

Smoothing/accommodating *Smoothing* does not lead to a permanent solution. It's a temporary way to resolve conflict where the areas of agreement are emphasized over the areas of difference so the real issue stays buried. Smoothing can also occur when someone attempts to make the conflict appear less important than it is. Everyone looks at each other and scratches their head and wonders why they thought the conflict was such a big deal anyway. As a result, a compromise is reached, and everyone feels good about the solution until they get back to their desk and start thinking about the issue again. When they realize that the conflict was smoothed over and really is more important than they were led to believe, or that they never dealt with the real issue at hand, they'll be back at it, and the conflict will resurface. This is an example of a lose-lose conflict resolution technique because neither side wins. Smoothing is also known as accommodating.

Compromise *Compromise* is achieved when each of the parties involved in the conflict gives up something to reach a solution. Everyone involved decides what they will give on and what they won't give on, and eventually through all the give and take, a solution is reached. Neither side wins or loses in this situation. As a result, neither side is really gung ho about the decision that was reached. They will drag their feet and reluctantly trudge along. If, however, both parties make firm commitments to the resolution, then the solution becomes a permanent one.

Confrontation/problem solving *Confrontation* is also called *problem solving* and is the best way to resolve conflict. One of the key actions you'll perform with this technique is a fact-finding mission. The thinking here is that one right solution to a problem exists and the facts will bear out the solution. Once the facts are uncovered, they're presented to the parties and the decision will be clear. Thus, the solution becomes a permanent one and the conflict expires. This is the conflict resolution approach project mangers use most often and is an example of a win-win conflict resolution technique.

Collaborating *Collaborating* occurs when multiple viewpoints are discussed and shared and team members have the opportunity to examine all the perspectives of the issue. Collaborating will lead to true consensus where team members commit to the decision.

Withdrawal/avoidance *Withdrawal* or avoidance never results in resolution. This occurs when one of the parties gets up and leaves and refuses to discuss the conflict. It is probably the worst of all the techniques because nothing gets resolved. This is an example of a lose-lose conflict resolution technique

Exam Spotlight

Know each of the conflict resolution techniques for the exam. Also remember that these techniques will not necessarily yield long-term results. The smoothing and withdrawal techniques have temporary results and aren't always good techniques to use to resolve problems. Resolutions reached through forcing, compromise, and confrontation techniques might not always be satisfying for all parties, but they tend to produce longer-lasting results. Collaborating techniques are often successful and produce commitment to the decision provided all parties believe they had opportunity to provide their opinions and ideas.

During the Manage Project Team process it's important to note that, as in any situation, you'll want to deal with conflict as soon as it arises. According to the *PMBOK® Guide*, when you have successfully resolved conflict, it will result in increased productivity and better, more positive working relationships.

Most conflicts come about in the Manage Project Team process as a result of schedule issues, availability of resources (usually the lack of availability), or personal work habits. When project team members are having a conflict, address them first in private with the person who has the issue. Work in a direct and collaborative manner, but be prepared to escalate the issue into a more formalized procedure (potentially even disciplinary action) if needed.

If conflicts exist between the team members, encourage resolution between them without intervention on your part. The best conflict resolution will come about when they can work out the issues between them. When that isn't possible, you'll have to step in and help resolve the matter.

Remember that solid ground rules and established policies and procedures will help mitigate conflict before it arises.

Issue Log

The issue log is a place to document the issues that keep the project team from meeting project goals. These can range from differences of opinion to newly surfaced responsibilities that need to be assigned to a project team member. Each issue should be recorded in the log along with the person responsible for resolving it. You should also note the date the resolution is needed.

Interpersonal Skills

We talked about interpersonal skills in the Develop Project Team process, but you should know for the exam that the *PMBOK® Guide* points out three types of interpersonal skills used most often in this process. They are leadership, influencing, and effective decision making. We've already covered leadership and influencing. Effective decision making concerns making decisions in a timely manner and making decisions that reflect and support the goals of the project. Effective decisions should bring about a good result for the project, the stakeholders, and the team members. They also help you take advantage of opportunities and minimize negative risks. As project managers, and good leaders, we have a responsibility to put the good of project and the organization over our own needs, so use sound judgment when making decisions.

NOTE I have seen many project managers in the course of my career drag their feet when it comes to making a decision or downright refuse to make a decision. No decision is a decision—in effect, you're choosing to do nothing. This can have disastrous consequences for your project. Sometimes, it's better to make a misguided decision than no decision at all. Make certain to examine all the information known at the time, consult your experts, and finally, make the decision.

Managing Project Team Outputs

The outputs of the Manage Project Team process are the result of the conversations, performance appraisals, and conflict resolution I've talked about previously. This process has four outputs:

- Enterprise environmental factors updates
- Organizational process assets update

- Change requests
- Project management plan updates

Remember that the elements of these outputs pertain to human resources. For example, change requests might come about as a result of a change in staffing, corrective actions might come about because of disciplinary actions or training needs, and preventive actions might be needed to reduce the impact of potential human resource issues. Any of these actions might cause changes to the staffing management plan or the human resource plan, which means you should update the project management plan.

The enterprise environmental process updates has two components that may need updating as a result of this process. They are input to organizational performance appraisals and personnel skill updates. The input to organizational performance appraisals comes from team members with significant interactions with the project and each other.

The organizational process asset updates output has three components: historical information/lessons learned documentation, templates, and organizational standard processes.

Lessons learned encompasses everything you've learned about the human resources aspect during this project, including documentation that can be used as templates on future projects (such as org charts, position descriptions, and the staffing management plan), techniques used to resolve conflict, the types of conflict that came up during the project, ground rules, when and how virtual teams were used on the project and the procedures associated with them, the staffing management plan, special skills needed during the project that weren't known about during the Planning processes, and the issue log.

In the next chapter, we'll wrap up the Executing process group and examine the processes associated with conducting procurements, providing quality assurance, distributing information, and managing the expectations of stakeholders.

Real World Scenario

Project Case Study: New Kitchen Heaven Retail Store

You are in Dirk's office giving him some good news.

"The lease is signed and the work of the project has started. Ricardo has several of his staff members assigned to perform tasks related to the information technology deliverables, as do Jill and Jake for their areas.

I held a kick-off meeting with all the key project team members. We started out with some team-building exercises and I explained the five stages of team development. It's normal to have some conflict as we're starting out, and I let them all know my door is always open and if they have issues they can't resolve, they can come to me directly. I explained the goals of the project, laid some ground rules for team interaction, and talked with them about the conflict resolution techniques we'll use as we get further into the project."

"I'm just glad to hear we're finally doing something," Dirk replies.

"Even though Gomez construction doesn't start until next week, they sent their crew leader to the kickoff meeting. I was impressed with that."

Dirk asks, "Why isn't Gomez starting work now?"

"They aren't scheduled to start until Sept 20 and we need to get our procurement documents signed. We have a week to finish up the signatures before they get here, so we're in fine shape. But Ricardo's group has already prepared their procurement documents to purchase the switches and other equipment they need to start work. Bryan, Ricardo's team lead, finished his other project sooner than anticipated, and since they have Ethernet cable on hand, he started running cable today."

The key stakeholder from the marketing department peeks her head in Dirk's door. "I saw you both in here and thought I'd ask you when someone from the project team is going to work with me on the website announcement? I haven't heard anything, and I don't want to cut this so close that we put up something subpar on the website. The 50th anniversary deserves a little splash."

"OK," you reply. "I'll set up a meeting with you to get more information, and then I'll work with Ricardo to determine who is the best fit. I've noted we need to assign someone to this activity in the issue log. The person he thought he was going to assign to this task is out on family leave and we don't know when he's expected back."

"Thanks," the stakeholder replies. "I also heard you lost a valuable team member last week. I was really sorry to see Madelyn go. What happened? And will her loss impact the project?"

"I don't want to go into all the details, but she violated our Internet acceptable use policy. She was placed on disciplinary action on this very issue once before. This may impact the project schedule because her activities were on the critical path. I've already interviewed two internal candidates who've expressed interest in working on the project. I believe either one would work out nicely. They have the skills we need and are very interested. However, there is some ramp-up time needed. I've added this to the risk list because we could have an impact to the schedule if we don't get Madelyn replaced by the end of this week. I've got a change request ready also in case there is a schedule impact. I won't know more until next week."

Dirk glances at his desk clock.

You stand and on your way to the door tell him, "Next week I'll hold a formal status meeting with all the stakeholders and will begin distributing written weekly status reports."

Project Case Study Checklist

The processes and concepts discussed in the case study include:

- Direct and Manage Project Execution
  - Deliverables
  - Work results
  - Work performance information
- Develop Project Team
  - Interpersonal skills
  - Team-building
  - Ground rules
  - Team performance assessments
- Acquire Project Team
  - Negotiation
  - Acquisition
  - Resource calendars
- Manage Project Team
  - Observation and conversation
  - Conflict management
  - Issue log
  - Change requests

Understanding How This Applies to Your Next Project

The topics in this chapter are some of my favorites because this is where project management shines—dynamic teams working under the direction of a capable, responsible leader who can effectively balance the needs of the team with the needs of the project (and ultimately the organization) and pull it all off successfully. There aren't many things better in an organization than a high-performing team working together to accomplish a well-understood goal. And it doesn't really matter whether the team members are all in the same company, department, or country. When they're working toward a common goal and functioning at the performing level, there's almost nothing they can't accomplish. The movies *Ocean's Eleven, Ocean's Twelve,* and *Ocean's Thirteen* are good examples of strong leadership and dynamic teamwork at play. Although I'm certainly not advocating you turn to a life of crime, you can pick up a few pointers on how effective teams work from George Clooney and the gang.

So, how does this apply? As the project manager, it's your responsibility, and dare I say duty, to acquire the best team members possible for your project. In my experience, this doesn't always mean all my team members are highly qualified. To me, team fit and team dynamics are as important as the team members' skills. I know some will disagree with me on this next point, but I believe it's easier to train someone on a new skill (given they have the aptitude) than it is to take on a team member with an abrasive personality who is imminently qualified but can't get along with anyone else on the team. Sometimes you really don't have much choice when it comes to picking team members, as referenced in the sidebar "The Only Candidate" earlier in this chapter. When you find yourself in this situation, I recommend you lay down clear ground rules for communication, problem escalation, work assignments, and so on.

Make it a habit to read at least a couple of leadership books a quarter. You may already be familiar with the topic and think there isn't anything new to learn. However, staying current on the topic will reinforce concepts that you already know and will remind you of other points that you forgot about and haven't yet developed but know you should. And occasionally, you will pick up a gold nugget of information that is new and immediately applicable to your situation.

Leadership skills are invaluable, but communication skills are just as important. In my opinion, it's difficult to be an effective leader without also being an effective communicator. My guess is that if you take a close look at the leaders you respect and admire, you'll discover they are also good communicators. And communication is mostly listening—not talking. I make it a habit to practice active listening. It's amazing what people will tell you when you smile politely and ask an open-ended question or two.

Let me stress again that you cannot successfully manage a project team without communicating with them on a regular basis. The last thing you want is for a stakeholder to follow you into the elevator to inform you about a major problem with the project that you weren't aware of. That will happen if you haven't established a relationship with your team. If they don't believe you're trustworthy or they don't know you well enough to know whether you'll stand by them, you'll be one of the last people to find out what's happening. I know managers and project managers who subscribe to the "don't get too close to your team" theory. I subscribe to the "all things in moderation" theory. You do want to establish relationships and prove your loyalty to the team, but you also have to know where to draw the line. When it comes time to hold a team member accountable, it can be difficult to do if you have become very close on a personal basis. But I advocate erring on the side of developing a relationship with the team. My teams have to trust me to the point that they know they can come to me—at any time, with all types of news, good or bad—and I'll help them resolve the problem.

Summary

This chapter described four processes from the Executing process group: Direct and Manage Project Execution, Acquire Project Team, Develop Project Team, and Manage Project Team.

In Direct and Manage Project Execution, the project plans come to life. Activities are authorized to begin and the product, result, or service of the project is produced. Status review meetings are held to inform stakeholders of project progress and updates.

Acquire Project Team involves negotiation with other functional managers, project managers, and organizational personnel to obtain human resources to complete the work of the project. The project manager might not have control over who will be a part of the team. Availability, ability, experience, interests, and costs are all enterprise environmental factors that should be considered when you are able to choose team members.

Develop Project Team involves creating an open, inviting atmosphere where project team members will become efficient and cooperative, increasing productivity during the course of the project. It's the project manager's job to bring the team together into a functioning, productive group.

Team development has five stages, according to the Tuckman-Jensen model: forming, storming, norming, performing, and adjourning. All groups proceed through these stages, and the introduction of a new team member will always start the process over again.

Co-location is physically placing team members together in the same location. This might also include a common meeting room or gathering area where team members can meet and collaborate on the project.

Several motivational theories exist, including reward and recognition, Maslow's hierarchy of needs, the Hygiene Theory, the Expectancy Theory, and the Achievement Theory. These theories conjecture that motivation is driven by several desires, including physical, social, and psychological needs, anticipation of expected outcomes, or needs for achievement, power, or affiliation. The Hygiene Theory proposes that hygiene factors prevent dissatisfaction.

Leaders inspire vision and rally people around common goals. Theory X leaders think most people are motivated only through punishment, money, or position. Theory Y leaders think most people want to perform the best job they can. The Contingency Theory says that people naturally want to achieve levels of competency and will continue to be motivated by the desire for competency even after competency is reached.

Leaders exhibit five types of power: reward, punishment, expert, legitimate, and referent power.

Communication skills are the most important skills a project manager exercises. People who send messages are responsible for making sure the messages are clear, concise, and complete. Receivers are responsible for understanding the messages correctly and making sure they've received all the information.

Listening skills put speakers at ease. Several techniques tell your speaker you're listening attentively, including making eye contact, nodding, asking clarifying questions, and limiting interruptions.

Manage Project Teams involves tracking and reporting on project team member performance. Performance appraisals are performed during this process and feedback is provided to the team members.

Exam Essentials

Be able to identify the distinguishing characteristics of Direct and Manage Project Execution. Direct and Manage Project Execution is where the work of the project is performed, and the majority of the project budget is spent during this process.

Be able to name the five stages of group formation. The four stages of group formation are forming, storming, norming, performing, and adjourning.

Be able to define Maslow's highest level of motivation. Self-actualization occurs when a person performs at their peak and all lower-level needs have been met.

Be able to name the five types of power. The five levels of power are reward, punishment, expert, legitimate, and referent.

Be able to identify the five styles of conflict resolution. The five styles of conflict resolution are forcing, smoothing, compromise, confrontation, and withdrawal.

Be able to name the tools and techniques of the Manage Project Team process. The tools and techniques of Manage Project Team are observation and conversation, project performance appraisal, conflict management, issue log, and interpersonal skills.

Key Terms

I've discussed in detail the processes you'll use while developing your project team. You need to understand each of these processes to effectively build your team and know them by the names used in the *PMBOK® Guide* to be successful on the exam:

Acquire Project Team

Develop Project Team

Direct and Manage Project Execution

Manage Project Team

You learned a lot of new key words in this chapter. PMI has worked hard to develop and define standard project management terms that apply across industries. Here is a list of some of the terms you came across in this chapter:

Achievement Theory	Motivation-Hygiene Theory
collaborating	politics
co-location	power
conflict	preassignment
confrontation	recognition and rewards
corrective actions	team building
Expectancy Theory	Theory X
Hygiene Theory	Theory Y
Theory Z	virtual teams
Maslow's hierarchy of needs	

Review Questions

1. You are a project manager for a growing dairy farm. It offers its organic dairy products regionally and is expanding its operations to the West Coast. It is in the process of purchasing and leasing dairy farms to get operations underway. You are in charge of the network operations part of this project. An important deadline is approaching that depends on the successful completion of the testing phase. You've detected some problems with your hardware in the testing phase and discover that the hardware is not compatible with other network equipment. You take corrective action and exchange the hardware for more compatible equipment. Which of the following statements is true?

   A. This is not a corrective action because corrective action involves human resources, not project resources.

   B. Corrective action is taken here to make sure the future project outcomes are aligned with the project management plan.

   C. Corrective action is not necessary in this case because the future project outcomes aren't affected.

   D. Corrective action serves as the change request to authorize exchanging the equipment.

2. You are a project manager for a growing dairy farm. It offers its organic dairy products regionally and is expanding its operations to the West Coast. It's in the process of purchasing and leasing dairy farms to get operations underway. The subproject manager in charge of network operations has reported some hardware problems to you. You're also having some other problems coordinating and integrating other elements of the project. Which of the following statements is true?

   A. You are in the Direct and Manage Project Execution process.

   B. Your project team doesn't appear to have the right skills and knowledge needed to perform this project.

   C. You are in the Information Distribution process.

   D. Your project team could benefit from some team-building exercises.

3. Which of the following processes serve as inputs to each other?

   A. Executing, Monitoring and Controlling

   B. Executing, Closing

   C. Planning, Monitoring and Controlling

   D. Executing, Initiation

4. Your team members have just completed training on specialized equipment. This is one of the work results you've gathered and recorded. Which of the following outputs of the Direct and Manage Project Execution process does this describe?

   A. Work performance information

   B. Deliverable

   C. Preventive action

   D. Project document updates

5. You are reporting on project elements such as schedule status, deliverables completion, lessons learned, and resource utilization. Which of the following outputs of the Direct and Manage Project Execution does this describe?

   A. Project management plan updates

   B. Deliverable

   C. Preventive action

   D. Work performance information

6. You are in the process of making project staff assignments. You have several candidates for a position on the project team that requires specific qualifications. All the candidates seem to meet the qualifications. You also consider prior experience, their interest in the project, cost rates, and availability of these potential candidates. Which of the following is true?

   A. You are considering the resource calendars input of the Develop Project Team process.

   B. You are considering the project staff assignments input of the Develop Project Team process.

   C. You are considering the enterprise environmental factors input of the Acquire Project Team process.

   D. You are considering the project management plan input of the Acquire Project Team process.

7. During a recent team meeting, you reached a resolution to a problem that's been troubling the team for several weeks. It turned out that there was a problem with one of the manufactured parts required for the project. Once this was corrected, the remaining production run went off without a hitch. You took responsibility for searching out the facts of this problem and implemented a change request to resolve the issue. Which of the following is true regarding this question? Choose the best response.

   A. This is a defect repair, which is performed during the Direct and Manage Project Execution process.

   B. This is a corrective action, which is performed during the Direct and Manage Project Execution process.

   C. This is a preventive action, which is performed during the Direct and Manage Project Execution process.

   D. This is an unapproved change request and must first go through the Perform Integrated Change Control process.

8. You are the project manager for a cable service provider. Your team members are amiable with each other and are careful to make project decisions jointly. Which of the following statements is true?

   A. They are in the forming stage of team development.

   B. They are in the norming stage of team development.

   C. They are in the storming stage of team development.

   D. They are in the adjourning stage of team development.

9. You are the project manager for a cable service provider. Your project team is researching a new service offering. They have been working together for quite some time and are in the performing stage of team development. A new member has been introduced to the team. Which of the following statements is true?

A. The team will start all over again with the storming stage.

B. The team will continue in the performing stage.

C. The team will start all over again with the forming stage.

D. The team will start all over again at the storming stage but quickly progress to the performing stage.

10. You are the project manager for a cable service provider. Your project team is researching a new service offering. They have been working together for quite some time and are in the performing stage of team development. This stage of team development is similar to which of the following?

A. Smoothing

B. Achievement Theory

C. Hygiene Theory

D. Self-actualization

11. You've promised your team two days of paid time off plus a week's training in the latest technology of their choice if they complete their project ahead of schedule. This is an example of which of the following?

A. Achievement Theory

B. Expectancy Theory

C. Maslow's theory

D. Contingency Theory

12. Your team is split between two buildings on either side of town. As a result, the team isn't very cohesive because the members don't know each other very well. The team is still in the storming stage because of the separation issues. Which of the following should you consider?

A. Corrective action

B. Co-location

C. Training

D. Conflict resolution

13. Which conflict resolution technique offers project managers the best option for resolution?

A. Smoothing

B. Collaborating

C. Confronting

D. Forcing

14. You are a fabulous project manager, and your team thinks highly of you. You are well respected by the stakeholders, management team, and project team. When you make decisions, others follow your lead as a result of which of the following?

A. Referent power

B. Expert power

C. Legitimate power

D. Punishment power

15. Theory Y managers believe which of the following?

A. People are motivated only by money, power, or position.

B. People will perform their best if they're given proper motivation and expectations.

C. People are motivated to achieve a high level of competency.

D. People are motivated by expectation of good outcomes.

16. When working in a matrix environment, all of the following are true regarding the Manage Project Team process except for which one? Choose the least correct response.

A. Improving competencies, team interactions, and the team environment can help enhance project performance.

B. Managing project teams in a matrix environment is often a critical success factor for the project.

C. It's the project manager's responsibility to make certain this dual reporting relationship is managed effectively.

D. Loyalty issues might arise when managing projects in a matrix environment.

17. You are preparing project performance appraisals and have decided you'd like each team member to get feedback regarding their performance from several sources, including peers, superiors, and subordinates. Which of the following is true?

A. This is called *360-degree feedback* and is part of the input to the organizational project performance appraisals, which is part of the organizational process assets updates input of the Manage Project Team process.

B. This is called *360-degree feedback* and is considered part of the team performance assessment input of the Manage Project Team process.

C. This is called *360-degree feedback* and is considered part of the work performance information input of the Manage Project Team process.

D. This is called *360-degree feedback* and is part of the project performance appraisals tool and technique of the Manage Project Team process.

18. Specific team members were promised for your project as part of the project proposal. You speak with the functional managers to assure their availability. All of the following are true regarding this question except for which one?

   A. This is a preassignment, which is a tool and technique of the process this question refers to.

   B. Team members promised as part of the project proposal should be noted in the project charter.

   C. The other tools and techniques of the process this question refers to are negotiation, virtual teams, and resource availability.

   D. Team members might be promised as part of a project that's put out for bid or of internal projects.

19. These two conflict resolution techniques are known as lose-lose techniques.

   A. Accommodating and forcing

   B. Smoothing and withdrawal

   C. Compromise and confronting

   D. Avoidance and forcing

20. You are a project manager who believes people will have high productivity, morale, and satisfaction if offered a job for life. Which theory do you subscribe to?

   A. Theory X

   B. Hygiene Theory

   C. Theory Y

   D. Theory Z

Answers to Review Questions

1. B. Corrective action brings anticipated future project outcomes back into alignment with the project management plan. Since there is an important deadline looming that depends on a positive outcome of this test, the equipment is exchanged so that the project plan and project schedule are not impacted.

2. A. The most difficult aspect of the Direct and Manage Project Execution process is coordinating and integrating all the project elements. The clue to this question is in the next-to-last sentence.

3. A. The Executing process group and Monitoring and Controlling process group serve as inputs to each other.

4. B. This question describes the deliverable output. Deliverables can be intangibles, such as the completion of training.

5. D. Work performance information includes elements such as schedule status, the status of deliverables completion, lessons learned, and resource utilization.

6. C. The enterprise environmental factors input of the Acquire Project Team process considers elements such as prior experience, interest in working on the project, cost rates, and availability of potential team members.

7. A. This question describes a defect repair that was discovered and implemented. Defect repairs come about as a result of approved changes. Approved changes are implemented in the Direct and Manage Project Execution process. The question implies that the change request was approved because the problem was corrected and the rest of the production run went smoothly.

8. B. Teams in the norming stage of team development exhibit affection and familiarity with one another and make joint decisions.

9. C. The introduction of a new team member will start the formation and development of the team all over again with the forming stage.

10. D. The performing stage is similar to Maslow's self-actualization. Both involve team members at the peak of performance, concerned with doing good and being the best.

11. B. The Expectancy Theory says that people are motivated by the expectation of good outcomes. The outcome must be reasonable and attainable.

12. B. Co-location would bring your team members together in the same location and allow them to function more efficiently as a team. At a minimum, meeting in a common room, such as a war room, for all team meetings would bring the team closer together.

13. C. Confronting is a problem-solving technique that seeks to determine the facts and find solutions based on the facts. That results in a win-win resolution for all parties.

14. A. Referent power is power that is inferred on a leader by their subordinates as a result of the high level of respect for the leader.

15. B. Theory Y managers believe that people will perform their best if they're provided with the proper motivation and the right expectations.

16. A. Improving competencies, team interactions, and the team environment are characteristics of the Develop Project Team process, not the Manage Team Process.

17. D. This technique is called *360-degree feedback*. It's part of the project performance appraisals tool and technique of the Manage Project Team process.

18. C. This question refers to preassignments, which are a tool and technique of the Acquire Project Team process. The other tools and techniques of this process are negotiation, acquisition, and virtual teams.

19. B. Smoothing (also known as accommodating) and withdrawal (also known as avoidance) are both lose-lose techniques. Forcing is a win-lose technique. Compromise is where neither side wins or loses.

20. D. Theory Z encourages employee loyalty because jobs are offered for life. This leads to increased productivity, morale, and high employee satisfaction.

Chapter 9

Conducting Procurements and Sharing Information

THE PMP EXAM CONTENT FROM THE EXECUTING THE PROJECT PERFORMANCE DOMAIN COVERED IN THIS CHAPTER INCLUDES THE FOLLOWING:

- ✓ **Execute Tasks Defined in Project Plan**
- ✓ **Ensure Common Understanding and Set Expectations**
- ✓ **Implement the Procurement of Project Resources**
- ✓ **Implement Quality Management Plan**

This chapter wraps up the Executing process group. We'll look at four processes in this chapter: Conduct Procurements, Perform Quality Assurance, Distribute Information, and Manage Stakeholder Expectations.

Most of these processes aren't related to each other, but all are necessary to conduct the work of the project. They work in coordination with all the other Executing processes and are all extensions of the Planning processes that preceded them (like Plan Procurements, Plan Quality, and so on). Conduct Procurements, and Perform Quality Assurance in particular, work hand in hand with their Monitoring and Controlling processes (Administer Procurements and Perform Quality Control) to implement, measure, and report services and results.

Conduct Procurements is where sellers respond to the bids we prepared in the Plan Contracting process. Contract awards are made here also. In Perform Quality Assurance, we'll look at several techniques to audit the project's quality requirements against the quality results. Distribute Information will cover more communication topics, including status reports, and last but not least we'll talk about Managing Stakeholder Expectations, which is critical during the Executing processes. Grab your favorite beverage and let's get started.

Conducting Procurements

Many times project managers must purchase goods or services to complete some or all of the work of the project. Sometimes the entire project is completed on contract. The *Conduct Procurements* process is concerned with obtaining responses to bids and proposals from potential vendors, selecting a vendor, and awarding the contract.

This process has several inputs:

- Project management plan (procurement management plan)
- Source selection criteria
- Qualified seller list
- Seller proposals
- Project documents
- Make-or-buy decisions
- Teaming agreements
- Organizational process assets

I've talked about most of these inputs in previous chapters. Procurement documents include requests for proposals (RFPs), requests for information (RFIs), requests for quotations (RFQs), and so on. The responses to those proposals become inputs to this process. Source selection criteria was defined in the Plan Procurements process that we talked about in Chapter 7. In the tools and techniques section for this process, we'll talk more about how seller proposals are evaluated.

Qualified sellers lists are lists of prospective sellers who have been preapproved or prequalified to provide contract services (or provide supplies and materials) for the organization. For example, your organization might require vendors to register and maintain information regarding their experience, offerings, and current prices on a qualified seller list. Vendors must usually go through the procurement department to get placed on the list. Project managers are then required to choose their vendors from the qualified seller list published by the procurement department. However, not all organizations have qualified seller lists. If a list isn't available, you'll have to work with the project team to come up with your own requirements for selecting vendors.

NOTE The Conduct Procurements process is used only if you're obtaining goods or services from outside your own organization. If you have all the resources you need to perform the work of the project within the organization, you won't use this process.

In the following sections, you'll examine some new tools and techniques that will help vendors give you a better idea of their responses, and then you'll move on to the outputs of this process, two of which are the selected seller and procurement contract award.

Conduct Procurements Tools and Techniques

Remember that the purpose of the Conduct Procurements process is to obtain responses to your RFP (or similar procurement document), select the right vendor for the job, and award the contract. The tools and techniques of this process are designed to assist the vendors in getting their proposals to you and include techniques for evaluating those proposals. The tools and techniques are as follows:

- Bidder conferences
- Proposal evaluation techniques
- Independent estimates
- Expert judgment
- Advertising
- Internet search
- Procurement negotiations

We'll look at each of these tools and techniques next with the exception of expert judgment.

Bidder Conferences

Bidder conferences (also known as vendor conferences, prebid conferences, and contractor conferences according to the *PMBOK® Guide*) are meetings with prospective vendors or sellers that occur prior to the completion of their response proposal. You or someone from your procurement department arranges the bidder conference. The purpose is to allow all prospective vendors to meet with the buyers to ask questions and clarify issues they have regarding the project and the RFP. The meeting is held once, and all vendors attend at the same time. The bidder conference is held before the vendor prepares their responses so that they are sure their RFP response will address the project requirements.

Proposal Evaluation Techniques

There are several techniques you might use to evaluate proposals. Simple procurements may not need much more than a quick check against the statement of work or a price comparison. Complex procurements may need several rounds of evaluation to begin narrowing the list of sellers. This is where you might use one or more of the following evaluation techniques to get to the final winner.

You can use source selection criteria as one method of rating and scoring proposals. We discussed source selection criteria in Chapter 6. You may recall that this includes several elements such as an understanding of the work, costs, technical capability, risk, warranty, and so on. We'll get into more detail on some of these criteria here. Keep in mind this is an input to the Conduct Procurements process, not a tool and technique, even though you'll be using it as you would a tool and technique.

The types of goods and services you're trying to procure will dictate how detailed your evaluation criteria are. (Of course, if your organization has policies in place for evaluating proposals, then you'll use the format or criteria already established.) The selection of some goods and services might be price driven only. In other words, the bidder with the lowest price will win the bid. This is typical when the items you're buying are widely available.

When you're purchasing goods, you might request a sample from each vendor in order to compare quality (or some other criteria) against your need. For example, perhaps you need a special kind of paper stock for a project you're working on at a bank. This stock must have a watermark, it must have security threads embedded through the paper, and when the paper is used for printing, the ink must not be erasable. You can request samples of stock with these qualities from the vendors and then test them to see whether they'll work for your project.

It's always appropriate to ask the vendor for references, especially when you're hiring contract services. It's difficult to assess the quality of services because it's not a tangible product. References can tell you whether the vendor delivered on time, whether the vendor had the technical capability to perform the work, and whether the vendor's management approach was appropriate when troubles surfaced. Create a list of questions to ask the references before you call.

You can request financial records to assure you—the buyer—that the vendor has the fiscal ability to perform the services they're proposing and that the vendor can purchase whatever equipment is needed to perform the services. If you examine the records of the company and find that it's two steps away from bankruptcy, that company might not be a likely candidate for your project. (Remember those general management skills? Here's another example where they come into play.)

One of the most important criteria is the evaluation of the response itself to determine whether the vendor has a clear understanding of what you're asking them to do or provide. If they missed the mark (remember, they had an opportunity at the bidder conferences to ask clarifying questions) and didn't understand what you were asking them to provide, you'll probably want to rank them very low.

Now you can compare each proposal against the criteria and rate or score each proposal for its ability to meet or fulfill these criteria. This can serve as your first step in eliminating vendors that don't match your criteria. Let's say you received 18 responses to an RFP. After evaluating each one, you discover that six of them don't match all the evaluation criteria. You eliminate those six vendors in this round. The next step is to apply the tools and techniques of this process to further evaluate the remaining 12 potential vendors.

Weighting Systems

Weighting systems assign numerical weights to evaluation criteria and then multiply them by the weights of each criteria factor to come up with total scores for each vendor. This technique provides a way to quantify the data and assist in keeping personal biases to a minimum. Weighting systems are useful when you have multiple vendors to choose from because they allow you to rank the proposals to determine the sequence of negotiations.

You'll find an example of a weighted scoring system in Chapter 2. These systems are commonly used to evaluate vendor proposals.

Screening Systems

Screening systems use predefined performance criteria or a set of defined minimum requirements to screen out unsuitable vendors. Perhaps your project requires board-certified engineers. One of the screening criteria would be that vendors propose project team members who have this qualification. If they don't, they're eliminated from the selection process.

Screening systems can be used together with some of the other tools and techniques of this process, weighting systems and independent estimates, to rank vendor proposals.

Seller Rating Systems

Seller rating systems use information about the sellers—such as past performance, delivery, contract compliance, and quality ratings—to determine seller performance. Your organization might have seller rating systems in place, and you should check with your procurement department to see whether they exist for the bidders on your project. Part of the Administer Procurement process (I'll talk about this in Chapter 10) concerns gathering and recording this type of information. Don't use seller rating systems as your sole criteria for evaluating vendors.

NOTE Proposal evaluation techniques are a combination of all the techniques I've discussed in this section. All techniques use some form of expert judgment and evaluation criteria—whether it's objective or subjective criteria. The evaluation criteria are usually weighted, much like a weighted scoring system, and those participating as reviewers provide their ratings (usually to the project manager) to compile into a weighted proposal to determine an overall score. Scoring differences are also resolved using this technique. Some or all of the evaluation techniques described here can be used in combination with the remaining tools and techniques of this section to evaluate seller responses.

Independent Estimates

Your procurement department might conduct *independent estimates* (also known as *should cost estimates*) of the costs of the proposal and compare these to the vendor prices. If there are large differences between the independent estimate and the proposed vendor cost, one of two things is happening: either the statement of work (SOW) or the terms of the contract or both are not detailed enough to allow the vendor to come up with an accurate cost. Or the vendor simply failed to respond to all the requirements laid out in the contract or SOW.

Advertising

Advertising is letting potential vendors know that an RFP is available. The company's Internet site, professional journals, or newspapers are examples of where advertising might appear.

Internet Search

Internet searches have several useful features in this process. You can use Internet searches to find vendors, perform research on their past performance, and compare prices. You can also use the Internet to purchase items that are readily available and are generally offered for a fixed price. Internet searches are probably not useful when you're conducting high-risk or complex procurements, but you could do some research on company performance and reputation to help in choosing a vendor.

Procurement Negotiation

In *procurement negotiation*, both parties come to an agreement regarding the contract terms. Negotiation skills are put into practice here as the details of the contract are ironed out between the parties. At a minimum, contract language should include price, responsibilities, regulations or laws that apply, and the overall approach to the project.

The complexity of the contract will determine how extensive the contract negotiations will be. Simple contracts may have predetermined, nonnegotiable elements that only require seller acceptance. Complex contracts may include any number of elements, including financing options, overall schedule, proprietary rights, service level agreements, technical aspects, and more. In either case, once agreement is reached and the negotiations are finished, the contract is signed by both buyer and seller and is executed.

You might see the term *fait accompli* show up on the exam. Fait accompli tactics are used during contract negotiation when one party tries to convince the other party discussing a particular contract item that it is no longer an issue. It can be a distraction technique, when the party practicing fait accompli tactics is purposely trying to keep from negotiating an issue and claims the issue cannot be changed. For example, during negotiations the vendor tells you that the key resource they're assigning to your project must start immediately or you'll lose that resource and they'll get assigned work elsewhere. However, you don't know—because the vendor didn't tell you—that the vendor can reserve this resource for your project and hold them until the start date. In this instance, they used fait accompli tactics to push you into starting the project, or hiring this resource, sooner than you would have otherwise.

The literal translation of fait accompli into English is *fact realized or accomplished*. And this tactic does not always produce a negative result. For example, when then President Elect Obama was running for the White House, he promised his daughters that if he won the election, they could get a dog. Once he won the election, getting a dog was no longer in question; it became a fact realized or a done deal you might say.

Exam Spotlight

Procurement negotiations, according to the *PMBOK® Guide*, can be performed as a process itself with inputs and outputs.

Real World Scenario

Vendor Selection for Fitness Counts HR System

Amanda Jacobson is the project manager for Fitness Counts, a nationwide chain of gyms containing all the latest and greatest fitness equipment, aerobics classes, swimming pools, and such. Fitness Counts is converting its human resources data management system. The RFP addressed several requirements, including the following:

- The new system must run on a platform that's compatible with the company's current operating system.
- Hardware must be compatible with company standards.
- Data conversion of existing HR data must be included in the price of the bid.
- Fitness Counts wants to have the ability to add custom modules using internal programmers.
- Training of Fitness Counts programmers must be included in the bid.

The project team is in the Conduct Procurements process and has received bids based on the RFP published earlier this month. Fitness Counts is using a combination of selection criteria and a weighted scoring model to choose a vendor.

One of the evaluation criteria said that the vendor must have prior experience with a project like this. Four vendors met that criteria and proceeded to the weighted scoring selection process.

Amanda is one of the members of the selection committee. She and four other members on the committee rated the four vendors who met the initial selection criteria. They read all of the proposals and rated the criteria using factors they had predetermined for each. For example, vendors who proposed a SQL database as part of the "Platform" criteria (along with the other predetermined factors) should receive a total weighted score of 5. Table 9.1 shows their results.

Vendor C is the clear winner of this bid. Based on the weighted scoring model, their responses to the RFP came out ahead of the other bidders. Amanda calls them with the good news and also calls the other vendors tc thank them for participating in the bid. Vendor C is awarded the contract, and Amanda moves on to the Contract Administration process.

TABLE 9.1 Example Weighted Scoring Model

	Platform	Hardware	Data Conversion	Custom Modules/ Training	Totals
Weighting Factor *	5	4	5	4	
Vendor A					
Raw Score	*3*	*3*	*3*	*4*	
Weighted Score	15	12	15	16	**58**
Vendor B					
Raw Score	*2*	*3*	*4*	*3*	
Weighted Score	10	12	20	12	**54**
Vendor C					
Raw Score	*4*	*4*	*4*	*3*	
Weighted Score	20	16	20	12	**68**

TABLE 9.1 Example Weighted Scoring Model *(continued)*

	Platform	Hardware	Data Conversion	Custom Modules/ Training	Totals
Vendor D					
Raw Score	*3*	*3*	*2*	*4*	
Weighted Score	15	12	10	16	**53**

*1–5, with 5 being highest

Conduct Procurements Outputs

The Conduct Procurements process has six outputs:

- Selected sellers
- Procurement contract award
- Resource calendars
- Change requests
- Project management plan updates
- Project document updates

The selected sellers output is obvious; you choose the seller (or sellers) to whom you'll award the project and execute the contract. I'll talk more about the procurement contract award next. I've discussed all the other outputs previously.

NOTE

According to the *PMBOK® Guide,* a negotiated draft contract is one of the requirements of the selected sellers output. Also note that senior management signatures may be required on complex, high-risk, or high-dollar contracts. Make certain to check your organization's procurement policies regarding the authority level and amounts you are authorized to sign for. In my organization, not only do our contracts require senior management signature, they also require signatures from two other external departments. We have to account for the multiple reviews, signatures, and question and answer sessions required to get to contract signature. This has a definite impact on the project schedule and must be accounted for in time estimates for these tasks.

Elements of a Procurement Contract Award

You might recall that a contract is a legally binding agreement between two or more parties, typically used to acquire goods or services. Contracts have several names, including agreements, memorandums of understanding (MOUs), subcontracts, and purchase orders.

The type of contract you'll award will depend on the product or services you're procuring and your organizational policies. I talked about the types of contracts—fixed price, cost reimbursable, and so on—in Chapter 6 if you need a refresher. If your project has multiple sellers, you'll award contracts for each of them.

The contract should clearly address the elements of the SOW, time period of performance, pricing and payment plan, acceptance criteria, warranty periods, dispute resolution procedures, and so on.

Since contracts are legally binding and obligate your organization to fulfill the terms, they'll likely be subject to some intensive review, often by several different people. Be certain you understand your organization's policies on contract review and approval before proceeding.

Contracts, like projects, have a life cycle of their own. You might encounter questions on the exam regarding the stages of the contract life cycles, so we'll look at this topic next.

Contract Life Cycles

The contract life cycle consists of four stages:

- Requirement
- Requisition
- Solicitation
- Award

These stages are closely related to the following Project Procurement Knowledge Area processes from the *PMBOK® Guide*:

- Plan Procurements
- Conduct Procurements

A description of each of the contract life cycles follows.

Requirement The requirement stage is the equivalent of the Plan Procurements process I discussed in Chapter 7. You establish the project and contract needs in this cycle, and you define the requirements of the project. The SOW defines the work of the project, the objectives, and a high-level overview of the deliverables. You develop a work breakdown structure (WBS), a make-or-buy analysis takes place, and you determine cost estimates.

The buyer provides the SOW to describe the requirements of the project when it's performed under contract. The product description can serve as the SOW.

Requisition In the requisition stage, the project objectives are refined and confirmed. Solicitation materials such as the request for proposals (RFP), request for information (RFI), and request for quotations (RFQ) are prepared during this phase. Generally, the project manager is the one responsible for preparing the RFP, RFI, and RFQ. A review of the potential qualified vendors takes place, including checking references and reviewing other projects the vendor has worked on that are similar to your proposed project. Requisition occurs during the Plan Procurements process.

Solicitation The solicitation stage is where vendors are asked to compete for the contract and respond to the RFP. You can use the tools and techniques of the Conduct Procurements process during this contract stage. The resulting output is the proposals. Solicitation occurs during the Conduct Procurements process.

Award Vendors are chosen and contracts are awarded and signed during the award stage. The Conduct Procurements process is the equivalent of the award phase.

The project manager—or the selection committee, depending on the organizational policy—receives the bids and proposals during the award phase and applies evaluation criteria to each in order to score or rank the responses. After ranking each of the proposals, an award is made to the winning vendor, and the contract is written.

Once you have a contract, someone has to administer it. In large organizations, this responsibility will fall to the procurement department. The project manager should still have a solid understanding of administering contracts because that person will work with the procurement department to determine the satisfactory fulfillment of the contract.

Now we're going to switch courses and discuss the quality assurance aspects of the project. We discussed the Plan Quality process back in Chapter 7, which prepared us for the Perform Quality Assurance process that's conducted during the Executing process group. We'll look at it next.

Laying Out Quality Assurance Procedures

The Plan Quality process laid out the quality standards for the project and determined how those standards are satisfied. The *Perform Quality Assurance* process involves performing systematic quality activities and uses quality audits to determine which processes should be used to achieve the project requirements and to assure they are performed efficiently and effectively.

The project team members, the project manager, and the stakeholders are all responsible for the quality assurance of the project. Continuous process improvement can be achieved through this process, bringing about improved process performance and eliminating unnecessary actions.

A quality assurance department or organization may be assigned to the project to oversee these processes. In that case, quality assurance might be provided to (rather than by) the project team. The project manager will have the greatest impact on the quality of the project during this process.

You'll review the inputs to this process next and then spend some time exploring a few new tools and techniques for assuring a quality product and project.

Inputs to Perform Quality Assurance

The inputs to Perform Quality Assurance are what you use to measure the organizational project quality management processes against. The quality management processes were defined during Quality Planning. The inputs to the Perform Quality Assurance process are as follows:

- Project management plan
- Quality metrics
- Work performance information
- Quality control measurements

You've heard about the inputs to Perform Quality Assurance before, so we'll move right into the tools and techniques of this section.

Exam Spotlight

The most important point to remember about Perform Quality Assurance is that quality management processes are what you use to make certain the project satisfies the quality standards laid out in the project management plan.

Perform Quality Assurance Tools and Techniques

The Perform Quality Assurance process has three tools and techniques: Plan Quality and Perform Quality Control tools and techniques, quality audits, and process analysis.

I discussed Plan Quality planning tools and techniques during the Quality Planning process in Chapter 7. You'll recall that the tools and techniques are cost-benefit analysis, cost of quality, control charts, benchmarking, design of experiments, statistical sampling, flowcharting, proprietary quality management methodologies, and additional quality planning tools. When we discuss the Perform Quality Control process in Chapter 11, "Controlling Work Results," we'll add even more tools to our quality tool bag with some Perform Quality Control tools and techniques. All of these tools and techniques from both the Plan Quality and Perform Quality Control processes can be used during the Perform Quality Assurance process as well to measure project performance.

We'll look at the remaining tools and techniques in the following sections.

Quality Audits

Quality audits are independent reviews performed by trained auditors or third-party reviewers. The purpose of a quality audit is the same as the purpose of the Perform Quality Assurance process—to identify ineffective and inefficient activities or processes used on the project. These audits might examine and uncover inefficient processes and procedures as well as processes that are not in compliance with organizational practices.

You can perform quality audits on a regular schedule or at random depending on the organizational policies. Quality audits performed correctly will provide the following benefits:

- The product of the project is fit for use and meets safety standards.
- Applicable laws and standards are adhered to.
- Corrective action is recommended and implemented where necessary.
- The quality plan for the project is adhered to.
- Quality improvements are identified.
- The implementation of approved change requests, corrective actions, preventive actions, and defect repairs are confirmed.
- Gaps or shortcomings in the process are identified.

Quality improvements come about as a result of the quality audits. During the course of the audit, you might discover ways of improving the efficiency or effectiveness of the project, thereby increasing the value of the project and more than likely exceeding stakeholder expectations.

Quality improvements are implemented by submitting change requests and/or taking corrective action. Quality improvements interface with the Monitoring and Controlling processes because of the need to submit change requests.

NOTE

You'll look at change requests and change request procedures in Chapter 10, "Measuring and Controlling Project Performance."

Experienced specialists generally perform quality audits. The specialist's job is to produce an independent evaluation of the quality process. Some organizations are large enough to have their own quality assurance departments or quality assurance teams; others might have to hire contract personnel to perform this function. Internal quality assurance teams report results to the project team and management team of the organization. External quality assurance teams report results to the customer.

Process Analysis

Process analysis looks at process improvement from an organizational and technical perspective. According to the *PMBOK® Guide*, process analysis follows the steps in the process improvement plan and examines the following:

- Problems experienced while conducting the project
- Constraints experienced while conducting the work of the project
- Inefficient and ineffective processes identified during process operation

One of the techniques of process analysis includes performing root cause analysis. (I talked about root cause analysis in the Identify Risks process in Chapter 6.) While you're examining problems and constraints, for example, you should look for what's causing the problem. The result of this exercise will allow you to develop preventive actions for problems that are similar to the problem you're examining or that have the similar root causes.

Perform Quality Assurance Outputs

The Perform Quality Assurance process has four outputs:

- Organizational process assets updates
- Change requests
- Project management plan updates
- Project document updates

These aren't new, but there is one new idea embedded in the change requests output. During this process, any recommended corrective actions, whether they are a result of a quality audit or process analysis, should be acted upon immediately. Let's say you're manufacturing parts for one of the deliverables of your project. Obviously, the moment you discover that the parts are not correct, you'd correct the process by calibrating the machine perhaps, or by using different raw materials, to make certain the parts are produced accurately.

Quality Improvements

Although it isn't stated as an output, one of the overarching goals of the Perform Quality Assurance process is to provide a foundation for continuous process improvements. As the name implies, continuous improvements are iterative. This process of continuous improvements sets the stage, so to speak, for improving the quality of all the project processes. This can mean project management processes, but it also means the processes and activities involved in accomplishing the work of the project.

The advantage of continuous process improvement is that it reduces the time the project team spends on ineffective or inefficient processes. If the activities don't help you meet the goals of the project or, worse yet, hinder your progress, it's time to look at ways to improve them.

Once again we're going to shift gears and talk about a new process. We'll look at best practices regarding sharing and distributing information next.

Distributing Project Information

The *Distribute Information* process is concerned with getting stakeholders information about the project in a timely manner. This can come about in several ways: status reports, project meetings, review meetings, and so on. Status reports are actually part of the work performance information you saw in the output of the Direct and Manage Project Execution process. Status reports inform stakeholders about where the project is today in regard to project schedule and budget, for example. They also describe what the project team has accomplished to date. This might include milestones completed to date, the percentage of schedule completion, and what remains to be completed. The Distribute Information process describes how this report, and other information, are distributed and to whom.

In the Distribute Information process, the communications management plan that was defined during the Plan Communications process is put into action. Remember that this plan is a subsidiary of the project management plan, which is an input to this process. The other inputs include performance reports and organizational process assets. Plan Communications and Distribute Information work together to report the progress of the project team.

Distribute Information has some new tools and techniques, which we'll look at next.

Tools and Techniques of Distribute Information

The tools and techniques of this process are as follows:

- Communication methods
- Information distribution tools

Communication methods include all means feasible to communicate project information to the appropriate recipients, such as meetings, email, videoconferences, conference calls, and so on.

Communication skills are probably the single most important skill in your project management toolbox. You can't employ communication methods without some sound communication skills, so let's take a look at this topic next.

Developing Great Communication Skills

Every aspect of your job as a project manager will involve communications. It has been estimated that project managers spend as much as 90 percent of their time communicating in one form or another. Therefore, communication skills are arguably one of the most important skills a project manager can have. They are even more important than technical skills. Good communication skills foster an open, trusting environment, and excellent communication skills are a project manager's best asset.

Throughout this book I've emphasized how important good communication skills are. Now I'll discuss the act of communication, listening behaviors, and conflict resolution. You'll employ each of these techniques with your project team, stakeholders, customers, and management team.

Information Exchange

Communication is the process of exchanging information. All communication includes three elements:

Sender The sender is the person responsible for putting the information together in a clear and concise manner. The information should be complete and presented in a way that the receiver will be able to correctly understand it. Make your messages relevant to the receiver. Junk mail is annoying, and information that doesn't pertain in any way whatsoever to the receiver is nothing more than that.

Message The message is the information being sent and received. It might be written, verbal, nonverbal, formal, informal, internal, external, horizontal, or vertical. Horizontal communications are messages sent and received to peers. Vertical communications are messages sent and received down to subordinates and up to executive management.

NOTE Make your messages as simple as you can to get your point across. Don't complicate the message with unnecessary detail and technical jargon that others might not understand. A simple trick that helps clarify your messages, especially verbal messages, is to repeat the key information periodically. Public speakers are taught that the best way to organize a speech is to first tell the audience what you're going to tell them; second, tell them; and third, tell them what you just told them.

Receiver The receiver is the person for whom the message is intended. They are responsible for understanding the information correctly and making sure they've received all the information.

Keep in mind that receivers filter the information they receive through their knowledge of the subject, culture influences, language, emotions, attitudes, and geographic locations. The sender should take these filters into consideration when sending messages so that the receiver will clearly understand the message that was sent.

NOTE This book is an example of the sender-message-receiver model. I'm the sender of the information. The message concerns topics you need to know to pass the PMP exam (and if I've done my job correctly, is written in a clear and easily understood format). You, the reader, are the receiver.

METHODS OF INFORMATION EXCHANGE

Senders, receivers, and messages are the elements of communication. The way the sender packages or encodes the information and transmits it and the way the receiver unpacks or decodes the message are the methods of communication exchange.

Senders encode messages. Encoding is a method of putting the information into a format the receiver will understand. Language, pictures, and symbols are used to encode messages. Encoding formats the message for transmitting.

Transmitting is the way the information gets from the sender to the receiver. Spoken words, written documentation, memos, email, and voicemail are all transmitting methods.

Decoding is what the receiver does with the information when they get it. They convert it into an understandable format. Usually, this means they read the memo, listen to the speaker, read the book, and so on.

FORMS OF COMMUNICATION

Communication occurs primarily in written or verbal form. Granted, you can point to something or indicate what you need with motions, but usually you use the spoken or written word to get your message across.

Verbal communication is easier and less complicated than written communication, and it's usually a fast method of communication. Written communication, on the other hand, is an excellent way to get across complex, detailed messages. Detailed instructions are better provided in written form because it gives the reader the ability to go back over information they're not quite sure about.

Both verbal and written communication might take a formal or an informal approach. Speeches and lectures are examples of formal verbal communication. Most project status meetings take more of a formal approach, as do most written project status reports. Generally speaking, the project manager should take an informal approach when communicating with stakeholders and project team members outside of the status meetings. This makes you appear more open and friendly and easier to approach with questions and issues.

Effective Listening Skills

What did you say? Often we think we're listening when we really aren't. In all fairness, we can take in only so much information at one time. But it's important to perform active listening when someone else is speaking. As a project manager, you will spend the majority of your time communicating with team members, stakeholders, customers, vendors, and others. This means you should be as good a listener as you are a communicator.

You can use several techniques to improve your listening skills. Many books are devoted to this topic, so I'll try to highlight some of the most common techniques here:

- Appear interested in what the speaker is saying. This will make the speaker feel at ease and will benefit you as well. By acting interested, you become interested and thereby retain more of the information being presented.
- Making eye contact with the speaker is another effective listening tool. This lets the speaker know you are paying attention to what they're saying and are interested.
- Put your speaker at ease by letting them know beforehand that you're interested in what they're going to talk about and that you're looking forward to hearing what they have to say. While they're speaking, nod your head, smile, or make comments when and if appropriate to let the speaker know you understand the message. If you don't understand something and are in the proper setting, ask clarifying questions.
- Another great trick that works well in lots of situations is to recap what the speaker said in your own words and tell it back to them. Start with something like this, "Let me make sure I understand you correctly, you're saying...," and ask the speaker to confirm that you did understand them correctly.
- Just as your mother always said, it's impolite to interrupt. Interrupting is a way of telling the speaker that you aren't really listening and you're more interested in telling them what you have to say than listening to them. Interrupting gets the other person off track, they might forget their point, and it might even make them angry.

Not to disagree with Mom, but there probably are some occasions where interrupting is appropriate. For example, if you're in a project status meeting and someone wants to take the meeting off course, sometimes the only way to get the meeting back on track is to interrupt them. You can do this politely. Start first by saying the person's name to get their attention. Then let them know that you'd be happy to talk with them about their topic outside of the meeting or add it to the agenda for the next status meeting if it's something everyone needs to hear. Sorry, Mom.

Resolving Conflicts

We discussed conflict resolution techniques in Chapter 8. These are also a form of communication skills. You may recall the conflict resolutions techniques:

- Forcing
- Smoothing/accommodating
- Compromise
- Confrontation/problem solving
- Collaborating
- Withdrawal/avoidance

Keep in mind that group size makes a difference when you're trying to resolve conflict or make decisions. Remember the channels of communication you learned about in Chapter 5? The larger the group, the more lines of communication and the more difficult it will be to reach a decision. Groups of 5 to 11 people have a manageable number of participants and have been shown to make the most accurate decisions.

Use communication, listening, and conflict resolution skills wisely. As a project manager, you'll find that your day-to-day activities encompass these three areas the majority of the time. Project managers with excellent communication skills can work wonders. Communication won't take the place of proper planning and management techniques, but a project manager who communicates well with their team and the stakeholders can make up for a lack of technical skills any day, hands down. If your team and your stakeholders trust you and you can communicate the vision and the project goals and report on project status accurately and honestly, the world is your oyster.

Information Distribution Tools

Information distribution tools are ways of getting the project information to the project team or stakeholders. As the name implies, these are ways to distribute the information and might include email, hard copy, voicemail, videoconferencing, and so on. It also includes electronic project management tools like schedules and meeting software for maintaining project records.

Exam Spotlight

According to the *PMBOK® Guide*, it's a project manager's professional obligation to hold lessons learned meetings.

NOTE I'll talk more about lessons learned in Chapter 11.

Output of Distribute Information

The output of the Distribute Information process is organizational process assets updates. The updates here consist of six elements:

Stakeholder notifications Remember that the focus of this process is distributing information. Stakeholder notifications involve notifying stakeholders when you have implemented solutions and approved changes, have updated project status, have resolved issues, and so on.

Project reports *Project reports* include the project status reports and minutes from project meetings, lessons learned, closure reports, and other documents from all the process outputs throughout the project. If you're keeping an issue log, the issues would be included with the project reports as well.

Project presentations *Project presentations* involve presenting project information to the stakeholders and other appropriate parties when necessary. The presentations might be formal or informal and depend on the audience and the information being communicated.

Project records *Project records* include, as you might guess, memos, correspondence, and other documents concerning the project. The best place to keep information like this is in a project notebook or in a set of project notebooks, depending on the size of the project. The project notebooks are ordinary three-ring binders where project information gets filed. They are maintained by the project manager or project office and contain all information regarding the project. You could also keep the information on a project website, the company intranet, or CDs. If you're keeping the information electronically, make certain it's backed up regularly. Individual team members might keep their own project records as well in notebooks or electronically. These records serve as historical information once the project is closed.

Feedback from stakeholders This one ties into lessons learned. Feedback you receive from the stakeholders that can improve future performance on this project or future projects should be captured and documented. If the information has an impact on the current project, distribute it to the appropriate team members so that future project performance can be modified to improve results.

Lessons learned documentation *Lessons learned* are information that you gather and document throughout the course of the project that can be used to benefit the current project, future projects, or other projects currently being performed by the organization. Lessons learned might include positive as well as negative lessons.

During the Distribute Information process, you'll begin conducting lessons learned meetings focusing on many different areas, depending on the nature of your project. These areas might include project management processes, product development, technical processes, project team performance, stakeholder involvement, and so on.

Lessons learned meetings should always be conducted at the end of project phases and at the end of the project at minimum. Team members, stakeholders, vendors, and others involved on the project should participate in these meetings. It's important to understand, and to make your team members understand, that this is not a finger-pointing meeting. The purpose of lessons learned is to understand what went well and why—so you can repeat it on future projects—and what didn't go so well and why—so you can perform differently on future projects. These meetings can make good team-building sessions because you're creating an atmosphere of trust and sharing and you're building on each other's strengths to improve performance.

You should document the reasons or causes for the issues, the corrective action taken and why, and any other information that future projects might benefit from.

We're making one last switch of focus in this chapter and will examine how to manage stakeholder expectations next.

Managing Stakeholder Expectations

In my experience, managing stakeholder expectations is much more difficult than managing project team members. Stakeholders are often managers or directors in the organization who might be higher in the food chain than the project manager and aren't afraid to let you know it. Having said that, you *can* manage stakeholder expectations and you do this using communication.

NOTE If you need a refresher on the definition and role of stakeholders, please see Chapter 1, "What Is a Project?"

The *Manage Stakeholder Expectations* process is about satisfying the needs of the stakeholders by managing communications with them, resolving issues, improving project performance by implementing requested changes, and managing concerns in anticipation of potential problems.

Stakeholders need lots of communication in every form you can provide. If you are actively engaged with your stakeholders and interacting with them, providing project status, and resolving issues, your chances of a successful project are much greater than if you don't do these things.

Exam Spotlight

According to the *PMBOK® Guide*, it's the project manager's responsibility to manage stakeholder expectations. By doing so, it will decrease the potential for project failure. Managing the expectations of your stakeholders will also increase the chance of meeting the project goals because issues are resolved in a timely manner and disruptions during the project are limited.

Manage Stakeholder Expectations Inputs

The inputs of Manage Stakeholder Expectations include the following:

- Stakeholder register
- Stakeholder management strategy
- Project management plan
- Issue log
- Change log
- Organizational process assets

We have discussed each of these inputs previously with the exception of change log. One thing to note about the issue log in this process is that it acts more like an action item log where you record the actions needed to resolve stakeholder concerns and project issues they raise. Issues should be ranked according to their urgency and potential impact on the project. As with the issue log in the Manage Project Team process, you'll assign a responsible party and a due date for resolution.

Exam Spotlight

According to the *PMBOK® Guide,* the issue log (or action item log) can be used to promote communication with stakeholders and to ensure that stakeholders and the project team have the same understanding of the issues.

We'll look more closely at change logs in the next chapter, but for purposes of this process, understand that this is a log that documents all the changes made during the course of the project. In terms of stakeholder expectations, you'll want to keep stakeholders updated on changes and their impacts to the project.

Tools and Techniques for Manage Stakeholder Expectations

The tools and techniques of this process include communication methods, interpersonal skills, and management skills. It's been a while since we talked about management skills, but for purposes of this process, they refer primarily to presenting, negotiating, writing, and public speaking skills. Keep in mind that face-to-face communications are the most effective with stakeholders.

Manage Stakeholder Outputs

The outputs of the Manage Stakeholder process are organizational process assets updates, change requests, project management plan updates, and project document updates.

The project documents that may need an update as a result of this process include the stakeholder management strategy, the stakeholder register, and the issue log.

You've successfully completed the Executing process group. Remember that the Executing processes and Monitoring and Controlling processes serve as inputs to each other and that Executing and Monitoring and Controlling are both iterative process groups. As your project progresses and it becomes evident that you need to exercise controls to get the project back on track, you'll come back through the Executing process group and then proceed through the Monitoring and Controlling processes again. You'll move on to the Monitoring and Controlling process group now and find out what it's all about.

Real World Scenario

Project Case Study: New Kitchen Heaven Retail Store

Dirk Perrier logs on and finds the following status report addressed to all the stakeholders and project team members from you:

Project Progress Report

Project Name Kitchen Heaven Retail Store

Project Number 081501-1910

Prepared By Project manager

Date October 8, 2010

Section 1: Action Items

- *Action Item 1*: Call cable vendor. Responsible party: Ricardo. Resolution date: 9/14
- *Action Item 2*: Check T1 connection status. Responsible party: Ricardo. Resolution date: Pending
- *Action Item 3*: Build-out begins. Responsible party: Jake. Resolution date: Pending

Section 2: Scheduled and Actual Completion Dates

- *Sign lease*: Scheduled: 8/21/06. Completed: 8/21/06
- *Gomez contract signed*: Scheduled: 9/12/06. Completed: 9/12/06
- *Ethernet cable run*: Scheduled: 9/18/06. Completed: 9/19/06
- *Build-out started*: Scheduled: 9/20/06. Completed: In progress

Section 3: Activity That Occurred in the Project This Week

The Ethernet cable run was completed without a problem.

Section 4: Progress Expected This Reporting Period Not Completed

None. Project is on track to date.

Section 5: Progress Expected Next Reporting Period

Build-out will continue. Jake reports that Gomez expects to have electrical lines run and drywall started prior to the end of the next reporting period.

Ricardo should have a T1 update. There's a slim possibility that the T1 connection will have occurred by next reporting period.

Section 6: Issues

We had to start the build-out on the last day of the cable run (this is called *fast tracking*) to keep the project on schedule. Jake and Ricardo reported only minor problems with this arrangement in that the contractors got into each other's way a time or two. This did not impact the completion of the cable run because most of day two this team was in the back room and Gomez's crew was in the storefront area.

A key member of the Gomez construction crew was out last week because of a family emergency. Gomez assures us that it will not impact the build-out schedule. They replaced the team member with someone from another project, so it appears so far that the build-out is on schedule.

Ricardo is somewhat concerned about the T1 connection because the phone company won't return his calls inquiring about status. We're still ahead of the curve on this one because hardware isn't scheduled to begin testing until January 21. Hardware testing depends on the T1 connection. This is a heads-up at this point, and we'll carry this as an issue in the status report going forward until it's resolved.

One of the gourmet food item suppliers Jill uses regularly went out of business. She is in the process of tracking down a new supplier to pick up the slack for the existing stores and supply the gourmet food products for the new store.

Status Meeting in Early December

"Thank you all for coming," you begin. You note those stakeholders who are present and pass out the agendas. "First, we have a contract update. Jake, would you give us the update, please?"

"Gomez Construction has submitted a seller payment request for the work completed through November 30. Shelly in our contract management office manages the payment system and handles all payment requests. She'll get a check cut and out to Gomez by the end of this month. They are doing an outstanding job as always. As you know, I've also hired an independent inspector, aside from the city and county types, so that we make sure we're up to code before the city types get there. I don't want to get caught in that trap and end up delaying the project because we can't get the city inspector back out to reinspect quickly enough."

"Thank you, Jake. Any problems with those inspections so far?"

Jake clears his throat. "It turned out to be a good move because the contractor did find some things that we were able to correct before bringing out the official inspectors."

"Ricardo, do you have a contract update for us today?"

"Yes. The contract management office used a fixed-price contract on the hardware and IT supplies order. That contract is just now making its way through the sign-off processes. My group will manage the quality control and testing once all this equipment arrives."

"Jill, can you give us the update on the store?" you ask.

"I've ordered all the retail products, have ordered the cookware line, and have lined up the chef demos. The costs for the new gourmet supplier we're using are higher than our original vendor. This impacts ongoing operations, but the hit to the project budget is minimal. I should also mention that a change request was submitted."

You point everyone's attention to the issues list. "In the last meeting I reported that Gomez had an important crew member out on a family emergency. Gomez was able to replace the team member with no impact to the schedule. The next issue was the T1 connection—I reported that Ricardo was not receiving return phone calls. Good news—that issue has been cleared, the date has been set, and we can close this issue. Are there any new issues to be added this week?"

There were no additional issues reported.

"What's the forecast?" Dirk asks. "Are we on track for meeting the grand opening date given all these issues?"

"I'll have performance figures for you at the next status meeting, and I have some ideas on how we can make up this time other ways so that we still meet the date."

You thank everyone for coming and remind them of the next meeting time.

Project Case Study Checklist

- Conduct Procurements
  - Contract documentation
  - Seller invoices
  - Payment systems
  - Records management system
- Perform Quality Assurance
  - Quality audits
  - Making certain the project will meet and satisfy the quality standards of the project

- Distribute Information
  - Project information is delivered to stakeholders in a timely manner.
  - The Distribute Information method is status reports via email and project meetings.
  - The status report is part of the project reports filed in the project notebook or filed for future reference as historical information.
- Manage Stakeholder Expectations
  - Communications methods
  - Issue log
  - Resolved issues

Understanding How This Applies to Your Next Project

This chapter is jammed with information you need to know for the exam as well as on the job. But depending on the size of your organization, many of the processes I discussed in the Executing process group might actually be handled by another department in your organization. I've worked in small companies (fewer than 100 people) and very large companies and have always had either a person or a department that was responsible for the vendor selection, contract negotiation, and contract administration. In all these situations and in my current role as project manager, I have significant input to these processes, but the person or department responsible for procurement has the ultimate control. For example, we use only RFPs (and occasionally RFIs) to solicit vendors. We typically use a weighted scoring model in combination with a screening and rating system to choose a vendor. For small projects, we have a list of prequalified vendors from which to choose.

Someone who is skilled at writing contracts can best handle the contracts, which ideally should be reviewed by the legal team. The legal team should also review changes proposed by the vendor before signing on the dotted line. Clear, concise, and specific contracts, in my experience, are a critical success factor for any project. I've too often seen contract issues bring a project to a sudden halt. Another classic contract faux pas allows the vendor to think the work is complete while the buyer believes the vendor is weeks or months away from meeting the requirements. These types of disputes can almost always be traced back to an unclear, imprecise contract. It's important to be specific in your statement of work. Make sure that the project requirements are clear and broken down far enough to be measurable and that deliverables are defined with criteria that allow you to inspect for contract compliance prior to final acceptance.

I'll emphasize one last time the importance of communication, good communication skills, and getting that information into the appropriate hands at the right time. Enough said.

Managing your stakeholder's expectations is as important as managing the project team. Stakeholders need plenty of communication, and issues need to be discussed and resolutions agreed upon. Remember the old adage that most people need to hear the same information six times before it registers with them. Stakeholders, understandably, are notorious for hearing what they want to hear. Here's an example: If I asked you to picture an elephant, you would likely picture an elephant in your mind. It might be live or the stuffed variety and it could be gray, brown, or pink, but you'd clearly understand the concept. *Elephant* is a word that's pretty hard to misinterpret. But what if I asked you to picture a three-bedroom house? There's lots of room for interpretation there. When I said *three-bedroom house*, I meant ranch style with the master on one end of the house and the other two bedrooms at the other end of the house. What did you picture? Make certain you're using language your stakeholders understand, and repeat it often until you're certain they get it.

Summary

This chapter finished up the Executing process group. We looked at Conduct Procurements, Perform Quality Assurance, Distribute Information, and Manage Stakeholder Expectations.

Conduct Procurements involves obtaining responses to bids and proposals from potential vendors, selecting a vendor, and awarding the contract. In this process, the selection committee will use proposal evaluation techniques to prioritize the bids and proposals, and the outcome is that a seller (or sellers) is selected and contracts awarded.

Contracts have cycles of their own, much like projects. Phases of the contracting life cycle include requirement, requisition, solicitation, and award. Changes to the contract are managed with change requests.

Changes that cannot be agreed upon are contested changes. These take the form of disputes, claims, or appeals. They might be settled among the parties directly, through a court of law, or through arbitration.

During the Perform Quality Assurance process, quality audits are performed to ensure that the project will meet and satisfy the project's quality standards set out in the quality plan.

Distribute Information is concerned with making certain project information is available to stakeholders at the right time and in the appropriate format. Distribute Information is performed throughout the life of the project.

The Manage Stakeholder Expectations process concerns making certain communication needs and expectations of the stakeholders are met, managing any issues stakeholders might raise that could become future issues, and resolving previously identified issues.

Exam Essentials

Be able to describe the purpose of the Conduct Procurements process. Conduct Procurements involves obtaining bids and proposals from vendors, selecting a vendor, and awarding a contract.

Be able to name the tools and techniques of the Conduct Procurements process. The tools and techniques of the Conduct Procurements process are weighting systems, independent estimates, screening systems, contract negotiation, seller rating systems, expert judgment, and proposal evaluation techniques.

Be able to name the contracting life cycle stages. Contracting life cycles include requirement, requisition, solicitation, and award stages.

Be able to describe the purpose of the Perform Quality Assurance process. The Perform Quality Assurance process is concerned with making certain the project will meet and satisfy the quality standards of the project.

Be able to differentiate between senders and receivers of information. Senders are responsible for clear, concise, complete messages, while receivers are responsible for understanding the message correctly.

Be able to describe the purpose of the Manage Stakeholder Expectations process. Manage Stakeholder Expectations concerns satisfying the needs of the stakeholders and successfully meeting the goals of the project by managing communications with stakeholders.

Key Terms

I've discussed the processes you'll use while measuring and evaluating project performance. You need to understand each of these processes to effectively evaluate progress, recognize variances from the plan, and make adjustments to keep the project on track. Know them by the names used in the *PMBOK® Guide* so you'll recognize them on the exam.

Conduct Procurements	Manage Stakeholder Expectations
Distribute Information	Perform Quality Assurance

You learned a lot of new key words in this chapter as well. PMI has worked hard to develop and define terms that apply across industries. Here is a list of some of the terms you came across in this chapter:

advertising	procurement negotiations
arbitration	project presentations
bidder conferences	project records
communication	project reports
fait accompli	qualified sellers lists
independent estimates	quality audits
information distribution tools	screening systems
lessons learned	seller rating systems
process analysis	should cost estimates

Review Questions

1. You have been hired as a contract project manager for Grapevine Vineyards. Grapevine wants you to design an Internet wine club for its customers. Customers must register before being allowed to order wine over the Internet so that legal age can be established. You know that the module to verify registration must be written and tested using data from Grapevine's existing database. This new module cannot be tested until the data from the existing system is loaded. You are going to hire a vendor to perform the programming and testing tasks for this module to help speed up the project schedule. You decide to use an IFB and include a detailed SOW. This is an example of which of the following?

   A. Standard form

   B. Make-or-buy analysis

   C. Advertising

   D. Procurement documents

2. Receivers in the communication model filter their information through all of the following except _______________.

   A. culture

   B. knowledge of subject

   C. habits

   D. language

3. You have accumulated project information throughout the project and need to distribute some important information you just received. Which of the following is not an information distribution tool?

   A. Project reports

   B. Electronic databases

   C. Electronic mail

   D. Manual filing system

4. You know that the next status meeting will require some discussion and a decision for a problem that has surfaced on the project. To make the most accurate decision, you know that the number of participants in the meeting should be limited to _______________.

   A. 1 to 5

   B. 5 to 11

   C. 7 to 16

   D. 10 to 18

5. You are holding end-of-phase meetings with your team members and key stakeholders to learn what has hindered and helped the project team's performance of the work. All of the following are true regarding this situation except for which one? Choose the least correct answer.

   A. These meetings are called lessons learned meetings. Lessons learned documentation is an output of the Distribute Information process. These meetings are also a good team-building activity.

   B. The information learned from these meetings concerns processes and activities that have already occurred, so it will be most useful to document the lessons learned for future projects.

   C. The project reports component of the organizational process assets updates output includes status meetings and lessons learned.

   D. These meetings should be documented and should always include the cause of the issue, the reasons for corrective actions, and other appropriate information about the issues.

6. You are a project manager for Dakota Software Consulting Services. You're working with a major retailer that offers its products through mail-order catalogs. The company is interested in knowing customer characteristics, the amounts of first-time orders, and similar information. As a potential bidder for this project, you worked on the RFP response and submitted the proposal. When the selection committee received the RFP responses from all the vendors bidding on this project, they used a weighted system to make a selection. Which tool and technique is this a part of?

   A. A proposal evaluation technique in the Conduct Procurements process

   B. A seller proposal technique in the Conduct Procurements process

   C. A make-or-buy decision technique in the Conduct Procurements process

   D. A procurement negotiations technique in the Conduct Procurements process

7. You have been asked to submit a proposal for a project that has been put out for bid. First you attend the bidder conference to ask questions of the buyers and to hear the questions some of the other bidders will ask. Which of the following statements is true?

   A. Bidder conferences are a component of the procurement negotiations tool and technique of the Conduct Procurements process.

   B. Bidder conferences are an input of the Conduct Procurements process.

   C. Bidder conferences are an output of the Conduct Procurements process.

   D. Bidder conferences are a tool and technique of the Conduct Procurements process.

8. You have been asked to submit a proposal for a project that has been put out for bid. Prior to submitting the proposal, your company must register so that its firm is on the qualified seller list. Which of the following statements is true?

   A. The qualified seller list provides information about the sellers and is a tool and technique of the Conduct Procurements process.

   B. The qualified seller list provides information about the project and the company that wrote the RFP and is an output of the Conduct Procurements process.

   C. The qualified seller list provides information about the project and the company that wrote the RFP and is a component of the procurement documents input of the Conduct Procurements process.

   D. The qualified seller list provides information about the sellers and is an input to Conduct Procurements.

9. Which of the following tools and techniques of the Conduct Procurements process is used to check proposed pricing?

   A. Screening systems

   B. Seller rating systems

   C. Independent estimates

   D. Proposal evaluation technique

10. During the opening rounds of contract negotiation, the other party uses a fait accompli tactic. Which of the following statements is true about fait accompli tactics?

    A. One party agrees to accept the offer of the other party but secretly knows they will bring the issue back up at a later time.

    B. One party claims the issue was documented and accepted in the issue log but they're willing to reopen it for discussion.

    C. One party claims the issue under discussion has already been decided and can't be changed.

    D. One party claims to accept the offer of the other party, provided a contract change request is submitted describing the offer in detail.

11. The tools and techniques of the Conduct Procurements process include all of the following except which one?

    A. Bidder conferences

    B. Make-or-buy analysis

    C. Advertising

    D. Internet search

12. The purpose of a quality audit includes all of the following except which one?

    A. To determine which project processes or activities are inefficient or ineffective

    B. To examine the work of the project, or the results of a process, and formally accept the work results

    C. To improve processes and reduce the cost of quality

    D. To improve processes and increase the percentage of product or service acceptance

13. You are a contract project manager for a wholesale flower distribution company. Your project involves developing a website for the company that allows retailers to place their flower orders online. You will also provide a separate link for individual purchases that are ordered, packaged, and mailed to the consumer directly from the grower's site. This project involves coordinating the parent company, growers, and distributors. You've discovered a problem with one of the technical processes needed to perform this project. You decide to perform root cause analysis to determine the cause of this problem and recommended preventive actions. Which of the following is true? Choose the most correct response.

A. You are using the process analysis technique.

B. You are using the quality audit technique.

C. You are using the root cause identification technique.

D. You are using a design of experiments tool and technique.

14. The tools and techniques of the Perform Quality Assurance process include all of the following except which one?

A. Quality audits

B. Process analysis

C. Proprietary quality management methodologies

D. Plan quality and perform quality control tools and techniques

15. You are working on a project and discover that one of the business users responsible for testing the product never completed this activity. She has written an email requesting that one of your team members drop everything to assist her with a problem that could have been avoided if she would have performed the test. This employee reports to a stakeholder, not to the project team. All project team members and stakeholders are co-located. Since your team needs her to also participate in an upcoming test, you decide to do which of the following?

A. You decide to record the issue in the issue log and bring it up at the next status meeting. Everyone can benefit from understanding the importance of stakeholders fulfilling their roles and responsibilities on the project.

B. You decide to record the issue in the issue log and then phone the stakeholder to explain what happened. You know speaking with the stakeholder directly is the most effective means for resolving issues.

C. You decide to have a face-to-face meeting with the stakeholder because this is the most effective means for resolving issues with them.

D. You decide to email the stakeholder and explain what happened in a professional manner so you can incorporate their response in the next status report.

16. Your project is progressing as planned. The project team has come up with a demo that the sales team will use when making presentations to prospective clients. You will do which of the following at your next stakeholder project status meeting?

A. Preview the demo for stakeholders, and obtain their approval and sign-off.

B. Report on the progress of the demo, and note that it's a completed task.

C. Review the technical documentation of the demo, and obtain approval and sign-off.

D. Report that the demo has been noted as a completed task in the information retrieval system.

17. Negotiated contracts that will be used as the final contract are a requirement of which of the following outputs of the Conduct Procurements process?

    A. Independent estimates

    B. Project document updates

    C. Procurement contract award

    D. Selected sellers

18. According to the *PMBOK® Guide*, this party is responsible for managing stakeholder expectations.

    A. Project manager, because actively managing stakeholder expectations will reduce project risk and help unresolved issues get resolved quickly.

    B. Project sponsor, because the overall success or failure of the project rests on this individual.

    C. All stakeholders have responsibility to make sure their expectations are managed and they receive the proper information at the right time.

    D. Project manager and the project team members together have the responsibility because the project manager alone cannot manage all the stakeholders on a large, complex project.

19. This activity can become its own process with inputs and outputs on large or complex projects.

    A. Seller selections

    B. Procurement negotiations

    C. Procurement contract awards

    D. Proposal evaluations

20. Which of the following statement is true regarding contract life cycles?

    A. The requirement phase is the first contract life cycle phase and is performed during the Plan Procurements process. The buyer prepares the SOW during this phase.

    B. The award phase is the fourth contract life cycle phase and is performed during the Conduct Procurements process. The buyer awards the contract in this phase.

    C. The solicitation phase is the third contract life cycle phase and is performed during the Conduct Procurements process. This phase receives the bids and proposals and applies evaluation criteria to each in order to score or rank the responses.

    D. The requisition phase is the second contract life cycle phase and is performed during the Plan Procurements process. The buyer prepares the SOW during this phase.

Answers to Review Questions

1. D. Procurement documents include bids, quotations, RFIs, IFBs, RFPs, RFQs, and so on as you learned in the Plan Procurements process. They are an input of the Conduct Procurements process.

2. C. Receivers filter information through cultural considerations, knowledge of the subject matter, language abilities, geographic location, emotions, and attitudes.

3. A. Project reports describe project status and are an item that is distributed, not a distribution tool.

4. B. Group sizes of 5 to 11 participants make the most accurate decisions.

5. B. Lessons learned (which is what this question describes) are useful for activities and processes for the current project as well as future projects.

6. A. Weighted systems are a type of proposal evaluation technique, which is one of the tools and techniques of this process used to evaluate vendors based on selection criteria defined by the organization.

7. D. Bidder conferences are a tool and technique of the Conduct Procurements.

8. D. Qualified seller lists are an input of Conduct Procurements. Their purpose is to provide information about the sellers.

9. C. Independent estimates, also called *should cost estimates*, are a way to check proposed pricing.

10. C. Fait accompli is a tactic used during contract negotiations where one party convinces the other that the particular issue is no longer relevant or cannot be changed.

11. B. Make-or-buy analysis is an input of the Conduct Procurements process and a tool and technique of the Plan Procurements process.

12. B. The acceptance of work results happens later during the Verify Scope process, not during Perform Quality Assurance.

13. A. The process analysis technique in the Perform Quality Assurance process includes root cause analysis to analyze a problem and solution and to create preventive actions.

14. C. Proprietary quality management methodologies are a tool and technique of the Plan Quality process.

15. C. Face-to-face meetings are the most effective means for resolving stakeholder issues provided these meetings are practical.

16. B. Status meetings are to report on the progress of the project. They are not for demos or show-and-tell. Option C is not correct because stakeholders are not concerned about the content of the technical documentation; they need to know that a qualified technician has reviewed the technical documentation and that the documentation task is accurate and complete.

17. D. The selected sellers output requires a negotiated contract. Independent estimates are a tool and technique of this process.

18. A. The project manager alone is responsible for managing stakeholder expectations.

19. B. Procurement negotiations, a tool and technique of Conduct Procurements, can become its own process with inputs and outputs for large or complex projects.

20. C. The solicitation phase is where bids and proposals are prepared. The award phase of the contract life cycle is where bids and proposals are received and evaluation criteria used to determine a winner.

Chapter 10

Measuring and Controlling Project Performance

THE PMP EXAM CONTENT FROM THE EXECUTING THE PROJECT PERFORMANCE DOMAIN COVERED IN THIS CHAPTER INCLUDES THE FOLLOWING:

- ✓ **Implement Approved Actions and Workarounds**
- ✓ **Measure Project Performance**
- ✓ **Verify and Manage Changes to the Project**

This chapter introduces the Monitoring and Controlling process group. The Monitoring and Controlling process group involves taking measurements and performing inspections to find out whether there are variances in the plan. If you discover variances, you need to take corrective action to get the project back on track and repeat the affected project Planning processes to make adjustments to the plan as a result of resolving the variances.

We'll start with the Monitor and Control Project Work process. This involves tracking, reviewing, and adjusting and controlling progress to meet the project performance objectives. We'll also look at Administer Procurements, Report Performance, and Perform Integrated Change Control.

Administer Procurements is where contract performance is monitored, procurement relationships are managed, and corrections or changes are implemented where needed.

Performance reports are an output of the Report Performance process and are used during the Monitoring and Controlling processes, along with tools and techniques, to measure project performance. These measurements and control tools allow the project manager to take corrective action during the Monitoring and Controlling processes to remedy wayward project results and realign future project results with the project management plan.

Perform Integrated Change Control lays the foundation for all the control processes that we'll talk about in Chapter 11, such as Monitor and Control Risk, Control Costs, Control Schedule, and more. I'll take the time during this discussion to explain how change control and configuration management works. Remember when you're reading these sections that the information from the Perform Integrated Change Control process applies to all the control processes we'll talk about in Chapter 11.

You've learned a lot about project management by this point and have just a few more topics to add to your study list. Keep up the good work. You're getting closer to exam day.

Monitoring and Controlling Project Work

The processes in the Monitoring and Controlling process group concentrate on monitoring and measuring project performance to identify variances from the project plan and get it back on track.

The *Monitor and Control Project Work* process is concerned with monitoring all the processes in the Initiating, Planning, Executing, and Closing process groups. Collecting data, measuring results, and reporting on performance information are some of the activities you'll perform during this process.

According to the *PMBOK® Guide*, the Monitor and Control Project Work process involves the following:

- Reporting and comparing actual project results against the project management plan
- Analyzing performance data and determining whether corrective or preventive action should be recommended
- Monitoring the project for risks to make certain they're identified and reported, their status is documented, and the appropriate risk response plans have been put into action
- Documenting all appropriate product information throughout the life of the project
- Gathering, recording, and documenting project information that provides project status, measurements of progress, and forecasting to update cost and schedule information that is reported to stakeholders, project team members, management, and others
- Monitoring approved change requests

Monitor and Control Project Work Inputs

The inputs of this process include project management plan, performance reports, enterprise environmental factors, and organizational process assets. The enterprise environmental factors input in this process includes elements like standards, work authorization systems, risk tolerances of your stakeholders, and project management information systems. Let's look briefly at work authorization systems.

NOTE A curious thing happens here. The *PMBOK® Guide* lists work authorization systems as a tool in its glossary but it's noted as an enterprise environmental factor input in the Monitor and Control Project Work process. I recommend that you understand what a work authorization system is for the exam and how you use it. And for the record, you'll use these systems during the Executing processes.

A *work authorization system* is a subsystem of the project management system. This is a formal, documented procedure that describes how to authorize work and how to begin that work in the correct sequence and at the right time. This system describes the steps needed to issue a work authorization, the documents needed, the method or system you'll use to record and track the authorization information, and the approval levels required to authorize the work. You should understand the complexity of the project and balance the cost of instituting a work authorization system against the benefit you'll receive from it. This might be overkill on small projects, and verbal instructions might work just as well. For purposes of the exam, understand that project work is assigned and committed via a work authorization system.

Work is usually authorized using a form that describes the task, the responsible party, anticipated start and end dates, special instructions, and whatever else is particular to the activity or project. Depending on the organizational structure, the work is generally assigned and authorized by either the project manager or the functional manager. Remember that the system includes documentation on who has the authority to issue work authorization orders.

The only tool and technique of this process is expert judgment, so we'll move right into the outputs next.

Monitor and Control Project Work Outputs

The outputs of the Monitor and Control Project Work process will also look familiar. They are as follows:

- Change requests
- Project management plan updates
- Project document updates

Remember from Chapter 9 that change requests may take the form of corrective actions, preventive actions, or defect repairs. Corrective actions bring the work of the project into alignment with expected future performance. Preventive actions are implemented to help reduce the probability of negative project risks. Defect repairs either correct or replace components that are substandard or malfunctioning.

Project management plan updates may include updates to one or more of the management plans, including schedule, cost, or quality, and may require updates to the baselines, including scope, schedule, and cost performance.

Project document updates may include updates to forecasts, performance reports, and the issue log.

NOTE You'll examine several formulas and other tools and techniques that will help you do update forecasts in the next chapter.

Administering Procurements

We'll now take another look at the procurement arena. We learned about Conduct Procurements in Chapter 9. Now that the contract has been awarded, you need to administer it.

The *Administer Procurements* process concerns monitoring the vendor's performance and ensuring that all the requirements of the contract are met. When multiple vendors are providing goods and services to the project, Administer Procurements entails coordinating the interfaces among all the vendors as well as administering each of the contracts. If vendor A has a due date that will impact whether vendor B can perform their service, the management and coordination of the two vendors become important. Vendor A's contract and due dates must be monitored closely because failure to perform could impact another vendor's ability to perform, not to mention the project schedule. You can see how this situation could multiply quickly when you have six or seven or more vendors involved.

NOTE It's imperative that the project manager and project team are aware of any contract agreements that might impact the project so the team does not inadvertently take action that violates the terms of the contract.

Depending on the size of the organization, administering the contract might fall to someone in the procurement department. This doesn't mean you're off the hook as the project manager. It's still your responsibility to oversee the process and make sure the project objectives are being met, regardless of whether a vendor is performing the activities or your project team members are performing the activities. You'll be the one monitoring the performance of the vendor and informing them when and if performance is lacking. You'll also monitor the contract's financial conditions. For example, the seller should be paid in a timely manner when they've satisfactorily met the conditions of the contract, and it will be up to you to let the procurement department know it's OK to pay the vendor. If administering the contract is your responsibility, you might have to terminate the contract when the vendor violates the terms or doesn't meet the agreed-upon deliverables. If the procurement department has this responsibility, you'll have to document the situation and provide this to the procurement department so that they can enforce or terminate the contract.

Administering the contract is closely linked with project management processes. You'll monitor the progress of the contract, execute plans, track costs, measure outputs, approve changes, take corrective action, and report on status, just as you do for the project itself. According to the *PMBOK® Guide*, you must integrate and coordinate the Direct and Manage Project Execution, Report Performance, Perform Quality Control, Perform Integrated Change Control, and Monitor and Control Risk processes during the Administer Procurements process.

Exam Spotlight

Buyers and sellers are equally responsible for monitoring the contract. Each has a vested interest in ensuring that the other party is living up to their contractual obligations and that their own legal rights are protected.

Contracting Inputs

Administer Procurements has six inputs:

- Procurement documents
- Project management plan
- Contract
- Performance reports
- Approved change requests
- Work performance information

Procurement documents and project management plan are outputs from previous processes. We will cover performance reports in more detail in the section "Establishing Performance Measurements" later in this chapter. Performance reports for the Administer Procurements process include information related to the seller (or vendor).

Approved Change Requests

Sometimes as you get into the work of the project, you'll discover changes need to be made. This could entail changes to the contract as well. Approved change requests are used to process the project or contract changes and might include things such as modifications to deliverables, changes to the product or service of the project, changes in contract terms, or termination for poor performance. Contracts can be amended at any time prior to contract completion provided the changes are agreed to by all parties and conform to the change control processes outlined in the contract.

Exam Spotlight

Work performance information is an output of the Direct and Manage Project Execution process. The results you gather in the Administer Procurements process are actually collected as part of the Direct and Manage Project Execution work result output.

Work Performance Information

Work performance information concerns monitoring work results and examining the vendor's deliverables. This includes monitoring their work results against the project management plan and making certain activities are performed correctly and in sequence. You'll need to determine which deliverables are complete and which ones have not been completed to date. You'll also need to consider the quality of the deliverables and the costs that have been incurred to date.

Vendors request payment for the goods or services delivered in the form of *seller invoices*. Seller invoices should describe the work that was completed or the materials that were delivered and should include any supporting documentation necessary to describe what was delivered. The contract should state what type of supporting documentation is needed with the invoice.

Administering Procurements Tools and Techniques

The Administer Procurements process has several tools and techniques:

- Contract change control system
- Procurement performance reviews
- Inspections and audits
- Performance Reporting

- Payment systems
- Claims administration
- Records management system

You will look at each of these in the following sections.

Contract Change Control System

Much like the management plans found in the Planning processes, the *contract change control system* describes the processes needed to make contract changes. Since the contract is a legal document, changes to it require the agreement of all parties. A formal process must be established to process and authorize (or deny) changes. (Authorization levels are defined in the organizational policies.)

The purpose of the contract change control system is to establish a formal process for submitting change requests. It documents how to submit changes, establishes the approval process, and outlines authority levels. It includes a tracking system to number the change requests and record their status. The procedures for dispute resolution are spelled out in the contract change control system as well.

The change control system, along with all the management plan outputs, becomes part of the Perform Integrated Change Control process that I'll discuss later in this chapter.

Procurement Performance Reviews

Procurement performance reviews examine the seller's performance on the contract to date. These reviews can be conducted at the end of the contract or at intervals during the contract period. Procurement reviews examine the contract terms and seller performance for elements such as these:

- Meeting project scope
- Meeting project quality
- Staying within project budgets
- Meeting the project schedule

The performance reviews themselves might take the form of quality audits or inspections of documents as well as the work of the product itself. The point of the review is to determine where the seller is succeeding at meeting scope, quality, cost, and schedule issues, for example, or where they're not measuring up. If the seller is not in compliance, action must be taken to either get them back into compliance or terminate the contract. The yardstick you're using to measure their performance against is the contract SOW and the terms of the contract. When the RFP is included as part of the contract, you might also use it to determine contract compliance.

Inspections and Audits

I talked about quality audits as part of the Perform Quality Assurance process. The idea is the same here. The buyer, or some designated third party, will physically inspect the work of the seller and perform audits to determine whether there are any deficiencies in the seller's product or service.

Performance Reporting

Performance reporting is a large part of project management. This tool and technique entails providing your managers and stakeholders with information about the vendor's progress in meeting the contract objectives. This information is also part of the Report Performance process that I'll discuss in depth later in this chapter.

Payment Systems

Vendors submit seller invoices as an input to this process, and the *payment systems* tool and technique is used to issue payments. The organization might have a dedicated department, such as accounts payable, that handles vendor payments, or it might fall to the project manager. In either case, follow the policies and procedures the organization has established regarding vendor payments and make certain the payments themselves adhere to the contract terms.

Claims Administration

Claims administration involves documenting, monitoring, and managing contested changes to the contract. Changes that cannot be agreed upon are called *contested changes*. Contested changes usually involve a disagreement about the compensation to the vendor for implementing the change. You might believe the change is not significant enough to justify additional compensation, whereas the vendor believes they'll lose money by implementing the change free of charge. Contested changes are also known as *disputes*, *claims*, or *appeals*. These can be settled directly between the parties themselves, through the court system, or by a process called arbitration. *Arbitration* involves bringing all parties to the table with a third, disinterested party who is not a participant in the contract to try to reach an agreement. The purpose of arbitration is to reach an agreement without having to go to court.

Exam Spotlight

According to the *PMBOK® Guide*, when the parties cannot reach an agreement themselves, they should use an alternative dispute resolution (ADR) process, like arbitration. Also note that the preferred method of settling disputes is negotiation.

Records Management System

It has been a while since I've talked about documentation, but discussing the *records management system* reminds me of the importance of having an organized system for contract documentation. A records management system involves not just documentation, but policies, control functions, and automated tools. These can all be considered part of the project management information system you use to manage project documents and should include your contract documents. Records management systems typically index documents for easy filing and retrieval.

Managing Contract Outputs

The outputs to the Administer Procurements process are as follows:

- Procurement documentation
- Organizational process asset updates
- Change requests
- Project management plan updates

These outputs relate to the tools and techniques just talked about and in practice, work hand in hand with them. I've talked about project management plan updates before and I don't have anything new to add here. The remaining outputs have some additional information you need to know.

Procurement Documentation

Here's your favorite topic again. This output includes (but isn't limited to) all of the following:

- Contract
- Performance information
- Warranties
- Financial information (such as invoices and payment records)
- Inspection and audit results
- Supporting schedules
- Approved and unapproved changes

The records management system I talked about earlier is the perfect place to keep all these documents.

Organizational Process Asset Updates

Organizational process assets updates consist of organizational policies, procedures, and so on. Three elements of this output relate to contracts:

Correspondence Correspondence is information that needs to be communicated in writing to either the seller or the buyer. Examples include changes to the contract, clarification of contract terms, results of buyer audits and inspections, and notification of performance issues. You'll use correspondence to inform the vendor if their performance is unsatisfactory. If they don't correct it, you'll use correspondence again to notify a vendor that you're terminating the contract because performance is below expectations and is not satisfying the requirements of the contract.

Payment schedules and requests Many times, contracts are written such that payment is made based on a predefined performance schedule. For example, perhaps the first payment is made after 25 percent of the product or service is completed. Or maybe the payment schedule is based on milestone completion. In any case, as the project manager, you will verify that the vendor's work (or delivery) meets expectations before the payment is authorized. It's almost always your responsibility as the project manager to verify that the terms of the contract to date have or have not been satisfied. Depending on your organizational policies, someone from the accounting or procurement department might request written notification from you that the vendor has completed a milestone or made a delivery. Monitoring the work of the vendor is as important as monitoring the work of your team members.

If the procurement department is responsible for paying the contractor, then that department manages the payment schedule (which is one of the terms of the contract). The seller submits a payment request, an inspection or review of their performance is conducted to make certain the terms of the contract were fulfilled, and the payment is made.

Seller performance evaluation Seller performance evaluation is a written record of the seller's performance on the contract and is prepared by the buyer. It should include information about whether the seller successfully met contract dates, whether the seller fulfilled the requirements of the contract and/or contract statement of work, whether the work was satisfactory, and so on. Seller performance evaluations can be used as a basis for terminating the existing contract if performance is not satisfactory. It can also be used to determine penalty fees in the case of unsatisfactory performance or incentives that are due according to the terms of the contract. They should also indicate whether the vendor should be allowed to bid on future work. Seller performance evaluations can also be included as part of the qualified sellers lists.

Change Requests

Requested contract changes are coordinated with the Direct and Manage Project Execution and Perform Integrated Change Control processes so that any changes impacting the project are communicated to the project team and appropriate actions are put into place to realign the objectives. This might also mean you'll have to change or modify the project management plan, the cost baseline, or the project schedule. That requires you to jump back to the Planning process group to bring the project management plan, or other documents, up-to-date. Once the plan is updated, the Direct and Manage Project Execution process might require changes as well to get the work of the project in line with the new plan. Remember that project management is an iterative process, and it's not unusual to revisit the Planning or Executing processes, particularly as changes are made or corrective actions are put into place.

Contract changes will not always impact the project management plan, however. For example, late delivery of key equipment probably would impact the project management plan, but changes in the vendor payment schedule probably would not. It's important that you are kept abreast of any changes to the contract so that you can evaluate whether the project management plan needs adjusting.

Exam Spotlight

I recommend remembering the inputs, tools and techniques, and outputs of the contracting processes, including Plan Procurements, Conduct Procurements, and Administer Procurements. Be certain you understand the purposes of these processes and don't simply memorize their components. Here's a brief recap:

- Plan Procurements: Preparing the SOW and procurement documents and determining source selection criteria
- Conduct Procurements: Obtaining bids and proposals from potential vendors, evaluating proposals against predetermined evaluation criteria, selecting vendors, and awarding the contract
- Administer Procurements: Monitoring vendor performance to ensure that contract requirements are met

Establishing Performance Measurements

As mentioned, the Monitoring and Controlling process group concentrates on monitoring and measuring project performance to identify variances from the project plan. *Report Performance* is the process where the collection of baseline data occurs and is documented and reported. Report Performance is part of the Communications Management Knowledge Area, as is the Manage Stakeholder Expectations process. Thus, it involves collecting information regarding project progress and project accomplishments and reporting it to the stakeholders. This information might also be reported to project team members, the management team, and other interested parties. Reporting might include information concerning project quality, costs, scope, project schedules, procurement, and risk, and it can be presented in the form of status reports, progress measurements, or forecasts.

Exam Spotlight

According to the *PMBOK® Guide*, the performance reports produced as a result of this process should include project completion forecasts. We'll talk about forecasting methods as a tool and technique of this process.

Report Performance Inputs

You've examined most of the inputs to the Report Performance process previously. They are as follows:

- Project management plan
- Work performance information
- Work performance measurements
- Budget forecasts
- Organizational process assets

The project management plan contains the project management baseline data (typically cost, schedule, and scope factors), which you'll use to monitor and compare results. Deviations from this data are reported to management. Work performance measures are taken primarily during the Control Cost, Control Schedule, and Perform Quality Control processes, which we'll look at in the next chapter.

Report Performance Tools and Techniques

The following are tools and techniques of this process:

- Variance analysis
- Forecasting methods
- Communication methods
- Reporting systems

We will talk in depth about variance analysis in Chapter 11, and we'll examine the remaining tools and techniques next.

Forecasting Methods

Forecasting involves examining the actual project performance data to date and making predictions about future project performance based on this data. According to the *PMBOK® Guide*, forecasting methods fall into four different categories and each category has several types of forecasting methods. We'll look at a brief description of each of the categories next. The methods listed within these categories are beyond the scope of this book to describe.

Time series methods This forecasting method uses historical data to predict future performance. Earned value, moving average, extrapolation, trend estimation, linear prediction, and growth curve are some of the methods the *PMBOK® Guide* states fall into this category. We'll cover earned value in Chapter 11.

Causal/econometric methods Causal methods are based on the ability to identify variables that may cause or influence the forecast. A drop in interest rates, for example, may spur an increase in home sales. The methods included in this category are regression analysis, autoregressive moving average (ARMA), and econometrics.

Judgmental methods If your mom is anything like mine, judging others was an activity we were forbidden to participate in. This category of forecasting does just that, only it doesn't judge people. It uses opinions, intuitive judgments, and probability estimates to determine possible future results. Methods within this category include composite forecasts, the Delphi method, surveys, technology forecasting, scenario building, and forecast by analogy.

Other methods Other types of forecasting methods include simulation (like Monte Carlo analysis), probabilistic forecasting, and ensemble forecasting.

Communication Methods

Communication methods in this process include *status review meetings*. Status meetings are a type of push communication and are important functions during the course of the project. (I introduced status review meetings with the Information Distribution Process in the previous chapter.) The purpose of the status meeting is to provide updated information regarding the progress of the project. These are not show-and-tell meetings. If you have a prototype to demo, set up a different time to do that. Status meetings are meant to exchange information and provide project updates. They are a way to formally exchange project information. I've worked on projects where it's not unusual to have three or four status meetings conducted for different audiences. They can occur between the project team and project manager, between the project manager and stakeholders, between the project manager and users or customers, between the project manager and the management team, and so on.

Notice that the project manager is always included in status review meetings. Take care that you don't overburden yourself with meetings that aren't necessary or meetings that could be combined with other meetings. Having any more than three or four status meetings per month is unwieldy.

NOTE Regular, timely status meetings prevent surprises down the road because you are keeping stakeholders and customers informed of what's happening. Team status meetings alert the project manager to potential risk events and provide the opportunity to discover and manage problems before they get to the uncontrollable stage.

The project manager is usually the expediter of the status meeting. As such, it's your job to use status meetings wisely. Don't waste your team's time or the stakeholders' time either. Notify attendees in writing of the meeting time and place. Publish an agenda prior to the meeting, and stick to the agenda during the meeting. Every so often, summarize what has been discussed during the meeting. Don't let side discussions lead you down rabbit trails, and keep irrelevant conversations to a minimum. It's also good to publish status meeting notes at the conclusion of the meeting, especially if any action items resulted from the meeting. This will give you a document trail and serves as a reminder to the meeting participants of what actions need to be resolved and who is responsible for each action item.

It's important that project team members are honest with the project manager and that the project manager is in turn honest about what they report. A few years ago, a department in my agency took on a project of gargantuan proportions and unfortunately didn't employ good project management techniques. One of the biggest problems with this project was that the project manager did not listen to the highly skilled project team members. The team members warned of problems and setbacks, but the project manager didn't want to hear about it. The project manager took their reports to be of the "Chicken Little" ilk and refused to believe the sky was falling. Unfortunately, the sky *was* falling! Because the project manager didn't believe the reports, she refused to report the true status of the project to the stakeholders and oversight committees. Millions of dollars were wasted on a project that was doomed for failure while the project manager continued to report that the project was on time and activities were completed when in fact they were not.

There are hundreds of project stories like this, and I'll bet you've got one or two from your experiences as well. Don't let your project become the next bad example. Above all, be honest in your reporting. No one likes bad news, but bad news delivered too late along with millions of dollars wasted is a guaranteed career showstopper.

Reporting Systems

Reporting systems are used to record, store, and distribute information about the project, including cost, schedule progress, and performance information. According to the *PMBOK® Guide*, spreadsheet analysis, presentations, table reporting, and graphic capabilities are types of distribution formats.

Report Performance Outputs

The Report Performance process has several outputs:

- Performance reports
- Organizational process assets updates
- Change requests

Performance reports are the primary output of this process. It's here that performance information is documented and reported to the stakeholders as outlined in the communication management plan. These reports might take many forms, including S curves (cost baselines are recorded this way), bar charts, tables, and histograms. Earned value information and variance analysis is often reported during this process as well. We'll examine the earned value topic in the next chapter during the discussion of the Cost Control process.

Performance reports may range from simply stated status reports to highly detailed reports. Dashboards are an example of a simple report that may use indicators like red-yellow-green to show the status of each area of the project at a glance. Red means the item being reported is in trouble or behind schedule, yellow means it's in danger and corrective action should be taken, and green means all is well.

More detailed reports may include the following elements according to the *PMBOK® Guide*:

- Analysis of project performance for previous periods
- Risk and issue status
- Work completed in the current reporting period

- Work expected to be completed during the next reporting period
- Changes approved in the current reporting period (or a summary if there are numerous changes)
- Results of variance analysis
- Time completion forecasts and cost forecasts
- Other information stakeholders want or need to know

The updates needed to the organizational process assets output won't be a surprise. They include lessons learned documentation, report formats, causes of issues, and corrective actions taken. The change requests process includes recommended corrective actions to bring performance in alignment with the project management plan and preventive actions to reduce probable future negative performance.

Managing Perform Integrated Change Control

The *Perform Integrated Change Control* process serves as an overseer, so to speak, of the Monitoring and Controlling processes. This is where you establish the project's change control process. Changes, which encompass corrective actions, preventive actions, and defect repair, are common outputs across all the Monitoring and Controlling processes. (And don't forget that change requests are also an output of the Direct and Manage Project Plan Execution process, which is an Executing process.) Both processes can generate the change requests that are managed through the Perform Integrated Change Control process.

You're likely to see exam questions on several topics that involve change and the Perform Integrated Change Control process. Configuration management, for example, isn't listed as a tool and technique of this process, but you really can't perform the Perform Integrated Change Control process without it. I'll discuss this shortly. First, though, you'll look at change, what it is, and how it comes about.

Changes come about on projects for many reasons. It's the project manager's responsibility to manage these changes and see to it that organizational policies regarding changes are implemented. Changes don't necessarily mean negative consequences. Changes can produce positive results as well. It's important that you manage this process carefully, because too many changes—even one significant change—will impact cost, schedule, scope, and/or quality. Once a change request has been submitted, you have some decisions to make. Ask yourself questions such as these:

- Should the change be implemented?
- If so, what's the cost to the project in terms of project constraints: cost, time, scope, and quality?
- Will the benefits gained by making the change increase or decrease the chances of project completion?

Just because a change is requested doesn't mean you have to implement it. You'll always want to discover the reasons for the change to determine whether they're justifiable, and you'll want to know the cost of the change. Remember that cost can take the form of increased time. Let's say the change you're considering will result in a later schedule completion date. That means you'll need human resources longer than expected. If you've leased equipment or project resources for the team members to use during the course of the project, a later completion date means your team needs the leased equipment for a longer period of time. All this translates to increased costs. Time equals money, as the saying goes, so manage time changes wisely, and dig deep to find the impacts that time changes might make on the budget.

How Change Occurs

As the project progresses, the stakeholders or customers might request a change directly. Team members might also recommend changes as the project progresses. For example, once the project is underway, they might discover more efficient ways of performing tasks or producing the product of the project and recommend changes to accommodate the new efficiencies. Changes might also come about as a result of mistakes that were made earlier in the project in the Planning or Executing processes. (However, I hope you've applied all the great practices and techniques I've talked about to date and you didn't experience many of these.)

Changes to the project might occur indirectly as a result of contingency plans, other changes, or team members performing favors for the stakeholders by making that one little change without telling anyone about it. Many times, the project manager is the last to know about changes such as these. There's a fine line here because you don't want to discourage good working relationships between team members and stakeholders, yet at the same time, you want to ensure that all changes come through the change control process. If a dozen little changes slip through like this, your project scope suddenly exits stage left.

Change Control Concerns

Perform Integrated Change Control, according to the *PMBOK® Guide*, is primarily concerned with the following:

- Influencing the factors that cause change control processes to be circumvented
- Promptly reviewing and analyzing change requests
- Managing approved changes
- Maintaining the integrity of the project baselines (including scope, quality, schedule, cost, and performance measurement baseline) and incorporating approved changes into the project management plan and other project documents
- Promptly reviewing and analyzing corrective and preventive actions
- Coordinating and managing changes across the project
- Documenting requested changes and their impacts

Factors that might cause change include project constraints, stakeholder requests, team member recommendations, vendor issues, and many others. You'll want to understand the factors that are influencing or bringing about change and how a proposed change might impact the project if implemented. Performance measures and corrective actions might dictate that a project change is needed as well.

NOTE

Modifications to the project are submitted in the form of change requests and managed through the change control process. Obviously, you'll want to implement those changes that are most beneficial to the project. I'll talk more about change requests later in this chapter.

Managing changes might involve making changes to the project scope, schedule, or cost baseline, also known as the *performance measurement baseline*. This baseline might also involve quality or technical elements. The performance measurement baseline is the approved project management plan that describes the work of the project. This is used through Executing and Monitoring and Controlling to measure project performance and determine deviations from the plan. It's your responsibility to maintain the reliability of the performance measurement baselines. Changes that impact an existing or completed project management process will require updates to those processes, which might mean additional passes through the appropriate Planning and Executing processes.

The management plans created during the Planning process group should reflect the changes as well, which might require updates to the project management plan or the project scope statement. This requires a close eye on coordination among all the processes that are impacted. For example, changes might require updates to risk response alternatives, schedule, cost, resource requirements, or other elements. Changes that impact product scope always require an update to the project scope.

Exam Spotlight

Managing changes involves maintaining accurate and reliable performance measurement baselines; coordinating all processes impacted as a result of the change, including revisiting Planning and Executing processes where needed; and updating project scope to reflect any changes in product scope.

I caution you to not change baselines at the drop of a hat. Examine the changes, their justification, and their impacts thoroughly before making changes to the baselines. Make certain your project sponsor approves baseline changes and that the project sponsor understands why the change occurred and how it will impact the project. And be sure to keep a copy of the original baseline for comparison purposes and for lessons learned.

Configuration Management

Configuration management is generally a subsystem of the project management information system. It involves managing approved changes and project baselines. I'll talk about each of these topics later in this chapter.

The following items are what the *PMBOK® Guide* notes as activities associated with configuration change management in the Perform Integrated Change Control process:

Configuration identification Configuration identification describes the characteristics of the product, service, or result of the project. This description is the basis that's used to verify when changes are made and how they're managed. Configuration identification is also used to label products or documents, manage changes, and verify changes.

Configuration status accounting This activity doesn't really have to do with financials as you might guess from its title. It's about accounting for the status of the changes by documenting and storing the configuration information needed to effectively manage the product information. This includes the approved configuration identification, the status of proposed changes, and the status of changes currently being implemented.

Configuration verification and auditing Verification and audits are performed to determine whether the configuration item is accurate and correct and to make certain the performance requirements have been met. It assures that changes are registered in the configuration management system and that they are assessed, approved, tracked, and implemented correctly.

Exam Spotlight

Understand for the exam that configuration management involves identifying the physical characteristics of the product, service, or result of the project (or its individual components); controlling changes to those characteristics; and documenting changes to verify that requirements are met. It also includes the change management system and documents the process for requesting, tracking, and determining whether change requests should be approved or denied.

Change Control System

If you were to allow changes to occur to the project whenever requested, you would probably never complete the project. Stakeholders, the customer, and end users would continually change the project requirements if given the opportunity to do so. That's why careful planning and scope definition are important in the beginning of the project. It's your job as project manager to drive out all the compelling needs and requirements of the project during the Planning process so that important requirements aren't suddenly "remembered" halfway through the project. However, we're all human, and sometimes things are not known, weren't thought about, or simply weren't discovered until a certain point during the project. Stakeholders will probably start thinking in a direction they weren't considering during the Planning process, and new requirements will come to light. This is where the *change control system* comes into play.

The Purpose of the Change Control System

Change control systems are documented procedures that describe how the deliverables of the project and associated project documentation are controlled, changed, and approved. It also often describes how to submit change requests and how to manage change requests. They may include preprinted change request forms that provide a place to record general project information such as the name and project number, the date, and the details regarding the change request. Change control systems are usually subsystems of the configuration management system.

The change control system also tracks the status of change requests, including their approval status. Not all change requests will receive approval. Those changes that are not approved are also tracked and filed in the change control log for future reference.

The change control system might define the level of authority needed to approve changes, if it wasn't previously defined in the configuration management system. Some change requests could receive approval based on the project manager's decision; others might need a review and formal approval by the project sponsor, executive management, and so on.

NOTE The change control system is a subset of the configuration management system.

Procedures should be defined that detail how emergency changes are approved as well. For example, you and your team might be putting in some weekend hours and are close to the completion of a deliverable when you discover that thing 1 will not talk to thing 2 no matter what you do. The team brainstorms and comes up with a brilliant solution that requires a change request. Do you stop work right then and wait until the change control board or committee can meet sometime next week and make a decision, or do you—the project manager—make the decision to go forward with this solution and explain the change to the appropriate parties later? That answer depends on the change procedures you have in place to handle situations like this and on the authority you have to make emergency changes as outlined in the change control system.

Many organizations have formal change control or change request systems in place. If that's the case, you can easily adopt those procedures and use the existing system to manage project change. But if no procedures exist, you'll have to define them.

Exam Spotlight

The change control system and configuration management system together identify, document, and control the changes to the performance baseline.

The *PMBOK® Guide* states three objectives you should know about for implementing and using configuration management systems and change control processes:

- Establish a method to consistently identify changes, request changes to project baselines, and analyze and determine the value and effectiveness of the changes.
- Continuously authenticate and improve project performance by evaluating the impact of each change.
- Communicate all change requests—whether approved, rejected, or delayed—to all the stakeholders.

Real World Scenario

But I Thought You Said

Marcus is working on a web redesign project for a division of the marketing department in his organization. The project started out as a simple redesign of the look and feel of the site. Marcus made the mistake of not defining change control procedures for the project from the beginning because he reasoned that the project was small, the design changes were well understood by all, and the project could be finished in a matter of weeks.

After the work of the project started, Marcus's team showed the initial design results to the business lead, Kendra. Kendra asked for a few modifications that seemed minor, and Marcus was happy to accommodate. When his team finished the work and turned the site over for initial testing, Kendra created a list of changes that extended beyond the initial scope of the project. Marcus thought everyone had agreed that the project involved only an update to the look and feel of the site, but Kendra was now requesting changes to the applications people used to order products from the website. Marcus knew that application changes need their own set of requirements and testing. Changing the look of the site is a lot different from changing the way an application works and the results it produces. Kendra and Marcus were in disagreement over what the changes entailed. Kendra thought she had carte blanche to make changes until she was satisfied with the project. Marcus knew that the projects waiting in the queue were going to suffer because of the never-ending stream of changes to Kendra's project. The additional time her project was taking already had pushed the deliverable of the next project on their list by two weeks.

To resolve the dilemma, Marcus had to negotiate with Kendra on the list of changes she had requested. He agreed to all changes that required less than four hours to complete, and the remaining changes were moved to a new project request. Marcus also vowed to implement change control procedures for all projects from this point forward, no matter what the size or complexity of the project.

Requirements for Change

You should require two things at the beginning of all projects regarding change. First, require that all change requests be submitted in writing. This is to clarify the change and make sure there's no confusion about what's requested. It also allows the project team to accurately estimate the time it will take to incorporate the change.

Second, all change requests must come through the formal change control system. Make sure no one is allowed to go directly to team members and request changes without the project manager knowing about them. Also make certain your stakeholders understand that this can cause schedule delays, cost overruns, and sacrifices to quality and that it isn't good change management practice. Encourage them from the beginning of the project to use the formal procedures laid out in the change control system to request changes.

NOTE

It's good practice to require all change requests in writing. This should be a documented procedure outlined in your change control system. Beware! Stakeholders are notorious for asking for changes verbally even when there is a detailed process in place. If they don't want to follow the process, someone on the project team should have the responsibility for documenting and logging the change requests for future reference.

Change Control Board

In some organizations, a *change control board (CCB)* is established to review all change requests. The board is given the authority to approve or deny change requests as defined by the organization. It's important that its authority is clearly defined and that separate procedures exist for emergency changes. The CCB might meet only once a week, once every other week, or even once a month, depending on the project. When emergencies arise, the preestablished procedures allow the project manager to implement the change on the spot. This always requires follow-up with the CCB and completion of a formal change request, even though it's after the fact.

CCB members might include stakeholders, managers, project team members, and others who might not have any connection to the project at hand. Some organizations have permanent CCBs that are staffed by full-time employees dedicated to managing change for the entire organization, not just project change. You might want to consider establishing a CCB for your project if the organization does not have one.

Exam Spotlight

For purposes of the exam, note that the *PMBOK® Guide* states that the CCB is made up of a group of stakeholders who review and then approve, delay, or reject change requests.

Some organizations use other types of review boards that have the same responsibilities as the CCB. Some other names you might see are technical assessment board (TAB), technical review board (TRB), engineering review board (ERB), and configuration control board (CCB).

Perform Integrated Change Control Inputs, Tools and Techniques, and Outputs

The inputs for the Perform Integrated Change Control process are as follows:

- Project management plan
- Work performance information
- Change requests
- Enterprise environmental factors
- Organizational process assets

Remember that the project management plan includes all the documents together that make up that plan—the project schedule, budget, scope statement, and so on.

You've seen all the tools and techniques for Perform Integrated Change Control in previous processes:

- Expert judgment
- Change control meetings

The outputs of the Perform Integrated Change Control process are as follows:

- Change request status updates
- Project management plan updates
- Project document updates

Project management plan updates are typically required as a result of an approved change or corrective action, especially those changes that impact a project baseline. It may sound obvious, but I'll tell you anyway: changes made to baselines should reflect changes from the current point in time forward. You cannot change past performance. These changes are noted in the change control system or the configuration management system, and stakeholders are informed at the status meetings of the changes that have occurred, their impacts, and where the description of the changes can be found.

You should document all the actions taken in the Perform Integrated Change Control process (whether implemented or not) as part of the project document updates output. You should also record the reason for the change request. In other words, how did this particular change request come about? How did it change the original project management plan? Is this something you could or should have known about in the Planning processes? You should note the corrective action taken and the justification for choosing that particular corrective action as part of lessons learned also. You can use the information you capture here in your configuration management system as lessons learned for future projects. When you take on a new project, it's a good idea to review the lessons learned from similar projects so that you can plan appropriately and avoid, where possible, the variances that occurred in those projects.

In the next chapter, you'll explore the individual change control processes (like Control Cost and Control Schedule) and the measurement tools you'll use to provide the variance measurements that are gathered and reported to the stakeholder via the Report Performance process that we discussed earlier in this chapter.

Real World Scenario

Project Case Study: New Kitchen Heaven Retail Store

Your regularly scheduled status meeting is in progress. Let's see how it's progressing.

Your next agenda item is an update on change requests. Ricardo submitted a change request regarding the hardware installation at the new store site. A new, much anticipated operating system was just released, and Ricardo has plans to upgrade the entire company to the new operating system. Since he must purchase new equipment for this store anyway, he contends that it makes sense to go ahead and purchase the hardware with the newest operating system already loaded. His staff won't have to upgrade this store as part of the upgrade project because the store will already have the new operating system.

Ricardo's change request was submitted in writing through the change control system. A CCB was set up during the Planning stages of this project to handle change requests. At the CCB meeting, the following questions come up regarding Ricardo's request: Has the new operating system been tested with the existing system? Are there compatibility problems? If so, what risks are associated with getting the problems resolved and the equipment installed by opening day? Is the vendor ready to ship with the new operating system?

The CCB defers their decision for this request until Ricardo gives them answers to these questions.

During the next CCB meeting, the board reviews a change request from Jill. The gourmet food supplier she used went out of business and Jill contracted with a new vendor. She received a sample shipment from the new vendor and was very unhappy with the results. Upon inspecting the products, she found broken containers and damaged packaging. Meanwhile, Jill found another vendor, who has sent her a sample shipment. She is very pleased with the new vendor's products and service. However, this vendor's prices are even higher than the first replacement vendor she contracted with. Jill submitted a cost change request to the CCB because of the increased cost of the gourmet food product shipment. The change in cost does not have a significant impact on the budget.

Jake reported that payments have been made to the vendor supplying the store's display cases and shelving and also gave an update on the vendor supplying the lighting for the store. Both vendors met or exceeded performance requirements and he's happy with their service.

You hold a seat on the CCB and are aware of the change requests and their impacts to the project. Ricardo satisfactorily answered all the questions the CCB had, so his request and Jill's request were both approved during the meeting.

"Now I'd like to give a brief update on the project forecast," you tell the group. "Based on the preliminary data I've gathered, we are somewhat behind schedule but budget appears to be on track. I will have some forecast numbers for you at the next meeting."

Project Case Study Checklist

- Administer Procurements
  - Monitor vendor performance
  - Document vendor performance
  - Monitor payments to seller
- Perform Integrated Change Control
  - Review and approve changes
  - Document changes in change log
- Configuration management systems
  - Configuration identification
  - Configuration status accounting
  - Configuration verification and auditing
  - Change control system
- Report Performance
  - Performance reports (status meetings)
  - Forecasts

Understanding How This Applies to Your Next Project

I've learned from experience the value of having a change control process in place for all projects. I've never managed a project that didn't encounter change. And there are hundreds of reasons that bring about change. One of the ways to help reduce the amount of change you might experience is to make certain you've documented the requirements of the project accurately and have obtained sign-off from the stakeholders. Be aware—just because the stakeholders have agreed to the requirements doesn't mean they won't want change. As you elaborate the deliverables and requirements, the product or end result becomes clearer, and that means some elements not previously known or at least not known in their entirety early in the planning process will require change.

If you don't already have a change control process in place, I recommend setting one up before you begin your next project. Document the procedures for requesting, tracking, and approving or denying changes. Make them one of the agenda items for discussion at your project kickoff meeting. It's easier to enforce change procedures (and deny changes that are out of scope) if the process is discussed with the stakeholders early in the project. You will likely want to include important stakeholders on the change control board, and that gives you another great opportunity to discuss and reinforce the process.

Administering contracts and procurements, as I mentioned earlier, may be managed by someone in your procurement department. In my experience, there is always someone from this department involved from the request process through contract administration. However, it will likely be up to you to monitor vendor performance, make sure deliverable dates are met, and verify timecards against the submitted invoice.

Summary

This chapter examined several change control processes starting with the Monitor and Control Project Work process. This process is responsible for reviewing, tracking, and controlling project progress. It ensures that the performance objectives outlined in the project management plan are met.

The Administer Procurements process is concerned with managing vendor relationships, monitoring performance, and implementing changes or corrections when necessary. Both buyer and seller are responsible for administering the contract (or other procurement vehicle) to assure that contractual obligations are being met.

Perform Integrated Change Control is an important part of the project process. It's your responsibility as project manager to manage change and implement corrective action where needed to keep the project on track with the plan. Perform Integrated Change Control concerns influencing the things that cause change and managing the change once it has occurred. One or more of the project baselines may be affected when change occurs. Managing change might involve changes to the project plan, the project schedule, the project budget, project scope, and so on. Changes that impact processes you've already completed require updates to those processes. Corrective action is often a result of a change and ensures that the future performance of the project lines up with the project management plan.

Configuration management systems typically include change control systems that document the procedures to manage change and how change requests are implemented. Change requests might come in written or verbal forms, but ideally you should ask for all your change requests in writing. Change requests are processed through a formal change control system, and configuration control boards have the authority to approve or deny change requests.

Exam Essentials

Name the outputs of the Monitor and Control Project Work process. The outputs are change requests (which includes corrective action, preventive action, and defect repair), project management plan updates, and project document updates.

Name the processes that integrate with the Administer Procurement process. Direct and Manage Project Execution, Report Performance, Perform Quality Control, Perform Integrated Change Control, and Monitor and Control Risk.

Describe the purpose of the Report Performance process. Report Performance concerns collecting and distributing performance information about the project, including status reports, progress to date, and forecasts.

Name the purpose of the Perform Integrated Change Control process. Perform Integrated Change Control is performed throughout the life of the project and involves reviewing all the project change requests, establishing a configuration management and change control process, and approving or denying changes.

Be able to define the purpose of a configuration management system. Configuration management systems are documented procedures that describe the process for submitting change requests, the processes for tracking changes and their disposition, and the processes for defining the approval levels for approving and denying changes. The configuration management system also includes a process for authorizing the changes. Change control systems are generally a subset of the configuration management system. Configuration management also describes the characteristics of the product of the project and ensures accuracy and completeness of the description.

Be able to describe a CCB. The change control board (CCB) has the authority to approve or deny change requests. Their authority is defined and outlined by the organization. A CCB is made up of stakeholders.

Key Terms

The processes introduced in this chapter give you the tools and techniques you need to keep your projects on track and to manage change. Know these processes by the PMI terms if you want to be successful in obtaining your PMP certification.

Administer Procurements

Monitor and Control Project Work

Perform Integrated Change Control

Report Performance

You've learned a lot of new key words in this chapter. PMI has worked hard to develop and define standard project management terms that apply across industries. Here is a list of some of the terms you came across in this chapter:

change control board (CCB)	disputes
change control system	forecasting
claims	performance measurement baselines
claims administration	performance review
configuration management	seller invoices
contested changes	status review meetings
contract change control system	

Review Questions

1. You are a project manager for an international marketing firm. You are ready to assign resources to your new project using a work authorization system. Which of the following statements is not true?

   A. Work authorization systems clarify and initiate the work for each work package.

   B. Work authorization systems are written procedures defined by the organization.

   C. Work authorization systems are used throughout the project Execution processes.

   D. Work authorization systems are a tool and technique of the Monitor and Control Project Work process.

2. You are working on a project and discover that one of the business users responsible for testing the product never completed this activity. She has written an email requesting that one of your team members drop everything to assist her with a problem that could have been avoided if she would have performed the test. This employee reports to a stakeholder, not to the project team. You estimate that the project might not be completed on time as a result of this missed activity. All of the following are true except for which one?

   A. You should recommend a corrective action to bring the expected future project performance back into line with the project management plan because of this employee's failure to perform this activity.

   B. You should recommend a preventive action to reduce the possibility of future project performance veering off track because of this employee's failure to perform this activity.

   C. You should recommend a change request, which is an output of the Monitor and Control Project Work process, to get the project performance back in alignment with the project management plan.

   D. You might have to request a change to the project schedule as a result of this missed activity.

3. Which one of the following is the most preferred method of settling claims and disputes according to the *PMBOK® Guide*?

   A. Arbitration

   B. Collaboration

   C. ADR

   D. Negotiation

4. Which option includes all of the tools and techniques of the Administer Procurements process?
   - A. Contract change control system, expert judgment, inspection and audits, performance reporting, payment systems, claims administration, and records management system.
   - B. Contract change control system, procurement performance reviews, inspection and audits, performance reporting, payment systems, claims administration, configuration management system, and records management system.
   - C. Contract change control system, expert judgment, inspection and audits, performance reporting, payment systems, claims administration, configuration management system, and records management system.
   - D. Contract change control system, procurement performance reviews, inspection and audits, performance reporting, payment systems, claims administration, and records management system.
5. You are a project manager for an engineering company. Your company won the bid to add ramp-metering lights to several on-ramps along a stretch of highway at the south end of the city. You subcontracted a portion of the project to another company. The subcontractor's work involves digging the holes and setting the lamp poles in concrete. The subcontractor's performance is not meeting the contract requirements. Which of the following is not a valid option?
   - A. You document the poor performance in written form and send the correspondence to the subcontractor.
   - B. You terminate the contract for poor performance and submit a change request through Administer Procurements.
   - C. You submit a change request through Administer Procurements demanding that the subcontractor comply with the terms of the contract.
   - D. You agree to meet with the subcontractor to see whether a satisfactory solution can be reached.
6. The Administer Procurements process is closely integrated with all of the following processes except for which one?
   - A. Direct and Manage Project Execution
   - B. Perform Quality Assurance
   - C. Integrated Change Control
   - D. Performance Reporting
7. You are holding a regularly scheduled status meeting for your project. You know all of the following are true regarding status meetings except which one?
   - A. Status meetings are a type of interactive communication.
   - B. Status meetings are a type of communication method, which is a tool and technique of the Report Performance process.
   - C. Status meetings are a way to formally exchange information and update the stakeholders project status.
   - D. Status meetings should be held throughout the project and regularly scheduled intervals.

8. You are performing actions such as analyzing past performance, assessing the current status of risks and issues, describing the work completed this period, and summarizing the changes approved this period. Which process are you performing?

   A. Report Performance

   B. Integrated Change Control

   C. Monitor and Control Project Work

   D. Administer Procurements

9. All of the following are tools and techniques of the Report Performance process except which one?

   A. Records management system

   B. Communication methods

   C. Variance analysis

   D. Forecasting methods

10. The Delphi method, technology forecasting, and forecast by analogy are examples of what category of forecasting methods?

    A. Time series

    B. Judgmental

    C. Causal

    D. Econometric

11. Your project is progressing as planned. The project team has come up with a demo that the sales team will use when making presentations to prospective clients. You will do which of the following at your next stakeholder project status meeting? Choose the best answer.

    A. Preview the demo for stakeholders, and obtain their approval and sign-off.

    B. Report on the progress of the demo, and note that it's a completed task.

    C. Review the technical documentation of the demo, and obtain approval and sign-off.

    D. Report that the demo has created a change request that's been documented in the change control system.

12. All of the following statements are true regarding forecasting except which one?

    A. Forecasting predicts future project performance based on actual performance to date.

    B. Forecasting is a Monitor and Control Project Work tool and technique.

    C. Causal/econometric methods and judgmental methods are two categories of forecasting.

    D. Time series methods is one category of forecasting.

13. You are a project manager for Bluebird Technologies. Bluebird writes custom billing applications for several industries. A schedule change has been requested. You know change from the perspective of the Perform Integrated Change Control is concerned with all of the following except which one?

A. Influencing factors that circumvent the change control process

B. Issuing change requests

C. Reviewing change

D. Maintaining the integrity of baselines

14. You are a project manager for Bluebird Technologies. Bluebird writes custom billing applications for several industries. One of your users verbally requests changes to one of the screen displays. You explain to her that the change needs to go through the change control system, which is a subset of the configuration management system. You explain that a change control system does all of the following except for which one?

A. Documents procedures for change requests

B. Tracks the status of change requests

C. Describes the management impacts of change

D. Determines whether changes are approved or denied

15. You are a project manager for Star Light Strings. Star Light manufactures strings of lights for outdoor display. Its products range from simple light strings to elaborate lights with animal designs, bug designs, memorabilia, and so on. Your newest project requires a change. You have documented the characteristics of the product and its functionality using which of the following tools and techniques?

A. Change control system

B. Corrective action

C. Configuration management

D. Updates to the project management plan

16. You are a project manager for Star Light Strings. Star Light manufactures strings of lights for outdoor display. Its products range from simple light strings to elaborate lights with animal designs, bug designs, memorabilia, and so on. Your newest project requires a change. One of the business unit managers submitted a change through the change control system, which utilizes a CCB. Which of the following is true regarding the CCB?

A. The CCB describes how change requests are managed.

B. The CCB requires all change requests in writing.

C. The CCB approves or denies change requests.

D. The CCB requires updates to the appropriate management plan.

17. All of the following are activities of the configuration management system except for which one?

A. Variance analysis

B. Identification

C. Status accounting

D. Verification and auditing

18. According the *PMBOK® Guide*, this system centrally manages approved changes and baselines within a project.

A. Records management system

B. Change control system

C. Work authorization system

D. Configuration management system

19. You are performing the following activities: comparing actual performance against the project plan, assessing performance to determine if a corrective action is necessary, identifying new risks, providing forecasts to update current cost and schedule data, and monitoring implementation of approved changes. Which process are you in?

A. Perform Integrated Change Control

B. Report Performance

C. Monitor and Control Project Work

D. Monitor and Control Risks

20. All of the following are acronyms for other boards that fulfill the same responsibilities as a change control board except for which one?

A. TAB

B. TRB

C. ARB

D. ERB

Answers to Review Questions

1. D. Work authorization systems are a tool used during Project Execution processes and are a subset of the project management information system considered part of the enterprise environmental factors input of the Monitor and Control Project Work process. They formally initiate the work of each work package and clarify the assignments.

2. B. You are in the Monitor and Control Project Work process and should recommend a change request that can take the form of a corrective action. Preventive actions reduce the possibility of negative impacts from risk events and do not apply to this situation.

3. D. Negotiation is the preferred method of settling claims or disputes in the Administer Procurements process.

4. D. The tools and techniques of the Administer Procurements process are contract change control system, procurement performance reviews, inspection and audits, performance reporting, payment systems, claims administration, and records management system.

5. C. The contract change control system describes the processes you'll use to make changes to the contract; it is not a means of communication. The changes might include contract term changes, date changes, and termination of a contract.

6. B . According to the *PMBOK® Guide*, the Contract Administration process is closely coordinated with the Direct and Manage Project Execution, Report Performance, Perform Quality Control, Perform Integrated Change Control, and Monitoring and Control risk processes.

7. A. According to the *PMBOK® Guide*, status meetings are a form of push communication.

8. A. This question describes the Report Performance process, which is concerned with collecting and reporting information regarding project progress and project accomplishments to the stakeholders.

9. A. The tools and techniques of the Report Performance process are variance analysis, forecasting methods, communication methods, and reporting systems.

10. B. The Delphi method, technology forecasting, scenario building, and forecast by analogy are all in the judgmental methods category of forecasting.

11. B. Status meetings are to report on the progress of the project. They are not for demos or show-and-tell. Option D could be correct but there isn't enough information in the question to know that a change request was submitted.

12. B. Forecasting is a tool and technique of the Report Performance process.

13. B. Change requests are submitted through other process like the Monitor and Control Project Work process and are reviewed, tracked, managed, analyzed, and documented in this process.

14. D. Change control systems are documented procedures that describe how to submit change requests. They track the status of the change requests, document the management impacts of change, track the change approval status, and define the level of authority needed to approve changes. Change control systems do not approve or deny the changes—that's the responsibility of the change control board (CCB).

15. C. The key to this question was that the characteristics of the product were documented with this tool. Configuration management documents the physical characteristics and the functionality of the product of the project.

16. C. Change control boards (CCBs) review change requests and have the authority to approve or deny them. Their authority is defined by the configuration control and change control process.

17. A. The three activities associated with configuration management are configuration identification, configuration status accounting, and configuration verification and auditing.

18. D. Configuration management systems are a way to manage approved changes and baselines.

19. C. These are elements the Monitor and Control Project Work process is concerned with.

20. C. The TAB stands for technical assessment board, TRB is a technical review board, and ERB is an engineering review board.

hapter 11

Controlling Work Results

THE PMP EXAM CONTENT FROM THE MONITORING AND CONTROLLING THE PROJECT PERFORMANCE DOMAIN COVERED IN THIS CHAPTER INCLUDES THE FOLLOWING:

- ✓ **Ensure Project Deliverables Conform to Quality Standards**
- ✓ **Measure Project Performance**
- ✓ **Verify and Manage Changes to the Project**
- ✓ **Monitor All Risks**

You've almost made it to the homestretch. This chapter covers the last group of project processes in the Monitoring and Controlling group. There's a significant amount of information packed into this chapter, and I recommend you memorize all the formulas presented here for the exam.

I'll cover the Monitor and Control Risks, Control Costs, Control Schedule, Perform Quality Control, Verify Scope, and Control Scope processes in this chapter.

Monitor and Control Risks monitors the project for risks and monitors the risk response plans that have been put into action or might need to be put into action. The Control Cost and Control Schedule processes are similar to Perform Integrated Change Control, which we discussed in the last chapter. Remember when you're reading these sections that the information from the Perform Integrated Change Control process applies to these areas as well.

The Perform Quality Control process involves several new tools and techniques that might show up on the exam. Take some time here to understand the tools and techniques in the Perform Quality Control process and to differentiate them from the tools and techniques associated with the Plan Quality and Perform Quality Assurance processes.

Verify Scope involves verifying and accepting work results. Control Scope is like the change control processes I discussed in Chapter 10 and is concerned with controlling changes to project scope.

Monitoring and Controlling Risk

The *Monitor and Control Risks* process involves implementing response plans, tracking and monitoring identified risks, and identifying and responding to new risks as they occur. You will examine performance information, and use the tools and techniques of this process, to analyze and implement other functions of this process, including the following:

- Evaluating risk response plans that are put into action as a result of risk events
- Monitoring the project for risk triggers
- Reexamining existing risks to determine if they have changed or should be closed out
- Monitoring residual risks
- Reassessing project assumptions and determining validity
- Ensuring that policies and procedures are followed
- Ensuring that risk response plans and contingency plans are put into action appropriately and are effective

- Ensuring that contingency reserves (for schedule and cost) are updated according to the updated risk assessment
- Evaluating the overall effectiveness of the Risk processes

Monitor and Control Risks is a busy process. During the course of the project, risk responses, which were developed during the Planning process group, have been implemented and have reduced or averted the impact of risk events (or you hope they did).

Monitor and Control Risks Inputs

This process has four inputs:

- Risk register
- Project management plan
- Work performance information
- Performance reports

You'll recall that the risk register tracks and ranks individual risks, identifies the risk owner, describes risk triggers and residual risks, and lists the response plans and strategies you should implement in the event of an actual risk event. Keep in mind that some risk events identified in risk planning will happen and some will not. You will have to stay alert for risk event occurrences and be prepared to respond to them when they do occur. This means you should monitor the risk register regularly.

Work performance information includes information that may help you identify that a new risk event is about to occur, or it may assist you in monitoring previously identified risks. Work performance information includes elements such as the status of deliverables, costs to date, cost changes, schedule progress to date, schedule changes, and/or scope changes.

Performance reports include information such as status reports, performance measurements, and forecasts. These should also be examined from the perspective of risks or risk response plans that might need close monitoring or changes to the response plans to coincide with the performance reports data.

Additional risk response planning might be needed to deal with the new risks or with expected risks whose impact might be greater than expected. This might require repeating the Plan Risk Responses process to create new contingency plans or alternative plans to deal with the risk, or it might require modification to existing plans.

Monitor and Control Risks Tools and Techniques

The tools and techniques of Monitor and Control Risks are used to monitor risks throughout the life of the project. You should perform periodic reviews, audits, and new earned value analyses to check the pulse of risk activity and to make certain risk management is enacted effectively.

The tools and techniques of this process are as follows:

- Risk reassessment
- Risk audits
- Variance and trend analysis
- Technical performance measurement
- Reserve analysis
- Status meetings

You'll look at risk reassessment, risk audits, and technical performance measurements next. You've examined all the other tools and techniques of this process in discussions of previous processes.

Risk Reassessment

Periodic, scheduled reviews of identified risks, risk responses, and risk priorities should occur during the project. The idea here is to monitor risks and their status and determine whether their consequences still have the same impact on the project objectives as when they were originally planned. Every status meeting should have a time set aside to discuss and review risks and response plans.

Risk identification and monitoring is an ongoing process throughout the life of the project. Risks can change, and previously identified risks might have greater impacts than originally thought as more facts are discovered. Reassessment of risks should be a regular activity performed by everyone involved on the project. Monitor the risk register, including those risks that have low scores, and risk triggers. You should also monitor the risk responses that have been implemented for their effectiveness in dealing with risk. You might have to revisit the Perform Qualitative and Perform Quantitative Risk Analysis processes when new risk consequences are discovered or risk impacts are found to be greater than what was originally planned.

Risk Audits

Risk audits are carried out during the entire life of the project by risk auditors. Risk auditors are not typically project team members and are expertly trained in audit techniques and risk assessment. Risk audits are specifically interested in examining the implementation of response plans and their effectiveness at dealing with risks and their root causes.

Technical Performance Measurements

This tool and technique compares the technical accomplishments of project milestones completed during the Executing processes to the technical milestones defined in the project Planning processes. Variances might indicate that a project risk is looming, and you'll want to analyze and prepare a response to it if appropriate. For example, a technical milestone for a new computer software project might require that the forms printed from a particular module include a bar code at the bottom of the page. If the bar code functionality does not work once the module is coded, a technical deviation exists, which means you should reexamine project risks. In this particular example, project scope is likely at risk.

Monitor and Control Risks Outputs

Monitor and Control Risks should occur throughout the life of the project. Identified risks are monitored and plans are reexamined to determine whether they will adequately resolve the risk as it approaches during this process. Several outputs might come about as a result of monitoring risks:

- Risk register updates
- Organizational process assets updates
- Change requests (recommended corrective and preventive actions)
- Project management plan updates
- Project document updates

I've discussed these outputs before, so I'll just bring to your attention the new points you need to know here about risk register updates and change requests.

Risk Register Updates

The risk register should be updated under two conditions. The first condition is when a risk audit or risk reassessment concludes that some element of the original risk information has changed—for example, the impact or probability scores are updated to reflect new conditions, the priority of the risk has changed, or the response plan has been updated. The second condition for updating the risk register is when the risk needs to be closed. If a risk event occurs, you'll record that in the risk register along with the effectiveness of the response plan. This information becomes an input to the Close Project Process, which I'll cover in the next chapter.

Change Requests

Change requests must be processed through the Perform Integrated Change Control process. You might find that a workaround is needed when implementing a requested change or recommended corrective action. A *workaround* is an unplanned response to a negative risk event. It attempts to deal with the risk in a productive, efficient manner. If no risk response plan exists (this might be the case when you accept a risk event during the Planning process) or an unplanned risk occurs, workarounds are implemented to deal with the consequences of the risk.

Managing Cost Changes

The *Control Costs* process monitors the project budget and manages changes to the cost baseline. It's concerned with monitoring project costs to prevent unauthorized or incorrect costs from being included in the cost baseline. This means you'll also use Control Costs to assure that the project budget isn't exceeded (resulting in cost overruns). If a change is implemented, you'll have to make certain the budget for the changed item stays within acceptable limits. All budget changes should be agreed to and approved by the project sponsor where applicable (the criteria for approvals should be outlined in the change control system documentation). Stakeholders should also be made aware of budget changes.

The following list includes some of the activities you'll be involved in during this process:

- Monitoring changes to costs or the cost baseline and understanding variances from the baseline
- Monitoring change requests that affect cost and resolving them in a timely manner
- Informing stakeholders of approved changes and their costs
- Assuring the project budget does not exceed acceptable limits by taking action when overruns are imminent

Control Costs Inputs

The Control Costs process includes the following inputs:

- Project management plan
- Project funding requirements
- Work performance information
- Organizational process assets

These inputs are examined using the tools and techniques of this process to determine whether revised cost estimates or budget updates are required. One thing you should note regarding the project management plan input is that it includes the cost performance baseline and the cost management plan. You'll use the cost performance baseline to compare actual expenditures to date on the project to the baseline. The cost management plan details how costs should be monitored and controlled throughout the life of the project. I've covered each of these inputs in previous chapters.

Control Costs Tools and Techniques

The tools and techniques of the Control Costs process are as follows:

- Earned value measurement (EVM)
- Forecasting
- To-complete performance index (TCPI)
- Performance reviews
- Variance analysis
- Project management software

We'll look at each of these next with the exception of project management software. This output has been discussed previously, but you should know that in this process it can help automate and calculate the formulas we're going to examine next. It can also display the results in graphical form for status reporting purposes.

Earned Value Management

You can accomplish performance measurement analysis using a technique called *earned value measurement (EVM)*. Simply stated, EVM compares what you've received or produced to what you've spent.

The EVM continuously monitors the planned value, earned value, and actual costs expended to produce the work of the project (I'll cover the definition of these terms shortly). When variances that result in cost changes are discovered (including schedule variances and cost variances), those changes are managed using the project change control system. The primary function of this analysis technique is to determine and document the cause of the variance, to determine the impact of the variance, and to determine whether a corrective action should be implemented as a result. We'll walk through various examples of how to determine these variances later in this section.

EVM looks at schedule, cost, and scope project measurements together and compares them to the actual work completed to date. It is the most often used performance measurement method. EVM is performed on the work packages and the control accounts of the WBS. To perform the EVM calculations, you need to first gather the three measurements mentioned earlier: the planned value (PV), actual cost (AC), and earned value (EV).

NOTE

If you do any research on your own regarding these values, you might come across acronyms that are different from what you see here. I've included their alternate names and acronyms at the end of each description. They are also noted in the glossary of the *PMBOK® Guide*. I recommend you memorize planned value (PV), actual cost (AC), and earned value (EV) and make certain you understand the meaning of each before progressing.

Let's take a look at some definitions of these key measurements before diving into the actual calculations:

Planned value The *planned value (PV)* is the cost of work that has been authorized and budgeted for a schedule activity or WBS component during a given time period or phase. These budgets are established during the Planning processes. PV is also called *budgeted cost of work scheduled (BCWS)*.

Exam Spotlight

Remember to read exam questions carefully. PV might mean present value (as I talked about in Chapter 2) or planned value, as defined here.

Actual cost *Actual cost (AC)* is the cost of completing the work component in a given time period. Actual costs might include direct and indirect costs but must correspond to what was budgeted for the activity. If the budgeted amount did not include indirect costs, do not include them here. Later you'll see how to compare this to PV to come up with variance calculation results. AC is also called *actual cost of work performed (ACWP).*

Earned value *Earned value (EV)* is the value of the work completed to date as it compares to the budgeted amount (PV) assigned to the work component. EV is typically expressed as a percentage of the work completed compared to the budget. For example, if our budgeted amount is $1,000 and we have completed 30 percent of the work so far, our EV is $300. Therefore, EV cannot exceed the PV budget for the activity. EV is also called *budgeted cost of work performed (BCWP).*

Exam Spotlight

PV, AC, and EV are really easy to mix up. In their simplest forms, here's what each means:

- *PV*: The approved budget assigned to work to be completed during a given time period
- *AC*: Money that's actually been expended during a given time period for completed work
- *EV*: The value of the work completed to date compared to the budget

According to the earlier definition, EV is the sum of the cumulative budgeted costs for completed work for all activities that have been accomplished as of the measurement date. For example, if your total budget is $1,000 and 50 percent of the work has been completed as of the measurement date, your EV would equal $500. You can plot all the PV, AC, and EV measurements graphically to show the variances between them. If there are no variances in the measurements, all the lines on the graph remain the same, which means the project is progressing as planned. Figure 11.1 shows an example that plots these three measurements.

FIGURE 11.1 Earned value

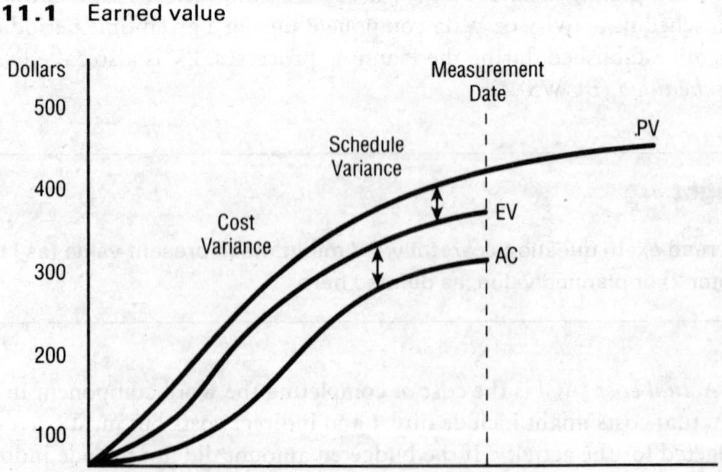

All of these measurements include a cost component. Costs are displayed in an S curve because spending is minimal in the beginning of the project, picks up steam toward the middle, and then tapers off at the end of the project. This means your earned value measurements will also take on the S curve shape.

Now you can calculate whether the project is progressing as planned or if variances exist in the approved baseline by using a variety of formulas discussed in the following sections. Use Figure 11.1 as your example for the formulas that follow. The Figure 11.1 totals are as follows: PV = 400, EV = 375, AC = 325.

Cost Variance

Cost variance is one of the most popular variances that project managers use, and it tells you whether your costs are higher than budgeted (with a resulting negative number) or lower than budgeted (with a resulting positive number). It measures the actual performance to date or during the period against what's been spent.

The *cost variance (CV)* is calculated as follows:

CV = EV – AC

Let's calculate the CV using the numbers from Figure 11.1:

375 – 325 = 50

The CV is positive, which means you're spending less than what you planned for the work that you have completed as of July 1 (which Figure 11.1 shows because AC is less than EV).

If you come up with a negative number as the answer to this formula, it means that costs are higher than what you had planned for the work that was completed as of July 1 and these costs are often not recoverable.

Schedule Variance

Schedule variance, another popular variance, tells you whether the schedule is ahead or behind what was planned for this period. This formula is most helpful when you've used the critical path methodology to build the project schedule. The *schedule variance (SV)* is calculated as follows:

SV = EV – PV

Let's plug in the numbers:

375 – 400 = –25

The resulting schedule variance is negative, which means you are behind schedule, or behind where you planned to be as of July 1.

Together, the CV and SV are known as *efficiency indicators* for the project and can be used to compare performance of all the projects in a portfolio.

Performance Indexes

Cost and schedule performance indexes are primarily used to calculate performance efficiencies, and they're often used to help predict future project performance.

The *cost performance index (CPI)* measures the value of the work completed against actual cost. It is the most critical of all the EVM measurements according to the *PMBOK®*

Guide because it tells you the cost efficiency for the work completed to date, or at the completion of the project. If CPI is greater than 1, your spending less than anticipated. If CPI is less than 1, you are spending more than anticipated for the work completed.

The schedule performance index (SPI) measures the progress to date against the progress that was pianned. This formula should be used in conjunction with an analysis of the critical path activities to determine if the project will finish ahead or behind schedule. If SPI is greater than 1, you are ahead of schedule. If SPI is less than 1, you are behind schedule.

The cost performance index (CPI) is calculated this way:

CPI = EV / AC

Let's plug in the numbers and see where you stand:

375 / 325 = 1.15

This means cost performance is better than expected. You get an A+ on this assignment!

Cumulative CPI is a commonly used calculation to predict project costs at the completion of the project. It also represents the cumulative CPI of the project at the point the measurement is taken. First you need to sum the earned value calculations taken to date, or cumulative EV, and the actual costs to date, or cumulative AC. The formula looks just like the CPI formula only it uses the cumulative sums as follows:

Cumulative CPI = cumulative EV / cumulative AC

The difference between this and the CPI formula earlier is that the CPI formula is used for a single work period whereas the cumulative CPI is calculated using the sum of all the costs of every work component for the project. Additionally, you might also use cumulative CPI to calculate the total cost of a work component such as a deliverable, for example. Let's say you have a deliverable that has five work packages. You would total the EV and AC at the measurement date for all five work packages to determine the cost performance index for the deliverable.

The schedule performance index (SPI) is calculated this way:

SPI = EV / PV

Again, let's see where you stand with this example:

375 / 400 = .94

Uh-oh, not so good. Schedule performance is not what you expected. Let's not grade this one.

Cumulative SPI predicts schedule performance at the completion of the project. Like cumulative CPI, it also represents the cumulative SPI of the project at the point the measurement is taken. The formula is as follows:

Cumulative SPI = cumulative EV / cumulative PV

Forecasting

Forecasting uses the information you've gathered to date and estimates the future conditions or performance of the project based on what you know when the calculation is performed. Forecasts are based on work performance information (an output from the Executing process group) and your predictions of future performance.

The forecasting formulas you'll see later in this section are called *estimate at completion (EAC)*. EAC estimates (or forecasts) the expected total cost of a work component, a schedule activity, or the project at its completion. This is the probable final value for the work component (or project). EAC is most often calculated by using actual costs incurred to date plus a bottom-up ETC estimate. The formula for the most typical EAC looks like this:

EAC = AC + bottom-up ETC

The bottom-up *estimate to complete (ETC)* is an estimate provided by the members of the project team actually working on the project activities. They provide the project manager with an estimate of the amount of effort remaining (and therefore the cost of the effort) based on the activities they have completed to date and what they believe will occur in the future. Their estimates are summed to come up with a total ETC. We'll look at two other ETC formulas at the end of this section.

There are three EAC forecasting formulas outlined in the *PMBOK® Guide* that we'll look at next. They reference a new parameter you haven't seen yet called *budget at completion (BAC)*. BAC is the sum of all the budgets established for all the work in the work package, control account, schedule activity, or project. It's the total planned value for the work component or project.

The first EAC formula is called "EAC forecast for ETC work performed at the budgeted rate." I know that's a mouthful. Here's what you should know. This formula calculates EAC based on the actual costs to date and the assumption that ETC work will be completed at the budgeted rate. The formula looks like this:

EAC = AC + BAC – EV

Let's assume your AC to date is $800, BAC is $1,200, and EV is $600. EAC, assuming work ETC will be completed at the budgeted rate, is as follows:

$800 + $1,200 – $600 = $1,400

In English, you'll spend $1,400 to complete this work component, assuming the remaining work is performed at the budgeted rate.

The next EAC formula is called "EAC forecast for ETC work performed at the present CPI." I didn't make up these titles! Here's what you need to know. This forecast assumes that future performance will be just like the past performance for the project. The formula looks like this:

EAC = BAC / cumulative CPI

For this example, let's assume that BAC is $2,200 and cumulative CPI is 1.2. The formula looks like this:

$2,200 / 1.2 = $1833.33

This formula predicts you will spend less than the originally budgeted amount for the project.

The last formula is called "EAC forecast for ETC work considering both SPI and CPI factors." This formula assumes two things: there is a negative cost performance to date and the project schedule dates must be met. The formula looks like this:

EAC = AC + [(BAC – EV) / (cumulative CPI * cumulative SPI)]

Let's assume AC is $1,000, BAC is $1500, EV is $900, cumulative CPI is .97, and cumulative SPI is 1.05. Here's the resulting EAC:

$1,000 + [($1,500 – $900) / (.97 * 1.05)] = $1,598.10

Based on the assumption that cost performance to date is negative and we must meet the project schedule date, EAC is $1,598.10.

Exam Spotlight

For study purposes, the EAC formula and the three EAC calculations are shown together here:

The EAC formula

EAC = AC + bottom-up ETC

EAC using actual costs to date and assuming ETC uses budgeted rate

EAC = AC + BAC – EV

EAC assuming future performance will behave like past performance

EAC = BAC / cumulative CPI

EAC when cost performance is negative and schedule dates must be met

EAC = AC + [(BAC – EV) / (cumulative CPI * cumulative SPI)]

In addition to the bottom-up ETC, there are two other formulas for calculating ETC that you should be aware of for the exam. They are discussed next.

When you believe that future cost variances will be similar to the types of variances you've seen to date, you'll use this formula to calculate ETC:

ETC = (BAC – cumulative EV) / cumulative CPI

Assuming your cumulative earned value (cumulative EV) is 725, cumulative CPI value is 1.12, and BAC is 1,000, plug in the numbers:

(1,000 – 725) / 1.12 = 245.5

Therefore, at the measurement date, you need $245.50 to complete all the remaining work of this work component (or project if you're using project totals), assuming variances in the future will be the same as they have been to date.

When you believe that future cost variances will *not* be similar to the types of variances you've seen to date, you'll use this formula to calculate ETC:

ETC = (BAC – cumulative EV)

Now calculate your value:

(1,000 – 725) = 275

In this case, you need $275 to complete all the remaining work of this work component, assuming variances in the future are different than they have been to date.

Exam Spotlight

For study purposes, the ETC formulas are shown here.

Bottom-up ETC

Summation of the costs of the remaining work based on estimates from the project team members working on these activities

ETC when future cost variances will be similar to past variances

ETC = (BAC – cumulative EV) / cumulative CPI

ETC when future cost variances are expected to be atypical

ETC = (BAC – cumulative EV)

To-Complete Performance Index

To-complete performance index (TCPI) is the projected performance level the remaining work of the project must achieve in order to meet the BAC or EAC. It's calculated by dividing the work that's remaining by the funds that are remaining.

The formula for TCPI when using the BAC is as follows:

(BAC – EV) / (BAC – AC)

Assume for this example that BAC is $1,000, EV is $700, and AC is $800.

($1,000 – $700) / ($1,000 – $800) = 1.5

This means you'll need to reach a CPI rate that's 1.5 times what you've experienced to date in order to meet the BAC goal. If the result is less than one, future work does not have to be performed as efficiently as past performance.

When the BAC is no longer attainable, the project manager should calculate a new EAC and this new estimate becomes the goal you'll work toward once it's approved by management. The TCPI formula when EAC is the goal you're aiming for is as follows:

(BAC – EV) / (EAC – AC)

We'll use the same assumptions as we did in the formula earlier and note that EAC is $1,200. The formula looks like this:

($1,000 – $700) / ($1,200 – $800) = .75

There is one last thing to note regarding this formula. If cumulative CPI falls below one, all future project work must be performed at the TCPI

Performance Reviews

Performance reviews compare cost performance over time and the estimates of funds needed to complete the remaining work. Three types of analyses are associated with performance reviews: variance analysis, trend analysis, and earned value performance.

According to the *PMBOK® Guide*, trend analysis determines whether project performance is improving or worsening over time by periodically analyzing project results. These results are measured with mathematical formulas that attempt to forecast project outcomes based on historical information and results. You can use several formulas to predict project trends, but it's outside the scope of this book to go into them. For the exam, you're expected to understand the concept behind trend analysis, not the formulas used to calculate it. You'll want to remember that you can use the results you've analyzed using trend analysis formulas to predict future project behavior or trends.

I've already covered earned value performance and variance analysis is its own technique, so we'll look at it next.

Variance Analysis

Variance analysis in the Control Costs process examines the difference between the performance cost baseline and actual performance. One formula you can use with this technique is called *variance at completion (VAC)*. This calculates the difference between the budget at completion and the estimate at completion. It looks like this:

VAC = BAC – EAC

If the result is a negative number, it means you're not doing as well with costs as you anticipated and that variance exists. Assuming your project performance is improving, as the project progresses, variances will become smaller.

NOTE You'll be given some scratch paper when you go into the exam. I recommend that you write these formulas down on a piece of your scratch paper before you start the exam and keep it handy. That way, the formulas are off your mind and you've got them in front of you to reference when you get to the portion of the exam where these questions appear. You might want to use this tip for other items you've memorized as well. If you write them down before you begin, you don't have to jog your memory on every question. If you forget something, leave a blank space where it goes and as soon as you remember it or see a question that reminds you what it is, fill in the blank.

Control Costs Outputs

The Control Costs process has six outputs:

- Work performance measurements
- Budget forecasts
- Organizational process assets updates
- Change requests
- Project management plan updates
- Project document updates

I've discussed most of these before, or they are self-explanatory.

Recap of Formulas

You have a lot of formulas to memorize. Keep in mind that you'll be given a calculator when you take the exam, so you don't have to do the math manually. Variance and trend analysis are part of the project performance reviews tool and technique. Here are the formulas I've covered in this chapter:

- **Performance measurements**

  Cost variance: CV = EV – AC

  Schedule variance: SV = EV – PV

- **Performance indexes**

  Cost performance index: CPI = EV ÷ AC

  Cumulative cost performance index: Cumulative CPI = cumulative EV / cumulative AC

  Schedule performance index: SPI = EV / PV

  Cumulative schedule performance index: Cumulative SPI = cumulative EV / cumulative PV

- **Forecasting**

  EAC formula: EAC = AC + bottom-up ETC

  EAC using actual costs to date and assuming ETC uses budgeted rate: EAC = AC + BAC – EV

  EAC assuming future performance will behave like past performance: EAC = BAC / cumulative CPI

  EAC when cost performance is negative and schedule dates must be met: EAC = AC + [(BAC – EV) / (cumulative CPI * cumulative SPI)]

  Bottom-up ETC: Summation of the costs of the remaining work based on estimates from the project team members working on these activities

  ETC when future cost variances will be similar to past variances: ETC = (BAC – cumulative EV) / cumulative CPI

  ETC when future cost variances are expected to be atypical: ETC = (BAC – cumulative EV)

- **Variance analysis**

  Variance analysis: VAC = BAC – EAC

NOTE

Problems with costs come about for many reasons, including incorrect estimating techniques, predetermined or fixed budgets with no flexibility, schedule overruns, inadequate WBS development, and so on. Good project management planning techniques during the Planning processes might prevent cost problems later in the project. At a minimum, proper planning will reduce the impact of these problems if they do occur.

Always inform appropriate stakeholders of revised budget or cost estimates and any changes of significant impact to the project. Keep them updated on changes, status, and risk conditions during regularly scheduled project meetings.

Real World Scenario

Mustang Enterprises's New Accounting System

You are a stakeholder of the New Accounting System project for Mustang Enterprises. The existing accounting system resides on a mainframe, and some of the programs used to process data are more than 15 years old. Your company decided to hire a contract software services firm to write a thin-client, browser-based version of the accounting system so that the mainframe programs could be retired. You've also assigned a senior programmer to act as the project manager on behalf of your organization.

The project is in the Monitoring and Controlling process group, and the project manager keeps reporting that everything is OK and on schedule. When you asked him detailed questions and requested performance data, the project manager patted you on the back and said, "Don't worry, I've got everything under control."

You are a little worried because some of the key project team members have come to you confidentially to inform you of the progress of the project.

After further investigation, you discover that the project manager changed the database from SQL to Oracle midway through the project and didn't tell anyone except the project team. The project scope stated specifically that project development required a SQL database. The change in database products changed the project scope and product scope without letting the stakeholders know.

This change has caused schedule delays because the project team members have told you they need training in the new database development tools before they can proceed. Additionally, many of the programs have already been written to interface with SQL, not Oracle, and will have to be modified. To add insult to injury, the database switch will impact the project budget in two ways. First, purchasing the Oracle database involves substantially more money than purchasing the SQL database, and it requires the purchase of new development tools for the programming team. Second, several members of the programming staff will have to attend multiple training sessions on the new database product to fully integrate the programs and system. Training is currently running $2,200 per session per person.

Since you're a key stakeholder, you decide to bring this information out into the open at the next project status meeting. Additionally, you plan to meet with the project sponsor and the procurement department to determine what alternatives you have to request that the contracting firm realign the project to meet the original contractual requirements. However, you fear that since the project manager is the one who gave the orders to change the database, your organization might not have a lot of recourse. You will also make the project sponsor aware that the project manager doesn't have the skills needed to conduct this project and a new project manager should be hired as soon as possible. The project manager is invaluable to the organization as a programmer, but he doesn't have the project management experience needed to conduct a project of this size and complexity. This might cause further setback to the project, but the project management plan and project schedule will require updates anyway as a result of the existing project manager's decisions. You also determine to document all that has happened as a lesson learned and to set up a change control process to prevent this from happening in the future.

Monitoring and Controlling Schedule Changes

The *Control Schedule* process involves determining the status of the project schedule, determining whether changes have occurred or should occur, and influencing and managing schedule changes. In the following sections, you'll look at this process's inputs, tools and techniques, and outputs.

Control Schedule Inputs

Control Schedule inputs include the following:

- Project management plan
- Project schedule
- Work performance information
- Organizational process assets

I've covered each of these inputs previously. Keep in mind that the Control Schedule process works hand in hand with the Perform Integrated Change Control process we covered in Chapter 10 (as all the change control processes do).

NOTE Keeping the schedule on track means you're monitoring and controlling time—one of the classic triple constraints.

Schedule and Control Tools and Techniques

The tools and techniques of the Control Schedule process are as follows:

- Performance reviews
- Variance analysis
- Project management software
- Resource leveling
- What-if scenario analysis
- Adjusting leads and lags
- Schedule compression
- Scheduling tool

We've covered all of these tools and techniques previously. I'll give you a few new points you should know regarding performance reviews.

Performance reviews in this process examine elements such as actual start and end dates for schedule activities and the remaining time to finish uncompleted activities. If you've taken earned value measurements, the SV and SPI will be helpful in determining the impact of the schedule variations and in determining if corrective actions are necessary.

The *PMBOK® Guide* notes that if you're using the critical chain method to construct the schedule, you should compare the amount of buffer needed to the amount of buffer remaining to help determine if the schedule is on track. This will also indicate whether corrective actions are necessary to adjust the schedule.

In the Control Schedule process, because you're dealing with time issues, it's imperative that you act as quickly as possible to implement corrective actions so that the schedule is brought back in line with the plan and the least amount of schedule delay as possible is experienced.

NOTE

Schedule changes might be potential hot buttons with certain stakeholders and can burn you if you don't handle them correctly. No one likes to hear that the project is going to take longer than originally planned. That doesn't mean you should withhold this information, however. Always report the truth. If you've been keeping your stakeholders abreast of project status, they should already know that the potential for schedule changes exists. Nevertheless, be prepared to justify the reason for the schedule change or start dusting off your résumé—maybe both, depending on the company.

Make sure to examine the float variance of the critical path activities when monitoring the schedule. Thinking back to the Develop Schedule process, you'll recall that float is the amount of time you can delay starting an activity without increasing the amount of time it takes to complete the project. Because the activities with the least amount of float have the potential to cause the biggest schedule delay, examine float variance in ascending order of critical activities.

Keep in mind that not all schedule variances will impact the schedule. For example, a delay to a noncritical path task will not delay the overall schedule and might not need corrective action. Use caution here, though—if a delay occurs on a noncritical path task or its duration is increased for some reason, that task can actually become part of the critical path. Delays to critical path tasks will *always* cause delays to the project completion date and require corrective action. Careful watch of the variances in schedule start and end dates helps you control the total time element of the project.

Control Schedule Outputs

The Control Schedule process has the following outputs:

- Work performance measurements
- Organizational process assets updates
- Change requests
- Project management plan updates
- Project document updates

Project management plan updates include making updates to the schedule baseline and the cost baseline. Changes to the cost baseline may be necessary when you've used a schedule compression or crashing technique. Changes to approved schedule start and end dates in the schedule baseline are called *revisions*. These generally occur as a result of a project scope change, or changes to activity estimates, and might result in a schedule baseline update. Schedule baseline updates occur when significant changes to the project schedule are made like the changes just mentioned. This means a new schedule baseline is established that reflects the changed project activity dates. Once the new baseline is established, it is used as the basis for future performance measurements. Never rebaseline a schedule without first having it approved by the project sponsor and archiving a copy of the original baseline and schedule.

NOTE

Take care when rebaselining a project schedule. Don't lose the original baseline information. Why do you care? Because the original baseline serves as historical information to reference for future projects. Make a backup copy of the original schedule so that you have a record of the original baseline as a reference. Even though some project management software allows you to save several baselines plus the original, it's still good practice to make a backup copy of the original.

Changes to the project schedule might or might not require updates to other elements of the project plan as well. For example, extending a schedule activity involving a contractor might impact the costs associated with that activity.

The project document updates output may require updates to either the schedule data or project schedule or both. For example, project schedule network diagrams require updates as a result of schedule model data updates. Don't forget to document these changes and inform your stakeholders.

Utilizing Perform Quality Control Techniques

Plan Quality, Perform Quality Assurance, and Perform Quality Control are part of the project Quality Management Knowledge Area. These processes work together to define and monitor the work of the project and to make certain the quality activity results meet the quality requirements laid out in the plan.

Perform Quality Control is specifically concerned with monitoring work results to see whether they comply with the standards set out in the quality management plan. You should practice Perform Quality Control throughout the project to identify and remove the causes of unacceptable results. Remember that Perform Quality Control is concerned with project results both from a management perspective, such as schedule and cost performance, and from a product perspective. In other words, the end product should conform to the requirements and product description defined during the Planning processes.

Perform Quality Control Inputs

Perform Quality Control includes the following inputs:

- Project management plan
- Quality metrics
- Quality checklists
- Work performance measurements
- Approved change requests
- Deliverables
- Organizational process assets

I've discussed each of these inputs previously, so I'll move on to tools and techniques.

Perform Quality Control Tools and Techniques

The tools and techniques in the Perform Quality Control process are as follows:

- Cause-and-effect diagram
- Control charts
- Flowcharting
- Histogram
- Pareto chart
- Run chart
- Scatter diagram

- Statistical sampling
- Inspection
- Approved change requests review

NOTE The first seven Perform Quality Control tools and techniques are collectively known as Ishikawa's seven basic tools of quality. We talked about the fishbone diagram (a cause-and-effect diagram), also known as the Ishikawa diagram, in Chapter 6, "Risk Planning." You recall that the fishbone diagram is used to help determine root causes. Kaoru Ishikawa is not known only for the fishbone diagram, he was also a significant contributor in the realm of quality.

The primary purpose of each of these tools is to examine the product, service, or result as well as the project processes for conformity to standards. If the results fall within the tolerance range specified, the results are acceptable. Alternatively, if the results fall within the control limits set for the product (as defined by the various tools and techniques I'll discuss in the following sections), the process you are examining is said to be *in control*. Spend time understanding these tools and techniques and their individual uses because you might see exam questions about each of them.

I talked about cause-and-effect diagrams as a diagramming technique in the Risk Identification process in Chapter 6. This technique helps identify root causes. If you need a refresher, refer to Figure 6.2 in that chapter.

I also discussed flowcharts in the same section of Chapter 6. Flowcharts are diagrams that show the logical steps that must be performed in order to accomplish an objective. They can also show how the individual elements of a system interrelate. Flowcharting can help identify where quality problems might occur on the project and how problems happen. This is important because it gives the project team the opportunity to develop alternative approaches for dealing with anticipated quality problems identified with this tool and technique. Refer to Figure 6.3.

Histograms are typically bar charts that depict the distribution of variables over time. Chapter 7, "Planning Project Resources," contains an example histogram. In Perform Quality Control, the histogram usually depicts the attributes of the problem or situation. (I'll discuss attributes shortly.)

We will look at the other tools and techniques in more detail in the following sections.

Control Charts

Control charts measure the results of processes over time and display the results in graph form. Control charts are a way to measure variances to determine whether process variances are in control or out of control.

A control chart is based on sample variance measurements. From the samples chosen and measured, the mean and standard deviation are determined. Perform Quality Control is usually maintained—or said to be in control—within plus or minus three standard deviations. In other words, Perform Quality Control says that if the process is in control (that is, the measurements fall within the control limits), you know that 99.73 percent of the parts going through the process will fall within an acceptable range of the mean. If you discover a part outside of this range, you should investigate and determine whether corrective action is needed.

Figure 11.2 illustrates an example control chart.

FIGURE 11.2 Control chart

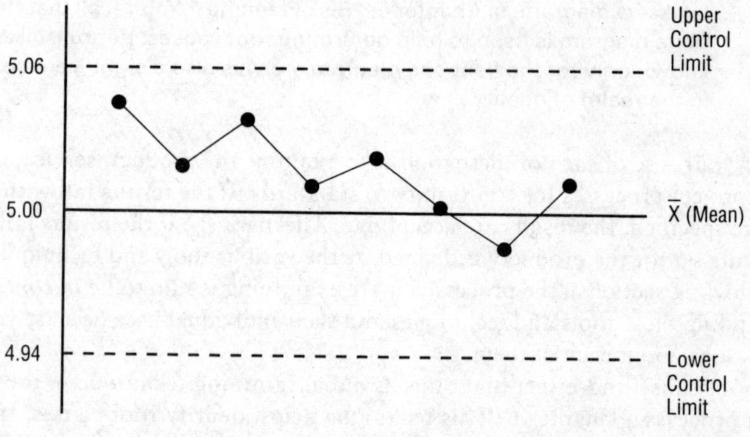

Let's assume you've determined from your sample measurements that 5 mm is the mean in the example control chart. One standard deviation equals 0.02. Three standard deviations on either side of the mean become your upper and lower control points on this chart. Therefore, if all control points fall within plus or minus three standard deviations on either side of the mean, the process is in control. If points fall outside the acceptable limits, the process is not in control and corrective action is needed.

Control charts are used most often in manufacturing settings where repetitive activities are easily monitored. For example, the process that produces widgets by the case lot must meet certain specifications and fall within certain variances to be considered in control. However, you aren't limited to using control charts only in the manufacturing industry. You can use them to monitor any output. You might consider using control charts to track and monitor project management processes. You could plot cost variances, schedule variances, frequency or number of scope changes, and so on to help monitor variances.

Pareto Chart

You have probably heard of the 80/20 rule. Vilfredo Pareto is the person credited with discovering this rule. He observed that 80 percent of the wealth and land ownership in Italy was held by 20 percent of the population. Over the years, others have shown that the 80/20 rule applies across many disciplines and areas. As an example, generally speaking, 80 percent of the deposits of any given financial institution are held by 20 percent of its customer base.

Let's hope that rule doesn't apply to project managers, though, with 20 percent of the project managers out there doing 80 percent of the work!

The 80/20 rule as it applies to quality says that a small number of causes (20 percent) create the majority of the problems (80 percent). Have you ever noticed this with your project or department staff? It always seems that just a few people cause the biggest headaches. But I'm getting off track.

Pareto charts are displayed as histograms that rank-order the most important factors—such as delays, costs, and defects, for example—by their frequency over time. His theory is that you get the most benefit if you spend the majority of your time fixing the most important problems. The information shown in Table 11.1 is plotted on an example Pareto chart shown in Figure 11.3.

TABLE 11.1 Frequency of Failures

Item	Defect Frequency	Percent of Defects	Cumulative Percent
A	800	.33	.33
B	700	.29	.62
C	400	.17	.79
D	300	.13	.92
E	200	.08	1.0

FIGURE 11.3 Pareto chart

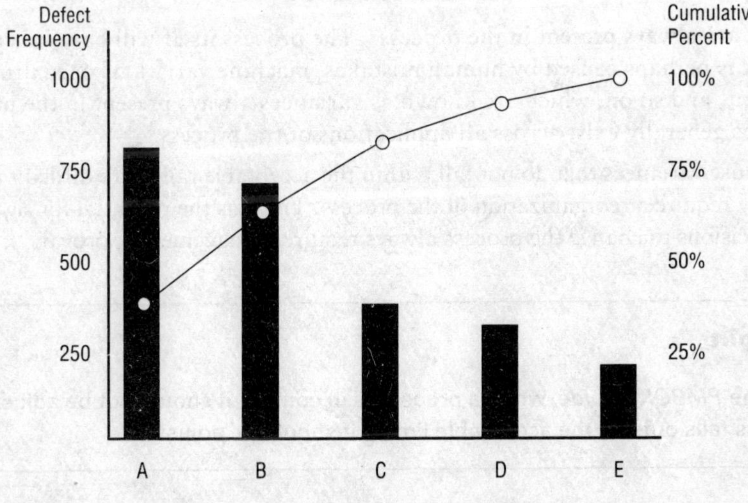

The problems are rank-ordered according to their frequency and percentage of defects. The defect frequencies in this figure appear as black bars, and the cumulative percentages of defects are plotted as circles. The rank-ordering of these problems shows you where corrective action should be taken first. You can see in Figure 11.3 that problem A should receive priority attention because the most benefit will come from fixing this problem.

Run Charts

Run charts are used to show variations in the process over time or to show trends (such as improvements or lack of improvements) in the process. Differences in results will occur in processes because there is no such thing as a perfect process. When processes are considered in control, differences in results might occur because of common causes of variances or special-cause variances.

Common causes of variances come about as a result of circumstances or situations that are relatively common to the process you're using and are easily controlled at the operational level. *Special-cause variances* are variances that are not common to the process. For example, perhaps you have very detailed processes with specific procedures that must be followed in order to produce the output and a process gets missed. Or maybe your project requires the manufacturing of a certain part and a machine on the line has a problem and requires a special calibration. This is an easy set of terms to remember because their names logically imply their definitions.

For the exam, you should understand the three types of variances that make up common causes of variances:

Random variances Random variations might be normal, depending on the processes you're using to produce the product or service of the project, but they occur as the name implies, at random.

Known or predictable variances Known or predictable variances are variances that you know exist in the process because of particular characteristics of the product, service, or result you are processing. These are generally unique to a particular application.

Variances that are always present in the process The process itself will have inherent variability that is perhaps caused by human mistakes, machine variations or malfunctions, the environment, and so on, which are known as variances always present in the process. These variances generally exist across all applications of the process.

Common cause variances that do not fall within the acceptable range are difficult to correct and usually require a reorganization of the process. This has the potential for significant impact, and decisions to change the process always require management approval.

Exam Spotlight

According to the *PMBOK® Guide*, when a process is in control, it should not be adjusted. When a process falls outside the acceptable limits, it should be adjusted.

Trend analysis is another technique that's carried out using run charts. Trend analysis in the Perform Quality Control process is a mathematical technique that uses historical results to predict future outcomes. Trend analysis often tracks variances in cost and schedule performance by monitoring the number of activities completed with significant variances within a certain time period. This information can then be used to forecast future performance. Trend analysis also tracks technical performance by determining the number of defects observed and the number of defects not corrected. *Technical performance measurements* compare the technical accomplishments of project milestones completed to the technical milestones defined in the project Planning process group.

Scatter Diagrams

Scatter diagrams use two variables, one called an *independent* variable, which is an input, and one called a *dependent* variable, which is an output. Scatter diagrams display the relationship between these two elements as points on a graph. This relationship is typically analyzed to prove or disprove cause-and-effect relationships. As an example, maybe your scatter diagram plots the ability of your employees to perform a certain task. The length of time (in months) they have performed this task is plotted as the independent variable on the X axis, and the accuracy they achieve in performing this task, which is expressed as a score—the dependent variable—is plotted on the Y axis. The scatter diagram can then help you determine whether cause-and-effect (in this case, increased experience over time versus accuracy) can be proved. Scatter diagrams can also help you look for and analyze root causes of problems.

The important point to remember about scatter diagrams is that they plot the dependent and independent variables, and the closer the points resemble a diagonal line, the closer these variables are related. Figure 11.4 shows a sample scatter diagram.

FIGURE 11.4 Scatter diagram

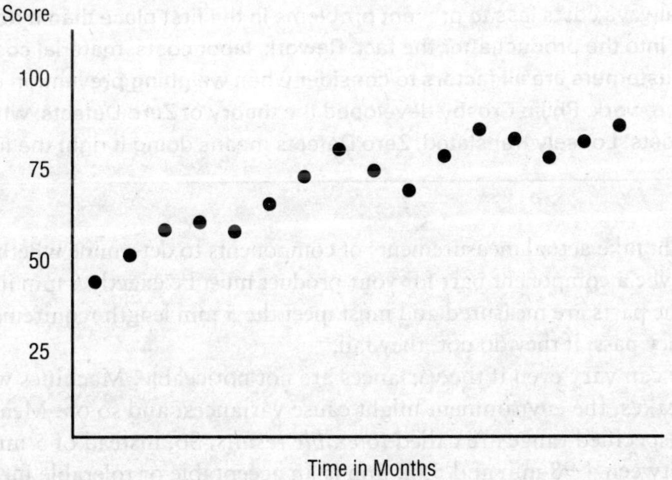

Statistical Sampling

Statistical sampling involves taking a sample number of parts from the whole population and examining them to determine whether they fall within acceptable variances. The formula to calculate the correct sample size is beyond the scope of this book. However, Creative Research Systems has an online calculator and an explanation of statistical sampling that you might find useful. You can find them at `http://www.surveysystem.com/sscalc.htm`.

Perhaps you determine to statistically sample 25 parts out of a lot or run. The quality plan outlines that the lot will pass if four parts or fewer fall outside the allowable variance.

Statistical sampling might also involve determining the standard deviation for a process, as discussed in the control chart tool and technique. The quality plan determines whether plus or minus two standard deviations—95.44 percent of the population—is adequate or whether plus or minus three standard deviations—99.73 percent—is adequate.

Inspection

Inspection involves physically looking at, measuring, or testing results to determine whether they conform to the requirements or quality standards. It's a tool used to gather information and improve results. Inspections might occur after the final product is produced or at intervals during the development of the product to examine individual components. Acceptance decisions are made when the work is inspected and the work is either accepted or rejected. When work is rejected, it might have to go back through the process for rework. Inspection is also known as *reviews* or *peer reviews*.

Exam Spotlight

Don't confuse inspection with prevention; they're two different tools. Inspection keeps errors in the product from reaching the customer. *Prevention* keeps errors from occurring in the process. It always costs less to prevent problems in the first place than it does to fix problems built into the product after the fact. Rework, labor costs, material costs, and potential loss of customers are all factors to consider when weighing prevention costs versus the cost of rework. Philip Crosby developed the theory of Zero Defects, which deals with prevention costs. Loosely translated, Zero Defects means doing it right the first time.

Inspection might take actual measurements of components to determine whether they meet requirements. Maybe a component part for your product must be exactly 5 mm in length. To pass inspection, the parts are measured and must meet the 5 mm length requirement. If they measure 5 mm, they pass; if they do not, they fail.

Measurements can vary even if the variances are not noticeable. Machines wear down, people make mistakes, the environment might cause variances, and so on. Measurements that fall within a specified range are called *tolerable results*. So, instead of 5 mm exactly, maybe a range between 4.98 mm and 5.02 mm is an acceptable or tolerable measurement for the component. If the samples that are measured fall within the tolerable range, they pass; otherwise, they fail inspection.

One inspection technique uses measurements called *attributes*. The measurements taken during attribute sampling determine whether they meet one of two options, conforming or nonconforming. In other words, the measurements conform or meet the requirement or they do not conform. This can also be considered a pass/fail or go/no-go decision.

Attribute conformity and inspections are not necessarily performed on every component part or every end product that's produced. That's time-consuming and inefficient when you're producing numerous components. Inspection in cases like this is usually performed on a sampling of parts or products where every x number of parts is tested for conformity or measurement specifics.

Inspection will tell you where problems exist and gives you the opportunity to correct them, thus leading to quality improvements. The other tools and techniques I'll talk about in these sections also lead to quality improvements in the product or process or in both.

Real World Scenario

An Ounce of Prevention

One of the main thoroughfares into your city requires a bridge replacement. You were appointed the project manager for the city and have managed this project since its initiation 15 months ago.

The project entailed hiring a contractor to build the new bridge and manage the contract and the work of the contracting agency to bring the project to a successful completion.

Approximately 28,000 vehicles travel across this bridge on a daily basis, carrying commuters and college students back and forth to the downtown area. One of the requirements was the closure of no more than three of the six lanes of traffic at one time during construction. Each piece of steel was required to be painted (two coats) before bringing it on-site. A third coat of paint was to be applied at the site after construction. The paint was to be guaranteed to last 25 to 30 years.

An on-site quality control inspection revealed that some of the paint was peeling. After further investigation, you discovered that the contractor did not allow the first coat of paint to cure properly, so when the second coat was applied, it peeled and flaked.

You've instructed the contractor that, according to the terms of the contract and the SOW specifications, they're required to apply three coats of paint to the bridge, and the paint is required to last 25 to 30 years. Paint that peels before construction is completed does not comply with specifications. Corrective action is needed. As a result, the contract company decides to subcontract out the painting work to another company while they finish up their remaining tasks on the project.

Unfortunately, the subcontractor who was hired found they were in way over their heads and were not able to complete the paint job. Several months have passed, and the original project completion date was missed long ago. Obviously, revisions to the project schedule were required when it became clear that the subcontractor wasn't going to make the date. Now another revision to the project schedule is necessary because of the subcontractor's failure to complete the painting task.

The original contractor did some searching and found another subcontractor capable of completing the painting job. It's now the middle of winter. Because the temperatures are cold, the painting crew must hang insulated tarps between the bays on the bridge and use heaters to warm up small areas of steel to the proper temperature to apply the paint. This process extended the completion date by more than three times its original estimate and ultimately delayed the completion of the project by two years. Additional costs were incurred to hire the subcontractor and rent the heaters.

Corrective action was taken as a result of the inspection, and eventually the project was completed, but not without schedule delays, schedule changes, scope changes, and rework—not to mention the increased cost to the original contractor. Since the contract was a fixed-price contract, the contractor's profit was eaten away paying for the painting job. The cost to correct the quality issue did not impact the city, but it did impact the contractor. This is a case where an ounce of prevention would have been worth several gallons of cure, as the old saying goes.

Perform Quality Control Outputs

Quality improvements, as mentioned in the Perform Quality Assurance process discussed in Chapter 9, are a primary goal of the quality processes. Failure to meet quality requirements can have a significant impact on the project and the project team and might result in rework. *Rework* causes a project to take longer and cost more than originally planned because the project team has to repeat processes to correct the work. You should try to keep rework to a minimum so as not to impact the project schedule and budget. Rework has the potential to cause morale issues as well, especially if the team members thought they were doing a good job all along. Rework might require the project team to put in extra long hours, which in turn might cause more errors or other negative consequences. Monitor quality periodically so that rework is kept to a minimum.

NOTE Perform Quality Assurance is concerned with assuring that the project is using the correct and most efficient processes to meet the project requirements; Perform Quality Control is concerned with the accuracy of the project results.

Perform Quality Control has several outputs:

- Quality control measurements
- Validated changes
- Validated deliverables
- Organizational process assets updates
- Change requests
- Project management plan updates
- Project document updates

I've already discussed many of these outputs, but I'll add a few quick notes here.

Validated changes are the results of changes, defect repairs, or variances that have been inspected and corrected. The resulting change, particularly corrective and preventive actions, can contribute to overall quality improvements and should be noted in the lessons learned documentation. Remember that processes that are in control should not be adjusted. Processes out of control might require adjusting, but this should occur only as a result of a management decision.

Validating deliverables involves using the tools and techniques of this process to determine if the deliverable is correct and accurate. This output becomes an input to the next process we'll discuss, Verify Scope, which entails accepting the deliverables.

Completed checklists become part of the project's documentation and are included as part of the organizational process asset updates. Lessons learned should include the causes of variances found during this process and why the corrective actions were recommended.

Updates to the quality management plan and the process improvement plan may be required as part of the project management plan updates output of this process. Quality standards may also need updating as a result of this process, and they are included in the project document updates output.

Verifying Project Scope

Managing and reporting on project progress make up the primary focus of the Monitoring and Controlling processes. One of the Monitoring and Controlling processes that helps manage and control project progress is the *Verify Scope* process. The primary purpose of the Verify Scope process is to formally accept completed deliverables and obtain sign-off that the deliverables are satisfactory and meet stakeholders' expectations.

The inputs of the Verify Scope are the project management plan, requirements documentation, requirements traceability matrix, and validated deliverables. This process involves evaluating these inputs to determine whether the work is complete and whether it satisfies the project objectives. Evaluation is performed using inspection, which is the only tool and technique of this process. You should perform Verify Scope even if the project is canceled to document the degree to which the project was completed. This serves as historical information, and if the project is ever started up again, you've got documentation that tells you what was completed and how far the project progressed.

Exam Spotlight

The most important fact you should know about the Verify Scope process is that Verify Scope formalizes the acceptance of the project scope and is primarily concerned with the acceptance of work results. Don't confuse this process with the Perform Quality Control process I just discussed.

You can remember the difference between Verify Scope and Perform Quality Control this way:

- Perform Quality Control = *checking* for correct work results and assuring that the quality requirements are met
- Verify Scope = *accepting* work results

The outputs of Verify Scope are accepted deliverables, change requests, and project document updates. Accepted deliverables is concerned with the formal acceptance of the work by the stakeholders. Remember that stakeholders include customers, the project sponsor, the project team, the management team, and so on. Document their acceptance with formal sign-off, and keep this with your project documents.

Controlling Scope

The Scope Management Knowledge Area includes Collect Requirements, Define Scope, Create WBS, Verify Scope, and Control Scope. You'll recall that project scope describes the work required to produce the product, service, or result of the project. This broad statement usually includes the product scope statement and the product description, which describes the characteristics, features, and functionality of the product, service, or result. The *Control Scope* process involves monitoring the status of both the project and the product scope, monitoring changes to the project and product scope, and monitoring work results to ensure that they match expected outcomes. Any modification to the agreed-upon WBS is considered a scope change. (It has been eons ago that you looked at this, so remember that the work breakdown structure is a deliverables-oriented hierarchy that defines the total work of the project.) This means the addition or deletion of activities or modifications to the existing activities on the WBS constitute a project scope change.

Changes in product scope require changes to the project scope as well. Let's say one of your project deliverables is the design of a piece of specialized equipment that's integrated into your final product. Now let's say that because of engineering setbacks and some miscalculations, the specialized equipment requires design modifications. The redesign of this equipment impacts the end product or product scope. Since changes to the product scope impact the project requirements, which are detailed in the scope document, changes to project scope are also required. This change, along with recommended corrective actions, should be processed through the Perform Integrated Change Control process.

Unapproved or undocumented changes that sometimes make their way into the project are referred to as *scope creep*. How often have you overheard a stakeholder speaking directly with a project team member asking them to make "this one little change that doesn't impact anybody…really, no one will notice." Make certain your project team members are well versed in the change control process and insist that they inform you of shenanigans like this. Scope creep can kill an otherwise viable project. Little changes add up and eventually impact budget, schedule, and quality.

Control Scope Inputs

The Control Scope process has five inputs, all of which you've seen before:

- Project management plan
- Work performance information
- Requirements documentation
- Requirements traceability matrix
- Organizational process assets

There isn't any new information you need to know about these inputs for this process, so let's move on to tools and techniques.

Control Scope Tools and Techniques

The Control Scope process has one tool and technique: variance analysis. Variance analysis includes reviewing project performance measurements to determine whether there are variances in project scope. It's also important to determine and document the cause of variances and examine those against the scope baseline so that you can implement corrective actions if needed.

NOTE

If you are using a configuration management system to control product scope, the change control system must also integrate with it. The configuration management system manages changes to product and project scope and ensures that these changes are reasonable and make sense before they're processed through the Perform Integrated Change Control process.

Control Scope Outputs

The outputs of the Control Scope process are as follows:

- Work performance measurements
- Organizational process assets updates

- Change requests
- Project management plan updates
- Project document updates

Changes to scope will likely require that you repeat some of the project Planning processes and make any needed adjustments, including updating the project documents. Scope changes require an update to the project scope statement. This may require an update to the WBS and WBS dictionary as well. Pop quiz: what are the scope statement, WBS, and WBS dictionary collectively known as? Answer: the scope baseline. Scope baseline updates are part of the project management plan updates output of this process.

Scope changes include any changes to the project scope as defined by the agreed-upon WBS. This in turn might require changes or updates to project objectives, costs, quality measures or controls, performance measurements baselines, or time in the form of schedule revisions. Scope changes almost always affect project costs and/or require schedule revisions.

NOTE

Schedule revisions are almost always needed as a result of scope changes. But not all scope changes lengthen the project schedule. Some scope changes (a reduction in overall project requirements, for example) might reduce the number of hours needed to complete the project, which in turn might reduce the project budget. This most often occurs when the schedule is the primary constraint on the project and the start or end dates cannot be changed.

When scope changes are requested, all areas of the project should be investigated to determine what the changes will impact. The project team should perform estimates of the impact and of the amount of time needed to make the change. Sometimes, however, the change request is so extensive that even the time to perform an estimate should be evaluated before proceeding. In other words, if the project team is busy working on estimates, they aren't working on the project. That means extensive change requests could impact the existing schedule because of the time and effort needed just to evaluate the change. Cases like these require you to make a determination or ask the change control board (CCB) to decide whether the change is important enough to allow the project team time to work on the estimates.

Always remember to update your stakeholders regarding the changes you're implementing and their impacts. They'll want to know how the changes impact the performance baselines, including the project costs, project schedule, project scope, and quality.

This process concludes the Monitoring and Controlling process groups. You'll look at the Closing processes in the next chapter.

Real World Scenario

Project Case Study: New Kitchen Heaven Retail Store

Stakeholders have asked for an updated status on the project schedule as well as a remaining cost projection. You decide to provide several cost and schedule performance figures for the project on the status report.

"Build-out is behind schedule. They were scheduled to be completed by the 15th of January, but they aren't going to finish up until the 24th."

"What's that going to do to my schedule?" Jill asks. "I'm starting interviews for the store positions on the 16th. I hope to have that wrapped up by the 19th. As long as I have the majority of the staff hired by the 20th, we can have them stocking shelves starting the 22nd."

"Let's finish up the status of the other items, and I'll come back to that."

You've calculated some performance measurements, including earned value measures, and you show them to Jill and Dirk (all figures are in millions of dollars):

- BAC = 2; PV = 1.86; cumulative EV = 1.75; cumulative AC = 1.70
- Cumulative CPI is 1.03 (1.75 / 1.70)
- SPI is .94 (1.75 / 1.86)
- EAC is 1.94 (1.70 + ((2 – 1.75) / 1.03)))
- ETC is .25 (2 – 1.75)

"What is all this telling us?" Dirk asks.

"The cost performance index tells us we're getting a good return for the money spent on the project so far. In other words, we've experienced a $1.03 value for every dollar spent to date," you respond.

"The schedule performance index isn't as cheery, but it's not dreadful news either. This performance indicator says that work is progressing at 94 percent of what we anticipated by this point.

"The estimate at completion tells us that based on what we know today, the total project will cost $1.94 million. That's coming in under the original $2 million we had budgeted for completion, so we're on track with the project budget. The last figure is the estimated cost of the remaining work."

"It looks like we're a little behind schedule based on what you have figured here," Dirk says.

"Yes, that's correct," you reply. "That brings us back to Jill's question. I have two alternatives to propose. One, we overlap the schedule and allow Gomez's crew to complete their work while Jill's staff starts stocking shelves."

Jill says, "I don't like this option. We'll be tripping over each other, and I don't want merchandise damaged by workers who are still dragging equipment around inside the store. What's your other option?"

"We could ask Gomez to increase the crew size so that they complete on time according to the contract. We have a provision in the contract that stipulates they add crew members if it looks as though they'll miss the scheduled completion date. I will instruct the contract management department to inform Gomez that we're requiring additional crew members."

"That will do the trick," Jill says. "We need the storefront to ourselves when stocking and preparing for opening. I'm glad you had that stipulation in the contract."

You report that sign-off has been obtained for the completed deliverables to date. Quality inspections and comparisons of the deliverables to the acceptance criteria were completed to Jill and Ricardo's satisfaction on the work performed to date.

Project Case Study Checklist

- Control Costs
  - Cost change control system
  - Performance measurement analysis
  - Forecasting
- Control Schedule
  - Schedule compression
- Verify Scope
  - Verified work results
- Perform Quality Control
  - Assured quality requirements were met

Understanding How This Applies to Your Next Project

With the exception of the Perform Integrated Change Control process, we covered the meaty portion of the Monitoring and Controlling process group in this chapter. It's critical to monitor every process we discussed in order to keep the project in alignment with the objectives and to be able to take corrective action as soon as possible.

Monitoring and Controlling Risk is a process you'll perform once the work of the project begins throughout the remainder of the project. Just like change, risk is something that will occur on most every project you undertake. I've never managed a project (except for projects that were started and finished within a matter of days) that didn't encounter risk. And I'd say my experience has been that most risks are unknown, which makes contingency reserves (both time and money) essential on any project. For example, during the writing of this book, we moved to a new home. I did the smart thing and got three estimates from three reputable moving companies in the area. The estimates are based on an hourly rate for a certain number of movers. Two estimates came back very close to each other and the third was more than double the other estimates. So I picked the company that said they could get us moved in two days rather than the three their competitor quoted. Fortunately, we don't move very often. Unfortunately, I didn't realize moving companies woefully underbid the amount of time it actually takes to pack you up, load the truck, and unload at the other end. By the third day, I had to insist they complete the job in four hours because we were at more than double the original quote at that point. It's a good thing I had a reserve tucked away for the unexpected, but this overrun wiped out the entire contingency fund! Taking on a project without knowing that risks will occur and without having some contingency set aside is a huge gamble because even the smallest projects have risks.

Earned value measurement is a tool you can't live without for measuring performance on your project, particularly the cost and schedule variance and the cost and schedule performance indexes. The size and complexity of the project will dictate how often you should run the performance measurements. The mantra of stakeholders everywhere is "on time and on budget." Therefore, controlling the project budget and the schedule will likely be two of your most time-consuming project management tasks. Use the tools we discussed in this chapter to keep yourself and your stakeholders informed of what's happening regarding these two important areas. If cost or schedule changes must occur, it's imperative you communicate what happened, why it happened, and if it's expected to happen again and that you realign stakeholders' expectations with the new forecasted estimates.

Perform Quality Control and Verify Scope work together to measure, inspect, and accept the project deliverables. Verifying and accepting the work of the project shouldn't be a mind-boggling task at this point if you've been following the project management processes all along. For example, you should monitor and inspect deliverables as they're completed. At project's end, there might be additional testing or inspection needed to be certain all the deliverables work together (if they're required to do so), but many issues or problems you've discovered regarding the deliverables should have been discovered by now. However, I know that exceptions do exist. It isn't always possible to inspect the work of the project as it progresses because some projects aren't complete until the last piece of the puzzle is put into place. In that case, inspection, testing, and deliverables acceptance won't occur until the end of the project. But again, if you've used sound Monitoring and Controlling tools and techniques to monitor the processes, ideally you won't encounter any big surprises at this stage.

Control Scope is absolutely essential for all projects. Time and again I've seen changes to scope end up pitting stakeholders against the project team because the requirements weren't defined adequately in the first place and because neither party clearly understood what was being requested. Scope changes can kill a project by significantly delaying the finish date or by so drastically modifying the original objective of the project that it no longer resembles what it set out to accomplish. I try to keep the questions regarding scope change simple, as in "Do you absolutely have to have this to meet the objective of this project?" That isn't always easy for people to understand because we often confuse wants with needs. So, I might come up with an analogy they can relate to—something like this: "Let's say your one and only culinary skill is boiling water. Do you really need a designer stove with dual fuel options and a built-in warming oven to boil water? Wouldn't a simple store brand work in that case?"

Summary

We covered a lot of material in this chapter, and we also closed out the Monitoring and Controlling process group.

Monitor and Control Risks responds to risks as they occur and implements workarounds for unplanned risk events. Some risks planned for during the Plan Risk Responses process will occur, and some will not. Perhaps risks that were previously identified do occur, and their impacts are much greater than anticipated during the Plan Risk Responses process. These will require updates to the risk management plan or workarounds.

Cost Control involves managing changes to project costs. It's also concerned with monitoring project budgets to prevent unauthorized or incorrect costs from getting included in the cost baseline. Cost Control uses tools and techniques such as earned value measurement (such as CV, SV, CPI, SPI), forecasting (ETC and EAC), and project performance reviews (variance analysis, trend analysis, and EVM) to monitor costs.

Schedule Control involves determining the status of the project schedule, determining whether changes have occurred or should, and influencing and managing schedule changes.

Perform Quality Control monitors work results to see whether they fulfill the quality standards outlined in the quality management plan. Perform Quality Control should occur throughout the life of the project. It uses many tools and techniques. Inspection measures results to determine whether the results conform to the quality standards. Attributes are measurements that either conform or do not conform. Control charts measure the results of processes over time, and Pareto charts are histograms that rank-order the most important quality factors by their frequency over time. You should not adjust processes that are in control; however, you can change these processes to realize improvements.

Verify Scope involves verifying and accepting work results, while Control Scope is concerned with controlling changes to project scope.

Exam Essentials

Describe the purpose of Monitor and Control Risks. Monitor and Control Risks involves identifying and responding to new risks as they occur. Risk monitoring and reassessment should occur throughout the life of the project.

Name the purpose of the Control Costs process. The Control Costs process is concerned with monitoring project costs to prevent unauthorized or incorrect costs from getting included in the cost baseline.

Be able to describe earned value measurement techniques. Earned value measurement (EVM) monitors the planned value (PV), earned value (EV), and actual costs (AC) expended to produce the work of the project. Cost variance (CV), schedule variance (SV), cost performance index (CPI), and schedule performance index (SPI) are the formulas used with the EVM technique.

Be able to name the tools and techniques of the Control Costs process. The tools and techniques of the Control Costs process are earned value measurement, forecasting, to-complete performance index, performance reviews, variance analysis, and project management software.

Be able to name the purpose of the Perform Quality Control process. The purpose of the Perform Quality Control process is to monitor work results to see whether they comply with the standards set out in the quality management plan.

Name the purpose of the Verify Scope process. The purpose of Verify Scope is to determine whether the work is complete and whether it satisfies the project objectives.

Be able to describe product verification. Product verification confirms that all the work of the project was completed accurately and to the satisfaction of the stakeholder.

Key Terms

I've discussed in detail the processes you'll use to monitor your project progress. You need to understand and use each of these processes to be an effective project manager. You'll need to know them by the names used in the *PMBOK® Guide* to be successful on the exam.

Control Costs

Control Schedule

Control Scope

Monitor and Control Risks

Perform Quality Control

Verify Scope

You've learned a lot of new key words in this chapter. PMI has worked hard to develop and define standard project management terms that apply across industries. Here is a list of some of the terms you came across in this chapter:

actual cost (AC)

attributes

budget at completion (BAC)

common causes of variances

control charts

cost performance index (CPI)

cost variance (CV)

cumulative CPI

cumulative SPI

earned value (EV)

earned value measurement (EVM)

efficiency indicator

estimate at completion (EAC)

estimate to complete (ETC)

inspection

planned value (PV)

prevention

revisions

rework

run chart

scatter diagrams

Pareto charts

schedule performance index (SPI)

schedule variance (SV)

statistical sampling

technical performance measurements

tolerable results

variance at completion (VAC)

workaround

Review Questions

1. You are working on a project that was proceeding well until a manufacturing glitch occurred that requires corrective action. It turns out the glitch was an unintentional enhancement to the product, and the marketing people are absolutely crazy about its potential. The corrective action is canceled, and you continue to produce the product with the newly discovered enhancement. As the project manager, you know that a change has occurred to the product scope because the glitch changed the characteristics of the product. Which of the following statements is true?

   A. Changes to product scope should be reflected in the project scope.

   B. Changes to product scope should be documented in the scope management plan.

   C. Changes to product scope will result in cost changes.

   D. Changes to product scope are a result of corrective action.

2. You are working on a project that was proceeding well until a manufacturing glitch occurred that requires corrective action. It turns out the glitch was an unintentional enhancement to the product, and the marketing people are absolutely crazy about its potential. The corrective action is canceled, and you continue to produce the product with the newly discovered enhancement. As the project manager, you know that a variance has occurred. Which of the following is true?

   A. Common causes of variance, also known as special-cause variances, are situations that are unique and not easily controlled at the operational level.

   B. Random variances, known or predictable variances, and variances that are always present in the process are known as common causes of variance.

   C. Attribute inspection determines whether measurements fall within tolerable results.

   D. Scatter diagrams display the relationships between an independent and a dependent variable to show variations in the process over time.

3. Your project has experienced some changes to the agreed-upon WBS elements. The changes were approved through the proper change control process. The WBS changes might in turn require which of the following? Choose the best answer.

   A. Scope changes

   B. Cost changes

   C. Schedule revisions

   D. Risk response changes

4. You are a project manager for Dakota Software Consulting Services. You're working with a major retailer that offers its products through mail-order catalogs. It is interested in knowing customer characteristics, the amounts of first-time orders, and similar information. The stakeholders have accepted the project scope. Work has begun on the project, and you're confirming some of the initial work results with the stakeholders. You've asked for acceptance of the work results. Which process are you in?

   A. Monitor and Control Risks
   B. Perform Quality Control
   C. Verify Scope
   D. Control Scope

5. You are the project manager for a top-secret software project for an agency of the United States government. Your mission—should you choose to accept it—is to complete the project using internal resources. The reason is that getting top-secret clearances for contractors takes quite a bit of time and waiting for clearances would jeopardize the implementation date. Your programmers are 80 percent of the way through the programming and testing work when your agency appoints a new executive director. Your programmers are siphoned off this project to work on the executive director's hot new project. Which of the following addresses the purpose of Verify Scope in this case?

   A. Verify Scope determines the correctness and completion of all the work.
   B. Verify Scope documents the level and degree of completion.
   C. Verify Scope determines whether the project results comply with quality standards.
   D. Verify Scope documents the correctness of the work according to stakeholders' expectations.

6. Which of the following statements is true regarding schedule variances?

   A. Schedule variances impact scope, which impacts the schedule.
   B. Schedule variances sometimes impact the schedule.
   C. Schedule variances always impact the schedule.
   D. Schedule variances never impact the schedule.

7. You are a project manager for Laurel's Theater Productions. Your new project is coming in over budget and requires a cost change through the cost change control system. You know all of the following statements are true regarding Control Costs except for which one?

   A. A description of how cost changes should be managed and controlled is found in the cost management plan.
   B. Cost changes are reflected in the cost baseline.
   C. EVM is used to determine the cost performance that must be realized for the remaining work of the project to meet the goal.
   D. This equation, EAC = BAC / cumulative CPI, is used to forecast an estimate at completion assuming future project performance will be the same as past performance.

8. Which of the following might require rebaselining of the cost baseline?
   - **A.** Corrective action
   - **B.** Revised cost estimates
   - **C.** Updates to the cost management plan
   - **D.** Budget updates

9. What are the performance measurements for the Control Schedule process?
   - **A.** SV = (EV – PV) and SPI = (EV / PV)
   - **B.** SV = (EV – AC) and SPI = (EV / AC)
   - **C.** SV = (EV – BAC) and SPI = (EV / BAC)
   - **D.** SV = (PV – EV) and SPI = (PV / EV)

10. This measurement is the value of the work that has been completed to date compared to the budget.
    - **A.** PV
    - **B.** AC
    - **C.** EV
    - **D.** EAC

11. You are a contract project manager for a wholesale flower distribution company. Your project is to develop a website for the company that allows retailers to place their flower orders online. You will also provide a separate link for individual purchases that are ordered, packaged, and mailed to the consumer directly from the grower's site. This project involves coordinating the parent company, growers, and distributors. You are preparing a performance review and have the following measurements at hand: PV = 300, AC = 200, and EV = 250. What do you know about this project?
    - **A.** The EAC is a positive number, which means the project will finish under budget.
    - **B.** You do not have enough information to calculate CPI.
    - **C.** The CV is a negative number in this case, which means you've spent less than you planned to spend as of the measurement date.
    - **D.** The CV is a positive number in this case, which means you're under budget as of the measurement date.

12. A negative result from an SV calculation means which of the following?
    - **A.** PV is higher than EV.
    - **B.** PV equals 1.
    - **C.** EV is higher than PV.
    - **D.** EV is higher than AC.

13. You are a contract project manager for a wholesale flower distribution company. Your project is to develop a website for the company that allows retailers to place their flower orders online. You will also provide a separate link for individual purchases that are ordered, packaged, and mailed to the consumer directly from the grower's site. This project involves coordinating the parent company, growers, and distributors. You are preparing a performance review and have the following measurements at hand: PV = 300, AC = 200, and EV = 250. What is the CPI of this project?

A. 0.80

B. 1.25

C. 1.5

D. 0.83

14. You accept project costs to date and assume future work (ETC) will be performed at the budgeted rate. If BAC = 800, ETC = 275, PV = 300, AC = 200, EV = 250, and cumulative CPI = 1.25, what is the EAC?

A. 640

B. 750

C. 600

D. 550

15. You know that BAC = 375, PV = 300, AC = 200, and cumulative EV = 250. Variances that have occurred on the project to date are not expected to continue. What is the ETC?

A. 75

B. 50

C. 125

D. 150

16. You expect future project performance to be consistent with the project performance experienced to date. If BAC = 800, ETC = 275, PV = 300, cumulative AC = 200, EV = 250, and cumulative CPI = 1.25, what is the EAC?

A. 640

B. 750

C. 600

D. 550

17. You know that BAC = 500, PV = 325, AC = 275, CPI = .9, and EV = 250, and you are using actual costs to date and assuming ETC uses the budgeted rate. Variance at completion tells you which of the following?

A. 25

B. –52

C. 52

D. –25

18. You know that BAC = 500, PV = 325, cumulative AC = 275, and cumulative EV = 250 and that you are experiencing typical variances. What is ETC?

A. 227.3

B. 250

C. 274.7

D. 525

19. Your project progressed as planned up until yesterday. Suddenly, an unexpected risk event occurred. You quickly devised a response to deal with this negative risk event using which of the following outputs of Monitor and Control Risks?

A. Risk management plan updates

B. Workarounds

C. Corrective action

D. Additional risk identification

20. Which of the following is considered the most critical EVM metric?

A. CPI

B. CV

C. SPI

D. SP

Answers to Review Questions

1. A. Changes to product scope should be reflected in the project scope.

2. D. Scatter diagrams display the relationship between an independent and dependent variable over time.

3. C. WBS element changes are scope changes. According to the *PMBOK® Guide*, schedule revisions are often required as a result of scope changes.

4. C. The Verify Scope process is concerned with the acceptance of work results. It also formalizes the acceptance of the project scope.

5. B. Verify Scope should document the level and degree of completion of the project given the circumstances in this question. If you come back at a later date and restart this project, Verify Scope will describe how far the project progressed and give you an idea of where to start.

6. B. Schedule variances will sometimes—but not always—impact the schedule. Changes to noncritical path tasks will not likely impact the schedule, but changes to critical path tasks will always impact the schedule.

7. C. To-complete performance index determines the cost performance that must be realized for the remaining work of the project to meet a goal such as BAC or EAC.

8. D. Budget updates might require cost rebaselining.

9. A. Schedule variance is (EV – PV) and schedule performance index is (EV / PV).

10. C. Earned value is referred to as the value of the work that's been completed to date compared to the budget.

11. D. The CV is a positive number and is calculated by subtracting AC from EV as follows: 250 – 200 = 50. A positive CV means the project is coming in under budget, meaning you've spent less than you planned as of the measurement date.

12. A. The SV calculation is EV – PV. If PV is a higher number than EV, you'll get a negative number as a result.

13. B. CPI is calculated as follows: EV / AC. In this case, 250 / 200 = 1.25.

14. B. When you accept project performance to date and assume future ETC work will be performed at the budgeted rate, EAC is calculated as follows: AC + BAC – EV. Therefore, the calculation for this question looks like this: (200 + 800) – 250 = 750.

15. C. The correct formula for ETC for this question is as follows: BAC – cumulative EV. Therefore, ETC is as follows: 375 – 250 = 125.

16. A. When project performance is expected to behave like past performance, EAC is calculated as follows: EAC = BAC / cumulative CPI. Therefore, the calculation for this question looks like this: 800 / 1.25 = 640.

17. D. You first have to calculate EAC in order to calculate VAC. EAC for variances that are atypical is AC + BAC – EV. So our numbers are 275 + 500 – 250 = 525. VAC is calculated this way: BAC – EAC. Therefore, 500 – 525 = –25. Our costs are not doing as well as anticipated.

18. C. You must first calculate cumulative CPI in order to calculate ETC. Cumulative CPI is cumulative EV / cumulative AC. We have 250 / 275 = .91. ETC with typical variances is (BAC – cumulative EV) / cumulative CPI. Our numbers are (500 – 250) / .91 = 274.7.

19. B. Workarounds are unplanned responses. They deal with negative risk events as they occur. As the name implies, workarounds were not previously known to the project team. The risk event was unplanned, so no contingency plan existed to deal with the risk event, and thus it required a workaround.

20. A. CPI is considered the most critical EVM metric. It measures the cost efficiency of the project work completed at the measuring date.

Chapter 12

Applying Professional Responsibility

THE PMP EXAM CONTENT FROM THE CLOSING THE PROJECT PERFORMANCE DOMAIN COVERED IN THIS CHAPTER INCLUDES THE FOLLOWING:

- ✓ Obtain Final Acceptance for the Project
- ✓ Obtain Financial, Legal, and Administrative Closure
- ✓ Release Project Resources
- ✓ Identify, Document, and Communicate Lessons Learned
- ✓ Create and Distribute Final Project Report
- ✓ Archive and Retain Project Records
- ✓ Measure Customer Satisfaction

THE PMP EXAM CONTENT FROM THE PROFESSIONAL AND SOCIAL RESPONSIBILITY PERFORMANCE DOMAIN COVERED IN THIS CHAPTER INCLUDES THE FOLLOWING:

- ✓ Ensure Individual Integrity
- ✓ Contribute to the Project Management Knowledge Base
- ✓ Enhance Personal Professional Competence
- ✓ Promote Interaction Among Stakeholders

Congratulations! You've made terrific progress and after finishing this chapter will be well equipped to take the Project Management Professional (PMP) exam.

The last process group we'll cover is the Closing process group, and it has two processes: Close Project or Phase and Close Procurements. The Close Project or Phase process is concerned with verifying that the work of the project was completed correctly and to the stakeholders' satisfaction. Close Procurements supports the Close Project or Phase process and also verifies that the work of the project was completed correctly and the deliverables accepted.

Once you've obtained the PMP designation, you have an obligation to maintain integrity, apply your subject matter knowledge and project management knowledge, and maintain the code of conduct published by the PMI. You'll also be required to balance the interests and needs of stakeholders with the organization's needs. The exam might include questions on any of these topics.

As a project manager, you'll find yourself in many unique situations, different organizations, and possibly even different countries. Even if you never get involved in international project management, you will still come in contact with people from different cultures and backgrounds than yours. If you work as a contract project manager, you'll be exposed to many different organizations that each has its own culture and ways of doing things. You should always strive to act in a professional, courteous manner in these situations.

I'll talk about each of these topics in this chapter.

Formulating Project Closeout

All good projects must come to an end, as the saying goes. Ideally, you've practiced all the topics I've talked about that have led up to this point, and you've delivered a successful project to the stakeholders and customers. You've also put some of the vital tools of project management into play—planning, executing, controlling, and communicating—to help you reach that goal.

But how do you know when a project has ended successfully? Delivering the product or service of the project doesn't mean it has been completed satisfactorily. Remember back to the opening chapters, I said a project is completed successfully when it meets or exceeds stakeholders' expectations and satisfies the goals of the project. During the Closing processes—Close Project or Phase and Close Procurements—you'll document the acceptance of the product of the project with a formal sign-off and file it with the project records for future reference. The formal sign-off is the way stakeholders indicate that the goals have been met and that the project meets or exceeds their expectations so that the project ends.

Characteristics of Closing

A few characteristics are common to all projects during the Closing processes. One is that the probability of completing the project is highest during this process and risk is lowest. You've already completed the majority of the work of the project—if not all of the work—so the probability of not finishing the project is very low.

Stakeholders have the least amount of influence during the Closing processes, while project managers have the greatest amount of influence. Costs are significantly lower during this process because the majority of the project work and spending has already occurred. Remember those cost S curves we talked about in the Cost Budgeting process? This is where they taper off as project spending comes to an end.

One last common characteristic of projects during closing is that weak matrix organizations tend to experience the least amount of stress during the Closing processes. This is because, in a weak matrix organization, the functional manager assigns all tasks (project-related tasks as well) so the team members have a job to return to once the project is completed and there's no change in reporting structure.

All projects do eventually come to an end. You'll now examine a few of the reasons for project endings before getting into the Close Project or Phase and Close Procurements processes.

Project Endings

Projects come to an end for several reasons:

- They're completed successfully.
- They're canceled or killed prior to completion.
- They evolve into ongoing operations and no longer exist as projects.

Four formal types of project endings exist that you might need to know for the exam:

- Addition
- Starvation
- Integration
- Extinction

You'll look at each of these ending types in detail in the following sections.

Addition

Projects that evolve into ongoing operations are considered projects that end because of *addition*; in other words, they become their own ongoing business unit. An example of this is the installation of an enterprise resource planning system. These systems are business management systems that integrate all areas of a business, including marketing, planning, manufacturing, sales, financials, and human resources. After the installation of the software, these systems can develop into their own business unit because ongoing operations, maintenance, and monitoring of the software require full-time staff. These systems usually evolve into an arm of the business reporting system that no one can live without once it's installed.

A project is considered a project when it meets these criteria: it is unique, has a definite beginning and ending date, and is temporary in nature. When a project becomes an ongoing operation, it is no longer a project.

Starvation

When resources are cut off from the project or are no longer provided to the project, it's starved prior to completing all the requirements, and you're left with an unfinished project on your hands. *Starvation* can happen for any number of reasons:

- Other projects come about and take precedence over the current project, thereby cutting the funding or resources for your project.
- The customer curtails an order.
- The project budget is reduced.
- A key resource quits.

Resource starving can include cutting back or withholding human resources, equipment and supplies, or money. In any case, if you're not getting the people, equipment, or money you need to complete the project, it's going to starve and probably end abruptly.

This is one of those cases where documentation becomes your best friend. Organizations tend to have short memories. As you move on to bigger and better projects, your memory regarding the specifics of the project will fade. Six months from now when someone important wonders why that project was never completed and begins the finger-pointing routine, the project documents will clearly outline the reasons why the project ended early. That's one of the reasons project documentation is such an important function. I'll talk more about documenting project details shortly.

Integration

Integration occurs when the resources of the project—people, equipment, property, and supplies—are distributed to other areas in the organization or are assigned to other projects. Perhaps your organization begins to focus on other areas or other projects, and the next thing you know, functional managers come calling to retrieve their resources for other, more important things. Again, your project will come to an end due to lack of resources because they have been reassigned to other areas of the business or have been pulled from your project and assigned to another project.

NOTE The difference between starvation and integration is that starvation is the result of staffing, funding, or other resource cuts while integration is the result of reassignment or redeployment of the resources.

Again, good documentation describing the circumstances that brought about the ending of a project because of integration should be archived with the project records for future reference.

Extinction

This is the best kind of project end because *extinction* means the project has been completed and accepted by the stakeholders. As such, it no longer exists because it had a definite ending date, the goals of the project were achieved, and the project was closed out.

Real World Scenario

Pied Piper

Jerome Reed is the project manager for Pied Piper's newest software project. His team is working on a program that will integrate the organization's human resource information, including payroll records, leave-time accruals, contact information, and so on. His top two programmers, Brett and Kathy, are heading up the coding team and are in charge of the programming and testing activities.

Pied Piper recently hired a new CIO who started working with the company just a few weeks ago. Jerome is concerned about his human resources project. It was the former CIO's pet project, but he's not sure where it falls on the new CIO's radar screen.

Jerome is in the computer room checking out the new hardware that just arrived for his project. Liz Horowitz, the director of network operations, approaches Jerome.

"That's a nice piece of hardware," Liz comments.

"It sure is. This baby is loaded. It's going to process and serve up data to the users so fast they'll be asking us to upgrade all the servers."

Liz replies, "You're right about that. I've asked Richard to burn it in and load the software."

"What software?" Jerome asks.

"You know, the new customer relationship management software. The CIO hired some vendor she has worked with before to come in and install their CRM system here. She said it was our top priority. I knew this new server was already on order, and it happens to be sized correctly for the new CRM system."

"I purchased this server for the human resources project. What am I supposed to use for that?"

Liz answers, "I've got a server over there on the bottom of the third rack that might work, or maybe you can order another one. But you should take this up with the CIO. All I know is she authorized me to use this server. She understood I was taking it from your project, so maybe she's thinking about going another direction with the human resources project.

"You probably should know I also asked to have Brett and Kathy assigned to the CRM project. Even though it's a vendor project, it still requires some of our coders. The CIO wanted the best, and they're the best we've got. It shouldn't take them long to make the changes I need, and then you can have them back for your project. In the meantime, they can give directions to your other programmers so they can keep working."

"I'm going to go see whether the CIO is in," Jerome replies.

This is a case where Jerome's project ends by integration because of the reassignment of resources. The new CIO came on board and changed the direction and focus of the project priorities, making her new project a higher priority than the previous project. As a result, Jerome's hardware and his top two resources were reassigned to the new project. Had the CIO cut the resources and equipment on the original project altogether, it would have ended because of starvation.

Closing Out the Project

The key activity of the *Close Project or Phase* process is concerned with gathering project records and disseminating information to formalize the acceptance of the product, service, or result as well as to perform project closure. You'll want to review the project documents to make certain they are up-to-date. For example, perhaps some scope change requests were implemented that changed some of the characteristics of the final product. The project information you're collecting during this process should reflect the characteristics and specifications of the final product. Don't forget to update your resource assignments as well. Some team members will have come and gone over the course of the project; you need to double-check that all the resources and their roles and responsibilities are noted.

Once the project outcomes are documented, you'll request formal acceptance from the stakeholders or the customer. (I'll cover formal acceptance later when I talk about the outputs.) They're also interested in knowing whether the product or service of the project meets the goals the project set out to accomplish. If your documentation is up-to-date, you'll have the project results at hand to share with them.

The Close Project or Phase process is also concerned with analyzing the project management processes to determine their effectiveness and to document lessons learned concerning the project processes. And one of the other key functions of the Close Project or Phase process is to archive all project documents for historical reference. You can probably guess that Close Project or Phase belongs to the Project Integration Management Knowledge Area since this process touches so many areas of the project.

Every project requires closure. According to the *PMBOK® Guide*, the completion of each project phase requires project closure as well.

Exam Spotlight

Project closure occurs at the end of each phase of the project in order to properly document project information and keep it safe for future reference. You shouldn't wait until project completion to perform the Close Project or Phase process but rather perform it at the end of every phase, no matter whether the project phase was completed successfully or ended for some other reason.

Close Project or Phase Inputs

The Close Project or Phase process gathers all the project records and verifies that they are up-to-date and accurate. The project records must correctly identify the final specifications of the product or service the project set out to produce. Close Project or Phase is the place to ensure that this information accurately reflects the true results of the project.

The inputs to the Close Project or Phase process are as follows:

- Project management plan
- Accepted deliverables
- Organizational process assets

I've talked about all of these inputs previously.

Close Project or Phase Tools and Techniques

The only tool and technique of Close Project or Phase is expert judgment. When you're conducting administrative closure activities, which we'll discuss next, the subject matter experts can help assure that the process is performed according to the organization's and to project management standards.

Administrative closure procedures involve collecting all the records associated with the project, analyzing the project success (or failure), documenting and gathering lessons learned, and archiving project records. Keep in mind that when projects are performed under contract, the archiving of financial records is especially important. These records might need to be accessed if there are payment disputes, so you need to know where they are and how they were filed. Projects with large financial expenditures also require particular attention to the archiving of financial records for the same reasons. Financial information is especially useful when estimating future projects, so again, make sure to archive the information so it's easily accessible.

All of these documents should be indexed for reference and filed in a safe place. Don't forget to include electronic databases and electronic documents as part of your project archives as well. These records can be stored on a network drive or copied onto a CD that's kept with the project binder.

Administrative closure procedures also document the project team members' and stakeholders' roles and responsibilities in performing this process. According to the *PMBOK® Guide*, this should include the processes and methodologies for defining the following:

- Approval requirements of the stakeholders for project deliverables and changes to deliverables.
- Assuring and confirming that the project meets the requirements of the stakeholders, customers, and sponsor. This includes documenting necessary actions to verify that the deliverables have been accepted and exit criteria have been met.
- Assuring and confirming that the exit criteria for the project are satisfied.

Close Project or Phase Outputs

Sometimes you'll work on projects where everything just clicks. Your project team functions at the performing stage, the customers and stakeholders are happy, and things just fall into place according to plan. I often find it difficult to perform Close Project or Phases on projects that have progressed particularly well, just because I don't want them to end. Believe it or not, the majority of your projects can fall into this category if you practice good project management techniques and exercise those great communication skills.

The Close Project or Phase process has the following outputs:

- Final product, service, or result transition
- Organizational process assets updates

We'll take a brief look at each in the following sections.

Final Product, Service, or Result

The name of this output is somewhat misleading. This actually refers to the acceptance of the final product, service, or result and the turnover of the product to the organization. This usually requires a formal sign-off (I'll talk about that next), and in the case of a project performed on contract, it definitely requires a formal sign-off or receipt indicating acceptance of the project.

Formal acceptance includes distributing notice of the acceptance of the product or service of the project by the stakeholders, customer, or project sponsor to stakeholders and customers. You should require formal sign-off indicating that those signing accept the product of the project.

NOTE

The final product, service, or result is concerned with obtaining formal acceptance; organizational process assets involves documenting and archiving formal acceptance.

Organizational Process Assets Updates

The organizational process assets output is where the formal sign-off of the acceptance of the product is documented, collected, and archived for future reference. Documenting formal acceptance is important because it signals the official closure of the project, and it is your proof that the project was completed satisfactorily.

Another function of sign-off is that it kicks off the beginning of the warranty period. Sometimes project managers or vendors will warranty their work for a certain time period after completing the project. Projects that produce software programs, for example, might be warranted from bugs for a 60- or 90-day time frame from the date of implementation or acceptance. Typically in the case of software projects, bugs are fixed for free during the warranty period. Watch out, because users will try to squeeze new requirements into the "bug" category mold. If you offer a warranty, it's critical that the warranty spells out exactly what is covered and what is not.

This is also where the other project records and files are collected and archived. This includes the project planning documents (project scope statement, budget, schedule, risk responses, quality plan and baselines, and so on), change records and logs, issue logs, and so on.

Project or phase closure documents are included in this output. These include documentation showing that the project or phase is completed and that the transfer of the product of the project to the organization (or department responsible for ongoing maintenance and support) has occurred. In the case of a phase completion, the transfer would be the official hand-off to the next phase of the project rather than to an operations or maintenance group. If your project is canceled or ends prematurely, you should document the reasons for its premature end as well as the procedures for transferring the completed and uncompleted deliverables.

Historical information and lessons learned are used to document the successes and failures of the project. As an example, lessons learned document the reasons specific corrective actions were taken, their outcomes, the causes of performance variances, unplanned risks that occurred, mistakes that were made and could have been avoided, and so on.

Unfortunately, sometimes projects do fail. You can learn lessons from failed projects as well as from successful projects, and you should document this information for future reference. Most project managers, however, do not document lessons learned. The reason for this is that employees don't want to admit to making mistakes or learning from mistakes made during the project. And they do not want their name associated with failed projects or even with mishaps on successful projects.

NOTE

Lessons learned can include some of the most valuable information you'll take away from a project. We can all learn from our experiences, and what better way to have even more success on your next project than to review a similar past project's lessons learned document? But lessons learned will be there only if you document them now. I strongly recommend you not skip this step.

You and your management team will have to work to create an atmosphere of trust and assurance that lessons learned are not reasons for dismissing employees but are learning opportunities that benefit all those associated with the project. Lessons learned allow you to carry knowledge gained on this project to other projects you'll work on going forward.

They'll also prevent repeat mistakes in the future if you take the time to review the project documents and lessons learned prior to undertaking your new project.

Post-implementation audits aren't an official output, but they are a good idea. These go hand in hand with lessons learned because they examine the project from beginning to end and look at what went right and what went wrong. They evaluate the project goals and determine whether the product or service of the project satisfies the objectives. Post-implementation audits also examine the activities and project processes to determine whether improvements are possible on future projects.

Organizations might conduct post-implementation audits instead of lessons learned sessions. Documenting and gathering information during this procedure can serve the same function as lessons learned if you're honest and include all the good, the bad, and the ugly. Let's hope there's very little ugly.

Real World Scenario

Cimarron Research Group

The Cimarron Research Group researches and develops organic pesticides for use on food crops. It is a medium-sized company and has established a project management office (PMO) to manage all aspects of project work. The PMO consists of project managers and administrative staff who assist with information handling, filing, and disbursement.

Terri Roberts is the project manager for a project that has just closed. Terri diligently filed all the pertinent project documents as the project progressed and has requested the research files and engineering notes from the director of engineering to include them with the project archives as well. All information regarding the research on this project is included with the project archives. The engineering department chooses to keep its own set of research records as well, but it's important to keep a copy of these notes with the project archives so that all the information about the project is in one place.

Terri's assistant has indexed all the project documents and recently sent notice of formal acceptance and approval of this project to the stakeholders, project sponsor, and management team. This notice officially closes the project. The next step is to archive the files onto CDs and store them.

Closing Out the Procurements

Procurements have life cycles of their own—just like projects. I talked about the contract life cycles in Chapter 9. As such, procurements and contracts come to a close just as projects come to a close. As you might guess, there is a process that deals with procurement closings; it's called Close Procurements.

The *Close Procurements* process is concerned with completing and settling the terms of the procurement. It supports the Close Project or Phase process because the Close Procurements process determines whether the work described in the procurement documentation or contract was completed accurately and satisfactorily. This is called *product verification*. Projects that have multiple deliverables may have procurements for some of the deliverables but not all. Obviously, this process applies only to those phases, deliverables, or portions of the project that were performed under some form of procurement.

Close Procurements updates records and archives the information for future reference. These records detail the final results of the work of the project. I'll talk about the specifics of this when I cover the Close Procurements outputs.

Procurement documents might have specific terms or conditions for completion and closeout. You should be aware of these terms or conditions so that project closure isn't held up because you missed an important detail. If you are not administering the procurement yourself, be certain to ask your procurement department whether there are any special conditions that you should know about so that your project team doesn't inadvertently delay contract or project closure.

NOTE

Close Project or Phase verifies and documents the project outcomes just like the Close Procurements process. Keep in mind that not all projects are performed under contract, so not all projects require Close Procurements. However, all projects do require the Close Project or Phase process. Since verification and documentation of the project outcomes occur in both of these processes, projects that are performed under contract need to have project results verified only one time.

Exam Spotlight

For the exam, remember that product verification, which determines whether all of the work of the project was completed correctly according to the contract or other procurement terms and satisfactory according to stakeholder expectations, is performed during the Closing processes. Product documentation is verified and accepted during the Verify Scope process. One more note: when projects end prematurely, the Verify Scope process is where the level of detail concerning the amount of work completed gets documented.

Close Procurements Inputs

The Close Procurements process has two inputs:

- Project management plan
- Procurement documentation

I've discussed both these inputs before, but you should know a few more things about procurement documentation for this process. Procurement documentation includes the contract itself (or other procurement form) and all the supporting documents that go along with it. These might include things such as the WBS, the project schedule, change control documents, technical documents, financial and payment records, quality control inspection results, and so on. This information—along with all the other information gathered during the project—is filed once the project is closed out so that anyone considering a future project of similar scope can reference what was done.

Close Procurements Tools and Techniques

The Close Procurements process has three tools and techniques: procurement audits, negotiated settlements, and records management system. The records management system here serves the same function as the records management system I talked about in the discussion of the Contract Administration process in Chapter 9. *Procurement audits* are reviews of procurement processes to determine whether they are meeting the right needs and are being performed correctly and according to standards. The *PMBOK® Guide* says procurement audits are concerned with reviewing the procurement process, starting with the Plan Procurements process through Administer Procurements

The primary purpose of the procurement audit is to identify lessons learned during the procurement process. Procurement audits examine the procurement process to determine areas of improvement and to identify flawed processes or procedures. This allows you to reuse the successful processes on other procurement items for this project, on future projects, or elsewhere in the organization. It also alerts you to problems in the process so that you don't repeat them.

Procurement audits might be used by either the buyer or the vendor, or by both, as an opportunity for improvement. Documenting the lessons learned—including the successes and failures that occurred—allows you to improve other procurement processes currently underway on this project or other projects. It also gives you the opportunity to improve the process for future projects.

Negotiated settlements occur when using an alternative dispute resolution (ADR) technique due to disagreements about deliverables, payments, performance, and so on. Reaching a negotiated settlement through the aid of ADR techniques is the most favorable way to resolve the dispute.

Close Procurements Outputs

One of the purposes of the Close Procurements process is to provide formal notice to the seller—usually in written form—that the procurement is complete. The output of Close Procurements that deals with this is called *closed procurements*. This is a *formal acceptance and closure* of the procurement. It's your responsibility as project manager to document the formal acceptance of the procurement. Many times the provisions for formalizing acceptance and closing the procurement are spelled out in the procurement documents.

If you have a procurement department that handles contract administration, they will expect you to inform them when the procurement is completed and will in turn follow the formal procedures to let the seller know it's complete. However, you'll still note the procurement completion in your copy of the project records.

NOTE Depending on the terms of the procurement, early termination (whether by agreement, via default, or for cause) might result in additional charges to the buyer. Be certain to note the reasons for early termination in your procurement documentation.

The other output of Close Procurements is organizational process updates. This includes updating the procurement file, deliverables acceptance, and lessons learned. The *procurement file* is simply a file of all the procurement records and supporting documents. These records should be indexed for easy reference and included as part of the project files in the Close Project or Phase process.

Exam Spotlight

The *PMBOK® Guide* does not state in which order these processes should be performed. In practice, you will likely close out the procurement before closing the project and archiving the project documents. However, in prior editions of the *PMBOK® Guide*, the Close Procurements process (or its equivalent name in previous editions) was performed last.

This process is your organization's way of formally accepting the product of the project from the vendor and closing out the procurement. The deliverable acceptance portion of the organizational process updates includes the formal written notice from the buyer that the deliverables are acceptable and satisfactory or have been rejected. If the product or service does not meet expectations, the vendor will need to correct the problems before you issue a formal acceptance notice. Ideally, quality audits have been performed during the course of the project, and the vendor was given the opportunity to make corrections earlier in the process than the closing stage. It's not a good idea to wait until the very end of the project and then spring all the problems and issues on the vendor at once. It's much more efficient to discuss problems with your vendor as the project progresses because it provides the opportunity for correction when the problems occur.

Lessons learned include information and documentation about what worked well and what didn't work well regarding the procurement processes. You can use this information on future projects to improve performance and prevent inefficiencies.

Celebrate!

I think it's a good idea to hold a celebration at the conclusion of a successfully completed project. The project team should celebrate their accomplishment, and you should officially recognize their efforts and thank them for their participation. Any number of ideas come to mind here—a party, a trip to a ball game, pizza and sodas at lunchtime. This shouldn't be the only time you've recognized your team, as discussed during the Team Development process, but now is the time to officially close the project and thank your team members. Even if no funds are available for a formal celebration, your heartfelt "thank you" can go a long way with the members of your team. It's tough for team members to remain disgruntled, and it's easier to revive them, when they know their efforts are appreciated.

A celebration helps team members formally recognize the project end and brings closure to the work they've done. It also encourages them to remember what they've learned and to start thinking about how their experiences will benefit them and the organization during the next project.

Releasing Project Team Members

Releasing project team members is not an official process. However, it should be noted that at the conclusion of the project, you will release your project team members, and they will go back to their functional managers or be assigned to a new project if you're working in a matrix type organization.

You will want to keep the functional managers or other project managers informed as you get closer to project completion so that they have time to adequately plan for the return of their employees. Start letting them know a few months ahead of time what the schedule looks like and how soon they can plan on using their employees on new projects. This gives the other managers the ability to start planning activities and scheduling activity dates.

In all the excitement of wrapping up the project we shouldn't forget about our stakeholders. Let's take a look at balancing the stakeholders' interests and assuring we've met their expectations in the next section.

Balancing Stakeholders' Interests at Project Close

I know we discussed Managing Stakeholder Expectations in Chapter 9. Since stakeholder satisfaction is the key to project success and acceptance, I want to add some closing thoughts on this topic and discuss a few new concepts.

Projects are undertaken at the request of customers, project sponsors, executive managers, and others. You'll recall that stakeholders are those who have something to gain or lose by implementing the project. As such, stakeholders have different interests and needs, and one of your jobs is to balance the needs of the stakeholders.

Customer satisfaction is probably the primary goal you're striving for in any project. If your customer is satisfied, it means you've met or exceeded their expectations and delivered the product or service they were expecting. You've got a winning combination when the customer is satisfied with the product, and you've also provided excellent customer service along the way. Satisfied customers tell others about your success and will most likely use your services in the future.

One of the key ways to assure that customer satisfaction is achieved is to apply appropriate project management techniques to your project. This includes taking the time to discover all the requirements of the project and documenting them in the scope statement. You will find that stakeholders who have a clear understanding of the requirements and have signed off on them won't suffer from faulty memory and pull the ever-famous "I thought that *was* included" technique. Take the time to define your requirements and get stakeholder sign-off. You can't forget or fudge what's written down.

In the following sections, I'll discuss how to juggle the competing needs of stakeholders, how to handle the issues and problems with stakeholders, and finally, how to balance project constraints against stakeholder needs.

Competing Needs

Stakeholders come from all areas of the organization and include your customer as well. Because stakeholders do not all work in the same areas, they have competing needs and interests. One stakeholder's concern on a typical IT project might take the form of system security issues, while another stakeholder is concerned about ease of use. As the project manager, you will have situations in which stakeholder needs compete with each other, and you'll have to decide between them and set priorities. Sometimes you'll be able to accommodate their needs, and sometimes you'll have to choose. You want to examine the needs against the project objectives and then use your negotiation and communication skills to convince the stakeholders of priorities.

Individual stakeholders might or might not have good working relationships with other stakeholders. Because of this, office politics come into play. I advise you to stay away from the politics game but get to know your stakeholders. You'll want to understand their business processes and needs in order to make decisions about stakeholder requirements.

Dealing with Issues and Problems

Problems will occur on your project—it's part of the process. I've talked throughout this book about how to deal with problems and risks and how to use conflict resolution techniques in handling problems. Balancing stakeholder needs comes into play here also.

You'll have to determine alternatives that will meet the key requirements of the project without jeopardizing the competing needs of stakeholders. Once you're into the Executing processes of the project and beyond, redefining scope becomes less and less of an option. So your responsibility is to resolve issues and determine alternative solutions to problems as they occur without changing the original objectives of the project. Enlist the help of your project team members and stakeholders during these times. Use some of the techniques I talked about in Chapter 6 such as brainstorming and the Delphi technique, to find solutions.

You might also have difficulty trying to make stakeholders understand your decision or the technical nature of a problem. Again, this is where communication skills help you immensely. Take the case of a technical problem that's cropped up on your project. You should not expect your stakeholder to understand the technical aspects of rocket science if they work in the finance department, for example. It's up to you to keep the explanation at a level they can understand without loading them down with technical jargon and specifications. Keep your explanations simple, yet don't skip important details they'll need to make decisions.

Balancing Constraints

Your toughest issues will almost always center on the triple constraints: time, cost, and scope. Because of the nature of the constraints, one of these is the primary driver, and one is the least important. Keep a close eye on stakeholders who want to switch the priority of the constraints for their own purposes. Let's say the project sponsor already told you that time is the primary constraint. Another stakeholder tells you that a requirement of the project is being overlooked and quality is suffering. Be careful that the stakeholder isn't trying to divert the primary constraint from time to quality to suit their own objectives.

Real World Scenario

The Geographic Information System

Ryan Loveland is a project manager for a multinational company. He's working on a complex software project that involves rewriting the organization's mainframe accounting system to become a browser-based system running on thin-client architecture. A major problem with the existing system occurs when new accounts are entered into the system or account information changes. The accounts are tied to geographic areas, which are assigned to individual sales associates. Sales commissions are paid based on where the account resides. To date, the process of determining which territory an account belongs to has been done manually by looking at a map.

The project sponsor, Victor, requested a geographic information system (GIS) as part of the requirements of this project. The hope is that errors will be eliminated and commissions will be processed correctly. The sponsor is hoping that Ryan's internal team can write the GIS that will tie to the accounting system. Let's drop in on Ryan and Victor's conversation.

"I just don't understand," Victor says. "I can go onto that Internet site and plug in an address and get directions and a map detailing those directions from my house to anywhere in the country. It seems easy enough to me. Why can't your team write code like that?"

"It isn't that we can't write a program to do that. But there are several issues surrounding this request that I'd like to explain to you. I'd like you to understand why I'm asking to purchase a software product from an external vendor that will take care of these functions for us."

"Let's hear it," Victor says.

"One of the first problems is that our sales force is multinational. It would take us months just to obtain address information to populate the program. The second issue is that our sales districts are not divided by any known boundaries. Most GIS systems work off of latitude and longitude or geographic boundaries such as county borders or zip code boundaries."

Victor interrupts, "Well, here's what we do. You give me a set of maps, I'll hand-draw in the sales districts, and then you can scan it into the system."

"Unfortunately, it's not that easy. Our sales district boundaries are not consistent with known boundaries, and our existing address database is not standardized. For example, some addresses use the word *Street* spelled out; some use the abbreviation *St.* All of the addresses need to be standardized, and then we have to figure out which addresses belong to which territory.

"This process could take a great deal of time. There are vendors that specialize in GIS that could have us operational in a matter of weeks. I've already checked on a couple of the top vendors, and there aren't any problems interfacing with our new system. The time we'd save in the long run far outweighs the cost associated with purchasing this system from a vendor. And one last point: if I were to build this system internally, I'd have to take our top programming team off of existing project priorities to put them on this. GIS is extremely complicated. We're talking several months delay —if not a year or more—to get our programmers up to speed on GIS techniques and then write the programs."

Victor says, "If we're talking about a major delay in the schedule as you say, we can at least look at what these vendors have to offer. It's important that this system is accurate as well, and I think I hear you saying, 'Why reinvent the wheel?' Let's have a look at the costs."

We have officially closed out the project and hopefully satisfied our stakeholders' expectations. We have also completed our study of all of the project management processes from Initiating to Closing. But there's one more area you need to know about for the exam. We'll look at it next.

Professional Responsibility

As a certified Project Management Professional, you are required to adhere to the *PMI Code of Ethics and Professional Conduct*. You can find a copy of this code inside the *PMP Handbook*.

You should read and understand this code because you will be agreeing to adhere to its terms as part of the certification process. The *PMI Code of Ethics and Professional Conduct* outlines four areas of responsibility:

- Responsibility
- Respect

- Fairness
- Honesty

Exam Spotlight

Each of these areas is described in the code, along with sections called "Aspirational Standards" and "Mandatory Standards" for each one. We will not cover every standard in this chapter, so I recommend you read them and understand them for the exam.

You will find at least a few exam questions regarding professional responsibility on the exam, so we'll look at each of these areas and a few others for good measure.

Responsibility

Responsibility is the act of making decisions that are for the good of the organization rather than ourselves, admitting our mistakes, being responsible for the decisions we make and the consequences that result, along with other actions. We'll look at several elements that fall within the responsibility arena.

Ensuring Integrity

As a project manager, one of your professional responsibilities is to ensure integrity of the project management process, the product, and your own personal conduct. I've spent the majority of this book discussing how to achieve project management integrity by following the project management processes.

NOTE A product that has integrity is one that is complete and sound or fit for use.

Correctly applying the project management processes you've learned will ensure the integrity of the product. The effective execution of the Planning, Executing, and Monitoring and Controlling processes, including documenting scope, performing quality inspections, measuring performance, and taking corrective actions, will ensure that a quality product is produced that satisfies the requirements of the stakeholders (and the project plan). And as you learned earlier, you will seek acceptance of the product from the stakeholders and customer during the Closing process group.

Accepting Assignments

This topic, as well as many of the others discussed in these sections, cross two of the areas noted in the *PMI Code of Ethics and Professional Conduct*—responsibility and honesty. You should always honestly report your qualifications, your experience, and your past performance of services to potential employers, customers, PMI, and others. You should not knowingly accept assignments that are beyond your capabilities or experience.

Be honest about what you know and what you don't know as it relates to your experience. For example, the Control Quality processes as described in the *PMBOK® Guide* are used extensively in the manufacturing industry. However, the information technology field looks at quality issues in different ways. If you're a project manager in the information technology field, you've probably never used control charts and cause-and-effect diagramming techniques. Don't lead others to believe that you have used techniques you haven't used or that you have experience you don't have.

Emphasize the knowledge you do have and how you've used it in your specific industry, and don't try to fudge it with processes and techniques you've never used. Potential clients and employers would much rather work with you and provide training where you might need it than think they've got someone fully experienced with the project or industry techniques needed for a project when they don't.

If you're working on contract or you're self-employed, you have a responsibility to ensure that the estimates you provide potential customers are accurate and truthful. Make certain you clearly spell out what services you're providing and let the customer know the results they can expect at the end of the project. Accurately represent yourself, your qualifications, and your estimates in your advertising and in person.

Laws and Regulations Compliance

This might seem obvious, but as a professional, you're required to follow all applicable laws and rules and regulations that apply to your industry, organization, or project. This includes PMI organizational rules and policies as well. You should also follow any ethical standards and principles that might govern your industry or the state or country in which you're working. Remember that rules or regulations you're used to in the United States might or might not apply to other countries and vice versa.

Confidential Information

Many project managers work for consulting firms where their services are contracted out to organizations that need their expertise for particular projects. If you work in a situation like this, you will likely come across information that is sensitive or confidential. Again, this might seem obvious, but as part of the *PMI Code of Ethics and Professional Conduct*, you agree not to disclose sensitive or confidential information or use it in any way for personal gain.

Often when you work under contract, you'll be required to sign a nondisclosure agreement. This agreement simply says that you will not share information regarding the project or the organization with anyone—including the organization's competitors—or use the information for your personal gain.

However, you don't have to work on contract to come into contact with sensitive or private information. You might work full-time for an organization or a government agency that deals with information regarding its customer base or citizens. For example, if you work for a bank, you might have access to personal account information. If you work for a government agency, you might have access to personal tax records or other sensitive material. It would be highly unethical and maybe even illegal to look up the account information of individuals not associated with the project at hand just to satisfy your own curiosity. In my organization, that is grounds for dismissal.

NOTE Don't compromise your ethics or your organization's reputation by sharing information that is confidential to the organization or would jeopardize an individual's privacy.

Company Data

Although it might seem obvious that you should not use personal information or an organization's trade secrets for personal gain, sometimes the organization has a legitimate need to share information with vendors, governmental agencies, or others. You need to understand which vendors or organizations are allowed to see sensitive company data. In some cases, you might even need to help determine which individuals can have access to the data. When in doubt, ask.

Here are some examples. Maybe the company you're working with has periodic mailings it sends to its customer base. If one of your project activities includes finding a new vendor to print the mailing labels, your organization might require the vendor to sign a nondisclosure agreement to guard the contents of the customer lists. Discovering just who should have access to this information might be tricky.

Another example involves data on citizens that is maintained by the government. You might think that because the data belongs to one agency of the government—say the Internal Revenue Service—any other agency of the government can have access to it. This isn't the case. Some agencies are refused access to the data even though they might have good reason to use it. Others might have restricted access, depending on the data and the agency policy regarding it. Don't assume that others should have access to data because it seems logical.

Most organizations require vendors or other organizations to sign nondisclosure agreements when the vendors or others will have access to sensitive company data. It's your responsibility to ensure that the proper nondisclosure agreements are signed prior to releasing the data. The procurement department often handles this function.

Intellectual Property

You are likely to come into contact with intellectual property during the course of your project management career. Intellectual property includes items developed by an organization that have commercial value but are not tangible and copyrighted material such as books, software, and artistic works. It might also include ideas or processes that are patented. Or it might involve an industrial process, business process, or manufacturing process that was developed by the organization for a specific purpose.

Intellectual property is owned by the business or person who created it. You might have to pay royalties or ask for written permission to use the property. Intellectual property should be treated just like sensitive or confidential data. It should not be used for personal gain or shared with others who should not have access to it.

Respect

Respect involves several areas as well, including the way we conduct ourselves, the way we treat others, listening to other viewpoints, conducting ourselves in a professional manner, and so on. We'll look at some of the elements of respect next.

Professional Demeanor

Acting in a professional manner is required of most everyone who works in the business world. Although you are not responsible for the actions of others, you are responsible for your own actions and reactions. Part of acting professionally involves controlling yourself and your reactions in questionable situations. For example, a stakeholder or customer might lash out at you but have no basis for their outburst. You can't control what they said or did, but you can control how you respond. As a professional, your concern for the project and the organization should take precedence over your concern for your own feelings. Therefore, lashing out in return would be unprofessional. Maintain your professional demeanor, and don't succumb to shouting matches or ego competitions with others.

As project manager, you have a good deal of influence over your project team members. One of the items on the agenda at the project team kickoff meeting should be a discussion of where the team members can find a copy of organizational policies regarding conflict of interest, cultural diversity, standards and regulations, and customer service and standards of performance. Better yet, have copies with you that you can hand out at the meeting or have available the addresses of website where they can find these documents.

When you see project team members acting out of turn or with less-than-desirable customer service attitudes, coach and influence those team members to conform to the standards of conduct expected by you and your organization. Your team members represent you and the project. As such, they should act professionally. It's your job as the project leader to ensure that they do.

Reporting Ethics Violations

As a PMP, one of the responsibilities that falls into this category is your responsibility to report violations of the PMP code of conduct. To maintain integrity of the profession, PMPs must adhere to the code of conduct that makes all of us accountable to each other.

When you know a violation has occurred and you've verified the facts, notify PMI. Part of this process—and a requirement of the code of conduct—is that you'll verify that an ethics violation has occurred (in other words, don't report bogus or unsubstantiated reports) and will assist PMI in the investigation by supplying information, confirming facts and dates, and so on. This includes anything listed as violations in the *PMI Code of Ethics and Professional Conduct*, such as conflicts of interest, untruthful advertising, and false reporting of PMP experience and credentials, appearances of impropriety, and so on. This one calls for some judgment on your part, but it's mostly based on common sense. For example, a PMP in most situations should not have a family member working on the project team reporting to them (unless they own and run a family business).

Cultural Awareness

More and more companies compete in the global marketplace. As a result, project managers with multinational experience are increasingly in demand. This requires a heightened awareness of cultural influences and customary practices of the country where they're temporarily residing.

If you are used to working in the United States, for example, you know that the culture tends to value accomplishments and individualism. U.S. citizens tend to be informal and call each other by their first names, even if they've just met. In some European countries, people tend to be more formal, using surnames instead of first names in a business setting, even when they know each other well. Their communication style is more formal than in the United States, and although they tend to value individualism, they also value history, hierarchy, and loyalty. The Japanese, on the other hand, tend to communicate indirectly and consider themselves part of a group, not as individuals. The Japanese value hard work and success, as most of us do.

One thing I've witnessed when working in foreign countries is U.S. citizens trying to force their own culture or customs on those with whom they're visiting or working. That isn't recommended, and it generally offends those you're trying to impress. Don't expect others to conform to your way of doing things, especially when you're in their country. You know the saying "When in Rome, do as the Romans do"? Although you might not want to take that literally, the intent is good. For example, a quick kiss on both cheeks is a customary greeting in many countries. If that is the case and it's how you're greeted, respond with the same.

Culture Shock

Working in a foreign country can bring about an experience called *culture shock*. When you've spent years acting certain ways and expecting normal, everyday events to follow a specific course of action, you might find yourself disoriented when things don't go as you expected.

One of the ways you can avoid culture shock is to read about the country you're going to work in before getting there. The Internet is a great resource for information such as this. Your local library is another place to research customs and acceptable practices in foreign countries.

When in doubt about a custom or what you should do in a given situation, ask your hosts or a trusted contact from the company you'll be working with to help you. People are people all over the world, and they love to talk about themselves and their culture. They're also generally helpful, and they will respect you more for asking what's expected rather than acting as though you know what to do when you clearly do not.

Diversity Training

Sometimes you might find yourself working with teams of people from different countries or cultures. Some team members might be from one country and some from another. The best way to ensure that cultural or ethical differences do not hinder your project is to provide training for all team members.

Team-building activities are ways to build mutual trust and respect and bond team members with differing backgrounds. Choose activities that are inoffensive and ones in which everyone can participate.

Diversity training makes people aware of differences between cultures and ethnic groups, and it helps them to gain respect and trust for those on their team. Provide training regarding the project objectives and the company culture as well.

NOTE Remember that project objectives are why you are all together in the first place. Keeping the team focused on the objectives cuts across cultural boundaries and will help everyone concentrate on the project and tasks at hand rather than each other.

Respecting Your Neighbors

Americans tend to run their lives at high speed and get right down to business when working with vendors or customers. It isn't unusual for a businessperson to board a plane in the morning, show up at the client site and take care of business, and hop another flight to the next client site that night.

You'll find that this is not that common in many other countries. People in other countries will often expect you to take time to get to know them first, building an atmosphere of trust and respect. Some cultures build relationships first and then proceed to business. And don't expect to do that relationship building in a few hours. It could take several days, depending on the culture. They might even want you to meet their family and spend time getting to know them. Resist the urge to get right down to business if that's not customary in the culture because you'll likely spoil the deal or damage relationships past the point of repair.

NOTE Spend time building relationships with others. Once an atmosphere of mutual trust and cooperation is established, all aspects of project planning and management—including negotiating and problem solving—are much easier to navigate.

Perceiving Experiences

All of us see the world through our own experiences. Your experiences are not someone else's experiences, and therefore what you perceive about a situation might be very different from what others believe. Keep this in mind when it appears that a misunderstanding has occurred or that someone you're working with didn't respond as you expected. This is especially true when you're working with someone from another country. Always give others the benefit of the doubt and ask for clarification if you think there is a problem. Put your feelings in check temporarily, and remember that what you think the other person means is not necessarily as it appears.

Fairness

Fairness includes avoiding favoritism and discrimination against others, avoiding and reporting conflict of interest situations, and maintaining impartiality in our decision making process. We'll focus on conflict of interest in this section.

Conflict of Interest

The *PMI Code of Ethics and Professional Conduct* discusses your responsibility to report to the stakeholders, customers, or others any actions or circumstances that could be construed as a *conflict of interest*.

A conflict of interest is when you put your personal interests above the interests of the project or when you use your influence to cause others to make decisions in your favor without regard for the project outcome. In other words, your personal interests take precedence over your professional obligations, and you make decisions that allow you to personally benefit regardless of the outcome of the project. Let's look at a few examples.

Associations and Affiliations

Conflicts of interest might include your associations or affiliations. For example, perhaps your brother-in-law owns his own construction company and you are the project manager who has just published an RFP. Your brother-in-law bids on the project and ends up winning the bid.

If you sit on the decision committee and don't tell anyone about your association with the winning bidder, that is clearly a conflict of interest. If you influence the bid decision so that it goes to your brother-in-law, he benefits from your position—again, a conflict of interest. You put your personal interests, or in this case the interests of your associations, above the project outcome. Even if you did not influence the decision in any way, when others on the project discover the winning bidder is your brother-in-law, they will assume a conflict of interest occurred. This could jeopardize the awarding of the bid and your own position as well.

The correct thing to do in this case would be to, first, inform the project sponsor and the decision committee that your brother-in-law intends to bid on the project. Second, refrain from participating on the award decision committee so as not to unduly influence others in favor of your brother-in-law. And last, if you've done all these things and your brother-in-law still wins the bid, appoint someone else in your organization to administer the contract and make the payments for the work performed by him. Also, make certain you document the decisions you make regarding the activities performed by him and keep them with the project files. The more documentation you have, the less likely someone can make a conflict of interest accusation stick.

Vendor Gifts

Some professionals work in situations where they are not allowed to accept gifts in excess of certain dollar amounts. This might be driven by company policy, the department manager's policy, and so on. I have worked in organization where it was considered a conflict of interest to accept anything from a vendor, including gifts (no matter how small), meals, or even a cup of coffee. Vendors and suppliers often provide their customers and potential customers with lunches, gifts, ballgame tickets, and the like. It's your responsibility to know whether a policy exists that forbids you from accepting these gifts. It's also your responsibility to inform the vendor if they've gone over the limit and you are unable to accept the gift.

The same situation can occur here as with the brother-in-law example earlier. If you accept an expensive gift from a vendor and later award that vendor a contract or a piece of the project work, it looks like and probably is a conflict of interest. This violates PMI guidelines and doesn't look good for you personally either.

NOTE

Using the "I didn't know there was a policy" reasoning probably won't save you when there's a question of conflict of interest. Make it your business to find out whether the organization has a conflict of interest policy and understand exactly what it says. Get a copy, and keep it with your files. Review it periodically. Put a note on your calendar every six months to reread the policy to keep it fresh in your mind. This is a case where not knowing what you don't know can hurt you.

Don't accept gifts that might be construed as a conflict of interest. If your organization does not have a policy regarding vendor gifts, set limits for yourself depending on the situation, the history of gift acceptance by the organization in the past, and the complexity of the project. It's always better to decline a gift you're unsure about than to accept it and later lose your credibility, your reputation, or your PMP status because of bad judgment.

Stakeholder Influence

Another potential area for conflict of interest comes from stakeholders. Stakeholders are usually folks with a good deal of authority and an important position in the company. Make certain you are not putting your own personal interests above the interests of the project when you're dealing with powerful stakeholders. They might have the ability to promote you or reward you in other ways. That's not a bad thing, but if you let that get in the way of the project or let a stakeholder twist your arm with promises like this, you're getting mighty close to a conflict of interest. Always weigh your decisions with the objectives of the project and the organization in mind—not your own personal gain.

Keep in mind that you might not always be on the receiving end of the spectrum. You should not offer inappropriate gifts or services or use confidential information you have at your disposal to assist others because this can also be considered a conflict of interest.

Real World Scenario

The Golf Trip

Amanda Lewis is a project manager for a network upgrade project for her organization. This project will be outsourced to a vendor. Amanda will manage the vendor's work. She also wrote the RFP and is a member of the selection committee.

The project consists of converting the organization's network from 100MB Ethernet to Gigabit Ethernet. This requires replacing all of the routers and switches. Some of the cabling in the buildings will need to be replaced as well. The RFP requires that the vendor who wins the bid install all the new equipment and replace the network interface cards in each of the servers with Gigabit Ethernet cards. The grand total for this project is estimated at $1.2 million.

Steve James is a vendor with whom Amanda has worked in the past. Steve is very interested in winning this bid. He drops in on Amanda one day shortly after the RFP is posted.

"Amanda, it's good to see you," Steve says. "I was in the neighborhood and thought I'd stop in to see how things are going."

"I'm great" Amanda replies. "I'll bet you're here to talk to me about that RFP. You know I can't say anything until the whole process closes."

"You bet we bid on the project. I know you can't talk about the RFP, so I won't bring it up. I wanted to chat with you about something else. My company is sending 15 lucky contestants and one friend each to Scottsdale, Arizona, for a 'conference.' The conference includes the use of the Scottsdale Golf Club (green fees paid, of course), and all the hotel and meal expenses are on us for the length of the trip. I know Scottsdale is one of your favorite places to golf, so I thought of you. What do you say?"

Amanda sits forward in her chair and looks at Steve for a minute. "That sounds fabulous, and I do love Scottsdale. But you and I both know this isn't a conference. I wouldn't feel right about accepting it."

"Come on, Amanda. Don't look a gift horse in the mouth. It is a conference. I'll be there and so will the top brass from the company. We have some presentations and demonstrations we'd like to show you while you're there, no obligation of course, and then you're free to spend the rest of the time however you'd like."

"I appreciate the offer. Thanks for thinking of me, but no thanks. I'm on the selection committee for the RFP, and it would be a conflict of interest if I attended this conference. Besides, the value of the conference is over the $100 limit our company sets for vendor gifts and meals," Amanda says.

"OK, we'll miss you. Maybe next time."

Honesty

Honesty can include a lot of topics: reporting the truth regarding project status, being honest about your own experience, not deceiving others, not making false statements, and so on.

One of the aspects of honesty includes your truthfulness about your PMP application and certification, your qualifications, and the continuing reports you provide to PMI to maintain your certification. Let's look at a few others.

Personal Gain

Honesty involves not only information regarding your own background and experience, but information regarding the project circumstances as well. For example, let's say you're a project manager working on contract. Part of your compensation consists of a bonus based on total project billing. Now let's suppose your project is finishing sooner than anticipated, and this means your personal profit will decrease by $1,500. Should you stretch the work to meet the original contracted amount so that your personal bonus comes in at the full amount even though your project team is finished? I think you know the answer is of course not.

Your personal gain should never be a consideration when billing a customer or working on a project. Personal gain should never be a factor in any project decision. If the project finishes sooner than planned, you should bill the customer according to the terms of the procurement agreement. Compromising the project for the sake of your personal gain shows a lack of integrity, which could ultimately cost you your PMP status and even your job.

Truthful Reporting

As a project manager, you are responsible for truthfully reporting all information in your possession to stakeholders, customers, the project sponsor, and the public when required. Always be up front regarding the project's progress.

NOTE

Nothing good will come of telling stakeholders or customers that the project is on track and everything looks great when in fact the project is behind schedule or several unplanned risk events have occurred that have thrown the project team a curveball. I've personally witnessed the demise of the careers of project managers who chose this route.

Tell the truth regarding project status, even when things don't look good. Stakeholders will likely go to great lengths to help you solve problems or brainstorm solutions. Sometimes, though, the call needs to be made to kill the project. This decision is usually made by the project sponsor or the stakeholders based on your recommendation and predictions of future project activities. Don't skew the reporting to prevent stakeholders from making this decision when it is the best solution based on the circumstances.

Truthful reporting is required when working with the public as well. When working in situations where the public is at risk, truthfully report the facts of the situation and what steps you're taking to counteract or reduce the threats. I recommend you get approval from the organization regarding public announcements prior to reporting the facts. Many organizations have public relations departments that will handle this situation for you.

> **NOTE** You probably remember something your mother always told you: Actions speak louder than words. Always remember that you lead by example. Your team members are watching. If you are driven by high personal ethics and a strong desire for providing excellent customer service, those who work for you will likely follow your lead.

Role Delineation Study

In addition to the areas covered in the *PMI Code of Ethics and Professional Conduct*, you should be aware of four other focus areas that PMI discusses in its role delineation study. This study was published in PMI's publication *Project Management Professional (PMP®) Examination Specification*. The four focus areas are as follows:

- Ensure Personal Integrity and Professionalism
- Contribute to the Project Management Knowledge Base
- Enhance Personal Professional Competence
- Promote Interaction Among Team Members & Other Stakeholders

I've covered most of the concepts surrounding these focus areas throughout this chapter with the exception of contributing to the project management knowledge base. We'll look at that topic next.

Applying Professional Knowledge

Professional knowledge involves the knowledge of project management practices as well as specific industry or technical knowledge required to complete an assignment.

As a PMP, you should apply project management knowledge to all your projects. Take the opportunity to educate others by keeping them up-to-date on project management practices, training your team members to use the correct techniques, informing stakeholders of the correct processes, and then sticking to those processes throughout the course of the project. This isn't always easy, especially when the organization doesn't have any formal processes in place. But once the stakeholders see the benefits of good project management practices, they'll never go back to the "old" way of performing their projects.

One way to apply professional knowledge is to become and remain knowledgeable in project management best practices techniques. I'll cover this topic next along with how to become a PMI education provider and the importance of having industry knowledge.

Project Management Knowledge

Project management is a growing field. Part of your responsibility as a PMP is to stay abreast of project management practices, theories, and techniques. You can do this in many ways, one of which includes joining a local PMI chapter. There are hundreds of local chapters throughout the United States and in other countries as well. You can check the PMI website (`www.pmi.org`) to find a chapter near you.

Chapter meetings give you the opportunity to meet other project managers, find out what techniques they're using, and seek advice regarding your project. Usually guest speakers appear at each chapter meeting and share their experiences and tips. Their stories are always interesting, and they give you the opportunity to learn from someone else's experiences and avoid making wrong turns on your next project. You might have a few stories of your own worth sharing with your local chapter. Volunteer to be a speaker at an upcoming meeting, and let others learn from your experiences.

One of the things you'll get when you join the PMI organization and pay your yearly dues is its monthly magazine. This publication details real-life projects and the techniques and issues project managers have to deal with on those projects. Reading the magazine is a great way to learn new project management techniques or reinforce the information you already know. You might discover how to apply some of the knowledge you've already learned in more efficient ways as well.

PMI offers educational courses through their local chapters and at the national level as well. These are yet another way for you to learn about project management and meet others in your field.

Education Providers

PMI has a program that allows you or your organization to become a Registered Education Provider (REP). This enables you—once you're certified—to conduct PMI-sanctioned project management training, seminars, and conferences. The best part is that your attendees are awarded professional development units (PDUs) for attending the training or seminar. As a PMP, and especially as an REP, you have a responsibility to the profession and to the PMI to provide truthful information regarding the PMI certification process, the exam applications, the PDU requirements, and so on. Keep up-to-date on the PMI's certification process by periodically checking the website.

Industry Knowledge

Contributing and applying professional knowledge goes beyond project management experience. You likely have specific industry or technical experience as well. Part of applying your professional knowledge includes gaining knowledge of your particular industry and keeping others informed of advances in these areas.

Information technology has grown exponentially over the past several years. It used to be that if you specialized in network operations, for example, it was possible to learn and become proficient in all things related to networks. Today that is no longer the case. Each specialized area within information technology has grown to become a knowledge area in and of itself. Many other fields have either always had individual specialties or just recently experienced this phenomenon, including the medical field, bioengineering, manufacturing, and pharmaceuticals, to name a few. You need to stay up-to-date regarding your industry so that you can apply that knowledge effectively. Today's fast-paced advances can leave you behind fairly quickly if you don't stay on top of things.

I mentioned in the beginning of the book that as a project manager you are not required to be a technical expert, and that still holds true. But it doesn't hurt to stay abreast of industry trends and knowledge in your field and have a general understanding of the specifics of your business. Again, you can join industry associations and take educational classes to stay on top of breaking trends and technology in your industry.

Real World Scenario

Project Case Study: New Kitchen Heaven Retail Store

Dirk strolls into your office maintaining his formal and dignified manners as always and then sits down in the chair beside your desk.

"I just want to congratulate you on a job well done," he says. "The grand opening was a success, and the store had a better-than-expected week the first week. I'm impressed you were able to pull this off and get the store opened prior to the Garden and Home Show. That was the key to the great opening week."

"Thank you, Dirk. Lots of people put in a lot of hard work and extra hours to get this job done. I'm glad you're happy with the results."

"I thought the banner with our logo, 'Great Gadgets for People Interested in Great Food,' was a wonderful touch."

"That was Jill's idea. She had some great ideas that made the festivities successful. As you know, though," you continue, "we did have some problems on this project. Fortunately, they weren't insurmountable, but I think we learned a thing or two during this project that we can carry forward to other projects."

"Like what?" Dirk asks.

"We should have contracted with Gomez Construction sooner so that we didn't have to pay overtime. We had a very generous budget, so the overtime expense didn't impact this project, but it might impact the next one.

"And we came fairly close to having a hardware disaster on our hands. Next time, we should order the equipment sooner, test it here at headquarters first, and then ship it out to the site after we know everything is working correctly."

"Good ideas. But that's old news. Now that this project is over, I'd like to get you started on the next project. We're going to introduce cooking classes in all of our retail stores. The focus is the home chef, and we might just call the classes the Home Chef Pro series. We'll offer basic classes all the way to professional series classes if the project is a hit. We'll bring in guest chefs from the local areas to give demos and teach some of the classes as well."

"I'm very interested in taking on this project and can't wait to get started. I'm thrilled that you want me to head this up. But I do have a few things here to wrap up before I start work on the new project," you reply.

Dirk says, "The project is over. The grand opening was a success. It's time to move on. Let Jill take over now; the retail stores are her responsibility."

"Jill has taken over the day-to-day operations. However, I've got to finish collecting the project information, close out the contract with Gomez, and make the final payment. Jake verified that all the work was completed correctly and to his satisfaction. Then I need to publish the formal acceptance notice to all of the stakeholders via email. I will also create a document that outlines those things I told you earlier that we should remember and reference during the next project; that document is called *lessons learned*. Then after all those things are completed, all of the project records need to be indexed and archived. I can have all that done by the end of the week and will be free starting Monday to work on requirements gathering and the charter document for the new project."

"This is just like the planning process discussion we got into with the tree, the breakdown structure thing, and all the planning, I suspect. I do have to admit all the planning paid off. I'll give you until the end of the week to close out this project. Come see me Monday to get started on Home Chef Pro."

Jill Overstreet thought you did such a great job of managing this project that she has offered to buy you lunch at one of those upscale, white tablecloth–type French restaurants. The iced teas have just been delivered, and you and Jill are chatting about business.

"I'm impressed with your project management skills. This store opening was the best on record. And you really kept Dirk in line—I admire that. He can be headstrong, but you had a way of convincing him what needed doing and then sticking to it."

"Thanks," you reply. "I've got several years of project management experience, so many of those lessons learned on previous projects helped me out with this project. I enjoy project management and read books and articles on the subject whenever I get the chance. It's nice when you can learn from others' mistakes and avoid making them yourself."

Jill takes a long drink of tea. She glances at you over the top of her glass and pauses before setting it down. "You know," Jill starts, "we almost didn't hire anyone for your position. Dirk wanted to do away with the project management role altogether. He had a real distaste for project management after our last project."

"Why is that?"

"The last project manager got involved in a conflict of interest situation. She was working on a project that involved updating and remodeling all the existing stores. Things like new fixtures, signs, shelving, display cases, and such were up for bid. And it was a very sizable bid. Not only did she accept an all-expenses-paid weekend visit to a resort town from one of the vendors bidding on the contract, she also revealed company secrets to them, some of which leaked to our competitors."

Your mouth drops open. "I can't believe she would accept gifts like that from a vendor. And revealing company secrets is even worse. Conflict of interest situations and not protecting intellectual property violate the code of professional conduct that we agree to adhere as certified PMPs. I can understand why Dirk didn't want to hire another project manager. Behavior like that makes all project managers look bad."

"I'm glad you kept things above board and won Dirk back over. The project management role is important to Kitchen Heaven, and I know your skills in this discipline are what made this project such a success."

"Jill, not only would I never compromise my own integrity through a conflict of interest situation, I would report the situation and the vendor to the project sponsor and to the PMI as an ethics violation. It's better to be honest and let the project sponsor or key stakeholders know what's happening than to hide the situation or, even worse, compromise your own integrity by getting involved in it in the first place. You have my word that I'll keep business interests above my own personal interests. I'll report anything that even looks like it would call my actions into question just to keep things honest and out in the open."

"That's good to hear," Jill replies. "Congratulations on your new assignment. Dirk and I were discussing the new Home Chef Pro project yesterday. We're venturing into new territory with this project, and I'm confident you'll do an excellent job heading it up. Dirk made a good choice."

Project Case Study Checklist

- Close Project or Phase
  - Product verification (work was correct and satisfactory)
  - Collecting project documents
  - Disseminating final acceptance notice
  - Documenting lessons learned
  - Archiving project records
- Close Procurements
  - Product verification (work was correct and satisfactory)
  - Formal acceptance and closure

- Adhering to the *PMI Code of Ethics and Professional Conduct*
  - Ensuring personal and professional integrity
  - Not placing personal gain above business needs
  - Avoiding conflict of interest situations
  - Truthfully reporting questionable situations and maintaining honesty
  - Protecting intellectual property

Understanding How This Applies to Your Next Project

Closing out the project should always include a formal sign-off (from the project sponsor and key stakeholders at a minimum) that the work of the project is acceptable and complete. Also, you've probably experienced, as I have, stakeholders with short-term memory lapses. For example, I'll get to the end of the project and find the stakeholder has a list of additional requirements longer than their arm. Some of this goes back to assuring that requirements are accurately defined during the Planning processes and that ongoing communication regarding project status, along with feedback from the stakeholders, is occurring on a regular basis. Another key here is making certain you are managing stakeholder expectations throughout the project. You might indeed have identified all the requirements and accurately documented the objective of the project. But if the stakeholder had expectations that weren't captured or that took shape after the work of the project began, you could end up with a very unhappy stakeholder on your hands and, potentially, a failed project. In my experience, stakeholder expectations tend to stray midway through the project. That's because they are beginning to see nearly completed deliverables and new possibilities for the product begin to develop that they hadn't thought of during the Planning stage. It's similar to buying a new house based on blueprints and then going on that first walk-through when the framing is finished. It's during walk-through that you think, "Gee, I thought that closet was bigger than this." Tune in to what your stakeholders are saying and get at the basis of their questions (dig deep) so that there are no hidden expectations and you're able to manage any new expectations that pop up.

The professional responsibility section of this chapter can easily be boiled down to the golden rule, "Do unto others as you would have them do unto you." I wish I could tell you that everything I talked about here is practiced by all project managers everywhere. But you've likely read, as I have, the endless stories in the news of this corporate exec or the other acting in their own best interest rather than that of the organization. Project managers make the news as well, especially when they're working on projects that involve public funds or charitable organizations. In my humble opinion, ignoring the practices and advice in this chapter isn't worth the damage it might cause to my organization, to the project, or to my career.

I'd also add that if your first thought on a new project is what a great résumé builder it's going to be for you and how you'll likely score that next big promotion after the project is complete, you've started off on the wrong foot. Although I'm the first to admit big projects (when they are executed well and satisfy the stakeholder expectations) *are* résumé builders, it's the wrong reason to take on a project. Consider your experience level and how and what you'll be able to contribute to the project to make it a success. It's OK if the project is a stretch for you—you can't grow your experience without taking on more complex projects as your career progresses. But also be wise enough to know when you might be in over your head.

There's no substitute for integrity and honesty when conducting your projects. Once you've tarnished your integrity, whether intentional or not, it's almost impossible to regain the trust of your stakeholders and management staff. Because of this, I'm never afraid of telling anyone, "I don't know," but I always follow it up with, "But I'll find out." You're a project manager, not a miracle worker. No one expects you to have all the answers any-more than they expect you to perform every single task on the project.

I've had the unfortunate experience of being instructed to lie about project status and to purposely withhold project information from oversight boards. I spent a few sleepless nights worrying about where I'd find my next job because I immediately disobeyed those orders and reported the truth. I knew it would cost me my job. But I also knew it was better for me to lose the job than to compromise my integrity. As it turned out, I found a new job quickly. And in retrospect, if I had not left the position when I did, my reputation would have taken a hit—not because of anything I had done but through association with the people on the project who had compromised when they shouldn't have.

I hope you've found this study guide helpful both for your studies for the PMP exam and for your next project. Thank you for spending some time with me in the pages of this book. I wish you the best of luck in your project management endeavors.

Summary

Project closure is the most often neglected process of all the project management processes. The two processes in the Closing process group are Close Project or Phase and Close Pro-curements. The four most important tasks of closure are as follows:

- Checking the work for completeness and accuracy
- Documenting formal acceptance
- Disseminating project closure information
- Archiving records and lessons learned

Close Project or Phase involves checking that the work of the project was completed cor-rectly and to the satisfaction of the stakeholders. Documenting formal acceptance of the product of the project is an important aspect of project closure as well. This assures that the stakeholder or customer is satisfied with the work and that it meets their needs.

Projects come to an end in one of four ways: addition, starvation, integration, or extinction. Addition is when projects evolve into their own business unit. Starvation happens because the project is starved of its resources. Integration occurs when resources are taken from the existing project and dispersed back into the organization or assigned to other projects. And extinction is the best end because the project was completed, accepted, and closed.

Close Project or Phase is performed at the end of each phase of the project as well as at the end of the project. Close Project or Phase involves documenting formal acceptance and disseminating notice of acceptance to the stakeholders, customer, and others. All documentation gathered during the project and collected during this process is archived and saved for reference purposes on future projects.

Close Procurements is concerned with settling the contract and completing the contract according to its terms. Its primary outputs include the contract file and formal acceptance and closure (both are components of the organizational process assets update).

Lessons learned document the successes and failures of the project and of the procurement processes. Many times lessons learned are not documented because staff members do not want to assign their names to project errors or failures. You and your management team need to work together to assure employees that lessons learned are not exercises used for disciplinary purposes but benefit both the employee and the organization. Documenting what you've learned from past experiences lets you carry this forward to new projects so that the same errors are not repeated. It also allows you to incorporate new methods of performing activities that you learned on past projects.

Project management professionals are responsible for reporting truthful information about their PMP status and project management experience to prospective customers, clients, and employers and to the PMI. As a project manager, you're responsible for the integrity of the project management process and the product. In all situations, you are responsible for your own personal integrity.

Personal integrity means adhering to an ethical standard. As a PMP, you'll be required to adhere to the *PMI Code of Ethics and Professional Conduct* established by the PMI. Part of this code involves avoiding putting your own personal gain above the project objectives.

As a professional, you should strive to maintain honesty in project reporting. You're required to abide by laws, rules, and regulations regarding your industry and project management practices. You should also report any instances that might appear to be a conflict of interest. It's always better to inform others of an apparent conflict than to have it discovered by others and have your methods called into question after the fact.

You will likely come across confidential information or intellectual property during your project management experiences. Respect the use of this information and always verify who might have permission to access the information and when disclosures are required.

Stakeholders have competing needs and business issues and as such will sometimes cause conflict on your project. You will be required to balance the needs and interests of the stakeholders with the project objectives.

Many project managers today are working in a global environment. It's important to respect and understand the cultural differences that exist and not try to impose your cultural beliefs on others. Culture shock is an experience that occurs when you find yourself in a different cultural environment than you're familiar with. Training is a good way to provide project team members with relationship management techniques regarding cultural and ethnic differences.

Exam Essentials

Be able to name the primary activity of the Closing processes. The primary activity of the Closing processes is to distribute information that formalizes project completion.

Be able to describe when the Close Project or Phase process is performed. Close Project or Phase is performed at the close of each project phase and at the close of the project.

Be able to define the purpose for lessons learned. The purpose of lessons learned is to describe the project successes and failures and to use the information learned on future projects.

Be able to name the publication that describes the ethical standard to which PMPs are required to adhere. The ethical standard PMPs are required to adhere to is described in the *PMI Code of Ethics and Professional Conduct*.

Describe the areas in which PMPs must apply professional knowledge. PMPs must apply professional knowledge in the areas of project management practices, industry practices, and technical areas.

Know the key activity that ensures customer satisfaction. The key activity that ensures customer satisfaction is documenting project requirements and meeting them.

Define how multinational project managers must manage relationships. Multinational project managers manage relationships by building relationships based on mutual trust and acceptance and recognizing and respecting diverse cultures and ethnic beliefs.

Key Terms

We discussed two processes in this chapter that you need to understand for the exam.

Close Procurements

Close Project or Phase

Once again, you've learned some new key words in this chapter. PMI has worked hard to develop and define standard project management terms that apply across industries. Here are the terms you came across in this chapter:

addition

conflict of interest

culture shock

formal acceptance and closure

extinction

integration

PMI Code of Ethics and Professional Conduct

procurement audits

procurement file

product verification

starvation

Review Questions

1. You are the project manager for a top-secret software project for an agency of the United States government. Your mission—should you choose to accept it—is to complete the project using internal resources. The reason is that finding contractors with top-secret clearances takes quite a bit of time, and waiting for clearances would jeopardize the implementation date. Your programmers are 80 percent of the way through the programming and testing work when your agency appoints a new executive director. Slowly but surely your programmers are taken off this project and reassigned to the executive director's hot new project. Which of the following type of project ending is this?

   A. Starvation

   B. Extinction

   C. Addition

   D. Integration

2. You are a project manager for Cinema Snicker Productions. Your company specializes in producing comedy films for the big screen. Your latest project has just been canceled because of budget cuts. Which of the following statements is true?

   A. This project ended due to starvation because the funding was cut off.

   B. This project ended due to integration because the resources were distributed elsewhere.

   C. This project ended due to starvation because the resources were distributed elsewhere.

   D. This project ended due to integration because the funding was cut off.

3. You are a project manager for Cinema Snicker Productions. Your company specializes in producing comedy films for the big screen. Your latest project has just been completed and accepted. You've been given your next project, which starts right away. Which of the following statements is true?

   A. This project ended due to extinction because it was completed and accepted.

   B. This project ended due to integration because it was completed and accepted and the project manager moved on to a new project.

   C. This project ended due to addition because it was completed and accepted and archived into the company's catalog of available films.

   D. This project ended due to integration because it was completed and accepted.

4. You are a project manager for Dutch Harbor Consulting. Your latest project involves the upgrade of an organization's operating system on 236 servers. You performed this project under contract. You are in the Close Procurements process and know that you should document which of the following? (Choose the best response.)

   A. Administrative closure procedures

   B. Close Procurements procedures

   C. Formal acceptance

   D. Product verification

5. You are a project manager for Dutch Harbor Consulting. Your latest project involves the upgrade of an organization's operating system on 236 servers. You performed this project under contract. You are in the Close Procurements process and have reviewed the contracting process to identify lessons learned. What is the name of the tool and technique you used to perform this function?
   - A. Procurement audits
   - B. Performance reviews
   - C. Performance audits
   - D. Procurement reviews
6. Your project was just completed. Because of some unfortunate circumstances, the project was delayed, causing cost overruns at the end of the project. Which of the following statements is true?
   - A. You should document the circumstances as lessons learned.
   - B. You should pay particular attention to archiving the financial records for this project.
   - C. Your project ended because of starvation because of the cost overruns.
   - D. You should document the circumstances surrounding the project completion during the Scope Verification process.
7. Procurement audits review which of the following?
   - A. The procurement processes from Plan Procurements through Administer Procurements
   - B. The procurement processes from Plan Procurements through Close Procurements
   - C. The Plan Procurements and Conduct Procurements processes
   - D. The procurement processes from Plan Procurements through Close Project or Phase process
8. As a project manager, you're responsible for maintaining and ensuring integrity for all of the following except which one?
   - A. Personal integrity of others
   - B. Project management process
   - C. Personal integrity
   - D. Product integrity
9. You are a project manager working on contract. You've performed earned value analysis and discovered that the project will be completed on time and under the original estimated amount. This means the profit to your company will decrease as will your personal bonus. Which of the following should you do?
   - A. Add activities to the project to increase the cost enough to meet the original estimated amount.
   - B. Tell the customer you're adding requirements to the project that were originally cut because of cost constraints.
   - C. Upon completion, inform the customer the project has come in under budget.
   - D. Bill the customer for the full amount of the contract because this was the original agreed-upon price.

10. You are a project manager for a manufacturing firm that produces Civil War–era replicas and memorabilia. You discover a design error during a test production run on your latest project. Time is a critical constraint on this project. Which of the following is the most likely response to this problem?
   A. Reduce the technical requirements so that the error is no longer valid.
   B. Go forward with production, and ignore the error.
   C. Go forward with production, but inform the customer of the problem.
   D. Develop alternative solutions to address the error.

11. You are a project manager for a telecommunications firm. You're working on a project that entails upgrading technical hardware and equipment. The estimated cost of the hardware and equipment is $1,725,000. You are reviewing products from three different vendors. One of the competing vendors invites you to lunch. What is the most appropriate response?
   A. Thank them, but let them know this could be a conflict of interest since you haven't made a decision about which vendor you're going to choose.
   B. Thank them, and decline. You know this could be considered personal gain, which could call your integrity into question.
   C. Thank them, and accept. You don't believe there is a conflict of interest or a personal integrity issue.
   D. Thank them, and decline. You believe this could be a conflict of interest on the part of the vendor, and you don't want to encourage that behavior.

12. You are a project manager for a telecommunications firm. You're working on a project that entails upgrading technical hardware and equipment. The estimated cost of the hardware and equipment is $1,725,000. You are reviewing products from three vendors. One of the vendors offers you and your family the use of the company yacht for the upcoming three-day weekend. What is the most appropriate response?
   A. Thank them, and accept. You don't believe there is a conflict of interest or an integrity issue at stake.
   B. Thank them, and decline. You know this could be considered personal gain, which could call your integrity into question.
   C. Thank them, and accept. Immediately report your actions to the project sponsor so that your motives are not called into question after the fact.
   D. Thank them, and decline. You know this could be considered an integrity issue on the part of the vendor.

13. You are a project manager working on contract with a company in a foreign country. At the project kickoff meeting, you are given an expensive-looking gift. The person who presented this to you said that it is customary in their country to give their business partners gifts. What is the most appropriate response?

    A. Thank them, and decline. Explain that this is considered personal gain, which is unacceptable in your country.

    B. Thank them, and accept. You don't believe there is a conflict of interest or an integrity issue at stake.

    C. Thank them, and decline. Explain that this is considered a conflict of interest, which is unacceptable in your country.

    D. Thank them, and accept since you know that it would be considered offensive to decline the gift in their culture. Immediately report the acceptance of the gift to the appropriate parties at your company so that your actions are not called into question later.

14. Life seems to be going very well for your close friend, a fellow PMP. She has taken a trip to France, bought a new car, and stocked her wine cellar with a couple dozen expensive bottles of wine, all within the last six months. After a few cocktails one evening, she tells you her secret. The vendor she's working with on the $4 billion project she's managing has given her all of these items as gifts. Which scenario is the most appropriate? (Choose the best answer.)

    A. You tell your friend these gifts probably aren't appropriate and leave it at that.

    B. You and your friend have a long conversation about the gifts, and she decides to return them (with the exception of the trip) and not accept any more gifts in the future.

    C. You're happy for your friend and say nothing.

    D. Your friend doesn't see a problem with accepting these gifts at all. You know this is a conflict of interest situation and should be reported as an ethical violation.

15. As a project manager, you know that the most important activity to ensure customer and stakeholder satisfaction is which of the following?

    A. Documenting and meeting the requirements

    B. Documenting and meeting the performance measurements

    C. Reporting changes and updating the project plan and other project documents where appropriate

    D. Reporting project status regularly and in a timely manner

16. Your upcoming project includes project team members from a foreign country. To make certain that cultural differences don't interfere with team performance, thereby affecting the success of the project, your first course of action is to do which of the following?

    A. Provide diversity training to all the team members.

    B. Co-locate the project team.

    C. Perform team-building exercises.

    D. Inform the team members of the organization's rules and standards.

17. You are a contract project manager working with the State of Bliss. Your latest project involves rewriting the Department of Revenue's income tax system. One of the key stakeholders is a huge movie buff, and she has the power to promote you into a better position at the conclusion of this project. She has discovered that one of her favorite superstars lives in the State of Bliss and therefore must file income tax returns in that state. She asks you to look up the account of this movie star. What is the most appropriate response?

A. Report her to the management team.

B. Refuse to comply with the request, citing conflict of interest and violation of confidential company data.

C. Look up the information she has requested. Since the data is considered part of the project, there is no conflict of interest.

D. You believe that tax records are public information, so you comply with the request.

18. You are a contract project manager working with the State of Bliss. Your latest project involves rewriting the Department of Revenue's income tax system. As project manager, you have taken all the appropriate actions regarding confidentiality of data. One of the key stakeholders is a huge movie buff, and she has the power to promote you into a better position at the conclusion of this project. She's reviewing some report data that just happens to include confidential information regarding one of her favorite movie superstars. What is the most appropriate response?

A. Report her to the management team.

B. Request that she immediately return the information, citing conflict of interest and violation of confidential company data.

C. Do nothing, because she has the proper level of access rights to the data and this information showed up unintentionally.

D. Request that she immediately return the information until you can confirm that she has the proper level of access rights to the data.

19. You are a project manager with several years of experience in project management. You've just accepted your first project in a foreign country. You've been in the country a week or two and are experiencing some disorientation. This is known as which of the following?

A. Co-location

B. Diversity shock

C. Global culturing

D. Culture shock

20. You are a project manager for a software manufacturing firm. The project you've just finished created a new software product that is expected to become a number-one seller. All prerelease of software is handled through the marketing department. A friend of yours is a certified software instructor. They have asked you for a copy of the software prior to the beta release so they can get familiar with it. What is the most appropriate response?

    A. Decline the request because the software is the intellectual property of the company.

    B. Ask them to sign a nondisclosure agreement before releasing a copy of the software.

    C. Decline the request since you stand to gain from this transaction by receiving free training.

    D. Since your friend is certified to teach your company's brand of software, provide them with a copy of the software.

Answers to Review Questions

1. D. Integration occurs when resources, equipment, or property are reassigned or redeployed back to the organization or to another project.

2. A. Starvation occurs because the project no longer receives the resources needed to continue. Resources could include people, equipment, money, and the like.

3. A. Extinction is the best type of project end because it means the project was completed successfully and accepted by the sponsor or customer.

4. C. The project manager is responsible for documenting the formal acceptance of the work of the contract. This should be done during Close Procurements when projects are performed under contract or during Close Project or Phase if no work was performed under contract. In cases where part of the work was performed under contract and part with in-house staff, formal acceptance should occur in both of these processes.

5. A. Procurement audits are used to review the procurement process and identify and document any lessons learned during the procurement process for future reference.

6. A. Lessons learned document the experiences, successes, and failures that occurred during this project for future reference. There isn't enough information in the question to determine whether B or D is correct. C is not correct because the project was completed.

7. A. According to the *PMBOK® Guide*, the procurement audit examines the procurement processes from Plan Procurements through Administer Procurements.

8. A. You are not responsible for the personal integrity of others, but as project manager you do have influence over others, such as your project team members.

9. C. Integrity means you'll honestly report project outcomes and status. Your personal gain should not be placed above the satisfaction of the customer.

10. D. The best answer to this problem is to develop alternative solutions to address the design error. Reducing technical requirements might be an alternative solution, but it's not one you'd implement without looking at all the alternatives. Ignoring the error and going forward with production will result in an unsatisfactory product for the customer.

11. A. A luncheon date could be considered a conflict of interest prior to awarding a contract to a vendor. Consider what a competitor of this vendor would think if they spotted you having lunch together.

12. B. The best response to this situation is to thank the vendor and decline based on the fact that this could be considered personal gain on your part. Option D might seem correct, but remember, you're not responsible for the integrity of others. And it's often common business practice for vendors to offer gifts to potential customers.

13. D. The best response in this case is to accept the gift because it would cause great offense to the other party if you were to decline. Report the gift and the circumstances as soon as possible to the appropriate parties at your company.

14. D. This is a conflict of interest situation, and you should report it as a violation of the *PMI Code of Ethics and Professional Conduct*.

15. A. Documenting the requirements and meeting them is one of the key things you can do to ensure customer satisfaction. The requirements describe what the customer is looking for, and the final product is compared against them to determine whether all of the requirements were met.

16. A. The most correct response is to first provide training to your team members to teach them how to respect and work with others from different cultures. Co-location might not be possible when you're working with team members from two different countries. Team-building exercises are a good idea as well but are not your first course of action.

17. B. The situation presented here requires you to put the interest of the company and the confidentiality of the data above your own personal interests or those of your stakeholders. D is not the most correct response because it says you believe the information is public. This implies you haven't verified whether the data is private or public. Until you know, treat the data as confidential. In this case, the information is confidential and should be shared only with those who have a valid reason for using it.

18. C. As project manager, it's your responsibility to make sure the people you will be sharing data with have the proper permissions to see the data; this question indicated that you did that. In this case, D is not correct because it implies that you did not verify ahead of time that the stakeholder had the proper level of approvals to use the data.

19. D. Culture shock is the disoriented feeling that people might experience when working in a foreign country.

20. A. The most appropriate response is to deny the request. Software is considered intellectual property and should not be used for personal gain or given to others without prior consent from the organization. This question states that the release of the beta software is handled through the marketing department, so you should not give your friend a copy of the software outside of this process.

Appendix A

Process Inputs and Outputs

Throughout this book, *PMP: Project Management Professional Study Guide*, I've discussed the inputs and outputs to the PMI processes. In this appendix, you'll find the inputs, tools and techniques, outputs, and Knowledge Areas of the project management processes listed by process in the order they appear in the text. I think you'll appreciate the convenience of having all this information in one location. Enjoy!

Initiating Processes

Table A.1 lists the inputs, tools and techniques, outputs, and Knowledge Areas for the Initiating process group.

TABLE A.1 Initiating Processes

Process Name	Inputs	Tools and Techniques	Outputs	Knowledge Area
Develop Project Charter	Project statement of work	Expert judgment	Project charter	Integration
	Business case			
	Contract			
	Enterprise environmental factors			
	Organizational process assets			
Identify Stakeholders	Project charter	Stakeholder analysis	Stakeholder register	Communication
	Procurement documents	Expert judgment	Stakeholder management strategy	

TABLE A.1 Initiating Processes *(continued)*

Process Name	Inputs	Tools and Techniques	Outputs	Knowledge Area
	Enterprise environmental factors			
	Organizational process assets			

Planning Processes

Table A.2 lists the inputs, tools and techniques, outputs, and Knowledge Areas for the processes in the Planning process group.

TABLE A.2 Planning Processes

Process Name	Inputs	Tools and Techniques	Outputs	Knowledge Area
Develop Project Management Plan	Project charter	Expert judgment	Project management plan	Integration
	Outputs from planning processes			
	Enterprise environmental factors			
	Organizational process assets			
Collect Requirements	Project charter	Interviews	Requirements documentation	Scope
	Stakeholder register	Focus groups	Requirements management plan	
		Facilitated workshops	Requirements traceability matrix	

TABLE A.2 Planning Processes *(continued)*

Process Name	Inputs	Tools and Techniques	Outputs	Knowledge Area
		Group creativity techniques		
		Group decision-making techniques		
		Questionnaires and surveys		
		Observations		
		Prototypes		
Define Scope	Project charter	Expert judgment	Project scope statement	Scope
	Requirements documentation	Product analysis	Project document updates	
	Organizational process assets	Alternatives identification		
		Facilitated workshops		
Create WBS	Project scope statement	Decomposition	Work breakdown structure	Scope
	Requirements documentation		WBS dictionary	
	Organizational process assets		Scope baseline	
			Project document updates	
Define Activities	Scope baseline	Decomposition	Activity list	Time
	Enterprise environmental factors	Rolling wave planning	Activity attributes	

TABLE A.2 Planning Processes *(continued)*

Process Name	Inputs	Tools and Techniques	Outputs	Knowledge Area
	Organizational process assets	Templates	Milestone list	
		Expert judgment		
Sequence Activities	Activity list	Precedence diagramming method (PDM)	Project schedule network diagrams	Time
	Activity attributes	Dependency determination	Project document updates	
	Milestone list	Applying leads and lags		
	Project scope statement	Schedule network templates		
	Organizational process assets			
Estimate Activity Resources	Activity list	Expert judgment	Activity resource requirements	Time
	Activity attributes	Alternatives analysis	Resource breakdown structure	
	Resource calendars	Published estimating data	Project document updates	
	Enterprise environmental factors	Bottom-up estimating		
	Organizational process assets	Project management software		
Estimate Activity Durations	Activity list	Expert judgment	Activity duration estimates	Time
	Activity attributes	Analogous estimating	Project document updates	
	Activity resource requirements	Parametric estimating		

TABLE A.2 Planning Processes *(continued)*

Process Name	Inputs	Tools and Techniques	Outputs	Knowledge Area
	Resource calendars	Three-point estimates		
	Project scope statement	Reserve analysis		
	Enterprise environmental factors			
	Organizational process assets			
Develop Schedule	Activity list	Schedule network analysis	Project schedule	Time
	Activity attributes	Critical path method	Schedule baseline	
	Project schedule network diagrams	Critical chain method	Schedule data	
	Activity resource requirements	Resource leveling	Project document updates	
	Resource calendars	What-if scenario analysis		
	Activity duration estimates	Applying leads and lags		
	Project scope statement	Schedule compression		
	Enterprise environmental factors	Scheduling tool		
	Organizational process assets			
Estimate Costs	Scope baseline	Expert judgment	Activity cost estimates	Cost
	Project schedule	Analogous estimating	Basis of estimates	

TABLE A.2 Planning Processes *(continued)*

Process Name	Inputs	Tools and Techniques	Outputs	Knowledge Area
	Human resource plan	Parametric estimating	Project document updates	
	Risk register	Bottom-up estimating		
	Enterprise environmental factors	Three-point estimate		
	Organizational process assets	Reserve analysis		
		Cost of quality		
		Project management estimating software		
		Vendor bid analysis		
Determine Budget	Activity cost estimates	Cost aggregation	Cost performance baseline	Cost
	Basis of estimates	Reserve analysis	Project funding requirements	
	Scope baseline	Expert judgment	Project document updates	
	Project schedule	Historical relationships		
	Resource calendars	Funding limit reconciliation		
	Contracts			
	Organizational process assets			
Plan Communications	Stakeholder register	Communication requirements analysis	Communications management plan	Communications

TABLE A.2 Planning Processes *(continued)*

Process Name	Inputs	Tools and Techniques	Outputs	Knowledge Area
	Stakeholder management strategy	Communication technology	Project document updates	
	Enterprise environmental factors	Communication models		
	Organizational process assets	Communication methods		
Plan Risk Management	Project scope statement	Planning meetings and analysis	Risk management plan	Risk
	Cost management plan			
	Schedule management plan			
	Communications management plan			
	Enterprise environmental factors			
	Organizational process assets			
Identify Risks	Risk management plan	Documentation reviews	Risk register	Risk
	Activity cost estimates	Information gathering techniques		
	Activity duration estimates	Checklist analysis		
	Scope baseline	Assumptions analysis		
	Stakeholder register	Diagramming techniques		
	Cost management plan	SWOT analysis		

TABLE A.2 Planning Processes *(continued)*

Process Name	Inputs	Tools and Techniques	Outputs	Knowledge Area
	Schedule management plan	Expert judgment		
	Quality management plan			
	Project documents			
	Enterprise environmental factors			
	Organizational process assets			
Perform Qualitative Risk Analysis	Risk register	Risk probability and impact assessment	Risk register updates	Risk
	Risk management plan	Probability and impact matrix		
	Project scope statement	Risk data quality assessment		
	Organizational process assets	Risk categorization		
		Risk urgency assessment		
		Expert judgment		
Perform Quantitative Risk Analysis	Risk register	Data gathering and representation techniques	Risk register updates	Risk
	Risk management plan	Quantitative risk analysis and modeling techniques		
	Cost management plan	Expert judgment		

TABLE A.2 Planning Processes *(continued)*

Process Name	Inputs	Tools and Techniques	Outputs	Knowledge Area
	Schedule management plan			
	Organizational process assets			
Plan Risk Responses	Risk register	Strategies for negative risks or threats	Risk register updates	Risk
	Risk management plan	Strategies for positive risks or opportunities	Risk-related contract decisions	
		Contingent response strategies	Project management plan updates	
		Expert judgment	Project document updates	
Plan Procurements	Scope baseline	Make-or-buy analysis	Procurement management plan	Procurement
	Requirements documentation	Expert judgment	Procurement statements of work	
	Teaming agreements	Contract types	Make-or-buy decisions	
	Risk register		Procurement documents	
	Risk-related contract decisions		Source selection criteria	
	Activity resource requirements		Change requests	
	Project schedule			
	Activity cost estimates			

TABLE A.2 Planning Processes *(continued)*

Process Name	Inputs	Tools and Techniques	Outputs	Knowledge Area
	Cost performance baseline			
	Enterprise environmental factors			
	Organizational process assets			
Develop Human Resource Plan	Activity resource requirements	Organization charts and position descriptions	Human resource plan	Human Resource
	Enterprise environmental factors	Networking		
	Organizational process assets	Organizational theory		
Plan Quality	Scope baseline	Cost-benefit analysis	Quality management plan	Quality
	Stakeholder register	Cost of quality	Quality metrics	
	Cost performance baseline	Control charts	Quality checklists	
	Schedule baseline	Benchmarking	Process improvement plan	
	Risk register	Design of experiments	Project document updates	
	Enterprise environmental factors	Statistical sampling		
	Organizational process assets	Flowcharting		

TABLE A.2 Planning Processes *(continued)*

Process Name	Inputs	Tools and Techniques	Outputs	Knowledge Area
		Proprietary quality management methodologies		
		Additional quality planning tools		

Executing Processes

Table A.3 lists the inputs, tools and techniques, outputs, and Knowledge Areas for the processes in the Executing process group.

TABLE A.3 Executing Processes

Process Name	Inputs	Tools and Techniques	Outputs	Knowledge Area
Direct and Manage Project Execution	Project management plan	Expert judgment	Deliverables	Integration
	Approved change requests	Project management information system	Work performance information	
	Enterprise environmental factors		Change requests	
	Organizational process assets		Project management plan updates	
			Project document updates	
Acquire Project Team	Project management plan	Pre-assignment	Project staff assignments	Human Resource

TABLE A.3 Executing Processes *(continued)*

Process Name	Inputs	Tools and Techniques	Outputs	Knowledge Area
	Enterprise environmental factors	Negotiation	Resource calendars	
	Organizational process assets	Acquisition	Project management plan updates	
		Virtual teams		
Develop Project Team	Project staff assignments	Interpersonal skills	Team performance assessments	Human Resource
	Project management plan	Training	Enterprise environmental factors update	
	Resource calendars	Team-building activities		
		Ground rules		
		Co-location		
		Recognition and rewards		
Manage Project Team	Project staff assignments	Observations and conversation	Enterprise environmental factors updates	Human Resource
	Project management plan	Project performance appraisals	Organizational process assets update	
	Team performance assessments	Conflict management	Change requests	
	Performance reports	Issue log	Project management plan updates	
	Organizational process assets	Interpersonal skills		

TABLE A.3 Executing Processes *(continued)*

Process Name	Inputs	Tools and Techniques	Outputs	Knowledge Area
Conduct Procurements	Project management plan	Bidder conferences	Selected sellers	Procurement
	Procurement documents	Proposal evaluation techniques	Procurement contract award	
	Source selection criteria	Independent estimates	Resource calendars	
	Qualified sellers list	Expert judgment	Change requests	
	Seller proposals	Advertising	Project management plan updates	
	Project documents	Internet search	Project document updates	
	Make-or-buy decisions	Procurement negotiations		
	Teaming agreements			
	Organizational process assets			
Perform Quality Assurance	Project management plan	Plan Quality and Perform Quality Control tools and techniques	Organizational process assets updates	Quality
	Quality metrics	Quality audits	Change requests	
	Work performance information	Process analysis	Project management plan updates	
	Quality control measurements		Project document updates	
Distribute Information	Project management plan	Communication methods	Organizational process assets updates	Communications
	Performance reports	Information distribution tools		

TABLE A.3 Executing Processes *(continued)*

Process Name	Inputs	Tools and Techniques	Outputs	Knowledge Area
	Organizational process assets			
Manage Stakeholder Expectations	Stakeholder register	Communication methods	Organizational process assets updates	Communications
	Stakeholder management strategy	Interpersonal skills	Change requests	
	Project management plan	Management skills	Project management plan updates	
	Issue log		Project document updates	
	Change log			
	Organizational process assets			

Monitoring and Controlling Processes

Table A.4 lists the inputs, tools and techniques, outputs, and Knowledge Areas for the Monitoring and Controlling group processes.

TABLE A.4 Monitoring and Controlling Processes

Process Name	Inputs	Tools and Techniques	Outputs	Knowledge Area
Monitor and Control Project Work	Project management plan	Expert judgment	Change requests	Integration
	Performance reports		Project management plan updates	

TABLE A.4 Monitoring and Controlling Processes *(continued)*

Process Name	Inputs	Tools and Techniques	Outputs	Knowledge Area
	Enterprise environmental factors		Project document updates	
	Organizational process assets			
Perform Integrated Change Control	Project management plan	Expert judgment	Change request status updates	Integration
	Work performance information	Change control meetings	Project management plan updates	
	Change requests		Project document updates	
	Enterprise environmental factors			
	Organizational process assets			
Administer Procurements	Procurement documents	Contract change control system	Procurement documentation	Procurement
	Project management plan	Procurement performance reviews	Organizational process assets updates	
	Contract	Inspections and audits	Change requests	
	Performance reports	Performance reporting	Project management plan updates	
	Approved change requests	Payment systems		
	Work performance information	Claims administration		
		Records management system		

TABLE A.4 Monitoring and Controlling Processes *(continued)*

Process Name	Inputs	Tools and Techniques	Outputs	Knowledge Area
Report Performance	Project management plan	Variance analysis	Performance reports	Communications
	Work performance information	Forecasting methods	Organizational process assets updates	
	Work performance measurements	Communication methods	Change requests	
	Budget forecasts	Reporting systems		
	Organizational process assets			
Monitor and Control Risks	Risk register	Risk reassessment	Risk register updates	Risk
	Project management plan	Risk audits	Organizational process assets updates	
	Work performance information	Variance and trend analysis	Change requests	
	Performance reports	Technical performance measurement	Project management plan updates	
		Reserve analysis	Project document updates	
		Status meetings		
Control Costs	Project management plan	Earned value measurement	Work performance measurements	Cost
	Project funding requirements	Forecasting	Budget forecasts	
	Work performance information	To-complete performance index (TCPI)	Organizational process assets updates	

TABLE A.4 Monitoring and Controlling Processes *(continued)*

Process Name	Inputs	Tools and Techniques	Outputs	Knowledge Area
	Organizational process assets	Performance reviews	Change Requests	
		Variance analysis	Project management plan updates	
		Project management software	Project document updates	
Control Schedule	Project management plan	Performance reviews	Work performance measurements	Time
	Project schedule	Variance analysis	Organizational process assets updates	
	Work performance information	Project management software	Change requests	
	Organizational process assets	Resource leveling	Project management plan updates	
		What-if scenario analysis	Project document updates	
		Adjusting leads and lags		
		Schedule compression		
		Scheduling tool		
Perform Quality Control	Project management plan	Cause-and-effect diagrams	Quality control measurements	Quality
	Quality metrics	Control charts	Validated changes	
	Quality checklists	Flowcharting	Validated deliverables	
	Work performance measurements	Histogram	Organization process assets updates	

TABLE A.4 Monitoring and Controlling Processes *(continued)*

Process Name	Inputs	Tools and Techniques	Outputs	Knowledge Area
	Approved change requests	Pareto chart	Change requests	
	Deliverables	Run chart	Project management plan updates	
	Organizational process assets	Scatter diagram	Project document updates	
		Statistical sampling		
		Inspection		
		Approved change requests review		
Verify Scope	Project management plan	Inspection	Accepted deliverables	Scope
	Requirements documentation		Change requests	
	Requirements traceability matrix		Project document updates	
	Validated deliverables			
Control Scope	Project management plan	Variance analysis	Work performance measurements	Scope
	Work performance information		Organizational process assets updates	
	Requirements documentation		Change requests	
	Requirements traceability matrix		Project management plan updates	
	Organizational process assets		Project document updates	

Closing Processes

Table A.5 lists the inputs, tools and techniques, outputs, and Knowledge Areas for the processes in the Closing process group.

TABLE A.5 Closing Processes

Process Name	Inputs	Tools and Techniques	Outputs	Knowledge Area
Close Project or Phase	Project management plan	Expert judgment	Final product, service, or result transition	Integration
	Accepted deliverables		Organizational process assets updates	
	Organizational process assets			
Close Procurements	Procurement management plan	Procurement audits	Closed procurements	Procurement
	Procurement documentation	Negotiated settlements	Organizational process assets updates	
		Records management system		

Appendix B

About the Companion CD

IN THIS APPENDIX:

- ✓ What you'll find on the CD
- ✓ System requirements
- ✓ Using the CD
- ✓ Troubleshooting

What You'll Find on the CD

The following sections are arranged by category and summarize the software and other goodies you'll find on the CD. If you need help with installing the items provided on the CD, refer to the installation instructions in the "Using the CD" section of this appendix.

Some programs on the CD might fall into one of these categories:

Audio files are MP3 files that can be played on your computer, on music listeners such as iTunes, or burned to a CD and played on an MP3 player.

Shareware programs are fully functional, free, trial versions of copyrighted programs. If you like particular programs, register with their authors for a nominal fee and receive licenses, enhanced versions, and technical support.

Freeware programs are free, copyrighted games, applications, and utilities. You can copy them to as many computers as you like—for free—but they offer no technical support.

GNU software is governed by its own license, which is included inside the folder of the GNU software. There are no restrictions on distribution of GNU software. See the GNU license at the root of the CD for more details.

Trial, *demo*, or *evaluation* versions of software are usually limited either by time or by functionality (such as not letting you save a project after you create it).

Sybex Test Engine

For Windows

The CD contains the Sybex test engine, which includes two bonus exams located only on the CD.

PDF of Glossary of Terms

For Windows

We have included an electronic version of the Glossary in `.pdf` format. You can view the electronic version of the Glossary with Adobe Reader.

Adobe Reader

For Windows

We've also included a copy of Adobe Reader so you can view PDF files that accompany the book's content. For more information on Adobe Reader or to check for a newer version, visit Adobe's website at `www.adobe.com/products/reader/`.

Electronic Flashcards

For PC, Pocket PC, and Palm

These handy electronic flashcards are just what they sound like. One side contains a question or fill-in-the-blank question, and the other side shows the answer.

System Requirements

Make sure your computer meets the minimum system requirements shown in the following list. If your computer doesn't match up to most of these requirements, you may have problems using the software and files on the companion CD. For the latest and greatest information, please refer to the ReadMe file located at the root of the CD-ROM.

- A PC running Microsoft Windows 98, Windows 2000, Windows NT4 (with SP4 or later), Windows Me, Windows XP, or Windows Vista
- An Internet connection
- A CD-ROM drive

Using the CD

To install the items from the CD to your hard drive, follow these steps:

1. Insert the CD into your computer's CD-ROM drive. The license agreement appears.

> **NOTE** *Windows users*: The interface won't launch if you have autorun disabled. In that case, click Start > Run (for Windows Vista, Start > All Programs > Accessories > Run). In the dialog box that appears, type `D:\Start.exe`. (Replace *D* with the proper letter if your CD drive uses a different letter. If you don't know the letter, see how your CD drive is listed under My Computer.) Click OK.

2. Read the license agreement, and then click the Accept button if you want to use the CD.

The CD interface appears. The interface allows you to access the content with just one or two clicks.

Troubleshooting

Wiley has attempted to provide programs that work on most computers with the minimum system requirements. Alas, your computer may differ, and some programs may not work properly for some reason.

The two likeliest problems are that you don't have enough memory (RAM) for the programs you want to use or you have other programs running that are affecting installation or running of a program. If you get an error message such as "Not enough memory" or "Setup cannot continue," try one or more of the following suggestions and then try using the software again:

Turn off any antivirus software running on your computer. Installation programs sometimes mimic virus activity and may make your computer incorrectly believe that it's being infected by a virus.

Close all running programs. The more programs you have running, the less memory is available to other programs. Installation programs typically update files and programs; so if you keep other programs running, installation may not work properly.

Have your local computer store add more RAM to your computer. This is, admittedly, a drastic and somewhat expensive step. However, adding more memory can really help the speed of your computer and allow more programs to run at the same time.

Customer Care

If you have trouble with the book's companion CD-ROM, please call the Wiley Product Technical Support phone number at (800) 762-2974. Outside the United States, call +1(317) 572-3994. You can also contact Wiley Product Technical Support at `http://sybex.custhelp.com`. John Wiley & Sons will provide technical support only for installation and other general quality-control items. For technical support on the applications themselves, consult the program's vendor or author.

To place additional orders or to request information about other Wiley products, please call (877) 762-2974.

Glossary

Numbers

360-degree review This is a form of project performance appraisal (a tool and technique of the Manage Project process) that solicits feedback from everyone the team member interacts with, including the stakeholders, customers, project manager, peers, subordinates, and others.

A

acceptance Acceptance is a strategy for threats or opportunities and is part of a tool and technique of the Plan Risk Responses process. This strategy implies that the organization is willing to accept the consequences of the risk should it occur.

acceptance criteria Acceptance criteria refers to the product of the project and includes the process and the criteria that will be used to determine whether the deliverables and the final product or service of the project are acceptable and satisfactory.

Achievement Theory This motivational theory says people are motivated by the need for three things: achievement, power, and affiliation.

Acquire Project Team This process involves attaining human resources and assigning them to the project. Human resources may come from inside or outside the organization. Acquire the Project Team belongs to the Executing process group.

activity attributes Activity attributes describe the characteristics of activities, such as the activity identifier or code, descriptions, constraints and assumptions associated with the activity, predecessor activities, successor activities, resource requirements, the individual responsible for completing the work, and so on. The activity attributes are an extension of the activity list and are used in the schedule model tool and technique of the Develop Schedule process.

activity duration estimates Activity duration estimates are quantifiable estimates of the number of work periods needed to complete the schedule activities listed. They are an output of the Estimate Activity Durations process.

activity list This is an extension of the WBS that contains all the activities of the project and a description of each activity. The activity list is an output of the Define Activities process.

activity on arrow (AOA) This is a diagramming method that places activities on arrows, which connect to dependent activities using nodes. This is also known as the *arrow diagramming method*.

activity on node (AON) This is a diagramming method that places activities on nodes, which connect to dependent activities using arrows. This is also known as the *precedence diagramming method*.

actual cost (AC) This is the actual cost of work to date or during a given time period, including direct and indirect costs.

addition This is a type of project ending where the project evolves into an ongoing operation.

Administer Procurements This process involves monitoring vendor performance and ensuring that all the requirements of the contract are met.

advertising This is the act of informing potential vendors that an RFP, RFQ, and so on is available. This is a tool and technique of the Conduct Procurements process.

alternatives identification This is a technique used to discover different methods or ways of accomplishing the project. Alternatives identification is a tool and technique of the Define Scope process.

analogous estimating This technique uses the actual duration of a similar, completed activity to determine the duration of the current activity. This is also called *top-down estimating* and uses both expert judgment and historical information.

appeals See *contested changes*.

appraisal costs Appraisal costs are the costs expended to examine the product or process and make certain the requirements are being met. Appraisal costs might include costs associated with aspects such as inspections and testing.

approval requirements Approval requirements refer to how the objectives, deliverables, project management documents, and other outcomes and results of the project will be approved.

arbitration This is a negotiation technique used to settle contract disputes. All parties come to the table with a third, disinterested party who is not a participant in the contract to try to reach an agreement. The purpose of arbitration is to reach an agreement without having to go to court.

arrow diagramming method (ADM) This is a diagramming method that places activities on arrows, which connect to dependent activities using nodes. This is also known as *activity on arrow*.

assumption This is an event or action believed to be true. Project assumptions should always be documented.

attributes These are measurements of deliverables (or certain characteristics of the deliverable) that meet one of two options: conforming or nonconforming. Conforming meets the requirement; nonconforming does not. This is an inspection technique (which is a tool and technique) of the Perform Quality Control process.

avoid The avoid strategy is used for risks that pose threats to the project or have negative impacts. It's part of a tool and technique of the Plan Risk Responses process. This strategy requires changes to the project plan in order to avoid or eliminate risk events and their impacts to the project objectives.

B

backward pass This is a calculation used in CPM to determine late start and late finish dates for activities.

balanced matrix This is a type of organizational structure where power is balanced between project managers and functional managers.

bar charts This is a method of displaying schedule activities. See also *Gantt charts.*

benchmarking Benchmarking is a process of comparing previous similar activities to the current project activities to provide a standard to measure performance against.

benefit measurement methods This is a category of project selection methods, which are a tool and technique of the Develop Project Charter process. They employ various forms of analysis and comparative approaches to make project decisions and include cost-benefit analysis, scoring models, benefit contribution methods, and economic models.

bidder conferences Meetings with prospective vendors or sellers are held prior to the completion of their response proposal to clarify project objectives and answer questions. Bidder conferences are a tool and technique of the Conduct Procurements process.

brainstorming This is an information-gathering technique that is a tool and technique of the Identify Risks process. It involves assembling in one place subject matter experts, team members, risk management team members, and anyone else who might benefit from the process and querying them on possible risk events.

budget at completion (BAC) This is the sum of all the budgets established for all the work of the project, the work package, the control account, or the schedule activity. It's the total planned value for the work component or project. This figure is used in earned value analysis calculations.

buffer See *reserve time.*

C

calculation methods This is a category of selection methods outlined in the project selection methods tool and technique of the Initiation process. Calculation methods provide a way to calculate the value of the project. This value is used in the project selection decision-making process.

cardinal scale This is a scale of values that are linear or nonlinear and referenced in the Perform Qualitative Risk Analysis process.

cause-and-effect diagram This diagram shows the relationship between the effects of problems and their causes. It depicts every potential cause and subcause of a problem and the effect that each proposed solution will have on the problem. This diagram is also called a *fishbone diagram* or an *Ishikawa diagram.*

change control board (CCB) This is a team of stakeholders that is established by the organization and given the authority via the configuration management system to review all change requests and approve them or deny them.

change control system This includes documented procedures that describe how to submit change requests and how to manage change requests. The change control system tracks the status of change requests and defines the level of authority needed to approve changes. It describes the management impacts of the changes as they pertain to project performance. Change control systems are a subset of the configuration management system.

chart of accounts The organization's accounting system. Control accounts associated with the WBS are linked to the chart of accounts.

checklists Checklists can be used with the Plan Quality, Perform Quality Control, and Identify Risk process. They outline a series of required steps a particular process must follow.

claims See *contested changes*.

claims administration Claims administration involves documenting, monitoring, and managing contested changes to the contract.

Close Procurements This process is concerned with completing and settling the terms of the contract and determines whether the work described in the contract was completed accurately and satisfactorily. This process is performed after Close Project or Phase, but its output (contract file) becomes an input to the Close Project or Phase process (contract documentation).

Close Project or Phase This process is concerned with gathering and disseminating information to formalize project closure. The completion of each project phase requires that Close Project or Phase is performed as well.

close project procedures Close project procedures is a document that outlines how Close Project or Phase procedures will occur on the project, the activities needed to perform the close procedures, and the essential roles and responsibilities. This is an output of the Direct and Manage Project Execution process.

Closing This is the last of the five project management process groups. Closing brings a formal, orderly end to the activities of a project phase or to the project itself. All the project information is gathered and archived for future reference. Contract closeout occurs here, and formal acceptance and approval are obtained from project stakeholders.

code of accounts These are unique identifiers assigned to each level of the WBS that are associated with the corporation's chart of accounts. The chart of accounts tracks project costs by category.

collaborating This is a conflict resolution technique that allows multiple viewpoints to be discussed and all perspectives of an issue examined. Collaborating can lead to true consensus and commitment when performed correctly.

Collect Requirements The purpose of the Collect Requirements process is to define and document the project sponsor, customer, and stakeholder's expectations and needs for meeting the project objective. You will use requirements to manage customer expectations throughout the project.

co-location Team members physically working at the same location or holding project meetings in a common area such as a war room.

common causes of variances These are process variances seen during the Perform Quality Control process that result in random variances, known or predictable variances, or variances that are always present in the process.

communication This is the process of exchanging information. There are three elements to all communication: the sender, the message, and the receiver. Communication can be written or verbal and formal or informal. A project manager spends 90 percent of their time communicating.

communications management plan This plan documents the types of stakeholder information needs, when and how frequently the information should be distributed, and the method of communication.

compromise Compromise is a conflict resolution technique. Compromise is achieved when each of the parties involved in the conflict gives up something to reach a solution.

Conduct Procurements This process involves obtaining bids and proposals from vendors in response to RFPs and similar documents prepared during the Plan Procurements process.

configuration management Configuration management is concerned with centrally managing approved changes and project baselines. It is concerned with the specifications of the deliverables and processes.

conflict Conflict is the incompatibility of goals, which often leads to one party resisting or blocking the other party from attaining their goals.

conflict of interest Conflict of interest occurs when personal interests are put above the interests of the project. It also occurs when personal influence is used to cause others to make decisions in favor of the influencer without regard for the project outcome.

confrontation This conflict resolution technique, also known as *problem solving*, is the most often used conflict resolution technique by project managers. This is a win-win technique because it concentrates on finding all the facts about the issue and continues to examine solutions until the right one surfaces.

constrained optimization methods See *mathematical models*.

constraint This is anything that either restricts the actions of the project team or dictates the actions of the project team.

contested changes These are contract changes that cannot be agreed upon. They usually involve a disagreement about the compensation to the vendor for implementing the change.

contingency planning This is a risk response strategy that involves planning alternatives to deal with the risks should they occur. The contingent response strategy, which uses contingency planning, is a tool and technique of the Plan Risk Responses process.

contingency reserves Contingency reserves hold project funds, time, or resources in reserve to offset any unavoidable threats that might occur to project scope, schedule, cost overruns, or quality. This is a tool and technique of the Plan Risk Responses process. Contingency reserves are also taken into consideration in the Determine Budget process.

contingency time See *reserve time*.

continuous improvement Continuous improvement involves everyone in the organization watching for ways to improve quality, whether incrementally or by incorporating new ideas into the process. This involves taking measurements, improving processes by making them repeatable and systemized, reducing variations in production or performance, reducing defects, and improving cycle times. TQM and Six Sigma are examples of continuous improvement. The Kaizen approach is a quality technique from Japan (*Kaizen* means continuous improvement in Japanese).

contract This is a legally binding agreement between two or more parties used to acquire products or services. Contracts can be made between two or more parties, and money is typically exchanged for goods or services. They are enforceable by law and require an offer and an acceptance.

contract change control system This describes the processes needed to make contract changes and is a tool and technique of the Administer Procurements process.

contract statement of work (SOW) This is a detailed, concise description of the work of the project included with the contract. Either the buyer or the seller can write this. See also *statement of work*.

control accounts A control account is where factors such as actual cost, schedule, and scope can be measured using earned value performance measures. Control accounts are assigned to various levels of the WBS.

control chart This is a tool and technique of the Perform Quality Control process that measures the results of processes over time and displays them in graph form. Control charts measure variances to determine whether process variances are in control or out of control.

Control Costs This process manages the changes to project costs using the cost change control system.

Control Schedule This process involves documenting and managing changes to the project schedule.

Control Scope This process involves documenting and managing changes to project scope. Any modification to the agreed-upon WBS is considered a scope change. Changes in product scope will require changes to the project scope. See also *product scope* and *project scope.*

corrective actions This is when you take action to align the anticipated future project outcomes with the project plan.

cost of quality (COQ) This is the total cost to produce the product or service of the project according to the quality standards.

cost performance baseline This is the authorized time-phased budget for the project using the budget at completion earned value management formula. Cost performance baselines represented as S curves.

cost performance index (CPI) This is an earned value analysis technique that is used to calculate cost performance efficiencies: CPI = EV / AC.

cost plus fee (CPF) Cost plus fee contracts reimburse the seller for all allowable costs and include a fee that's calculated as a percentage of total costs. This is also called a *cost plus percentage of cost contract (CPCC).*

cost plus fixed fee (CPFF) Cost plus fixed fee contracts charge back all allowable project costs to the seller and include a fixed fee upon completion of the contract.

cost plus incentive fee (CPIF) This type of contract charges the allowable costs associated with producing the goods or services of the project to the buyer and includes an incentive for exceeding the performance criteria laid out in the contract.

cost plus percentage of cost (CPCC) See *cost plus fee (CPF).*

cost reimbursable contract This type of contract charges the allowable costs associated with producing the goods or services of the project to the buyer.

cost variance (CV) This is an earned value analysis technique that determines whether costs are higher or lower than budgeted during a given period of time: CV = EV – AC.

cost-benefit analysis This compares the financial benefits to the company of performing the project to the costs of implementing the project.

crashing Crashing is a compression technique that looks at cost and schedule trade-offs. One of the things you might do to crash the schedule is add resources, from either inside or outside the organization, to the critical path tasks.

critical chain This is the new critical path formed as a result of constrained resources.

critical chain method This tool and technique from the Develop Schedule process modifies the project schedule by accounting for limited or restricted resources. This is a technique that's designed to help manage the uncertainties of a project. It combines deterministic and probabilistic approaches. The critical chain method often changes the critical path.

critical path (CP) This is the longest path through the project. It's made up of activities with zero float.

Critical Path Method (CPM) This determines a single early and late start date and early and late finish date for each activity on the project to determine both the longest path of the project schedule network diagram and the finish date of the project.

critical success factors These are the elements that must be completed in order for the project to be considered complete.

culture shock This is a disorienting experience that occurs when working in foreign surroundings or cultures that you are not familiar with.

cumulative cost performance index (CPI^C) This is an earned value analysis technique that is used to calculate cost performance efficiencies: cumulative CPI = cumulative EV / cumulative AC.

D

decision models This is a category of selection methods outlined in the project selection methods tool and technique of the Develop Project Charter process. Decision models are used to examine different criteria to help make a decision regarding project selection. See also *calculation methods*.

decision trees These are diagrams that show the sequence of interrelated decisions and the expected results of choosing one alternative over the other. This is a Perform Quantitative Risk Analysis modeling technique, which is a tool and technique of this process.

Define Activities This process identifies the activities of the project that need to be performed to produce the product or service of the project.

Define Scope This Planning process further elaborates the objectives and deliverables of the project into a project scope statement that's used as a basis for future project decisions.

deliverable This is a measurable outcome, measurable result, or specific item that must be produced to consider the project or project phase completed. Deliverables are tangible and can be measured and easily proved.

Delphi technique This is an information gathering technique in the Identify Risks process used to gather information. Similar to brainstorming, except participants don't usually know each other, and they don't have to be present at the same location.

dependencies See *logical relationships*.

design of experiments (DOE) Design of experiments (DOE) is a statistical technique that identifies the elements—or variables—that will have the greatest effect on overall project outcomes.

Determine Budget This process creates the cost performance baseline, which measures the variance and performance of the project throughout the project's life.

Develop Human Resource Plan This process documents the roles and responsibilities of individuals or groups for various project elements and then documents the reporting relationships for each.

Develop Project Management Plan This is the first process in the Planning process group. The purpose of this process is to define, coordinate, and integrate all subsidiary project plans. The subsidiary plans might include the following: project scope management plan, schedule management plan, cost management plan, quality management plan, process improvement plan, staffing management plan, communication management plan, risk management plan, procurement management plan, milestone list, resource calendar, schedule baseline, cost baseline, quality baseline, and risk register.

Develop Project Team This process concerns creating an open, encouraging environment for team members as well as developing them into an effective, functioning, coordinated group.

Develop Schedule This process calculates and prepares the schedule of project activities, which becomes the schedule baseline. It determines activity start and finish dates, finalizes activity sequences and durations, and assigns resources to activities.

Direct and Manage Project Execution This process involves carrying out the project plan. Activities are clarified, the work is authorized to begin, resources are committed and assigned to activities, and the product or service of the project is created. The largest portion of the project budget will be spent during this process.

discounted cash flow This compares the value of the future cash flows of the project to today's dollars using time value of money techniques.

discretionary dependencies These are dependencies defined by the project management team. Discretionary dependencies are usually process or procedure driven. They are also known as *preferred logic*, *soft logic*, and *preferential logic*. See also *logical relationships*.

disputes See *contested changes*.

Distribute Information This process is concerned with providing stakeholders with information regarding the project in a timely manner via status reports, project meetings, review meetings, email, and so on. The communications management plan is put into action during this process.

E

earned value (EV) This is a measurement of the project's progress to date or the value of the work completed to date.

earned value management (EVM) This is the most commonly used performance measurement method. It looks at schedule, cost, and scope project measurements and compares their progress as of the measurement date against what was expected. The three measurements needed to perform earned value analysis are *planned value (PV)*, *actual cost (AC)*, and *earned value (EV)*.

efficiency indicators Cost variance and schedule variance together are known as efficiency indicators.

enhance Enhance is a Plan Risk Responses strategy used for risks that pose an opportunity to the project.

Estimate Activity Durations This process assesses the number of work periods needed to complete the project activities. Work periods are usually expressed in hours or days. Large projects might express duration in weeks or months.

Estimate Activity Resources This process determines the types of resources needed (both human and materials) and in what quantities for each schedule activity within a work package.

estimate at completion (EAC) This is an earned value analysis technique that forecasts the expected total cost of a work component, the schedule activity, or the project at its completion.

Estimate Costs This process develops an approximation of the costs of each project activity.

estimate to complete (ETC) This is an earned value analysis technique that determines the additional expected costs to complete the schedule activity, WBS component, or control account (or project). This is most typically calculated in a bottom-up manner.

evaluation criteria This is a method of rating and scoring vendor proposals. Evaluation criteria are an output of the Conduct Procurements process.

Executing This is the third of the project management process groups. The Executing process group involves putting the project management plan into action, including coordinating and directing project resources to meet the objectives of the project plan. The Executing processes ensure that the project plan stays on track and that future execution of project plans stays in line with project objectives.

Expectancy Theory This is a motivational theory that states that the expectation of a positive outcome drives motivation and that people will behave in certain ways if they think there will be good rewards for doing so. The strength of the expectancy drives the behavior.

expected monetary value (EMV) EMV is a statistical technique that calculates the anticipated impact of the decision. This is a Perform Quantitative Risk Analysis modeling technique, which is a tool and technique of this process.

expected value This is the value calculated by using the three-point estimates for activity duration (most likely, pessimistic, and optimistic) and then finding the weighted average of those estimates.

expert judgment Expert judgment is a tool and technique of several processes. Expert judgment relies on individuals or groups of people who have training, specialized knowledge, or skills about the inputs you're assessing.

exploit Exploit is a Plan Risk Responses strategy used for risks that pose an opportunity to the project.

external dependencies These are the dependencies that are external to the project. See also *logical relationships.*

extinction This is a type of project ending where the work of the project is completed and accepted by the stakeholders.

F

failure costs Failure costs are the cost associated with nonconformance when products or services do not meet specifications. There are two types of failure costs, internal and external. Failure costs are also know as cost of poor quality.

fait accompli Fait accompli happens during contract negotiation when one party tries to convince the other party discussing a particular contract term that it is no longer an issue. It's a distraction technique because the party practicing fait accompli tactics is purposely trying to keep from negotiating an issue and claims the issue cannot be changed.

fast tracking This is a schedule compression technique where two activities that were previously scheduled to start sequentially start at the same time. Fast tracking reduces schedule duration if applied to the critical path.

feasibility study Feasibility studies are undertaken to determine whether the project is a viable project, the probability of project success, and the viability of the product of the project.

firm fixed-price contract (FFP) This type of contract sets a specific, firm price for the goods or services rendered based on a well-defined deliverable agreed upon by the buyer and seller. The biggest risk is borne by the seller with a fixed-price contract.

fitness for use Joseph Juran is noted for this theory, which means that stakeholders and customers expectations are met or exceeded.

fixed-price plus incentive contract (FPIF) This type of contract sets a specific, firm price for the goods or services rendered (like the fixed-price contract) and includes an extra incentive for exceeding agreed-upon performance criteria.

fixed-price with economic price adjustment (FP-EPA) This contract sets a firm price for the goods or services rendered and includes an adjustment that's tied to a reliable financial index. FP-EPA contracts are used when the contract period extends several years.

float The amount of time you can delay the early start of a task without delaying the finish date of the project. This is also known as *slack time*, *total float*, *total slack*, or *path float*.

float time See *float*.

forecasting Forecasting examines the actual project performance data to date and makes predictions about future project performance based on this data.

force majeure Catastrophic risk events that are outside the scope of Project Risk Management, such as earthquakes, meteorites, volcanoes, floods, civil unrest, and terrorism. This is referenced in the risk categories section of the Identify Risks process.

forcing This is a conflict resolution technique where one person forces a solution on the other parties.

formal acceptance and closure Formal acceptance and closure involves providing formal notice to the seller—usually in written form—that the contract is complete. It's the organization's way of formally accepting the product of the project from the vendor and closing out the contract. This is an element of both the Close Project or Phase and Close Procurements processes.

forward pass A calculation used in CPM to determine early start and early finish dates for activities.

free float This is the amount of time the start of a task can be delayed without delaying the early start of a successor task.

functional organization This is a form of organizational structure. Functional organizations are traditional organizations with hierarchical reporting structures. The functional manager traditionally has more authority in this type of organization than the project manager has.

G

Gantt charts Gantt charts display schedule activities. They might also show activity sequences, activity start and end dates, resource assignments, activity dependencies, and the critical path.

H

hammocks These are summary-level activities or aggregate activities shown as a summary activity on a project schedule network diagram.

handoffs This is the process of ending one project life cycle phase and beginning the next.

hard dependencies See *mandatory dependencies.*

hard logic See *mandatory dependencies.*

historical information This is an input to several Planning processes that refers to information or records regarding past projects and their performance. Records are available for reference on the existing project.

Hygiene Theory Fredrick Herzberg developed this theory. It's also known as the Motivation-Hygiene Theory. Hygiene factors and motivators contribute to motivation. Hygiene factors prevent dissatisfaction and deal with work environment issues.

I

Identify Risks This process identifies the potential project risks and documents their characteristics.

Identify Stakeholders The Identify Stakeholders process involves identifying and documenting all the stakeholders on the project, including their interests, impact, and potential negative impacts on the project. Information regarding the stakeholders is recorded in the stakeholder register, the only output of this process.

impact This is the amount of damage or opportunity a risk event poses to a project.

impact scale This is a scale in which a value is assigned to depict the severity of a potential risk impact using a cardinal value or actual numeric value.

independent estimates This is the process of comparing the costs of a vendor proposal with outside sources or other vendor prices to determine whether estimates are reasonable. This is a tool and technique of the Conduct Procurements process.

influence diagrams This is a diagramming technique referenced in the Identify Risks process that shows the causal influences among project variables, the timing or time order of events, and the relationships among other project variables and their outcomes.

information distribution tools This tool and technique of the Distribute Information process involves methods for distributing the project information to the project team or stakeholders.

Initiating This is the first project management process group and generally the first phase of a project life cycle. It acknowledges that the project, or the next phase in an active project, should begin.

inspection This tool and technique of the Verify Scope and the Perform Quality Control processes involves physically looking at, measuring, or testing results to determine whether they conform to the requirements or quality standards.

integration This is a type of project ending where the financial or human resources assigned to the project are diverted or reassigned elsewhere in the organization.

internal rate of return (IRR) This is the discount rate when the present value of the cash inflows equals the original investment. Projects with higher IRR values are generally considered better than projects with lower IRR values. IRR assumes that cash inflows are reinvested at the IRR value.

interviews Interviews are question-and-answer sessions held with other project managers, subject matter experts, stakeholders, customers, the management team, project team members, and users. Typically these folks have previous experience on projects similar to the current project, or they have specialized knowledge or industry expertise.

iterative This describes processes that are repeated. The five process groups are repeated throughout the project's life because of change requests, responses to change, corrective action, and so on.

K

Kaizen approach Kaizen is a cost of quality technique. When this technique is used, all team members and managers should be constantly watching for quality improvement opportunities. *Kaizen* means continuous improvement in Japanese.

L

lags Lags occur when time elapses between two activities; the result is time being added to the start date or the finish date of the schedule activity.

leaders Leaders impart vision, gain consensus for strategic goals, establish direction, and inspire and motivate others.

leads Leads speed up successor activities and result in time being subtracted from the start date or the finish date of the dependent activity.

lessons learned These consist of information gained throughout the course of the project that can be used to benefit the current project, future projects, or other projects currently being performed by the organization. Lessons learned should be documented and might include positive as well as negative lessons.

lines of communication This is the total number of communication channels among a group of participants. The formula to calculate lines of communication is n (n – 1) / 2.

logical relationships These are dependencies between two project activities whereby one activity must do something (finish or start) before another activity can do something (start or finish). Logical relationships can also exist between an activity and a milestone. These are also known as *precedence relationships*. The four types of logical relationships are finish-to-start, finish-to-finish, start-to-start, and start-to-finish.

lump-sum contracts See *firm fixed-price contracts (FFP)*.

M

make-or-buy analysis This tool and technique of the Plan Procurements process determines whether it's more cost effective for the organization to purchase goods and services or to produce the goods and services itself. Make-or-buy analysis can also include capacity issues, skills, availability, trade secrets, and so on.

Manage Project Team Manage Project Team is concerned with tracking and reporting the performance of individual team members and preparing performance appraisals.

Manage Stakeholder Expectations Manage Stakeholder Expectations is concerned with satisfying the needs of the stakeholders by managing communications with them, resolving issues, and improving project performance by implementing requested changes.

managers Managers focus on results and are concerned with getting the job done according to the requirements.

mandatory dependencies These are dependencies that are directly related to the nature of the work being performed. This is also known as *hard dependencies* or *hard logic*. See also *logical relationships*.

Maslow's Hierarchy of Needs This is a motivational theory that hypothesizes that people have five basic needs and they fall in hierarchical order: basic physical needs, safety and security needs, social needs, self-esteem needs, and self-actualization.

mathematical models Mathematical models, also called *constrained optimization methods*, are a category of project selection methods. They are complex mathematical models that use linear, dynamic, integer, nonlinear, and/or multi-objective programming in the form of algorithms, or in other words, a specific set of steps to solve a particular problem.

matrix organization This is a form of organizational structure. Employees in a matrix organization report to one functional manager and at least one project manager. Functional managers assign employees to projects and carry out administrative duties, while project managers assign tasks associated with the project to team members and execute the project.

milestone This is a major deliverable or key event in a project used to measure project progress.

milestone chart This is a method to display project schedule information that shows the start and/or finish date of milestones.

mitigate This is a strategy for negative risks or threats, which is a tool and technique of the Plan Risk Responses process. Mitigation reduces the probability of a risk event and its impacts to an acceptable level.

Monitor and Control Project Work Monitor and Control Project Work is concerned with monitoring all the processes in the Initiating, Planning, Executing, and Closing process groups. Collecting data, measuring results, and reporting on performance information are some of the activities performed during this process.

Monitor and Control Risks This process involves responding to risks as they occur. The risk management plan details how risk is managed, and the risk response plan details how risk response strategies are implemented in the event of an actual risk event. This process implements risk response according to the plan.

Monitoring and Controlling This is the fourth project management process group. The Monitoring and Controlling process group involves taking performance measurements and analyzing them to determine whether the project is staying true to the project plan. Corrective action is applied where necessary to get the project activities realigned with the project plan.

Monte Carlo analysis This is a simulation technique that is discussed in the modeling and simulation tool and technique of the Perform Quantitative Risk Analysis and Develop Schedule processes. Monte Carlo typically simulates schedule and cost variables many times to calculate a distribution of probable cost or duration results.

motivational theories Motivational theories present ideas on why people act the way they do and how they can be influenced to act in certain ways to get the results desired.

Motivation-Hygiene Theory See *Hygiene Theory.*

N

net present value (NPV) Net present value evaluates the cash inflows using the discounted cash flow technique, which is applied to each period the inflows are expected. The total present value of the cash flows is deducted from the initial investment to determine NPV. NPV assumes that cash inflows are reinvested at the cost of capital. This is similar to *discounted cash flow.*

Nominal Group Technique This is an information-gathering technique similar to brainstorming that can be used during the Identify Risks process.

O

objectives These describe the results and/or the product or service the project intends to produce. They are the quantifiable criteria used to measure project success. All project work is directed at completing the objective of the project. Objectives should be stated in tangible terms that are specific, measurable, accurate, realistic, and time bound.

operational definition An operational definition is also known as a quality metric and it describes what is being measured and how it will be measured during the Perform Quality Control process.

operations These are ongoing endeavors typically involving repetitive processes that produce the same results.

ordinal scale These are values that are rank-ordered as, for example, high, medium, or low. They are referenced in the Perform Qualitative Risk Analysis process.

organization breakdown structure (OBS) This relates the WBS elements to the organizational unit responsible for completing the work.

P

parametric estimating Parametric estimating is a quantitatively based estimating method that multiplies the quantity of work by the rate.

Pareto charts Pareto charts are a tool and technique of the Perform Quality Control process. They rank-order the most important factors, such as delays, costs, or defects, by their frequency over time and are displayed as histograms.

passive acceptance Passive acceptance means that plans will not be made to avoid, transfer, or mitigate a negative risk, nor will plans be made to share, exploit, or enhance a positive risk. The consequences of the risk event are accepted should the risk event occur.

payback period This is the length of time it takes a company to recover the initial cost of producing a product or service of a project.

payment system A payment system is the tool and technique of Administer Procurements that is used to issue payment based on the input of seller invoices.

Perform Integrated Change Control This process is concerned with influencing the things that cause change, determining that change is needed or has happened, and managing change. All other change control processes are integrated with this process.

Perform Qualitative Risk Analysis This process determines what impact the identified risks will have on the project and the probability that they'll occur, and it puts the risks in priority order according to their effect on the project objectives.

Perform Quality Assurance This process involves performing systematic quality activities and uses quality audits to determine which processes should be used to achieve the project requirements and to assure that they are performed efficiently and effectively.

Perform Quality Control This process is concerned with monitoring work results to see whether they fulfill the quality standards set out in the quality management plan. The Perform Quality Control process determines whether the end product conforms to the requirements and product description defined during the Planning processes.

Perform Quantitative Risk Analysis This process assigns numeric probabilities to each identified risk and examines their potential impact to the project objectives.

performance measurement baselines The project plan baseline, schedule baseline, and cost baseline are collectively known as the performance measurement baselines.

performance review Performance reviews examine schedule activities, work packages, or cost account status and their progress to date. The three types of analyses associated with performance reviews are variance analysis, trend analysis, and earned value technique.

Plan Procurements This process involves identifying the goods or services that will be purchased from outside of the organization, the quantity needed, and when they need to be purchased. It also involves identifying the project needs that can be met by the project team.

Plan Quality This process is concerned with targeting quality standards that are relevant to the project at hand and devising a plan to meet and satisfy those standards.

Plan Risk Responses This process defines what steps to take to reduce threats and take advantage of opportunities and assigns departments or individual staff members the responsibility of carrying out the risk response plans developed in this process.

planned value (PV) This is the cost of work that has been budgeted for an activity during a certain time period. (Note: *PV* also stands for *present value*.)

Planning This is the second project management process group. The Planning process group consists of processes that involve formulating and revising project goals and objectives and creating the project management plan that will be used to achieve the goals the project was undertaken to address. Planning involves determining alternative courses of action and selecting from among the best of those to produce the project's goals. The Planning process group is where the project requirements are determined and stakeholders are identified.

PMI Code of Ethics and Professional Conduct This is an ethical code established by PMI to ensure personal and professional conduct on the part of PMPs.

politics This is a technique used to influence people to perform. It involves getting groups of people with different interests to cooperate creatively even in the midst of conflict and disorder.

portfolio This is a collection of projects or programs that meet a specific business goal or objective.

portfolio management This is the management of collections of programs and projects to meet and maximize the strategic objectives of the business. It involves monitoring active projects, balancing the portfolio among other investments, assuring efficient use of resources, and assessing the value of projects and potential projects against the portfolio's strategic objectives.

power This is a technique used to influence people to perform. It's the ability to get people to do things they wouldn't do otherwise, to change minds and the course of events, and to influence outcomes.

preassignment This is a tool and technique of the Acquire Project Team process. This occurs when a project is put out for bid and specific team members are promised as part of the proposal or when internal project team members are promised and assigned as a condition of the project.

precedence diagramming method (PDM) This is a diagramming method that places activities on nodes, which connect to dependent activities using arrows. This is also known as *activity on node*.

precedence relationships See *logical relationships*.

preferential logic See *discretionary dependencies*.

preferred logic See *discretionary dependencies*.

prevention This keeps errors from occurring in the process. Prevention is a quality concern.

preventive action Preventive action involves anything that will reduce the potential impacts of risk events should they occur. Contingency plans and risk responses are examples of preventive action. These are inputs to the Direct and Manage Project Execution process.

probability This is the likelihood that a risk event will occur.

probability and impact matrix The probability and impact matrix defines the combination of probability and impact that helps determine which risks need detailed risk response plans. It's defined during the Project Risk Management process and included in the risk management plan. The matrix is used in the Perform Qualitative Risk Analysis process to assign an overall risk rating to each of the project's identified risks. The combination of probability and impact results in a classification usually expressed as high, medium, or low. High risks are considered a red condition, medium risks are considered a yellow condition, and low risks are considered a green condition.

process analysis Process analysis is a tool and technique of the Perform Quality Assurance process. It looks at process improvement from an organizational and technical perspective. Process analysis steps are documented in the process improvement plan and examine problems experienced while conducting the project, the constraints of the project, and inefficient and ineffective processes identified during process operation.

process improvement plan The process improvement plan focuses on finding inefficiencies in a process or activity and eliminating them. It is an output of the Plan Quality process.

procurement audits This tool and technique of the Close Procurements process examines the procurement processes to determine their effectiveness. Procurement audits are performed on Plan Procurements, Conduct Procurements, and the Administer Procurements processes.

procurement documents Procurement documents are prepared in the Plan Procurements process and are used to solicit vendors and suppliers to bid on project procurement needs. A procurement document might be called *request for proposal* (RFP), *request for information* (RFI), *invitation for bid* (IFB), or *request for quotation* (RFQ).

procurement file This is a file of all the contract records and supporting documents. This is part of the organizational process asset output of the Close Procurements process.

procurement management plan This details how the procurement process will be managed throughout the project and includes elements such as the types of contracts used, the authority of the project team, and where to find standard procurement documents.

procurement negotiations Procurement negotiation occurs when all parties discuss the terms of the contract, or procurement document, and reach an agreement. This is a tool and technique of the Conduct Procurements process.

procurement statement of work See *statement of work*.

product analysis This is a description of the product of the project that might include performing value analysis, function analysis, quality function deployment, product breakdown analysis, systems engineering techniques, value engineering, and function deployment techniques to further define and better understand the product or service of the project. This is a tool and technique of the Define Scope process.

product description See *product scope description*.

product scope See *product scope description.*

product scope description This is a description of the product features and functionality that describes the characteristics of the end product.

product verification This determines whether the work described in the contract was completed accurately and satisfactorily. It's one of the purposes of the Close Procurements process.

Program Evaluation and Review Technique (PERT) PERT uses expected value—or weighted average—of critical path tasks to determine project duration by establishing three estimates: most likely, pessimistic, and optimistic. The formula for PERT is optimistic + pessimistic + (4 * most likely) / 6. PERT is used when activity duration estimates are highly uncertain.

program This is a grouping of projects that are managed together. The individual projects are usually part of one bigger project and are therefore related.

program management Program management is the central management and coordination of groups of related projects and operations work to obtain benefits and administer controls that aren't possible when the projects and operations are managed individually to achieve the program's strategic objectives.

progressive elaboration This is the process of taking incremental steps to examine and refine the characteristics of the product of the project. Processes may be progressively elaborated as well.

project Projects are temporary in nature; have definite start and end dates; create a unique product, service, or result; and are completed when the goals and objectives of the project have been met.

project boundaries These define what is and what is not included in the work of the project. They should specifically state what is excluded from the work of the project. This is an element of the project scope statement.

project calendars Project calendars are an input to the Develop Schedule process. They define the organization's working calendar of holidays, shift schedules, and so on.

project charter This is an official, written acknowledgment and recognition that a project exists. The project charter is issued by senior management and gives the project manager the authority to assign organizational resources to the work of the project.

Project Communications Management This is one of the nine Knowledge Areas of project management. Project Communications Management ensures proper and timely communications and includes these processes: Identify Stakeholders, Plan Communications, Distribute Information, Manage Stakeholder Expectations, and Report Performance.

Project Cost Management This is one of the nine Knowledge Areas of project management. Project Cost Management ensures proper cost planning, budgets, and controls and includes these processes: Estimate Costs, Determine Budget, and Control Costs.

Project Human Resource Management This is one of the nine Knowledge Areas of project management. Project Human Resource Management ensures effective use of human resources and includes these processes: Develop Human Resource Plan, Acquire Project Team, Develop Project Team, and Manage Project Team.

Project Integration Management This is one of the nine Knowledge Areas of project management. Project Integration Management involves coordinating all aspects of the project and includes these processes: Develop Project Charter, Develop Project Management Plan, Direct and Manage Project Execution, Monitor and Control Project Work, Perform Integrated Change Control, and Close Project or Phase.

project life cycle This is the grouping of project phases in a sequential order from the beginning of the project to the close.

project management This is the process that's used to initiate, plan, execute, monitor, control, and close out projects by applying skills, knowledge, and project management tools and techniques to fulfill the project requirements.

project management Knowledge Areas These nine project management groupings—known as *Knowledge Areas*—bring together common or related processes.

project management office (PMO) This is the office established by organizations to create and maintain procedures and standards for project management methodologies to be used throughout the organization.

project management plan This plan defines how the project is executed, how it's monitored and controlled, and how it's closed and also documents the outputs of the Planning group processes. The size and complexity of the project will determine the level of detail contained in this plan.

project management information system (PMIS) The PMIS is incorporated as part of the enterprise environmental input to several processes. It is an automated or manual system used to document the project management plan and subsidiary plans, to facilitate the feedback process, and revise documents.

project manager This is the person responsible for applying the skills, knowledge, and project management tools and techniques to the project activities in order to successfully complete the project objectives.

project plan This is an assortment of documents (outputs from the Planning process group) that constitutes what the project is, what the project will deliver, and how all the processes will be managed. The project plan is used as the guideline throughout the project Executing and Controlling process groups to track and measure project performance and to make future project decisions. It's also used as a communication and information tool for stakeholders, team members, and the management team.

project presentations Project presentations are part of the organizational process assets updates, which is an output of the Distribute Information process. These concern presenting project information to the stakeholders and other appropriate parties.

Project Procurement Management This is one of the nine Knowledge Areas of project management. Project Procurement Management concerns procurement and contract oversight. The processes included in this Knowledge Area are Plan Procurements, Conduct Procurements, Administer Procurements, and Close Procurements.

Project Quality Management This is one of the nine Knowledge Areas of project management. Project Quality Management ensures that the quality requirements of the project are satisfied. The processes included in this Knowledge Area are Plan Quality, Perform Quality Assurance, and Perform Quality Control.

project records Project records include all information regarding the project, including project reports, memos, project schedules, project plans, and other documents. This is an element of the organizational process assets update output of the Distribute Information process.

project reports This is an element of the organizational process assets update output of the Distribute Information process that includes project information such as the project status reports and minutes from project meetings.

Project Risk Management This process determines how risks will be managed for a project.

Project Risk Management Knowledge Area This is one of the nine Knowledge Areas of project management. Project Risk Management is concerned with identifying and planning for potential risks that may impact the project. Its processes include Project Risk Management, Identify Risks, Perform Qualitative Risk Analysis, Perform Quantitative Risk Analysis, Plan Risk Responses, and Monitor and Control Risks.

project schedule The project schedule determines the start and finish dates for project activities and assigns resources to the activities.

project scope The project scope describes the work required to produce the product or the service of the project. This includes the requirements of the product, which describe the features and functionality of the product or service.

Project Scope Management This is one of the nine Knowledge Areas of project management. Project Scope Management is concerned with the work of the project and only the work that is required to complete the project. Its processes include Collect Requirements, Define Scope, Create WBS, Verify Scope, and Control Scope.

project scope management plan The project scope management plan has a direct influence on the project's success and describes the process for defining project scope and verifying the work of the project. It facilitates the creations of the WBS, describes how the product or service of the project is verified and accepted, and documents how changes to scope will be handled.

project scope statement The project scope statement documents the project objectives, deliverables, and requirements, which are used as a basis for future project decisions. It also includes other elements, such product scope description, project boundaries, product acceptance criteria, constraints, assumptions, project organization, risks, milestones, fund limitations, cost estimate, configuration management requirements, project specifications, and approval requirements.

project sponsor This is usually an executive in the organization. The project sponsor has the authority to assign resources and enforce decisions regarding the project. They are typically the escalation path for issues on a project.

project statement of work (SOW) This describes the product or service the project was undertaken to complete. It is an input to several processes. See also *contract statement of work (SOW).*

Project Time Management This is one of the nine Knowledge Areas of project management. Project Time Management is concerned with estimating the duration of the project plan activities, devising a project schedule, and monitoring and controlling deviations from the schedule. Its processes include Define Activities, Sequence Activities, Estimate Activity Resources, Estimate Activity Durations, Develop Schedule, and Control Schedule.

projectized organization This is a type of organizational structure focused on projects. Project managers generally have ultimate authority over the project. Sometimes, supporting departments such as human resources and accounting might report to the project manager. Project managers are responsible for making project decisions and acquiring and assigning resources.

Q

qualified sellers lists These are lists of prospective sellers who have been preapproved or prequalified to provide contract services (or provide supplies and materials) for the organization. Qualified seller lists are part of the selected sellers output of the Conduct Procurements process.

quality audits Quality audits are independent reviews performed by trained auditors or third-party reviewers. The purpose of a quality audit is to identify ineffective and inefficient activities or processes used on the project. Audits may also examine and uncover inefficient processes and procedures.

quality baseline The quality baseline is the quality objective of the projects and is what's used to measure and report quality against throughout the project.

quality metric See *operational definition.*

R

RACI chart This is a matrix-based chart that shows types of resources and their responsibility on the project. RACI stands for *responsible*, *accountable*, *consult*, and *inform*. This is a tool and technique of the Develop Human Resource Plan process.

recognition and rewards This is a tool and technique of the Develop Project Team process; recognition and rewards systems are formal ways for the management team and the project manager to recognize and promote desirable behavior.

records management system A records management system is a tool and technique of the Administer Procurements process and involves documenting policies, control functions, and automated tools used to manage project documents and contract documents. A records management system is part of the project management information system.

regulation A regulation is mandatory and typically imposed by governments or institutions.

Report Performance This process concerns collecting information regarding project progress and project accomplishments and reporting it to the stakeholders, project team members, management team, and other interested parties. It also makes predictions regarding future project performance.

requirements These are the specifications of the objective or deliverable that must be met in order to satisfy the needs of the project. Requirements might also describe results or outcomes that must be produced in order to satisfy a contract, specification, standard, or other project document (typically the scope statement). Requirements quantify and prioritize the wants, needs, and expectations of the project sponsor and stakeholders.

reserve time This is the practice of adding a portion of time (percentage of total time or number of work periods) to an activity to account for schedule risk.

residual risk This is a risk that remains after implementing a risk response strategy.

resource-based method See *resource leveling.*

resource breakdown structure (RBS) This is a hierarchical chart of resources that breaks down the work of the project according to the types of resources needed.

resource calendars Calendars are an input to the Develop Schedule process. Resource calendars refer to specific resources—or categories of resources—and their individual (or group) availability.

resource leveling Resource leveling is used when resources are overallocated. It attempts to smooth out the resource assignments so that tasks are completed without overloading the individual and without negatively affecting the project schedule. Some ways to perform resource leveling include delaying the start of a task to match the availability of a key team member or giving more tasks to underallocated members. Resource leveling is also known as the *resource-based method*.

resources Resources include the people, equipment, and materials needed to complete the work of the project.

responsibility assignment matrix (RAM) The RAM ties roles and responsibilities with the WBS elements to ensure that each element has a resource assigned.

reverse resource allocation scheduling This is a resource-leveling technique used when key resources are required at a specific point in the project and they are the only resources available to perform these activities. Reverse resource allocation scheduling requires that the resources be scheduled in reverse order, that is, from the end date of the project rather than from the beginning, in order to assign key resources at the correct time.

revisions These are adjustments to approved schedule start and end dates for activities to coincide with approved changes and/or corrective actions. This is another term for *schedule updates*.

rework Failing to meet quality requirements or standards might result in rework (performing the work again to make it conform). Rework might increase the project schedule.

risk breakdown structure (RBS) An RBS is a graphical way to display risk categories and their subcategories. The RBS is an element of the risk management plan.

risk categories Risk categories systematically identify risks and provide a foundation for understanding. The use of risk categories helps improve the Identify Risks process by giving everyone involved a common language or basis for describing risk. Risk categories are an element of the risk management plan.

risk management plan This describes how risks are defined, monitored, and controlled throughout the project. The risk management plan is a subsidiary of the project management plan, and it's the only output of the Project Risk Management process.

risk register This is the output of the Identify Risks process that contains the list of identified risks. The risk register is updated, and its update becomes an output of every remaining Risk process.

risk tolerance Risk tolerance is the level at which stakeholders are comfortable taking a risk because the benefits to be gained outweigh what could be lost or the level at which risks are avoided because the potential loss is too great.

rolling wave planning This is a process of fully elaborating near term WBS work packages and waiting to elaborate later term work packages until more information is known. It involves elaborating the work of the project to the level of detail known at the time.

run chart A run chart is a tool and technique of the Perform Quality Control process that is used to show variations in the process over time. A run chart might also show trends in the process.

S

Scatter diagrams Scatter diagrams are a tool and technique of the Perform Quality Control process. They use two variables—an independent variable, which is an input, and a dependent variable, which is an output—to display the relationship between these two elements as points on a graph.

schedule baseline The approved project schedule serves as the schedule baseline that will be used in the Executing and Monitoring and Controlling processes to measure schedule process.

schedule change control system This defines how changes to the schedule are made and managed. This tracks and records change requests, describes the procedures to follow to implement schedule changes, and details the authorization levels needed to approve the schedule changes.

schedule compression This is a form of mathematical analysis that's used to shorten the project schedule without changing the project scope. Compression is simply shortening the project schedule to accomplish all the activities sooner than estimated. Crashing and fast tracking are two examples of schedule compressions.

schedule network analysis This technique of Develop Schedule creates the project schedule. It uses a schedule model and other analytical techniques such as critical path and critical chain method, what-if analysis, and resource leveling (all of which are other tools and techniques in this process) to help calculate these dates and the project schedule.

schedule performance index (SPI) This is a performance index that calculates schedule performance efficiencies: SPI = EV / PV.

schedule updates Schedule updates are an output of the Control Schedule process and involve adjusting activities and dates to coincide with approved changes and/or corrective actions.

schedule variance (SV) This is an earned value analysis technique that determines whether the project schedule is ahead or behind what was planned for a given period of time: SV = EV – PV.

scope Scope includes all of the components that make up the product or service of the project and the results the project intends to produce. See also *product scope* and *project scope.*

scope creep This is changing the project or product scope without considering the impacts it will have to the project schedule, budget, and resources.

scope management plan See *project scope management plan.*

scope statement See *project scope statement.*

scoring model This is a project selection method used to score and rank project proposals. Scoring models might also be used in the Conduct Procurements process.

screening systems This is a set of predetermined performance criteria used to screen vendors. Screening systems are a proposal evaluation technique, which is a tool and technique of the Conduct Procurements process.

secondary risks These are risks that come about as a result of implementing a risk response.

seller invoices These are requests for the payment of goods or services that should describe the work that was completed or the materials that were delivered. Seller invoices are part of the Administer Procurements process.

seller rating systems Seller rating systems are part of the proposal evaluation tool and technique of the Conduct Procurements process. These systems use information about the sellers—such as past performance, delivery, contract compliance, and quality ratings—to determine seller performance.

sensitivity analysis This is a quantitative method of analyzing the potential impact of risk events on the project and determining which risk events have the greatest potential for impact by examining all the uncertain elements at their baseline values. This is a Perform Quantitative Risk Analysis modeling technique.

Sequence Activities This process sequences activities in logical order and determines whether dependencies exist among the activities.

share Share is a Plan Risk Responses strategy for risks that pose an opportunity to the project.

should cost estimates See *independent estimates*.

Six Sigma Six Sigma is a measurement-based strategy that focuses on process improvement and variation reduction by applying Six Sigma methodologies to the project. Six Sigma is a quality management approach that is similar to TQM and is typically used in manufacturing and service-related industries.

slack time This is the amount of time you can delay the early start of a task without delaying the finish date of the project. This is also known as *float time*.

smoothing Smoothing is a conflict resolution technique that is a temporary way to resolve conflict where someone attempts to make the conflict appear less important than it is.

soft logic See *discretionary dependencies*.

stakeholder This is an organization or person who has a vested interest in the project and stands to gain or lose something as a result of the project.

standard A standard employs rules, guidelines, or characteristics that should be followed. They are not mandatory but should be considered when developing the quality management plan.

starvation This is a type of project ending where financial or human resources are cut off from the project.

statement of work (SOW) The statement of work describes the product, service, or result the project was undertaken to complete. If the project is performed internally to the organization, this document is usually written by either the project sponsor or the initiator of the project. When the project is external to the organization, the buyer typically writes the SOW. The SOW should consider the business need for the project, the product scope description, and the organization's strategic plan.

statistical sampling This means making a sample number of parts from the whole population and examining them to determine whether they fall within the variances outlined in the quality management plan. Statistical sampling is a tool and technique of the Perform Quality Control process.

status review meetings Status meetings are a component of the Report Performance process. The purpose of status meetings is to provide updated information regarding the progress of the project. They are not show-and-tell meetings.

steering committee This is a group of high-level managers or executives in the organization who manage project prioritization and various project decisions. The steering committee typically represents functional areas or departments within the organization.

successor activities These are activities that follow predecessor activities.

T

tailoring This means determining which processes and process groups should be performed for the project. The project manager and project team should take into consideration the size and complexity of the project and the various inputs and outputs of each of the processes when determining which ones to perform. It's generally accepted that performing all five process groups is good practice for any project.

team building Team building activities are a tool and technique of the Develop Project Team process. They involve getting a diverse group of people to work together in the most efficient and effective manner possible.

technical performance measurements These measurements are usually determined during trend analysis (which is used with the run chart tool and technique of the Perform Quality Control process) to compare the technical accomplishments of project milestones completed to the technical milestones defined in the project Planning processes.

Theory X This is a motivational management theory that proposes that most people do not like work and will try to steer clear of it. It postulates that people have little to no ambition, need constant supervision, and won't actually perform the duties of their job unless threatened.

Theory Y This is a motivational management theory that proposes that people are interested in performing their best given the right motivation and proper expectations.

three-point estimates Three-point estimates are a tool and technique of the Estimate Activity Durations process used to determine activity estimates. The three estimates are the most likely estimate, an optimistic estimate, and a pessimistic estimate.

time and materials (T&M) contract This is a type of contract that is a cross between the fixed-price contract and the cost-reimbursable contract. Preset unit rates are agreed to at contract signing, but costs are charged to the buyer as they're incurred.

time-phased budget The cost performance baseline is the authorized time-phased budget for the project. Time-phased budgets disburse funds at different periods throughout the life of the project.

to-complete performance index (TCPI) The to-complete performance index (TCPI) is the projected performance level the remaining work of the project must meet in order to satisfy a management goal such as meeting BAC or EAC.

tolerable results These are quality measurements that fall within a specified range. Tolerable results are a concern of the Perform Quality Control process. These are also known as *tolerances*.

top-down estimating See *analogous estimating*.

tornado diagram This is a diagramming method for sensitivity analysis data. The variables with the greatest effect on the project are displayed as horizontal bars at the top of the graph and decrease in impact as they progress down through the graph. This gives a quick overview of how much the project can be affected by uncertainty in the various elements and which risks have the greatest impact on the project.

total float This is the amount of time the earliest start of a task can be delayed without delaying the ending of the project.

Total Quality Management (TQM) W. Edwards Deming is considered the founder of TQM. This quality theory states that the process is the problem, not people. TQM stipulates that quality must be managed in and that quality improvement should be a continuous process, not a one-time task.

training This tool and technique of the Develop Project Team process improves the competencies of the project team members.

transfer Transference is a strategy for negative risks or threats, which is a tool and technique of the Plan Risk Responses process. This strategy transfers the consequences of a risk to a third party. Insurance is an example of transference.

triggers These are risk symptoms that imply a risk event is about to occur. Triggers can also be referred to as symptoms or warning signs.

V

variance at completion (VAC) This is an earned value analysis technique that calculates the difference between the budget at completion (BAC) and the estimate at completion (EAC): VAC = BAC – EAC.

Verify Scope This process formalizes the acceptance of the project scope and is primarily concerned with the acceptance of work results.

virtual teams Virtual teams are teams that don't necessarily work in the same location but all share the goals of the project and have a role on the project. This type of team allows the inclusion of resources from different geographic locations, those who work different hours or shifts from the other team members, those with mobility limitations, and so on.

W

weighted scoring model See *weighting system*.

weighting system This is a way to rank and score vendor proposals or project proposals. Weighting systems assign numerical weights to evaluation criteria and then multiply this by the weight of each criteria factor to come up with total scores for each project or vendor. These systems keep personal biases to a minimum.

withdrawal This conflict resolution technique occurs when one of the parties gets up and leaves and refuses to discuss the conflict. This never results in resolution.

work authorization systems Work authorization systems clarify and initiate the work of each work package or activity. This is a formal procedure that authorizes work to begin in the correct sequence and at the right time. Work authorization systems are usually written procedures defined by the organization. These are used in the Executing processes of the project.

work performance information Work performance information is an input to the Administer Procurements process. Work performance information is used to monitor work results and examine the vendor's deliverables and compares their work results against the project management plan. It also makes certain activities are performed correctly and in sequence.

workaround This is an unplanned response to a risk event that was unknown and unidentified or an unplanned response to a risk that was previously accepted. Workaround plans are an element of the Monitor and Control Risks process.

Z

zero defects Zero defects is a quality theory attributed to Philip B. Crosby. Zero defects means perform the task right the first time to avoid engaging in rework, loss of productivity, and increased costs.

ETC = estimate to complete

$$ETC = \frac{BAC - \text{cumulative } EV}{\text{cumulative } CPI}$$ if future cost variance similar to types of variances to date

$$ETC = (BAC - \text{cumulative } EV)$$ if future cost variances not similar to prev variances.

$$TCPI = \frac{BAC - EV}{BAC - AC}$$

$$TCPI \text{ for } EAC = \frac{BAC - EV}{EAC - AC}$$

variance analysis = BAC − EAC

Initiating → Planning

M&C
Initiating → Planning → executing

Executing → M&C → Planning
Executing

Planning
M&C → Executing → Closing
M&C

M&C → Closing

handoffs – sequential phase proj

fast tracking – overlapping

handoff – technical transfer.

phase-end reviews – phase exits, phase gates, milestones, decision gates, stage gates, kill pts

Index

Note to the reader: Throughout this index **boldfaced** page numbers indicate primary discussions of a topic. *Italicized* page numbers indicate illustrations.

Numbers

A

B

D

E

F

G

H

I

J

K

L

M

N

O

P

Q

R

T

Wiley Publishing, Inc.
End-User License Agreement

READ THIS. You should carefully read these terms and conditions before opening the software packet(s) included with this book "Book". This is a license agreement "Agreement" between you and Wiley Publishing, Inc. "WPI". By opening the accompanying software packet(s), you acknowledge that you have read and accept the following terms and conditions. If you do not agree and do not want to be bound by such terms and conditions, promptly return the Book and the unopened software packet(s) to the place you obtained them for a full refund.

1. License Grant. WPI grants to you (either an individual or entity) a nonexclusive license to use one copy of the enclosed software program(s) (collectively, the "Software," solely for your own personal or business purposes on a single computer (whether a standard computer or a workstation component of a multi-user network). The Software is in use on a computer when it is loaded into temporary memory (RAM) or installed into permanent memory (hard disk, CD-ROM, or other storage device). WPI reserves all rights not expressly granted herein.

2. Ownership. WPI is the owner of all right, title, and interest, including copyright, in and to the compilation of the Software recorded on the physical packet included with this Book "Software Media". Copyright to the individual programs recorded on the Software Media is owned by the author or other authorized copyright owner of each program. Ownership of the Software and all proprietary rights relating thereto remain with WPI and its licensers.

3. Restrictions On Use and Transfer.

(a) You may only (i) make one copy of the Software for backup or archival purposes, or (ii) transfer the Software to a single hard disk, provided that you keep the original for backup or archival purposes. You may not (i) rent or lease the Software, (ii) copy or reproduce the Software through a LAN or other network system or through any computer subscriber system or bulletin-board system, or (iii) modify, adapt, or create derivative works based on the Software.

(b) You may not reverse engineer, decompile, or disassemble the Software. You may transfer the Software and user documentation on a permanent basis, provided that the transferee agrees to accept the terms and conditions of this Agreement and you retain no copies. If the Software is an update or has been updated, any transfer must include the most recent update and all prior versions.

4. Restrictions on Use of Individual Programs. You must follow the individual requirements and restrictions detailed for each individual program in the About the CD-ROM appendix of this Book or on the Software Media. These limitations are also contained in the individual license agreements recorded on the Software Media. These limitations may include a requirement that after using the program for a specified period of time, the user must pay a registration fee or discontinue use. By opening the Software packet(s), you will be agreeing to abide by the licenses and restrictions for these individual programs that are detailed in the About the CD-ROM appendix and/or on the Software Media. None of the material on this Software Media or listed in this Book may ever be redistributed, in original or modified form, for commercial purposes.

5. Limited Warranty.

(a) WPI warrants that the Software and Software Media are free from defects in materials and workmanship under normal use for a period of sixty (60) days from the date of purchase of this Book. If WPI receives notification within the warranty period of defects in materials or workmanship, WPI will replace the defective Software Media.

(b) WPI AND THE AUTHOR(S) OF THE BOOK DISCLAIM ALL OTHER WARRANTIES, EXPRESS OR IMPLIED, INCLUDING WITHOUT LIMITATION IMPLIED WARRANTIES OF MERCHANTABILITY AND FITNESS FOR A PARTICULAR PURPOSE, WITH RESPECT TO THE SOFTWARE, THE PROGRAMS, THE SOURCE CODE CONTAINED THEREIN, AND/OR THE TECHNIQUES DESCRIBED IN THIS BOOK. WPI DOES NOT WARRANT THAT THE FUNCTIONS CONTAINED IN THE SOFTWARE WILL MEET YOUR REQUIREMENTS OR THAT THE OPERATION OF THE SOFTWARE WILL BE ERROR FREE.

(c) This limited warranty gives you specific legal rights, and you may have other rights that vary from jurisdiction to jurisdiction.

6. Remedies.

(a) WPI's entire liability and your exclusive remedy for defects in materials and workmanship shall be limited to replacement of the Software Media, which may be returned to WPI with a copy of your receipt at the following address: Software Media Fulfillment Department, Attn.: *PMP: Project Management Professional Exam Study Guide, Fifth Edition*, Wiley Publishing, Inc., 10475 Crosspoint Blvd., Indianapolis, IN 46256, or call 1-800-762-2974. Please allow four to six weeks for delivery. This Limited Warranty is void if failure of the Software Media has resulted from accident, abuse, or misapplication. Any replacement Software Media will be warranted for the remainder of the original warranty period or thirty (30) days, whichever is longer.

(b) In no event shall WPI or the author be liable for any damages whatsoever (including without limitation damages for loss of business profits, business interruption, loss of business information, or any other pecuniary loss) arising from the use of or inability to use the Book or the Software, even if WPI has been advised of the possibility of such damages.

(c) Because some jurisdictions do not allow the exclusion or limitation of liability for consequential or incidental damages, the above limitation or exclusion may not apply to you.

7. U.S. Government Restricted Rights. Use, duplication, or disclosure of the Software for or on behalf of the United States of America, its agencies and/or instrumentalities "U.S. Government" is subject to restrictions as stated in paragraph (c)(1)(ii) of the Rights in Technical Data and Computer Software clause of DFARS 252.227-7013, or subparagraphs (c) (1) and (2) of the Commercial Computer Software - Restricted Rights clause at FAR 52.227-19, and in similar clauses in the NASA FAR supplement, as applicable.

8. General. This Agreement constitutes the entire understanding of the parties and revokes and supersedes all prior agreements, oral or written, between them and may not be modified or amended except in a writing signed by both parties hereto that specifically refers to this Agreement. This Agreement shall take precedence over any other documents that may be in conflict herewith. If any one or more provisions contained in this Agreement are held by any court or tribunal to be invalid, illegal, or otherwise unenforceable, each and every other provision shall remain in full force and effect.

TCPI => To complete performance index.

$$TCPI = \frac{BAC - EV}{BAC - AC}$$

$$TCPI \text{ for } EAC = \frac{BAC - EV}{EAC - AC}$$

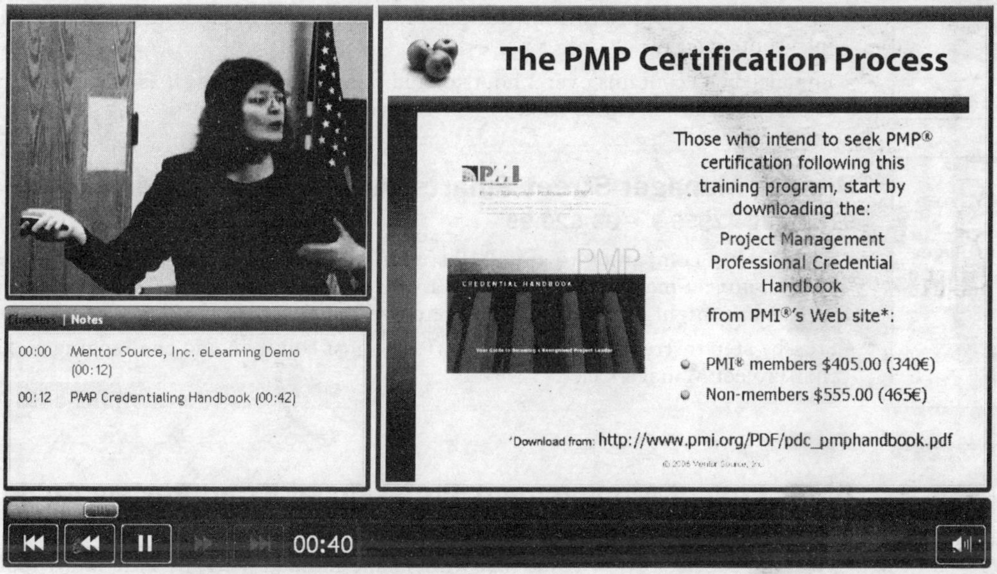

The PMP Certification Process
Those who intend to seek PMP® certification following this training program, start by downloading the:
Project Management Professional Credential Handbook
from PMI®'s Web site*:
PMI® members $405.00 (340€)
Non-members $555.00 (465€)
*Download from: http://www.pmi.org/PDF/pdc_pmphandbook.pdf
CREDENTIAL HANDBOOK
Notes
00:00 Mentor Source, Inc. eLearning Demo (00:12)
00:12 PMP Credentialing Handbook (00:42)
00:40

23 T
te, et fructus fácite : Pro-
FERIA TERTIA
III classis
AD MATUTINUM
De Isaía Prophéta
Erumpant montes iu-
cunditátem, et colles iustí-
tiam : * Quia lux mundi
Dóminus cum poténtia ve-
Lectio iii Cap. 14, 12-15
Quómodo cecidísti de
cælo, lúcifer, qui mane
oriebáris? corruísti in ter-
ram, qui vulnerábas gentes ?
qui dicébas in corde tuo :
cient exactóres suos.
Montes Israel, ramos
vestros expándite, et floré-

CROIRE EN LIBERTÉ

CROIRE EN LIBERTÉ

SOUS LA DIRECTION DE

Jean-François Malherbe
et Jean Desclos

TEXTES DE

Jean Desclos
Marie Gratton
Jean-François Malherbe
Martine Pelletier
Patrick Snyder
Raymond Vaillancourt

SUPERVISION ÉDITORIALE

Daniel Sylvestre

DESSINS

André Bergeron

FIDES

Données de catalogage avant publication (Canada)

Vedette principale au titre :

Croire en liberté

Comprend des réf. bibliogr.

ISBN 2-7621-1957-X

1. Liberté - Aspect religieux - Christianisme.
2. Religion et sciences.
3. Religion et morale.
4. Religion et politique.
5. Médiations.
I. Malherbe, Jean-François, 1950-
II. Desclos, Jean.

BV4637.C76 1999 234'.23 C99-940354-0

Dépôt légal : 2e trimestre 1999
Bibliothèque nationale du Québec

Les Éditions Fides remercient le ministère du Patrimoine canadien du soutien qui leur est accordé dans le cadre du Programme d'aide au développement de l'industrie de l'édition. Les Éditions Fides remercient également le Conseil des Arts du Canada et la Société de développement des entreprises culturelles du Québec (SODEC).

AVANT-PROPOS

Au XIXe siècle, le philosophe Friedrich Nietzsche a proclamé la mort de Dieu. Au XXe, siècle par excellence de l'indécision spirituelle, on a prêté à André Malraux l'idée que le XXIe siècle serait religieux ou ne serait pas.

La question abordée de front dans cet ouvrage par une équipe d'enseignants de la Faculté de théologie, d'éthique et de philosophie de l'Université de Sherbrooke est celle-ci : *sera-t-il absurde de croire en Dieu au XXIe siècle ?* La réponse est négative, c'est clair. Toutefois, elle ne tiendra qu'au prix d'une révision substantielle de nos préjugés en matière de foi religieuse. Croire reste possible. Mais pas dans la naïveté d'une pensée prête-à-porter. Pas dans la soumission à des doctrines déformées par les routines ecclésiastiques.

Croire a toujours été et restera toujours un des actes les plus purs de la liberté d'être, même si, trop souvent, il est apparu comme un acte de sujétion.

C'est que Dieu, autant qu'Il puisse « vouloir » quoi que ce soit, ne peut que vouloir la liberté des humains. C'est dire que lorsque nous exerçons notre liberté, de façon responsable et créative, c'est la volonté de Dieu que nous accomplissons.

Dans cette perspective, l'acte de croire revêt explicitement une dimension de libération que tant les institutions religieuses que les destitutions athées de Dieu tolèrent assez mal. Et pourtant, c'est l'essence même de la foi en Dieu qui s'exprime dans cette liberté que l'on perçoit souvent encore comme une fronde. C'est que la foi en actes, la foi véritable, renvoie dos à dos l'athéisme et le fidéisme à leurs préjugés.

Tenter de dire à haute et intelligible voix quelques éléments essentiels de la foi chrétienne à l'intention d'un public aussi vaste que possible, composé, tel que nous nous le figurons, à la fois de chrétiens pratiquants inquiets, de croyants d'autres religions, de chrétiens non pratiquants, d'ex-chrétiens, d'agnostiques et d'athées, tel est le défi que nous avons voulu relever.

Et pour nous, ce travail fut un plaisir, car approfondir notre propre foi nous libère de préjugés restés jusqu'ici inaperçus. Mettre ensemble nos idées sur papier, les confronter, les discuter, les reformuler nous a été une grande joie.

L'acte de croire est un acte de profonde confiance. C'est ce que je tente d'indiquer dans le premier chapitre. Mais l'acte de foi est aussi un acte de liberté qui n'est lisible dans son intelligibilité intrinsèque qu'avec les lunettes de la foi. C'est ce que je souligne dans le chapitre suivant intitulé *Des lunettes pour lire la foi.*

Dans des chapitres subséquents, Raymond Vaillancourt nous propose une méditation sur les temps qui nourrissent l'acte de croire. Des étapes dans l'année aux âges dans la vie, il parcourt avec nous la structuration chrétienne de la temporalité qui confère à nos existences le sens de leur pèlerinage dans la durée.

Mais l'acte de croire n'est pas un acte d'un monde autre que le nôtre. C'est une prise de position souvent radicale face aux multiples défis que nous pose le projet de bâtir un monde plus humain. Que ce soit dans l'ordre de la sexualité, du rapport entre science et foi, de l'action politique ou des rapports entre cultures, l'acte de foi ne reste pas lettre morte.

Marie Gratton s'interroge sur les malentendus et les incompréhensions qui hantent les doctrines ecclésiastiques sur la sexualité et la procréation. Elle y décèle une réelle difficulté de l'Église à « faire confiance aux ventres des femmes, ces creusets de l'amour » (comme dit Christiane Singer) alors même que la foi chrétienne affirme que Dieu lui-même a pris chair des entrailles d'une femme.

Ensuite, je m'interroge sur l'« affaire Galilée » et tente de montrer que le véritable problème n'est peut-être pas celui qu'on croit habituellement. En deçà de l'*opposition* radicale de la science et de la foi, chère à l'athéisme rationaliste hérité du siècle des Lumières, semble se dessiner, à la suite de Teilhard de Chardin, mais aussi en toute indépendance à son égard, un courant qui fonde sur l'éthique la possibilité d'une rigoureuse *articulation* de la science et de la foi. Telle est la perspective que je m'attache à esquisser.

L'éthique, toutefois, ne suffit pas à la construction d'une société plus humaine. Elle en appelle donc aussi à la politique, c'est-à-dire à l'art de gouverner la Cité, aussi éthiquement qu'il est possible. C'est Jean Desclos qui aborde cette délicate question. Il rappelle que servir le monde n'est jamais sans risque et que si l'Église, parfois, n'a pas les mains immaculées, c'est sans doute qu'elle les a mises à la pâte de nos réalités sociales et économiques. Il réaffirme toutefois la nécessité d'une vigilante lucidité pour éviter que l'Église n'emboîte le pas, comme ce fut parfois le cas, à des mouvements totalitaires.

Une autre question très délicate nous a préoccupés : celle des rapports entre unité et pluralité. C'est devenu un lieu commun que d'affirmer que nous vivons aujourd'hui, à l'aube du XXIe siècle, dans un monde pluriel, dans une société pluraliste, tant au niveau des valeurs de référence que des pratiques sociales.

Comment, à travers cette légitime diversité, construire une unité qui respecte les différences et, même, en fasse le principe de notre enrichissement mutuel ? Telle est la question qu'aborde Marie Gratton dans une réflexion à la fois exigeante et novatrice.

À propos de la question très controversée des rapports de la conscience morale à la loi je rappelle que la loi n'est jamais un absolu mais toujours un repère destiné à éclairer la conscience. Comme le disait d'ailleurs l'ancienne scolastique tant décriée de nos jours : la dernière règle pratique (c'est-à-dire celle qui exprime la décision en situation) est dictée non pas par la loi mais par la conscience en référence à la loi.

Le volume se termine par une brève méditation en forme d'action de grâce. Je tente d'y dénouer un possible malentendu au sujet de la liberté dont il se sera agi tout au long de l'ouvrage. Qu'en est-il de la supposée rivalité entre notre liberté d'humains et celle de Dieu, rivalité que tant d'athées considèrent implicitement comme la pierre angulaire de leur position ? Je tente d'esquisser à ce sujet un point de vue inspiré du mystique Eckhart : la liberté humaine, lorsqu'elle est affranchie de tous ses leurres, c'est tout uniment la liberté de Dieu.

En achevant cet avant-propos, je souhaite exprimer la reconnaissance des auteurs à toute l'équipe des Éditions Fides. Sous la conduite lucide et décidée de leur directeur général, Antoine Del Busso, à qui l'on doit d'ailleurs l'idée de ce volume, elle a réalisé un travail technique à la hauteur des relations amicales qui sont nées entre nous.

Jean-François Malherbe

ACCÈS

LA FOI : UNE EXPÉRIENCE DE LIBERTÉ

JEAN-FRANÇOIS MALHERBE

La foi est une expérience — littéralement une mise à l'épreuve — de la liberté à laquelle tout sujet humain est convié.

Chacun de nous, lorsqu'il prend conscience de son appartenance à l'humanité, se découvre héritier d'un patrimoine qu'il n'a pas choisi. Sa langue maternelle véhicule une culture qui, pour une part au moins, façonne l'existence qui lui est donnée au départ et dans laquelle il s'est trouvé inséré sans avoir pu y consentir ni s'y soustraire.

Cet héritage, toutefois, n'est pas une fatalité qui dirigerait sa vie selon une causalité irréfragable. C'est plutôt un point d'appui, un roc, sur lequel construire sa propre destinée. Toute existence humaine n'est-elle pas mémoire de l'héritage en direction d'un à-venir à vivre ?

Souvent, les humains ont peur de la liberté et se racontent des histoires pour se persuader que leur vie est toute tracée d'avance. Mais qui veut ouvrir les yeux, les oreilles, le nez, la bouche et les mains s'aperçoit vite des choix que lui apporte la vie.

La liberté est une épreuve que nous dénions ou que nous accueillons, une grâce qui nous est offerte et que nous refusons ou recevons, une dimension de la création que nous récusons ou célébrons.

Toute forme de culture, à cet égard, montre son ambivalence. Chacun, selon son désir, y trouve de quoi colmater les brèches de la liberté et se rassurer en remplaçant ses incertitudes par de fausses vérités ou, tout au contraire, y crée des occasions d'avancer pas à pas à la découverte d'une vérité que construit son propre cheminement. Ulysse ou Abraham. Faire le tour de la question et retrouver la sécurité de son point de départ. Ou, tout à l'opposé, partir en compagnie du Dieu inconnu, à la recherche de sa propre identité, une recherche qui construit l'identité plus qu'elle ne la trouve. N'est-ce pas cette confiance au Dieu inconnu, à chaque pas renouvelée, qui, seule, nous apporte la sécurité de vivre en bonne compagnie avec les incertitudes de l'existence ?

La foi se présente souvent comme une réponse préfabriquée à nos questions de toujours. C'est une tendance perpétuelle de l'esprit humain que de vouloir récupérer jusqu'à la transcendance elle-même dans les leurres qu'il se construit pour se rassurer. La foi se transforme alors en superstition, en idéologie, en rationalisation. C'est pourquoi nombre d'esprits libres la rejettent.

Mais ce qui est ainsi rejeté, ce n'est pas la foi elle-même. Ce n'en est qu'un simulacre, que l'absolutisation des traces sédimentées des démarches de ceux et celles qui nous ont précédés. Car la transcendance n'est pas un objet saisissable. C'est plutôt cette irrécupérable différence qui marque l'excès de notre désir d'être sur tous les avoirs que nous pouvons accumuler. Et la foi, loin de faire taire nos désirs, nos questions et nos incertitudes, les avive et nous brûle de les combler. Elle les porte à l'incandescence, à ce point de non-retour où, se retournant un bref instant sur le chemin parcouru, désirs, questions et incertitudes s'aperçoivent qu'ils sont les symptômes de la vie en nous de la transcendance. Les signes de la naissance en nous de la divinité.

Alors, la foi devient épreuve du vide plutôt que comblement, accueil de l'inconnu plutôt que répétition du trop connu, jouissance de la création plutôt que souffrance de la destinée. Le sujet de foi, d'un même mouvement, découvre ainsi en lui un Dieu qui le jette hors de lui, hors de son passé auquel il s'identifie. Un Dieu qui lui confirme que sa condition humaine n'est pas fermée sur elle-même mais ouverte à la condition divine. Un Dieu qui l'affranchit de toute malédiction.

Et la bénédiction de Dieu, alors, se fait ainsi chair en chacun des sujets de foi pour se diffuser à travers sa vie en direction de tous ses semblables humains, comme du cosmos tout entier.

La théologie, lorsqu'elle renonce à n'être que l'écho des paroles d'autrefois qui, en leur temps, furent vives, mais ont fini par s'user à force de répétition, passe par l'épreuve d'un long et tragique silence, d'une parole en souffrance. De n'être pas reprise prématurément, cette parole mûrit comme le bon vin, à l'abri des lumières trop fortes, puis finit par se laisser tirer hors de l'obscure protection du chêne et jaillit en paroles vives...

Tel est le sens de ce livre à plusieurs voix. Tel est l'espoir de ce jeu « re-créatif » que nous avons voulu risquer ensemble : esquisser une *mémoire prospective* de l'héritage. Pour apporter un peu d'air frais à la petite étincelle divine qui couve sous la cendre de nos certitudes toutes faites comme de nos frustrations scandalisées, à la petite étincelle inextinguible, mais souvent négligée, ignorée, voire déniée dont la reconnaissance fait de nous des affranchis.

LE « CROIRE » ET LE « CRU »

Le « croire » survient inévitablement dans le contact, la rencontre, la relation à d'autres. Il surgit rarement dans la solitude silencieuse du cœur qui se recentre sur soi. Il naît en terrain communautaire, dans l'attention à l'Autre et aux autres qui disent et agissent selon leur foi.

Le « cru » est visiblement plus fragile que le « croire ». Je ne sais pas de certitude absolue que Dieu existe, que les anges et les archanges peuplent le ciel, que les livres saints sont inspirés, que Jésus est le Fils de Dieu, que l'Esprit agit dans les cœurs. Mais je sais que j'y crois, et que je ne suis pas le seul à y croire. Que cela plaise ou non, les croyants ont d'abord accès aux *représentations* qu'ils se font de Dieu, et non à Dieu lui-même. C'est très bien ainsi, et fort cohérent avec ce que l'Écriture nous enseigne sur Dieu que l'on ne peut voir sans mourir. Tous les « crus » nous renvoient donc aux « croires » multiples, à ces lieux et médiations de nos recherches de Dieu avec d'autres. Et c'est pourquoi la foi doit se dire, se partager, se vivre en dialogue des cœurs et des esprits.

L'UNIVERS DE LA FOI

L'univers de la foi est un immense construit symbolique, non par défaut de l'intelligence humaine qui serait incapable de saisir la transcendance, mais d'abord par chance, voire par nécessaire cohérence avec la dimension « angélique » de l'humain. Comment, en effet, penser une vie spirituelle, c'est-à-dire essentiellement libre, ouverte, disponible à la nouveauté, à l'inconnu, au bien, à l'Autre et à l'Être, autrement que sur la corde de la libre interprétation, laissée à l'intelligence, par une référence qui « donne à penser » sans limites ? Les mots de la foi chrétienne, à la manière des paraboles de Jésus, interpellent chacune et chacun à faire sa propre lecture, et à revivre, à partir des objets, à partir des « crus » soumis à son attention croyante, la démarche d'une adhésion de foi, d'un « croire » authentiquement solidaire et authentiquement libre. Et c'est en se partageant ces diverses lectures que surgit, dans une chimie dont l'Esprit a la recette, la communion à une même doctrine, à un même « cru ».

La foi se transmet, comme la culture, la langue. Elle s'apprend et elle s'oublie. Elle est un héritage, une réalité que l'on reçoit, ou un cadeau. Elle est également un choix, un projet personnel, une option. La foi tient sur le registre du religieux socialement manifesté et vérifiable, le religieux en son sens commun de mythes, de rites, de règles fixés par le groupe. Elle se comprend aussi comme attitude intérieure tissée discrètement dans le patient travail pour se libérer de soi, se détacher de soi pour adhérer à plus que soi. ◇

Jean Desclos

DES LUNETTES POUR LIRE

LIRE LA PRÉSENCE DE DIEU

Jean-François Malherbe

À un jeune couple déçu qui revenait de l'hôpital suite à un espoir avorté d'avoir un enfant, un ami religieux demanda s'ils n'en voulaient pas trop à Dieu. « Mais Dieu n'a rien à se reprocher dans cette histoire ! Ni nous non plus. C'est le hasard de la nature. Dieu n'est pas contre nous, mais avec nous ! » lui répondit le mari, tandis que son épouse esquissait un sourire aussi douloureux qu'approbateur.

La foi consiste-t-elle à imputer à Dieu la responsabilité de tout ce qui nous arrive, surtout de ce qui survient par hasard ? Ou bien consiste-t-elle à vivre en compagnie de Dieu tout ce qui nous arrive, les souffrances comme les jouissances ?

Deux lectures divergentes entrent en collision dans ce bout de conversation. Selon la première, celle du religieux, la foi demanderait à ces jeunes parents d'accepter leur déception comme un châtiment mérité ou, à tout le moins, comme une épreuve voulue par Dieu qui leur donne ainsi l'occasion de croître en sainteté. Selon la seconde, celle du couple, la foi est vécue comme proximité de Dieu dans l'événement malheureux lui-même.

La première lecture s'inscrit dans une perspective que Jésus lui-même, selon ce qu'en raconte Jean l'Évangéliste, récusait sans ambages. À ses disciples qui lui demandaient si c'était l'aveugle-né ou ses parents qui avaient péché pour qu'il soit venu au monde ainsi, le Fils de l'homme répondit : « Ce n'est ni lui ni ses parents, c'est pour que se manifestent en lui les travaux de Dieu » (*Jn* 9).

La seconde lecture, par contre, se trouve en harmonie avec l'enseignement de Jésus : quoi qu'il arrive, Dieu est avec nous. Pour un jeune couple qui se réjouit d'attendre un enfant,

ANGE

Du grec *angelos*, qui signifie « messager », les anges étaient et sont toujours considérés dans l'imaginaire collectif comme des envoyés invisibles de Dieu.

Saint Thomas d'Aquin soutient, dans l'un de ses plus beaux traités de la *Somme théologique*, celui sur *Les Anges*, qu'il y a des bons et des mauvais anges. Selon lui, les mauvais anges, qui ont volontairement et librement péché contre Dieu, incitent à faire le mal. Pour leur part, les bons anges, que saint Thomas décrit comme d'une nature spirituelle supérieure à la nôtre, ont comme vocation de nous venir en aide ici-bas par leur protection bienveillante.

À l'aube du XXIe siècle, dans un univers technicien, les anges sont encore très en vogue. En fin de compte, la croyance à l'existence des anges ou à celle des anges-gardiens ne reflète-t-elle pas encore aujourd'hui le besoin de se donner des signes de la proximité et de l'action de Dieu dans le monde ? Habituellement, le nom qu'on donne aux anges : Raphaël, Gabriel, Michel, inclut la terminaison EL, c'est-à-dire le nom hébreu *Elohim* signifiant Dieu*. ◇

* Sauf indication contraire, les textes en retrait sont de Patrick Snyder, chargé de cours à la Faculté de théologie, d'éthique et de philosophie de l'Université de Sherbrooke.

Feria secunda ad Completorium
163
In manus tuas, Dómine, commendo spíritum meum, * Allelúia, allelúia. In manus tuas. ℣. Redemísti nos, Dómine, Deus veritátis. Allelúia, allelúia. Glória Pa-
Sub umbra alárum tuárum prótege nos, allelúia.
secúndum verbum tuum in pace.
ante fáciem ómnium populórum,
custódi nos dormiéntes; ut vigilémus cum Christo et requiescámus in
manes, et stella maris,
succúrre cadénti,

apprendre qu'il est atteint d'une malformation mortelle et le perdre représente une grande déception, une souffrance difficile à vivre, une contradiction absurde. La foi ne soustrait rien à la douleur, n'enlève pas un iota à la frustration, ne console nullement la détresse que vivent ces parents « désenfantés ». Leur foi, c'est leur expérience qu'en dépit de leur malheur, ils sont aimés de Dieu.

Cette foi qu'ils portent et qui les porte apparaît aux yeux du monde comme une illusion qu'ils déploient pour vivre malgré tout, comme une béquille sur laquelle ils s'appuient pour continuer à marcher, comme un trompe-l'œil qui les rend étrangers à leur propre réalité.

Mais eux-mêmes, tout au contraire, éprouvent leur foi comme une réalité nourrissant à chaque étape leur faim de pèlerins, comme un chemin construit par leurs propres pas, comme un avenir ouvert qui les appelle à se révéler à eux-mêmes.

La foi qui engendre

Un ami m'a raconté que sa mère lui avait un jour envoyé pour son anniversaire, peu de temps après son divorce, dans un épisode de sa vie marqué par de profondes perturbations et une grande solitude, une carte postale qui illustrait l'histoire de Théophile. Théophile (nom grec qui signifie : ami de Dieu), arrivé au soir de sa vie, rencontra Dieu face à face qui lui demanda comment il avait vécu sa vie. Il répondit : « Ça n'a pas toujours été facile, car tu m'as faussé la route, me semble-t-il, aux moments les plus pénibles. Regarde la trace de mes pas dans le monde, elle chemine côte à côte avec celle de tes propres pas. Mais, aux passages les plus pénibles de l'itinéraire, ta trace disparaît. » Dieu lui répondit : « Mais Théophile, s'il n'y a qu'une trace de pas en ces pénibles passages, c'est la mienne ; c'est moi qui te portais ! »

L'histoire est jolie et plusieurs lecteurs la connaissaient sans doute déjà. Mais elle ne s'arrête pas ici.

En effet, mon ami ajouta que quelques années plus tard, sa mère mourante se plaignit à lui d'avoir été abandonnée par son mari, mort quelques jours plus tôt. Il me confia l'avoir apaisée en lui répondant ceci. « Mais maman, te souviens-tu de l'histoire de Théophile que tu m'as envoyée autrefois pour mon anniversaire ? Ne penses-tu pas que papa, loin de t'avoir abandonnée, a pu prendre un peu d'avance pour t'ouvrir la porte ? »

Cet ami prenait-il son propre père pour Dieu ? Voulait-il rendre à sa mère « la monnaie de sa pièce » ? pourrait demander un esprit fort. Je l'ignore. Nul ne peut jamais prétendre ses actions exemptes de toute ambivalence. Mais ce n'est pas ce qui importe ici. L'essentiel est, en effet, de saisir que la foi, par le témoignage, engendre la foi.

Nul sujet de foi n'est en effet isolé. La foi qu'il vit, il l'a reçue en partage d'autres sujets de foi qui le précédaient sur ce chemin où l'on devient soi dans la mesure où l'on se laisse déprendre de ces fausses images de soi auxquelles on tient tant. Ces images sont l'héritage que nous recevons de la culture qui est la nôtre. Elles nous façonnent dès avant que nous puissions le savoir. Elles font de nous leurs complices dès que nous voulons plaire. Elles nous persuadent qu'elles détiennent notre identité alors même qu'elles nous enserrent dans les lourds vêtements qui entravent notre pèlerinage.

Si la vie en compagnie de Dieu — qu'on appelle ici « la foi » — se nourrit de symboles (tels les traces de pas) comme de paraboles (telle l'histoire de Théophile), c'est tout simplement parce que les symboles comme les paraboles crient leur inadéquation en même temps qu'ils signifient leur vérité. La présence active de Dieu dans la vie quotidienne est, en effet, une expérience à proprement parler indicible. Et toute image qui prétendrait l'exprimer ne pourrait être que blasphématoire, c'est-à-dire faire injure à Dieu. La seule issue possible qui à la fois respecte Dieu et nous-mêmes est donc d'en parler en symboles et paraboles.

Mais si telle est notre condition — notre finitude, disent les philosophes —, n'est-ce pas le signe que toute foi qui prétend à l'authenticité se doit d'être iconoclaste? N'est-il pas interdit, aujourd'hui encore, dans la religion juive, de représenter Dieu, fût-ce en prononçant son nom? Mais, ce que la mort de Jésus en croix nous a révélé, c'est que l'iconoclasme divin conduit à l'iconoclasme humain. Ne sont-ce pas, en effet, tout à la fois les fausses images de l'homme et les fausses images de Dieu qui sont mortes sur la croix?

La foi, c'est l'expérience de la vie qui tente, dans le récit qu'elle se fait de son propre cheminement, de se laisser déprendre des pièges de son propre héritage. Ce sont les moments de crise de la vie qui sont les plus difficiles à raconter, car ils ne s'inscrivent pas, précisément parce qu'ils sont des crises, dans la logique des épisodes antérieurs. Ils en défient l'intelligibilité acquise. Ils en défont les images toutes faites. Ils en détruisent les certitudes. Les moments de crise sont donc les moments favorables de la foi, les moments de liberté.

Ce n'est pas parce qu'une crise apporte avec elle son lot de souffrances qu'elle prend de la valeur, c'est parce qu'elle accule à un discernement, à séparer le faux du vrai, à discriminer l'image et le symbole. Une crise provoque toujours la fissure, voire le déchirement de nos images de Dieu comme de nos images de nous-mêmes. C'est pourquoi les crises sont souffrantes. Mais nous ne sommes pas seuls dans la souffrance si nous lisons en toute chose la présence de Dieu. D'autant moins seuls que cette présence prend souvent le visage d'un autre humain.

Ce qui est en jeu ici, c'est ma capacité de me faire illusion à moi-même en me racontant une histoire qui n'est pas vraiment celle de ma vie en présence de Dieu ; c'est que je mette en scène soit un faux Dieu, soit un faux moi. Comment donc raconter en vérité l'histoire de sa vie en présence de Dieu ? Il n'y a de récit vrai de ma vie que dans la parole qui se donne à interpréter à l'oreille d'un autre qui sache me désarçonner de mes propres illusions en

APOCALYPSE

Le mot apocalypse a pour plusieurs une signification négative. Il est souvent employé pour désigner ou annoncer de grandes catastrophes, voire la fin du monde. Pourtant, ce mot, du latin *apocalypsis* et du grec *apokalupsis*, signifie tout simplement « révélation ». Il peut s'agir de révélations sur le jugement divin de la fin des temps ou sur la personne de Jésus.

Le *Livre de l'Apocalypse*, ou « Révélation », attribué par l'Église à l'apôtre Jean, n'a pas comme objectif d'annoncer les grands cataclysmes qui marqueront la fin des temps. Ce livre veut nous faire saisir, dans un genre littéraire bien particulier, que le salut se réalise dans l'histoire à travers l'action de multiples acteurs. L'auteur veut aussi témoigner que le Christ et l'Église ont, après des luttes terribles, triomphé des forces du mal. Ce message d'espérance étant destiné aux nouveaux chrétiens menacés par la persécution, on peut comprendre que l'auteur ait choisi, dans un contexte particulièrement dramatique, un style d'écriture adapté aux circonstances.

À l'approche du troisième millénaire, il est tentant pour de nombreux leaders et groupes religieux d'utiliser l'Apocalypse pour annoncer une fin du monde violente et imminente. Cela est en soi une fausse utilisation de cette œuvre. Si l'arrivée du troisième millénaire représente une date importante pour les chrétiens et les chrétiennes, c'est qu'il commémore la naissance de Jésus et la perspective du salut pour tous. ◇

écoutant, au travers des mots de l'histoire, la souffrance secrète qui l'habite. Un autre qui, par la vertu de son oreille, pratique en moi cette brèche par laquelle je serai délivré, petit à petit, de mes terreurs les plus enfouies comme de mes espoirs les plus cachés. Finalement, cette délivrance sera accomplie quand il s'avérera qu'elle est elle-même illusoire et que la seule chose qui compte, en définitive, c'est le mouvement même de la parole à la recherche de sa propre vérité. C'est dire qu'il n'y a pas de foi vivante sans altérité, sans un autre à qui puisse se dire cette recherche qui trouve son objet dans son mouvement même.

Étincelle de Dieu

Un maître de vie est un autre pèlerin qui marche avec nous quelques pas et disparaît quand nous le reconnaissons. Le Dieu de la foi est comme l'amant du *Cantique des cantiques* : lorsque son aimée le rejoint, il manque à l'appel.

Une telle perspective est-elle absurde en philosophie ? Mais non ! La raison humaine, lorsqu'elle tente de penser ses propres limites, s'aperçoit aisément que les principes de certaines options de vie sont indémontrables. S'il n'est pas possible de démontrer l'existence de Dieu, il est tout aussi impossible de démontrer son inexistence, c'est logique[1]. L'existence du mal est sans doute la plus forte objection contre l'existence d'un Créateur bon et tout-puissant[2]. Mais l'idée d'un Dieu bon et tout-puissant n'implique pas qu'il soit directement responsable de tout ce qui survient dans sa création. Il se pourrait, en effet, que Dieu ait créé l'univers

1. Voir Emmanuel KANT : *Critique de la raison pure* (1781), multiples traductions françaises.

2. Voir Paul RICŒUR : *Le Mal, défi à la philosophie et à la théologie*, Labor et Fides, Genève, 1985.

indéterminé et que celui-ci ait donné naissance à un animal doué de liberté, appelé à répondre de son monde comme de lui-même. Et si cet animal, c'était l'humain ?

La foi n'est lisible qu'avec les lunettes de la foi. Autrement dit, la foi ne se démontre pas. Mais se communique et peut s'avérer féconde. On la juge d'ailleurs aux fruits dont elle se nourrit. Mais à nouveau, ceux-ci ne sont lisibles, comme fruits de la foi tout autant que sa nourriture, que par les lunettes de la foi. Est-ce à dire que la foi est, de part en part, subjective ? Assurément, puisque ce sont des sujets qui la vivent. Mais ne vaut-il pas mieux une subjectivité vécue qui soit libératrice qu'une objectivité réductrice ?

YAHVÉ

L'innommable a-t-il un nom ? Selon *Exode* 3,14, Moïse entend Dieu se présenter ainsi : « Je suis celui qui suis », en hébreu, *hâwah* ou *hâyah*, qui se traduit par arriver, devenir, être et être agissant. Il ne faut pas entendre cette formule comme une définition métaphysique de Dieu, mais comme l'assurance d'une présence fidèle passée, actuelle et à venir. La transcription du mot hébreu donne Yahvé ou Jéhovah. Les juifs ne prononcent jamais le nom de Yahvé et le remplacent par un respectueux silence. ◇

Il était une fois un peintre passionné qui, depuis de longues années, s'efforçait de faire le portrait de Dieu. Il progressait. Lorsqu'il croyait avoir achevé son œuvre, il s'en allait prendre un peu de repos. Au retour, il trouvait toujours un défaut à son tableau et le brûlait. Toutefois, il ne désespérait pas car, au fil des années, il éprouvait une familiarité de plus en plus intense avec la vie qu'il tentait d'exprimer dans ses toiles.

Un matin, après une nuit de repos qu'il s'était accordée plus longue que d'habitude, il fut surpris par la qualité de son travail de la veille. Il s'extasia et, fou de joie, se prit à rire et à pleurer tout à la fois. Il fit venir son ami pour lui partager son bonheur. Ce dernier applaudit, chanta la réussite. Ensemble, ils célébrèrent le chef-d'œuvre.

Au moment où son hôte allait prendre congé, le peintre lui posa cette question : « Qu'est-ce qui te frappe le plus dans ce portrait ? » L'autre lui répondit, enthousiaste : « Tu es vraiment très ressemblant, c'est magnifique ! »

Cette remarque laissa le peintre aussi seul que désemparé. Ainsi donc, son fameux portrait de Dieu, si réussi, n'était que son autoportrait ! Il était désespéré et allait, comme d'habitude, brûler la toile, mais il ne put s'y résoudre, car elle était vraiment très ressemblante. Il avait réussi à rendre avec ses pinceaux cette lumière intérieure qu'il avait observée parfois chez ces gens tout simples qui semblaient voir au-delà des apparences.

Il conserva donc la toile, mais arrêta de peindre. Il n'en avait plus le goût. Cependant, il n'était pas malheureux. Il ressentait à certains moments une sorte de chaleur en lui, qui le brûlait doucement. Il se sentait calme et ouvert, faisait de longues marches dans la montagne et revenait le soir à son atelier rempli d'air, de parfums de fleurs et de soleil. Souvent, il méditait.

Un soir, en rentrant d'une randonnée particulièrement agréable, il s'assit, épuisé, face à son propre portrait et, levant doucement les yeux sur son œuvre, il vit, au-delà des apparences, la petite étincelle divine qui brûlait au fond de ses yeux. Il sut que son œuvre n'était pas une image, mais un symbole. Le lendemain, il écrivit à son ami et lui confia que la présence de Dieu peut prendre n'importe quel visage, mais toujours le transfigure. Puis, il reprit son travail.

DES TEMPS POUR NOURRIR LA FOI

DES ÉTAPES DANS L'ANNÉE

Raymond Vaillancourt

Le temps, avec l'espace, constitue l'une des deux dimensions fondamentales de l'univers. Le temps situe et structure la vie humaine, ne serait-ce qu'en délimitant sa durée par la naissance et la mort. Les sociétés et les cultures structurent le temps chacune à leur façon. Dans notre culture, on parle du temps des fêtes, des vacances, des mois d'école, etc. Il en est de même dans l'univers chrétien : les chrétiens, catholiques, protestants et orthodoxes, se situent dans le temps à travers une série de fêtes et de périodes liées à des moments de la vie de Jésus (l'Avent, Noël, le Carême, Pâques, la Pentecôte) ou des personnes qui ont été des témoins exemplaires de foi (fête des saints et des saintes). La façon chrétienne de structurer le temps se reflète au niveau de l'année, de la semaine et de la journée.

L'histoire nous montre une relation étroite entre les temps liturgiques et les temps sociaux et culturels. On peut même affirmer que le temps liturgique chrétien, à l'instar du temps liturgique juif, s'est moulé sur le temps social fortement lié aux cycles de la nature. Aujourd'hui, avec la forte urbanisation des sociétés, une distance de plus en plus grande apparaît entre le temps liturgique et le temps social. On constate même une pluralité de structures du temps social : année scolaire, année fiscale, année pastorale distincte de l'année liturgique. La structuration du temps chrétien n'est plus la seule référence dans les sociétés actuelles, même si elle garde encore une influence principalement avec Noël et Pâques. Cette nouvelle situation manifeste une restructuration de notre rapport au temps qui bouscule la logique des temps liturgiques et peut en voiler la signification spirituelle.

Même si elle côtoie d'autres façons de structurer le temps, la structure chrétienne du temps a sa logique propre. Nous la présenterons dans ce chapitre à travers les cycles annuels, hebdomadaires et quotidiens qui commémorent les grands moments de la révélation en Jésus Christ.

L'année liturgique

Au plan religieux, on divise l'année en cinq temps : le temps de l'Avent, le temps de Noël, le temps du Carême, le temps de Pâques et le temps dit ordinaire. Dans ces temps s'insèrent les grandes fêtes liturgiques et les fêtes des saints et des saintes. En raison de l'influence du christianisme dans la société, ces expressions font encore généralement partie du langage courant en Occident.

Pour comprendre le sens de ces temps liturgiques, il faut se situer dans la tradition juive, reprise et transformée par la tradition chrétienne. Ce qui les caractérise toutes deux, c'est la conviction que, pour les croyants et les croyantes, Dieu est intervenu dans l'histoire. L'année liturgique veut rappeler à la conscience chrétienne les grands événements de l'intervention de Dieu dans l'histoire humaine. Les croyants se réfèrent donc à l'histoire du salut. Comme dans l'Ancien Testament, le culte consistait à faire mémoire des interventions de Dieu dans la vie du peuple d'Israël, dans la Nouvelle Alliance, les célébrations des temps liturgiques font mémoire des principaux faits et gestes de Jésus, révélation de Dieu. Le culte a aussi d'autres fonctions. Il rappelle à la conscience chrétienne les événements fondateurs du christianisme, il montre la portée actuelle de ces événements historiques, tant au plan moral que doctrinal, et, comme l'histoire est en marche, il montre la direction de l'histoire. Pour reprendre une formulation théologique classique, le culte est signe *commémoratif* d'événements passés, *démonstratif* d'une réalité en réalisation et *préfiguratif* d'événements à venir.

Dans une société sécularisée, les temps liturgiques ne correspondent plus entièrement aux temps sociaux. Nous reviendrons sur quelques questions posées par ce nouveau contexte socioculturel après avoir brièvement exposé la symbolique chrétienne du cycle annuel.

Dans l'univers chrétien catholique, l'année liturgique commence avec le premier dimanche de l'Avent. Suivent les temps de Noël, du carême, de Pâques et le temps dit ordinaire. Si le temps de l'Avent commence l'année liturgique, cela ne signifie pas que la fête de Noël à laquelle il prépare soit la plus importante. Historiquement, la célébration de Pâques a été à l'origine des temps liturgiques et est la fête la plus importante de l'année liturgique. Ici, nous présenterons les temps liturgiques en respectant l'ordre historique et l'importance théologique et spirituelle, soit le temps de Pâques avec sa préparation, le Carême, les temps de Noël et de l'Avent, et le temps dit ordinaire.

Pâques

Même si l'année liturgique commence avec l'Avent, il ne faut pas oublier qu'historiquement toute la liturgie chrétienne prend naissance avec la célébration de la Pâque du Christ. Les premières prédications font référence au mystère de la mort et de la résurrection du Christ. Le culte chrétien est né de Pâques. Dans les premiers temps, on ne célébrait pas *les* mystères du Christ, mais *le* mystère du Christ, c'est-à-dire son passage de la mort à la vie. Et cette célébration se renouvelait chaque dimanche. Mais très tôt, sans doute sous l'influence du culte juif, on fit d'un dimanche particulier la grande célébration de la Pâque du Seigneur, précédée de trois jours de jeûne et de prières, appelés un *Triduum*. Par la suite, voulant contempler et revivre chaque moment de la passion du Christ, on fit précéder cette fête de la Pâque de la commémoration du dernier repas de Jésus, de sa passion et de sa mort ; ce qui a donné naissance aux jours saints et, plus tard, à la semaine sainte. On faisait ainsi mémoire des derniers moments de la vie de Jésus. La célébration de la Pâque exprimait donc une vérité historique et doctrinale.

C'est autour de la fête de Pâques, spécialement au cours de la nuit pascale, que s'instaura tout le processus de l'initiation chrétienne. C'était normal, puisque l'adhésion au Christ par le baptême impliquait la référence à la mort et à la résurrection du Christ, comme le dit saint Paul aux Romains (*Rm* 6,4).

Précédé des quarante jours du carême, le temps pascal se prolonge cinquante jours après la fête de Pâques. On y rappelle d'abord les récits des apparitions du Christ ressuscité pour ensuite faire mémoire de deux événements ou expériences des apôtres, l'Ascension du Christ au mont Thabor et l'expérience des apôtres prenant conscience d'une nouvelle présence du Christ par son Esprit au jour de la Pentecôte, fête qui met un terme au cycle pascal.

Le Carême

Ce temps est bien connu. L'expression même fait partie de notre culture malgré un mouvement de sécularisation grandissant. On dit populairement d'une personne triste qu'elle a une « face de carême ». Le mercredi des cendres, qui inaugure le Carême, donnait un ton à la fois d'humilité et de pénitence, voire de tristesse.

Il est assez difficile d'établir, surtout en détail, l'origine exacte de ce temps précédant la fête de Pâques. Nous savons seulement que ce temps s'est développé progressivement puisqu'on en repère des traces au IVe siècle, tant en Orient qu'en Occident. Déjà, au IIe siècle, on relève l'existence d'une période de pénitence préparatoire à la fête de Pâques. Mais c'est plus tard, vers le IVe siècle, qu'on en distingue nettement les contours : la période de quarante jours et le caractère pénitentiel. D'ailleurs, le vocabulaire latin parle de la *quadragésime*, en référence au chiffre quarante, d'inspiration biblique. On sait que, dans la tradition biblique, le chiffre quarante a une signification religieuse et non mathématique. Jésus a jeûné pendant quarante jours dans le désert avant de commencer sa vie publique. Le peuple d'Israël a marché quarante ans dans le désert avant d'arriver à la terre promise. De son côté, Moïse jeûna pendant quarante jours sur le Sinaï avant de recevoir les tables de la loi, et le prophète Élie marcha pendant quarante jours dans le désert pour rencontrer Dieu sur le mont Horeb. Dans ces références, le chiffre quarante signifie un temps de purification, de tentation, de pénitence et de préparation en vue d'une profonde expérience spirituelle.

Il semble que le Carême se soit implanté dans l'Église dans le contexte de l'initiation chrétienne et, plus tard, de la pénitence imposée aux grands pécheurs publics qui avaient apostasié leur foi, commis un meurtre ou un adultère. On imposait à ces derniers un long temps de pénitence qui prenait une forme particulière pendant quarante jours avant la réconciliation le Jeudi saint. Quant aux catéchumènes qui se préparaient au baptême lors de la vigile pascale, cette période de quarante jours comprenait pour eux des pratiques spéciales, en plus évidemment de longues catéchèses quotidiennes. Quant aux fidèles, on les invitait à redoubler de ferveur tant dans la piété que dans la pratique de la charité chrétienne en vue de donner aux nouveaux convertis l'image d'une communauté signifiante. D'où le caractère ecclésial de ce temps liturgique.

Dans la tradition, le Carême n'a pas été inspiré par les pratiques ascétiques des religions de l'époque, mais il se voulait un temps où on fait une expérience plus vive de la participation au mystère pascal du Christ. « Nous souffrons avec lui pour être glorifiés avec lui » (*Rm* 8,17). Tel est l'esprit du Carême. En somme, le Carême a un caractère fondamentalement baptismal auquel s'ajoute un caractère pénitentiel. Malheureusement, c'est ce dernier aspect qui a marqué la mentalité chrétienne populaire. Au cours de cette période, l'Église a proposé divers moyens pour atteindre ses objectifs baptismaux, pénitentiels et ecclésiaux. Elle recommande la lecture et l'écoute plus attentive et assidue de la Parole de Dieu, invite à une prière plus intense, au jeûne et à une pratique plus authentique de la charité chrétienne.

Noël et l'Avent

C'est vers le IVe siècle que les communautés chrétiennes ont commencé à faire mémoire de la naissance de Jésus, indépendamment des fêtes pascales. Cette innovation voulait faire contre-pied aux fêtes religieuses de l'époque, considérées idolâtriques par les chrétiens, du soleil invaincu (*sol invictus*), qui avaient lieu au solstice d'hiver. Au moment des journées les plus courtes de l'année, au moment où l'on attend que les journées s'allongent, certaines cultures avaient établi des fêtes pour célébrer cette nouvelle force du soleil. En situant la célébration de la naissance du Christ au même moment, il s'agissait moins de commémorer un anniversaire au sens strict que de combattre les fêtes, considérées idolâtriques, du solstice d'hiver, qui étaient célébrées à Rome, le 25 décembre, et, en Égypte, le 6 janvier. Cette fête de la naissance du Christ Soleil et de son épiphanie, c'est-à-dire la manifestation humaine du Christ, fut accueillie avec d'autant plus d'enthousiasme qu'elle constituait, face à l'hérésie du moine Arius (280-336), une proclamation du dogme de Nicée (en 325) qui affirmait la divinité du Christ.

À Rome, le mémorial de la naissance du Christ fut célébré le 25 décembre. Et cela, dès l'an 330. Par contre, en Égypte, on en fit mémoire le 6 janvier en mettant l'accent non plus sur le fait de la naissance, mais sur la manifestation de Dieu dans l'histoire. Ce qui explique qu'au lieu de la fête de la nativité, on parle de l'épiphanie, c'est-à-dire de la révélation du Christ au monde en exploitant surtout le récit de l'adoration des mages.

Le temps de Noël ne se limite pas à la fête de la nativité. Il comprend une série de célébrations relatives aux principaux événements qui ont entouré la naissance de Jésus. C'est ainsi qu'on souligne la circoncision de Jésus et la maternité de Marie le 1er janvier, la fête de l'Épiphanie le 6 janvier, le baptême de Jésus le dimanche suivant et qu'on termine avec la fête de la lumière, autrefois appelée la Chandeleur, pour rappeler la purification de Marie, son retour à la vie sociale le quarantième jour après la naissance de son enfant, selon le rite juif.

Vers la fin du IVe siècle, à l'instar du Carême précédant la fête de Pâques, on a instauré à Rome une période préparant la fête de Noël qu'on a appelée Avent, du nom latin *Adventus*. Très tôt, on a donné une triple signification à ce temps liturgique. En premier lieu, il voulait commémorer la venue historique du Christ incluant le temps d'attente du peuple d'Israël, ce qui justifie la lecture du prophète Isaïe au cours des liturgies de ce temps ainsi que le rappel de Jean Baptiste et des autres prophètes. En second lieu, il veut faire prendre conscience de l'actuelle venue de Dieu dans l'histoire humaine. Et en dernier lieu, le temps de l'Avent rappelle l'espérance de la venue du Christ glorieux à la fin du monde. Par ailleurs, la fête de l'Immaculée-Conception, le 8 décembre, s'est insérée dans ce parcours liturgique.

En soi, l'Avent célèbre la triple venue de Dieu dans l'histoire humaine. Cette signification est affirmée dans la liturgie du premier dimanche de l'Avent au 16 décembre. Par la suite, l'accent est mis sur la préparation à Noël en en faisant pratiquement un temps de pénitence assimilé au Carême. Cette dimension qui est secondaire dans le temps de l'Avent a pris le dessus dans la conscience chrétienne populaire. Le renouveau liturgique de Vatican II a conservé les deux caractères de ce temps, soit la préparation à Noël et la triple venue du Christ, spécialement sa venue eschatologique, c'est-à-dire à la fin des temps. C'est un appauvrissement, même une déviation, que de ne considérer ce temps que comme un temps de préparation à la fête de Noël assimilé au Carême. D'ailleurs, le nom même de l'Avent indique son orientation. Il ne s'agit pas de « l'avant », c'est-à-dire ce qui précède, mais bien d'une venue en présence dans l'histoire : l'*adventus, ce qui advient*.

Le temps ordinaire

Les temps commémorant les grands moments de la vie de Jésus terminés, commence un nouveau temps que la liturgie appelle le temps ordinaire et qu'on appelait autrefois le temps après la Pentecôte. Il débute par deux fêtes tardives, la fête de la Sainte-Trinité et celle du Saint-Sacrement, auxquelles on ajouta la fête du Sacré-Cœur. Il existait bien une dévotion au cœur de Jésus dès le

XIIIe siècle et plus tard chez les mystiques rhénans, mais c'est au XVIIe qu'on développa un culte au Cœur de Jésus. C'est à Jean Eudes que reviendra l'initiative d'instaurer une fête publique au Cœur de Marie en 1647 et au Cœur de Jésus en 1672. Par contre, il reviendra à une religieuse visitandine de Paray-le-Monial, sainte Marguerite-Marie Alacoque, de populariser cette dévotion.

En somme, ces dernières fêtes veulent souligner la présence sacramentelle du Christ après avoir célébré les grands moments de sa vie terrestre.

Après ces fêtes, le temps ordinaire occupe le reste de l'année liturgique jusqu'au premier dimanche de l'Avent. Au cours de ce temps, la liturgie de chaque dimanche veut rappeler aux fidèles l'enseignement de Jésus. Avec la réforme liturgique de Vatican II, on a étalé sur un cycle de trois ans la lecture de la Parole de Dieu pour permettre aux fidèles d'entrer en contact avec un plus large éventail de textes bibliques.

Fêtes de Marie et des saints et saintes (le sanctoral)

Avec le temps, la piété des fidèles et l'évolution de la théologie chrétienne ont incité les Églises à instaurer d'autres fêtes pour mettre en évidence certaines dimensions des dogmes chrétiens ou le témoignage exemplaire de personnes reconnues pour leur doctrine, leur sainteté et leur charisme prophétique. C'est ainsi que l'année liturgique se trouve parsemée de fêtes concernant la mère de Jésus et de nombreux saints et saintes.

On sait qu'à partir du Moyen Âge, la piété mariale a pris une grande importance dans la religion populaire. C'est ainsi que, progressivement, on a instauré des fêtes liturgiques pour souligner la nativité de Marie le 8 septembre, l'annonciation de l'ange à Marie le 25 mars, la visitation de Marie à sa cousine Élisabeth le 31 mai, l'Assomption de Marie le 15 août, celle de Notre-Dame des Sept Douleurs le 15 septembre, la fête de Notre-Dame du Rosaire le 7 octobre, la Présentation de Marie le 21 novembre pour terminer par l'Immaculée-Conception le 8 décembre. Cette nomenclature indique clairement l'importance de la dévotion mariale dans la piété et même dans le dogme chrétien. Sans faire disparaître ces fêtes, la réforme liturgique de Vatican II a recentré, à juste titre, le culte chrétien sur le Christ en mettant au second plan ces nombreuses fêtes mariales et, comme on le verra, les fêtes des saints et des saintes.

Avec le temps, on a ajouté à l'année liturgique des fêtes pour rappeler à la conscience chrétienne le rôle de nombreux témoins de la foi et de l'engagement. C'est ainsi qu'apparaissent des fêtes liturgiques à portée universelle pour rappeler le témoignage inspirant des apôtres, des fondateurs et fondatrices des grandes communautés religieuses, et des docteurs de l'Église. Signalons ici, à titre d'exemple, saint Benoît (les bénédictins), saint François d'Assise (les franciscains), saint Dominique (les dominicains), saint Ignace de Loyola (les jésuites) sans oublier tous les autres, plus récents. Les docteurs de l'Église sont aussi fêtés : saint Ambroise, saint Jean Chrysostôme, saint Augustin, saint Thomas d'Aquin, sainte Catherine de Sienne, sainte Thérèse d'Avila, sainte Thérèse de Lisieux et combien d'autres. Comme on ne pouvait pas inscrire au calendrier liturgique tous les noms des saintes et saints reconnus, l'Église institua, le 1er novembre, une fête commune appelée la Toussaint, suivie de celle de tous les fidèles défunts, le jour suivant.

À cela, on peut ajouter de nombreuses fêtes à portée plus restreinte. Il s'agit de commémoration de saints et de saintes dont l'influence et la réputation se limitent à un pays ou à une région. Ainsi, on souligne au Canada français la fête des Saints-Martyrs canadiens, de Marguerite d'Youville, de Marguerite Bourgeoys et de quelques autres.

Par les diverses célébrations de l'année liturgique, l'Église veut assurer la mémoire des grands moments de la vie de Jésus et des témoins les plus significatifs de la foi chrétienne. Un certain nombre de fêtes, très à l'honneur autrefois, n'ont plus aujourd'hui autant de signification qu'elles en avaient dans le passé. Par sa réforme liturgique, le concile Vatican II a voulu montrer clairement dans son calendrier liturgique que l'essentiel est la foi en Jésus Christ, une foi à vivre et à célébrer dans le temps qui marque les chrétiens et chrétiennes.

Avent	
• Immaculée-Conception	8 décembre
Temps de Noël	
• Noël (solstice d'hiver)	25 décembre
• Circoncision de Jésus et maternité de Marie	1er janvier
• Épiphanie	6 janvier
• baptême de Jésus	
Carême	
• mercredi des Cendres	
• semaine sainte	
Temps pascal	
• Pâques	
• Ascension du Christ	
• Pentecôte	
Temps ordinaire	
• Trinité	
• Saint-Sacrement	
• Sacré-Cœur	

Sanctification de la semaine : le dimanche

Les *Actes des apôtres* nous rapportent que, dès le début du christianisme, on avait adopté la division du temps en sept jours, selon la manière juive de compter. « Le premier jour » de la semaine se voulait la célébration chrétienne de la résurrection du Christ. Dans sa *première lettre aux Corinthiens*, Paul situe la collecte pour les frères de Jérusalem au cours de la réunion hebdomadaire, ce premier jour de la semaine (*1 Cor* 16,2). Les *Actes* nous racontent les événements qui se sont déroulés lors de la réunion autour de Paul à Troas en commençant de la façon suivante : « Le premier jour de la semaine, nous étions réunis pour rompre le pain... » (*Ac* 20,7).

Avec l'*Apocalypse*, on voit apparaître une nouvelle désignation de ce jour : « Je tombai en extase, le "jour du Seigneur", et j'entendis derrière moi une voix clamer, comme une trompette... » (*Ap* 1,10). « Le jour seigneurial », tel est le nom qui se répandit dans les communautés chrétiennes. Les communautés latines d'Occident le traduisent littéralement par *dominicus dies*. Bientôt on fit disparaître le substantif pour ne laisser place qu'à l'adjectif devenu lui-même substantif. En français : dimanche.

Très tôt, le dimanche devint une réalité importante dans la vie des premières communautés chrétiennes. Citons deux témoignages. Le premier vient d'Ignace d'Antioche (début du IIe siècle) : « Ceux qui vivaient selon l'ancien ordre des choses sont venus à la nouvelle espérance, n'observant plus le sabbat, mais le dimanche, jour où notre vie s'est levée par le Christ et par sa mort[1]. » Le second vient d'un non-chrétien, Pline le Jeune (61-114), gouverneur de Bithynie. Il déclare que les chrétiens arrêtés

1. Ignace d'ANTIOCHE, *Épître aux Magnésiens 9*, éd. Camelot (SC 10) 2e éd., 1951, p. 102.

« affirmaient que toute leur faute ou leur erreur s'était bornée à se réunir habituellement à jour fixe, avant l'aube, pour chanter entre eux un chant au Christ comme à un dieu[2] ». Il n'y a pas de doute que le « jour fixe » dont parle Pline le Jeune est le dimanche.

Sur la base de nombreux témoignages, on déduit facilement que le dimanche s'était fortement implanté chez les chrétiens comme célébration de la résurrection du Christ à la fin de l'ère des persécutions. L'empereur Constantin (début du IVe siècle) va donner un élan nouveau à l'implantation de ce jour dans la culture occidentale en imposant le chômage le jour qui était en même temps célébration du culte du dieu Soleil et du Christ. Les conciles qui légiféreront par la suite sur le sens de ce jour férié et qui rappelleront périodiquement la nécessité de participer à l'assemblée chrétienne n'ajouteront rien à la signification de ce jour.

Le dimanche se distingue nettement du sabbat juif. Alors que le sabbat consistait d'abord en une cessation de travail, ne prenant sa signification religieuse qu'en référence à l'alliance de Moïse, le dimanche, de son côté, consiste essentiellement dans le mémorial et la célébration de la résurrection du Seigneur par l'assemblée et dans l'attente de son retour. Trois caractéristiques marqueront profondément les premiers disciples du Christ. Le dimanche, c'est d'abord le mémorial de la Résurrection que les disciples célèbrent dans la foi ; c'est l'affirmation du retour du Seigneur qui est célébré dans l'espérance et, enfin, c'est le rassemblement des disciples du Christ qui, dans le partage de la Parole, du Pain et d'autres biens terrestres, actualisent la charité. Avec le temps, deux traits vont caractériser le dimanche, la célébration eucharistique et le repos dominical.

2. Pline LE JEUNE, *Epistolarum Liber*. 10. 96.

Le dimanche n'était pas seulement un jour de prière et d'activités religieuses. Il a joué un grand rôle dans la vie sociale, puisque c'était le jour des rassemblements de famille, de voisins et d'amis. Il est bon de souligner ici que dès la reconnaissance du christianisme par l'empereur Constantin, on fit une loi qui demandait aux fidèles de chômer le jour du Seigneur. Cette loi avait pour but de permettre aux fidèles de participer à l'assemblée de la communauté et de donner aux esclaves une journée de repos. D'où l'expression de s'abstenir des « œuvres serviles », c'est-à-dire des travaux accomplis par les esclaves, les *servus*.

Aujourd'hui, plusieurs fidèles se posent la question concernant l'obligation de l'assistance à la messe le dimanche. On sait que, dans le passé, c'était une obligation très stricte, puisqu'on l'imposait sous peine de péché mortel dans le cas d'un manque sans raison valable. En soi, il n'y a pas eu de nouvelle législation concernant le précepte de l'assistance à l'Eucharistie dominicale comme il y en a eu sur d'autres sujets tel le jeûne eucharistique. Et il y a de fortes probabilités qu'il n'y en aura pas dans le contexte actuel. L'Église invite toujours fortement les chrétiens et les chrétiennes à se rassembler pour sanctifier le jour du Seigneur. Cette invitation pressante prend son sens même en dehors du contexte légaliste : la force de l'invitation dépend de la relation avec Dieu et de l'expérience spirituelle de chaque personne.

Le précepte de l'assistance à l'Eucharistie pose un grave problème aux communautés chrétiennes en raison du manque de présidents d'assemblée. Pour apporter un correctif, l'Église propose des assemblées dominicales en l'absence de prêtres. Les fidèles se rassemblent, écoutent la Parole de Dieu, prient ensemble et se partagent le pain eucharistique. Une telle situation exceptionnelle est appelée à se répandre de plus en plus en raison de la diminution croissante du nombre de prêtres. Cette situation soulève une question importante : peut-on priver des communautés chrétiennes de la célébration eucharistique sous prétexte de sauvegarder un modèle unique de président d'assemblée, le prêtre « classique », homme, célibataire et ordonné à vie ? Cette nouvelle forme de rassemblement sans prêtre soulève une autre question. Cette pratique ne risque-t-elle pas de dévaloriser la célébration eucharistique même pour ne mettre l'accent que sur la communion ? C'est un danger qui est réel parce qu'il repose sur un présupposé profondément ancré dans la conscience catholique. Malgré une tradition théologique remise en évidence concernant la présence du Christ dans la communauté et dans la Parole, plusieurs fidèles n'accordent encore d'importance qu'à la présence du Christ dans l'hostie consacrée. Par ailleurs, ce type de célébration ne pourrait-il pas aider à faire prendre conscience de la priorité du rassemblement des fidèles le jour du Seigneur ? Rencontre à multiples finalités, allant du partage de la Parole à l'action eucharistique, en passant par des rassemblements à caractère uniquement caritatif. N'y aurait-il pas plusieurs manières de sanctifier le jour du Seigneur par une diversité d'activités répondant à divers types de communautés ?

La journée

La tradition montre que les communautés chrétiennes ont inscrit des activités et des célébrations non seulement au cours de l'année et de la semaine, mais également au cœur de chaque journée. Cette façon de faire n'était pas une nouveauté radicale, puisque des activités semblables se trouvaient déjà dans le judaïsme. De fait, les juifs se rassemblaient le matin pour la prière et pour la lecture des Écritures. Les communautés chrétiennes ont sanctifié le jour de multiples façons, surtout par la prière des heures, plus communément appelée le bréviaire, par la prière du matin et du soir et par la récitation de l'*Angelus*.

Le bréviaire ou la prière des heures

Sans doute inspirées par la tradition juive, les premières communautés se rassemblaient à certaines heures pour la prière. Les *Actes des Apôtres* attestent cette expérience de prière : « Pierre et Jean montaient au Temple pour la prière de la neuvième heure » (*Ac* 3,1) et « Le lendemain, tandis qu'ils faisaient route et approchaient de la ville, Pierre monta sur la terrasse, vers la sixième heure, pour prier » (*Ac* 10,9).

Chez les juifs, cette prière consistait surtout dans la récitation des psaumes. Mais très vite, les communautés chrétiennes ont manifesté une certaine originalité en empruntant au monde grec le genre littéraire des hymnes.

Dans les premiers siècles, cette forme de prière avait une grande liberté. Elle était considérée comme prière liturgique, non par une réglementation, mais par le fait qu'elle était accomplie par l'*Ecclesia* sous la présidence du chef de la communauté. Cette liberté eut comme conséquence une grande diversité. Chaque communauté avait sa formule. Avec le temps, se constitua peu à peu un corpus comprenant des hymnes, un choix de lectures bibliques et, évidemment, les psaumes.

Le christianisme emprunta aux Romains la répartition de la journée en tranches de quatre heures (*prima, tertia, sexta* et *nona*) et la nuit en quatre veilles : la première veille le soir, le seconde à minuit, la troisième au chant du coq et la quatrième à l'aurore. Ce sera l'origine de ce qu'on appellera plus tard les heures canoniales, c'est-à-dire récitées par les chanoines dans les églises cathédrales.

Vers l'an mil, on fit une synthèse de divers recueils qu'on appela *Breviarum*, cette synthèse se voulant un abrégé des différents éléments constituant la prière des heures, spécialement les lectures.

TEMPUS NATIVITATIS
DIE 25 DECEMBRIS
IN NATIVITATE DOMINI

Cette forme de prière pour sanctifier les heures du jour et de la nuit a des caractéristiques bien particulières. D'abord, c'est une célébration communautaire solennelle avec présidence, chants, lectures, homélies, hymnes et prières. De plus, elle n'est célébrée qu'en communauté, surtout dans les communautés monastiques et dans les églises cathédrales, là où l'évêque se réunit avec son clergé.

Au début du deuxième millénaire, spécialement au XIIe siècle, la prière des heures se modifia considérablement. La vie commune des clercs séculiers était peu pratiquée du fait qu'ils recevaient des bénéfices qui ne comportaient pas forcément de responsabilités pastorales et n'obligeaient pas à la résidence. L'Office demeurait obligatoire pour les chanoines réguliers, mais on s'en dispensait facilement tout en maintenant l'obligation de suppléer privément aux heures auxquelles on n'avait pas pu prendre part avec la communauté. C'est le début de la récitation privée de l'office des heures qui se répandit dans le clergé régulier et séculier. Plus tard, on lia l'obligation du bréviaire à l'ordination au moment de l'engagement dans le premier des ordres majeurs de la hiérarchie de l'Église, le sous-diaconat, ordre précédant le diaconat.

Dans le mouvement du concile Vatican II qui demandait une réforme de l'ensemble de la liturgie, on refit le bréviaire en autorisant la traduction dans les différentes langues des peuples et en le simplifiant. Ce mouvement de prière se répandit quelque peu chez des fidèles au point où on leur offrit une formule simplifiée pour la sanctification des heures.

Prières du matin et du soir et Angelus

Il n'est sans doute pas inutile de rappeler l'existence de la tradition populaire de la prière du matin et du soir. C'était une tradition bien ancrée chez les familles chrétiennes de réciter la prière du matin et du soir. À celle du soir, on ajoutait parfois le chapelet. On y récitait le « Symbole des apôtres », le « Notre Père », les actes de foi, d'espérance et de charité ainsi que d'autres prières incluant, le soir, celle demandant une bonne mort.

Matin, midi et soir, au son de la cloche du village, les fidèles s'arrêtaient pour réciter l'*Angelus*, prière faite à la mère de Jésus, du nom des deux premiers mots qui la composent : *Angelus Domini* (Ange du Seigneur). Cette prière est composée de trois versets, de trois *Ave Maria* et d'une oraison. Elle apparaît au XIIe siècle dans les monastères, mais ce n'est que vers le XVe siècle qu'elle trouva sa forme définitive. En pratique, c'est surtout à midi qu'on récitait cette prière de l'*Angelus*. Elle commémorait l'annonce faite à Marie par l'ange du Seigneur et l'Incarnation du Verbe de Dieu. Le son de la cloche invitait les fidèles à la sanctification du mitan du jour par la prière de l'*Angelus*.

Temps liturgique et temps social

L'éventail des nombreuses fêtes de l'année liturgique rappelle un passé de chrétienté. Dans ce contexte, la vie sociale s'organisait autour des grands temps liturgiques et de ses fêtes les plus marquantes. Ce qui contribuait à instaurer des liens étroits entre le sacré, le religieux et le profane. Le temps liturgique rythmait pour ainsi dire la vie des gens.

Cette société de chrétienté qui a permis l'instauration de si nombreuses fêtes et du calendrier liturgique est pratiquement devenue chose du passé. Notre contexte socioculturel marqué par la sécularisation est tout à fait différent de celui dans lequel est née et s'est développée l'année liturgique. D'une part, un grand nombre de fêtes n'ont plus d'impact sur la vie sociale tout en demeurant inscrites dans le calendrier. Elles ne sont célébrées que par des communautés restreintes. Par ailleurs, d'autres fêtes tels Noël, le jour de l'an et Pâques demeurent fortement inscrites dans le tissu social. Elles sont l'occasion de périodes de congés et de réjouissances particulières, mais elles sont souvent très éloignées de leur signification religieuse.

Une telle situation pose une sérieuse question à la pastorale de l'Église qui ne doit céder ni à une sécularisation extrême, ni à la tentation du maintien rigide des formes d'antan. Elle doit donc tenir compte de la présente évolution culturelle qui se fait en marge de la structure des temps et des fêtes liturgiques. Ne pouvant plus imposer à la société civile le temps de ses fêtes, l'Église apprend à composer dans le temps de la société. L'un des défis actuels des chrétiens et chrétiennes est de vivre une dissociation entre les temps liturgiques liés à leur pratique de foi et les temps de la vie sociale. C'est le défi d'une Église qui n'est plus la seule gérante de la vie sociale et qui apprend à s'inscrire dans une société pluraliste. Si ce défi peut faire regretter la belle harmonie passée, il est aussi l'occasion d'une prise de conscience plus vive de la différence de sa foi qui, éventuellement, peut se nourrir des autres pratiques.

DES ÂGES DANS LA VIE

Raymond Vaillancourt

Toute vie humaine est composée d'événements et d'étapes que les sociétés ont ritualisés selon leurs croyances et leurs cultures. Les ethnologues, les anthropologues et les sociologues proposent diverses définitions des rites tout en observant certains traits communs, qu'on pourrait résumer en parlant de pratiques sociales spécifiques à un événement, programmées, répétitives et symboliques. Certains de ces rites sont appelés « rites de passage[1] » parce qu'ils marquent une rupture à l'égard de l'étape antérieure et une intégration à la nouvelle situation.

L'évolution du christianisme en Occident montre qu'il s'est appuyé sur le besoin de ritualisation, tout en empruntant aux cultures ambiantes les éléments de leur ritualité propre. C'est ainsi que plusieurs rites de cultures qualifiées de païennes ont été intégrés dans la vie chrétienne, devenant ainsi les ancêtres de certains rites chrétiens.

1. « Ils s'inscrivent aux carrefours des changements d'état, d'occupation, de situation sociale, de statut et d'âge. Ils rythment le déroulement de la vie humaine, du berceau à la tombe. » Nicole Belmont, « La notion de rite de passage » dans *Les Rites de passage aujourd'hui* (Actes du colloque de Neuchâtel 1981), Lausanne, L'Âge d'homme, 1986, p. 11.

Les rites chrétiens n'ont pas tous la même importance. Au Moyen Âge, le Magistère de l'Église a identifié sept de ces rites comme étant porteurs d'une efficacité particulière et les a appelés « sacrements ». Ces sept sacrements sont bien connus : baptême, confirmation et eucharistie qui constituent les sacrements de l'initiation chrétienne ; le sacrement de la réconciliation et l'onction des malades qui concernent la fragilité humaine (morale ou physique) ; le mariage et l'ordre qui concernent des cadres de vie chrétienne. Mais il existe d'autres rites chrétiens qui sont importants même s'ils ne sont pas appelés sacrements. Pensons aux funérailles, aux liturgies de la Parole, aux bénédictions de toutes sortes, etc.

Plonger

Naissance et baptême sont très associés dans l'Occident chrétien. De fait, le baptême des nouveau-nés correspond à une pratique ancienne et répandue même si, théologiquement, le baptême s'adresse à des adultes qui adhèrent à la foi chrétienne. Ainsi, si le baptême correspond à la naissance du baptisé à la vie chrétienne, il ne correspond pas nécessairement à la naissance à la vie humaine. Cependant, la pratique généralisée dans l'Occident chrétien de baptiser les nouveau-nés a quasi presque réduit le baptême à un rite de la naissance humaine.

Le baptême chrétien a été l'objet d'un débat célèbre entre Pierre et Paul. Le problème venait du lien entre le baptême et l'exigence de la circoncision pour les hommes qui se convertissaient au christianisme sans avoir adhéré à la foi juive. Pierre tenait à ce que les nouveaux convertis soient circoncis, tandis que Paul ne jugeait pas cette exigence nécessaire à la foi chrétienne. Après de vives controverses, on choisit de ne pas imposer aux

Grecs et aux Romains qui se convertissaient au message de Jésus une pratique juive qui leur répugnait (*cf. Ac* 15,5-11). Cette décision a donné une impulsion déterminante pour le baptême chrétien qui signifiait à lui seul l'adhésion au message du Christ et l'entrée dans la nouvelle communauté de foi. Il était alors normal de préparer ces nouveaux adeptes par de longs enseignements, appelés catéchèses. C'est l'époque de la naissance de l'institution catéchuménale qui s'implanta jusqu'à la généralisation du baptême des enfants en bas âge, provoqué par un double facteur, la reconnaissance du christianisme comme religion d'État et la théorie du péché originel.

Dans l'Occident catholique, il a été de coutume et même d'obligation de faire baptiser les enfants dès la naissance. Cette pratique remonte aux débats de saint Augustin avec le moine Pélage concernant la nécessité du baptême (fin du IVe siècle). Augustin, s'appuyant sur certains textes bibliques et surtout sur son expérience personnelle, en vint à concevoir le baptême comme absolument nécessaire au salut. Par ailleurs, Pélage, beaucoup moins pessimiste sur la réalité humaine, n'y voyait pas une si grande nécessité. La condamnation de Pélage et le prestige toujours grandissant d'Augustin contribuèrent à implanter sa vision des choses dans l'univers chrétien et à imposer la pratique du baptême chez les enfants en bas âge. Vers la fin du premier millénaire, cette pratique, appelée pédobaptisme, était devenue une coutume généralisée. Au cours du Moyen Âge, l'Église en a fait une obligation stricte, soutenue, d'ailleurs, par les États, au point où certains pays ont imposé des peines aux parents dont les enfants mouraient sans avoir été baptisés. On est même allé jusqu'à la confiscation des biens.

Cette pratique justifiée par la théologie du péché originel s'est implantée dans la mentalité populaire au point de semer beaucoup d'inquiétude chez les parents qui perdaient un enfant avant qu'il n'ait été baptisé. Cette inquiétude, persistant dans l'inconscient collectif, pousse encore des parents à faire baptiser leur enfant quelque temps après la naissance en se disant : « On ne sait jamais. »

De nos jours, bon nombre de gens se posent la question concernant l'obligation et la signification du baptême d'un enfant quelques mois après la naissance. Et cela, pour bien des raisons, entre autres celle de laisser la liberté à l'enfant de choisir par lui-même son univers religieux. Ne va-t-on pas contre les droits de la personne en engageant ainsi son enfant dans un groupe religieux sachant qu'en raison du contexte actuel, le risque est réel qu'il reproche à ses parents d'avoir pris un tel engagement ? D'autant

LE SIGNE DE LA CROIX

Le signe de la croix est une expression du cœur de la foi chrétienne. En référence au Dieu de Jésus, Père, Fils et Esprit, il rappelle la mort et la résurrection du Christ. Les fidèles l'utilisent fréquemment dans leur prière personnelle. Toute liturgie commence et souvent se termine par ce signe de la croix. De plus, au cours de la célébration, le président fait des signes de croix sur les personnes et les objets du culte. De façon toute spéciale, il est utilisé lors de la bénédiction.

SE TENIR DEBOUT

C'est la position traditionnelle de la prière chrétienne. Elle se veut l'expression de la liberté des enfants de Dieu acquise par le baptême. Le Christ l'ayant libéré et délivré de la mort et du péché, le fidèle n'est plus un esclave. Il est un fils ou une fille de Dieu. Sans honte, il peut se tenir debout devant son Dieu. Cette position se réfère également à l'attitude de ceux et celles qui attendent la Parousie. Voilà pourquoi la liturgie invite l'assemblée à se lever pour la prière de la communauté. C'est aussi une attitude fondamentale de respect dans plusieurs cultures. On se lève devant une personne à qui l'on doit le respect, soit en l'accueillant, soit en l'écoutant. Ainsi, les fidèles se lèvent à l'entrée et à la sortie du président d'assemblée, de même que pendant la proclamation de l'Évangile, parole du Christ.

Avec le renouveau liturgique de Vatican II, les fidèles sont invités à recevoir debout le pain eucharistique, contrairement à la période précédente où ils le recevaient à genoux. On a voulu ainsi signifier que Dieu se rend présent à une personne ressuscitée, donc libre et non esclave. Une personne debout en train de peiner à la construction du royaume de Dieu.

S'AGENOUILLER

Dans la tradition primitive, la prière à genoux avait un caractère pénitentiel. Se mettre à genoux, c'était manifester que le péché nous avait jetés à terre. C'est aussi une expression de deuil, d'humilité, de repentir, incompatible avec la joie pascale, mais caractéristique des temps de pénitence. Cette attitude exprime aussi la supplication, la soumission, la dépendance et même l'adoration. À une époque fortement marquée par la conviction de l'indignité de l'homme devant Dieu, cette position a été largement répandue dans la prière chrétienne. On l'a introduite pour l'adoration de l'Eucharistie pendant le récit de l'institution, appelée consécration, et pour recevoir la communion. Une nouvelle anthropologie chrétienne valorise davantage l'attitude du fidèle debout plutôt qu'agenouillé.

SE PROSTERNER

Voici une attitude rarement utilisée à l'exception des célébrations des ordinations et du Vendredi saint. Elle comporte donc une exceptionnelle solennité. Au cours de ces liturgies, les ordinands s'allongent totalement sur le parquet en signe d'abandon total à Dieu. ◇

plus que la mentalité populaire affirmait que les parrains et marraines s'engageaient au nom de l'enfant. Sans doute, au cours des siècles, la théologie a-t-elle justifié cette perception. Mais depuis le renouveau conciliaire, l'Église, davantage consciente du contexte actuel, a modifié cette conception. Les parents, parrains et marraines ne prennent plus d'engagement au nom de l'enfant. Ils prennent un engagement pour eux-mêmes, soit de mettre leur enfant en contact avec la foi chrétienne ne pouvant présumer de l'accueil que celui-ci, une fois adolescent et adulte, réservera à cet univers spirituel.

Aujourd'hui, l'obligation du baptême à la naissance telle que la préconisait l'ancienne législation de l'Église de 1917 est mise de côté. De fait, l'Église propose trois temps et trois rites du baptême. Elle a gardé la possibilité du baptême à la naissance appelé le pédobaptisme. Elle a remis à l'honneur le baptême des adultes, pratique courante dans les premiers siècles et dans les pays de mission, et elle a instauré une nouvelle pratique, celle du baptême des enfants d'âge scolaire. Si la pratique du baptême des adultes ne pose pas de problème puisqu'il s'agit d'adultes qui consciemment optent pour l'univers chrétien catholique, il n'en va pas de même pour celle du baptême des enfants en âge de scolarité. Dans bien des cas, les enfants qui en font la demande sont plus souvent motivés par leur identification à un groupe de compagnons et de compagnes que par de véritables motivations spirituelles. L'Église invite donc à la prudence dans ces cas.

Il est facile de constater que le rite chrétien du baptême se détache progressivement de la naissance, se rapprochant en cela des pratiques des premières communautés chrétiennes. Il devient de plus en plus un rite d'intégration à l'univers religieux catholique comme il est une occasion pour l'Église d'exprimer sa conception de l'être humain. Créée à l'image de Dieu, toute per-

ENCENSER

Le fait de faire brûler de l'encens est une pratique fort ancienne, commune à plusieurs religions ; c'était une manière d'honorer les divinités. Les juifs avaient adopté cette coutume au temple de Jérusalem. Dans la liturgie chrétienne, ce geste est une marque d'honneur et de respect. Ainsi, au cours des célébrations liturgiques, on encense le livre de la Parole, les offrandes du pain et du vin, l'autel, la croix, le cierge pascal et même le président, les fidèles et le corps des défunts. La fumée symbolise la prière qui monte vers Dieu. Aujourd'hui, ce geste qui parfume l'atmosphère est fort répandu dans la vie courante, sans qu'on y attache une signification religieuse.

OINDRE

Le geste de l'onction prend également ses racines dans la tradition biblique, et même dans les milieux profanes, comme symbole de joie, de bonheur et d'hospitalité. Dans l'Ancien Testament, il signifie surtout une consécration à Dieu. On faisait des onctions avec l'huile bénite sur des personnes, les prêtres, les prophètes et les rois, et sur des objets, tel l'autel. Le Christ lui-même se présentera comme consacré par l'onction de l'Esprit de Dieu (*Lc* 4,18). La liturgie chrétienne est restée fidèle à cette tradition. Pour certains sacrements, l'onction constitue le rite essentiel, telle l'onction des malades, et pour d'autres, il s'agit d'un rite important et significatif, mais secondaire. C'est le cas du baptême et de l'ordination. On en fait aussi un rite de consécration à Dieu ou de bénédiction. C'est une coutume de consacrer les églises, les autels, les cloches, etc.

Le symbolisme de l'huile prend racine dans sa nature même. Autrefois comme aujourd'hui, on utilise l'huile pour certains traitements, la cuisson, les soins de beauté, pour assouplir le corps et, lorsqu'elle est parfumée, pour embaumer les lieux. On s'en sert également pour l'éclairage. Dans la liturgie chrétienne, l'onction avec l'huile parfumée reprend ces valeurs. Elle veut signifier que l'Esprit de Dieu s'empare d'une personne, la pénètre en quelque sorte, pour la rendre apte à une mission. ◇

sonne est appelée à bâtir un monde plus humain et à continuer l'œuvre de la création.

Communier

L'Eucharistie est le rassemblement de la communauté ecclésiale au cours duquel deux gestes essentiels sont faits. D'une part, on proclame des textes de la Bible, Parole de Dieu, en les réécrivant en quelque sorte pour aujourd'hui et, d'autre part, on partage le pain et le vin en mémoire du dernier repas de Jésus.

L'Eucharistie chrétienne a subi une double influence. Elle s'enracine dans le repas pascal juif. Au cours de ce repas, les juifs faisaient mémoire de la grande merveille de Yahvé dans son histoire, la libération de la servitude des pharaons d'Égypte. En plus, elle a accueilli une autre pratique du peuple d'Israël, celle de la prière et de la lecture de la Parole de Dieu à la synagogue. Ce qui donnera naissance aux deux grandes parties de l'Eucharistie, la liturgie de la Parole qui consiste à proclamer et à comprendre pour aujourd'hui cette Parole de Dieu, et la liturgie de l'action de grâce qui reprend à son compte la grande bénédiction du repas pascal juif.

S'appuyant sur le commandement de Jésus lui-même qui, au cours du repas pascal, a invité ses apôtres à refaire ce geste en mémoire de lui, les premières communautés chrétiennes se sont rassemblées pour faire mémoire de la mort et de la résurrection du Christ. Cette célébration a vite pris le nom d'Eucharistie, mot grec qui signifie « action de grâces » pour ensuite prendre le nom de messe, du mot latin *missa*, substantif de *mittere* signifiant *envoyer*. Dans la tradition chrétienne, l'Eucharistie a été considérée comme l'expérience sommet de l'existence chrétienne communautaire. Très tôt, on l'a imposée à l'ensemble des fidèles.

Il est sans doute intéressant de constater qu'au tout début du christianisme, l'obligation portait davantage sur le rassemblement que sur le partage du pain eucharistique. Ce type de rassemblement était l'expression d'une réelle solidarité entre les fidèles, particulièrement avec les personnes dans le besoin. La société du temps ne bénéficiant bien sûr pas des services sociaux d'aujourd'hui, les communautés chrétiennes ont pris en charge les nécessiteux, spécialement les veuves et les orphelins. Au cours de ce rassemblement, on partageait la Parole de Dieu dans une perspective d'enseignement et d'engagement, et on partageait également des biens matériels avec les gens dans le besoin pour terminer par le partage du pain et du vin.

Avec le temps, la dimension du partage matériel s'est estompée. La parole de Dieu proclamée en latin, langue devenue hermétique pour l'ensemble du peuple chrétien, n'avait plus le même impact sur la vie des fidèles. Le partage du pain et de la coupe s'est réduit au minimum avec une petite hostie. Et même, à partir du Moyen Âge, le partage du pain, appelé la « communion », s'est raréfié au point où l'Église a dû imposer la communion une fois par année à l'occasion de Pâques. L'Eucharistie avait perdu sa dimension fondamentale de rassemblement dans la foi d'une communauté pour rendre grâce à Dieu de sa présence bénéfique auprès de l'humanité dans l'histoire. Elle était devenue un rite d'obligation pour les chrétiens. En raison d'autres facteurs, dont le fait de multiplier les eucharisties pendant les jours de la semaine, elle est presque devenue, pour un certain nombre de bonnes gens, une dévotion.

Qu'en est-il donc aujourd'hui de cette obligation et quelle peut être sa signification ? Le caractère d'obligation n'a évidemment plus le même impact que dans le passé. Il faut bien reconnaître que, jusqu'à tout récemment, la liberté des fidèles était fort limitée, puisque l'obligation d'assister à la messe était imposée sous peine de péché grave avec tout ce que cela signifiait, c'est-à-dire l'exclusion du paradis. Heureusement, l'Église n'utilise plus ce langage. Elle invite toujours les fidèles à se rassembler le jour du Seigneur, pour partager la Parole et communier à la présence du Christ, sans imposer de peine à ceux et celles qui s'en abstiennent.

Malheureusement, pour un grand nombre de fidèles, l'importance ne porte pas tellement sur un rassemblement de foi de la communauté dans le partage de la Parole, mais elle se concentre encore sur la communion au Christ dans l'hostie consacrée. Il y a donc lieu d'élargir la notion de présence du Christ, qu'avec le temps on a réduite à un seul rite, celui de la communion. Les chrétiens ont toujours reconnu la présence du Christ dans le rassemblement, dans le partage de la Parole et dans les œuvres de charité, au même titre que celle dans l'hostie consacrée en s'appuyant sur la parole de Jésus: « Là où deux ou trois sont rassemblés en mon nom, je suis au milieu d'eux » (*Mt* 18,20).

Être relevé

Le sacrement de la réconciliation porte différents noms: la pénitence, le pardon, la confession et la réconciliation. Évidemment, cette nomenclature indique les soubresauts de l'histoire de ce rite et cette diversité d'approches témoigne d'une pratique à la recherche de son identité. Pourtant, malgré les difficultés de sa pratique (ou de sa non-pratique), aujourd'hui comme à certaines périodes de son histoire, une réalité humaine profonde est touchée par ce sacrement. Les difficultés du sacrement de la réconciliation indiquent aussi sa pertinence fondamentale.

Il faut bien reconnaître que la pratique du sacrement de pénitence a subi au cours des siècles une très grande évolution.

Elle est passée d'un extrême à l'autre. Dans les premiers siècles, on l'avait pensée comme une reprise de l'option du baptême. Après la ferveur qui suivait le baptême, certaines communautés ont été confrontées à la réalité de l'apostasie et à des crimes qui dénaturaient la vocation de sainteté que voulait se donner la communauté, tels le meurtre et l'adultère. On s'est même demandé s'il ne fallait pas dans certains cas graves renouveler le baptême. Très vite, les responsables des Églises en sont arrivés à la conclusion que le baptême signifiait l'option pour Dieu dans une mission. Si l'être humain peut ne pas être fidèle à son engagement, Dieu reste fidèle. C'est alors qu'est apparue une pratique semblable au baptême, mais avec des exigences très grandes : un long temps de pénitence et de réflexion suivi d'une cérémonie d'accueil, le jeudi précédant la fête de Pâques. À l'instar du baptême, cette célébration était présidée une fois l'an par l'évêque. C'était la dernière chance pour les grands pécheurs. La sévérité de cette pratique (dont les exigences pénitentielles étaient maintenues même après la réconciliation) a conduit à une première crise où la pratique a été presque totalement abandonnée ou repoussée aux limites de la vie. C'est alors que, vers le VIe siècle, des moines irlandais, en mission dans une grande partie de l'Europe, se firent les promoteurs d'une toute nouvelle forme de pénitence inspirée de leur pratique de se confesser mutuellement leurs fautes en vue de se soutenir dans la vie monastique. Changement radical, puisque cette nouvelle pratique s'étendait à tous les fidèles, à toutes leurs fautes, et pouvait être renouvelée à volonté. Cette nouvelle pratique ne s'est pas imposée sans heurts, elle fut à la fois appuyée et condamnée (Tolède, 589) par des conciles. On a appelé cette forme la *pénitence tarifée* du fait qu'on imposait une pénitence (un *tarif*, une satisfaction) correspondant à la faute. Ce qui donna naissance aux livres pénitentiels, qui étaient en fait des répertoires de fautes et des tarifs pénitentiels correspondants.

Vers le XIIIe siècle, on imposa, au IVe concile du Latran, l'obligation de la confession annuelle des péchés graves au prêtre. Ce sera le début d'une pratique qui s'implantera dans l'Église jusqu'à tout récemment. On l'appela la *pénitence individuelle.* Si on compare cette forme aux précédentes, on constate les caractéristiques suivantes : elle est renouvelable à volonté et elle s'étend à toute faute, même à des imperfections. Les longues et sévères pénitences imposées dans les régimes précédents, jeûnes et aumônes, se spiritualisent. On impose des prières. Et, fait le plus caractéristique, l'aveu, donc la confession, prend une si grande importance qu'il donne son nom à l'ensemble de la démarche.

Il est facile de constater les changements considérables dans la conception de cette pratique. Une démarche qui se voulait, après de graves écarts, une reprise sérieuse de son option baptismale s'est progressivement transformée en une demande de pardon à Dieu pour des fautes graves mais aussi pour des fautes très légères. De la conversion au pardon, tel est le chemin parcouru par le sacrement de pénitence à tel point qu'on nomme fréquemment aujourd'hui cette démarche le sacrement du pardon. Jamais dans l'histoire de cette pratique on n'avait fait appel à cette dénomination.

Avec le concile Vatican II, une nouvelle forme rituelle est apparue : le sacrement de la réconciliation sans aveu personnel et avec absolution collective. Cette pratique n'est pas aussi nouvelle qu'elle ne paraît : elle avait fait l'objet d'une lettre du pape Innocent XI (1679). Sa pratique a été relancée lors de deux guerres mondiales. Même si les textes officiels indiquent que cette pratique doit être autorisée par les évêques dans des cas précis, elle introduit une nouvelle forme rituelle où l'accent est mis sur la réconciliation, sans qu'il y ait eu aveu personnel.

On sait que la pratique du sacrement de la réconciliation est quasi abandonnée. Ce qui n'est pas vraiment nouveau dans l'histoire de ce sacrement. Quel est l'avenir du sacrement de la réconciliation ? Est-il réaliste de prévoir son évolution ? Il semble qu'on peut poser quelques conditions pour que cette pratique retrouve une place significative dans l'expérience chrétienne. Il faut sans doute revenir à l'intuition originelle. La pratique de la pénitence avait pour but d'aider un fidèle à reprendre son option face à l'expérience chrétienne à cause de fautes très graves qui ont été commises. Par conséquent, il faut remettre l'accent sur la conversion avec tout ce que cela implique. Le sacrement de pénitence n'est pas une dévotion. Pour cela, il faut recentrer la démarche sur le sens de sa responsabilité face à soi et aux autres. Par conséquent, il faut mettre au second plan la crainte que Dieu ne pardonne pas et insister sur le retour intérieur vers Dieu. Le pardon de Dieu n'est pas lié aux œuvres des hommes. On n'achète pas le pardon. Dieu pardonne de toute éternité. Mais chaque chrétien est appelé à se laisser « relever » dans sa foi, par Dieu et avec le soutien de la communauté. Être réconcilié, c'est être gracié et libéré des conséquences des fautes commises. Le sacrement de la réconciliation indique qu'aucun péché ne peut enfermer définitivement le croyant qui désire faire à nouveau une place à Dieu dans sa vie.

Une telle approche questionne la démarche d'initiation des enfants au cours des premières années du primaire. Le but n'est pas tellement de leur faire « trouver » des péchés, mais de les aider à identifier leur propre responsabilité dans les situations conflictuelles et avilissantes de leur milieu. N'y aurait-il pas une autre façon, dans le processus éducatif actuel, d'éveiller un enfant à sa responsabilité et à un regard lucide sur soi dans un monde qui accuse trop facilement la société de tous les malheurs ? Au niveau de la pratique de ce sacrement, nous sommes encore sous l'influence des pratiques passées. Mais plusieurs signes indiquent que nous sommes à un moment charnière où de nouvelles pratiques semblent naître.

Être confirmé

L'importance de la confirmation est liée à la pratique largement répandue du pédobaptisme. Dans les premiers siècles de l'Église, l'initiation chrétienne rejoignait majoritairement des adultes. Cette célébration qui se vivait à la veillée pascale comprenait trois rites : le rite de l'eau présidé par un diacre ou une diaconesse pour les femmes, le rite de l'onction et le repas eucharistique, présidés par l'évêque entouré de son *presbyterium*, c'est-à-dire l'ensemble de son clergé. On appelait cette célébration, le baptême. La confirmation était ainsi l'un des rites baptismaux[2].

Avec le temps, dû à la pratique généralisée du baptême des nouveau-nés, on assista à un étalement dans le temps des trois rites de l'initiation chrétienne. Le fait que le christianisme se soit répandu dans les campagnes rendait impossible la présence des évêques à toutes les célébrations baptismales. C'est alors que s'implantèrent dans l'Église deux pratiques. En Orient, on permit aux prêtres de procéder à l'ensemble de la démarche de l'initiation chrétienne dans ses trois rites, le rite de l'eau, le rite de l'onction et celui du partage eucharistique dans la même célébration. Le lien avec l'évêque étant sauvegardé par une grande importance accordée à l'huile qu'il bénissait. Il en est encore ainsi dans la tradition orientale. Par contre, la tradition occidentale voulut garder à tout prix l'intervention de l'évêque dans le processus de l'initiation chrétienne, ce qui a conduit à différer l'eucharistie et

2. On ne peut parler de « sacrement » puisque ce n'est qu'au Moyen Âge (XIIe-XIIIe siècles) que ce terme désignera les sept rites chrétiens que nous connaissons.

la confirmation. Ce qui fait que, dans notre contexte, le rite de la confirmation est présidé par l'évêque ou, actuellement, par un prêtre qui occupe dans le diocèse une fonction importante au nom de l'évêque.

Malgré les discussions théologiques entourant le sens de la Confirmation, cette démarche trouve une signification quand on prend en compte l'étalement des rites de l'initiation chrétienne. En raison du baptême des enfants quelques mois après la naissance, il va de soi que l'Église et les parents offrent aux enfants la possibilité de faire un choix réel face à l'option chrétienne et surtout d'en découvrir la portée sociale et ecclésiale. Car, dans la vision de l'Église, l'expérience chrétienne ne se limite pas à une dimension de salut personnel. Elle engage la personne dans le devenir de son milieu. Elle a donc une perspective communautaire : ecclésiale et sociale. Ce qui explique que, traditionnellement, la catéchèse a toujours fait valoir cette perspective en privilégiant tantôt le témoignage, tantôt la force pour le combat. Cela était exprimé rituellement par le soufflet que l'évêque donnait à l'enfant au moment de l'onction.

Il faut ajouter à cela que le sacrement de Confirmation se réfère à la présence de l'Esprit saint. L'Église veut signifier par là que la vie et la mission du croyant ne se calquent pas sur une idéologie, mais qu'elles sont animées par la présence dynamique, libératrice et prophétique de l'Esprit saint, l'Esprit de Jésus.

Dans ce contexte, on s'interroge dans plusieurs communautés ecclésiales sur la question de l'âge de la Confirmation. On a vérifié, ici et là, plusieurs hypothèses, allant de la fin du primaire à la fin des études secondaires, soit à l'occasion de l'entrée dans l'enseignement supérieur ou sur le marché du travail. Les résultats ne semblent pas encore des plus concluants. On constate cependant un intérêt de moins en moins marqué pour la Confirmation au point que dans certains pays d'Europe, il n'y a qu'un très petit nombre de baptisés qui se font confirmer. Même la législation de l'Église catholique romaine dans *Le code de droit canonique* n'en fait pas une condition essentielle pour le mariage chrétien, bien qu'elle la recommande toujours.

S'unir

Parmi les grandes étapes de la vie, il y a sans contredit celle où les jeunes adultes décident de vivre leur propre expérience conjugale. Saisissant ce passage, l'Église a progressivement institué au fil des siècles le rite du mariage qui est devenu dans tous les pays d'inspiration chrétienne un rite obligatoire pour ceux qui forment un couple.

Le mariage est sans doute un des rites de passage les plus significatifs. C'était, dans la majorité des cas, l'occasion de quitter formellement la maison familiale et de fonder son propre foyer. Dans un passé encore récent, mariage, couple et famille formaient socialement et ecclésialement un tout. Il était impensable de vivre en couple sans être marié, et encore moins d'avoir un enfant. Une pression sociale et ecclésiale mettait à l'écart quiconque enfreignait ces règles.

Depuis quelques décennies, il n'en est plus de même. On forme un couple sans nécessairement vouloir se marier, comme on peut vouloir un enfant sans nécessairement former une famille. Le tout harmonieux s'est disloqué. Le mariage est souvent lié au désir du couple d'avoir des enfants ou après les avoir eus. Pour d'autres, le lien du mariage n'est pas jugé nécessaire à la vie de couple et de famille.

Dans ce contexte, que signifie le mariage s'il n'est plus considéré, surtout socialement, comme le point de départ obligé pour former un couple et fonder une famille ?

BÉNIR

Du latin *benedicere*, dire du bien, le geste de bénir s'inscrit dans la tradition juive et chrétienne. D'une part, le rituel du repas juif comportait de nombreuses bénédictions et, de son côté, les communautés chrétiennes ont fait un grand usage des bénédictions. Dans la Bible, les bénédictions consistaient dans des prières d'action de grâce et de louange pour reconnaître que tout vient de Dieu. Elles s'adressaient à Yahvé au sujet des biens matériels comme des biens spirituels. La liturgie chrétienne en fait un grand usage. Le rituel des bénédictions affirme que l'Église «a institué toutes sortes d'expressions de bénédiction, par lesquelles elle invite les fidèles à louer Dieu, les incite à demander sa protection, les exhorte à gagner sa miséricorde par la sainteté de vie, et leur offre des prières pour demander ses bienfaits, pour qu'ils aient le bonheur d'obtenir ce qu'elle implore». Le rituel comporte un riche éventail de bénédictions pour plusieurs catégories de personnes, pour des activités humaines, pour des objets de culte et de dévotion ainsi que pour diverses circonstances. On les utilise fréquemment dans les actes de culte.

Malheureusement, on doit constater qu'il existe, dans la mentalité populaire, une certaine crispation sur une fonction de la bénédiction, soit celle d'implorer Dieu pour obtenir des bienfaits et surtout pour se préserver de certains malheurs. On l'utilise parfois comme gage de protection contre les accidents et les incendies, un peu à la manière d'une police d'assurance. C'est réduire le sens théologique de ce geste. La bénédiction d'un objet étant plutôt une action de grâce à Dieu pour les biens qu'il nous donne. ◇

Face à cette situation, on rencontre deux types de réactions. D'une part, certains considèrent désastreuse la situation actuelle, estimant que c'est le résultat d'un manque de sérieux, de la peur de l'engagement face aux échecs de nombreux couples et le fruit d'une jeunesse sans principes chrétiens. Par contre, d'autres considèrent la situation comme positive, y voyant même, pour l'Église, une chance de redécouvrir le sens chrétien de l'expérience conjugale.

Dans la société de chrétienté, le mariage était souvent perçu comme le permis de vivre sa sexualité en vue de la procréation dans le seul contexte autorisé, celui d'un couple uni pour la vie. Or la société accepte une autre vision de la sexualité, vision qui s'impose dans la pratique des chrétiens malgré la rigidité des discours officiels. Ainsi, au niveau de la pratique chrétienne, un déplacement s'opère. Le mariage n'est plus perçu comme la seule possibilité de licence sexuelle. Il est centré davantage sur l'engagement qui confère une stabilité à la relation conjugale et à une éventuelle vie de famille.

L'histoire du mariage dans la tradition chrétienne nous révèle que c'est progressivement qu'on a reconnu une dimension spirituelle à la réalité humaine du mariage au point de le considérer parmi les sept sacrements. On a longuement hésité à le faire en raison du regard soupçonneux porté par les autorités ecclésiales sur la sexualité humaine. C'est après un long débat que des théologiens du Moyen Âge, entre autres Albert le Grand et Thomas d'Aquin, firent école en imposant un nouveau courant de pensée qui insistait sur la bonté de la nature parce que créée par Dieu, même si elle se trouve blessée par le péché. Dans cette perspective, le mariage est lui aussi un don de Dieu. Et le plaisir qui accompagne l'acte conjugal participe également à la sainteté du mariage. C'est en se sens que le mariage a été reconnu sacrement au Moyen Âge, après dix siècles de vie ecclésiale.

L'histoire nous montre que, dans le contexte de la société de chrétienté, les responsables de l'Église s'étaient en quelque sorte accaparé tout le pouvoir concernant cette réalité humaine. Tel n'est plus le cas. La plupart des pays, considérant que la vie de famille et de couple peut avoir une répercussion sociale, ont légiféré sur la réalité civile du mariage, laissant aux Églises le soin d'exprimer et de faire vivre à leur façon la dimension religieuse de cette expérience humaine.

Au lieu de déplorer cette situation, l'Église doit saisir cette occasion comme une chance pour mieux faire voir la signification chrétienne de l'expérience conjugale. Le mariage n'étant plus nécessairement le point de départ de la vie commune, il y a donc lieu de découvrir la dimension de foi de cette expérience dégagée de contraintes morales et civiles. L'Église présente aujourd'hui le mariage comme le projet de bâtir une communauté profonde de vie et d'amour, c'est-à-dire une cellule familiale, au service de la vie, celle des conjoints eux-mêmes et celle d'enfants à naître, de la société par leur implication, au service des valeurs de l'Évangile et, éventuellement, au service de leur communauté chrétienne. On a donc pris une distance par rapport à la présentation classique du mariage qui le définissait en termes de finalité. On y voyait une fin première, la procréation, et deux fins secondaires, l'entraide mutuelle et le remède à la concupiscence. Dans le contexte actuel, les couples veulent d'abord se réaliser eux-mêmes et consolider leur vie de couple avant de décider d'avoir un enfant.

Si on ajoute à cela une nouvelle approche de toute la réalité sacramentelle, on découvre que le mariage ne se limite pas au rite et à la célébration. C'est toute la vie conjugale dans toutes ses dimensions, affective, intellectuelle et corporelle, qui est lieu de réciprocité, d'amour, d'entraide et de fécondité, donc de salut.

Accompagner

Pour exister, toute société a besoin de structures et de serviteurs de l'institution. Comme la société, l'Église a ses rites d'investiture pour souligner la désignation des serviteurs que sont les diacres, les prêtres et les évêques. Ils ont pour rôle d'animer les communautés, d'en assumer l'accompagnement.

L'histoire de ces services, appelés ministères dans l'Église, révèle une institutionnalisation progressive, influencée très souvent par les modes de gouvernement du pouvoir civil.

À l'origine du christianisme, les apôtres ont fondé de petites communautés lors de leurs voyages missionnaires. Très tôt, ils ont établi un peu partout des responsables qu'on a appelés presbytres, d'un mot grec signifiant anciens, ou épiscopes, également d'un mot grec signifiant superviseurs. Les presbytres étaient des anciens choisis dans la communauté. C'est à partir de cette fonction que s'est développée la fonction du prêtre que nous connaissons. Quant aux épiscopes, ils jouaient un rôle semblable dans les « communautés de communautés ». Le mot se réfère à la fonction de surveillance. Leur fonction a conduit à la fonction d'évêque. Presque en même temps, les premières communautés ont choisi un certain nombre de personnes honnêtes pour s'occuper du service caritatif de la communauté. On les a appelés « diacres » (du grec *diaconos* qui veut dire serviteur). Par la suite, en raison de leur importance et de leur expansion, les communautés ecclésiales ont mis en place un certain nombre de services qu'on a appelés « ordres mineurs ».

Depuis Vatican II, l'Église a quelque peu modifié l'organisation des ministères en supprimant le sous-diaconat et certains ministères, traditionnellement appelés ordres mineurs, qui n'avaient plus de signification, tels l'ordre de portier et d'exorcisme. Par contre, elle a retenu et réaffirmé les ministères de l'épiscopat et du presbytérat et réinstauré un ministère ancien, celui du diaconat permanent. Depuis le Moyen Âge jusqu'au concile Vatican II, le diaconat était une étape obligatoire pour devenir prêtre. Tout en gardant cette étape, le dernier concile a remis en honneur, pour des hommes mariés, le service des diacres. C'est une nouveauté dans l'Église qui n'est pas sans soulever une importante question du fait que ce service n'est pas accessible aux femmes à qui on demande de suivre, autant que possible, la formation de leur époux.

IMPOSER LES MAINS

Le geste de l'imposition des mains s'apparente à celui du symbolisme de l'onction avec l'huile. Enraciné dans la tradition biblique, il signifie en priorité la transmission d'un pouvoir ou l'emprise de l'Esprit pour une mission. Ainsi, dans les Actes, on voit que les apôtres ont imposé les mains pour transmettre l'Esprit. Celui qui est oint est pénétré de l'Esprit de Dieu. La liturgie chrétienne utilise ce rite dans presque tous les sacrements. Au baptême, le ministre fait l'onction avec l'huile bénite par l'évêque pour signifier que le nouveau fidèle est prophète, prêtre et roi, comme les prophètes, les prêtres et les rois du peuple d'Israël étaient oints lors de leur consécration ou de leur sacre. À la confirmation, à l'onction des malades et à l'ordination, c'est même le rite essentiel. Dans les autres sacrements, tels la pénitence, l'eucharistie, le mariage, on impose les mains sans toutefois utiliser l'huile bénite. ◇

Dans le contexte nord-américain, la même interrogation se pose concernant les prêtres. Jusqu'à présent, le Magistère de l'Église maintient sa discipline d'exclure les femmes des fonctions de gouvernement dans l'Église en s'appuyant sur trois arguments majeurs : le fait que Jésus n'a pas choisi de femmes parmi ses apôtres ; la tradition qui démontre que l'Église n'a jamais autorisé de femmes à prendre ces responsabilités ; et un argument de type symbolique. Jésus étant un homme, il ne convient qu'à un homme de symboliser le Christ présent dans la communauté.

Évidemment, dans une société qui fait de plus en plus de place aux femmes dans presque tous les secteurs de la vie sociale, il va de soi qu'une telle discipline est loin de recueillir l'assentiment de la population. On ne reconnaît pas la valeur de ces arguments, d'autant plus que l'Église anglicane et d'autres Églises, telle l'Église luthérienne, admettent des femmes dans tous ces ministères, y compris à l'épiscopat.

Dans l'Église, l'évêque joue un rôle important. Il préside à la bonne marche de son diocèse, unité civile et religieuse qui comprend un ensemble de communautés chrétiennes appelées paroisses. En plus, il a comme fonction de réaliser la communion de son Église avec les autres Églises de sa province, de son pays, et même dans certains cas avec l'ensemble des Églises du monde entier par des institutions, tels les synodes romains, les conciles, et surtout leurs visites quinquennales à Rome, appelées visites *ad limina*.

De son côté, l'évêque de l'Église de Rome, qu'on appelle le Pape, a une fonction de service, de rassemblement et de communion de toutes les Églises catholiques du monde entier. Il ne faut pas oublier qu'en soi il ne s'agit pas d'un pouvoir supérieur à celui des évêques qui, comme le pape, sont les successeurs des apôtres. Avec le temps, suite à des controverses et à plusieurs facteurs, le pape s'est accaparé une grande partie des responsabilités et pouvoirs qui relevaient des évêques eux-mêmes. Alors qu'au cours du premier millénaire, sa fonction se concentrait surtout sur la communion des Églises locales entre elles, avec le temps, il en est venu à se considérer comme l'évêque de chaque fidèle du monde entier, faisant ainsi des évêques des porte-parole du Pape. Par contre, les Églises orientales ont mieux conservé les structures de l'Église primitive, ce qui leur confère une plus grande autonomie. Cela constitue d'ailleurs un obstacle majeur à l'effort œcuménique contemporain.

Pour accéder aux trois fonctions mentionnées, l'Église a institué trois rites : l'ordination diaconale l'ordination presbytérale l'ordination épiscopale. Par ces rites, l'Église confère une fonction ecclésiale et un pouvoir juridique aux ordonnés et les invite à considérer ces fonctions comme un service à la communauté au nom du Christ lui-même.

Faiblir et approcher la mort

Parmi les étapes de la vie, il y a lieu de signaler les moments de crise de l'existence, soit par la maladie grave, soit par l'imminence ou le risque de la mort. L'Église propose un rite sacramentel qui aide à vivre dans la foi ces moments où la personne éprouve la précarité de son être. Ce sacrement s'appelle l'onction des malades.

Beaucoup gardent en mémoire ces tristes moments où le prêtre est venu accomplir auprès d'une personne chère, en danger de mort, un ensemble de rites la préparant au grand passage. Jusqu'au concile Vatican II, on appelait cet ensemble de rites l'extrême-onction parce que, effectivement, c'était la dernière onction. Dans la mentalité populaire, ce sacrement correspondait à la fin de la vie. Ces rites étaient perçus comme un moyen d'effacer les conséquences du péché et de préparer à la vie éternelle. Ils avaient une grande importance dans la mentalité populaire chrétienne. À la mort d'un proche, on se consolait en se disant : « Au moins, il a reçu les derniers sacrements. » Et on trouvait déplorable que des personnes meurent accidentellement sans avoir reçu ces rites de l'Église.

Le renouveau ecclésial a considérablement modifié la perception et la finalité de ces rites. L'extrême-onction est devenue l'onction des malades avec tout ce que peut suggérer ce changement de nom. Ce rite ne s'adresse plus aux mourants. Il s'offre aux malades dont la vie est menacée dans sa qualité et dans sa durée. Il veut favoriser une démarche spirituelle en vue de les aider à vivre lucidement dans l'ouverture et la foi ces moments où la vie est éprouvée. Le rite de l'onction des malades pointe ainsi la question de la mort et de l'au-delà. Il propose l'espérance chrétienne du salut réalisé en Jésus Christ.

Vivre la mort

Les rites funéraires font partie de toutes les cultures. On n'y échappe pas même si on relève, depuis tout récemment, une évolution dans les mœurs funéraires. Depuis plusieurs siècles, l'Église offrait un ensemble de rites entourant la mort : les veillées auprès du défunt, la fermeture du cercueil, la messe des funérailles, le transport au cimetière et les prières finales sur la tombe du défunt. Ces rites s'imposaient socialement et ecclésialement.

La célébration des funérailles n'a pas le statut de sacrement tout en étant un rite chrétien. Cette célébration fait la boucle avec le baptême : le parcours temporel du baptisé est arrivé à son terme. Cette célébration est l'occasion pour la communauté ecclésiale de rendre grâce à Dieu pour la vie du défunt ou de la défunte et, dans la foi, de Le prier de l'accueillir dans son Royaume.

Actuellement, il y a émergence de diverses pratiques funéraires. Dans la société actuelle, qui a tendance à faire comme si la mort n'existait pas, on ne sait trop que penser de la réalité de la mort. On retrouve aussi une prolifération, parfois fantaisiste, de conceptions de l'au-delà qui n'est pas sans révéler à sa façon un déni de la mort en apportant des réponses à des questions sans réponse définitive. Il est loisible de penser qu'à travers la diversité des nouvelles pratiques, certaines s'imposeront par leur pertinence

367*
Dómini nostri Iesu Christi...;
et in ultimo cubiculo ad-
dat versum : Dóminus vobís-
cum, cum suo responsorio, et
cum sequenti oratione plurali
numero dicenda : Dómine,
pyxide velo humerali cooper-

et seront peut-être intégrées aux pratiques chrétiennes. Seul l'avenir le dira.

Appartenir à l'humanité et au royaume de Dieu : rites chrétiens

Toutes les sociétés, les plus anciennes comme les plus modernes, ont leurs propres rites qui viennent scander les étapes marquantes des individus et des groupes humains. Profondément ancrés dans la mentalité de chaque culture, ces rites jouent un rôle important dans l'identité personnelle et collective. Les chrétiens ne sont pas

ASPERGER ET IMMERGER

Les gestes avec l'eau bénite sont fréquents dans la liturgie. C'est même le rite essentiel du baptême. D'ailleurs, le mot baptême vient d'un mot grec qui signifier immerger. Au début du christianisme, le baptistère, lieu du baptême, consistait en une mini piscine dans laquelle plongeaient réellement les baptisés. On l'appelait baptême par immersion. Avec le temps, et surtout en raison de l'expansion du christianisme dans les pays nordiques et de l'imposition du baptême des petits enfants, ce rite de l'immersion devint désuet. On le remplaça par le rite de l'infusion qui consiste à verser un peu d'eau sur la tête du baptisé.

Par ailleurs, on utilise aussi ce geste de l'aspersion sur les fidèles et sur certains objets. Autrefois, la célébration solennelle de l'eucharistie débutait par ce rite avec le chant du psaume *Asperges me*. Disparu avec la réforme liturgique, il demeure possible au début de l'eucharistie. Il veut rappeler aux fidèles que s'ils sont réunis pour l'eucharistie, c'est qu'un jour, lors de leur baptême, ils ont été accueillis dans la communauté chrétienne. Il est aussi généralement associé aux divers rites de bénédiction. C'est un rappel du baptême et une marque de respect. ◇

soustraits à ce jeu rituel. Ils le vivent dans la foi chrétienne qui consiste à vivre sa vie d'homme et de femme « en compagnie de Dieu », compagnie médiatisée par la communauté ecclésiale.

Au cours des siècles, le défi de l'Église a porté sur le besoin de signifier, à travers ses propres rites, la double appartenance des chrétiens à l'humanité et au Royaume de Dieu en le préfigurant, en l'annonçant et en l'anticipant dès aujourd'hui. Avec le temps, l'Église a proposé des rites pour permettre aux croyants et aux croyantes de saisir leur double appartenance et d'en découvrir leurs rapports réciproques et féconds. Cela est particulièrement évident dans les sept sacrements, mais cela s'est réalisé aussi avec d'autres rites dont l'importance est variable. De ces rites non sacramentels, les funérailles ont un statut particulier puisqu'elles encadrent la fin de vie d'une personne. Mais il y a aussi de nombreux rites, comme les liturgies de la Parole, où des groupes se rassemblent pour entendre des extraits bibliques, les comprendre et les commenter, les prier et en inspirer leur vie. Le chapelet, pratique de prière surgi de la dévotion populaire, relève aussi de ces rites. La prière est aussi une pratique rituelle importante, qu'elle se fasse dans des formules toute faites ou dans le silence du retrait. Il existe une autre pratique rituelle chrétienne fort ancienne, les pèlerinages. Le pèlerinage implique toujours un parcours plus ou moins long pour se rendre à un sanctuaire. Le parcours géographique est lié au parcours spirituel souhaité lors de la visite du sanctuaire en question. Les rites chrétiens, dans leur diversité, sont autant de façon de vivre pleinement la vie humaine dans la proximité du Dieu de Jésus Christ.

MÉDIAS ET FOI CHRÉTIENNE, DEUX MONDES ?

Qu'en a dit l'Église catholique romaine ?

L'évolution de la pensée de l'Église catholique en matière de médias de masse démontre bien un déplacement entre deux visions, c'est-à-dire de l'une, pessimiste voire moralisatrice, vers l'autre, optimiste colorée de providentialisme et surtout d'utilitarisme.

L'expansion de l'imprimerie de Gutenberg qu'a vu le xve siècle ne laisse pas les autorités pontificales indifférentes. Une surveillance rigoureuse des fruits de cette invention durcira le jugement de la papauté, notamment sous Léon X (1515) qui impose de fait un contrôle absolu sur tous documents imprimés. Méfiante, l'Église considère les médias de son temps comme une menace pour l'intégrité de la doctrine qu'elle entend promouvoir. Deux siècles plus tard, Pie VI (1791) s'en prend, pour sa part, à la liberté de la presse qu'il considère comme « un droit monstrueux ». Il faudra attendre le second concile du Vatican pour sentir une ouverture significative aux médias. Entre-temps, elle aura développé ses propres médias : son journal *L'Osservatore Romano* en 1860, et sa *Radio vaticane* en 1931. De plus, près de 300 interventions officielles de l'Église ont été faites à ce sujet à travers des lettres pastorales, des messages et des instructions.

Une sorte d'ouverture, donc, où l'Église saisit les médias comme « signes des temps » et avec lesquels elle peut et doit composer pour réaliser sa mission d'évangélisation. Avec le décret conciliaire *Inter Mirifica* (1963), l'Église transforme sa vision des choses malgré une certaine réserve. Bien qu'ils soient considérés comme des « dons de Dieu », les médias sont tout de même entre des mains humaines et peuvent tout autant être outils du bien que du mal. L'Église mesure bien l'énorme influence des médias, elle en appelle donc à la vigilance des fidèles. L'instruction pastorale *Ætatis Novæ* (1992) de Jean-Paul II fait justement la promotion de la formation aux médias pour favoriser une conscience sensible et éclairée autour de ces réalités incontournables qui caractérisent notre siècle.

Au nom de la foi, Jean-Paul II prend le risque des médias

Jean-Paul II est sans contredit le pape le plus médiatisé et aussi le plus médiatique de l'histoire. Reconnu pour son talent d'animateur de foules, soutenu par son expérience du théâtre, il s'engage dans le monde des médias sans doute par choix mais aussi porté par la conviction qu'il a d'utiliser stratégiquement ces moyens.

Parce que Jean-Paul II se rend accessible au monde médiatique, il crée une révolution autour de l'image du pouvoir de la papauté. Cette implication comporte des risques, entre autres celui de réduire le message central de l'Évangile au profit d'une image, en faisant du serviteur de Pierre une vedette médiatique. En d'autres mots, c'est encourir l'idolâtrie. Reproche fait d'ailleurs par l'Église aux moyens de communication. Mais l'Église n'est pas dupe, elle sait que les médias peuvent servir tout autant que détruire l'idéal qu'elle porte, soit de tendre davantage vers la communion humaine. C'est pourquoi elle s'applique à bien comprendre leur fonctionnement. Car la tension et le risque de distorsion sont toujours présents entre l'image voulue par l'Église, celle que les médias projettent d'elle et celle qui est retenue par le public. On peut se demander si c'est la façon dont le message est transmis qui gêne, ou bien si c'est le message en lui-même qui dérange...

Foi et médias, un chemin de plus vers la liberté ?

L'infiltration des médias dans le quotidien de la vie ne se fait pas sans laisser de traces. Au-delà de leur efficacité technique, ils sont reconnus comme des moyens qui fournissent à des millions de gens un système de valeurs, un guide de comportement, une conception du monde qui les influencent profondément. Il est fort pertinent alors de s'interroger, comme croyant et comme croyante, sur ce que nous cherchons à faire de ces instruments, fruits du génie humain. Y a-t-il une manière chrétienne d'agir dans ce monde médiatique ? Sommes-nous des consommateurs passifs ou des personnes engagées dans une attitude critique face à cette présence technologique ? Comment les valeurs évangéliques, qui animent la foi chrétienne, nous placent-elles précisément devant ces réalités techniques ? Sans répondre directement à ces questions, bien sûr, les récits bibliques ne manquent toutefois pas de suggestions. Le refus des idoles, le souci pour les pauvres, le respect de la dignité humaine, l'ambition d'un projet pour l'ensemble de l'humanité, voilà quelques balises qui permettent d'orienter des actions qualifiables d'attitudes chrétiennes. On peut donc penser que la « manière chrétienne » d'agir dans ce monde des médias doit porter le souci de libérer la personne de certaines tendances narcissiques qui risquent de rendre désuet le sens de la solidarité. Nous devons, si nous nous reconnaissons comme chrétiens et comme chrétiennes, mettre à contribution nos talents afin de faire en sorte que les médias soient des outils au service de cette quête continuelle de la liberté et la réalisation pleine du potentiel humain. ◇

Martine Pelletier

DES DÉFIS
POUR BÂTIR LA FOI

ENGENDRER : SEXUALITÉ ET FÉCONDITÉ

Marie Gratton

Allez donc savoir pourquoi ! Certains sujets ont le don d'émoustiller le commun des mortels et de stimuler leur verve. Le sexe, à d'autres époques on disait « la chose », puisque le mot faisait presque aussi peur que la réalité qu'il évoquait, le sexe, donc, obsède bien des esprits, à tort ou à raison, pour des motifs différents, que ce soit du côté des laïcs, des clercs ou des autorités ecclésiales. La tournure prise par trop de confessions, le contenu de tant de sermons ne sont sans doute pas étrangers à l'affaire. De nos jours, les homélies ont changé de ton, les gens ne se confessent plus guère, et ce sont les thérapeutes de tout acabit qui semblent avoir hérité de l'obsession. Et ils ne manquent pas d'alliés pour la propager, c'est bien connu. Au milieu du chahut, les plus hautes autorités de l'Église continuent d'élever la voix, alors que de nombreux prêtres ont baissé les bras et laissé à Dieu seul le soin de juger ce que les gens faisaient dans leur chambre à coucher, se contentant de rappeler à tous, sans entrer dans les détails, que le respect de soi et des autres devrait toujours être au rendez-vous dans leurs amours.

La voie étroite de la tradition catholique

La tradition catholique officielle limite la légitimité des relations sexuelles à l'intérieur d'un mariage sanctionné par l'Église, symbole de l'amour indéfectible du Christ pour elle, et de ce fait réputé indissoluble. La fidélité en pensée et en acte y est de rigueur. Ce mariage trouve normalement son accomplissement idéal dans la fécondité du couple dont chaque échange sexuel doit être « ouvert à la vie ». Aucune religion, ni aucune culture, ne semble avoir jamais aussi étroitement encadré l'exercice de la sexualité.

Pour les catholiques, sexualité et fécondité sont présentées comme indissociables. Une question monte à l'esprit : en soutenant pareille opinion, les autorités ecclésiales traduisent-elles la volonté divine du créateur ou trahissent-elles plutôt, par la sévérité de leur doctrine, une méfiance presque maladive à l'égard de la sexualité, méfiance dont il serait d'ailleurs assez aisé de retracer les causes humaines, très humaines ?

Le lien entre sexualité et procréation est si évident qu'il serait carrément stupide de nier que la propagation de la vie est l'une des fins de l'union charnelle. Le tout est de savoir si c'est la seule. L'Église a reconnu, il y a longtemps, qu'à l'intérieur du mariage, les relations sexuelles avaient deux autres fins : soutenir l'amour mutuel des époux et être le seul légitime « remède à la concupiscence ». La formule donnait à penser que le désir est une sorte de maladie dont la seule thérapie admissible serait le mariage. Aujourd'hui on ne conserve plus, dans la formulation officielle à tout le moins, que la procréation et l'amour mutuel des conjoints comme fins du mariage ; ainsi l'a voulu le concile Vatican II (1962-1965).

On ne peut que s'étonner du paradoxe que constitue dans l'Église catholique la tenace méfiance que lui inspire la sexualité, étant donné qu'elle proclame du même souffle la bonté et la beauté de la création. Après avoir créé l'être humain, femme et homme, le texte biblique nous affirme que Dieu trouva cela « très bon » (*Gn* 1,31). Voilà un passage que les catholiques n'ont pas cru devoir censurer. La création est sortie sexuée des mains de Dieu, s'il est permis de s'exprimer ainsi. Il aurait pu, il faut le croire, trouver d'autres moyens de prolonger son œuvre. Il aurait pu, de surcroît, n'attacher aucun plaisir à la rencontre sexuelle. Et personne n'aurait songé à s'en plaindre dans l'ignorance de ce qu'elle ou de ce qu'il manquait. Dieu, visiblement, ne semble pas s'être méfié de la sexualité ni être jaloux de nos plaisirs. Comment en sommes-nous donc venus à lui prêter de tels sentiments ?

Cherchez l'homme...

Pour trouver la réponse à la question que je viens de poser, je propose de chercher l'humain, le trop humain qui se drape de l'autorité divine, pour résoudre l'énigme. Les chrétiens, normalement, se tournent vers le Nazaréen comme vers un guide capable, à travers ses paroles et les gestes de sa vie, d'éclairer leur conscience et d'orienter leur agir moral. Jésus toutefois semble avoir attaché bien peu d'importance à la réglementation de « la chose ». Pas un mot sur la contraception, ni sur l'avortement, ni sur l'homosexualité, ni sur les relations préconjugales, ni sur l'inceste ou autres « abominations » que saint Paul, quant à lui, dénoncera alors qu'il sera confronté aux mœurs du milieu gréco-romain. Jésus se contente, pour sa part, d'une recommandation sur le mariage : « Que l'homme ne sépare pas ce que Dieu a uni » (*Mt* 19,6), et semble ne retenir que l'adultère comme motif légitime de divorce (*Mt* 19,9). Avec lui, fini le temps où un mari pouvait renvoyer sa femme pour un repas brûlé, désastre domestique aisément évitable, ou pour cause de rencontre d'une femme plus belle ou plus jeune, incident de parcours qui ne peut, fatalement, jamais longtemps tarder.

C'est à saint Augustin (354-430) qu'il faut remonter pour voir se dessiner dans la tradition chrétienne le lien exclusif entre sexualité et procréation. Ce Père de l'Église, dont l'influence a sans doute été la plus décisive en regard de cette question, était un converti. Pendant neuf ans il avait été membre de la secte des Manichéens. Ceux-ci prétendaient qu'il fallait s'abstenir de procréer pour éviter d'enfermer dans la chair une parcelle de la lumière divine. Mais, singulièrement, ils ne condamnaient pas les relations sexuelles. Le moyen de s'en sortir? La contraception, évidemment. L'Antiquité connaissait tout un arsenal de méthodes tantôt contraceptives, tantôt abortives, dont l'efficacité variait considérablement. Certaines étaient inoffensives et d'autres dangereuses. Si le port d'un grigri au moment des relations sexuelles n'a jamais empêché un enfant de naître ni mis en péril la vie d'un couple, l'absorption de certaines potions a expédié des femmes et des fœtus de vie à trépas.

Les Manichéens, quant à eux, avaient recueilli chez les Égyptiens la méthode du rythme. Ils savaient que la femme n'est féconde que quelques jours à chaque cycle menstruel, et conseillaient à leurs adeptes de s'abstenir de relations sexuelles durant ce temps-là. Augustin connaissait cette méthode, et c'est sans doute grâce à elle qu'il réussit à n'engendrer qu'un seul fils dans la première année d'une liaison qui devait durer quatorze ans. Adeodatus — Dieudonné — voilà comment il nommera ce fils « né contre tout désir », avouera-t-il plus tard, mais qui une fois né s'est fait « de force chérir ». Une erreur de calcul ! Au XXe siècle, la méthode Ogino-Knaus, fondée sur des calculs à peine plus raffinés, en produira bien d'autres.

On connaît la réaction de nombreux convertis : « brûler ce qu'ils avaient adoré et adorer ce qu'ils avaient brûlé ». Après avoir

MARIE

La Très Sainte Vierge, voilà pour plusieurs le vocable associé à la personne de Marie, au point de donner l'impression que toute la richesse de sa personnalité se réduit à cette dimension. Une telle réduction ne rend pas compte de la profondeur du bouleversement que Dieu a produit en s'associant personnellement à notre monde à travers cette Nazaréenne. Elle ne rend pas justice à la grandeur particulière de cette croyante disponible, prête à faire naître une vie nouvelle extraordinaire par sa propre maternité ordinaire. ◇

reçu le baptême au début de la trentaine, et être devenu presque aussitôt après évêque, Augustin élaborera sa théologie du mariage en prenant le contre-pied de ce que prônaient les hérétiques manichéens. Seul l'enfant constitue pour lui « l'excuse » des relations sexuelles. La jouissance est une « dangereuse compagnonne » et un obstacle à la poursuite du bonheur, entendez ici Dieu, le souverain bien. Désormais, dans la tradition chrétienne, tout spécialement dans son expression catholique, sexualité et fécondité seront indissociablement liées. Si étroitement et exclusivement liées en fait, qu'on viendra à déclarer invalide et nul un mariage contracté alors que l'un des croyants ou les deux à la fois entretiennent la ferme intention de ne pas avoir d'enfants.

Fécondité : un but, plusieurs chemins ?

Cette fixation obstinée sur la fécondité physique est-elle défendable ? Après tout, l'Église permet le mariage de personnes dont la stérilité est avérée soit à cause d'une déficience organique, soit à cause de l'âge. L'amour des conjoints et le remède à la concupiscence sont apparus traditionnellement dans ces cas des motifs suffisants pour contracter mariage. Ne pourrait-on pas penser qu'un couple jeune, en santé et généreux de surcroît, mais certainement pas prêt à la chasteté perpétuelle, pourrait faire preuve d'un autre type de fécondité, en consacrant temps, énergie et créativité à des causes caritatives et sociales, voire en adoptant des enfants sans foyer, ou tout simplement en poursuivant des objectifs et une carrière qui leur paraissent plus en accord avec leurs dispositions naturelles et leurs goûts ? Le mariage ne rend pas automatiquement les femmes et les hommes aptes à devenir de bons parents. C'est une évidence que trop d'enfants malheureux illustrent, hélas.

Bien des gens s'imaginent que les femmes ne peuvent trouver leur plein épanouissement que dans la maternité. Pour les religieuses, qui par vœu y ont renoncé, on fait miroiter les joies incomparables de la maternité spirituelle. Pour les femmes, hors de la maternité, point de salut ? Est-ce si simple, est-ce si clair ?

Élargissons encore un peu la perspective. Pour l'ensemble des catholiques, est-ce si simple, est-ce si clair de croire qu'en dehors du mariage un, indissoluble et ouvert à la fécondité, il n'y ait point de salut, comme ils l'entendent si souvent répéter par l'autorité suprême de leur Église ? Rien n'est moins sûr, d'autant plus qu'ils savent, soit par expérience, soit par ouï-dire, que plusieurs pasteurs, confesseurs et directeurs spirituels manifestent plus d'ouverture d'esprit et de compréhension vis-à-vis des situations concrètes des personnes qui se confient à eux, et leur demandent conseil, pour les aider à vivre chrétiennement leur sexualité, même lorsqu'elles ne s'estiment pas capables de respecter à la lettre la doctrine catholique à cet égard.

Loin de nous l'idée de discréditer une loi sous le prétexte que beaucoup de gens y contreviennent. Néanmoins, ne faut-il pas consentir à la soumettre à un nouvel examen quand elle est systématiquement ignorée par une foule de gens, et ouvertement contestée, en théorie aussi bien qu'en pratique, par des personnes dont on ne peut par ailleurs sérieusement remettre en cause le sens moral, la bonne foi et l'attachement aux valeurs évangéliques ?

Pour ce qui est des gens mariés, la contestation de la discipline en matière d'éthique sexuelle tourne beaucoup autour du refus de l'Église de toute forme dite artificielle de contraception. Nous y reviendrons tout à l'heure. Mais arrêtons-nous pour l'instant à l'interdiction de toute relation sexuelle préconjugale, ainsi que de tout rapport charnel entre personnes du même sexe. Demeurer célibataire, par choix, ou parce que les circonstances particulières de la vie n'ont pas permis à quelqu'un de se marier, oblige aussi, selon la discipline officielle de l'Église, à la chasteté perpétuelle.

IMMACULÉE CONCEPTION

La croyance en la sainteté de Marie, la mère de Jésus, est très ancienne. Les théologiens des premiers siècles, ceux qu'on appelle les Pères de l'Église, et ceux du Moyen Âge, dits les Scolastiques, s'appuyaient sur la salutation de l'ange Gabriel: «Je te salue, pleine de grâce», pour étayer cette thèse. Néanmoins, il faudra attendre le XIXe siècle pour que l'Immaculée Conception de Marie devienne un dogme de l'Église catholique. Selon cette doctrine, Marie aurait été préservée du péché originel dès le premier instant de sa conception dans le ventre maternel.

La doctrine de l'Immaculée Conception est non seulement liée aux connaissances biologiques d'une époque, mais encore à la représentation qu'on se fait du péché originel. Si celui-ci est une tache, en être préservée a rendu Marie immaculée. Bien des gens confondent l'Immaculée Conception de Marie avec la conception virginale de Jésus. Erreur! Jésus conçu dans le sein de Marie par l'opération du Saint-Esprit, voilà ce qu'on appelle la conception virginale. ◇

Nous ne poserons pas la question théorique à savoir si ces exigences sont réalistes. Cela nous entraînerait dans des débats psychologiques sur le rôle de la volonté d'une part, et plus encore théologiques sur la puissance de la grâce divine d'autre part, capable de rendre possible ce qui apparaît humainement si terriblement exigeant. Nous nous contenterons d'observer ce qui se vit. Certaines personnes croient fermement, malgré toutes les difficultés qu'elles rencontrent dans l'observance stricte de la discipline de l'Église, que ses enseignements en matière sexuelle reflètent vraiment la volonté de Dieu et s'y soumettent. Un plus grand nombre, dirait-on, pense qu'il s'agit plutôt d'opinions humaines tout à fait discutables. De toute manière, les faits s'imposent : des célibataires sans projet de mariage ont une vie sexuelle active ; d'autres cohabitent avec la ferme intention d'en venir à un engagement nuptial, mais souhaitent, en vivant côte à côte, vérifier la profondeur de leur attachement réciproque avant de sceller leur union devant Dieu. Des personnes divorcées se remarient civilement, des hommes et des femmes entretiennent des relations homosexuelles, stables pour un certain nombre, passagères et occasionnelles pour d'autres.

Depuis longtemps les pasteurs ont pris conscience de la diversité des situations, des motivations qui conditionnent les conduites humaines en matière de sexualité. La psychologie et la sociologie les ont beaucoup éveillés à la nécessité d'adopter une approche qui fait plus de place au discernement qu'à la condamnation sans appel.

La façon dont plusieurs fidèles catholiques prennent leur distance à l'égard du Magistère, alors que ni leur sens moral ni leur attachement sincère à l'Évangile ne peuvent raisonnablement être mis en doute, invite, nous semble-t-il, à une reconsidération de la morale sexuelle catholique. Comment les autorités ecclésiastiques peuvent-elles ne pas prendre en compte toutes ces connaissances que nous possédons maintenant sur notre moi intime, et sur les façons si différentes qu'ont les diverses cultures de gérer les conduites sexuelles, quand on sait par ailleurs que Jésus s'est montré pour sa part si discret en ces matières qu'il est bien difficile d'en appeler à lui pour régler dans le détail tous nos comportement sexuels. Ce silence de Jésus ne peut certes pas justifier n'importe quelle pratique sexuelle, puisque la fidélité à son esprit exige que toutes nos conduites, quelles qu'elles soient, portent la marque de l'amour et du respect de soi-même et du prochain, mais il ouvre certainement la porte à un exercice de discernement, non seulement pastoral et pratique, mais aussi théorique et théologique.

L'interdiction de la « pilule » : un refus difficile à avaler

Mais revenons au problème de la contraception, un sujet qui a tant fait pour creuser le fossé entre le magistère de l'Église et les laïcs. En reprenant dans *Humanæ vitæ* (1968) l'interdiction qu'on trouvait déjà dans *Casti connubii* (1930), le pape Paul VI a déclenché chez les catholiques un vaste phénomène de rejet. À quels facteurs faut-il attribuer une réaction à la fois si vive et si négative ? D'abord au fait que l'expérience des personnes laïques et mariées semble n'avoir pas été retenue comme un élément important dans l'élaboration de la position de l'Église. C'est d'en haut et du dehors qu'on affirma avec une autoritaire assurance que les méthodes dites artificielles de contraception mettaient en péril la dignité de la femme et la fidélité conjugale. Comment s'étonner que des personnes, plongées dans le quotidien de la vie conjugale et familiale et de ses lourdes obligations matérielles et psychologiques, aient jugé quelque peu abusif que des clercs célibataires, et à l'abri des aléas familiaux, viennent décider pour eux des meilleurs moyens de mener une vie digne et harmonieuse aux yeux de Dieu, un Dieu dont ils seraient les seuls à connaître la volonté? La méthode du rythme, utilisée pour planifier les naissances, mais non pour les empêcher tout à fait, est retenue comme acceptable. L'ironie du sort veut que ce soit précisément la seule qu'Augustin ait nommément décrite et condamnée comme «abominable». Pour lui, le crime résidait dans la dissociation entre sexualité et procréation. La méthode importait moins que la fin poursuivie. Il dénonce celle qu'il connaît le mieux pour l'avoir lui-même pratiquée.

Augustin ne s'embarrasse pas de subtiles nuances entre méthodes dites «naturelles» et dites «artificielles». C'est sur la fin poursuivie: éviter une grossesse, dissocier donc sexualité et fécondité, qu'il fait peser sa condamnation. On comprend donc qu'aucun moyen si «naturel» qu'il puisse paraître ne peut trouver grâce à ses yeux. Dur, mais logique.

Le document pontifical, dont bien des gens n'ont retenu qu'une chose, à savoir qu'il était «contre la pilule», a souvent été l'objet d'un autre reproche. L'usage qu'il fait d'une certaine conception de la «loi naturelle» apparaît, à un grand nombre de philosophes et de théologiens, qu'ils soient hommes ou femmes, complètement dépassé et sans grande pertinence. Comme l'Église ne peut pas s'appuyer sur l'enseignement de Jésus pour interdire les méthodes contraceptives mécaniques, comme le condom ou le stérilet, ou chimiques, comme la pilule, c'est sur une conception de la nature empruntée à la philosophie grecque qu'elle fonde son rejet de la contraception dite «artificielle», mais aussi sur une vision particulière du Dieu créateur.

Il est clair que le débat, pour une grande majorité de personnes, semble se jouer autour des notions de naturel et d'artificiel. Se plier aux calculs de la méthode du rythme, ont-elles compris en lisant *Humanæ vitæ*, serait naturel, les périodes de fécondité et de stérilité étant inscrites dans la nature biologique des femmes; leur faire avaler une pilule ferait appel à un artifice. Mais, si on y pense bien, le raisonnement de Paul VI dans *Humanæ vitæ* ne peut pas s'arrêter là puisque les méthodes Ogino-Knaus, symptothermique, ou Billings, font appel au calendrier, au thermomètre ou à une éprouvette, toutes choses qu'on ne retrouve pas telles quelles dans la nature. Pourtant, toutes trois sont jugées acceptables par les autorités catholiques, à condition d'être utilisées pour des motifs raisonnables comme la préservation de la santé de la mère ou le désir de ne mettre au monde que les enfants dont on peut convenablement assurer la subsistance.

Il faut donc chercher ailleurs, dans une certaine conception du Dieu créateur, par exemple. Dieu est maître de la vie et de la mort. C'est ainsi que le conçoivent les chrétiens. Les catholiques en particulier s'attachent aujourd'hui à appliquer avec rigueur les conséquences ultimes de cette conviction en ce qui a trait à son surgissement et à son extinction. C'est ainsi que la morale catholique officielle se révèle rigoureuse en affirmant que rien ne doit s'interposer pour empêcher Dieu de faire surgir une vie par l'utilisation de pratiques comme la contraception et l'avortement, et que rien non plus ne doit hâter sa fin par le recours à l'euthanasie ou au suicide. Empêcher de naître, faire mourir apparaît de ce fait comme une sorte de sacrilège: empêcher Dieu d'être Dieu, l'empêcher d'exercer son pouvoir créateur et son empire sur toute vie.

La plupart des personnes qui pratiquent une forme ou l'autre de contraception, ou jugent acceptable l'euthanasie dans certains cas, seraient fort troublées d'apprendre qu'elles font ainsi injure à Dieu. En général, elles estiment plutôt que les interdictions romaines reposent sur un soupçon tenace à l'égard du plaisir, elles se sentent blessées de voir à quel point on sous-estime leur sens de la responsabilité en ce domaine. On peut les comprendre.

D'autant plus que le respect révérenciel qu'on manifeste ici vis-à-vis du Dieu créateur ne marque pas d'une manière aussi scrupuleuse le reste de l'activité humaine. Les progrès scientifiques et techniques en général sont salués comme de glorieux exploits, et si on refuse le clonage, ce dont il faut se réjouir, on admet pourtant la greffe d'organes. Remplacer un cœur, un rein, un foie, n'est-ce pas un peu, beaucoup, jouer au bon Dieu?

La position de l'Église catholique en ces matières force tout le monde à aborder avec gravité et révérence le mystère de la vie; il faut lui en savoir gré. Néanmoins, le débat, nous semble-t-il, doit rester ouvert.

Si Dieu, et nous sommes en droit de le présumer, ne s'estime pas offensé par le harnachement des cours d'eau qui nous permettent de fabriquer à bon compte l'électricité qui nous est si utile, ni par les greffes d'organes qui prolongent des vies autrement condamnées à une fin certaine, pourquoi le serait-il *gravement* quand un couple recourt à une méthode artificielle de contraception quand ses conditions de santé, de fortune ou d'équilibre psychologique ou social ne lui permettent plus raisonnablement de mettre un autre enfant au monde? *Humanæ vitæ* a été très mal accueillie; les motifs que je viens d'évoquer permettront de comprendre pourquoi. En des matières aussi complexes et aussi intimes, les nuances sont mieux reçues que les interprétations qui se veulent définitives et absolues.

Pour faire des enfants tous les moyens ne sont pas bons

Les sujets reliés à la sexualité suscitent souvent malaise et méfiance. La condamnation sans réserve et sans nuance qui a frappé l'utilisation des méthodes de procréation assistée illustre bien ce fait. Ici encore, comme le recours à Jésus est bien évidemment impossible — il n'a rien pensé ni rien dit, et pour cause, sur le sujet ! —, c'est une fois de plus sur la nature qu'on s'est rabattu. La « nature » a prévu comment on fabrique les enfants. Une femme et un homme font cela tout seuls, sans assistance. Ainsi les choses se sont-elles déroulées depuis la nuit des temps. Puis vinrent l'insémination artificielle, la fécondation *in vitro*, les banques de sperme, la congélation d'embryons, les mères porteuses, et j'en oublie sans doute. Pas besoin d'être un éthicien chevronné pour saisir la complexité des enjeux psychologiques, sociaux, génétiques, médicaux, économiques, juridiques et éthiques de pareilles technologies.

On peut avec raison, le sens commun y invite, s'inquiéter de leur développement échevelé, commandé davantage parfois par la mégalomanie des chercheurs et des médecins, en quête de gloire et de fortune, que par un souci désintéressé d'offrir à des couples « naturellement » infertiles l'enfant dont ils rêvent. Mais faut-il pour autant, au nom de la loi naturelle, associer dans une même condamnation le recours à l'insémination artificielle avec le sperme du conjoint — et non pas d'un parfait inconnu, rémunéré ou pas — avec l'embauche d'une mère porteuse ou la congélation d'embryons pour une future fécondation ou pour d'éventuelles expériences scientifiques ? Le bon sens suggère une réponse circonstanciée. Rome se retranche dans ses jugements absolus. Des esprits mal tournés ont trouvé une formule bien tournée pour résumer la position du Vatican sur la contraception et la procréation assistée : « Pas de sexe sans bébé, pas de bébé sans sexe ».

Refuser la vie : un pouvoir usurpé ?

Plus nos sociétés se sécularisent, moins Dieu y tient de place, plus l'être humain semble tenté de se prendre pour Dieu. Certes, tout ce qui est lié à la production de la vie confère à l'être humain un pouvoir qui l'associe au pouvoir divin. Contrôler la propagation de la vie, brimer son élan là où elle était « naturellement » généreuse et féconde, la faire jaillir là où « naturellement » elle se refusait à naître, c'est faire preuve d'un stupéfiant pouvoir. Il ne faut donc pas s'étonner que les sociétés et les religions aient cherché à légiférer sur ces questions. Les femmes encore plus que les hommes ont été l'objet de contrôles d'autant plus sévères qu'elles sont les plus proches du fascinant et redoutable pouvoir sur la vie, puisqu'elles portent et mettent au monde les enfants.

Ce qui constitue l'ultime exercice de ce pouvoir des femmes sur la vie, quand elles choisissent de lui dire non, c'est le recours à l'avortement. Il arrive que des femmes conçoivent sans l'avoir voulu, voire à leur corps défendant, dans le cas d'une grossesse survenue à la suite d'un viol par exemple. De tout temps, on le sait, les femmes ont eu recours à l'avortement, plus souvent qu'autrement au péril de leur vie, et le sachant. Si elles passaient à l'acte en dépit des risques qu'elles étaient conscientes d'encourir pour elles-mêmes, c'est qu'elles étaient désespérées. Il est trop commode de ne vouloir les considérer que comme des dévergondées méritant des châtiments, temporels et éternels.

Avorter est un geste grave qui ne devrait être envisagé, du moins le pensons-nous, que pour des motifs d'une extrême gravité. Attenter à la vie, même au tout premier stade de son développement, ne pourra jamais être raisonnablement considéré comme un geste anodin. Le magistère de l'Église fait ici encore preuve de grande rigueur, sans s'encombrer de nuances. Il condamne tout avortement, quel que soit le motif qui pousse une femme à y avoir recours. Cette intransigeance, argumente-t-il, lui est inspirée par le principe du respect dû à la vie, et tout particulièrement de la vie faible et innocente. Certes, une société se juge elle-même à la façon dont elle traite les personnes les plus fragiles et les plus démunies. Nous n'entrerons pas ici dans le débat philosophique de savoir si un embryon de quelques jours ou un fœtus de quelques semaines est une personne, avec tous les droits attachés à ce statut. Contentons-nous de dire que les autorités de l'Église soutiennent cette opinion alors que la *Charte des droits de la personne* a plutôt éludé la question.

Dans le débat qui oppose les individus favorisant le libre choix face à l'avortement et ceux qui s'y opposent totalement, ces derniers parlent volontiers de la vie humaine comme d'un absolu. Il faut oser se poser lucidement la question : pour les chrétiens en général, et pour les catholiques en particulier, la vie a-t-elle jamais été considérée comme un absolu ? La réponse est claire, c'est non.

ASSOMPTION

L'Assomption de Marie s'inscrit dans une tradition attestée vers le VIIe siècle et définie comme dogme le 1er novembre 1950 par le pape Pie XII. Selon cette doctrine, Marie « ayant achevé le cours de sa vie terrestre » fut glorifiée par Dieu dans toute sa personne. De touchantes légendes ont fleuri autour des circonstances de cette « montée au ciel » de Marie, où les anges et les apôtres jouent toutes sortes de rôles. Mais l'essentiel est ailleurs : comme Jésus, Marie est accueillie par le Père. Sa fidélité à la grâce de Dieu si généreusement répandue sur elle en fait le prototype de la personne sauvée. La mère se trouve associée à la gloire de son fils. Cette fête liturgique est célébrée le 15 août. ◇

La légitime défense, la « juste guerre », la peine de mort comme punition de crimes contre la société ou contre l'État ont été reconnue par l'Église comme des circonstances où l'on pouvait infliger la mort à autrui. Faut-il vraiment ajouter que la torture et la mort elle-même sont apparues pendant de trop longs siècles comme des méthodes acceptables pour combattre l'hérésie ? Faut-il aussi rappeler que si la vie était considérée comme un absolu par la tradition catholique, on comprendrait mal qu'elle ait si fort loué et vénéré les hommes et les femmes qui ont choisi de subir le martyre alors que, dans bien des circonstances, il leur aurait suffi de clamer moins haut leur foi pour avoir la vie sauve ?

En dépit de la position officielle de l'Église sur l'avortement, une femme, victime d'inceste ou de viol, et qui se trouve enceinte à la suite d'un pareil crime commis sur sa personne, bénéficiera vraisemblablement de la compréhension et de la compassion d'un grand nombre de pasteurs, si elle s'estime physiquement et surtout psychologiquement incapable de porter jusqu'à son terme l'enfant qui incarnera à jamais à ses yeux sa honte et son malheur. Saint Augustin, en son temps, désapprouvait les femmes qui avaient eu recours au suicide pour laver leur honneur à la suite du viol que leur avait fait subir l'armée déferlante des barbares envahissant l'Empire romain, mais il ajoutait, compatissant : « Quel cœur d'homme oserait le leur reprocher ? »

Certes, les circonstances auxquelles sont confrontées les femmes qui désirent mettre un terme à leur grossesse ne sont pas toujours aussi dramatiques. Et l'on peut juger futiles les motifs de certaines d'entre elles. Une approche pastorale, à l'écoute de la souffrance des êtres, réussira toujours mieux qu'une froide intransigeance à affiner les consciences et à éclairer les choix des femmes se retrouvant enceintes contre leur gré.

Ne pas procréer : faute ou vertu ?

Contrairement à ce qui se passe dans certaines cultures, l'Occident chrétien ne considère pas comme foncièrement asociales les personnes qui choisissent de ne pas procréer. Pour l'Église catholique, si elles prennent une telle décision tout en ayant des rela-

S. Petri Nolasci Conf., III classis.
Com. S. Agnetis Virg. et Mart., secundo.
29 S. Francisci Salesii Ep., Conf. et Eccl. Doct., III classis.
30 S. Martinæ Virg. et Mart., III classis.
31 S. Ioannis Bosco Conf., III classis.

tions sexuelles à l'intérieur du mariage, elles seront jugées comme trahissant les termes du contrat en choisissant de dissocier union conjugale et procréation. Si c'est à l'extérieur du mariage, la condamnation est plus rigoureuse, puisqu'elles font d'une pierre deux mauvais coups.

Toutefois, si le renoncement à procréer est vécu dans la chasteté, c'est-à-dire dans l'abstention de tout acte sexuel, mieux encore, dans le célibat consacré à l'intérieur d'un ordre religieux pour les femmes et les hommes, ou pour ces derniers seulement à l'intérieur du ministère ordonné, cette option apparaît aux yeux de l'Église comme le choix par excellence. L'idéal prôné par saint Augustin de renoncer aux plaisirs de la chair pour mieux se consacrer à la poursuite de Dieu est encore proposé de nos jours.

Toutes les Églises chrétiennes n'accordent pas au célibat consacré la même valeur. Les Églises protestantes l'ont abandonné, et il n'est guère que la secte des Shakers pour l'imposer à tous ses membres, ce qui ne va pas, bien sûr, sans danger d'extinction, si le recrutement ne se fait pas parmi les gens qui ont déjà des enfants pour assurer un temps la relève. L'Église orthodoxe accorde de l'importance à la vie monastique, mais n'impose pas nécessairement le célibat à son clergé. Encore une fois, l'Église catholique se singularise en liant sacerdoce et célibat. Il faut savoir toutefois qu'elle a mis beaucoup de temps pour en arriver là : dix siècles au moins. Néanmoins, la tâche de convaincre les clercs de renoncer au mariage, comme à tout concubinage, s'est révélée fort ardue pendant plusieurs siècles et elle n'est pas achevée puisque les remises en cause du lien obligatoire entre sacerdoce et célibat se multiplient encore de nos jours.

Aucun argument théologique décisif n'oblige l'Église à imposer le célibat à ses clercs, c'est une question de discipline ecclésiastique qui pourrait être révisée. Plusieurs souhaiteraient que les membres du clergé puissent exercer un libre choix face au mariage ou au célibat.

Quant à la vie religieuse et à la chasteté que les personnes qui s'y engagent promettent de respecter, elles auront toujours leur place dans l'Église. Mais à cause des renoncements considérables qu'elles impliquent, on peut penser qu'elles resteront toujours le choix d'une minorité que les grands défis attirent et stimulent.

Naître, un aller simple

Le christianisme estime que la vie qu'on reçoit est un billet d'aller simple. Ce qui confère à l'existence humaine une sorte de gravité. Tout se joue ici et maintenant. On ne peut pas écrire sa vie comme le brouillon d'un scénario qu'on pourrait au gré de réincarnations successives améliorer jusqu'à en faire un chef-d'œuvre. La vie est comme un examen sans possibilité de reprise. Voilà une perspective stimulante pour plusieurs, mais redoutable et décourageante pour d'autres. « L'homme est un roseau, le plus faible de la nature, disait Blaise Pascal, mais c'est un roseau pensant. » Un roseau pensant capable de donner un sens à sa vie, de choisir ou non de la prolonger dans d'autres êtres, d'y mettre volontairement un terme, de l'orienter vers Dieu. « L'homme, écrivait pour sa part Dostoïevski, est un animal qui s'habitue à tout », y compris, dirait-on, à la complexité de son propre mystère où coexistent dans un équilibre précaire l'expérience de la limite et la soif d'absolu. Pour la tradition judéo-chrétienne, la création de la femme et de l'homme comme personnes sexuées est une histoire sacrée, dont la suite est confiée à des êtres émerveillés et fragiles… Tout cela occupant l'espace de quelques grains de poussière dans l'immensité incalculable des galaxies.

COMPRENDRE ET EXPLIQUER : FOI ET SCIENCE

JEAN-FRANÇOIS MALHERBE

La façon dont se pose aujourd'hui la question des rapports entre les sciences et la foi chrétienne est tributaire du conflit qui a opposé l'Église à Galilée. C'est la raison pour laquelle il importe d'examiner l'« affaire Galilée » pour comprendre le rapport que l'on peut établir aujourd'hui entre la recherche scientifique et la foi chrétienne.

Le temps des ruptures

« L'affaire Galilée » n'est pas ce qu'on croit le plus souvent. Ce ne sont pas tant les théories astronomiques du savant italien qui ont été condamnées par l'Église que les positions qu'il tenait en théologie. Galilée (1564-1642) était un grand physicien, mais ce fut aussi un chrétien. Et c'est peut-être comme chrétien d'ailleurs qu'il a le plus à nous apprendre, car en définitive, au plan de l'astronomie, la plupart des idées qu'il défend sont empruntées explicitement à Nicolas Copernic.

S'interroger sur l'affaire Galilée, c'est s'interroger à la fois sur la naissance d'une certaine façon de faire la science, qui est très proche de la nôtre aujourd'hui, et sur une manière qu'a l'Église d'aujourd'hui de réagir par rapport à la science. Avant Galilée, la conception que les savants et les philosophes se faisaient du monde était très proche de la conception que l'on peut lire dans la Bible.

C'est pourquoi le véritable conflit entre la science et la foi n'est né qu'avec la science, c'est-à-dire au XVIe ou au XVIIe siècle ; avant, en effet, la science et la philosophie, c'était tout un.

Quand la science s'est développée, lorsqu'elle a commencé à prendre conscience qu'elle est « gardienne de ses propres lois », selon la belle expression de Kant, l'Église, qui estimait elle aussi être gardienne non seulement de ses propres lois mais de toutes les lois, a réagi d'une façon telle que nous pouvons éprouver aujourd'hui certaines difficultés à comprendre son attitude.

Galilée est le symbole de la rupture entre l'Église et la science parce qu'il a découvert des phénomènes astronomiques apparemment contradictoires avec les récits bibliques. C'est en utilisant d'une part les théories de Copernic (c'est-à-dire l'idée générale que c'est la terre qui tourne autour du soleil et non, comme le croyaient les Grecs et comme on le dit dans la Bible, le soleil qui tourne autour de la terre) et, d'autre part, la lunette astronomique mise au point par les opticiens hollandais, qu'il s'est rendu compte par exemple que la rotation des lunes de Jupiter autour de la planète fournissait une analogie pour concrétiser dans le mouvement des planètes ce que Copernic, un chanoine polonais, avait estimé, sans doute par diplomatie, n'être finalement qu'une entourloupette de mathématicien. Il était plus facile de prévoir les éclipses à l'aide des équations de Copernic qu'à l'aide de celles des astronomes grecs. Alors Galilée, qui était un chrétien convaincu, fut très embarrassé par sa propre découverte. Celle-ci, en effet, contredisait manifestement la Bible puisqu'en différents passages, la Bible contient des phrases attribuant au soleil un mouvement autour de la terre. Dans le livre de Josué, notamment, se trouve le passage célèbre où Josué prie Jahvé d'arrêter le soleil et la lune, le temps de gagner une bataille (*Jos* 10,12-13). Après la bataille, le soleil et la lune se sont remis à tourner. Mais si le soleil et la lune peuvent s'arrêter, c'est qu'ils tournent autour de la terre. D'autre part, on raconte, dans un des deux récits de la *Genèse* (1,14-17), que Dieu a mis des luminaires dans le ciel pour rythmer les jours et les nuits et les saisons ; mais si Dieu a accroché des luminaires dans le ciel, c'est parce que ceux-ci ne sont pas le centre du ciel mais bien la terre.

CIEL/PARADIS

Si l'on se réfère au mot latin *cælum*, le ciel devrait être défini comme l'inconnu. Il peut aussi désigner la zone visible qui se trouve au-dessus de nos têtes. Pour les anciens, le ciel était le lieu de la demeure de Dieu. Cette image pouvait aussi signifier que Dieu est hors de la portée des humains, qu'il ne peut être manipulé par eux. On utilise aussi le mot ciel comme une métaphore qui désigne non pas un lieu précis, mais la croyance à une vie possible après la mort. Pour les chrétiennes et les chrétiens, cette croyance puise sa source dans la foi en la victoire du Christ sur la mort et à son ascension auprès de son Père.

Les rédacteurs de l'Ancien Testament utilisent le mot persan *paridaëza*, c'est-à-dire terrain planté d'arbres, pour rendre compte de l'idée de paradis. Ainsi, dans la *Genèse*, l'Éden (*Gn* 2,15), désigne un lieu paradisiaque où Dieu aurait placé Adam et Ève au commencement du monde. Dans le Nouveau Testament, l'idée de paradis évoque plutôt la perspective d'une béatitude éternelle auprès de Dieu. « Je te le dis, aujourd'hui tu seras avec moi dans le paradis » (*Lc* 23,43). Malgré l'assurance qu'elle donne, cette affirmation ne précise pas ce qu'est le paradis qui, comme le ciel, relève de l'inconnu. ◇

L'attitude de Galilée a été de s'interroger sur la façon dont il avait appris à lire la Bible et il s'est rendu compte, après beaucoup de réflexion, qu'on lui avait appris à lire la Bible d'une façon qui n'était pas tout à fait correcte. C'est pourquoi il a proposé une distinction entre ce qu'on pourrait appeler une *lecture superficielle* de la Bible et une *lecture profonde* de la Bible. Selon la *lecture superficielle*, si la Bible dit que le soleil s'est arrêté, c'est que le soleil s'est vraiment arrêté. On prend le texte au pied de la lettre. La *lecture profonde* consiste à se demander ce que ça veut dire que « le soleil s'est arrêté au-dessus de la terre ».

Galilée a donc trouvé une manière de lire la Bible qui permettait d'éviter la contradiction flagrante entre la Bible et ses propres découvertes scientifiques.

Et le conflit s'est développé parce que Galilée a été dénoncé par ceux qui n'avaient vu dans ses découvertes et dans ses publications que les aspects négatifs. C'est particulièrement sensible dans un texte extrêmement intéressant reprenant les chefs de condamnation qui ont provoqué la mise à l'index d'un des livres de Galilée, le livre sur les mouvements des planètes. Les théologiens romains avaient repéré dans ce livre une série de propositions qui n'étaient pas compatibles avec la doctrine orthodoxe. C'est le 24 février 1616 que la commission de censure s'était réunie et avait, à l'issue de sa réunion, publié le protocole suivant : « Censure a été faite au Saint-Office de la ville le jour du mercredi 24 février 1616, en présence des Pères théologiens soussignés : "Le soleil est au centre du monde et concrètement immobile du mouvement local" ». C'est une phrase de Galilée qui est ainsi censurée. La censure étant commentée comme suit : « À l'unanimité, cette proposition est déclarée insensée et absurde en philosophie et formellement hérétique, en tant qu'elle s'oppose expressément aux sentences de la Sainte Écriture en plusieurs

CRÉATION

Les récits des chapitres 1 et 2 de la *Genèse* ne parlent pas d'une création à partir de rien. Dieu est plutôt présenté comme faisant régner l'ordre dans le chaos primitif. Il sépare la lumière des ténèbres, la terre de l'eau. Cela dit, ces récits ne doivent pas être compris comme retraçant l'emploi du temps de Dieu, au commencement du temps. Ils ont plutôt une visée théologique. Il n'y a qu'un Dieu et il est différent de sa création. La nature n'est pas Dieu. Les « païens » ont donc tort d'adorer le soleil, la lune ou les pierres. La rédaction de ces textes bibliques date d'une époque préscientifique (VIe et IXe siècles avant Jésus-Christ) et il ne faut pas les lire comme des traités de biologie ou d'astrophysique. La théorie du Big bang tente d'expliquer la naissance de l'univers à partir des connaissances dont nous disposons aujourd'hui, sans faire intervenir une foi religieuse, mais sans la discréditer non plus. Le prétendre, c'est confondre les genres, c'est reprocher au clinicien de jeter sur un corps un regard autre que celui de l'artiste ou de l'amant. ◇

endroits, soit sur le sens littéral des mots, soit sur l'interprétation commune des Saints-Pères et des docteurs en théologie. »

À première vue, on pourrait croire que les théologiens romains reprennent la distinction entre la lecture superficielle et la lecture profonde de la Bible. En fait, la distinction faite entre sens littéral et interprétation n'est qu'un artifice de langage, car « l'interprétation commune des Saints-Pères et des docteurs en théologie » était en fait soit une interprétation au pied de la lettre, soit, pour les plus astucieux, des interprétations de type symbolique. Il ne s'agissait pas, en tout cas, d'interprétations de type scientifique, c'est-à-dire d'interprétations visant à montrer une distinction des plans entre ce qu'on pouvait savoir par la simple observation humaine et ce qu'on pouvait savoir par la révélation.

Les théologiens ont donc utilisé un argument d'autorité contre Galilée. Ils ont tenté de s'abriter derrière les Saints-Pères et les Docteurs en théologie de l'histoire, derrière toute la tradition de l'Église, de façon à ne pas être seuls à protester.

Une deuxième proposition de Galilée a été condamnée : « La terre n'est pas au centre du monde ni immobile mais se meut d'un mouvement total », c'est-à-dire d'un mouvement de révolution et d'un mouvement diurne. Cet énoncé est censuré à l'aide d'un argument d'unanimité. La seconde proposition de Galilée relève donc du même type de censure que la précédente : « Quant à l'aspect théologique, il doit être considéré au moins comme erroné selon la foi », mais personne n'explique dans ce texte ce que veut dire « être erroné selon la foi ». Il convient de souligner que les censeurs ne discutent pas les arguments scientifiques de Galilée ; ils ne se placent pas sur le terrain de Galilée ; ils ne reprennent pas les distinctions subtiles qui lui permettaient d'articuler les deux terrains ; ils se placent dans l'ancienne formulation des problèmes et imposent à l'astronome une fin de non-recevoir.

Cependant, Galilée avait été averti, charitablement pourrait-on dire, par certains amis romains qu'il avait en haut lieu. Un de ces avertissements est resté célèbre : « Tant que vous traiterez du système de Copernic, écrit à Galilée le cardinal Robert Bellarmin, et de ses démonstrations sans y mêler les Écritures dont l'interprétation est réservée aux professeurs de théologie approuvés par l'autorité, tant que vous traiterez de cette façon-là de votre astronomie, vous ne rencontrerez aucune opposition, mais dans le cas contraire, on admettrait difficilement des déclarations de votre part sur les Écritures, pour ingénieuses qu'elles soient, si elles s'écartaient un tant soit peu de l'opinion commune des Pères de l'Église. »

Galilée a donc été condamné non pas à cause de ses déclarations scientifiques, mais à cause de l'effort qu'il a fait lui-même pour les rendre compatibles avec la Bible. Il a été condamné pour avoir mis en cause l'autorité de ceux qui imposaient une certaine lecture de la Bible et non pas pour avoir fait œuvre proprement scientifique. Il a été condamné finalement sur ses positions théologiques de chrétien plus que sur ses positions scientifiques de savant.

Cependant, Galilée n'a pas été condamné comme théologien, parce qu'il ne se prétendait pas tel ; mais il a été condamné comme chrétien, c'est-à-dire comme homme qui n'était pas partagé en tiroirs avec un tiroir astronomique, un tiroir de foi, un tiroir théologique, un tiroir biblique, etc. Galilée essayait de garder l'unité qu'il avait en lui et, pour garder cette unité, il s'est senti autorisé à mettre en cause un certain nombre de choses qu'il jugeait de moindre valeur que d'autres qu'il ne voulait pas mettre en cause. Il y avait donc là pour Galilée un conflit de valeurs entre ce qu'il croyait, ce qu'on lui enseignait dans l'Église et ce qu'il avait découvert à la suite de Copernic. Ce conflit, il l'a résolu en proposant une façon de distinguer ce qui était véritablement la sève des textes bibliques dont il nourrissait sa méditation d'une part et, d'autre part, les constructions théologiques qu'on en avait tirées. Du point de vue d'une analyse institutionnelle, si l'on veut, il a mis en cause un certain type d'autorité romaine beaucoup plus que la véracité des textes bibliques.

Ce n'est donc pas la science qui a été condamnée avec Galilée, mais une certaine façon de comprendre la foi. La science n'a donc pas perdu son autonomie dans l'affaire Galilée. Au contraire, elle l'a gagnée, car Galilée a fait de la science « la gardienne de ses propres lois ». La condamnation de Galilée forme, en effet, le principal argument d'un certain nombre d'athées positivistes : si l'Église a condamné Galilée, disent-ils, c'est bien qu'elle est obscurantiste. Cependant, une telle position néglige la différence considérable qui peut séparer la foi des chrétiens et l'autorité de l'Église.

La distinction des domaines

Après l'affaire Galilée, la science semblait définitivement s'opposer aux conclusions de la théologie. Cependant, un certain nombre d'esprits ont tenté de reprendre l'intuition fondamentale de Galilée en théologie et de montrer comment ces deux discours, qui paraissent complètement antagonistes, ne sont pas aussi contradictoires qu'on pouvait l'imaginer.

Ce n'était d'ailleurs pas la première fois que l'Église se trouvait face à un discours qu'elle croyait totalement opposé à sa foi.

Depuis bien longtemps déjà, en effet, l'Église avait dû se dire à elle-même comment la philosophie grecque, qui était la science de toute une époque, n'était pas incompatible avec la foi, et tout ce travail avait été mené à bien par de grands théologiens et, en particulier, par les maîtres du Moyen Âge dont Thomas d'Aquin fut l'un des plus éminents.

On distingua alors deux modes de connaissance. La connaissance que l'homme pouvait acquérir par ses propres forces, en réfléchissant sur lui-même, sur ce qui l'entourait ; et la connaissance que comporte la révélation. De tout temps, des chrétiens s'étaient posé la question de la compatibilité de ces deux sources de connaissance. Et de fait, ils ont mis au jour une articulation entre la démarche rationnelle purement humaine qu'était la philosophie et la démarche du croyant réfléchissant à sa propre foi, c'est-à-dire la démarche du théologien.

Ils partaient de l'hypothèse selon laquelle Dieu a créé le monde et l'homme, ce qui est un dogme de la foi. Et ils remarquaient que si Dieu a créé l'homme, c'est lui aussi qui a créé l'intelligence de l'homme. Par conséquent, ce que l'homme peut inventer, découvrir, construire avec son propre esprit est toujours déjà un prolongement de la création de Dieu. D'autre part, Dieu inspire aussi l'Écriture. Voilà un autre dogme. C'est donc Dieu, finalement, qui est à la source à la fois de la révélation et de la pensée purement autonome et rationnelle de l'homme. C'est Dieu qui a donné à l'homme la force de faire de la philosophie, c'est Dieu qui a donné à l'homme la force et le pouvoir de faire de la science et on ne comprend donc pas comment il pourrait y avoir jusqu'à la fin des temps une opposition radicale entre la science ou la philosophie et la foi. On peut se rendre compte qu'actuellement, on ne connaît pas tout, et qu'il peut donc y avoir sur tel ou tel point une incompatibilité entre la science actuelle et la formulation actuelle de la foi. Mais le chrétien peut aussi avoir confiance dans le fait qu'un jour viendra où science et foi, science et théologie seront entièrement conciliées.

Cependant, le débat science-foi, tel qu'il s'est formulé après l'affaire Galilée, n'a pas encore, pour ainsi dire, trouvé son Thomas d'Aquin. C'est pourquoi aujourd'hui, l'on vit toujours dans une situation où les domaines respectifs de la science et de la foi sont nettement séparés.

Il est admis qu'un chrétien puisse être un très grand savant et qu'un très grand savant puisse être un chrétien sans se renier lui-même en tant que savant. Mais être savant et être chrétien sont le plus souvent considérés comme deux dimensions différentes de la même personne sans qu'il y ait un véritable rapport entre elles.

Évidemment, un savant ne peut pas tenir à la fois une interprétation naïve de la Bible et une interprétation rigide de la science. Comme les croyants sont eux-mêmes des personnes non divisées, du moins en principe, il s'agit de trouver un principe d'unité. Et l'on pourrait avancer que celui-ci consisterait à reconnaître qu'en fait, de part et d'autre, il s'agit de la même chose. Dans les sciences, on parle du monde, et dans la Bible, on parle aussi du monde et c'est bien du même monde qu'il s'agit de part et d'autre parce que c'est du monde dans lequel on vit. Cependant, il y a deux points de vue différents sur ce monde : le point de vue de la foi et le point de vue de la science. Le point de vue de la foi n'est pas du tout le point de vue naïf opposé au point de vue critique que serait celui de la science. Car l'homme porte en lui une exigence de rationalité qui s'exerce tout aussi bien dans sa démarche de foi que dans sa démarche de science.

Cette exigence de rationalité s'est d'ailleurs exercée dans le domaine de la foi notamment sous la forme d'une réflexion critique sur la Bible. Cette réflexion partait de la question suivante : comment comprendre la Bible de façon à ce que la foi soit préservée et la science respectée pour ce qu'elle est. On reconnaît ici la question de Galilée. Répondre à cette question, c'est effectuer un travail éminemment philosophique qui consiste à tenter de saisir une cohérence qui n'apparaît pas explicitement au départ.

À partir du moment où la pensée scientifique s'est développée, elle n'a pas arrêté d'élargir ses champs d'application et si l'on s'est d'abord intéressé à l'astronomie, puis à la chimie, puis à la biologie, on est passé ensuite à la sociologie, etc. et, entre autres, on est passé à l'étude scientifique des textes que toutes les traditions, toutes les civilisations anciennes nous ont légués ; et la Bible est un de ces textes. Il y a donc une démarche de type scientifique qui s'applique à l'étude des textes les plus anciens et on a ainsi étudié la Bible sans supposer la foi. D'une certaine façon, on a entrepris une étude strictement scientifique de la Bible. Et cette démarche d'analyse scientifique de la Bible a eu un impact considérable sur la théologie, puis sur la pensée chrétienne en général, parce qu'on s'est rendu compte en étudiant soigneusement la Bible, sans présupposer la foi dans cette étude, qu'il y avait à l'intérieur de la Bible elle-même un certain nombre de raisons de penser qu'il n'y avait aucune possibilité de lire la Bible en prenant toutes ses phrases au pied de la lettre. On s'est rendu compte que la Bible elle-même, d'une certaine façon, est truffée de contradictions, qu'elle ne pouvait pas être lue comme un traité de zoologie, ni comme un traité d'évolution biologique. La Bible n'est même pas un simple livre d'histoire factuelle. Si c'est bien l'histoire du peuple d'Israël qui est racontée dans la Bible, elle n'est pas racontée à la manière d'un peuple qui tente à chacune de ses générations de comprendre ce qui s'est passé avant. Ce travail de compréhension spirituelle est très différent de celui qui préside à la rédaction d'un manuel d'histoire. Ce n'est pas une étude scientifique. On s'est rendu compte ainsi que le message de la Bible est à dégager des textes bibliques, non pas phrase par phrase, mais dans une lecture plus globale. Et qu'il est possible de comprendre véritablement la Bible en la respectant et en même temps en restant pleinement homme, c'est-à-dire sans renoncer à son intelligence.

On peut illustrer cela à partir du récit biblique de la création. La vision scientifique des origines du monde paraît plus fiable que la vision biblique, sans aucune discussion, et c'est un des apports de la pensée scientifique d'avoir montré cela même, en ce sens que si l'on fait des études historiques précises pour essayer de savoir quand ont été écrits les textes qui racontent la création du monde, on peut parfaitement se rendre compte que les deux récits de la création ont été écrits bien après l'époque où l'on a écrit l'Exode, par exemple. La question est de savoir qui a écrit cela et pourquoi il l'a écrit comme il l'a fait. L'analyse philosophique, historique et anthropologique permet de deviner, à travers le texte, la personnalité de celui qui l'a rédigé et c'est ainsi que pour l'un des deux récits, on peut se rendre compte qu'il a été écrit probablement par un paysan assez érudit de l'époque de Salomon. Ce paysan lettré s'est posé des questions comme celles-ci : « J'appartiens au peuple élu de Dieu, j'appartiens à ce peuple avec qui Dieu a conclu une alliance et je ne comprends pas pourquoi je dois travailler pour manger, je ne comprends pas pourquoi ma femme doit enfanter dans la douleur, je ne comprends pas pourquoi je dois souffrir toute ma vie pour finalement mourir. » Il ne comprenait rien de tout cela et essayait de s'expliquer à lui-même pourquoi la condition humaine est ce qu'elle est. Et l'on imagine bien ce philosophe ou ce théologien qui tente, avec tout ce qu'il a à sa disposition dans sa culture, de se forger à lui-même un récit qui lui permette de dire en symboles ce qu'il croit en fait et qu'il a découvert à la suite de ses pères et grands-pères.

Le récit de la création dans la Bible est donc plutôt le récit d'un homme qui essaye de dégager le sens de son expérience humaine et qui, pour dégager ce sens, le restitue dans une intention de Dieu à l'origine. Cela est extrêmement différent du récit scientifique qui, comme tel, décrit la mécanique, la naissance des choses dans leur fonctionnement.

Les propos de l'un et de l'autre discours sont totalement différents. Le propos du savant est d'expliquer la suite des liens de causalité entre les différentes étapes d'un développement cosmologique tandis que le propos du croyant, qui tente de réfléchir à sa situation dans le monde, est celui-ci : « Je suis dans une situation particulière et j'essaye de comprendre pourquoi j'en suis arrivé là. » Autrement dit, le savant ne s'interroge par sur son existence ; le savant s'interroge sur un monde par rapport auquel il prend une distance, tandis que le croyant s'interroge finalement sur lui-même, sur sa solidarité avec ses frères, sur sa solidarité dans un peuple et puis aussi sur cette espèce d'alliance incroyable qui est arrivée à ce peuple par la proposition d'un Dieu. Et il est clair que le récit des débuts du monde que l'on trouve dans la Bible a été écrit bien après que le peuple d'Israël ait reconnu la main de Dieu dans sa propre histoire. Le croyant fait l'expérience qu'il y a comme une espèce de double victoire de Dieu qui se passe dans sa vie, qui s'est passée auparavant et qui ne s'arrêtera pas. Il y a d'abord une victoire de Dieu sur le désordre cosmique qui fait précisément que le chaos est perpétuellement repoussé et que l'univers se construit, qu'il y a comme une mise en ordre de l'univers. Et ensuite, il y a la seconde victoire de Dieu ; en dépit de tous les ennemis de Dieu, un peuple s'est constitué et se reconnaît comme peuple des fils de Dieu. Cette seconde victoire, c'est ce que la Bible appelle l'alliance ; alors la création de Dieu telle qu'elle est comprise à l'intérieur de la démarche biblique elle-même est à la fois la célébration et le récit de la victoire de Dieu sur le chaos dont est tiré le monde et ceux de la victoire de Dieu sur les ennemis qui voulaient empêcher le peuple de se constituer, ces ennemis étant d'ailleurs, pour une part non négligeable, au sein du peuple lui-même, au cœur même de chacun des fils du peuple.

Cela implique que lorsqu'on entend parler de la création au sens biblique du terme, il ne faut pas du tout penser à une origine des choses, mais à leur signification dans ce qu'on pourrait appeler l'histoire du salut.

« Dieu a créé le monde », cela veut dire que Dieu tient le monde dans sa main, c'est-à-dire que c'est la main de Dieu qui tient le monde en ordre, que c'est la main de Dieu qui tient l'Histoire du peuple choisi dans la droite ligne ou qui tente de ramener le peuple de Dieu dans la fidélité à l'alliance. Cela veut dire que toute ma vie est en relation avec Dieu et dire cela ce n'est évidemment pas tenir le discours du savant. Car le discours du savant n'a que faire, à première vue, de savoir si toute sa vie est en relation avec Dieu ; le discours du savant consiste, en effet, à tenter de reconstruire un certain nombre d'enchaînements matériels qui se sont passés dans le monde par des processus physiques ou chimiques ou autres. Le travail du savant consiste à appréhender une évolution et pas seulement au plan purement biologique, l'évolution des animaux, mais aussi l'évolution historique, culturelle des peuples. Ça, c'est la tâche du savant. Ce qui est frappant, c'est l'analogie entre les deux préoccupations, la préoccupation du croyant qui reconnaît la main de Dieu dans son existence et la préoccupation du savant qui tente de reformuler en les expliquant les liens de causalité qui régissent l'univers.

Selon l'expérience du croyant, Dieu est la source de l'ordre du monde et, selon l'intention du savant, il s'agit de retrouver le principe de l'ordre qui est à l'œuvre dans le monde. Cela ne veut pas dire que le savant va découvrir Dieu à la fin de son enquête. Cela veut dire simplement que le savant va découvrir comment le monde est organisé, tandis que le croyant apprend pourquoi le monde est organisé. Au-delà de l'opposition d'un « comment » et d'un « pourquoi », il y a quelque chose de très frappant qui se manifeste dans la démarche de la foi et la démarche de la science. C'est que pour l'une comme pour l'autre, le monde est inachevé. Dieu n'a pas fini, même aujourd'hui, de tenir notre existence dans sa main, dit le croyant, et le savant constate que l'évolution n'est pas achevée ; le dernier mot n'est dit ni d'un côté ni de l'autre. On ne sait pas encore le dernier mot du « pourquoi », on ne sait pas encore le dernier mot du « comment ». Mais si l'on en croit les efforts que l'homme a pu faire dans sa réflexion au Moyen Âge, par exemple, on a un certain nombre de raisons d'espérer qu'un jour, le « comment » et le « pourquoi » ne seront

MYSTÈRE

Dans son sens fondamental le mot mystère désigne ce qui est secret, ce qui est caché, ce que l'on ne comprend pas. Saint Paul, dans ses lettres, nous parle du mystère de Dieu, du mystère du Christ et du mystère de la foi. Pour lui, le grand mystère, c'est la présence du « Christ parmi nous » (*Col.* 1,27). Si Dieu est Dieu, il restera toujours impossible à l'être humain de le définir parfaitement. Mais son mystère se laisse entrevoir à travers les merveilles de la création, la personne de Jésus, tout ce qui est beau et bon. Les mystères ne doivent donc pas être perçus comme des défis à l'intelligence, mais comme des chemins à emprunter pour poursuivre la quête d'absolu qui s'inscrit au plus profond de l'être humain. ◇

plus simplement deux façons d'interroger le monde qui peuvent coexister pacifiquement, mais deux façons d'interroger le monde qui pourront se compléter, s'enrichir profondément l'une l'autre.

Vers une articulation nouvelle

Après le temps de la rupture symbolisé par l'affaire Galilée, est venu le temps de la distinction des domaines et du respect mutuel. Peut-on espérer aujourd'hui dépasser cette coexistence silencieuse ? Le savant et le croyant ont-ils quelque chose à s'apprendre mutuellement ?

Aujourd'hui, on est dans une situation extrêmement confuse qu'il est difficile de dépeindre clairement, mais peut-être pourrait-on distinguer quelques axes essentiels. De nos jours, toutes sortes de gens interviennent dans le débat science-foi et ils se répartissent *grosso modo* en trois espèces différentes. Il y a ceux qui en sont encore à l'époque de Galilée, qu'ils soient savants ou qu'ils soient théologiens. Il y en a qui sont à l'époque de Kant et qui distinguent très soigneusement les deux plans sans trop se préoccuper de les nouer. Enfin, il y en a quelques autres qui tentent une articulation, qui tentent de nouer un nœud qui n'apparaît pas encore actuellement en pleine lumière, mais dont on pressent peut-être comment il pourrait se faire.

Dire qu'il y a des gens qui sont encore à l'époque de Galilée, c'est un reproche qu'on peut faire aussi bien à certains scientifiques qu'à certains théologiens. Pour nombre de savants, en effet, la question du rapport science-foi est totalement résolue, faute de combattants, étant donné que la foi ne serait qu'une illusion et que la science expliquerait tout. Ces gens-là sont ce qu'on appelle des positivistes. Finalement, ils commettent la même erreur que les théologiens qui considèrent que la question du rapport science-foi est tout à fait tranchée puisque de toute façon la science est perpétuellement faillible, que la science n'est jamais vraiment assurée de ses théories, qu'elle ne fait au mieux que diminuer la somme d'erreurs qu'elle a formulées jusqu'à maintenant et qu'après tout, elle n'est pas très sûre de sa vérité tandis que la foi, elle, est d'une certitude absolue. De part et d'autre, bien que de façons différentes, on observe une attitude dogmatique et un repli indigné sur les positions toutes faites.

D'autres en sont restés à l'époque qui a suivi immédiatement l'affaire Galilée. Ils en sont restés à cette espèce de distinction des domaines en séparant soigneusement le *comment* et le *pourquoi*. Ce sont eux qui s'efforcent, dans leur travail de savant, d'expliquer *comment* l'univers fonctionne et qui, dans leur vie religieuse, s'ils sont croyants, savent *pourquoi* ils sont ce qu'ils sont et *pourquoi* Dieu les a faits comme il les a faits.

Leur position n'est pas du tout méprisable, mais paraît incomplète parce qu'elle est statique ; la tension entre la science et la foi n'y est pas assumée comme un facteur de dynamisme.

Science et foi sont classées dans deux tiroirs différents et entre ces deux tiroirs, il y a une paroi étanche qui empêche la communication. Tout se passe comme s'il n'y avait aucune question commune aux deux terrains.

Actuellement, il semble qu'il y ait une série de questions communes aux deux terrains. Il y a à la fois dans le discours théologique et dans la science, comme une émergence du thème de l'*inachèvement.* Aux yeux d'un certain nombre de croyants en tout cas, la main de Dieu n'a pas fini d'agir dans l'existence des hommes, dans leur histoire. Et aux yeux de plus en plus de savants, l'évolution n'est pas terminée, l'évolution se continue toujours. Autrement dit, de part et d'autre, on se surprend à penser dans des catégories qui sont familières à l'autre : le dynamisme, le mouvement, le changement, le processus, le développement, le déploiement, l'évolution. Et l'on en vient à se demander dans cette nouvelle perspective si, finalement, science et foi ne sont pas plus proches qu'on ne l'avait cru jusqu'ici en distinguant soigneusement le *comment* et le *pourquoi*, distinction qui, par ailleurs, reste tout à fait pertinente. On se demande s'il n'y a pas une articulation possible du *comment* et du *pourquoi*, on se demande si science et foi n'auraient pas à se donner la main pour avancer ensemble. Pas du tout pour se confondre, pas du tout pour faire on ne sait quelle scientologie... Mais à se donner la main au nom de l'unicité de la destinée humaine parce que, si l'homme est un savant en même temps qu'un croyant, il s'agit bien du *même* homme qui vit dans l'univers qu'étudie le savant et du même homme qui, dans le cadre même de cet univers est, comme croyant, en relation avec Dieu.

Le lien entre la problématique scientifique et la problématique religieuse se trouve dans ce que l'on pourrait appeler la découverte par l'homme de ses *responsabilités* à l'égard de lui-même, à l'égard du prochain et à l'égard même du monde matériel. Dans la pensée théologique, comme dans la pensée scientifique, on se rend compte de plus en plus que l'homme est en situation de responsabilité. Dans la pensée scientifique, c'est très simple : le grand traumatisme de la communauté scientifique fut Hiroshima, la bombe atomique. On s'est rendu compte que la science n'était absolument pas neutre, que la science pouvait être au service de certaines puissances dominatrices, ou libératrices — je ne prends pas position dans cette affaire —, mais en tout cas de puissances politiques ou économiques et que, par conséquent, il y a une responsabilité éthique, voire une responsabilité politique de la communauté scientifique en tant qu'elle est une communauté scientifique.

À l'intérieur de tout son questionnement en termes de *comment*, « Comment cela se fait-il ? », « Comment cela fonctionne-t-il ? », le savant s'est rendu compte que cette interrogation en forme de *comment ?* suppose toujours des *pourquoi ?* Alors, bien entendu, il y a beaucoup de savants qui vous diront : « Non, non, non, la science est neutre, etc. » Je ne vais pas entrer dans le débat idéologique de savoir si la science est progressiste ou réactionnaire, ce n'est pas mon propos, mais je voudrais simplement attirer l'attention sur le fait que la communauté scientifique, pour une part au moins, commence à prendre conscience de ses responsabilités à l'égard du monde matériel et à l'égard de la science.

D'autre part, le théologien avait l'habitude de se poser uniquement des questions en termes de « pourquoi », schématiquement en tout cas ; et il s'est rendu compte que ces questions, il ne savait plus à propos de quoi il les posait. S'interrogeant sur la relation de l'homme à Dieu, sur la relation du peuple des chrétiens avec Dieu, le théologien s'est rendu compte que tous les *pourquoi* supposent des *comment*. Le deuxième concile du Vatican a servi, d'une certaine façon, de caisse de résonance à toute cette interrogation et lui a donné une force et un poids qui sont ceux que nous connaissons aujourd'hui : les théologiens, et plus généralement les croyants, se sont rendu compte qu'ils sont des croyants *dans le monde*, et que, finalement, ils connaissent très peu de ce monde. Si la main de Dieu est la main qui porte le monde et qui conduit l'histoire, non pas d'une façon déterministe en imposant ceci ou cela, mais qui fait que l'histoire peut se faire, que les hommes peuvent faire l'Histoire, et que cette Histoire ne se fait pas indépendamment de son décor. Auparavant, on était tenté de penser en termes d'acteurs et de décor. Le théologien s'occupait de l'acteur et le savant s'occupait du décor. Aujourd'hui, on se rend compte qu'en fait, si l'on change le décor, l'acteur change, et si l'on change d'acteur, le décor change parce que chaque acteur organise son décor et chaque décor, d'une certaine façon, déteint sur l'acteur.

La science pose donc de nouvelles questions aux théologiens. La génétique et la biologie, par exemple, ont fait d'énormes progrès et l'on connaît beaucoup mieux les mécanismes subtils par lesquels les cellules se reproduisent. On peut même, d'un point de vue purement technologique, intervenir dans la reproduction des cellules et modifier, du moins pour les bactéries, ce qu'on appelle le patrimoine génétique d'une cellule. On peut faire que la fille ne soit pratiquement pas de la même espèce que la mère. Mais dans la Bible, il est écrit : « Vous dominerez la terre. » Est-ce que cette affirmation implique que l'homme doive dominer tous les processus biologiques, et à sa guise créer un autre monde que le monde qui existe, ou bien est-ce que ça veut dire que l'homme doit simplement se contenter de ce qui existe ? Si un théologien tente de réfléchir sur les responsabilités de l'homme dans la création, il est évident qu'il ne peut pas ne pas tenir compte de la génétique, il ne peut pas ne pas tenir compte notamment des possibilités de manipulation génétique. Et cela n'est qu'un exemple.

ENFER

Voilà un mot qui a provoqué bien des angoisses. Chez de nombreux chrétiens, la menace de la damnation éternelle dont ont usé et abusé les prédicateurs au cours des siècles, en particulier au Moyen Âge, laisse encore planer la conviction que la vie chrétienne est plutôt guidée par la peur que par l'amour.

Du latin *infernus*, l'enfer désigne à proprement parler le « lieu d'en bas ». Même si sa représentation a évolué, une constante demeure, ce terme désigne la damnation éternelle. Par exemple, dans l'Ancien Testament, les enfers ou le *shéol* sont considérés comme une fosse ou un puits au plus profond de la terre où règne une obscurité totale. Voir s'ouvrir les portes du shéol, c'est être happé par les forces infernales sans espoir de louer à nouveau Dieu et d'espérer en sa justice. Dans la pensée religieuse israélite, le moyen le plus sûr de se préserver de l'abandon de Dieu, c'est de ne pas participer au désordre du monde, c'est-à-dire d'éviter le péché en respectant les préceptes divins.

L'idée de la mort dans le feu éternel, en se perpétuant sans fin sans la corruption, est une image de l'enfer qui est aussi présente dans le Nouveau Testament. Les Évangiles nous rapportent que Jésus a utilisé des images effroyables de l'enfer pour décrire les calamités qui attendent « les fauteurs d'iniquité » (*Mt* 13,41s) ; « les pleurs et les grincements de dents dans la fournaise ardente » (*Mt* 13,42) ; « la géhenne où le ver ne meurt point et où le feu ne s'éteint point » (*Mc* 9,43-48 ; *Mt* 5,22). Ceux qui n'obéissent pas à l'Évangile seront « châtiés d'une perte éternelle, éloignés de la face du Seigneur » (*2 Th* 1,8s). Ils rejoindront « dans l'étang de feu » la « Mort » (*Ap* 20,14). Voilà une conception de la damnation du pécheur qui est difficile à concilier avec l'accueil inconditionnel de celui en qui nous avons foi...

Consolons-nous, puisque aujourd'hui dans l'Église, on interprète l'utilisation de ces représentations de l'enfer par Jésus comme un moyen pédagogique pour faire saisir que l'enfer, c'est une vie sans Dieu, une vie sans Amour. Ce qui est proche de son enseignement qui puise sa source dans l'annonce du Salut et de la miséricorde de Dieu. Dans cette optique, le Christ nous invite à ne pas rater notre vie, à ne pas faire de celle-ci un enfer, en la fondant sur son amour, l'amour de soi et de l'autre.

Ainsi, le châtiment de l'enfer ne vient pas de Dieu, mais de nous-mêmes, de notre approche de la vie. Bernanos, dans *Journal d'un curé de campagne,* résume bien cette conception de l'enfer. « L'enfer, Madame, c'est de ne plus aimer. » Il faut interpréter la descente de Jésus aux enfers, telle que relatée dans le Nouveau Testament, comme une volonté de signifier la réalité de sa mort d'homme et son triomphe sur cette mort. Les auteurs veulent ainsi témoigner du fait que, par sa mort, le Christ a triomphé du dernier ennemi, la mort, et qu'il nous appelle à la récompense ultime, la vie éternelle. ◇

Toute la question pour le théologien est de savoir ce qu'il en est effectivement des nouvelles possibilités que la science donne à l'homme ; et pour le savant, le problème est de savoir à quoi il peut bien faire servir les nouvelles possibilités qu'il développe.

Mais cela, le théologien ne peut le faire seul, il doit s'agréger à une équipe interdisciplinaire. Évidemment, le travail interdisciplinaire est à la mode. Tout le monde fait du travail interdisciplinaire, et je suis certain que si vous prenez dans nos universités les départements qui ont été créés depuis dix ans, il y a plus de la moitié de ces départements qui sont « interdisciplinaires » dans leur titre. À la fois, c'est une mode et, comme toutes les modes, ça finit par devenir ridicule au bout d'un certain temps quand on passe à la mode suivante. Mais en même temps, cela exprime très fort un besoin, car chaque discipline se sent finalement très à l'étroit dans ses propres murs. Le savant se sent souvent débordé par ses propres découvertes, par les possibilités nouvelles qu'il acquiert et craint parfois de jouer à l'apprenti sorcier. Et comme la réalité est extrêmement complexe, le biologiste, s'il est vraiment conscient de son travail et des implications de ce travail, tentera de recourir aux lumières du physiologiste ou du psychologue, voire du sociologue, et de fil en aiguille, on en arrive à essayer (ce n'est pas encore fait) de faire une grande symphonie avec toutes ces disciplines. Ça, ce n'est pas pour demain, mais je pense qu'un certain nombre de gens travaillent dans ce sens-là. Il y a parmi les philosophes quelques esprits qui tentent, par un travail de réflexion sur les méthodes scientifiques propres à chacune des disciplines, de proposer aux savants un certain nombre de questions, un certain nombre de grilles de lecture, dirait-on aujourd'hui, qui leur permettraient de travailler ensemble un peu plus systématiquement.

Certains esprits donnent d'ailleurs l'impression d'avoir pu dominer en partie des problèmes d'articulation de ce genre.

À cet égard, un nom vient tout de suite en tête, surtout dans les milieux de langue française, c'est celui de Pierre Teilhard de Chardin. Voilà un homme qui a eu une destinée très curieuse. C'était un paléontologue, un savant qui s'occupait de la préhistoire de l'humanité et de la préhistoire de la vie sur terre. C'était en même temps un très grand croyant, un homme de foi et aussi, d'une certaine façon, un philosophe et un théologien, c'est-à-dire un homme qui avait une très grande soif de rationalité. Teilhard n'est certainement pas le seul ni même le premier qui ait tenté de réunir la science, la philosophie et la foi, mais en tout cas, il fut l'un des grands penseurs de notre époque à le faire.

Teilhard de Chardin a montré non seulement qu'on pouvait vivre sereinement en étant à la fois savant et croyant — ça, d'autres l'avaient déjà fait avant lui — mais il a été plus loin en ce sens qu'il a esquissé quelque chose comme une grande vision de l'histoire du Cosmos, de l'histoire de la destinée humaine où le regard que la foi peut porter sur l'évolution du monde et l'interrogation que le savant peut aussi faire porter sur l'évolution du monde, finalement, se complètent, où la science se nourrit de la foi et la foi se nourrit de la science. Mais la destinée de Teilhard a été d'une certaine façon tragique parce qu'il n'a été accepté pour ainsi dire par personne, du moins de son vivant, sauf par quelques amis très proches. Il a été rejeté par les théologiens parce qu'il n'était pas un théologien professionnel (il n'était pas docteur en théologie) et il a été rejeté par les philosophes parce que les philosophes trouvaient qu'il mélangeait tous les problèmes, qu'il ne respectait pas les sacro-saintes distinctions entre le *comment* et le *pourquoi,* et puis, il a été aussi en partie rejeté par la communauté scientifique parce qu'il ne sied pas qu'un savant de son rang se commette avec des philosophes et des théologiens. Alors, il a été rejeté par tout le monde et puis, maintenant, on se rend compte que peut-être ce n'était ni un philosophe ni un savant ni un théologien mais bien un poète visionnaire. Et ce qu'il a tenté de faire voir, me semble-t-il, c'est précisément qu'on n'a pas le droit d'en rester à une simple juxtaposition du *pourquoi* et du *comment* mais qu'il faut penser à une véritable collaboration entre ceux qui passent leur vie à poser principalement des pourquoi et ceux qui passent leur vie à poser principalement des *comment.*

Cette collaboration entre le savant et le croyant est nécessaire non seulement pour expliquer le monde mais aussi parce que l'homme moderne veut transformer ce monde ; parce qu'il veut changer le cours de l'Histoire pour l'améliorer ; parce qu'il s'affirme comme *créateur.*

L'homme contemporain, en effet, s'affirme comme créateur ; pas comme une espèce de créateur qui se poserait en rival du Créateur mais simplement comme un cocréateur. Le rapport de

Dieu à l'homme pourrait être considéré à l'avenir comme une responsabilité partagée. L'homme a précisément, à l'égard du monde qui l'entoure et à l'égard de lui-même, une responsabilité qui n'est pas exclusive, mais qui est en tout cas originale.

PARTICIPER : FOI ET POLITIQUE

Jean Desclos

Les religions ont-elles perdu leur force d'attraction ? Dans l'espace culturel occidental, marqué principalement par le modèle catholique romain, la vie semble désormais se dérouler quotidiennement sans référence aux énoncés dogmatiques et aux normes éthiques traditionnellement imposées par l'Église. Aujourd'hui, le souci de penser et d'agir en conformité à l'autorité romaine s'est largement estompé. Le pape est admiré et applaudi comme une vedette du grand théâtre de l'information-divertissement. Les évêques réussissent parfois à se faire remarquer sur un thème d'actualité, surtout éthique, et leur point de vue est rarement présenté sous un jour intéressant. Prêtres et laïcs ne savent plus tellement comment tricoter une pastorale qui ait une réelle emprise dans le vécu souffrant et aliénant de tant de groupes et de gens. En somme, l'impact de la foi chrétienne sur le bien de la cité et sur la « petite vie » du monde ordinaire apparaît plutôt mince. Risquons quelques explications.

Pour en finir avec l'éternité...

D'abord, ce monde en évolution ultra-rapide ne respire et n'inspire que la nouveauté, la primeur, l'inédit. La présentation des mêmes éternelles vérités, la répétition des mêmes sempiternelles formules rituelles, le recours à un système de pensée forgé dans une culture-du-lointain-passé-proche dépassé, donnent à l'univers religieux les couleurs délavées d'un horizon flou et ennuyeux. Alvin Tofler, le prophète du provisoire et du prêt-à-jeter, avait deviné à quel point les générations de cette fin de millénaire feraient une indigestion de tout ce qui sent l'éternité immuable et paralysante. Le bonheur des humains se vit au maintenant-présent-fragile, avec l'ambition de profiter au maximum de tous les instants. La cité des hommes et des femmes de ce temps n'est pas la Jérusalem éternelle, mais le camping imaginaire des innombrables déménagements : changements de conjoint, de profession, de réseau d'amis, de lieu de résidence, et même de Dieu. Tout change, tout doit changer. Le changement est la nouvelle divinité. Car Dieu aussi doit entrer dans cette frénésie de déplacement et de valorisation de tout ce qui a le courage de se faire en se défaisant, de s'affirmer en se reniant.

Les humains croient donc avoir raison de s'intéresser à autre chose qu'aux réalités éternelles, et d'investir rageusement dans la cité terrestre, avec leur seul courage et leurs étonnantes habiletés de ferrailleurs de la belle diatribe et d'architectes d'un vivre-ensemble-commode. Les nations de la terre ont tant d'intérêts contraires qu'il faut pourtant tisser sur le fragile métier de la paix et du respect de tous les humains. Quelle utilité peuvent bien avoir les prières et les naïves croyances ? Elles ressemblent à de fragiles fleurs facilement piétinées par les promeneurs distraits et affairés. À quoi sert le discours religieux dans l'aménagement de la vie en société ? Ou bien il distrait des vrais problèmes et des angoisses de la cité, et est donc anémiant ; ou bien il profite à certains habiles manipulateurs des consciences fragiles, à la solde d'un pouvoir concurrent et contraire aux vrais intérêts des gens, et est donc aliénant.

Dominica III Adventus
AD PRIMAM
AD SEXTAM
Osténde nobis.

CANONISATION (BÉATIFICATION)

C'est le souverain pontife qui, au terme d'une procédure rigoureuse, accorde à un fidèle défunt le titre de bienheureux ou de bienheureuse. Les fidèles peuvent lui vouer un culte seulement dans les endroits désignés par le Saint-Siège. Lorsqu'on a démontré que celui-ci ou celle-ci a vécu une vie qui répond pleinement à toutes les exigences de l'Église sur ce qu'est une vie de sainteté, on lui accorde le titre de sainte ou de saint et on l'inscrit au catalogue des saints. À partir de ce moment, on autorise son culte dans l'Église universelle. Pour faire de la bienheureuse ou du bienheureux une sainte ou un saint, l'Église, au-delà de la qualité de sa vie chrétienne, tient compte principalement de deux facteurs: le rayonnement spirituel après sa mort, c'est-à-dire le nombre de personnes qui rendent un culte au défunt et les miracles qui peuvent lui être attribués. Par la béatification ou la canonisation d'un défunt, l'Église veut donner un exemple et un témoignage au peuple chrétien d'une vie chrétienne vécue entièrement au service de l'Église et de Dieu. Outre les martyrs, ce sont des religieux ou des religieuses qui ont été, jusqu'à maintenant, le plus souvent reçus comme bienheureux ou comme saints. ◇

Pour en finir avec la gratuité...

Occupés fébrilement à leurs folles courses quotidiennes à la réussite scolaire, économique, médiatique, informatique, les citoyens et les citoyennes de nos sociétés de tradition chrétienne s'habillent sans gêne du manteau de l'athéisme quotidiennement banal et néolibéral d'une existence toute vouée aux intérêts de l'équilibre budgétaire, du déficit zéro, de la mondialisation des marchés, de la compétitivité économique. Nulle transcendance ne vient faire éclater ce paysage fermé sur lui-même et fermé sur l'humain individuel dans son individualité de consommateur-producteur. Les prophètes et les sibylles se recrutent dans les maisons de courtage, car les vraies valeurs sont mobilières et leurs cours incertains font désormais trembler le monde bien plus que les menaces de l'enfer.

Si Mammon est concurrent de Dieu, c'est parce qu'il réussit à dissoudre la pierre solide des solidarités en sable fin des égoïsmes individuels. Notre culture est trempée dans l'économisme, cet économisme atomisant qui mobilise les intelligences des jeunes dès l'école primaire, en leur mettant très tôt dans la tête que s'instruire, c'est s'enrichir, selon la rengaine bien connue. La richesse et l'abondance de nos sociétés développées fréquentent la cour de l'individu-roi et entretiennent son pouvoir discrétionnaire jusque sur le bien commun. L'argent achète tout, et bien plus que les consciences. Il entraîne à tricher et à tuer, la tricherie étant toujours le portique du meurtre.

Dans ce jeu violent des individualismes qui s'entrechoquent, l'État a plus que jamais mailles à tisser pour redonner sens à la vie en société. Les disparités sociales et économiques sont dénoncées, parfois avec vigueur, par des hommes et des femmes qui ont le courage de démasquer les hypocrisies d'une civilisation pas très civilisée, qui laisse les sans-abri à leur noire et froide errance, qui rétrécit l'emploi et le soutien aux sans-emploi, qui dévalorise et humilie les « bénéficiaires » d'une aide sociale qui est tout autant une forme de stigmatisation sociale. Tout se calcule à l'aune de la rentabilité, du PIB ou de la balance des exportations. Les gens n'ont plus le droit de simplement exister comme êtres humains dignes de respect. Ils doivent servir à quelque chose, qui n'est pas très clairement un projet de société humaine, mais le mythe-mirage d'un monde meilleur, suréquipé et surorganisé, plus asphalté, plus robotisé, plus « internetisé », plus pressé. Un monde plus rempli de tous les plus, y compris du « un peu plus inhumain ».

On comprend la difficile influence des références à la transcendance et à la dimension spirituelle de la vie humaine. Des phrases! Des mots! Du vent! La prise de parole des croyants et des croyantes sur le devenir de la cité humaine est précisément un vent à contresens, et une inspiration, une aspiration vers plus d'humanité dans nos rapports en société. La foi chrétienne dit gauchement la qualité extraordinaire de la vie humaine. Son Dieu est le Dieu de l'inutile, du gratuit, de la grâce, de la joie d'être, de la générosité sans calcul. Son modèle est celui du service humble du Fils de Marie. Son combat est la destruction de toutes les mesquineries et de toutes les injustices qui se drapent du manteau du plus fort.

INFAILLIBILITÉ

En 1870, à l'occasion du concile Vatican I, le pape Pie IX proclama le dogme de l'infaillibilité pontificale. Le climat révolutionnaire et le vent de démocratisation qui avaient balayé l'Europe, elle-même entraînée dans ce mouvement par la proclamation de l'indépendance des États-Unis en 1776 et la Révolution française de 1789, ne sont pas étrangers à cette initiative romaine. Réaffirmer l'attachement à la structure impériale et hiérarchique de l'Église et à la concentration du pouvoir dans la personne de l'Évêque de Rome était une tentative de résistance aux changements politiques et sociaux qui avaient, durant les cent années précédentes, transformé le visage de l'Occident.

Contrairement à ce que plusieurs personnes croient, il ne suffit pas que le pape énonce des opinions relatives à la foi et aux mœurs pour que la doctrine qu'il propose devienne «infaillible». Une seule fois depuis 1870, un pape, Pie XII en 1950, s'est prévalu de ce privilège en définissant le dogme de l'Assomption de Marie. Malgré la solennité de certains enseignements pontificaux, sur divers sujets, jamais les conditions n'ont été réunies depuis lors pour permettre la proclamation d'un enseignement dit «infaillible». Ces conditions sont: 1) une question touchant la foi et les mœurs, 2) l'expression de la foi du peuple chrétien et 3) que le pape fasse appel explicitement à son charisme d'infaillibilité. ◇

Pour en finir avec l'autorité...

Aussi longtemps que l'individu-roi peut compter sur la complicité de tous les autres individus-rois pour protéger son royaume, personne n'est maître de personne, et le respect mutuel bien calculé est au menu de la vie en société. Ce qui est bien, à condition que chacun soit un peu maître de soi, capable de gérer sa propre vie et ses propres pulsions. Mais aussi à condition que le respect de la personne soit d'une autre densité que l'abstention ou l'indifférence. Le respect de la personne humaine, si banalement proclamé dans toutes les rengaines à saveur pseudo-éthique ou pseudo-pédagogique, ressemble trop à un « tu fais ce que tu veux — je fais ce que je veux ». C'est un mur, non un pont. C'est une clôture, non un chemin. Le vrai respect de la personne a la fibre de l'engagement, de l'intérêt positif pour le bonheur de l'autre, et donc de la solidarité. Celle-ci, à son tour, a double visage. Elle a la couleur terne et un peu triste de la solidarité obligée, celle des naufragés qui doivent bien se serrer les coudes pour échapper à la noyade. Elle a surtout l'éclat de la solidarité offerte et ouverte, gratuite et généreuse, celle des bénévoles qui aident des malades ou des sinistrés. C'est alors que l'autre, mon prochain, devient mon maître, puisque je m'oblige pour lui, que j'inscris un devoir, une obligation à travailler à son bonheur. Le Je-Moi n'est que la pâle et fragile esquisse du vrai Je, qui est un Je-Nous.

L'homme n'est grand qu'en Je-Nous...

La fin de l'autorité, dans une société en révolte contre le père, selon l'interprétation de Freud, est un peu l'expression de ce refus du nous, et donc de *l'autre-qui-est-mon-frère* au risque du renfermement sur soi, de façon narcissique. Dans un tel contexte, l'Autre n'a pas de place. Le Dieu qui parle et interpelle à la justice pour les petits et les déshérités de la terre ne fait plus école. Il est remplacé par le Dieu-bonbon, le petit-papa-bon-Dieu, semblable au petit-papa-Noël, entouré d'anges joufflus qui sont le miroir de tous nos ego en mal d'une douce quiétude. Le nouvel âge cultive habilement ce repliement du sujet croyant sur sa petite planète intérieure et inhabitable par d'autres que lui-même. La foi nouvelâgiste idolâtre le croyant lui-même. Toutes les croyances se valent, bien sûr, sauf la croyance en soi-même. La vérité n'a pas d'importance. *L'effet* de la vérité en a. Ce qui procure un bien-être ressenti est sûrement vrai. Personne n'ose aujourd'hui questionner l'effet placebo des plus étranges doctrines...

On accorde d'ailleurs moins d'importance à l'appartenance religieuse bien identifiée, dans une confession de foi disciplinée. L'appartenance religieuse est élastique, imprécise, moins radicalement confessante et militante. Chacun fait « sa » religion, selon son propre code génétique, et n'a que faire des lignes de conduites « solidarisantes » et « culpabilisantes » venant des responsables religieux. Ni solidarité sociale, ni solidarité religieuse. Les Louis XIV ont bien appris : l'autorité, c'est moi. La société, c'est moi. Le monde, c'est moi.

En revisitant l'histoire

Mais ne serait-ce pas là tout simplement la rançon d'une histoire lourde de bien des péchés commis par le pouvoir religieux *contre l'humanité et la liberté*? Les chrétiens ne se battent plus, comme aux premiers siècles de l'histoire de l'Église, pour défendre un article du Credo ou pour protéger leurs pasteurs. Ils n'ont que du mal à dire des croisades, grandes ou petites, où s'emmêlaient et se confondaient des ambitions de belles conquêtes ou de joyeux pillages, des rêves de naïves évangélisations de pauvres païens risquant d'être exclus du ciel réservé aux seuls chrétiens validement baptisés. L'influence de l'Église s'est essoufflée. La sécularisation s'est infiltrée presque naturellement, sans grand heurt, dans un Occident chrétien qui a macéré longtemps dans l'eau bénite.

Certains regrettent ce temps de chrétienté; d'autres rendent grâce pour cette forme d'exil purificateur imposé à l'Église depuis plus d'un siècle. Certes, le modèle constantinien mis en place au début du IVe siècle n'a pas eu que des défauts. Le leadership exercé par la papauté, en Occident chrétien, le développement d'institutions ecclésiales fortes, bien structurées, la création d'écoles et d'universités sur le territoire européen comme lieux de haut savoir et de culture, et bien d'autres faits nous montrent la dimension nettement positive d'une présence forte de l'Église dans les affaires humaines.

Mais le modèle a produit ses excès. Mainmise des papes et des évêques sur des domaines fonciers, contrôle étroit de la vie des gens, intrigues de palais pontifical, luttes de papes et d'antipapes, guerres pas très saintes, prisons et inquisitions peu évangéliques... Le grenier des souvenirs catholiques est hanté par quelques sinistres fantômes. Et personne ne souhaite vraiment reconstituer un corps de zouaves pour défendre le pape contre ses ennemis, comme ce fut le cas en 1870. Pie IX, dernier souverain des États pontificaux, en fut dépossédé par Garibaldi et ses troupes. La cause de béatification du dernier pape-roi a été introduite au Vatican il y a quelques années. Il faudrait honnêtement examiner celle de son adversaire, qui au moins mérite une céleste mention pour avoir libéré l'Église catholique d'un pouvoir politique qui ne correspondait pas à sa mission.

Nous voilà donc mieux situés, en cette fin de XXe siècle, par rapport à la place de la religion dans la gouverne politique des sociétés. Les chefs religieux n'ont pas d'affaire là, sauf exceptions. La séparation du pouvoir religieux de l'Église et du pouvoir civil de l'État, jadis théologiquement discutable, voire impensable pour certains, fait maintenant l'unanimité dans les pays d'allégeance chrétienne. Mais quelle influence la foi peut-elle exercer, de façon concrète, dans la vie politique et économique?

Ambiguïtés des rapports du religieux au politique

La politique a mauvaise réputation. Le jeu politique, s'entend. Magouilles et tricheries partisanes, entourloupettes agiles de déclarations masquant l'impuissance et l'incompétence, langues de bois ronronnant les stériles évidences rassurantes du style « nous avons à cœur de servir les meilleurs intérêts de la population, gna gna... », scandales mal camouflés de chopes de bière et de pots de bon vin partagés entre amis savamment complices... De quoi déprimer tous les cœurs démocratiques qui veulent participer un peu naïvement à la construction d'un monde juste et meilleur.

Pourtant, le ferment évangélique est bien destiné à la pâte humaine, avec ses scories et ses poussières. Comment arrimer intelligemment le royaume de César et celui de Dieu qui, tout en étant bien distincts, ne sont pas obligatoirement concurrents ou contradictoires ?

Parfois, les gens d'Église se réclament du caractère surnaturel de leur mission pour s'élever au-dessus de la mêlée et fixer les yeux dans les nuages, vers le « Royaume » qui est ailleurs et nulle part. Nul besoin d'être disciple de Marx pour dénoncer les formes de désengagement social associées à une forme de mépris du monde présentée comme nécessaire pour l'obtention de la récompense céleste. Le concile Vatican II a tenté de corriger cette façon de dissocier la sainteté de la préoccupation des réalités terrestres, qu'il présente comme la « matière du Royaume des cieux », non comme un obstacle.

C'est donc en plongeant dans la vie humaine, dans les institutions, les cultures, les manières de penser et de vivre, en faisant siens les intérêts des humains et des sociétés que le croyant entre dans le projet évangélique d'être sel et lumière. Il fut un temps où l'on pensait se rapprocher de Dieu en s'éloignant des autres, en fuyant le monde au sens de la cité des hommes, des groupes humains. Jésus, le Fils de Dieu, habite ce monde concret et ne fait pas seulement en effleurer les contours. Il s'y incruste, prend part à la fête des noces, mange et boit au restaurant du coin, discute de fiscalité, débat des enjeux de certaines lois, se préoccupe de la faim et de la guérison des corps, prend du temps pour les déshérités et les pauvres.

On comprend mal la foi chrétienne si elle sert de caution à une fuite de nos responsabilités civiles ou professionnelles. La lettre à Diognète, écrite vers le IVe siècle, fait des chrétiens un portrait plutôt étonnant. Ils ressemblent à tout le monde, s'habillent et travaillent comme tout le monde. Ils sont totalement dans le monde et activement présents au cœur de la cité.

Sainte Église sale d'avoir servi le monde...

Vue sous cet angle, l'appartenance à l'Église ne sépare pas du monde, ne fait pas sortir de la vie concrète. Il n'y a pas de frontières étanches entre l'univers dit spirituel et l'univers dit matériel. Le travail, le métier, la profession, la participation au syndicat, la gestion de l'entreprise, le commerce, le loisir, l'activité physique, la lecture, les voyages, les réunions, les fêtes, les campagnes électorales, les diverses formes d'expression culturelle, la science, le progrès, rien n'est hors du champ d'intérêt des croyants, et nul territoire de l'expérience humaine ne doit échapper à l'influence évangélique qui est porteuse du maximum de respect de l'humanité.

On ne peut donc pas commodément vivre dans deux mondes séparés, l'un réservé aux belles activités pieuses et religieuses, l'autre destiné à la performance « profane ». Des gens s'imaginent être des bons chrétiens parce qu'ils fréquentent l'église et paient leur part pour son entretien, et ne s'inquiètent pas le moins du monde de tricher gentiment l'impôt, ou de sous-payer des employés à statut précaire... Certains travailleurs jouent un jeu semblable en ne méritant pas vraiment leur salaire, en se traînant les pieds et en mangeant de la procédure de griefs au moindre grognement d'un patron. On ne fabrique pas une société digne du Fils de Dieu en tricotant quotidiennement la mesquinerie, la tricherie, le mensonge.

TRINITÉ

Énorme problème théologique, souvent réduit à une gentille explication mathématique (un égale trois, comme les branches de l'unique fourchette, ou comme dans un triangle équilatéral). La Trinité est une façon de rendre compte du mystère de Dieu que Jésus nous présente sous trois « visages », sans que cela n'entraîne une division en trois divinités. Dieu est Père, Dieu est Fils, Dieu est Esprit. Dieu est richesse d'Être en relation d'éternelle réciprocité d'amour. Penser Dieu comme Trinité, c'est résumer en un mot l'expérience que Jésus veut nous communiquer de Celui qui est Source, Inspiration, Amour, Don de soi. Dans la catéchèse populaire, la Trinité a souvent l'air d'un mystère qu'on pourrait expliquer, en laissant entendre qu'un Dieu unique est aussi divisible en trois sous-divinités. Mais Dieu se révèle distinctement comme le Père, le Fils et l'Esprit saint. Chacune de ces personnes se distingue par rapport à l'autre, en se définissant par et dans sa relation à l'autre. La Trinité exprime symboliquement l'idée qu'une personne, homme et femme, ne peut pleinement vivre l'amour qu'en relation avec d'autres personnes qui sont aussi uniques qu'elle-même. ◇

L'Église n'est pas un corps étranger vivant en dehors du monde, à la manière d'une lune bien détachée de sa planète. L'Église n'est pas non plus un continent distinct des autres, ayant dérivé vers d'autres influences solaires plus saines. L'Église est intimement liée à toute la vie des humains de la terre, comme l'eau d'un ruisseau qui ira à la rivière puis au fleuve puis à la mer, et reviendra quelque part arroser et fertiliser un sol, pour rendre possible l'éclosion de multiples formes de la vie. Elle doit être toujours plus, par l'inspiration évangélique, une eau pure, limpide, fraîche, vivifiante. Mais aussi eau qui peut se salir en nettoyant les corps et les vêtements d'une humanité souvent blessée.

L'Église peut beaucoup avec des moyens très humbles. Elle peut arrêter la guerre, par le courage d'hommes et de femmes qui s'interposent hardiment entre belligérants. Elle peut contrer la violence faite aux femmes, en étant solidaire de marches silencieuses et de projets concrets de surveillance et de dénonciation. Elle peut améliorer les conditions de vie des détenus, des handicapés, des personnes âgées, en soutenant le respect inconditionnel des personnes, sans tapage, dans l'action bénévole quotidienne. Elle peut bouleverser des systèmes de lois et des organisations politiques devenues impersonnelles, en faisant retentir inlassablement les mêmes appels à se préoccuper des plus petits et à instaurer plus de justice.

L'Église se mêle des affaires du monde. C'est bien ainsi, aussi longtemps qu'elle n'y cherche pas le pouvoir, la domination, le prestige, mais la bonne influence, l'influence du bien, de la générosité gratuite, de la réconciliation à construire et à rebâtir sans cesse. Elle entretient la confiance dans la capacité qu'ont les humains de vouloir et de faire le bien.

On comprend donc que la religion ne se vit pas en dehors d'une attention réelle aux affaires du « siècle ». La foi, comme adhésion au Dieu de Jésus Christ, s'expérimente au cœur du monde créé et animé par l'Esprit de Jésus Christ. La foi nous engage à être d'excellents citoyens du monde et de bons artisans de la réussite de la vie politique, économique, sociale, culturelle de notre petit milieu.

Audaces et cohérences

Oui, mais... N'y a-t-il pas une sorte de jeu dangereux à courtiser en même temps Dieu et César ? Les règles de la vie politique ne s'accordent pas spontanément aux bonnes mœurs inspirées par l'Évangile. Les amis de Dieu peuvent-ils si facilement pactiser avec les puissants de ce monde ? Les chrétiens n'ont-ils pas la terrible mission d'être les chiens de garde et les dénonciateurs de tous les pouvoirs politiques ou économiques qui dévorent les petits et les pauvres ?

L'Église répète avec ferveur de bonnes et fortes déclarations en faveur de la justice et du respect des droits des plus petits, notamment depuis la célèbre encyclique de Léon XIII sur la question ouvrière (*Rerum novarum*, 1891). Elle est, sur ce point, souvent plus crédible et suivie que sur les questions touchant la morale individuelle, surtout en matière conjugale et sexuelle. Les interventions des papes et des conférences nationales pour la promotion de l'ouvrier, le soutien des handicapés, la consolidation des familles, le respect des droits fondamentaux de la personne en toute situation tracent un modèle d'Église audacieusement sensible aux misères concrètes du monde ordinaire.

Les chrétiens ne peuvent esquiver ici ce devoir de totale honnêteté et de totale cohérence avec leurs propres principes. Nous sommes parvenus, dans nos sociétés, à plus d'exigence de transparence en tous les domaines, dans l'administration des fonds publics, dans le respect des procédures établies, dans la mise au jour de défauts chroniques et d'injustices historiques. L'Église n'échappe pas à cette requête de faire la démonstration de sa volonté d'être irréprochable en tout. Elle doit corriger les abus auxquels elle a pu se prêter. Pourquoi n'accorderait-elle pas de justes conditions de salaires à ses propres employés ? Pourquoi hésiterait-on, en certains milieux ecclésiaux, à soutenir l'accréditation d'un syndicat d'employés de l'Église ? Les membres de l'Église sont-ils assez exigeants pour leurs responsables, et ceux-ci se donnent-ils des règles professionnelles claires et contraignantes ?

Plus grave encore est le fait, confirmé de temps à autre par des événements ou des crises politiques en pays dits catholiques, de la collusion de pasteurs et de groupes avec des régimes politiques opprimant les plus pauvres. Certains gouvernements n'hésitent pas, au nom de ce qu'ils nomment l'intérêt national ou la protection de la loi et de l'ordre, à soutenir des luttes sanglantes contre le petit peuple des paysans sans terre exploités par de riches propriétaires terriens, comme ce fut le cas au Brésil, ou à pratiquer la torture et l'assassinat de groupes contestataires, comme cela est arrivé en Argentine. Dans ces cas comme dans d'autres semblables, des gouvernements totalitaires ont reçu des appuis plus ou moins explicites d'évêques ou de chrétiens qui partageaient les mêmes ambitions de pouvoir et de richesse. Heureusement, d'autres chrétiens et d'autres évêques ont pris la parole pour dénoncer à la face du monde des gestes indignes de l'Évangile. Les révolutions et les grandes entreprises de lutte contre l'injustice faite aux hommes et aux femmes de la terre ne devraient jamais se vivre en l'absence d'une participation significative des disciples du Christ Jésus.

Cela est d'autant justifié que ce Jésus a été, dans l'ensemble de son action de brillant prophète, un dérangeur des consciences endormies dans le confort spirituel garanti par une fidélité superficielle à la volonté de Dieu exprimée dans sa loi. Les faux justes avaient par exemple élaboré un système qui les exemptait, légalement, du devoir d'aider matériellement leurs propres parents. Ils savaient se rendre agréables au pouvoir en place pour en retirer des honneurs et du prestige. Ils étaient méticuleux dans l'observance des prescriptions rituelles. Mais ils ne se laissaient pas rejoindre par la misère réelle du blessé laissé pour mort au bord du chemin.

Jésus fustige ceux qui ne font rien pour soulager la misère des autres, condamnés pour leur inertie bien plus que pour leurs mauvaises actions. Il dénonce les riches, ridiculise leur appétit insatiable de richesses qui ne les suivront pas en terre, décrit leur dureté de cœur inébranlable même par une apparition de revenants, leur promet tous les malheurs s'ils ne se convertissent pas. Pas étonnant que le dénonciateur soit à son tour dénoncé et mis à mort. Celui qui avait chassé les vendeurs du Temple en sera puni.

La foi chrétienne bien comprise et bien vécue ne s'accorde pas bien avec l'argent et le pouvoir. Aucune circonstance historique, aucune noble raison ne justifiera jamais que la foi au Fils de Dieu devienne le plat principal au menu des intrigues tricotées par les ambitions humaines, pour les justifier ou les recouvrir d'un manteau de légitimité. Et on aura toujours raison de questionner les groupes politiques qui se parent trop facilement de l'étiquette « chrétienne » pour servir en fait bien autre chose que les « intérêts de Dieu ». Ou les mouvements chrétiens organisés en vue d'une présence politique forte pour accomplir « l'œuvre de Dieu ».

Mais alors, comment les chrétiens doivent-ils participer à la chose publique ? À la manière de Jean-Paul II, par ses textes, ses discours, son influence personnelle sur les chefs politiques ? À la manière de l'Action catholique du début du siècle, qui mobilisait les jeunes et les adultes en les conscientisant sur les enjeux humains et chrétiens de situations sociales complexes ? Par une pastorale sociale bien structurée, en chaque milieu, de façon à développer une manière d'être proche des vrais problèmes des gens, en solidarité avec eux et avec les groupes communautaires non confessionnels ?

Les chrétiens seront toujours bien perçus tant qu'ils se présenteront comme partenaires engagés avec les pauvres, à leur service, dans la simplicité et le dépouillement. Jean XXIII avait rêvé d'un concile qui mettrait l'Église au diapason du monde et qui recentrerait son attention sur les pauvres. Le vrai fruit du concile Vatican II sera cueilli quand les chrétiens et les chrétiennes se reconnaîtront spontanément comme des pauvres marchant à la rencontre des autres pauvres de la terre.

DIFFÉRER : PLURALISME ET UNITÉ

Marie Gratton

« L'ennui, écrivait Jean de La Fontaine, naquit un jour de l'uniformité. » La formule devrait avoir de quoi nous rassurer vu le pluralisme culturel et religieux dans lequel nous baignons ! Pourtant, bien des gens seraient disposés à payer d'un peu d'ennui l'assurance d'une homogénéité culturelle et religieuse acquise et protégée aux couleurs de *leur* drapeau et à l'ombre de *leur* clocher. La création tout entière a beau nous renvoyer l'image d'une foisonnante diversité et nous la rendre belle et féconde, nous n'en tirons pas, hélas, toutes les leçons qu'elle semble se plaire à nous donner. Quel charme aurait l'aube si elle ne venait après la nuit ? Mais, nous le sentons bien, la question est futile, car sans la nuit, il n'y aurait point d'aube, ni de crépuscule sans le jour, ni de vallées sans montagnes. Et sans lacs comment penser les îles et sans les continents les rivages où puissent se briser les vagues de « la mer toujours recommencée » ? Cette diversité partout présente dans la nature et qui habituellement nous fascine et nous séduit, par quel singulier retournement de l'esprit en vient-elle à nous troubler et à nous effrayer si fort quand les êtres humains, d'abord façonnés par leur lieu d'origine, en poursuivent le déploiement à travers l'expression de leurs cultures particulières et de leurs quêtes multiformes de Dieu ?

Pourquoi la diversité culturelle nous fait-elle si souvent peur alors qu'elle devrait nous émerveiller ? Pourquoi le pluralisme religieux nous apparaît-il comme un mal et un scandale à extirper ? Compte tenu des limites de cet exposé, nous devrons nous contenter, pour essayer tant bien que mal de répondre à cette question, de nous placer du point de vue chrétien, et plus spécifiquement encore, catholique.

De l'universalité et de ses... limites

La diversité culturelle ne peut que poser problème à une tradition religieuse qui semble constamment oublier, dans la pratique, que sa prétention à l'universalité repose en même temps sur une base historique bien délimitée dans le temps et l'espace. Toutes les religions, bien entendu, se retrouvent exactement dans la même situation et il serait parfaitement aberrant de leur reprocher les limites inhérentes à ce fait. Toutefois, l'absolutisation d'un système religieux, à travers la dogmatisation de ses croyances, risque précisément de bloquer sa capacité à dépasser le cadre culturel qui l'a vu naître et lui a fourni les premiers outils qui lui ont permis de se créer un univers de concepts et de symboles capables de traduire sa foi et de célébrer son espérance.

L'étude comparée des religions nous apprend que les symboles auxquels nous identifions le plus étroitement une tradition religieuse et qui nous paraissent non seulement son signe distinctif, mais aussi sa caractéristique la plus originale, puisent souvent leurs racines dans un fonds commun de l'humanité. Les récits de conception virginale et de résurrection, avant d'encadrer l'essentiel du mystère chrétien et d'être présentés comme des vérités à croire, ont constitué pour bien des cultures antiques ou dites

HORS DE L'ÉGLISE...

La formule «Hors de l'Église point de salut» est née au IIIe siècle. À l'origine, elle se voulait un sévère avertissement lancé à toutes les personnes qui, baptisées dans la foi chrétienne, s'en détachaient pour se joindre à des sectes hérétiques, fort nombreuses à cette époque. Ce n'est que plus tard qu'on finit par l'entendre dans un sens strict et, il faut bien le dire, terrifiant, où se voyaient englobés dans une même perdition juifs, musulmans, chrétiens, protestants, «païens», bouddhistes, hindouistes, etc., indépendamment de la droiture de leur conscience ou de la pureté de leurs mœurs, en conformité avec leurs coutumes et leurs croyances. Cette interprétation abusive n'a plus court aujourd'hui et les plus hautes autorités de l'Église, notamment Pie IX, au XIXe siècle, et Pie XII, il y a une cinquantaine d'années, l'ont condamnée, tout en maintenant, il est vrai, que le baptême demeure la clé privilégiée et la foi chrétienne la voie royale pour aller vers Dieu. ◇

primitives des mythes porteurs de sens et d'espérance. Et la croix, arbre aux quatre branches, avant même que Jésus n'y soit cloué, parlait de vie et de salut cosmique depuis des temps immémoriaux.

Mais les systèmes dogmatiques se plaisent à revendiquer non seulement l'excellence, mais aussi l'exclusivité de leur vision du monde et, à la limite, de Dieu. Aussi une de leurs caractéristiques consiste à percevoir le pluralisme au mieux comme un problème à résoudre, au pire comme un scandale à éliminer.

La courtepointe chrétienne: déchirements et raccommodages

Considérons d'abord la chose à l'intérieur même du christianisme. Les chrétiens sont divisés depuis longtemps et pour des motifs qui ne peuvent souvent paraître que bizarres à des personnes non prévenues des subtiles arguties dont peuvent user et abuser des théologiens qui semblent avoir « connu Dieu tout petit » et qui, rendus audacieux par cette prétendue familiarité, « l'habillent de dogmes chaque matin », pour reprendre l'ironique formule de Marie Noël dans ses *Carnets intimes*. Or, osons le dire, même si la formule peut paraître choquante, les certitudes que la théologie dogmatique a acquises sur Dieu, certitudes qu'elle n'a pas hésité à défendre à certaines époques à coup d'anathèmes et de condamnations temporelles et éternelles, enferment Dieu dans un carcan et le rapetissent aux dimensions de notre esprit. Après s'être fait de Dieu une image, on l'impose à l'adoration comme si elle était Dieu même. Cela s'appelait déjà idolâtrie au temps de Moïse et des patriarches. N'y a-t-il pas en vérité quelque chose d'idolâtrique dans la manière obsessive, à force de vouloir être précise et exclusive de toute autre façon de penser, d'enfermer Dieu dans des définitions qui traduisent sans doute à merveille notre vanité intellectuelle, mais ne nous avancent guère dans la véritable connaissance de Celui dont nous tenons « la vie, le souffle et tout le reste », pour reprendre les mots de Paul prêchant aux Athéniens (*Ac* 17,25) ? Pour leur présenter son Dieu, leur « dieu inconnu », l'apôtre des Gentils n'hésitera pas par ailleurs à utiliser la formule du poète grec Épiménide, comme pour témoigner du respect qu'il éprouve pour leur culture et manifester la connaissance qu'il en a : « C'est en lui que nous avons la vie, le mouvement et l'être » (*Ac* 17,28). Expressions qui veulent aller à l'essentiel sans s'encombrer d'inextricables arguties.

On souhaiterait que cette leçon ne se soit jamais perdue, car elle aurait pu rendre, à certains tournants de l'histoire, de précieux services. Les péripéties de la fameuse « querelles des rites » nous serviront de premier exemple. Le jésuite italien Matteo Ricci est envoyé comme missionnaire en Extrême-Orient en 1577, et en 1600 il fonde avec quelques compagnons la première mission catholique en Chine. Ricci apprend le mandarin, s'habille comme les sages confucéens, étudie l'histoire du pays et publie, outre des ouvrages historiques, un traité sur la philosophie morale chinoise. Il a ses entrées à la cour de Pékin, où sa culture et sa science en mathématiques, en géométrie et en astronomie font grande impression sur les lettrés et sur la cour impériale. La voie est ouverte à un accueil de la religion que ces savants visiteurs ont apportée avec eux. Mais, bien sûr, il est une coutume du bouddhisme que la Chine n'est pas prête à abandonner, c'est le culte des ancêtres. Ricci estime que la difficulté n'est pas insurmontable, puisque les catholiques font une large part au culte des saints. Ne sont-ils pas un peu leurs « ancêtres » dans la foi ? Et ce n'est pas de l'idolâtrie que de célébrer solennellement leur mémoire par des cérémonies, des offrandes et des pèlerinages.

Les jésuites font donc preuve de tolérance à l'égard d'un certain nombre de coutumes locales. Ce qui facilite l'implantation de la foi catholique. Mais ils deviennent vite suspects aux yeux des dominicains et des franciscains qui les dénoncent à Rome. Il s'ensuivra une série de querelles théologiques à rebondissements multiples qui s'étendra sur un siècle et demi. Tantôt les jésuites sembleront prendre l'avantage, tantôt leurs ennemis triompheront. Les échanges épistolaires avec Rome se multiplient. Les papes se succèdent sur le trône pontifical, comme les empereurs de Chine. Tous ces débats irritent ces derniers. C'est ainsi qu'en 1724, l'empereur Yong-Tcheng interdit le christianisme. Certains missionnaires sont toutefois tolérés à Pékin. Par la bulle *Ex quo singulari*, en date du 9 août 1742, le pape Benoît XIV révoque toutes les concessions qui avaient été consenties aux jésuites durant le siècle et demi qu'avait duré la

« querelle des rites ». Dans les années qui suivirent, des missionnaires furent massacrés. D'accueillante, la Chine était devenue persécutrice. Le catholicisme avait, après bien des soubresauts, raté sa chance dans le Céleste empire.

Plus près de nous, on sait combien les théologiens venus d'Asie et d'Afrique, même ceux qui ont été formés en Occident, revendiquent en faveur d'une inculturation véritable en terres de mission. Il n'appartient pas seulement aux « indigènes », répètent-ils avec insistance, de s'ouvrir au catholicisme, à sa vision occidentale du monde et de l'être humain, il faut aussi que celui-ci puisse assimiler divers éléments des autres cultures, pour intégrer leurs concepts et leurs valeurs dans l'expression de sa foi, dans l'élaboration de son code de droit canon et dans sa liturgie. Des évêques africains ont consacré, depuis le concile Vatican II, beaucoup d'efforts pour convaincre Rome de permettre à leurs fidèles de rester eux-mêmes, si l'on peut dire, en devenant catholiques. Au plan liturgique, on a certes accepté que les instruments traditionnels remplacent l'orgue ou l'harmonium, et que la danse soit intégrée à certaines célébrations du culte. Mais on juge impensable de remplacer le froment dans la confection du pain eucharistique par du sorgho ou du mil en terre africaine, ou par du riz en Asie, là où les céréales constituent la nourriture de base. Dans des contrées où l'on ne produit pas de blé, mais où la culture et la consommation d'autres graminées sont sources de vie et de santé, ne conviendrait-il pas de les laisser transcender leur fonction profane pour devenir des signes sacrés de convivialité fraternelle et de vie éternelle auprès des fidèles croyants en Jésus Christ ?

En Amérique latine, la piété populaire fait une place souvent assez large à une sorte de syncrétisme où se mêlent, dans des cérémonies aussi colorées qu'exubérantes, le culte des saints et des réminiscences des cultes précoloniaux. Les canonistes et les liturgistes de stricte observance ne s'y retrouvent pas toujours. La superstition s'y glisse sans doute, mais la foi donne le courage d'espérer... Nous ne nous faisons pas ici l'avocate inconditionnelle de ces pratiques. Mais elles représentent une forme d'inculturation qu'il faut consentir à examiner de près.

N'y aurait-il pas lieu de reconsidérer aussi, en Afrique, là où il apparaît le plus culturellement difficile à justifier, le lien obligé entre sacerdoce et célibat ? Sur ce continent, ne pourrait-on pas permettre le mariage coutumier qui est, on le sait, une union qui ne se conclut pas en un jour, mais comporte plusieurs étapes et permet, avant qu'elle ne soit définitivement scellée, que les jeunes gens cohabitent ? L'effet pervers de ce refus, c'est que les Africains catholiques continuent néanmoins de se marier selon la manière coutumière, et se trouvent de ce fait tenus à l'écart du sacrement de l'Eucharistie aussi longtemps qu'ils n'ont pas régularisé leur situation à l'église, ce que certains ne font que très tardivement.

Le jour où on aura compris que l'unité n'appelle pas nécessairement l'uniformité, et que le catholicisme occidental n'est qu'une expression parmi d'autres de l'adhésion à Jésus Christ, on aura fait un pas de géant.

Saint Paul, qui sut adapter son message au monde grec, n'en a pas pour autant renoncé à présenter la vérité telle qu'il la comprenait, il a voulu la rendre la plus intelligible possible à celles et ceux qu'il voulait gagner à la cause du Christ. C'est la mission de la théologie, son défi, son risque et sa grandeur.

Il ne s'agit pas ici de dénigrer la démarche théologique, cette quête d'une intelligence de la foi qui doit nous apparaître comme une recherche légitime entre toutes, puisqu'elle s'applique à déchiffrer le mieux possible la rencontre de deux mystères qui sont au cœur de l'aventure humaine, celui de l'homme et celui de

Dieu. Mais les dogmatismes ont un effet pervers, ils enrayent le dynamisme de la recherche en donnant à penser que le trésor est trouvé et qu'on en a infailliblement et une fois pour toutes dressé l'inventaire. Saint Augustin, qui n'est guère suspect de laxisme en matière de respect de l'orthodoxie, manifestait pourtant, à l'occasion d'une prière, une attitude plus modeste quand il demandait à Dieu de lui donner le goût de le chercher comme s'il devait le trouver et, croyant l'avoir trouvé, de lui conserver l'appétit de le chercher encore.

Si l'objectif des fidèles d'une religion est la recherche de Dieu, la diversité des découvertes ne devrait troubler personne. Mais si l'on part du présupposé qu'on détient déjà la clé du mystère et de la vérité, alors toutes les discriminations se trouvent justifiées.

Ce sont souvent sur des théories indémontrables, et dont la formulation d'ailleurs a donné lieu à des débats épiques où la vanité des protagonistes et leurs intérêts politiques l'emportaient hélas sur une sereine recherche de la vérité, que les Églises chrétiennes se sont séparées. Le schisme d'Orient s'est consommé sur l'interprétation d'un article du Credo réglant les rapports du Père et du Fils dans la Trinité il y a plus d'un millénaire et demi. En 1054, il s'est fâcheusement aggravé quand Michel Cérulaire, patriarche de Constantinople, a remis en cause l'autorité du pontife romain. La Réforme protestante a amplifié encore le morcellement du christianisme. Mais cela est-il un drame, un scandale absolu ? Ce qui est triste, ce qui fait mal, ce ne sont pas les divergences d'opinion sur tel ou tel point de doctrine, de discipline ecclésiastique ou d'interprétation en matière d'éthique, ce sont les luttes acharnées allant, en certains cas, jusqu'à l'élimination physique des adversaires, pour soutenir la prétendue fidélité à la personne de Jésus. Alors que le choc des opinions est fécond à condition d'être vécu avec un cœur et un esprit ouverts, l'absolutisation d'un point de vue, par sa formulation dogmatique, ne peut que créer hargne et division.

Le pluralisme religieux : casse-tête et solution

Si les chrétiens qui se réclament d'un seul et même Seigneur peuvent si violemment se disputer l'exclusivité de l'interprétation correcte de sa nature et de sa volonté, on ne s'étonnera pas que le dialogue avec les autres grandes traditions religieuses de l'humanité n'aille pas sans anicroches. Des préjugés tenaces, des débats idéologiques acerbes, scandés dans les siècles passés par des luttes armées et des persécutions, ont laissé des blessures difficiles, sinon impossibles à cicatriser, entre les religions monothéistes. Quant aux autres, vite qualifiées d'idolâtriques, leurs fidèles étaient invités à écouter la « bonne parole »... Qui aurait songé, sinon à une époque très récente, à leur proposer de dialoguer ? Hormis chez quelques ethnologues et missionnaires aussi aventureux qu'avant-gardistes, les vertus du pluralisme religieux n'avaient guère droit de cité. On le jugeait plutôt comme un vice. Et encore aujourd'hui, il suscite plus de méfiance que d'enthousiasme. Voyons pourquoi. L'éloge du pluralisme religieux résonne en bien des milieux comme une profession de relativisme, ou pour dire les choses le plus simplement du monde : se réjouir plutôt que de s'affliger de la diversité des quêtes d'absolu signifierait que l'on juge que « toutes les religions sont bonnes ». Et cela, certaines personnes l'estiment insupportable parce qu'en contradiction avec les enseignements de leur tradition particulière.

Si nous prenons les choses autrement, et si nous considérons la quête religieuse comme une tentative pour tout humain d'accorder son être à l'Être, comment pourrions-nous ne pas nous incliner avec respect devant chacune de ces démarches ? Il n'est point nécessaire en l'occurrence d'obliger son intelligence et son cœur à trouver excellente chacune des doctrines qui sont proposées à l'intérieur des diverses voies, il suffit de reconnaître qu'elles puissent être une force capable d'entraîner l'être humain au-delà de lui-même pour le mener à sa Fin, quelque nom qu'il puisse lui donner.

L'attachement légitime que nous portons à notre tradition religieuse n'est en rien menacé par la reconnaissance que nous choisissons d'accorder à celle des autres. La coïncidence entre nos aspirations profondes et le message doctrinal et moral d'une religion particulière, le fait d'y avoir été initié dès l'enfance et d'avoir vécu et célébré les grands moments de notre vie au rythme de ses fêtes et aux accents de sa liturgie, tout cela crée des liens qui ne devraient jamais être dénoués à la légère. L'acceptation du pluralisme religieux n'a rien à voir avec l'indifférentisme, et s'accommode fort bien d'une profession de ferveur à l'égard d'un héritage particulier. Le respect pour la pluralité des cultes naît, nous n'en pouvons plus douter, d'une double exigence : une exigence éthique et une exigence psychologique.

« Comment les hommes peuvent-ils se connaître s'ils méprisent mutuellement leurs dieux ? » se demande Philippe Baud. Et s'ils ne se connaissent pas, comment peuvent-ils s'aimer, et s'ils ne s'aiment pas, comment peuvent-ils cohabiter ? Et s'ils ne peuvent cohabiter à une époque où des bouleversements politiques et des disparités économiques majeures et intolérables entraînent des déplacements massifs de populations d'un continent à l'autre, comment cette incapacité de vivre ensemble ne nous entraînerait-elle pas toujours plus inexorablement vers le chaos ? Comment ne pas saisir dans ce fait socio-politique banal, mais qui a valeur d'exemple, l'impératif éthique d'un mutuel respect interconfessionnel ?

37 T
FERIA TERTIA
FERIA QUARTA
II classis
Ant. 1 Prophétæ prædica-
Psalmi (cum ant.) de feria
2° loco 239 P.
Cum vénerit * Filius hó-
minis, putas, invéniet fi-
dem super terram?

Quand on demande au Dalaï Lama les conditions d'un dialogue interreligieux susceptible d'enrichir chacune des traditions en cause, il rappelle la nécessité de reconnaître la diversité qui existe dans l'humanité. Les êtres humains varient quant à leurs dispositions mentales, à leurs intérêts et à leurs inclinations spirituelles, et pourtant le but commun des traditions religieuses que sont par exemple le christianisme et le bouddhisme est de produire « une personne pleinement réalisée, spirituellement mature, bonne et généreuse ». Une fois admises la diversité des êtres, et la communauté des fins, pourquoi ne pas accepter sans se troubler, mais avec une sorte de candide reconnaissance, suggère le Dalaï Lama, que le christianisme propose la foi en un Dieu créateur à qui l'être humain soit redevable et devant qui il doive justifier ses actions, alors que le bouddhiste choisira de fonder son agir sur un sens aigu de sa responsabilité à l'égard de tout vivant, sans qu'il lui paraisse nécessaire de postuler l'existence d'un être transcendant ?

PARDON

Du latin *per*, qui signifie la perfection et *donare*, donner. Le pardon, c'est donc de donner à une personne qui nous a offensé la rémission de sa faute. C'est lui témoigner que l'on ne lui tient pas rancune. Pour qu'un don soit possible, quelqu'un doit consentir à l'accueillir. Ne pas reconnaître sa faute, c'est rendre inefficace en quelque sorte l'offre du pardon. Le Christ, qui nous a témoigné sur la croix jusqu'à quel point sa mission était œuvre de pardon (*Lc* 23,34), nous a invités dans son enseignement à nous pardonner mutuellement. Le pardon, Jésus nous invite même à le donner à ceux que nous considérons comme nos ennemis (*Mt* 5,44 ; *Lc* 6,27-36). L'appel de Jésus à remettre les péchés au nom de l'amour de Dieu ne trouve-t-il pas toute sa grandeur dans le pardon mutuel ? ◇

Certaines traditions orientales ont moins de peine que nous à imaginer la poursuite du souverain bien comme un itinéraire à voies multiples. Elles aiment se représenter les diverses démarches spirituelles en évoquant l'image d'une roue. À l'essieu central aboutissent plusieurs rayons séparés les uns des autres. Il serait mal venu d'en supprimer un certain nombre, comme de vouloir les amalgamer. Chacun, à sa place, remplit sa fonction, chacun, en son lieu, tend vers le centre. Ainsi chaque être, bien ancré dans une tradition particulière, devrait savoir, en suivant sa propre voie, aller vers la perfection de son être. L'obsession d'une vérité unique à posséder une fois pour toutes semble étrangère à ces traditions. Apprendre à vivre en paix avec soi-même et avec les autres, dans la compassion et la tolérance, accorder plus de poids au savoir-être qu'au savoir, et à la charité qu'à la foi.

Certes, les religions qui s'appuient sur un fort contenu doctrinal cherchent à répondre aux questions que se pose l'intelligence humaine face au mystère de Dieu, mais en réalité, nous le savons bien, elles sont condamnées à toujours se heurter aux portes du mystère, et leur insistance sur le contenu conceptuel de la foi masque mal leur impuissance à déchirer le voile et à conjurer l'angoisse existentielle. L'unique réponse possible à cette angoisse c'est l'amour, comme se plaît à le rappeler Eugen Drewermann dans un des ses récents ouvrages : *Dieu en toute liberté*.

Entre tous les noms dont il honore Allah, l'Islam privilégie « le Miséricordieux ». Le bouddhisme, qui ne connaît aucune divinité, prône comme vertu suprême la compassion à l'égard de tous les êtres du seul fait qu'ils soient vivants. Le christianisme nous dit que Dieu est amour et, avant que les philosophes et les savants ne se soient avisés de le définir moins simplement, Jésus avait choisi de nous le présenter ainsi. Vient-on à lui chargé d'angoisse, il rassure ; de souffrance, il soulage ; de culpabilité, il pardonne. Languit-on de faim, il nourrit ; est-on frappé d'exclusion, il accueille pour réintégrer aussitôt dans la société humaine.

À qui mise sur le sacrifice pour forger alliance avec Dieu, il propose la réconciliation avec le frère offensé ou offenseur, et quand il meurt victime de la révolution que ce message a amorcée dans les cœurs, il pardonne et s'abandonne dans les mains de Celui dont il se sait aimé.

Voilà sa vérité qui devrait être la nôtre. Cette vérité-là, loin de susciter divisions et querelles, ouvre un espace de liberté où peut se déployer le meilleur de l'aventure humaine acceptant d'assumer son mystère au sein d'un mystère plus insondable encore, et dont nous ne pourrons jamais ici-bas qu'esquisser maladroitement le visage et balbutier le nom.

Parce que la famille humaine est innombrable et bigarrée, parce qu'elle est appelée à créer entre ses divers clans des alliances que ni la géographie ni l'ethnologie ne semblaient avoir prévues, parce que tenaillée par l'angoisse elle aspire au bonheur, le respect devant sa quête multiforme d'absolu devrait constituer la pierre de touche, la pierre d'angle de toutes nos relations. Pour avoir trop longtemps méprisé mutuellement nos dieux, nous avons fait de notre diversité religieuse une pierre d'achoppement. Non seulement avons-nous fait avorter ainsi nos rêves de fraternité, de solidarité et de paix, mais pire encore, et cruel paradoxe, c'est au nom de la foi que nous avons saboté ce que les premiers nous nommons le « Royaume », ce rêve de Dieu.

DISCERNER : LOI ET CONSCIENCE[1]

JEAN-FRANÇOIS MALHERBE

Croire conduit à agir en toute liberté. Mais agir librement ne signifie pas pour autant n'en faire qu'à sa guise. Agir en chrétien exige que le croyant mette en jeu toutes ses capacités de discernement, de jugement et de créativité ; qu'il soupèse le pour et contre sur la balance de ses relations à lui-même, aux autres proches et plus lointains, et à ultimement Dieu. En un mot, croire implique l'exercice adulte de la liberté de conscience.

Mais la liberté de conscience, qu'est-ce que c'est ? Le droit de faire ce que je veux, quand je veux, comme je veux ? Je ne le pense pas, car dans la liberté de conscience s'exprime une dimension essentielle de notre « vivre ensemble » que contredirait, dénierait, refuserait cette référence à mon seul bon plaisir arbitraire. Est-ce alors le droit de penser comme je veux ? Évidemment, personne n'a le droit de me dénier ma liberté de penser, mais cela implique-t-il que l'on s'en tienne à ces positions résignées : « à chacun sa conscience », « à chacun sa morale », « à chacun sa religion », « à chacun sa culture », etc. ? La liberté de conscience est-elle à ce

1. Conférence prononcée le 16 mars 1997 à la basilique-cathédrale Notre-Dame de Québec dans le cadre des Grandes Conférences de carême.

point individualiste ? Je répondrai NON, parce que de nouveau la liberté de conscience implique la prise en considération de notre « vivre ensemble ».

La liberté de conscience est à la fois personnelle et sociale. Elle est personnelle parce que c'est la liberté de ma conscience et non celle de mon voisin. Mais en même temps, ma liberté de conscience est profondément sociale parce que je n'en suis pas le créateur. J'en ai hérité. Je l'ai reçue avec ma culture et mon éducation. Ce n'est que petit à petit que j'ai pris possession de cet héritage, au fur et à mesure que je suis devenu responsable de moi-même. Que ma liberté de conscience soit un héritage implique qu'elle est liée à l'existence d'autrui, qu'elle est sociale. En plus de cela, ma liberté de conscience se vit en interaction avec d'autres personnes qui, elles aussi, sont douées de liberté de conscience.

La question que je voudrais explorer est celle-ci : comment articuler ces deux dimensions de la liberté de conscience qui pourraient devenir contradictoires : la dimension personnelle et la dimension sociale ? Ces dimensions peuvent devenir contradictoires lorsqu'elles sont absolutisées, lorsque ma liberté de conscience s'érige en arbitraire absolu ou, au contraire, lorsque sa dimension sociale se mue en dictature de la pensée convenue. Notre époque connaît ces deux tendances à la fois : absolutisation de l'individu d'un côté et, de l'autre, la pensée unique, qui peut prendre la forme de l'intégrisme religieux, mais aussi du scientisme le plus dogmatique.

Comment articuler la dimension personnelle et la dimension sociale de la liberté de conscience ? Pour répondre à cette question, je voudrais vous proposer un petit détour du côté du dialogue. En effet, le dialogue est l'une des pratiques les plus humaines qui soit. On pourrait sans doute même définir l'humain comme un être-en-dialogue. Or, précisément, le dialogue est un événement qui s'inscrit, à l'instar de la liberté de conscience, dans la dimension de la personne comme dans celle de la société. Le dialogue est de part en part personnel et de part en part communautaire. Il n'y a pas de dialogue si personne n'est là pour dire *Je*. Mais il n'y a pas non plus de dialogue sans une interaction sociale : *Je-Tu-Il* ou *Elle*. *Je* et *Tu* s'adressent mutuellement la parole à propos de *Il* ou *Elle*, un sujet tiers (personne ou chose). Cette analogie entre la liberté de conscience et le dialogue, tous deux à la fois profondément personnels et sociaux, me suggère d'éclairer le moins connu, la liberté de conscience, par le plus familier, le dialogue. Le dialogue nous est familier parce que nous le pratiquons. Et si nous ne le pratiquons pas, nous avons au moins une idée de la manière dont il faudrait le pratiquer. Et même si nous sommes malhabiles à le pratiquer, nous savons ce qu'il devrait être puisque nous percevons notre maladresse. La liberté de conscience, par contre, nous apparaît comme un concept plus abstrait.

Un des professeurs que j'ai eu le privilège d'avoir autrefois à l'Université de Louvain, et qui est un philosophe célèbre, Paul Ricœur, nous disait que la vie humaine, c'est comme une réception où se rencontrent les uns et les autres autour d'un événement à célébrer. On y entre en ne sachant pas qui on va rencontrer ni de quoi l'on va parler. On se joint à un petit groupe et, tout en saluant les autres et en partageant avec eux quelques rafraîchissements et nourritures, on écoute ceux qui parlent. Au bout d'un temps, on croit saisir de quoi il s'agit et l'on se risque à participer à la conversation. Il se peut d'ailleurs que celle-ci prenne, suite à notre intervention, un tour différent de celui qui aurait été le sien en notre absence. Puis, la conversation se poursuit, de groupe en groupe, au gré des recoupements et des intérêts. Et à la fin, ajoutait-il malicieux, on se retire de l'assemblée sur la pointe des pieds... Une vie humaine, cela consiste à participer à une conversation qui a commencé avant notre arrivée et qui se poursuivra après notre départ. Nous n'inventons pas l'échange de paroles, le dialogue, nous en sommes les porteurs éphémères.

Qu'est-ce que cela peut nous apprendre sur la liberté de conscience ? Tout simplement que la liberté de conscience, comme le dialogue, ne sont possibles que si un certain nombre de conditions sont respectées, qui articulent entre elles leurs dimensions personnelle et sociale.

Principes universels

Ces conditions sont au nombre de trois. Elles sont très simples. Chacun les connaît déjà, mais n'a peut-être pas encore eu l'occasion de les mettre en ordre comme je le propose. Je voudrais présenter ces trois conditions sous la forme de principes, car nous réaliserons facilement qu'elles sont en réalité les trois principes fondamentaux de toute éthique.

Il n'est pas possible de dialoguer avec quelqu'un si vous parlez tout le temps, ou si l'on ne vous laisse jamais la parole. Il faut que les allocutaires se respectent mutuellement. Le respect de l'autre est d'ailleurs une forme de respect de soi. Empêcher l'autre de parler, c'est le tuer dans sa capacité de dialogue, c'est lui dénier sa propre humanité. Le premier principe universel de l'éthique, c'est *l'interdit de l'homicide* dont le respect mutuel des allocutaires est une forme dérivée. Ne jamais hésiter à s'exprimer et ne jamais empêcher l'autre de le faire.

Le dialogue n'est pas possible si vous êtes manipulé par l'autre ou si vous le manipulez. Si vous profitez des petites faiblesses de l'autre pour lui faire des petits (ou des gros) chantages et qu'ainsi vous le menez par le bout du nez parce qu'il craint ce que vous pourriez encore dire de lui pour lui nuire, ou si l'autre vous traite de cette façon, le dialogue n'est pas possible entre vous. Il nous arrive à tous d'être victimes de manipulations. C'est certain, mais il nous arrive également à tous d'être manipulateurs, c'est tout aussi certain, même si cela passe plus facilement inaperçu pour nous. Le second principe universel de l'éthique, c'est l'interdit de la manipulation d'autrui ou, si l'on préfère, l'interdit de l'instrumentalisation d'autrui. Ne pas se laisser utiliser par l'autre comme si l'on n'était qu'un simple outil, un simple objet. Ne pas non plus utiliser autrui de cette façon. En anthropologie, on appelle ce principe *l'interdit de l'inceste,* car l'inceste est le plus fort symbole de l'instrumentalisation d'autrui, de la réduction d'autrui à un objet dont on abuse sans aucun égard pour la subjectivité que l'on dénie ainsi. Finalement, instrumentaliser autrui, c'est bel et bien une façon de le tuer comme autre sujet dans la relation.

Mais le dialogue n'est pas non plus possible avec quelqu'un qui ment ou à qui l'on ment. Il peut arriver qu'on mente. Mais si cela se reproduit souvent, on finit par ne plus savoir si l'on est dans le vrai ou dans le faux, dans le délire ou dans la réalité, dans les nuages ou les deux pieds sur terre. Le mensonge tue le dialogue et, par conséquent, les interlocuteurs. Évidemment, il est toujours possible de pardonner à un menteur, pour autant qu'il s'engage à ne plus mentir. C'est même souvent une façon remarquable de relancer un dialogue enlisé, de revivifier une parole condamnée à mort par le mensonge. Le troisième principe universel de l'éthique est *l'interdit du mensonge.*

Remarquons au passage que je parle de principes universels de l'éthique. En effet, ce sont des principes qui définissent l'humanité de chacun de nous comme l'humanité qui nous est commune, quels que soient notre sexe, notre langue, notre culture, notre époque. De plus, ces principes universels valent autant pour le dialogue interpersonnel que pour le dialogue interculturel. Ces principes universels sont évidemment présents dans notre tradition chrétienne. Le décalogue les mentionne explicitement[2].

Tu ne tueras pas,
Tu ne commettras pas l'adultère[3],
Tu ne rendras pas de faux témoignage[4].

Ces principes universels de l'éthique, différentes cultures les ont énoncés à leur façon. Il se peut qu'ils ne soient pas présents dans toutes les cultures. Il se peut que certaines formes de cultures ne soient pas prêtes au dialogue interculturel. Mais ne nous imaginons pas trop vite que c'est seulement le cas d'autres cultures. La nôtre connaît aussi cet impérialisme. Ne prétendons-nous pas que notre religion catholique est la seule vraie religion ? Ne prétendons-nous pas que notre civilisation technicienne est la seule vraie civilisation ? Ne prétendons-nous pas que seule la morale chrétienne est la vraie morale ? Naturellement, nous ajoutons charitablement que la religion, la civilisation et la morale des autres peuvent être des approximations respectables de la vérité que nous prétendons détenir. Mais cela n'empêche pas nos

2. Bien que sous une forme parfois légèrement différente, ces différences étant précisément liées au contexte de leur énonciation, qui n'est plus le nôtre. Voir notes 3 et 4.

3. « Commettre l'adultère », cela consistait à s'accaparer l'épouse d'un autre, comme un objet que l'on aurait volé. La sexualité est de tous temps le lieu par excellence du risque d'instrumentalisation de l'autre.

4. Une autre façon d'énoncer l'interdit du mensonge est présente dans le décalogue : « Un seul Dieu tu adoreras ». Adorer un autre dieu, c'est adorer un faux dieu à la place du vrai, c'est se mentir à soi-même.

FONDAMENTALISME

Le premier ennemi de l'attitude croyante authentique se nomme le fondamentalisme. Il consiste à s'en remettre aveuglément à la lettre d'un texte, d'une écriture sainte ou d'un dogme, d'une déclaration papale ou d'une définition du catéchisme, et donc à s'interdire de réfléchir.

Les fondamentalismes ne se retrouvent pas seulement en territoire religieux, mais ils y sont plus visibles qu'ailleurs. Combien d'interprétations simplistes des écritures saintes ont été sources d'attitudes inacceptables et parfois mortifères (pour dominer la femme, pour justifier l'apartheid, pour mépriser les juifs, etc.). L'idolâtrie de textes mal compris, le recours à des anathèmes et à des dogmes élaborés à d'autres époques, et toutes les déformations du « croire » en mal de sécurité vont à l'encontre d'une minimale intelligence croyante ou d'une minimale foi intelligente. ◇

prétentions d'être incompatibles avec le dialogue, c'est-à-dire avec l'humanité de l'homme elle-même.

Dire que la vérité est unique et que je l'ai dans ma poche, c'est prononcer une parole qui enlève à l'autre son espace vital. C'est une parole mortifère, une parole de mort. Il est possible que la vérité soit unique. Il est possible que nous en ayons une part dans notre poche. Mais si nous voulons dialoguer avec autrui, il convient d'accepter qu'autrui peut lui aussi avoir dans sa poche une part de vérité. La pratique du dialogue exige que nous en espérions que la part de vérité dans notre poche croisse autant que la part de vérité dans la poche d'autrui. Pensons à cette poutre qui est dans notre œil avant de dénoncer la paille qui obscurcit le regard de l'autre.

Nous ne devenons plus humains que par le dialogue. Et le dialogue n'est possible que dans le respect de ces trois principes fondamentaux.

Il en va de même pour la liberté de conscience, car celle-ci s'exprime dans le dialogue. La liberté de conscience consiste à vivre selon les trois principes que je viens d'énoncer, en dépit de tout. Même si cette liberté nous met en contradiction avec ce que nous avons en poche et croyons vrai. Même si cette liberté nous met en contradiction avec la loi civile ou la loi morale religieuse ou laïque dont nous sommes les héritiers. C'est que ces trois principes sont, comme le proclame l'*Antigone* de Sophocle, *non écrits et imprescriptibles*. C'est à ces trois principes que nous sommes appelés à mesurer les morales dont nous sommes les héritiers. Sinon, nous absolutisons un héritage particulier et, implicitement, nous récusons à d'autres héritages le droit d'exister.

Archimède disait : donnez-moi un point d'appui assez solide et un levier assez long et je soulèverai le monde. Cette parabole est inspirante, car la liberté de conscience, c'est comme un levier que nous pouvons utiliser pour humaniser l'humain. Ce que nous pouvons bouger avec ce levier, c'est la réalité humaine trop humaine, la partie de l'humanité en nous personnellement et en nous socialement qui n'est pas encore assez humanisée. Mais quel est le point d'appui sur lequel on peut poser ce levier qu'est la liberté de conscience ? Ce point d'appui, c'est *la parole vive*.

Parole vive

L'exemple le plus extraordinaire de parole vive que je connaisse est cet épisode du *Livre des Rois* que nous connaissons sous le nom de Jugement de Salomon[5]. Deux prostituées qui vivaient dans la même maison avaient récemment donné toutes deux naissance à un fils. Une nuit, l'un des enfants meurt. Et les deux mères se disputent le survivant devant le souverain. Le roi demande qu'on

5. *1 Rois* 3,16-28.

JUGEMENT DERNIER

« Il reviendra dans la gloire pour juger les vivants et les morts et son règne n'aura pas de fin. » Cette parole du Credo, qui fait référence au retour du Christ et à son jugement, ne doit pas être comprise comme une sentence sans appel sur notre vie de pécheurs et de mortels. De fait, pour l'évangéliste Matthieu, celui qui sera sorti de lui-même et aura aidé les autres, celui-là s'est déjà jugé et s'est déjà ouvert au bonheur éternel. Même sans le savoir, il s'est ouvert à Dieu. Voilà de quoi nous convaincre que dans l'esprit évangélique le jugement dernier n'est pas si terrible puisqu'il nous permet surtout de réfléchir sur nos actes dans notre vie présente. Il est vrai que Michel-Ange, qui a peint son grandiose *Jugement dernier* (1534-1541) dans la chapelle Sixtine sous le pontificat du pape Paul III, nous donne une version plutôt terrifiante de cet événement. Il importe de comprendre cette représentation en lien avec la théologie de l'époque. Ce qu'il faut retenir du jugement dernier, c'est qu'il représente surtout un appel à la conversion, un appel à vivre selon les valeurs de l'Évangile. ◇

apporte une épée et qu'on donne à chacune des deux femmes une moitié de l'enfant vivant. Tandis que l'une d'elles s'écrie : « Il ne sera ni à toi ni à moi ; partagez », l'autre préfère céder l'enfant à la première. Salomon juge alors que la vraie mère est celle dont la parole fait vivre l'enfant et le lui donne.

L'intérêt du jugement de Salomon ne réside pas seulement dans son caractère astucieux. Il nous concerne ici parce que la parole du roi a provoqué les rivales à prononcer une parole de vie ou une parole de mort. Une parole vive ou une parole mortifère. La parole de la vraie mère vient de la vie et fait vivre. La parole de la malheureuse jalouse vient de la mort et fait mourir. La parole de mort procède du déni de la mort. La jalouse préfère deux morts plutôt que de reconnaître qu'elle a un deuil à accepter pour pouvoir vivre et contribuer à la vie autour d'elle. La parole vive, c'est d'accepter l'évidence. C'est cela le point d'appui sur lequel poser le levier de la liberté de conscience pour aller vers le plus humain : la parole vive.

La parole vive ne se trouve pas dans les livres de recettes. C'est la parole inattendue que la vie nous inspire pour que la vie s'épanouisse. C'est la parole inespérée qui débloque une situation inextricable. C'est la parole qui ranime la braise de la vie sous les cendres du désespoir. La parole vive, c'est la parole qui nous fait vivre et nous incite à dire d'autres paroles de vie qui, à leur tour, feront vivre.

La parole vive, c'est très exactement ce qui doit servir de principe pour guider notre liberté de conscience. La liberté de conscience, c'est cette vertu que nous possédons et qui nous permet de prendre distance à l'égard de la lettre de la loi héritée de notre tradition lorsque son application mécanique serait mortifère plutôt que vivifiante. La liberté de conscience, c'est cette responsabilité dont nous sommes investis de dénoncer les paroles mortifères et de leur substituer des paroles vivifiantes. Le critère de la liberté de conscience, c'est la parole vive. En principe, la loi de la morale héritée devrait être vivifiante. Mais lorsque son application s'annonce mortifère, nous portons cette responsabilité de transgresser la lettre au nom de l'esprit. C'est ce que le vieil Aristote[6] appelait la *phronèsis*, (que l'on traduit habituellement par *prudence*, mais que je préfère rendre par *discernement*).

6. Il se référait d'ailleurs à la transgression commise par Antigone lorsqu'elle avait donné symboliquement une sépulture à son frère, en dépit de l'interdiction du tyran, et qui respectait ainsi les lois non écrites et imprescriptibles des dieux plutôt que l'édit arbitraire d'un homme.

La liberté de conscience a pour responsabilité
de ne jamais permettre
que la loi devienne une parole de mort,
mais qu'elle soit toujours une parole vive.

Voilà qui est applicable dans tous les domaines de la vie des humains. Est-ce que cela signifie le retour de l'arbitraire ? Mais pas du tout. Car la liberté de conscience est autonome plutôt qu'arbitraire. Elle se donne à elle-même ses propres principes, certes. Mais à y bien penser, ceux-ci sont les conditions de possibilités de son propre exercice. Ils expriment la vérité la plus profonde du dialogue : les interdits de l'homicide, de l'instrumentalisation et du mensonge. Ses principes sont des balises qui ne sont pas infranchissables, puisqu'il peut survenir des situations où il est impossible de respecter les trois balises à la fois et où la conscience devra choisir le chemin de vie, l'itinéraire le moins mortifère.

La parole vive ne peut être mise en forme de loi. Elle reste définitivement non écrite. Elle procède de la résistance que la vie oppose à la peur de vivre. Je dis « peur de vivre » et non « peur de mourir », car la mort est une réalité de la vie. Mais il est des paroles inspirées par la peur de vivre la réalité telle qu'elle est, incluant la vraie mort qui viendra, inéluctablement, un jour. Et ces paroles sont des paroles de mort[7].

Il est un autre grand texte de l'Ancien Testament qui est très éclairant à ce sujet : le récit du sacrifice d'Isaac (*Gn* 22,1-19). Il s'agit d'une situation franchement paradoxale. Dieu vient à peine de promettre à Abraham une descendance aussi nombreuse que

7. En ce sens, accompagner un mourant, c'est entendre sa parole de vie et la soutenir jusqu'au bout dans la résistance qu'elle oppose à la peur de vivre la mort.

les étoiles du ciel, il vient à peine de lui donner un fils et voilà qu'il ordonne à son protégé de sacrifier la vie de ce fils pour lui rendre gloire. En langage d'aujourd'hui, on pourrait dire que Dieu soumet Abraham à des injonctions paradoxales. Mais Abraham ne se laisse pas démonter. Il n'hésite pas à donner la priorité à la parole vive qui s'exprime ici et maintenant et à mettre au second plan la promesse antérieure. C'est la présence active de la parole du Dieu vivant qui balise ses choix et non le souvenir d'une parole passée, aussi prometteuse fût-elle. Entre deux paroles de Dieu, Abraham choisit la plus vive, même si, paradoxalement, elle commande un sacrifice vital. C'est qu'il sait que son Dieu est le Dieu de vie. Il a foi que Dieu est plus vivant que le paradoxe auquel il est confronté. Sa foi va jusqu'à affronter l'absurde. Et cette foi, finalement, vivifie la vie d'Isaac comme la sienne.

Le Nouveau Testament connaît aussi des textes éclairants pour notre propos. Je pense notamment au récit des épis arrachés[8]. Ce passage relate la réponse de Jésus aux critiques qu'adressaient les pharisiens aux disciples qui arrachaient des épis un jour de sabbat. Jésus justifie la transgression de la lettre de la Loi en renvoyant les pharisiens à la transgression commise par leur père David lorsque ce dernier et ses compagnons, qui avaient faim, mangèrent les pains de proposition réservés aux prêtres. Non seulement de telles transgressions sont possibles, mais elles relèvent de la tradition d'Israël ! Et Jésus de conclure : « Le sabbat est fait pour l'homme et non l'homme pour le sabbat. En sorte que le fils de l'homme est maître du sabbat. »

La loi est un outil qui a pour fonction de nous soutenir dans notre effort de vie et non une contrainte qui nous apporte la mort. Et la liberté de conscience consiste précisément à écarter de nos pratiques les applications mortifères de la loi.

8. *Mc* 2,23-28.

L'adversaire des paroles vives, ce sont les paroles de mort. La loi est une parole de vie. C'est son application formaliste ou mécanique qui la transforme en parole de mort. Il y aurait d'ailleurs ici toute une méditation à entreprendre sur la personne même du Fils de Dieu dont l'évangéliste Jean nous dit qu'il est lui-même la parole vive incarnée. «Au commencement était la parole... »

Mais l'adversaire le plus commun de la parole vive, c'est la parole vide. Le baratin, le remplissage de l'espace de nos vies par toutes sortes de bavardages inutiles qui nous encombrent, nous étouffent et nous déconnectent de la parole vive. La grande leçon

MARTYR, MARTYRE

Déjà au IIe siècle, ceux et celles qui étaient morts pour leur foi chrétienne étaient considérés et vénérés comme martyrs, du grec *martus,* c'est-à-dire témoins privilégiés. C'est en période de persécution que le martyre apparut aux chrétiens et chrétiennes comme la forme la plus éminente de sainteté. Beaucoup de femmes et d'hommes sont morts martyrs, et cela dès les débuts du christianisme, puisque les premières persécutions ont eu lieu de 64 sous Néron à 180 sous Marc-Aurèle. Septime Sévère en 202, par un édit, interdit toute forme de prosélytisme pour les juifs et les chrétiens. Ce qui mena aussi au martyre de nombreux catéchumènes et de nouveaux baptisés. En 250, l'empereur Dèce, qui voulait maintenir l'unité romaine autour de la religion officielle, ordonna à tous les citoyens de participer à l'élimination des chrétiens. Aujourd'hui, témoigner de sa foi engage rarement à prendre en compte l'idée du martyre dans son sens plénier, soit celui de la perspective de tortures et de mort. Toutefois, on ne peut nier que des gens meurent encore sous diverses latitudes au nom de leur engagement chrétien ; d'autres personnes se font martyriser pour avoir milité en faveur de la justice et du respect des droits humains. ◇

du jugement de Salomon, c'est de manifester la force de la parole vive qui fait jaillir la vie du risque de mort.

La liberté de conscience, c'est la force de la parole vive, c'est la force que nous donne la parole par laquelle nous suscitons la vie là où il y a risque de mort. C'est la force qui nous donne de vivre.

Apprendre l'éthique

La liberté de conscience, c'est une possibilité dont nous héritons. Mais pour que cette possibilité se réalise, il faut un apprentissage. La liberté de conscience, cela s'apprend, le plus souvent avec l'aide d'un maître en éthique. Mais qu'est-ce qu'un maître en éthique ?

C'est tout simplement un apprenti expérimenté, un apprenti qui a quelques pas d'avance par rapport à d'autres sur le chemin de l'éthique. Il n'y a pas d'experts en éthique qui connaissent des choses éthiques qui seraient cachées aux autres. Et si quelqu'un se prétend expert en éthique au sens d'un sujet supposé savoir des choses que les autres ne savent pas et qu'il pourrait leur révéler, c'est un usurpateur. Un maître en éthique est simplement un humain qui a quelques longueurs d'avance sur ses apprentis ; mais lui-même reste un apprenti toute sa vie.

La plus belle comparaison que j'ai trouvée est celle de l'apprenti forgeron et du maître de forge. Un maître de forge a été apprenti forgeron. Il a acquis la maîtrise de son métier. Non seulement il est devenu habile à travailler le métal mais il a appris à faire lui-même ses outils et il est probable que, chemin faisant, il ait même créé de nouveaux outils. Il va enseigner son art à un apprenti en joignant le geste à la parole et la parole au geste. Il montre comment faire, il enseigne le tour de main par imitation. Et en même temps, il raconte ce qu'il montre. De plus, il a cette ouverture d'esprit qui le met en position de s'enrichir lui-même des progrès de son élève. Ce dernier va forcément, un jour ou l'autre, trouver quelque chose que le maître ne savait pas. Tout simplement parce qu'il est différent : il n'a pas les mêmes doigts, la même musculature, la même éducation, la même acuité visuelle, les mêmes désirs, les mêmes regrets, etc. Il a une façon de faire plier un clou en le chauffant juste assez pour qu'il ne perde pas trop sa rigidité et se fige rapidement et solidement dans la position voulue que son maître ne lui a pas apprise. Le véritable maître est toujours en situation d'apprentissage par rapport à son apprenti. Il va même souligner auprès de son apprenti et de l'entourage la contribution que ce dernier apporte à sa propre maîtrise. C'est d'ailleurs ainsi que l'apprenti finit par devenir lui-même un maître.

L'éthique, qui cultive la liberté de conscience, n'est pas un savoir cumulatif. Il ne s'agit pas d'avoir inventorié une galaxie de plus, ni de décrire une orchidée inconnue. Il s'agit véritablement de l'art de provoquer l'autre à accoucher de sa propre habileté, qu'il a en lui, mais qui est demeurée cachée. Il s'agit de provoquer l'autre à dévoiler sa propre humanité qui est encore cachée.

La liberté de conscience, c'est cette prérogative qui est la nôtre, qui est celle de tous les citoyens, de tous les humains, de tous les enfants de Dieu, de pouvoir juger avec discernement les circonstances dans lesquelles la loi, loin d'être vivifiante comme elle le devrait, risque de devenir mortifère et doit, par conséquent, être transgressée au nom d'une parole vive. « Une telle transgression implique une responsabilité personnellement assumée. » Jamais il n'est acceptable de prendre prétexte de la liberté de conscience pour justifier une telle transgression. C'est la responsabilité personnelle de l'auteur de la transgression, assumée dans la vivacité de sa parole, qui seule peut justifier une telle transgression. La liberté de conscience ne peut jamais être un prétexte pour agir arbitrairement. Elle est toujours une responsabilité d'agir dans la mouvance d'une parole vive.

Que faire pour bien faire dans une situation problématique ? On ne peut répondre que ceci : fais ce que te recommande la morale dont tu es l'héritier, à moins que d'agir ainsi ne vienne contredire l'un des trois principes fondamentaux de l'éthique universelle. Si tel devait être le cas, mieux vaudrait transgresser la morale héritée que de renier sa propre humanité. C'est le prix à payer personnellement pour devenir des enfants de Dieu véritablement adultes, qui grandissent en force et en sagesse. C'est le prix à payer socialement pour devenir ensemble les sujets de l'Histoire plutôt que d'en rester les jouets.

Avant de finir, je voudrais souligner que les perspectives que je propose permettent de construire une morale dans une société multiculturelle et pluraliste, mais à la condition expresse de mettre en question de façon assez radicale quelques-uns des préjugés qui sont le plus souvent les nôtres en matière d'éthique. Je les résumerai comme ceci :

> La *liberté de conscience* n'est pas la capacité de décider arbitrairement de notre action, mais bien de mesurer les morales héritées à l'aune des principes universels de l'éthique.
>
> Les *principes universels de l'éthique* ne sont pas des préceptes imposés de l'extérieur ; au-delà des essentialismes, ils expriment à l'apprenti les conditions pragmatiques de sa participation à la création des consensus nécessaires à la vie en société.
>
> Les *normes de la morale* dont il est l'héritier ne représentent plus des absolus pour l'apprenti, mais d'utiles contingences révisables qui facilitent la vie de son groupe social et en expriment les valeurs particulières.
>
> Les *maîtres en éthique* ne sont pas des sujets supposés détenir des recettes secrètes qu'ils pourraient révéler, mais de simples apprentis

qui ont pris quelques pas d'avance dans la création des « tiers-jeux » de l'éthique. Ils ne sont donc plus en position d'*autorité*. Ils visent au contraire à se rendre superflus. C'est d'ailleurs ce qui les distingue radicalement des *experts* en tous genres que cultive notre « société technicienne ».

Pour conclure, je me demande si la liberté de conscience, ce n'est pas, en définitive, la conscience en liberté ?

OUVERTURE

CROÎTRE ET CROIRE EN LIBERTÉ

JEAN-FRANÇOIS MALHERBE

Non, il n'est pas absurde de croire, même en passant dans le troisième millénaire de l'ère chrétienne. Mais la possibilité d'une foi chrétienne valide se paie du prix de la liberté. Il fut une époque où l'Église définissait « ce qu'il *faut* croire[1] ». Cette époque n'est peut-être pas révolue mais on constate que beaucoup de chrétiens qui se seraient contentés autrefois de recevoir passivement le message de l'Église, sont encouragés aujourd'hui, par leur présence dans une vie sociale de plus en plus « multiculturelle », à interroger ce message de façon décisive.

L'une des questions qui leur monte le plus clairement aux lèvres est celle-ci : comment serait-il possible que nous soyons vraiment libres si Dieu existe ? La question n'est pas nouvelle. Le plus souvent, elle s'est exprimée par la bouche des athées qui en ont fait un des arguments principaux de leur démonstration de l'absurdité de la foi en Dieu. Karl Marx, Friedrich Nietzsche et Sigmund Freud, pour ne citer que ces trois « Maîtres du soupçon », comme les appelle Paul Ricœur, en sont d'illustres témoins.

1. Un ouvrage demeuré célèbre de Mgr Garonne portait précisément ce titre.

Lorsqu'on analyse de près l'ensemble de ces positions athées, on repère assez aisément un point majeur qu'elles ont en commun. Toutes semblent s'articuler comme s'il existait une radicale rivalité entre la liberté humaine et la liberté divine ; comme s'il existait une balance de la liberté et que tout accroissement de liberté qui serait posé sur le plateau humain devait être enlevé au plateau divin et réciproquement. C'est soit Dieu, soit l'humain qui est libre mais pas les deux ensemble.

Confronté à cette façon de poser la question de la liberté de l'humain face au divin, plus d'un théologien a tenté d'expliquer que la liberté de l'humain est de se conformer à la volonté de Dieu, car celle-ci consiste à vouloir le vrai bien de l'humain. On voit immédiatement que cette explication ne fait que reporter le problème, car reste en suspens la question de savoir qui peut connaître la volonté de Dieu ?

La réponse classique comporte deux volets : la volonté de Dieu s'exprime dans la « Loi naturelle » et dans la « Révélation ». Mais de nouveau, la question est reportée : qui connaît la Loi naturelle et qui est autorisé à interpréter la Révélation ? Finalement, la question demeure en suspens ou bien alors elle est tranchée par recours à l'autorité.

Il faut avouer que choisir entre l'autorité et l'incertitude est pour le moins inconfortable. Et l'on comprend que de tout temps certains aient choisi la foi en l'autorité plutôt que le risque d'une incertitude à propos de Dieu lui-même. La plupart des croyants font le premier choix et les agnostiques le second. Quant aux athées, leur noble protestation contre l'argument d'autorité semble leur apporter une sorte de certitude pour ainsi dire inversée. Du Dieu qu'ils refusent, ils se font la même image que les croyants qui l'adorent. Athées et croyants semblent pour la plupart ratifier le même leurre que les uns rejettent tandis que les autres lui accordent leur confiance.

Mais trop rare est la démarche qui consiste à interroger la manière même dont est habituellement posée la question de la liberté de l'humain face au divin. Il se trouve pourtant certains esprits hardis qui s'y sont risqués et dont il vaut la peine de solliciter les avis. Parmi eux, les mystiques occupent une place de choix[2]. Et parmi les mystiques, ceux qui s'inscrivent dans la ligne de la « théologie négative[3] », et tout particulièrement Maître Eckhart (1260-1328)[4] que l'on considère à bon droit comme leur chef de file, ont abordé la question tout autrement.

Pour le maître dominicain, croître et croire sont une seule et même action. L'humain devient davantage humain en se laissant détacher par l'amour de Dieu de toutes les fausses images qu'il se forme des créatures, de lui-même et de Dieu. C'est en renonçant à nos idoles que nous sommes affranchis de notre condition d'esclaves. Et nos idoles sont légion : nous nous en formons de Dieu, de nous-mêmes et des choses. Et l'esclavage consiste à tenir davantage à ces images qu'aux réalités vivantes qu'elles tentent d'exprimer et qu'en réalité elles enferment dans les prisons de nos mots.

Ainsi, par exemple, nous nous sommes fabriqué une philosophie dans laquelle nous pensons qu'il nous faut conquérir notre liberté contre quelqu'un (un père, Dieu, ou les deux à la fois) ou contre quelque chose (la Nature, la Nécessité). Mais cette philo-

2. Voir à ce sujet, notamment, la collection « L'expérience de Dieu » aux Éditions Fides à Montréal.

3. C'est-à-dire un courant théologique regroupant des auteurs qui estiment mieux savoir ce que n'est pas Dieu que ce qu'Il est.

4. Voir à ce sujet *L'expérience de Dieu avec Maître Eckhart*, introduction et choix de textes par Jean-François Malherbe, Fides, Montréal, 1999 ; ainsi que mon livre *« Souffrir Dieu », la prédication de Maître Eckhart*, « Théologies », Cerf, Paris, 1992.

sophie nous enferme, nous rend étrangers à nous-mêmes. Et nous y tenons tellement que nous nous raidissons dès qu'il s'agit de la mettre en question.

Et pourtant, qui nous dit que loin de devoir l'arracher à un adversaire, nous n'aurions pas plutôt à la recevoir d'un proche ?

Dieu, observe le mystique rhénan, « nous est plus intime que nous-mêmes ». Et il suggère que c'est de Dieu lui-même que nous recevons notre liberté. Ce don nous est offert gracieusement mais nous lui opposons les certitudes de nos autorités, de nos idées héritées ou de nos illusions. Dès lors, loin de nous laisser affranchir par la présence de Dieu en nous, nous nous le représentons à l'extérieur de nous, enfermé dans un tabernacle, par exemple, et, en conséquence, nous nous éloignons de lui.

Mais si nous consentions à la présence active de Dieu en nous, nous ouvririons la porte de notre intimité au travail de la grâce. Et nous Le laisserions nous affranchir de l'intérieur. Nous Le laisserions nous rendre libres. Et nous-mêmes deviendrions *par grâce* ce qu'Il est *par nature* : Dieu. Et si cette grâce nous est offerte en Jésus Christ, vrai Dieu vrai homme, c'est précisément parce qu'en lui coïncident strictement la volonté de Dieu et la liberté humaine.

Dans cette perspective, la question d'une éventuelle rivalité entre notre liberté et celle de Dieu se pose tout autrement. Ou, même, ne se pose plus du tout. En effet, si c'est bien Dieu qui, de notre fond le plus intime, nous affranchit des fausses images que nous nous dessinons de Lui, de nous et des choses, alors, c'est nous qui, pour ainsi dire, donnerons figure concrète à la liberté de Dieu par l'exercice de la nôtre.

C'est comme si Dieu exerçait sa liberté en dégageant le terrain pour que nous y exercions la nôtre. C'est comme si notre propre volonté d'homme incarnait la volonté de Dieu. C'est comme si la liberté de Dieu ouvrait un espace à l'expression de la liberté humaine. Autrement dit : c'est comme si la liberté de Dieu avait besoin de la liberté de l'humain pour continuer à s'exprimer, pour achever son œuvre[5]. C'est d'ailleurs précisément cette « discrétion » de Dieu qui manifeste avec le plus d'éclat son indéchiffrabilité.

C'est dire que la voie la plus respectueuse, à la fois de Dieu et de l'humain, pour apprendre à connaître Dieu tel qu'il se donne et non pas tel que nous voudrions qu'il soit, c'est précisément d'assumer en toute liberté notre propre affranchissement.

Mais la liberté humaine dont il s'agit est une liberté affranchie de toute fausse image et non pas une volonté arbitraire dont l'exercice ne serait balisé que par l'illusion. C'est dire que l'humain ne devient véritablement humain, ne se laisse croître en humanité, qu'en se laissant désapproprier de ses illusion par le lent, tenace et bienveillant travail de Dieu en lui.

L'*arbitraire*, que la plupart des humains confondent avec la *liberté*, consiste à disposer de soi, des autres et des choses à sa propre guise, au gré de sa fantaisie, au bon plaisir de ses fantasmes. La liberté affranchie, ou vraie liberté, s'acquiert tout au contraire au fil d'un difficile travail sur soi qui consiste à « lâcher prise » de ses fausses certitudes, comme disent les maîtres zen, c'est-à-dire, en définitive, à laisser le travail à un Dieu inconnu et à se contenter d'accueillir dans la joie la grâce qu'Il nous fait de devenir fille et fils de Dieu.

5. Maître Eckhart, dont les formules audacieuses surprennent souvent ses lecteurs, disait, en ce sens-là précisément, que « l'homme libre commande à Dieu ». Cette hyperbole se comprend bien dans la perspective évoquée ici puisque c'est l'homme libre qui achève en quelque sorte, par l'exercice de sa propre volonté affranchie de toute fausse image, l'exercice de la volonté propre de Dieu.

L'exercice arbitraire de la liberté nous sépare de nous-mêmes ; la liberté affranchie, tout au contraire, nous rend présents à nous-mêmes, conscients de la présence de Dieu en nous.

C'est à ce prix, au prix de l'affranchissement, que croire ne sera pas absurde au troisième millénaire. C'est au prix de cette liberté vraie, reçue et non pas conquise, que l'humain fera l'épreuve que croître et croire sont deux balises sur le même chemin.

TABLE DES MATIÈRES

OUVERTURE

55 T
Ecce compléta sunt *
De Isaía Prophéta
Non erit
tristis, neque turbuléntus,
donec ponat in terra iudí-
cium, et legem eius ínsulæ
exspectábunt.
Nascetur nobis pár-
vulus, et vocábitur Deus,
potéstas super húmerum
tur omnes tribus terræ,
omnes gentes sérvient ei.
Ipse.
Dicit Dó-
regnum cælórum, allelúia.
Nolite timére : * quin-
ta enim die véniet ad vos
Dóminus noster.